CONSTRUCTION LAW

Law and Practice relating to the
Construction Industry

ELEVENTH EDITION

By
JOHN UFF

**CBE, QC, Ph.D, BSc.(Eng.)
FREng., FICE, FCIArb.**

*Chartered Engineer, Barrister,
Bencher of Gray's Inn,
Emeritus Professor of Engineering Law,
King's College, London*

 **SWEET & MAXWELL**

 **THOMSON REUTERS**

First Edition 1974
Second Edition 1978
Third Edition 1981
Fourth Edition 1985
Second Impression 1989
Fifth Edition 1991
Second Impression 1994
Sixth Edition 1996
Seventh Edition 1999
Reprinted 2000
Eighth Edition 2002
Ninth Edition 2005
Tenth Edition 2009
Eleventh Edition 2013

Published in 2013 by Sweet & Maxwell, 100 Avenue Road, London NW3 3PF part of
Thomson Reuters (Professional) UK Limited (Registered in England & Wales,
Company No 1679046.
Registered Office and address for service: Aldgate House, 33 Aldgate
High Street, London EC3N 1DL).
Computerset by LBJ Typesetting of Kingsclere. Printed and bound by
Ashford Colour Press, Gosport, Hants.

For further information on our products and services, visit
www.sweetandmaxwell.co.uk

No natural forests were destroyed to make this product;
only farmed timber was used and replanted.

British Library Cataloguing in Publication Data

A CIP catalogue record of this book
is available from the British Library.

ISBN 978-0-414-02319-2

For Diana

PREFACE

Construction Law is approaching its 40th anniversary and the 11th edition marks the now customary elapse of some four years, during which this ever-expanding and regularly changing subject calls for updating. While no dramatic innovations need be noted for this edition, there has been a steady stream of developments in both law and procedure. However, there is a textual change in this edition in the substitution at Ch.13 of a fuller commentary on the FIDIC (International) Conditions of Contract, which previously occupied a mere six pages within Ch.11. The previous coverage of the ICE Conditions of Contract, which can still be found in Ch.13 of the 10th edition, is correspondingly reduced and substituted for FIDIC in Ch.11. The reasons for this change are twofold: First the increasing international importance of contracts based on FIDIC, which dominates the international market on all continents; and secondly, an interregnum in the fortunes of the ICE Conditions of Contract, for which the ICE itself withdrew sponsorship in 2012 in favour of NEC 3. The ICE Conditions remain popular with contractors and consultants and thus its sponsorship has been taken over by the ACE and CECA, who have re-issued the form under the new title "The Infrastructure Conditions of Contract" (ICC). The edition published in 2012 was virtually a reprint of the ICE 7th edition, but a restructuring operation is currently underway through a committee which I have the privilege of chairing. The outcome will be a new set of ICC Conditions, to some extent radical but retaining much of the wording and "feel" of the ICE Conditions, designed to operate as an alternative both to NEC 3 domestically and FIDIC internationally. It is hoped that the new ICC Conditions will be completed during in 2013 and available the following year and will doubtless return as a full chapter in the next edition of *Construction Law.*

As regards changes to the law and practice in this edition, far reaching amendments to the civil litigation costs rules following the *Jackson Report* have finally reached the rule books. The progressive stripping away of supposed immunities has now been applied to expert witnesses in the Supreme Court's decision in *Jones v Kaney*.[1] In the field of arbitration, two more Supreme Court decisions call for mention: in *Hashwani v Jivraj*[2] it was decided that arbitrators were not *"employed"* so that restrictions on persons to be appointed did not offend anti-discrimination legislation; and in *Dallah v Pakistan*,[3] it was decided that the respondent was not a party to the arbitration agreement, reaching the opposite conclusion to that of the French courts. Investment treaty arbitrations continue to gain prominence and this is reflected in coverage of the important construction case of *Bayindir v Pakistan*.[4]

In the field of contract law the Supreme Court decision in *RTS v Molkerei*[5] is interesting, not just because a contract/no contract case had reached this level in the courts, but because it illustrates how entirely different conclusions can be reached from the same facts, even at the highest judicial level. In terms of the construing of contracts, the decision in *Belize Telecom*[6] has now been followed by *Rainy Sky*,[7] adding yet further Supreme Court authority to the impressive list of cases on the topic. On the construction-specific issue of extensions of time and concurrent delays, while the Scottish Appeal Court dismissed the appeal in *City Inn*,[8] the contrary view can be found in the TCC decision in *Walter Lilly v Giles Mackay*,[9] in the 9th edition of *Keating on Construction Contracts*[10] and, to add to the debate, in the updated SCL Paper of John Marrin QC, now entitled, *Concurrent Delay Revisited*.[11] The debate will doubtless continue.

While many other cases are noted in the text, it should be mentioned that the 10th edition of *Construction Law* unfortunately anticipated the bringing into effect of the Local Democracy, Economic Development and Construction Act 2009, which did not in fact come into force until October 1, 2011, some two years after the publication of the 10th edition.

---

[1] [2011] B.L.R. 283.
[2] [2011] UKSC 40.
[3] [2010] UKSC 56.
[4] ICSID case o.Arb/03/29.
[5] [2010] B.L.R. 337.
[6] [2009] 1 W.L.R. 1988.
[7] [2011] 1 W.L.R. 2900.
[8] [2010] B.L.R. 473.
[9] [2012] EWHC 1773 (TCC).
[10] Paragraph 8-026.
[11] SCL Paper 179, February 2013.

The Act as finally passed contains some further changes, all of which are now reflected in the current text.

As in all previous editions I remain grateful to my friends and colleagues at Keating Chambers, at the Centre of Construction law, King's College London and in The Society of Construction Law, The Society of Construction Arbitrators and The Worshipful Company of Arbitrators for many stimulating discussions. But above all, I am fortunate in the continuing flow of interesting professional cases, whether by arbitration, adjudication, expert determination, mediation, conciliation or Dispute Adjudication Board, all of which generate endless new points of interest which help to keep this lively subject regularly updated.

John Uff,
April 18, 2013,
Keating Chambers,
15 Essex Street,
London,
WC2R 3AA

ACKNOWLEDGMENTS

Grateful acknowledgment is made to the following authors and publishers for permission to quote from their works:

AC ARCHITECTS: PPC 2000 ACA Standard Partnering Form

LEXISNEXIS: All England Law Reports, Construction Law Reports and Local Government Reports, extracts reproduced by permission of Reed Elsevier (UK) Limited trading as LexisNexis.

FIDIC: FIDIC Conditions of Contract for Construction for Building and Engineering Works Designed by the Employer

HMSO: Controller of HMSO for extracts from Crown and Parliamentary copyright material

THE INCORPORATED COUNCIL OF LAW REPORTING FOR ENGLAND AND WALES: Law Reports and Weekly Law Reports

INFORMA LAW: Lloyd's Law Reports and Building Law Reports

ROSEMARY BEALES: ICC Conditions of Contract

SWEET & MAXWELL LTD: JCT Standard Form and Solicitor's Journal

THOMAS TELFORD PUBLISHING: NEC3 Engineering and Construction Contract

While every care has been taken to establish and acknowledge copyright, and contact copyright owners, the publishers tender their apologies for any accidental infringement. They would be pleased to come to a suitable arrangement with the rightful owners in each case.

CONTENTS

TABLE OF CASES

xxiii

TABLE OF STATUTES

TABLE OF STATUTORY INSTRUMENTS

CHAPTER 1

CONSTRUCTION LAW AND THE LEGAL SYSTEM

The term "construction law" is now universally understood to cover the whole field of law which directly affects the construction industry and the legal instruments through which it operates. However, Construction law extends well beyond the law as such. Efficient and workable construction contracts require that the needs of the construction process should be taken into account by applying the principles of management. Construction contracts must also take account of disputes and their resolution. Construction law is, thus, an interactive subject in which both lawyers and construction professionals, including managers, have an essential part to play. This has been the approach of different bodies concerned with the promotion and development of construction law, principally the Society for Construction Law (founded in 1983) and the Centre of Construction Law and Management at King's College, London (founded in 1987). Both bodies have emphasised the essential interaction of lawyers and construction professionals in the development and practice of construction law and their lead has been followed by other institutions and teaching establishments in different parts of the world.

Construction law and construction contracts

The term "construction contract" now has a statutory definition[1] covering most but not all types of construction work, and including both building and engineering work. Construction law, however, embraces all construction contracts, whether or not within the statute. Construction law and construction contracts have, for many years, been the subject of an unusual amount of attention in various official and semi-official inquiries and reports. These have included the Simon Report of 1944[2] and the Banwell Report of 1964.[3] These, now classic reports, were

---

[1] Housing Grants, Construction and Regeneration Act 1996 ss.104, 105.
[2] The placing and management of building contracts: HMSO.
[3] The placing and management of contracts for building and civil engineering work: HMSO.

concerned largely with public works undertaken by government and local authorities.

More recently, as private funding has grown in importance, inquiries and reports have concentrated on the efficiency of the construction industry. These have included the major study by a team lead by Sir Michael Latham, published in 1994.[4] This report in particular led to the setting up of a new tier of privately funded administration through the Construction Industry Board (CIB), which has been charged with implementation of the report through many new subsidiary bodies. These include the Construction Industry Council, the Construction Industry Employers' Council, the Construction Liaison Group, the Construction Clients' Forum and the Alliance of Construction Product Suppliers. Further reports have been produced under the direction of the CIB on a wide range of topics, including codes of practice for selection of sub-contractors and consultants and for education and training. The Latham Report led, via a further DOE consultation exercise, to the Housing Grants, etc. Act 1996 which contains new statutory rights and obligations in relation to construction contracts as defined in the Act. Many more references to this Act will appear later in this book. Other reports continue to appear, among which should be noted the report of Sir John Egan: "Re-thinking Construction".[5] Most recent is the *Government Construction Strategy*, launched in 2011 with the aim of securing a 15–20 per cent reduction in the cost of government construction projects. A *Construction Strategy Implementation Report* was issued in July 2012.[6] There have been a number of reviews of the working of the Housing Grants, etc., Act which led finally to the Local Democracy, Economic Development and Construction Act 2009,[7] which amends the mandatory payment measures and other provisions dealing with adjudication.[8]

Procurement and finance

At the root of all construction contract reform proposals lies procurement, that is, the methods by which construction projects are to be set up, financed and constructed. Procurement includes the separate or combined relationships between all or any of the participants, including promoters and financiers, designers and contractors. One aspect of procurement

---

[4] Constructing the Team: Joint review of procurement and contractual arrangements in the UK construction industry.
[5] Report of the Construction Task Force, 1998.
[6] *http://procurement.cabinetoffice.gov.uk/*.
[7] The 2009 Act came into force only on October 1, 2011.
[8] See Chs 2 (Adjudication) and 9 (Payment).

concerns the provision of design services, which are no longer to be assumed to emanate solely from separate consultants, but are increasingly combined with the construction process. Another aspect is the increasing insistence of financiers or funders on the minimisation of risk of cost or time over-runs, which had become a feature of construction projects. This aspect has been tackled in a number of ways, including the introduction of "partnering" arrangements, intended to exist alongside conventional legal obligations.[9] All procurement methods must now take account of the principles of project management, which is now to be seen as an addition to the traditional elements of design and construction.

Another generator of major change in construction contract practice during the last two decades has been the move from the financing of construction through capital investment to the new concept of "project finance". By this method an owner, instead of raising the capital and carrying out works on his own account, grants a "concession" to a project company, which then raises the finance and undertakes the project, taking the income over the concession period to repay the cost. Such projects thus include not just construction but the operation and management of facilities, which are notionally owned and operated by, but only later transferred to, the promoter (and thus known as Build-Own-Operate-Transfer or BOOT projects). Such schemes have proved popular in developing countries for the provision of major infrastrucure works. In the United Kingdom similar arrangements have been employed under the Private Finance Initiative (PFI) by which the user, generally a government department or public body, instead of paying the capital cost of the project, itself pays a fee for use of the facility over a defined concession period, usually including the provision of services which form part of the project. PFI is not free from controversy and concerns are now being raised as to the long-term cost compared to conventional funding based on government borrowing.[10]

A different approach, favoured by the United Kingdom government for maintenance and refurbishment work, is known as Prime Contracting, whereby a "contractor" undertakes single point responsibility, including management and design. All such new approaches, and more, must now be regarded as embraced within the term "construction contract", whether or not within the statutory definition. All of the aforementioned changes have resulted in much greater fluidity within the traditional parties to projects, with finance being provided sometimes by contractors and designers as well as the more conventional promoters, all of who then participate both in the risks and profits of a project. Those who provide

---

[9] See Ch.11.
[10] See Report of National Audit Office, *Lessons from PFI and other projects* (April 2011).

only finance, usually referred to as "lenders" or "funders", recover a pre-determined return on their investment, usually postponed until the project is completed and starting to earn revenue. They have a particular interest in ensuring that the project succeeds both technically and financially. A new generation of both ad hoc and standard form contracts now provides standard rights for funders, which will include the power to "step in" to the project in the event of non-performance by one of the primary contracting parties. The new fluidity in construction projects is also reflected in developments in the practice of assignment of rights and duties, particularly those in relation to design services.

With this brief introduction to the highlights of the world of construction law, this chapter now returns to basic matters and gives an account of the background legal systems on which construction law is founded. Later chapters will deal with more particular branches of the law including the principles of construction law and the various forms of contract which are used to regulate the performance of construction activities.

Nature of law

Many people now involved in construction law have no formal legal qualifications. It is appropriate therefore to include some general remarks about the nature of law and its underlying rules. Law is highly stratified, although there is much overlapping and many common principles. Thus, the same facts may give rise to issues under both civil law and criminal law. Civil law itself may involve disputes between individuals and issues which concern the State, for example where planning or tax matters are concerned. Health and safety involves both civil and criminal law.

A comparison of ways in which law differs from technology will also reveal some of the essential qualities of law. First, while there are always some technical problems which, for the time being perhaps, cannot be solved, the law must always find an answer to a dispute. No matter how complex the facts of a case, or how uncertain or novel the law, the appointed Tribunal must always provide an answer. Secondly, in engineering and building practice approximation and simplification play a large part: small light structures may be safely designed using approximate methods, while on large structures many more factors have to be taken into account. In law there is no such scale effect. The law applied to a claim for £100 is the same as that applied to a claim for £100 million. Simplification of the facts of a case does not simplify the law involved, and one may need to know every factual detail before any view can be given as to the probable legal result. Sometimes, cases heard by the House of Lords involve very modest sums of money, but turn on important issues of law.

STRATIFICATION OF LAW   5

Thirdly, while technology proceeds upon logical induction and deduction, the development of the common law is likely to be influenced by many other factors such as policy and practical considerations. Fourthly, while technical designs or construction will not always employ the latest theories and methods, legal rights and duties depend only upon what the law says at the relevant time. A change in statute law can mean that a man may do an act on one day with impunity but on the next at his peril. Common law, or case precedent, is rather different. In theory the judge states what the law is and has always been, so that a restatement applies retrospectively. The practical effect as to the future is, however, the same as a change in the law. Thus, when considering the law on some point, the very latest sources must be consulted and often likely future changes may need to be considered. It is by no means unknown for a court to come to a wrong decision because a recent change in statute law or recent case on the point was not brought to its attention.

STRATIFICATION OF LAW

English law is divided or stratified in a number of ways. It may be divided into substantive law and procedure. Substantive law refers to all the branches of law which define a person's rights and duties, such as contract, tort and crime. The substantive law determines in a particular case what rights a party possesses to recover a monetary loss which they have sustained. This may depend, for example, upon showing that the proposed defendant owed a duty in relation to that particular type of loss and was in breach of that duty (see Ch.14).

Procedure deals with the often complex rules by which the process of law is set in motion to enforce some substantive right or remedy. Procedure properly arises only when there is resort to legal action, but nevertheless it can be as important in practice as the substantive law. In the context of construction disputes, procedure includes arbitration and other dispute resolution processes, particularly now adjudication. A further division of law is into common law and statute law; that is, into judge-made law and legislation. Then there is another type of division between common law (used in a rather different sense) and equity, which is a distinction based upon the two great independent roots of English law. These latter two divisions are discussed separately in the following sections because they are fundamentally concerned with the sources of English law. While considering each of the divisions it should be borne in mind that they are not mutually exclusive. Statute law deals with procedure and substantive law; judge-made law comprises equity as well as common law, and so on.

Another division is between private law and public law, sometimes called administrative law. Private law relates to rights exercisable between individuals (including corporations and other legal entities). Public law, however, relates to the powers and duties exercisable by public bodies, which may affect the rights or expectations of individuals. The way in which public law rights may be enforced is significantly different to private rights, and consists essentially of applying to the courts for orders to review the actions of the public body in question. The enforcement of public law rights is dealt with below. Yet another division exists between so-called domestic and international law. International law itself falls into two distinct categories: private international law, which applies to disputes having an international character but concerning individuals or other legal entities; and public international law, which applies primarily to States. Private international law comprises the rules applied in a particular country to resolve conflict between the domestic law of that country and of other countries whose laws may affect a dispute. International law is discussed below.

The common law

English law is based upon the common law system. The common law means literally the law which was applied in common over all parts of the realm. It was created in the twelfth and thirteenth centuries by the King's judges and has been developed and handed down to the present time. The essential feature of the common law which distinguishes it from other legal systems, is that it is based on evolving precedent, with no written principles from which the precedent stems. The common law has thus been found to be a wonderfully flexible instrument, capable of rapid adaptation to wholly new circumstances without obvious strain. This is in contrast to problems which frequently occur under statutes, which may be found inadequate to cover some new situation. Likewise under the Civil Codes which constitute the basic laws of many foreign countries, it may be found that the code cannot be made to cover a new case, and the judge is unable to do anything other than to apply the existing code. The common law is fundamentally different in that judges in England and in other common law jurisdictions create law whenever they give a judgment. Successive cases thus progressively develop a body of "case law" on a particular topic. Judges under the common law system play a more significant constitutional role than under the civil law of other countries.

One effect of the spread of the English-speaking peoples from the sixteenth century onwards, was that they took with them their laws. As a result, by the nineteenth century there was established literally throughout the world, a greater common law, subject to the effect of local statute law in any particular state. Within the British Empire, and later the Commonwealth, this law was maintained as a common system by the establishment of the Privy Council (composed largely of members of the judicial committee of the House of Lords and Commonwealth judges) as the final court of appeal. This still applies in a limited number of countries although the major commonwealth countries have long since set up their own courts of final appeal, such as the High Court of Australia. This means that the law in such countries tends inevitably to diverge from English law with the passage of time. The United States, which has developed its own law for 200 years, has adopted some notable differences from English law, such as stricter liability under the law of tort. English courts will, however, take note of and draw guidance from decisions from other common law countries and, to an often greater extent, English decisions are regularly followed or adopted in many different countries. The common law can now be regarded as having many more sources than only English law.

In theory, the common law is not written down. It is stated each time a judgment is given at the end of a case, when the judge gives reasons for the legal principles embodied in his decision. In practice, the common law is found in the reports of judgments, and the law on any topic is to be discovered by reading those cases which turn on related facts. In some areas there will be only one or two cases, but in others there will be many dozens of cases, perhaps going back more than a century. There have been a number of attempts to "codify" the common law, that is, to write down in a statute the effect of the common law as it stands, with the object of making the law more accessible. This was done with considerable success at the end of the nineteenth century in a number of important commercial areas, including the of sale of goods (see Ch.7). In the twentieth century, codification and the general reform of areas of old and unsatisfactory law have generally been entrusted to the Law Commission. This is a statutory body which prepares reports, carries out consultations and makes proposals for amending legislation to codify and clarify the common law. It is then a matter for Parliament to accept their recommendations. One of the Law Commission Bills to be passed by Parliament in recent years is the Contracts (Rights of Third Parties) Act 1999.

Law reports

Not every case before the courts makes new law. Many cases depend simply upon conflicting versions of the facts. In the construction field, points of law are often involved, not least because the effect of complex conditions of contract is often uncertain. In addition to cases which turn on interpretation of contract conditions construction cases have, in recent years, become a major generator of new commercial law, having brought before the courts a number of new legal issues ranging from the application of the tort of negligence to defective buildings, to various principles of the law of contract, such as rights of third parties.

Judgments which do include issues of law or principle will usually be published in some form. This may be in one of the formal series of law reports, including those devoted to construction matters. A formal report will contain, verbatim, the essential parts (if not the whole) of the judge's decision, together with other information about the case. There may be a summary or headnote, and some reports provide a commentary on the case. It is, however, now increasingly common for judgments to be made available in their original form, exactly as delivered by the judges. Judgments in this form are widely available through various legal websites and can be traced and searched with ease. There are many such commercial websites and some free ones.

Given the importance of judgments it is curious that there is no official organisation to publish law reports. In mediaeval times official court "rolls" were maintained (in Latin) which are still the subject of legal research. From the sixteenth to the nineteenth century law reports were produced by private individuals, and published in series now know as the "English Reports". From about 1870 there has been a semi-official series called "The Law Reports," which are accepted as fully authoritative. There are several alternative series of formal "reports" such as the Weekly Law Reports (W.L.R.) and the All England Law Reports (All E.R.). Building cases will be found in many different series. In the formal Law Reports they may appear in Queen's Bench Reports (Q.B.), Chancery Reports (Ch.) or in Appeal Cases (A.C.). Commercial cases, including many important decisions in the field of arbitration and contract, appear in Lloyd's Reports (Lloyd's Rep.). The abbreviation in brackets is the proper citation for a particular series (the year, volume and page also being given) and this is how cases should be noted in formal or academic work.

In addition to these general reports, there are many reports and publications which contain cases relating to construction matters. Building Law Reports (B.L.R.) were the first, being issued since 1976, followed since 1985 by the Construction Law Reports (Con L.R.). Case reports in edited or summarised form appear in many periodicals such as the Construction Industry Law Letter (C.I.L.L.), Construction Law Journal (Const. L.J.) and Building Law Monthly (B.L.M.), as well as journals issued by professional institutions. Cases occasionally do not appear in any of the printed sources, but these may usually be found on one or more of the websites. All civil Court of Appeal cases and many High Court decisions are now reported on the internet with the citation EWCA or EWHC (England and Wales Court of Appeal or High Court) and can be accessed free on the BAILII (British and Irish Legal Information Institute) website at *http://www.bailii.org/ew/cases*. There is, in addition, increasing interest and interaction between UK and Commonwealth and other foreign sources. Cases from Australia, New Zealand, Canada Hong Kong and elsewhere regularly appear in the usual printed sources and are also easily accessible on the internet. Cases of current interest can be accessed free on the Commonwealth Legal Information Institute Website at *www.commonlii.org*, which also contains useful information about the different jurisdictions involved.

The now huge range of reported cases available raises the question of citation of authorities in textbooks. The leading texts on construction contracts are referred to below and these will provide guidance as to the leading authorities. However, an internet search will invariably produce many more cases and this may include cases on the specific point under consideration. For the text-book writer there has to be some limit and in this volume reference is made primarily to the leading cases which illustrate some point of importance. It should be noted, therefore, that more authorities will always be found in other textbooks and now on the internet.

A notable disadvantage of case law is that the law can change or develop only when a suitable case comes before the court. Thus, if a decision is given which is considered questionable, it remains an authority until reconsidered by a higher court, when it may be confirmed or over-ruled. Furthermore, the judges at all levels are concerned solely with stating what the common law is, and have no power to declare what it should be. Both these disadvantages are overcome by augmenting the common law through the separate system of statute law.

Statute law

While the judges declare and apply the common law, Parliament in its legislative capacity passes enactments to change the law. Since the seventeenth century Parliament has had supreme authority and can in theory make or unmake any law. The passing of a Bill through Parliament and the debate at different stages in its passage can be followed in the media and in *Hansard*. The end result is an officially printed document which states, in the words chosen by Parliament, the law on some topic or group of topics.

Once enacted and in force, the words of the statute are themselves law. However, there naturally arise situations where the words call for interpretation, and this is done by the courts. The opinions of the judges on the interpretation of statutes becomes a sub-branch of the common law, with which the statutes must be read to ascertain their meaning. A notable example of this process was s.1 of the Arbitration Act 1979 which, as drafted, appeared to be intended to facilitate appeals. The House of Lords, however, interpreted the section in *The Nema*[11] as restricting the right of appeal to exceptional cases. This piece of judicial interpretation or development is now codified in the Arbitration Act 1996 (see Ch.3). In the interpretation of statutory material the courts are not limited to the words of the statute itself. In *Pepper v Hart*,[12] the House of Lords confirmed that parliamentary debates and ministerial statements could be considered in order to determine the intention of the legislature, and recourse will often be had to the previous law to identify the "mischief" which the Act was intended to cure.[13]

Delegated legislation

In addition to statute law proper there has, particularly during the twentieth century, grown up a great body of delegated or sub-legislation. This is written not by Parliament itself, but by some other body or official to whom Parliament has given authority. The sub-legislators range from ministers of the government to statutory bodies such as local authorities. This delegated legislation goes under such names as rules, regulations or by-laws. It takes effect as though it were contained in the parent Act, which sets out the delegated power. As examples, the Building Act 1984 contains authority under which the Building Regulations are made; and the Housing Grants, Construction and Regeneration Act empowers the Minister to issue the Scheme for Construction Contracts. A great deal of day-to-day activity in industry generally and the construction industry in particular is covered by delegated legislation. In general this lays down more stringent and specific duties than those which are to be found in the common law.

Equity

In the division between common law and equity, each branch comprises both judge-made law (found in case reports) and statute law. The difference arises because before 1873, when the systems began to be jointly administered, there were two separate legal systems which operated in different courts. Equity was applied in the old Court of Chancery, located in Lincoln's Inn. Charles Dickens found much to criticise in the courts of early nineteenth century England but reserved the most biting

---

[11] *BTP Tioxide v Pioneer Shipping* [1982] A.C. 724.
[12] [1993] A.C. 593.
[13] *Heydon's Case* (1584) 3 Co. Rep 7a.

condemnation for the interminable delays of Chancery.[14] The delays in the Chancery Division are today no more than in the rest of the High Court.

The differences between law and equity are still of importance. One important distinction is that a common law remedy is said to be a right, whereas a remedy in equity is, theoretically, discretionary. It depends on the justice of the cause. The distinction may be illustrated by the consequences of a breach of contract. The common law remedy is damages, which will be awarded however unjustly the plaintiff has acted, and whether or not damages will make good the loss suffered. Alternatively, in equity the plaintiff can ask for the remedy of specific performance, that is, that the defendant be compelled to fulfil their obligation. But this will be available only under certain conditions, inter alia, that the plaintiff has acted fairly, that they have not delayed in seeking their remedy and that damages would not adequately compensate them.

Where to find the law

From the foregoing it may be said that the law proper is to be found only in law reports and in statutes, regulations and the like. However, textbooks and articles by academics, practitioners and (increasingly) by judges play an important part in stating the law. Legal writing has the function not only in presenting and commenting on source material, but of putting cases and legal materials in a wider context, perhaps an international one. Textbooks and articles published in reputable journals are often cited to the court and may be referred to in judgments with approval, giving the text added authority. The status of any book depends on the standing of its author and current editor. As a general rule, it is said that the courts pay less attention to the views of an author while they are still alive, although this rule is diminishing in importance as even legal writers live longer.

Legal textbooks are of several different kinds. Many were originally written by individuals on particular topics, although today it is rare for the original author or indeed any individual editor to be responsible for a complete textbook. In most fields there will be an authoritative text, often produced by a number or specialist editors. In the construction field, *Keating on Building Contacts* (currently the 9th edn) and *Hudson's Building and Engineering Contracts* (currently the 12th edn) are the best known and respected.[15] In the field of contracts, *Chitty on Contracts* (currently the 31st

---

[14] *Jarndyce v Jarndyce*, Bleak House.

[15] To these two major works, there should now be added texts by Richard Wilmot-Smith QC, *Construction Contracts, Law and Practice* and by Julian Bailey (CMS Cameron McKenna), *Construction Law*.

edn) has the advantage of being written by a large number of specialist in different fields and includes a chapter on "Construction Contracts".[16] Some works are published as a series, intended to create an encyclopaedia of law. The best known of these is *Halsbury's Laws of England*, first published in 31 volumes between 1907 and 1919. The current 5th edn is regularly updated with the addition of further volumes and annual supplements and is also available (as with many other texts) online. The companion work, *Halsbury's Statutes of England*, deals with legislation. Each topic in these works is written or edited by one or more specialist contributors. *Halsbury* is often cited in court as a convenient summary of the law.

THE COURTS

There are a number of different courts in which civil actions may be tried. A case will be heard at first instance in the High Court or in a County Court. Both the High Court and the County Court are to be found in different locations throughout the country. Appeals may then be brought to the Court of Appeal and finally to the Supreme Court (formerly House of Lords). The appeal courts generally sit only in London.

Courts of first instance

The High Court with its judges has three divisions: the Queen's Bench, the Chancery and the Family Division. Although each division adminis-ters the common law and equity and could theoretically deal with any matter, in practice a particular case will be assigned to one division. Matters concerning the construction industry come usually before the Queen's Bench Division, but occasionally before the Chancery Division. The Queen's Bench Division deals with most common law work, concerning claims based on contract and tort. The Chancery Division deals with contracts relating to land, company and partnership disputes, copyright and intellectual property.

Within the Queen's Bench Division of the High Court, there are two specialist divisions where construction cases may be found. The first is the Commercial Court where mercantile, banking, insurance and ship-ping cases are tried, before High Court judges assigned from the Queen's Bench Division. The second was for over a century known as the Official Referees' Court. In 1998 it was re-named the Technology and Construction Court (TCC). Here, matters specifically relating to the construction

---

[16] See Ch.37, by the author jointly with Vincent Moran QC.

industry are tried by judges appointed to deal with TCC business. In each case, an action may be started in the Commercial Court or in the TCC; or it may be started in the Queen's Bench Division and later transferred. For smaller civil cases trial may take place in the County Court by a Circuit Judge. Every district in the country has its local County Court. In the past, the County Courts have had a modest limit on their monetary jurisdiction. This has now gone and in theory the County Courts have unlimited jurisdiction. In practice, larger cases are started in the High Court, but may be transferred for trial. Government policy in recent years has been towards decentralisation with more civil work being tried in the County Courts. There are a number of provincial TCC courts where specialst judges will try TCC cases locally; and in London there has been established a "Business Court" at County Court level and a County Court Patents Court. While for many years distinct, the rules of procedure applied in the High Court and County Court have since 1999 been merged, the new rules being known as the Civil Procedure Rules (see Ch.2).

Appeals

After the hearing of a case at first instance either party may consider an appeal. From the High Court or the County Court there may be an appeal to the Court of Appeal. Changes to the rules introduced in 1998 mean that all appeals, whether on fact or law require permission (formerly called leave), either from the trial judge or from the Court of Appeal. This applies equally to TCC cases. An important difference between an appeal and the original trial or action, is that the appeal will usually be concerned solely with argument based on the submissions and evidence presented at the original trial. New evidence is admitted very rarely in the Court of Appeal. On an appeal, the court will give its own decision on matters of law. In issues of fact, however, while the Court of Appeal will review the written record of evidence given, it will usually attach weight to the trial judge's assessment of the witnesses.

After an appeal to the Court of Appeal, a further appeal may be available to the Supreme Court (formerly the Judicial Committee of House of Lords). Permission (or leave) is sparingly given. Supreme Court appeals are almost always on an important point of law. Where both the High Court and the Court of Appeal are bound by previous decisions it is possible to "leapfrog" by appealing direct from the High Court to the Supreme Court. Ordinarily, however, the Supreme Court requires issues to have been fully considered by the Court of Appeal and will not usually entertain a ground of appeal not raised in the court below.

Every court must apply statute law. However, with case law, courts are generally bound only by the decisions of higher courts, and to an extent by their own decisions. The Court of Appeal is bound by its own decisions (expressed in Latin as stare decisis). The same generally applies within a particular division of the High Court including the TCC. Where a court is bound by a previous decision, it may nevertheless be avoided if it is possible to "distinguish" the previous case from the one under consideration, or to confine its application to the particular facts of that case. This was done in the well-known case of *Junior Books v Veitchi*,[17] a decision of the House of Lords which was generally considered wrong but never overruled.

The law as stated by the Supreme Court is generally regarded as fixed and binding on all other courts in England and Wales (although not necessarily in Scotland or Northern Ireland which have their own courts and legal system). Nevertheless, in 1966, the House of Lords itself decided that it could depart from its own previous decisions. In the important case of *Murphy v Brentwood DC*[18] the House of Lords, consisting unusually in modern times of seven members including the then Lord Chancellor, decided to depart from the long-established authority of *Anns v London Borough of Merton*[19] and in doing so effectively reversed two decades of litigation. The House of Lords took another unprecedented step when it decided, in 1998, to set aside the decision of a different division of the House in the *Pinochet* case.[20] These were, however, exceptional events and, ordinarily, decisions of the House of Lords and now the Supreme Court are altered only by Statute.

PUBLIC LAW

Public law, sometimes called administrative law, concerns the exercise of powers and duties by public bodies, usually arising under statute. In some cases this may give rise to a direct right of action in civil law against the public body. For example, a claim for damages against a local authority alleging negligence in the enforcement of Building Regulations relates to such public law duties or powers. Where statutes do not provide expressly whether or not an individual who suffers damage may bring an action under the statute, it is necessary for the courts to decide whether the statute allows such a claim to be brought. The case of *Anns v London*

---

[17] [1983] A.C. 520.
[18] [1991] 1 A.C. 398.
[19] [1978] A.C. 728.
[20] *R v Bow Street Stipendiary Magistrate, ex p. Pinochet* [1999] 2 W.L.R. 272 and see *Dimes v Grand Junction Canal* below.

Borough of Merton[21] contains an analysis of whether the Building Regulations and their governing statutes create a right for individuals to sue. In that case the answer was affirmative but the question remains far from settled.

A different aspect of public law is the right of an individual who is affected by the exercise of such a power or duty to seek an order from the courts restraining or controlling the way in which the public body acts. This involves a distinct form of civil procedure known as Judicial Review. The law and procedure have become transformed in recent years. Formerly, only specific remedies were available but these have been enlarged by new statutory provisions and rules of court which now permit an individual to apply for the more general remedies of injunction or declaration. On an application for judicial review the court may also award damages to the applicant.[22]

Judicial review applies to an almost unlimited range of matters, including decisions of government ministers and local authorities, public bodies, inferior courts and tribunals, and covers all types of law, both civil and criminal, including, for example, the application of prison regulations. Perhaps the most numerous currently are claims relating to immigration decisions and to actions of local authorities in regard to housing or welfare. The procedure now laid down is straightforward. An applicant must first obtain permission of the court to proceed and this requires only the filing of a claim form. The decision to grant or refuse permission is now generally made by a single judge without a hearing, on a review of the papers. Where permission is refused, the application may be renewed in open court. If permission is granted, directions are given for a hearing against the body or authority which is the subject of the complaint and any other interested party. The rules require applications to be made promptly and in any event normally within three months of the relevant event. The court which deals with judicial review matters has been re-named the Administrative Court but is manned by judges from the High Court.

The principles of law which the courts apply on application for judicial review are common law principles developed by the courts themselves, principally in a series of cases following the introduction of the new procedure. On an application for judicial review, the court is not concerned with deciding whether it agrees with the decision or action of the relevant authority, nor is the process an appeal. The court is concerned only with restraining the wrongful exercise of public law powers and duties, and the grounds on which the court will intervene are limited. The principal grounds are the following:

[21] ibid.
[22] CPR, Pt.54.

(1) Want of excess of jurisdiction, which may include error of law.

(2) Irrationality, which is colloquially referred to as the "*Wednesbury*" principle following the leading case of *Associated Provincial Picturehouses v Wednesbury Corporation*.[23] In this case the local authority granted a licence for cinema performances on a Sunday on the condition that no children under 15 years of age should be admitted. The owners challenged the decision as an unreasonable exercise of discretion. Lord Greene M.R. said:

> "It is clear that the local authority are entrusted by Parliament with a decision on a matter which the knowledge and experience of that authority can best be trusted to deal with. The subject-matter with which the condition deals is one relevant for its consideration. They have considered it and come to a decision upon it. It is true to say that if a decision on a competent matter is so unreasonable that no reasonable authority could ever come to it, then the courts can interfere. ... It is not what the court considers unreasonable, a different thing altogether."

The principle is that the court will intervene if the decision is such that no authority properly directing itself on the relevant law and acting reasonably could have reached it.

(3) Procedural impropriety, which covers failure by a body to observe its own procedural rules. The main area of application here is in breach of the rules of natural justice. These rules broadly require public bodies to act fairly in the particular circumstances. For example, a person liable to be dismissed from a public office must be given a hearing, and must be notified of the allegations against them. A particular requirement of natural justice is that the person exercising a power or giving the decision must not have an interest in it. This was the subject of the celebrated case of *Dimes v Grand Junction Canal*[24] where, in the course of a long dispute between the company and an adjoining landowner, the Lord Chancellor gave a decision, after which it was found that he was a substantial shareholder in the company. The House of Lords subsequently expressed their views on the matter, Lord Campbell saying:

> "No one can suppose that Lord Cottenham could be, in the remotest degree, influenced by the interest that he had in this concern; but,

---

[23] [1948] 1 K.B. 223.
[24] (1852) 3 H.L. Cas. 794.

my Lords, it is of the last importance that the maxim that no man is to be a judge in his own cause should be held sacred. And that is not to be confined to a cause in which he is a party, but applies to a cause in which he has an interest. Since I have had the honour to be Chief Justice of the Court of Queen's Bench, we have again and again set aside proceedings in inferior tribunals because an individual, who had an interest in a case, took a part in the decision. And it will have a most salutary influence on these tribunals when it is known that this High Court of last resort, in a case in which the Lord Chancellor of England had an interest, considered that his decree on that account a decree not according to law, and was set aside. This will be a lesson to all inferior tribunals to take care not only that in their decrees they are not influenced by their personal interest, but to avoid the appearance of labouring under such an influence."

This case was applied in *Pinochet* (see above) where the House of Lords set aside their own judgment, holding that bias was not limited to financial interest but covered the situation of a judge who was a director of a charity controlled by a company which had an interest in the case before the court. The principles of judicial review are undergoing a general re-assessment by the courts in the light of the Human Rights Act 1998 and the above grounds will become modified in time.

There are many situations in which judicial review might be appropriate in the context of construction contracts, for example, decisions of local authorities regarding their tender lists. Such decisions are open to judicial review and may be set aside if appropriate grounds are established. For example, in *R. v London Borough of Enfield*[25] a decision to remove a contractor from the Council's tender list was set aside because the Borough had not complied with the appropriate procedural rules. In this case the contractor was under investigation for carrying out work to the house of a surveyor employed by Enfield, but no reasons had been given to the contractor. The decision about the tender list remained that of the Council and the court intervened only on the "*Wednesbury*" principle (see above). This area of law and practice has become greatly enlarged in the context of procurement, which is subject to European law.[26]

Proceeds of Crime Act 2002

While this book is concerned primarily with civil law, there are a number of areas in which construction activities may give rise to criminal sanctions. Health & Safety and Environment law are examples of this.

---

[25] (1989) 46 B.L.R. 1.
[26] See further Ch.6.

Construction projects, and particularly the management of construction claims and disputes, also involves financial transactions. It has always been the case that dishonesty concerning the pursuit of claims and other related activities may give rise to criminal liability, primarily under the law relating to bribery, deception or fraud (see below). These areas of law seemingly place no burden on practitioners beyond that of complying with normal professional and ethical standards. However, since February 2004, as a result of enactments following new European directives, all persons and bodies involved with financial transactions now owe positive duties to take action in relation to knowledge or suspicion of dealings in criminal property.

There are two relevant statutory measures: the Proceeds of Crime Act 2002 (POCA) and the Money Laundering Regulations 2003 (the Regulations), both of which came into force in early 2004. The POCA applies to all persons and provides as follows:

> "328(1) A person commits an offence if he enters into or becomes concerned in an arrangement which he knows or suspects facilitates (by whatever means) the acquisition, retention, use or control of criminal property by or on behalf of another person.
> (2)   That a person does not commit such an offence if:
> > (a)   He makes an authorised disclosure under Section 338 and (if the disclosure is made before he does the act mentioned in sub-section (1)) he has the appropriate consent. . . ."

Section 338 makes provision for authorised disclosure as mentioned in the section above, which means disclosure to the police through the National Criminal Investigation Service (NCIS) or to a Customs Officer. The fact that a person may know or suspect that particular property is criminal property by virtue of a confidential professional engagement is irrelevant for the purpose of the Act: POCA provides by s.338(4) that "an authorised disclosure is not to be taken to breach any restriction on the disclosure of information (however imposed)". Thus, the procedure envisaged by the Act is that where a person involved in a financial transaction suspects that sums of money may constitute crimnal property or the proceeds of crime, they may not continue their involvement in the transaction or arrangement without making an authorised disclosure and obtaining "appropriate consent" to proceed. Furthermore, while making the disclosure and seeking to obtain consent, the person concerned must not warn of their intention to make disclosure otherwise they commit an alternative offence under s.333 of POCA of "tipping off". The result is that a professional may find themselves obliged to suspend work without explanation while seeking consent to proceed.

In addition to POCA, the Regulations create a new "regulated" sector of businesses to which the Money Laundering Regulations apply. These include "legal services" which involve "participation" in financial transactions. The Regulations, where they apply, require adoption of detailed procedures for identification of clients, for record keeping and internal reporting. The application of the Regulations, which have become routinely familiar to all persons dealing with Bank accounts and any other financial transactions, are detailed and onerous. It is uncertain to what extent the Regulations (as opposed to POCA which applies to all persons) apply to Arbitrators, Mediators and Adjudicators. There is no doubt that they apply to legal practitioners and various professional bodies have responded to the new legislation by the issue of appropriate guidelines. Solicitors now regularly apply identification checks and maintain detailed records of financial transactions. The Bar Council has issued Guidance Notes by which barristers instructed by solicitors who comply with the regulations can themselves avoid further compliance. Whether arbitrators, adjudicators and mediators can rely on solicitors acting for the parties in the same way as barristers is uncertain. It is possible that an adjudicator, for example, may be obliged to suspend adjudication proceedings without explanation, pending application to NCIS, if they suspect that the subject matter of the Adjudication constitutes the proceeds of crime. A small number of cases have so far come before the courts through the Family Division, involving disputes about matrimonial property in which the claimant (wife) has disclosed to her solicitors the fact that part of the matrimonial property in dispute constitutes funds obtained by the defendant (husband) through VAT evasion. The question then arises whether the solicitor is obliged to suspend the proceedings and inform NCIS. Some relief was provided by the decision of the Court of Appeal in *Bowman v Fels*[27] where it was held that s.328 was not, in these circumstances, intended to affect the ordinary conduct of litigation by legal professionals; and if the section was applicable it did not override legal professional privilege. The position of other professionals, however, remains uncertain.

The Bribery Act 2010

This is another example of new UK legislation dealing with criminal law, following European directives, which persons and bodies involved in the construction industry must now become familiar with, particularly in relation to positive duties which it creates. The Bribery Act replaces all earlier laws concerning bribery and came into effect in July 2011. The Act creates the separate offences of bribery, being bribed, bribery of

[27] [2005] EWCA Civ 226.

foreign public officials and, perhaps having the most far reaching commercial effect, failure of a commercial organisation to prevent bribery on its behalf. Penalties, including imprisonment and unlimited fines, and follow the United Kingdom's ratification of the OECD Anti-Bribery Convention. The crime of bribery is defined as occurring when a person offers, gives or promises to give a "financial or other advantage" to another in exchange for improperly performing a "relevant function or activity".[28] The offence of being bribed is defined as requesting, accepting or agreeing to accept an advantage in exchange for improperly performing a function or activity.[29] Bribery of a foreign public official involves a promise or offer or giving of a financial advantage or other advantage to a foreign public official either directly or through a third party where such an advantage is not legitimately due.[30] In relation to a jurisdiction outside the United Kingdom, local practices or customs are to be disregarded unless they form part of the written law of the jurisdiction.[31]

The offence of failing to prevent bribery[32] applies to all commercial organisations which have business in the UK and applies not only to the organisation but to individuals and employees without the need to prove any intention or positive action. It is a defence, however, to show that the commercial organisation had in place "adequate procedures designed to prevent persons associated with (the organisation) from undertaking such conduct".[33] It is important to note that the Act covers offences committed anywhere in the world and allows for prosecution of an individual or company with links to the United Kingdom regardless of where the crime occurred. The Act undoubtedly imposes new burdens and duties on commercial companies, particularly those operating abroad where bribery and corruption are said to be common place. Bribery and corruption are also reported to have potentially devastating effects on the economies of poor countries particularly with reference to major construction projects supported by international finance arrangements.[34]

EUROPEAN COMMUNITY LAW

In addition to Common Law and Statute Law, the European Economic Community has, since 1973, formed a third independent and

---

[28] Section 1.
[29] Section 2.
[30] Section 6.
[31] Section 5.
[32] Section 7.
[33] Section 7(2).
[34] Refer particularly to the Transparency International Website.

increasingly major source of law applying throughout the United Kingdom. The foundation of the Community was and remains the Treaty of Rome, signed by the original six members in 1957. Membership of the Community has grown since then and continues to do so. Development in the 1980s was towards the Single European Market. This involved many radical harmonisation proposals, which included several related directly to construction. Among these were harmonising measures covering technical specifications and qualifications of professionals. The single market was implemented by the Maastricht Treaty, subsequently ratified (with some hesitation) by all Member States. The amendments to the Treaty of Rome included adoption of the new name of the European Community (EC). Successive treaties agreed in Amsterdam in 1997 and Nice in 2001 brought about further amendments to the Treaty of Rome which has (confusingly) had its articles regularly renumbered. The proposed European Constitution was rejected in referenda in 2004; some of these proposals are now embodied in the Lisbon Treaty, ratification of which was highly controversial.

The European treaties form a "framework" of measures, expressed as broad aims to be achieved, which are intended to be filled in by detailed measures. Areas for detailed legislation include: competition law and public procurement, health and safety, environment and consumer protection, and the more general harmonisation of the laws of Member States to the extent required for the functioning of the common market.

The EEC is unique in having achieved more in terms of inter-state integration than any comparable organisation in history. It operates in some ways as an international body and in other ways as a federal government although this concept is highly controversial in the United Kingdom. The principal institutions through which it operates are:

(1) The European Parliament, which is now a directly elected body which exercises defined powers, but falling far short of a full legislative assembly.

(2) The Council of Ministers, which is a fluctuating body of Ministers from individual Member States who meet when required and generally represent the interests of their own Governments. Presidency of the Council circulates among the Member States. When the Ministers are heads of state, the Council is referred to as the Council of Europe.

(3) The European Commission, which is the equivalent of the European Civil Service, headed by permanent Commissioners who, although drawn from the Member States, should

represent the interests of the Community, unlike the members of the Council. Every Member State contributes one Commissioner and the larger states, two.

(4) The European Court of Justice, which comprises judges appointed by each Member State and has the function of interpreting and applying Community law.

An early example of the effect of European law occurred in *Bulmer v Bollinger S.A.*[35] which became known as the *"Champagne"* case. The defendant French company claimed that the use of the word champagne to describe an English beverage contravened community law. The court was asked to refer the issue to the European Court of Justice under art.177 of the Treaty of Rome. Lord Denning prophetically described the effect of the new law:

> "The first and fundamental point is that the Treaty concerns only those matters which have a European element, that is to say, matters which affect people or property in the nine countries of the common market besides ourselves. The Treaty does not touch any of the matters which concern solely England and the people in it. These are still governed by English law. They are not affected by the Treaty. But when we come to matters with a European element, the Treaty is like an incoming tide. It flows into the estuaries and up the rivers. It cannot be held back. Parliament has decreed that the Treaty is henceforward to be part of our law. It is equal in force to any statute. . . . In future, in transactions which cross the frontiers, we must no longer speak and think of English law as something on its own. We must speak and think of the community law, of community rights and obligations, and we must give effect to them."

Lord Denning's judgment now requires qualification in two respects. First, community law is not simply of "equal force" to English statute or other law. It is clear that it must take precedence and any domestic rule running contrary to European law must give way to European law. Secondly, matters subject to Community law are not simply those where other members of the European Community are involved. Increasing areas of English domestic law and procedure are now governed or influenced by Community law. An important example of this is English domestic health and safety law relating to the design and construction of buildings (see Ch.16).

European legislation emanates from the Council and the European Commission, principally in the form either of a Regulation or a Directive. Regulations have direct binding force on all Member States and comprise fully detailed measures. Conversely, Directives specify the result to be achieved and are intended to be acted upon through individual legislation

[35] [1974] Ch. 401.

enacted in each Member State. Thus, in terms of English law, European Regulations comprise another category of delegated legislation which takes effect in England by virtue of s.2 of the European Communities Act 1972, which provides that rights and obligations created under the European treaties "are without further enactment to be given legal effect". In the case of Directives, however, they must be enacted by the United Kingdom Parliament in the form of a domestic Act. The fact that the United Kingdom Parliament has effectively bound itself by treaty to pass such enactments gives rise to the contention that Parliament has surrendered its power to Brussels. In legal terms, such powers were subordinated to the European legislative bodies upon accession to the Community, subject to the representation of the United Kingdom interests with the European Council and commission.

In later chapters reference is made to the principal elements of European Community law where they affect the construction industry, both here and within Europe.

HUMAN RIGHTS

This area of law has grown enormously in importance during the past two decades. The principal enactment covering the subject is the Human Rights Act 1998 which potentially affects all court proceedings and some other legal proceedings as well. The greatest impact of the new Act is in the field of criminal law, but the effects on civil court proceedings are still of great importance and the Act may also affect other forms of dispute resolution. In addition to human rights, current legislation also covers matters such as privacy, data protection and access to information.

Historically, the need to protect human rights has led to the adoption of written constitutions in civil law countries, and also in USA which has generated many "civil rights" issues. One of the early acts of the United Nations, in 1948, was the adoption of the Universal Declaration of Human Rights. In Europe, matters were taken further by establishing the Council of Europe, a body representing all European nations, separate from the European Community. The Council of Europe issued the European Convention on Human Rights, which was adopted by the United Kingdom in 1951 and is now incorporated into the constitution of most European countries. In the United Kingdom, however, no steps were taken to implement the Convention beyond the creation in 1966, of a direct right of action to the European Court of Human Rights in Strasbourg. As a result, judges in England began to apply, indirectly, the principles of the Convention as an aid to construction of legislation and the exercise of judicial discretion. It was not until 1998, however, that the Convention became part of English law. This posed a particular problem for the theory of parliamentary supremacy. A compromise was therefore adopted in the 1998 Act, by which statutes which were incompatible with the Convention were still be applied, but judges of the High Court (or above) were required to give a "declaration of incompatibility", in the expectation that Parliament would then amend the Act in question to conform with the Convention.

The Human Rights Act 1998 thus provides that a Court or Tribunal determining a question which has arisen in connection with Human Rights must apply the convention together with ECHR Case Law. Existing statutes, so far as possible are to be read and given effect in a way which is compatible with the Convention. For this purpose, the statutes are to be construed, not in accordance with existing principles of construction, where the words of the statute are pre-eminent, but in accordance with a "purposive" construction, having regard to the intentions of the Convention and construing it as a "living instrument". The interpretation of the Convention is intended to change with social requirements and not, as in the case of the Common Law, to remain fixed. Contrary to the position under the Common Law, older authority is given less, not more weight.

The Act provides that it is unlawful for a Public Authority to act in a way that is incompatible with a Convention right (s.6). "Public Authority" includes a Court or Tribunal. "Tribunal" is defined as meaning "any Tribunal in which legal proceedings may be brought". This may, therefore include both arbitration Tribunals and other Tribunals set up to determine legal rights. The Act primarily creates rights in favour of persons (which may include a company) against a Public Authority. The extent to which particular bodies are subject to rights under the convention is the subject of decisions in particular cases. Courts applying the Act have a wide range of remedies which they may grant, including damages in civil proceedings. Under the Convention, the ECHR may only deal with a matter after all domestic remedies, i.e. proceedings before the United Kingdom courts, have been exhausted.

The Human Rights Act 1998 incorporates the major parts (not the whole) of the original Convention together with subsequent protocols. The rights so incorporated include the right to liberty and security (art.5), the right to a fair trial (art.6), the right to respect for private and family life (art.8), the prohibition of discrimination (art.14) and the protection of property (First Protocol art.1).

The most important of these rights in civil law matters are arts 6 and 8. Article 6 expressly requires that, in the determination of their civil rights and obligations or of any criminal charge "everyone is entitled to a fair and public hearing within a reasonable time by an independent and impartial tribunal established by law". Article 8 provides that everyone has the right to respect for their private and family life, their home and correspondence. The following proviso is added:

> "There shall be no interference by a Public Authority with the exercise of this right except such as is in accordance with the law and is necessary in a democratic society in the interests of national security, public safety or the economic well-being of the country, for the prevention of disorder or crime, for the protection of health or morals, or for the protection of the rights and freedom of others."

Both the right to a fair trial and the right to privacy are qualified, not absolute, and issues concerning violation will involve balancing competing rights of the State and of other parties. For example, it has been held that the right to a fair trial was not violated by the German Federal Court of Justice when rejecting a civil appeal without an oral hearing and without giving judgment in open court, where this was expressly empowered by German law.[36]

In the case of privacy, the court held that there had been no breach of art.8 by the execution of a Search (Anton Pillar) Order made by the High Court in London against the complainant, requiring him to permit a search of his business premises (which were also his home) and to permit removal of films and documents in relation to an alleged breach of copyright.[37] Other, sometimes highly controversial cases, have held evidence obtained in breach of the Convention to be inadmissible. The Act and Convention have, so far, had no material effect on the processes of dispute resolution, primarily arbitration and adjudication, although the latter has survived more than one attempt to contend that the process was in breach of the respondent's human rights.[38] A challenge was brought to an arbitration clause contained in a license agreement issued by the FA to the agent representing Wayne Rooney. The agent contended the arbitration agreement did not comply with art.6 in that arbitration did not constitute a fair and public hearing (see above). The Court of Appeal rejected the challenge on the basis the agent had voluntarily entered into the agreement and had therefore waived the right to a public hearing.[39]

Data Protection

The Data Protection Act 1998 puts into effect European Directive 95/46/EC on the protection of individuals with regard to processing of

---

[36] *Axen v Germany* (1983) 6 EHRR 195, ECt HR.
[37] *Chappell v United Kingdom* (1989) 12 EHRR 1, ECt HR.
[38] See Ch.2.
[39] *Stretford v FA*, *The Times*, April 13, 2007.

personal data and the free movement of data. Schedule 1 to the Act sets out the eight "data protection principles" which include the requirement that personal data should be: (1) processed fairly and lawfully, (2) that personal data should be obtained only for one or more specified and lawful purposes, (3) that it should be adequate, relevant and not excessive, (4) where necessary, it should be kept up to date, (5) personal data is not to be kept for longer than necessary, (6) and is to be processed only in accordance with the Act, (7) measures are to be taken against unauthorised or unlawful processing, and (8) personal data is not to be transferred other than to countries having adequate protection of data. "Processing" of data refers to a wide range of operations but particularly to disclosure or dissemination. The control provided by the Act operates through "Data Controllers" who are the persons who determine the purposes for or the manner in which any personal data are to be processed. Data Controllers are required to be registered with the Data Protection Commissioner. Compliance with the Act is to be monitored by Data Protection Supervisors. Processing of data otherwise than as permitted by the Act or without proper registration is a criminal offence. Special safeguards are provided in respect of sensitive personal information such as that relating to political or religious opinions. The 1998 Act supersedes earlier legislation and now has a profound effect on the accumulation and use of data relating to individuals. In addition to control of processing, individuals are entitled to be informed about personal data held by Data Controllers. Wider rights of access to data affecting individuals have subsequently been created by other legislation, principally the Freedom of Information Act 2000 which creates a general right of access to information held by public authorities.

INTERNATIONAL CASES

International law has taken on new dimensions in the past two decades, in response to increasing international trade, such that a significant proportion of transactions is now no longer concerned only with English law. International law has two quite different roots: the first, sometimes called Public International Law, covers the legal principles applicable to a dispute between States, such as disagreement over off-shore oil and gas rights. The second, with which this section is concerned, is referred to as either Private International Law or Conflict of Laws, and deals with disputes between individuals or corporations involving different States, for example concerning a contract for construction work made with a foreign company to be performed in a third country. Public International Law was once regarded as having no connection with private international disputes. However, this is no longer so, and the principles and procedures of Public International Law may increasingly be found to apply in the case of ordinary commercial activities. Public International Law is dealt with principally in the context of international arbitration in a later chapter.[40]

Private international law issues usually raise one or more of three questions. First: does the forum chosen by the initiating party (claimant) have jurisdiction over the matter in issue; secondly, what national law should be applied to the merits of the dispute; and thirdly can the judgment, order or award of a foreign tribunal be enforced. In arbitration questions of procedure also arise and these are deal with later. This section deals with the first two questions. Enforcement internationally is dealt with in Ch.2. Matters of jurisdiction, choice of law and enforcement are part of the domestic law and therefore differences will exist between one state and another. It may be noted that in the context of international arbitration the questions of choice of law and enforcement remain of central importance; but issues of jurisdiction are usually concerned with the establishment of the tribunal rather than the forum.

Jurisdiction and procedure

The English courts normally assume jurisdiction to hear actions in contract and tort in three cases:

(1) where the defendant has been served with a claim form while present in England; a foreign company is regarded as being present if it carries on business here;

(2) where a defendant submits to the jurisdiction, for example, by bringing an action in the English courts;

(3) where the English court gives permission for a claim form to be served abroad so that the action can proceed, if necessary, in the absence of the defendant. The principal grounds on which permission to serve abroad may be given are:

  (i) that the defendant is normally resident in England;
  (ii) that the dispute arises from a tort where damage was sustained or the tort was committed in England; or

---

[40] See Ch.3.

(iii) that the dispute arises from a contract which was made or broken in England, governed by English law, or where the English courts are agreed to have jurisdiction.[41]

Where a foreign defendant is brought before the English courts they may apply for the proceedings to be stayed in favour of some more appropriate foreign court under the principle *forum non conveniens*. On such an application the court considers many matters including convenience to the parties and witnesses and the cost of the proceedings. In regard to disputes involving a party domiciled elsewhere in the European Community (and in some other European states) the question of jurisdiction is governed by the Civil Jurisdiction and Judgments Act 1982[42] which, inter alia, requires a defendant domiciled in a Member State to be sued in the courts of that state. Further, where proceedings are first brought in one Member State, the courts of a second Member State must stay any subsequent action, even where there is an exclusive jurisdiction agreement in favour of the second state.[43] The ECJ has held also that the same rule applies where the defendant is not based in a Member State, so that the English court could not stay an action brought in England in respect of an accident in Jamaica, where the courts of Jamaica would be more appropriate.[44]

If an English court accepts jurisdiction over a case, it will proceed to trial in the same way as a case with no foreign element, and generally English rules of procedure and evidence are applied. If it is an issue in the case, the court will decide which country's law is to be applied. If the applicable law is English law, the judge will treat the case as a domestic one and decide upon the law themselves. If the law to be applied is a foreign law, this is treated as a question of fact, the relevant provisions of that law being proved to the court by expert legal testimony. In the absence of proof to the contrary the English courts assume foreign law to be the same as English.

Choice of Law in international disputes

Despite a number of individual attempts, there has been no notable movement towards the harmonisation of different national laws. There have, however, been a number of initiatives aimed at identifying trans-national principles which can be applied to transactions between parties from different States. These include a now-published body of

---

[41] CPR Pt.6 III.
[42] Extended by the Civil Jurisdiction and Judgments Act 1991.
[43] *Erich Gasser v MISAT* (C-116/02) [2003] E.C.R.
[44] *Owusu v Jackson* (C-281/02) [2005] E.C.R.

general principles known as UNIDROIT[45] or trans-national commercial law. There have also been published "Principles of European Contract Law"[46] and there has been a separate initiative aimed at developing European construction law. All such principles or rules must be agreed by contract if they are to be applicable to a transaction and in the absence of agreement the ordinary rules of Conflict of Laws will apply. There are also international bodies which play a role in the law applicable to international transactions. As regards the United Kingdom, the most important is the European Community whose constitution and applicable legislation is dealt with above.[47] Despite the breadth of European Community law, contracts between community members remain essentially governed by the law of individual Member States and are tried in the courts of one of such Member States. The jurisdiction of the ECJ is limited to disputes concering European Community law and the "International Court of Justice", established under the UN Convention, deals only with disputes between states, according to public international law.

In the absence of choice of law by the parties, the Tribunal must determine what national law is to be applied to the merits of the dispute. This will depend on the nature of the dispute and different aspects may be governed by different laws. In the case of a dispute arising in contract, most aspects will be governed by the national law referred to as the "applicable law", the governing law or sometimes the "proper law" of the contract. This law is often specified in the contract as a specific national law such as the law of France or New York. Where the choice of the parties is unclear the court must interpret the contract to determine how it should be applied. In *Shamil Bank v Beximco Pharmaceuticals*[48] a loan contract was stated "subject to the principles of the glorious Sharia'a" to be governed by the laws of England. It was held that the reference to the Sharia'a was insufficiently specific and that the transaction was governed solely by English law. In the absence of express choice the proper law will be determined as the law of the country having the closest connection with the contract. This was formerly a matter of English common law but is now is governed by statute[49] which largely enacts the common law rule. The Act applies between EC States but the law so applied may be that of a non-EU State such as New York law. Ascertainment of the country having the closest connection depends on

[45] Roy Goode et al, *Transnational Commercial Law—International Instruments and Commentary*, 1st edn (2004).
[46] Prepared by the Commission on European Contract Law (1995), edited by Lando and Beale.
[47] See also Chs 6 and 16.
[48] [2004] 1 W.L.R. 1784.
[49] Contracts (Applicable Law) Act 1990.

various factors including where the contract was made, where it was to be performed and the place and currency of the payment. The applicable law, once identified, will determine such matters as whether a binding contract has been made, how the contract is to be construed, what is the effect of a misrepresentation, and whether an exclusion clause is valid. If a contract is illegal by the applicable law it is unenforceable in England. There are, however, matters which will be governed by a different law. A transfer of land is governed generally by the law of the place where the land is situated and many matters arising under a foreign construction contract will be subject to local laws, such as safety and employment regulations and taxation.

The FIDIC International Conditions of Contract provide for the national law governing the contract to be specified. It is now common for the governing law to be that of the promoter/owner, particularly where this is the location of the works. The choice of the law of a State within the developing world may itself pose problems if the particular law is silent as to principles of law assumed by the draftsmen of the contract. In such cases it may be necessary to add express provisions to the contract to attempt to ensure the enforceability of provisions intended to provide protection, such as clauses limiting the liability of the contractor or allowing the employer to deduct liquidated damages.

In the case of a dispute based on a duty in tort independent of contract, the conflict of laws arises only where the act complained of took place out of the jurisdiction. There is no concept of a "proper law" of tort. Under English law,[50] the law applied in a foreign tort action is an amalgam of the law of the place of commission and English law. In general, a tort committed abroad must be actionable both under English law and where the tort was committed. The law of the place of commission may affect the defences available but, more importantly, the damages recovered will be determined by English law. The same rule applies in the USA and explains why persons injured abroad by acts of US or British companies may seek to bring their claims in the US or English courts.

---

[50] See *Boys v Chaplin* [1971] A.C. 356.

CHAPTER 2

DISPUTE RESOLUTION—LITIGATION, ADJUDICATION AND ADR

Disputes in the construction industry can be resolved by a wide variety of means. Whatever means are employed, the coercive power of the courts always lies at the root, whether in terms of supporting the process or enforcing the result. This chapter therefore deals first with court procedure, and with the rules of evidence which apply to civil litigation. Chapter 3 covers Arbitration, which is the alternative means of final dispute resolution provided in the majority of construction contracts. Between these two formal systems lies a variety of procedures generally referred to as Alternative Dispute Resolution (ADR). These procedures are generally free from formal rules but can still generate a number of legal issues. Since 1998, construction contracts falling within the statutory definition have been subject to a mandatory right to have disputes resolved by rapid and temporarily binding adjudication. This right is available irrespective of any other provision in the contract and is used effectively to resolve a large proportion of construction disputes. Enforcement is, however, still subject to action in the courts.

COURT PROCEDURE

Procedure is a general term which covers the steps necessary to turn a legal right into a satisfied judgment of the court. Procedure can have a far-reaching effect on the course of an action, and the form of hearing may be dictated by the procedural steps which precede it. The pre-trial proceedings will usually extend over months, or even years. Appeals, enforcement of a judgment and the assessment and enforcement of costs orders may prolong the matter further after the trial. Procedure covers all these stages.

Procedure in the civil courts is governed by statutory rules. Those applying in the High Court since 1999 are known as the Civil Procedure Rules (CPR). The same Rules now apply throughout the civil courts, including the county courts. The rules themselves are contained in separate "Parts". The CPR implements recommendations of the Woolf report[1] and seeks to improve the accessibility, speed and efficiency of civil court procedure.

Basic steps in an action

The steps involved in a civil action in the Queen's Bench Division, where most cases concerning the construction industry will be brought, are as follows. An action is begun by the claimant issuing and serving a claim form (but subject to complying with the requirements of the pre-action protocol). The defendant must file a defence or an acknowledgement of service and also has the right to file a counterclaim. The claimant may then serve a reply and defence to any counterclaim. These are the pleadings in which the issues are defined. Disclosure and inspection of documents follows. Those preparing the case must collect the evidence which will be needed to prove the case or to discredit the opposing case. This will include both oral and documentary evidence. The culmination of this process is a hearing which results in a judgment. If there is no appeal, the matter is concluded by enforcement of the judgment and of any orders for the payment of costs. The principal steps are enlarged upon below.

Few actions proceed in the straightforward way suggested by the rules and in most cases there will be "interlocutory" battles over sensitive matters, often concerning the disclosure of documents. In fact the great majority of court actions which are commenced (well in excess of 90 per cent) are disposed of before reaching a hearing. Decisions by the court at an interlocutory stage are, in the Queen's Bench Division, given by a Master of the court. He is an official who exercises most of the powers of a judge including giving judgments and other decisions in advance of the hearing. This means that the judge often has no knowledge of a case until shortly before the trial. In cases before the Technology and Construction Court or in the Commercial Court, interlocutory orders are made by the trial judge, which has the advantage of ensuring familiarity with the issues before the start of the trial. The same advantage applies in an arbitration or adjudication.

Starting proceedings

A typical action is begun by issuing a claim form, which places the matter on the official record. This is, however, subject to compliance

---

[1] Access to Justice, 1994.

with any prescribed "pre-action protocol", which is dealt with further below. Particulars of the claim must either be contained within the claim form or served on the defendant within 14 days (CPR r.7.4). The Civil Procedure Rules are accompanied by detailed practice directions applying to each part of the rules. Since procedure in the High Court and County Court is now merged, the CPR practice direction provides for the appropriate court in which claims should be started. Claims are to be brought in the High Court only if they exceed a prescribed amount or in other special circumstances. Other rules provide for transfer between the courts. An innovation in the new rules is the requirement for a claim form and particulars to be accompanied by a "statement of truth" (CPR Pt 22) which may lead to sanctions in the case of a false statement made without honest belief in its truth. A copy of the claim form must be served on the defendant, either by delivering it to them personally, or by other means, such as service on their solicitor. It is now possible to "issue" a claim form through the internet via the Court Service website, which will effect service on the defendant. The general rule is that the defendant must be made aware of the proceedings against him. However, there is an important exception in respect of limited companies,[2] which may be served by leaving the writ at the registered office, or sending it there by post. A claim form must normally be served within the period of its initial validity, now four months from the date of issue. The court has power sparingly to extend the validity of a claim form. After they have been served with a claim the defendant must file either an admission, a defence or an acknowledgement of service. The defendant has the right to file a counterclaim with their defence, or it may be served later with the court's permission (CPR r.20.4).

Joinder of claims and parties

A particular advantage of litigation over arbitration and other dispute resolution methods is the ease with which other parties may be joined in an action. Arbitration proceedings are ordinarily limited to the two parties to the arbitration agreement (see Ch.3). Any number of claimants who have similar interests in the subject matter of the litigation may join together in a claim. Alternatively, they may issue separate claims which may be consolidated, that is, treated as a single action. Claims may be brought against two or more defendants. The general rule is that joinder is available where all the relevant claims can be conveniently disposed of in the same proceedings. The defendant may bring in another party as "sub-defendant" to the claim against them, and that party may similarly

---

[2] Companies Act 1985 s.725.

bring in other parties. All such subsidiary claims are known as "Pt 20 claims" under the CPR. Under this part of the rules, provision is also made for any party to bring counterclaims or claims for contribution or indemnity against any other party. The court then has an overriding discretion to decide, as part of the case management, which claims should be heard together and which should be severed and dealt with as separate proceedings. The important point is that all the parties who are ordered to take part in a hearing will be bound by the decision of the court. These advantages are not available in the case of arbitration.

Case management

At the heart of the new Civil Procedure Rules are extensive powers which the court is required to exercise in the interests of efficiency and expedition. Thus, at the outset of the proceedings, after the defendant has filed a defence, the court will inquire into the nature of the proceedings by issuing a questionnaire. The court has an initial power, whether on the application of a party or on its own initiative, to stay the proceedings for one month while the parties explore settlement. Thereafter the court will allocate the action (and may re-allocate if necessary) to one of the three "tracks" on the following basis:

(1) Small claims track (CPR Pt 27) is appropriate for claims not exceeding a prescribed amount.

(2) The fast track (CPR Pt 28) is the normal track for larger claims up to a prescribed amount where the trial is likely to last no more than one day and where expert evidence is limited to two experts per party.

(3) The multi-track (CPR Pt 29) is appropriate to any other claim.

Smaller and simpler claims are thus intended to be segregated off, leaving the bulk of substantial claims in the "multi-track". In relation to such claims, case management rules require the court to set up a time-table for steps leading up to the trial or to fix a case management conference for pre-trial review. The court is also required to fix the hearing date or the period in which the hearing is to take place as soon as practicable. These provisions are subject to the overriding case management powers of the court including general powers to decide which issues need full investigation and trial, and the order in which issues are to be resolved (CPR r.1.4). There is also power to strike out a statement of case where there has been a failure to comply with the rules and to the enter judg-ments in consequence (CPR r.3.4(2)). The stated objective of these procedural forms is to involve the court in a more pro-active role with a view to resolving the real issues between the parties quickly and efficiently.

Pleadings

The object of pleadings is to define the areas of dispute between the parties before the action comes to trial. A party will not normally be allowed to raise a matter at the trial unless they have pleaded it. Permission may be given to amend pleadings even during the trial, but this will invariably involve payment of the costs thrown away by the amendment; and an amendment may be refused where the other party will be prejudiced beyond the incurring of additional costs. The Civil Procedure Rules contain provisions as to the content of pleadings (CPR Pt 16). The claim should contain a concise statement of the facts relied upon, but not the evidence by which they will be proved; and matters of law should not normally be pleaded. These rules, however, are often difficult to satisfy and it is not uncommon in construction cases to find both matters of law and evidence included in pleadings. A useful rubric both for pleaders and for judges and arbitrators is that any matter which the opposing party needs to answer positively should be pleaded. Where a party contends that a pleading served on them does not disclose the case being made, there may be a request for "Further Information" or Clarification (CPR Pt 18).

Global claims

In construction cases it is often appropriate to plead facts in great detail. Often, there will be a dispute over the extent to which the party asserting a claim must give detailed information in advance of the hearing. This has given rise to a particular type of procedural dispute concerning "global" or "rolled up" claims. The issues often concern the extent to which the claiming party must specify in their pleading the causal connection alleged to exist between the causes of action relied upon and the damages or other relief (such as extension of time) claimed. In *Crosby v Portland UDC*[3] Donaldson J. upheld the award of an arbitrator on a global claim in the following terms:

> "Since, however, the extent of the extra cost incurred depends upon an extremely complex interaction between the consequences of the various denials, suspensions and variations, it may well be difficult or even

[3] [1967] 5 B.L.R. 121.

impossible to make an accurate apportionment of the total extra cost between the several causative elements. An artificial apportionment could of course have been made: but why (the contractor asks) should the arbitrator make an apportionment which has no basis in reality? I can see no answer to this question . . . provided (the arbitrator) ensures that there is no duplication, I can see no reason why he should not recognise the realities of the situation and make individual awards in respect of those parts of individual items of the claim which can be dealt with in isolation and a supplementary award in respect of the remainder of these claims as a composite whole."

This issue was taken up in a later Hong Kong case before the Privy Council. In *Wharf Properties v Eric Cumine*[4] it was said that the *Crosby* case had:

"no bearing upon the obligation of a plaintiff to plead his case with such particularity as is sufficient to álert the opposite party to the case which is going to be made against him at the trial. (The defendants) are concerned at this stage . . . with the specification of the factual consequences of the breaches pleaded in terms of periods of delay. The failure even to attempt to specify any discernible nexus between the wrong alleged and the consequent delay provides, to use Mr Thomas' phrase no agenda for trial."

The Privy Council upheld the decision that the claim be struck out as embarrassing the fair trial of the action or as an abuse of the process of the court. As a result of this decision, attempts are usually made to provide seemingly adequate details of the causation alleged between the individual grounds of claim and the damages or financial consequences alleged. This issue does, however, leave a number of matters still within the discretion of a tribunal dealing with such a claim. How far should the party asserting a claim be pressed to give information which it may be artificial or even impossible to give with precision? Also where full details are not given, should the party bringing the claim be permitted to call evidence or to "unroll" the claim at trial? The issue arose in the Scottish case of *John Doyle Construction v Laing Management*.[5] The court, while accepting the principle that a global claim would be undermined if an event which played a part in causation of the global loss was not proved to be the defendant's responsibility, held that the claim should not be struck out since it was possible that the claim might succeed, and if it did not a lesser claim might be open to the claimant within the existing pleadings. More recently in *Walter Lilly v Giles Mackay*,[6] Akenhead J. accepted that there was nothing objectionable to a global claim in principle and that such a claim could be founded on additional

[4] (1991) 52 B.L.R. 1.
[5] [2002] B.L.R. 393.
[6] *Walter Lilly v Giles Mackay and DMW Developments* [2012] EWHC 1773.

cost incurred, provided it was established that there were no other causes of the loss. Although the power to strike out an embarrassing pleading is available only in court,[7] global claims raise the same problems for arbitrators, whose powers include refusing to allow a party to introduce a case of which it has previously failed to give proper details.

Schedules and Annexures

A common feature of construction and other technical litigation, as well as arbitration, is the use of schedules to plead details. This covers both the pleading of facts and of damages or other quantum particulars. The point of a schedule is that it allows otherwise indigestible prose to be split into short entries under common headings. It can also be used to set out the case of two or more parties on the same sheet of paper. It is important to devise the most appropriate form for the schedule, but once set up, they can be of great use in collecting together details in the most convenient form. Schedules were first used in Official Referees' building defects cases and were named "Scott Schedules" after a former Official Referee. In modern use, schedules lend themselves well to production by word processors which can be used to produce conveniently formatted tables or spread sheets.

Pleadings in substantial cases, whether in court, arbitration or adjudication now tend to include details and significant documents in the form of Annexes. This is partly the product of the universal availability of electronic processing and copying. However, it offers the real advantage of providing much more information about a claim or response than has been possible in the past. Unfortunately this increased volume of paper has not diminished the appetite of opposing lawyers to request yet further information and "pleadings" and now tends to comprise substantial volumes of documentation. The advantage is that the judge, arbitrator or adjudicator will have a substantial knowledge of the case at the outset, once the pleadings have been read and digested.

Counterclaim and set-off

A defendant, in addition to serving a defence to the claim made against them, may serve a counterclaim against the party bringing the claim. The counterclaim need not relate to the subject matter of the original claim. Typically in construction litigation, a contractor's claim for payment may be met with a counterclaim for damages for delay; or for damages for defects in the work, which need not be that for which payment is

---

[7] CPR r.3.4 (2).

being claimed. An important question in relation to a counterclaim is whether it ranks merely as a separate cross-action or whether the defendant may rely on it as a defence to the original claim. A counter-claim which operates as a defence is called a set-off. A cross-claim need not arise out of the same transaction to rank as a set-off; but there must be a sufficiently close connection with the original claim. In *Hanak v Green*[8] a builder who was sued for defective work was held entitled to set-off a greater sum found due upon his counterclaim for payment and damages. Sellers L.J. said:

> "Some counter-claims might be quite incompatible with a plaintiff's claim, in no way connected with it and wholly unsuitable to be used as a set-off. But the present class of action involving building or repairs, extras and incidental work so often leads to cross-claims for bad or unfinished work, delay or other breaches of contract, that a set-off would normally prove just and convenient, and in practice, I should have thought, has often been applied, as indeed it was in the referee's report. It would serve to reduce litigation and the consequent costs. I would not be astute to restrict the right but rather to develop it and discourage litigation when no or little monetary benefit ensues on balance. It cannot, as I see it, make any difference which side commences proceedings in which cross-claims arise. If there is a set-off at all each claim goes against the other and either extinguishes it or reduces it."

This type of set-off is referred to as "equitable" set-off. In *Gilbert-Ash v Modern Engineering*[9] Lord Diplock described the different forms of set-off:

> "The principle is that when the buyer of the goods or the person for whom the work has been done is sued by the seller or contractor for the price it is competent for the defendant . . . not to set-off, by a proceeding in the nature of a cross-action, the amount of damages which he sustained by a breach of the contract, but simply to defend himself by showing how much less the subject matter of the action was worth by reason of the breach of contract . . .[10] This is a remedy which the common law provides for breaches of warranty and contracts for sale of goods and for work and labour. It is restricted to contracts of these types. It is available as of right to a party to such a contract. It does not lie within the discretion of the courts to withhold it. It is independent of the doctrine of equitable set-off developed by the court of Chancery to afford similar relief in appropriate cases to parties to other types of contract . . .".

Thus, a defendant may rely on a "common law" set-off to reduce or extinguish the value of the goods or services for which payment is

[8] [1958] 2 Q.B. 9.
[9] [1974] A.C. 689.
[10] *Mondel v Steel* (1841) 1 B.L.R. 108.

claimed in the action. Alternatively, they may bring a cross-action and rely on equitable set-off provided that the claim and cross-claim are sufficiently related. Where a claim in extinguished by set-off this may have an important effect on the right to recover costs, as in *Hanak v Green* where the defendant, who recovered more than the claimant, was awarded the costs. Another similar but distinct remedy occasionally relied on is abatement.[11] As an example of set-off in action, in *Safeway v Interserve*[12] a contractor was sued under a form of warranty by the owner for the cost of rectifying defects. The warranty limited the contractor's liability to that which was owed to the developer with whom the contractor had contracted, and who owed the contractor sums exceeding the owner's claims. The contractor was held to be entitled to set-off the unpaid sums to extinguish his liability under the warranty.

Where a contract is subject to the Housing Grants, etc. Act 1996, the right to withhold payment after the final date for payment is conditional upon notice being given as to the amount to be withheld and the grounds for withholding payment. Notice must be given within a prescribed period: in the absence of agreement, the Scheme for Construction Contracts provides for notice not later than seven days before the final date for payment, which is to be 17 days from the date that payment becomes due.[13] A number of enforcement cases have dealt with the question of whether there may be a set-off in the absence of withholding notice, where the contract so provides (see further below).

Remedies

The claim, and any counterclaim, must expressly state the remedy sought. In contract and tort actions the remedy is usually damages, that is, the payment of a sum of money in compensation. But there are other remedies, which may be appropriate in different circumstances, such as an injunction, specific performance, or rectification of a contract. Damages are sometimes categorised as general or special. General damages are claimed where the claimant has suffered loss which cannot be calculated in terms of money, for example, damages for pain and suffering. General damages must be assessed by the judge and, conventionally, no specific sum is claimed in the pleading (unlike the practice in USA where general damages are specified). Special damages are those which can be calculated in money as an actual or prospective loss. In construction cases it is rare to find claims for damages which cannot be

---

[11] See *Hutchinson v Harris* (1978) 10 B.L.R. 19.
[12] [2005] EWHC 3085.
[13] Scheme for Construction Contracts, Part II, paras 8, 10.

calculated. The difficulty is usually in terms of how the damages, for example for disruption of the progress of construction works, should be calculated.[14] There is no rule as to how a claim for damages should be assessed. There are often alternative approaches, for example, between claiming wasted expenditure or loss of anticipated profit. It is a matter for the claimant (or counter-claimant) to specify the claim they wish to pursue and there is nothing to prevent alternative damages claims being pleaded. The claimant must specify which is the primary claim, but may rely on a second or third alternative in the event that the preferred claim does not succeed. "Liquidated" damages, in the context of a construction contract, refers to specified sums payable in defined circumstances, particularly for delay in completion. They must be claimed by the employer as a specific remedy. The contractor, in such a case, may claim for an extension of time and for the consequent return of liquidated damages deducted.

Where the parties wish simply to establish their legal rights without claiming monetary relief, it may be appropriate to claim a "declaration". They may do so, for example, where there is a dispute as to the meaning of some term of the contract or as to whether some action taken by one party was contractually justified.

Injunction

This is an equitable remedy, granted in the discretion of the court, in circumstances where a party to existing or intended proceedings contends that the other party should be restrained from taking some threatened action or, rarely, ordered to take some action which it threatens not to take. The latter is called a "mandatory" injunction and, in the context of a contract, is equivalent to ordering specific performance, a remedy which is seldom granted. The procedure involves three stages: first there may be an application for an interim injunction which, in an emergency, may be made without notice to the other party; secondly, there must be an application on notice to continue the interim injunction; and thirdly there will be a full trial to determine whether a permanent injunction should be issued.

The leading case is the House of Lords' decision in *American Cyanamid v Ethicon*,[15] where it was held the court should reach its decision on the balance of convenience, and in doing so should consider whether damages would be an adequate remedy as an alternative to injunction, and this would include the ability of the respondent to pay

---

[14] See "global" claims above.
[15] [1975] A.C. 396.

damages if the claim ultimately succeeded. In *Redland Bricks v Morris*,[16] the House of Lords discharged an injunction which had been granted against the brick company whose excavations threatened the stability of Mr Morris' land. The injunction ordered the company to restore support to the land; but the court held the company had not behaved unreasonably, damages would be an adequate remedy and a mandatory injunction should not be ordered where the work required could not be specified precisely.

In *Ferrara Quay v Carillion Construction*,[17] the applicant employer under a JCT Design and Build Contract (which was a special purpose vehicle in receipt of outside of funding) obtained an interim injunction to restrain the contractor from terminating its employment where the employer had defaulted and appeared likely to default further in making interim payments due. On a full hearing of the application the court discharged the interim injunction, holding that it could not be concluded that Carillion would be acting unreasonably in terminating its employment; the employer remained un-creditworthy and the contractor should not be restrained.

Subsequent claims

It sometimes happens that a construction project leads to more than one set of proceedings being brought between the same parties, whether in the form of two separate arbitrations, two sets of court proceedings or some combination. A problem can arise where a decision is given in earlier proceedings which bears on matters in issue in subsequent proceedings. The same principle can apply where different claims in the same proceedings are dealt with by way of an interim award or judgment on preliminary issues.

The broad principle which applies in all these circumstances is that a claimant may not bring a subsequent claim which involves re-opening a matter already decided. This principle is referred to as issue estoppel or res judicata. Nor may a claimant bring a claim which seeks some relief which was or should have been included in the claim already decided. The application is often far from simple. In *Conquer v Boot*[18] the defendant builder had contracted to build a bungalow for the claimant, who brought an action for breach of contract to complete in a good and workmanlike manner. After recovering damages in this action, the claimant then brought another action in identical terms but alleging

[16] [1990] A.C. 652.
[17] [2009] B.L.R. 367.
[18] [1928] 2 K.B. 336.

failure to build with proper materials. The Divisional Court held the claimant not entitled to bring the second action. Talbot J. held:

> "The contract is an entire contract. No claim for payment could have been made by the defendant unless and until he had finished the bungalow. There is one contract and one promise to be performed at one time, although no doubt the defendant may have failed to perform it in one or in many respects. There may of course be many promises in one contract, the breach of each of which is a separate cause of action . . . here there is but one promise, to complete the bungalow."

Another consequence is that damages or relief arising from any cause of action must be claimed once and for all. It follows that any claim for damages whether in tort of for breach of contract, must claim for all future anticipated loss, which will be assessed at the date of the hearing. For example, in the case of *Batty v Metropolitan Realisations*[19] the court awarded damages in respect of a house which was deemed not fit for habitation because it had been built at the top of a potentially unstable slope. The claimant recovered for the anticipated loss even though it had not collapsed and, apparently, did not subsequently collapse. There is no mechanism whereby either claimant or defendant can ask for damages, once assessed, to be reassessed in the light of subsequent facts once a judgment becomes final. One of the few exceptions is in the case of claims for damages due to withdrawal of support to land where the rule is that the claimant may recover only the damage actually suffered, even though other damage may be imminent.[20] A further exception exists in respect of personal injury cases where the court can, in particular circumstances, defer final judgment until the extent of the claimant's injury is known.

When bringing claims under a construction contract, consideration must be given to whether different causes of action exist which allow separate claims to be brought. In many cases, the terms of the contract will permit such separate claims, but the claimant can recover their loss once only. If, therefore, the separate claims are simply alternative ways of recovering the same loss, they must be pleaded as alternatives. The claimant must also exercise caution in ensuring that all damages or remedies arising from the causes of action relied on are claimed for, otherwise they may be lost.

Another aspect of this issue arises when a claiming party elects to pursue some but not all of the parties who might potentially be liable for

---

[19] [1978] Q.B. 554.
[20] *Darley Main Colliery v Mitchell* (1886) 11 App. Cas. 127.

a loss. In *Aldi Stores v WSP Group and Aspinwall*[21] the claimant had previously brought an action against design and build contractors for settlement damage to a retail store. The action was pursued to judgment and subsequent enforcement against insurers. The defendant had joined specialist engineers and consultants as third parties but the claimant elected not to join them as defendants. When the insurers of the defendant successfully disputed liability to indemnify, the claimant sought to bring fresh proceedings against the third parties who could have, but had not been, joined in the first action. The judge struck the action out as an abuse, but the Court of Appeal reinstated the action, holding that the claimant had acted properly and that it was not abusive to bring a second action in the circumstances.

Judgments without trial

There are several instances in which the court may decide some issues in a case or may make orders, which have the effect of terminating the case, without waiting for the trial. First, there are a number of circum-stances in which one party may invoke the power of the court to terminate or strike out the case of the other party who is in default. For example, where the defendant fails to serve a defence to the claim,[22] judgment may be entered. Such "default" judgment may be set aside by the court, but but the need to comply with a pre-action protocol should reduce the number of claims to which there is no real defence. Where one party is ordered to do something, for example, to serve further information or to give disclosure, the court may in an appropriate case order that the claim or defence of that party be struck out in default. Where a claimant (or a defendant who has a counterclaim) fails to take any action to bring the claim to trial and the other party suffers prejudice, the court has an inherent power to strike out that claim for want of prosecution, which is backed up by rules of court.[23]

Summary judgment

The claimant may apply to the court for judgment on their claim (or the defendant on their counterclaim) on the ground that there is no sufficient defence. There are two sections of the CPR which may be relied on. Under CPR Pt 24, the claimant may apply for summary judgment on the claim or some particular part of it, on the ground that the

---

[21] [2007] EWCA Civ 1260.
[22] CPR r.15.3 and Pt 12.
[23] CPR r.3.4(2).

defendant has no real prospect of successfully defending the claim or issue. If the defendant fails to satisfy the court that there is an issue which ought to be tried, the claimant will be entitled to immediate judgment on the claim or part of the claim in question. Part 24 applies equally to the defendant, who may similarly apply to the court for judgment on the ground that the claimant has no real prospect of succeeding on the claim or issue.

Frequently, the only dispute on an application by a claimant for summary for judgment will be whether the defendant can establish a credible counterclaim which they are entitled to set-off against the sum otherwise due. In a construction dispute, where a valid certificate has been issued for payments to the contractor, the employer may seek to counter an application for summary judgment by setting up a counterclaim, for example, for delay or defects in the work done.[24] An alternative open to claimants is to apply for an interim payment under CPR Pt 25 if they can satisfy the court that, if the claim went to trial, there would be judgment for a substantial amount of money, after taking into account any cross-claim.[25]

The procedures under CPR Pts 24 and 25 are intended to facilitate "cash flow" and to avoid or deter fully contested litigation. These measures will usually take several months to reach court. In the case of construction contracts falling within the Housing Grants, Construction and Regeneration Act 1996, these procedures are effectively superseded by adjudication which will be conducted in accordance with a generally shorter timescale. A judgment of the court, however, is final (subject to any appeal) and more readily enforced than an adjudication decision.

Disclosure of documents

An important step in any proceedings, whether in court or arbitration, is disclosure and inspection of documents, when each side must disclose to the other documents which are relevant to the dispute. The Civil Procedure Rules require that a party disclose documents which are or have been in their custody or power. This includes documents which have been destroyed or may be in the physical custody of some other person. The obligation of disclosure may be backed up by orders of the court, which may relate to classes or specific documents.[26] The court also has powers to order pre-action disclosure.[27] The documents disclosed

---

[24] Subject to the payment provisions of the Housing Grants etc Act, as amended—see Ch.9.
[25] CPR r.25.7(1)(c).
[26] CPR r.31.12.
[27] CPR r 31.16 and s.33 of the Senior Courts Act 1981.

must be listed and described, even where they cannot be produced. Documents may be withheld on the ground of privilege. This covers documents which came into existence as a result of the dispute, including experts' reports, letters between the party and their solicitor and legal advice provided to the client. In the recent landmark decision of the House of Lords in *Three Rivers District Council v Bank of England*[28] it was held that privilege attached to advice previously given by solicitors to the Bank in relation to an earlier Inquiry into the collapse of BCCI, formed the background to the litigation. The decision reaffirms the broad scope of privilege which arises between the lawyer and their client.

Conversely, legal professional privilege is available only where legal advice is given by a professional who is engaged to act in that capacity. In *Walter Lilly v Giles Mckay*,[29] the defendant had engaged a firm of claims advisers who employed barristers and solicitors who had given advice in relation to a potential dispute. It was held in the TCC that documents exchanged with the claims adviser, including legal advice, did not attract legal professional privilege and must be disclosed.

One of the inherent problems created by the rules of discovery is the potentially huge burden of documentation which must be considered and copied in major commercial disputes, particularly those relating to construction projects. This may involve examining hundreds of files to extract relevant documents for disclosure and copying. The process is today made even more complex and lengthy by the need additionally to disclose electronic documents and records. Such disclosure is often requested in the form of access to the hard drive of the personal computers of particular individuals. The courts have in the past given a wide interpretation to the concept of "relevance". The current rules, however, generally require only "standard disclosure" which include the following:

(a) documents on which a party relies,

(b) documents which:

 (i) adversely affect their own case;
 (ii) adversely affect another party's case; or
 (iii) support another party's case.[30]

The CPR are also underpinned by the overriding objectives of proportionality and saving expense[31] which may lead the court to restrict the

[28] [2004] UKHL 48.
[29] [2012] EWHC 649.
[30] CPR r 31.6.
[31] CPR r.1.1.

extent of disclosure in appropriate cases. It is also provided that the court may order, or the parties agree, that disclosure be dispensed. This is, however, very rare and in most cases each party will wish to see the documents produced by the other in order to assess the strength of the case, prior to possible settlement.

There have been a number attempts to reduce the burden of discovery and the consequent costs of litigation. In arbitration, the former power of the court to order disclosure has been removed so that the extent of disclosure is now a matter for the discretion of the arbitrator or agreement of the parties. Civil law countries, that is most countries outside the Commonwealth and the United States of America, have no tradition of disclosure nor of conducting litigation by seeking to undermine the case of the adversary. In these jurisdictions, the parties are generally not obliged to produce documents which are against their interest and the documents produced are usually limited to those relied on to support the claim together with specified documents which may be ordered to be produced. These differences of approach explain why both litigation and arbitration under the civil law systems is said to be much quicker (and cheaper) than under the common law systems. None of the proposed civil justice reforms, including the Woolf report, have gone so far as to propose such fundamental changes.

As part of its inherent power to make orders for the production and preservation of documents, the court may make an order empowering the claimant to enter the defendant's premises to search for and seize material documents and articles. This is known as a Search Order (CPR r.25.1(h)).[32] Such an order may be made in circumstances where there is a real possibility that the defendant might destroy the material. The court will, if necessary, make an order before any proceedings are started so that the intended defendant has no notice of what is proposed. The claimant must make full disclosure of all material facts. The order usually requires the defendant to permit the claimant's representatives to enter, search for and remove to safe custody relevant documents or other evidence. Orders have been made in cases involving patent infringement and video piracy.

When each side has given disclosure it is necessary to collate the documents into a bundle for use at the trial. Increasingly, in order to save costs, the parties do not prepare a combined bundle but rely on the separate bundles generated as part of the case preparation. Different categories of documents may be put in separate bundles and frequently parties will rely on Annexures originally prepared as part of the pleadings. The objective should be to make the documents as accessible as

---

[32] Formerly known by the originating case of *Anton Piller K.G. v Manufacturing Processes* [1976] Ch. 55.

possible while avoiding unnecessary costs. Occasionally trial documents, both in court and in arbitration, are produced in electronic format. This requires the availability of appropriate hearing-room equipment and there are, currently, few locations which provide such a service.

The hearing

English trial procedure is still based on the adversary system. The court has no duty and very little power itself to investigate the issues. It is limited to making decisions on the cases presented by the parties. A hearing usually starts with the claimant's representative making an opening address outlining the case and the issues to be decided. It is invariably the practice to produce a written "skeleton" or note of the case for the assistance of the Tribunal, and the defendant may do likewise (for appeals this is expressly required by the rules[33]). Time limits are increasingly used in litigation at all levels as well as in arbitration and this is likely to apply to the opening address. After the claimant, the defendant's representative may be invited to open their case, and it is not unusual for the defendant to be asked to address the court (or arbitral tribunal) first. The modern principle of flexibility means that advocates must be prepared to accommodate the wishes of the Tribunal.

After the openings, the claimant must call their evidence, usually witnesses of fact first and then experts. Then the defendant calls their witnesses. Frequently the parties may agree or the Tribunal may direct that all factual witnesses are taken first, to be followed by expert witnesses. Statements of all witnesses are, today, invariably presented in writing. The way evidence is presented to a court or tribunal is enlarged on below. After the close of all the evidence, there are the closing addresses including submissions on the law, from the defendant's and then from the claimant's representative. These also may be supported by a written note and may also be time-limited.

During the course of the proceeding the parties' representatives and the judge must keep a note of the proceedings and particularly the evidence, sufficient to aid the submissions to be made at the end of the trial, and, in the case of the judge in order to prepare their judgment. Traditionally, this is done by taking, as rapidly as possible, a long-hand note. In larger cases, and more often in arbitration hearings, the parties may agree to provide a transcript at their own expense. The most useful form of transcript is "live note", which is transmitted direct onto laptop screens available to the parties and the judge as the case proceeds and can be annotated by individual recipients. The court also keeps a tape

[33] CPR, PD 52, para.5.9.

recording of all proceedings in open court, but these are usually only transcribed and made available to the parties for the purpose of an appeal.

Representation and duty of advocates

In most substantial civil litigation each party will instruct a firm of solicitors who will, at the appropriate time, instruct one or more specialist counsel. Barristers once had exclusive rights of audience in the High Court but the present rules allow parties to be represented in almost any manner they wish. The economics of litigation, however, mean that some parties cannot or do not wish to afford full legal representation and it is increasingly common, even in complex cases, to find parties wishing to represent themselves. A limited company must be legally represented, but this may be through an in-house lawyer; and any individual litigant is entitled to represent themselves in any court. An individual litigant is also entitled to be accompanied by a lay adviser who may be allowed to speak on behalf of the litigant in person.

Many of the larger construction companies maintain their own legal departments, staffed by solicitors or employed barristers. They do the same work as a private solicitor, including instructing barristers. Barristers in the past were only permitted to act on instructions from solicitors but this rule is also fast disappearing and for some years "direct professional access" to specialist barristers has been available to engineers, architects, surveyors and others. There are also measures which allow general direct access to the bar.

There is an important rule which binds professional advocates, which must be borne in mind by any Tribunal hearing a case presented by a non-professional advocate. When addressing the court (including an arbitral tribunal) it is the duty of a barrister or solicitor to put forward all the relevant facts and law, not just those favourable to their client. He or she will, as part of the skill of advocacy, seek to present the matters in the most favourable light, but all the facts and the law must be presented. This is particularly important when legally qualified advocates appear before a lay arbitrator. The relevant rule in the Code of Professional Conduct by which English barristers are bound, provides that the barrister must *"promote and protect fearlessly and by all proper and lawful means the client's best interest"* but also that:

> "A barrister has an overriding duty to the court to act with independence in the interests of justice: he must assist the court in the administration of justice and must not deceive or knowingly or recklessly mislead the court."[34]

[34] BSB Code of Conduct, paras 303, 302.

The advocate's "duty to the court" was thought to justify immunity from actions in negligence by unsuccessful clients. However, in the leading case of *Hall v Simons*[35] a seven-strong House of Lords decided that immunity, even in court, should be abolished, both in civil and criminal cases. This does not affect the duty of the advocate.

Judges, referees and court experts

The great majority of actions in the Queen's Bench Division of the High Court take place before a single judge who decides all matters of fact and law. Civil jury cases are extremely rare and are practically confined to actions in defamation. Cases which involve prolonged investigation into technical matters, such as building disputes, are tried in the Technology and Construction Court (TCC). The judges in these courts were, before 1998, known as Official Referees. Now they are designated judges appointed to deal with TCC business. TCC judges sit in London at the new Rolls Building in Fetter Lane. There are designated TCC judges in Birmingham, Bristol, Cardiff, Exeter, Leeds, Liverpool, Manchester and Newcastle as well as a county court trial centre in London. The TCC London judges are all now of High Court status and can sit elsewhere when appropriate.

In addition to the judge, court rules provide for the possibility of appointing an assessor in appropriate cases[36] although this is now rare. Following the Woolf Report, attention has been given to the use, as an alternative to experts being appointed by each party, of a single joint expert. Accordingly, the new Civil Procedure Rules contain express power by which the court may direct that evidence on a particular issue is to be given by one expert only. The rules provide that, where the parties cannot agree on a single expert, the court may direct the manner in which the expert is to be selected. Further powers allow the court to give directions about payment of the experts' fees and for any inspection, examination or experiment which the expert wishes to carry out.[37] Such procedures are already well known in arbitration and are becoming more familiar in court actions, in contrast to the traditional approach of relying on party-appointed experts.

TCC procedure

All TCC actions are automatically assigned to the multi-track under the CPR. There are a number of distinct features of TCC (formerly Official Referee) procedure which have evolved over many years and

---

[35] [2000] 3 W.L.R. 543.
[36] CPR r.35.15, Senior Courts Act 1981 s.70.
[37] CPR r.35.7, 35.8.

which are now applied throughout the civil courts system. The practice of exchanging experts' reports, now axiomatic in all types of action, originated in the Official Referee's Courts. This has been found to be of great use in informing each party of the case to be advanced by the other side, and in facilitating the narrowing of issues. Orders for experts to meet and discuss their differences on a without prejudice basis similarly originated with Official Referees and are now governed by formal rules.[38]

The former Official Referees led the way in use of computerised trial procedures. As well as widespread use of laptop computers, VDU screens have been introduced for the trial of large actions. The first "paperless" trial was conducted in the TCC using a fully developed electronic case management system with all documents stored on a retrieval system, the proceedings being recorded on a "live note" transcript system. This was provided as the case proceeded, both to those physically in court and to lawyers in offices served by a direct wired link to the proceedings. Such procedures are unusual but illustrate the types of procedure which may become more commonplace in future. Parallel reforms and developments have also been taking place in the field of arbitration which is described in the next chapter.

TCC practice has for many years included a pre-trial review meeting at which the parties, represented by counsel or solicitor, consider the form of the trial. This is now formally included in the CPR Practice Direction,[39] which requires the holding of both a case management conference and pre-trial review. In addition to court rules, there is a "Pre-Action Protocol" which applies to all construction and engineering disputes except those concerned with enforcement of the decision in a statutory adjudication or involving a claim for interim or summary relief. The objective of the protocol is to ensure that the prospective parties exchange information and avoid litigation if possible. The principal features of the Pre-Action Protocol are:

(i)   The claimant must send to each proposed defendant a letter of claim prior to commencing proceedings.

(ii) The defendants must acknowledge the letter within 14 days raising any preliminary objection, for example that the wrong defendant has been identified.

(iii) Within 28 days of receiving the claim letter, the defendants must outline their grounds of defence and counterclaim, if any, and give the names of experts already instructed.

---

[38] CPR r.35.12.
[39] Practice Direction TCC paras 8, 9.

(iv) The claimant must provide a similar response to any counterclaim.[40]

(v) After receipt of responses, there must be a pre-action meeting aimed at identifying the root cause of disagreement and considering whether all or any issues might be resolved without recourse to litigation. Further meetings should be held as necessary.

(vi) If the parties cannot agree upon a settlement they should consider the possible appointment of a joint expert, the extent of disclosure of documents needed and ways of minimising cost and delay in the action.

In *Cundall Johnson v Whipps Cross NHS Trust*[41] a TCC claim for professional fees by consulting engineers was stayed where the claimants had not, despite requests by the defendants, provided details of the claims. The stay was granted on the basis that there was a real chance of settlement if the parties complied with the protocol.

Judgment and enforcement

After the close of the hearing the judge must come to their decision on the facts and on the law. They give their decision in the form of a reasoned judgment. This can be delivered ex tempore at the end of the case, but is usually reserved to a later date. Judgments in cases of any substance are usually written. Copies are provided to the parties' representatives shortly before the judgment is to be given. After delivery of the judgment, the court proceeds immediately to consider the orders which ought to be made in consequence of the judgement, and further orders for interest and costs.

Interest

Where the sums in issue are substantial and time has elapsed since the incurring of loss or damage, the notional loss of interest on money can be very significant. The right to recover interest in court actions (and in arbitration) has been subject to progressive development, both statutory and through the cases, since the nineteenth century, when charging or claiming interest was still regarded as usury. The court is empowered to award interest under s.35A of the Senior Courts Act 1981 on any part

---

[40] CPR Section C—Pre-action conduct and protocols.
[41] (2007) C.I.L.L. 2516.

of a claim for debt or damages which is either included in a judgment or which is paid before judgment. Thus, even if the defendant pays all or part of the sum claimed after issue of proceedings but before trial, the court may still award interest on the sum so paid. The power is limited to awarding simple interest. The amount awarded should normally represent a realistic rate for the time during which the successful party has been wrongfully deprived of the sum awarded. This often results in an award of 1 or 2 per cent above bank lending rate over the period outstanding.

The Late Payment of Commercial Debts (Interest) Act 1998 (which came fully into force in 2002) allows recovery of statutory interest at bank rate plus 8 per cent on debts which are not paid by the agreed or customary credit period, usually 30 days. The Act now applies to most contracts encountered in the construction process, including contracts for professional services and contracts with public authorities. The Act operates by implying a term into the contract, which need not be in writing. There must, however, be a contract and the right to statutory interest applies only to a debt, not to a claim for damages. The Act does not apply if the contract itself provides a "substantial remedy" for late payment.

An alternative to the recovery of statutory interest, is to claim interest as damages. In *Wadsworth v Lydell*[42] the defendant had failed to pay an agreed sum which the plaintiff required to finance the purchase of a property. The plaintiff raised the necessary sum by borrowing on mortgage and claimed the interest payments from the defendant as special damages. The Court of Appeal held that the sum was recoverable, and the House of Lords have approved the decision.[43] Accordingly, by pleading the actual outlay of interest incurred, it is possible to recover the actual sum lost. Some forms of contract provide expressly for the payment of interest on overdue certificates.[44] Where a contract provides for the reimbursement of cost or loss there may be a right to include interest or "financing charges" in the amounts payable. The Court of Appeal so held in *Minter v W.H.T.S.O.*,[45] where the formula "direct loss and/or expense" under the JCT form of contract was held to include interest. This case should, in principle, apply to other forms of contract which provide for the recovery of claims based on actual loss or cost, including the ICE Conditions of Contract. The right to recover interest at common law has recently been comprehensively reviewed by the House

---

[42] [1981] 1 W.L.R. 461.
[43] *President of India v La Pintada* [1985] A.C. 104.
[44] e.g. ICC form, cl.60(7).
[45] (1980) 13 B.L.R. 1.

of Lords in *Sempra Metals v IRC*[46] which has established that interest at common law can now be awarded in the same way as any other damages and may include compound interest on damages or for late payment of a debt.

Recovery of costs

Prima facie, a successful party to litigation is entitled to an order for payment of their costs by the loser, who must also pay their own costs. The principle is shortly expressed as "costs follow the event". Owing to the high costs of litigation, it is important to examine the circumstances in which a successful party may not recover a full order for costs. The broad rules as to recovery and assessment of costs are set out in the CPR Pt 44. The award of costs is always in the discretion of the court or tribunal. The court is required to have regard to all the circumstances including:

(a) the conduct of all the parties;

(b) whether a party has succeeded on part of their case, if not the whole; and

(c) any payment into court or admissible offer to settle.[47]

The rules expressly provide that the conduct which the court can consider includes conduct before as well as during the proceedings, including the extent to which the parties followed the pre-action protocol; whether it was reasonable for a party to pursue or contest a particular issue; the manner in which a party pursued or defended their case; and whether the claim was exaggerated. The award of costs has become more controversial as a result of the impact of mediation. In *Dunnett v Railtrack*,[48] a successful party in the Court of Appeal was deprived of what would have been the normal order for costs in her favour, on the ground that she had refused offers of mediation. The court regarded the parties as bound to consider ADR methods to resolve their disputes. However, more recently, the Court of Appeal in *Halsey v Milton Keynes NHS Trust*[49] emphasised that, while the court had power to encourage the parties to mediate, there was no power to prevent a party bringing its case to court and it was for

[46] [2007] UKHL 34.
[47] CPR r.44.3(4).
[48] [2002] 1 W.L.R. 2434.
[49] [2004] EWCA Civ 576.

the unsuccessful party to show that there had been unreasonable conduct which should be reflected in the award of costs.

The award of costs becomes less clear when, in addition to (or in lieu of) a defence, the defendant has a counterclaim. If both claim and counterclaim succeed then each party may seek an order for costs, even where the defence operates as a set-off. The court, in awarding costs, will look at the issues which had to be litigated, not merely at the sums in dispute. In order to save the laborious process of assessing items of cost as between claim and counter claim, the court will often make a global order whereby one side is to pay a proportion of the full costs of the other side, and also to pay their own costs. However, the award of costs is not an exact science. The sums involved can be very large, even in relation to the substantial sums often in dispute in construction cases.

Where a party obtains an order for payment of its costs, the amount must be assessed by the court, unless the parties are able to agree the amount. There are two bases on which costs can be awarded, the "standard basis" or the "indemnity basis". Assessment involves ascertaining first whether the sums claimed for each element of costs are reasonable; and secondly, whether it was reasonable to incur the cost in question. Where there is doubt, on the standard basis of assessment the issue is resolved in favour of the paying party, whereas on an indemnity basis, it is resolved in favour of the receiving party. The net result is that an assessment on the standard basis usually results in recovery of not more than about two thirds of the actual outlay.

The court rules provide for either a detailed assessment of costs by a Costs Officer of the court, or for a summary assessment of costs by the judge. Summary assessment is appropriate for a fast-track trial or at the end of any other hearing which lasts less than a day. In such cases, the parties must be prepared to provide the judge with a note of all costs claimed, from which the summary assessment will be made after judgment has been given. In a more substantial trial the assessment of costs will be made at a later date, but the court has power to make an immediate order for an amount to be paid on account before the formal assessment.[50]

The recovery of costs in litigation involving individual parties has recently undergone a major change through the introduction of contingent or conditional fees, colloquially described as "no win, no fee". The practice has been familiar for many years in the USA and even in Scotland. This creates two particular problems: first, may the successful lawyer recover a premium or "success fee" on top of his normal fee; and secondly, how can the litigant be protected against an order that they should pay the

---

[50] CPR r.44.3(8).

costs of the defendant, if unsuccessful. The law applying up to April 1, 2013 was stated by the Court of Appeal in test cases[51] where it was held that the successful claimant was entitled to recover their lawyer's success fee of 20 per cent in a normal road accident case. In more complex cases, however, it might be reasonable for the lawyer to agree a much higher success fee, subject to reduction if the case settled within a short time. The percentage increase in fees recovered is subject to the discretion of the judge awarding costs.[52] Additionally, the successful claimant was entitled to recover the cost of after-the-event insurance (ATE) cover which would pay costs awarded in favour of the defendant. These principles have been extended to commercial litigation with the result that a number of commercial litigation funding companies have been set up. However in a comprehensive review of civil litigation costs,[53] Jackson L.J. recommended, inter alia, that success fees and ATE insurance premiums should cease to be recoverable from unsuccessful opponents in civil litigation; and that where a litigant engages a lawyer on a contingency fee basis, the unsuccessful party in the proceedings, should only required to pay a conventional amount of costs, not including any uplift to reflect the contingency fee agreement. These recommendations have now been given statutory effect which applies as from April 1, 2013.[53A]

Offers of settlement

Where the defendant considers that they are likely to be found liable in some degree they may obtain protection against liability for costs, both their own and those of the claimant, by making an offer of settlement. The rules allow the defendant to make a "payment into court"[54] of the sum offered. The claimant will be notified of the payment in, and may within a limited period of time accept the money in settlement of their claim, together with their costs on the claim. If the claimant chooses not to accept the payment in and fails to obtain judgment for more than that sum, they will normally be ordered to pay the defendant's costs and their own after the date of notification of the payment, even though they have won the action. The judge must not be told of the payment in until they have determined how much the claimant is to recover. A claimant may similarly pay money into court in respect of a counterclaim and the court rules now permit a claimant to make an offer in respect of the claim, which is intended to have similar consequences to a payment into court. The rules

[51] *Callery v Gray* [2001] 1 W.L.R. 2112.
[52] See *Buildability Ltd v O'Donnell Developments Ltd* [2010] B.L.R. 122.
[53] See *www.judiciary.gov/NR/rdonlyres/8EB9F3F3*.
[53A] Legal Aid, Sentencing and Punishment of Offenders Act 2012 (LAPSO Act) s.44–46.
[54] CPR Pt. 36.

are intended to encourage offers of settlement from any party, and accordingly, the court has power to take into account any offer (whether or not compliant with the rules) in the assessment of costs. The calculation of offers and the decision whether or not to accept may require very careful consideration in view of the large sums for costs which may be at risk. Costs protection in arbitration and other proceedings can be achieved by making an offer of settlement stated to be "without prejudice save as to costs". This is known as a *Calderbank*[55] offer and will be considered in the discretion of the court in the same way as an offer within the Rules.

From April 1, 2013 where a defendant rejects and then fails to beat an offer from the claimant, the defendant will be ordered to pay additional damages to the claimant, capped at £75,000.[55A] This is intended to encourage settlements. It has no application to arbitration unless adopted by agreement.

Enforcement

The final stage in the action is enforcement of the judgment. If the judgment debtor does not pay, there are a number of methods available to the judgment creditor by which they may obtain at least some payment. The most important of these are: seizure of the debtor's goods; charging the debtor's land; appointment of a receiver over the debtor's business; or obtaining an order that an identified debt owed to the debtor be paid to the judgment creditor instead. Where the debtor is a limited company there may be an application to the court for winding-up. However, if the threat does not produce payment, winding-up will not improve the position of the judgment creditor, who will rank equally with other unsecured creditors.

It is a fundamental principle of English law that a claimant bringing proceedings takes their chance as to whether there will be assets against which to enforce a judgment. However, in recent years the courts have evolved an important procedural device which, while it does not improve the claimant's position, prevents the defendant from worsening it. This is the "freezing injunction", formerly known as a "Mareva" order,[56] which prohibits the party against whom it is directed from disposing of or otherwise dealing with assets within the jurisdiction. Initially, this form of relief was granted against foreign defendants who might remove their assets from England, but developments in case law and now statutory backing[57] allow such injunctions to be granted against any party and in

---

[55]   *Calderbank v Calderbank* [1976] Fam. 93.
[55A] Legal Aid, Sentencing and Punishment of Offenders Act 2013 s.55.
[56]   *Mareva Compania v International Bulk Carriers* [1975] 2 Lloyd's Rep. 509.
[57]   CPR r.25.1(1)(f).

respect of assets within the jurisdiction or abroad. The claimant must show that they have a good arguable case against the defendant, and that there is a real risk that a judgment will be unsatisfied because the defendant will dispose of their assets in advance unless restrained from doing so.

Applications for freezing injunctions are now frequent, and the courts take a strict attitude. As with other forms of injunction, an order may be granted without notice to the defendant if necessary on very short notice; but the matter will be reconsidered at a hearing between the parties. The claimant must make full disclosure of all material facts. A freezing injunction does not give the claimant any preferential right over the assets restrained. However, a defendant will sometimes offer to put up security in lieu of the injunction, so as to permit them to use the assets in question. A freezing injunction may also be obtained in aid of arbitration proceedings.

Foreign judgments

A judgment may need to be enforced in a country other than that in which it was given. In every country enforcement depends solely on that country's internal laws. For enforcement in England, the courts must be satisfied that the foreign court had jurisdiction, that the judgment is final and for a fixed sum, and that it was properly obtained. If these conditions are satisfied, a foreign judgment may be enforced in England under various reciprocal statutory arrangements. These allow the foreign judgment to be registered and enforced as an English judgment. They similarly allow English judgments to be enforced abroad. Particular arrangements which apply to the enforcement of judgments throughout Europe (not limited to the European Community) are contained in the Civil Jurisdiction and Judgments Act 1982. A judgment from a country with which there is no statutory arrangement is treated in England as a simple contract debt, which may be enforced by suing in the English courts. Irrespective of the mode of enforcement, the English courts will not enforce a foreign judgment for multiple damages, which are expressly permitted under the laws of some foreign states. In *Lewis v Eliades*[58] the heavyweight boxer Lennox Lewis had obtained judgment in New York against his former managers for damages including triple damages for racketeering. In English proceedings, enforcement of the racketeering damages was refused in total, but the remainder of the judgment was enforced. Enforcement of an English judgment abroad, without the aid of reciprocal arrangements, depends on the internal law of the country

---

[58] [2004] 1 W.L.R. 692.

where enforcement is sought. Enforcement of arbitration awards in different countries is dealt with in Ch.3.

EVIDENCE AND WITNESSES

Evidence refers to the personal testimony and documents which each party must assemble to be put before a tribunal to prove the case it seeks to advance. In a civil action the relevant facts must be proved on a balance of probabilities, in contrast to the criminal standard of proof beyond reasonable doubt. The burden of proving a fact usually lies upon the party asserting it. When deciding how much evidence must be adduced, it must be considered that a judge, unlike an arbitrator cannot draw upon their own knowledge, except in very obvious matters, and therefore every fact relied on must be proved. In practice many facts may be admitted, either in pleadings, in witness statements or by formal admission. If one party refuses to admit some fact which, while likely to be true, would be expensive to prove formally (for example, that hundreds of day-work sheets were properly signed), the other party may serve a "notice to admit facts".[59] If not then admitted, the court may order the non-admitting party to pay the costs of proof, whoever wins the action.

Hearsay and opinion evidence

The question often arises as to what evidence a witness is entitled to give. Factual witnesses should normally be confined to relating facts they have themselves perceived and where the testimony goes outside this limit there may be objection from the opposing advocate on which the judge or tribunal must rule. Matters which a witness is aware of through being told by another person constitute "hearsay" which for many years was regarded as inadmissible both in courts and in other tribunals such as arbitrations. The rule against hearsay has been gradually eroded. The modern view is that a judge or tribunal can deal with any type of testimony by giving it appropriate weight. In arbitration and other less formal tribunals it is now generally accepted that there are no fixed rules governing what is admissible. In court the admission of hearsay evidence must still be dealt with on a formal basis. The relevant statute is the Civil Evidence Act 1995, under which a party proposing to adduce hearsay must give notice and provide particulars to the other

---

[59] CPR r.32.18.

party, including whether it is possible or convenient to call the maker of the original statement. These provisions may be excluded by agreement, or waived. However, it will be prudent, in potentially long cases, to take statements from elderly or infirm witnesses so that, should they subsequently be unfit to attend the trial, their evidence may be admitted under the Act.

A witness of fact may not normally give opinion evidence; and an expert is usually limited to giving their professional opinion on the facts on which they are instructed. This can create difficulty in construction and other technical cases, where the factual witnesses may wish, as part of their evidence, to give opinions on the matters in issue. Such difficulty can be resolved by agreement or ruling of the tribunal allowing technically qualified witnesses to give their opinion, where relevant to their evidence. Alternatively, there may be an application to admit the relevant witnesses as an expert (see below). Similarly, experts may need to be treated as witnesses of fact, for example, in relation to what they saw on site.

Giving evidence

The presentation of purely oral evidence in civil actions and arbitrations has been almost entirely superseded by the prior exchange of "witness statements", often of great length and prepared with the aid of lawyers. The provision of written statements is now enshrined in the Rules of Court,[60] which apply also to proceedings in the TCC and Commercial Court. Witness statements, like pleadings, are required to be supported by a "statement of truth". This is now a familiar procedural rule which tends to be applied also in arbitration and adjudication, although it is not required by their rules. There are various procedures for dealing with contentious parts of witness statements. In the Commercial Court, the practice is to require particular parts of the statement, if objected to by the opposing party, to be adduced by conventional question and answer. In arbitration, particularly in international cases, there is a strong trend towards limiting oral evidence to cross-examination and admitting the whole of the written statements subject to challenge. The Tribunal will then give such weight to the written statements as it thinks appropriate.

Evidence tendered on behalf of a party is known as evidence in-chief or, in more modern (American) terms, direct evidence. Where, occasionally, direct evidence is given orally there is a rule that the advocate should not "lead" the witness, i.e. suggest by the question what answer is

[60] CPR Pt.32.

being sought. Most oral evidence consists of cross-examination by the opposing advocate. This is regarded as a fundamental right and a witness who fails to appear for cross-examination will usually have their evidence disregarded by the tribunal. Cross-examination is not restricted to the matters on which the witness has given evidence in-chief. A witness may be questioned on any matter relevant to the case, including their truthfulness. Cross-examination may often have a material effect in exposing the truth. The right to cross-examine is more important when written statements are used, because of the temptation to include in the statements material which is not properly within the witness's knowledge.

A controversial issue, particularly in international cases involving advocates and witness from different countries, is witness preparation. Lawyers in the USA expect to rehearse witnesses as a matter of normal trial preparation. In the United Kingdom this is not permitted,[61] although it is not objectionable to familiarise intended witnesses with the process of trial so that they can prepare themselves. The problem for an international arbitration tribunal is to maintain a "level playing field" so that one side does not gain an unfair advantage.

A party may compel the attendance at the trial of any person whom they wish to give evidence or produce documents. Attendance is enforced by serving a witness summons.[62] In arbitration proceedings the High Court has power to issue a witness summons.[63] A person may be called to give evidence by either side. A person requested to give evidence is, however, entitled to refuse to give a statement in advance and a party is normally bound by the evidence of witnesses they choose to call. In the USA potential witnesses may be "deposed", i.e. required to attend for examination under oath in advance of the court proceedings to elicit whether they can provide relevant testimony or documents. No such procedures exist in the UK and parties are limited to persuading witnesses to co-operate by providing statements and subsequently attending the hearing.

Expert evidence

Evidence to be given by an expert is admissible only subject to court rules. These require permission to be obtained for the calling of such evidence, which will be conditional upon the exchange of reports between the parties in advance.[64] There is no precise definition of expert

---

[61] *R. v Momodou* [2005] EWCA Crim 177.
[62] CPR r.34.2.
[63] Arbitration Act 1996 s.43.
[64] CPR Pt.35.

evidence. Its function depends upon the tribunal before which it is to be adduced. In the High Court, expert evidence is necessary to explain technical features of a case. Conversely, in arbitration, expert evidence may be unnecessary where the arbitrator is appropriately qualified. Despite this, it is common for such evidence to be put forward. As in the case of factual evidence, expert reports will usually be read in advance by the tribunal and introduced briefly by each expert witness, before they are cross-examined. Both in court proceedings and in arbitration, the Tribunal may put questions to the expert and it is also common for opposed experts to give their evidence together. In such a case the Tribunal may also invite the experts to put questions to each other as a way of getting more rapidly to the essential matters of difference between them.

Until the report of an expert is exchanged, their views and opinions are technically privileged. If a party obtains an unfavourable opinion from one expert, they may go to another and rely exclusively upon the second opinion. A party who takes this course, however, runs a risk that the identity of the first expert may be discovered and the opposing party may then compel them to give evidence. Parties are usually well advised to accept the first opinion they are given. In some jurisdictions all reports of experts, including drafts are disclosable to the opposing side, thus depriving a party of the luxury of choosing what expert evidence it wishes to deploy. An expert should always give an independent and unbiased opinion on the issues. It is, however, quite proper for the expert, both in their report and in their evidence, to emphasise any technical points in their client's favour. Technical issues are often arguable in just the same way as legal issues are. The duty of an expert was discussed in *The Ikarian Reefer*,[65] where the expert's duty to the court was emphasised. More recently the Civil Procedure Rules have provided a Protocol for the instruction of experts to give evidence in civil claims,[66] which reflect best practice in the use of expert evidence.

Expert witnesses, together with counsel appearing in court, were supposed to enjoy immunity from suit at the hands of a dissatisfied client. This supposition and the reasoning behind it have been progressively stripped away by the courts, first in *Hall v Simons*,[67] when the House of Lords decided that barristers could be sued for actions in court; secondly in *GMC v Meadow*,[68] in which the Court of Appeal held that an expert in a criminal case had no immunity against disciplinary

---

[65] *National Justice Comp Naviera v Prudential Assurance* [1993] 2 Lloyd's Rep. 68, 81.
[66] CPR, para.36.16.
[67] [2000] UKHL 38.
[68] [2007] 1 Q.B. 462.

proceedings; and finally in *Jones v Kane*,[69] where the Supreme Court held that, despite an expert witness owing a duty to the court, there was no immunity in respect of a negligence action by the client. The expert is thus in the same position as regards potential liability as any other professional person.

Experts' costs

An important distinction between an expert and a witness of fact, is that the former is entitled to be paid a proper professional fee, which may be recovered as part of the assessed costs. This sometimes leads to disputes about whether a particular witness is an expert. In the case of *James Longley v S.W. Regional Health Authority*[70] the claimant contractor in an arbitration sought to include a substantial sum in the bill for costs in respect of the fees of a "claims consultant." The respondent objected that the consultant was not qualified to give expert evidence, and that his evidence was not admissible. On a review in the High Court, it was held that such evidence was admissible, and an expert might be appropriately qualified by skill and experience. It has also been held that, where a successful party in an arbitration is represented by a claims adviser rather than a solicitor, the costs of the adviser may be recovered.[71]

ALTERNATIVE DISPUTE RESOLUTION

The term ADR has been in circulation for some years, having been imported from the United States of America. There are different views as to what it includes. In the Woolf report ADR includes both arbitration and the "ombudsmen" system; but the more general view is that it refers to the various forms of ad hoc procedure which are all consensual and (unlike litigation and arbitration) are unsupported by any coercive or directive powers of the court, save to the extent of enforcing what the parties may agree.

ADR procedures tend to be relatively informal, but their range is very wide. At one extreme, the process usually described as mediation may consist essentially of settlement negotiation through an intermediary, from which either party can withdraw at any stage. At the opposite extreme are processes which may be referred to as contractual

---

[69] [2011] B.L.R. 283.
[70] (1983) 25 B.L.R. 56.
[71] *Piper Double Glazing v D.C. Contracts* (1992) 31 Con. L.R. 149.

adjudication, which have a formal structure and a decision which may become binding. There is considerable scope for confusion in the use of the terms and it is safer to define what is meant. A general distinction which needs to be drawn is between processes which (pursuant to the agreement of the parties) are mandatory, and those which are voluntary. A mandatory procedure is one that operates as a condition precedent to the pursuit of any further remedy, for example by arbitration or litigation. Such procedures will generally be enforced by the courts, as in the *Channel Tunnel* case. Here the employers had sought an injunction from the English court, despite the existence of an elaborate dispute resolution procedure involving an initial reference to a panel of three independent experts. Lord Mustill, holding that the agreed procedure should be enforced, said:

> "Having made this choice I believe that it is in accordance, not only with the presumption exemplified in the English cases cited above that those who make agreements for the resolution of disputes must show good reasons for departing from them, but also with the interests of the orderly regulation of international commerce, that having promised to take their complaints to the experts and if necessary to the arbitrators, that is where the (employers) should go. The fact that the (employers) now find their chosen method too slow to suit their purpose, is to my way of thinking, quite beside the point."[72]

The same principle applies whenever a customised dispute resolution procedure is provided in a contract and expressed in mandatory terms, and equally when the parties enter into an ad hoc agreement to pursue a particular procedure. Further, in *Cable & Wireless v IBM UK*[73] the parties had agreed, under a contract to provide IT services, that in the event of a dispute they should conduct non-binding ADR. Colman J. in the Commercial Court decided that the substantive claim should be adjourned pending reference to ADR, thereby effectively enforcing the agreed dispute resolution mechanism. The same result was achieved in *Shirayama Shokusan v Danovo*,[74] where the court ordered the parties to mediate despite one party being opposed to mediation.

The Woolf report stopped short of recommending court-annexed ADR but did recommend that parties to litigation should be required, at the pre-trial stage, to state whether they have discussed ADR. Such a provision is included in the TCC Pre-Action Protocol. This is in contrast to the position in the United States of America, where the courts are more pro-active in promoting ADR. Within the European Union a Directive

---

[72] *Channel Tunnel Group v Balfour Beatty* [1993] A.C. 334.
[73] [2003] B.L.R. 89.
[74] [2003] EWHC 3006.

(requiring implementation by Member States by 2011) was adopted in October 2008 for use of ADR in cross-border civil and commercial disputes. The intention is, as a minimum, to provide machinery for the encouragement of parties to adopt ADR methods and may include mandatory requirements. The general view is that ADR in the UK is already largely compliant with these requirements which will bring other Member States up to the same level. The following section reviews briefly the major forms of ADR, excluding arbitration (which is the subject of Ch.3).

Mediation and conciliation

These terms are often used interchangeably but they are two essentially different processes. Mediation, as the name implies, involves a neutral mediator finding middle ground between the position of the parties with the aim of achieving a negotiated solution acceptable to all parties. The role of the mediator includes separate and private negotiation with each party in order to discover, by a process of accelerated settlement discussions, at what figure (or on what terms) each party will settle. The actual settlement is achieved by a legally enforceable contract setting out the terms agreed. Once a settlement has been reached it will bind the parties as a contract, and will preclude the bringing of further proceeding in respect of the matter settled. The settlement may, in theory, be set aside on the same grounds which would allow a contract to be vitiated. In *Brennan v Bolt Burden*[75] a settlement compromising an action was set aside when the court found that the compromise was based on a common and fundamental mistake as to the law. In *Farm Assist v Minister for the Environment*[76] a party to a mediation sought to set aside the contract of settlement as having been entered into under economic duress. A witness summons was issued against the mediator to compel her to give evidence. This was resisted on the basis the mediator's agreement with the parties precluded her being called as a witness. It was held that the interests of justice prevailed over the mediators terms and the witness summons would not be set aside. It is central to the process of mediation that the mediator does not publicly express their view on the case. Their function is to achieve an acceptable settlement, using whatever grounds or issues appear most fruitful to bring the parties together, which will usually include the commercial aspects of the dispute. Mediation services are offered by a number of institutions, such as the Centre for Dispute Resolution (CEDR), and by most of the National and

---

[75] [2004] EWCA Civ 1017; [2004] 3 W.L.R. 1321.
[76] [2009] B.L.R. 399.

International arbitration bodies, such as the ICC and LCIA. There are many alternative sets of rules or procedures, but the essence of mediation remains its non-binding flexibility.

In contrast to the mediator, a conciliator may be empowered or required to express their provisional view on the merits of the case. The ICE Conciliation Procedure, which appears in cl.66 of the ICE Conditions of Contract, requires the conciliator initially to act in a mediating role, in the sense discussed above. If an agreed settlement is not achieved, the conciliator gives a recommendation which may become binding upon the parties if a notice to refer to arbitration is not given.[77]

Mini-trials

This refers to a form of aided settlement in which each side presents a summary of its case, in trial mode and using advocates and experts, before a tribunal composed a senior representative of each side and a neutral chairman. The objective is to demonstrate directly the strengths and weaknesses of the respective cases to those in a position of responsibility so that they may seek to negotiate an informed settlement, with the aid of the neutral chairman. The process is not inexpensive and necessarily involves preparation and the employment of professional advocates in order that the case of each side is seen in its best light.

Dispute Adjudication Board

Clause 20 of the FIDIC Conditions provides for a dispute under the Contract to be referred to a Dispute Adjudication Board (DAB) of three persons who are required to be appointed at the outset and to be available throughout the project to deal timeously with any disputes that may arise. The contract conditions require the parties to make available to the DAB information and access to the Site, and such facilities as the DAB may require. The DAB is deemed not to be acting as arbitrators. The conditions lay down a timetable for references and decisions, which the parties are required promptly give effect to it unless and until it shall be revised by an amicable settlement or an arbitral award. The DAB decision is to become final and binding upon both parties unless timely notice of dissatisfaction is given (see Ch.13 for further detail).

This procedure is typical of that found in numerous standard and ad hoc contracts for major projects in which it is now accepted good practice to appoint a DAB, sometimes called a Dispute Avoidance Board

---

[77] ICE Conditions cl.66 (5).

or Dispute Resolution Board at the start, and to operate throughout the project. The members are often required to attend the site, which may be in at remote location, on a regular basis to keep abreast of contractual developments and to head off potential disputes. Differences exist between the various forms of DAB or DRB in that the decision is sometimes advisory only and the procedure may be more or less formal, sometimes amounting to meetings and advice only. Where the decision is to be temporarily binding on a party, there may be a problem obtaining enforcement where the contract (as in the case of FIDIC) requires further disputes to be referred to arbitration[78].

Expert determination

A further analogous process closely related to the DAB procedure, is expert determination, by which any issue which the parties agree to refer is to be decided by an agreed expert whose opinion the parties agree to accept. The process resembles and can be conducted in exactly the same manner as an arbitration, but is not subject to any of the controls of the Arbitration Act, nor is it conventionally open to any form of appeal. In the leading case of *Jones v Sherwood Services*,[79] however, it was held that the expert's decision may, in the same way as the decision of an adjudicator, be set aside if it can be shown that the expert has departed from their mandate in a material respect, for example by answering the wrong question. Expert Determination has grown in its use and is now often found in commercial contracts as a convenient way of deciding matters of valuation. The increased use has also led to increased challenges. Thus, in a case where the parties agreed to accept an expert valuation where the expert was required to give reasons, the court decided that the reasons given were insufficient to explain the conclusions and remitted the decision to the expert.[80] In another case where the expert volunteered additional reasons, the court decided that while the original decision disclosed no error, the additional reasons showed that the decision was given on a mistaken basis and should not therefore be enforced,[81] and in *Barclays Bank v Nylon Capital*[82] it was suggested by Lord Neuberger M.R. that a decision could be challenged if it could be shown to have been arrived at on the basis of a mistake of law.

---

[78] See Ch.13 under cl.20 and *CRW v PT Perusahaan TBK* [2011] S.G.C.A. 33.
[79] [1992] 1 W.L.R. 277.
[80] *Halifax Life v Equitable Life* [2007] EWHC 503.
[81] *Homepace v SITA* [2008] EWCA Civ 1.
[82] [2011] B.L.R. 614 at [63].

ADJUDICATION

Statutory adjudication is presently the most widely used form of dispute resolution in the UK construction industry. The decision of an adjudicator is binding only until the dispute is finally resolved by other available means, but it appears that well over 90 per cent of decisions are either accepted or result in settlement and, in either event, do not lead on to further proceedings. Adjudication was recommended for all construction contracts in the Latham Report[83] and the right to refer a dispute to adjudication is now available under construction contracts falling within the Housing Grants, Construction and Regeneration Act, 1996 (the Act) as recently amended by the Local Democracy, Economic Development and Construction Act 2009.[84] The Acts contain no further definition of the process and it is instructive to recall the origin of adjudication and the intention behind its more general introduction.

The standard forms of contract, and particularly sub-contract, for some years contained provision for contractual adjudication.[85] Arbitration, however, remained the principal means of resolving construction disputes. By the 1990s arbitration was seen as unduly slow and expensive and incapable of providing an effective remedy for contractors and sub-contractors who were unable to obtain payment for work carried out. Adjudication was seen as a means of securing rapid payment of sums to which there was no serious challenge. The policy of adjudication has been characterised as "pay now, argue later". This has, to a large extent, been the result of the widespread adoption of adjudication. There have also been a substantial number of challenges to the enforcement of adjudicator's decisions, resulting in the development of a new jurisprudence, the effects of which are noted below. But the popularity of adjudication is such that, in a number of areas, contracts falling outside the Act now provide for a form of adjudication modelled on the statutory provisions with amendments, for example providing for a longer time-scale. For international contracts using the FIDIC form of contract[86] adjudication will be available through the Dispute Adjudication Board, which is intended to be available throughout the contract period.

The important distinction between adjudication and various forms of ADR is that adjudication is intended to result in a decision which is enforceable, if not complied with voluntarily. In the case of an arbitration

---

[83] *Constructing the Team* (1994).

[84] The Act came into force only on October 1, 2011.

[85] See generally Mark McGaw, "Adjudicators, Experts and Keeping out of Court" (1992) 8 Const. L.J. 332.

[86] See Ch.13.

award, enforcement has been provided for in successive Arbitration Acts, and enforcement in different countries is assisted by international conventions. This process is dependent on the decision to be enforced being recognised as having the status of an Award. In *Cameron v Mowlem*,[87] one of the first contract adjudication cases to come before the courts, the Court of Appeal held that the adjudicator's decision could not be enforced as an arbitration award and that it should be treated as a matter of contract. Cameron was a sub-contractor under Form DOM/1 who brought adjudication proceedings to recover payment alleged to be due. The adjudicator determined that the sum of £52,800 was due, which Mowlem resisted, relying on a right of set-off. The court held that the decision was not immediately enforceable, but was dependent on the terms of the contract. When translating contractual adjudication into a statutory right, the Housing Grants, etc. Act made clear that the adjudicator's decision is to be binding on the parties[88] and that intended to be withheld must be the subject of a timely notice.[89] As noted below, however, the Act does not deal with the status of the adjudicator's decision, which remains a matter of contract. Statutory adjudication has, since its introduction in the UK, been adopted in a number of other common law countries,[90] where alternative measures have been introduced, including giving the adjudicator's decision a defined status.

Housing Grants, etc. Act 1996

Following the Latham Report of 1994 and after a somewhat controversial[91] consultation process, a Bill was introduced dealing with a limited number of the report's recommendations, which was passed into law as Pt II of the Housing Grants, Construction and Regeneration Act 1996. The Act deals with three construction-related matters. First, there is an elaborate definition of the term "construction contract", to which the substantive provisions of Pt II are to apply. None of the provisions apply where the definition is not met. Secondly, there are measures providing for the mandatory availability of adjudication and its consequences. Thirdly, there are important provisions dealing with the right to payment under a construction contract, as defined. The first two matters are dealt with in this section and the third in Ch.9. As noted above the Housing Grants, etc. Act has been amended by the Local Democracy,

---

[87] (1990) 52 B.L.R. 24.
[88] Section 108(3).
[89] Section 111 as amended.
[90] These include Australia, New Zealand and Singapore.
[91] See John Uff QC, *Contemporary Issues in Construction Law, Construction Contract Reform: A Plea for Sanity*, Vol.2 (Construction Law Press, 1997).

Economic Development and Construction Act 2009,[92] which amends particular sections and adds new provisions. The following sections refer to the Housing Grants, etc. Act as amended as "the Act" and to the Local Democracy, etc., Act as "the 2009 Act".

"Construction contract" is defined in ss.104 and 105 of the Act as an agreement for carrying out construction operations (as defined), including sub-contracted work and architectural design or surveying work or advice on building, engineering, decoration or landscape.[93] Thus, in addition to contracts for construction, the Act extends to professional design contracts, including a potentially wide area of disputes involving both claims for fees and professional negligence claims. The term "construction operations" is widely defined but (significantly) excludes a long list of construction operations such as the extraction of oil, gas or minerals, installation of plant for nuclear processing, power generation or water or effluent treatment, bulk storage of chemicals, oil, gas, steel, or food or drink. Also excluded is the manufacture or delivery of components, materials, plant and machinery unless the contract also provides for installation.[94] The Act applies only to construction operations in England and Wales (and subsequently Scotland and Northern Ireland), whatever the applicable law of the contract. Accordingly, the Act will apply to an Italian sub-contractor supplying marble if it is also to be installed by the sub-contractor; but it will not apply to a United Kingdom supplier who merely delivers components for heating and ventilation, drainage or fire protection, etc.

There have been a number of disputed enforcement actions turning on whether the contract in question falls within the statutory definition. One issue was whether the contract in question fell within s.107 of the original Act which required the contract to be in writing or evidenced in writing. The 2009 Act repeals this section, with the effect that, if the contract does not contain written provisions for adjudication as set out in s.108 (see below), the Scheme for Construction Contracts applies.

The right to invoke adjudication is set out in s.108 of the Act which provides, as amended, as follows:

"108—Right to refer disputes to adjudication,

(1) A party to a construction contract has the right to refer a dispute arising under the contract for adjudication under a procedure complying with this section.

---

[92] See fn.61.
[93] Sections 104(1), (2).
[94] Sections 105(2).

For this purpose dispute includes any difference.

(2) The contract shall include provision in writing so as to—

  (a) enable a party to give notice at any time of his intention to refer a dispute to adjudication;

  (b) provide a timetable with the object of securing the appointment of the adjudicator and referral of the dispute to him within 7 days of such notice;

  (c) require the adjudicator to reach a decision within 28 days of referral or such longer period as is agreed by the parties after the dispute has been referred;

  (d) allow the adjudicator to extend the period of 28 days by up to 14 days, with the consent of the party by whom the dispute was referred;

  (e) impose a duty on the adjudicator to act impartially; and

  (f) enable the adjudicator to take the initiative in ascertaining the facts and the law

(3) The contract shall provide in writing that the decision of the adjudicator is binding until the dispute is finally determined by legal proceedings, by arbitration (if the contract provides for arbitration or the parties otherwise agree to arbitration) or by agreement. The parties may agree to accept the decision of the adjudicator as finally determining the dispute.

(3A) The contract shall include provision in writing permitting the adjudicator to correct his decision so as to remove a clerical or typographical error arising by accident or omission.

(4) The contract shall also provide in writing that the adjudicator is not liable for anything done or omitted in the discharge or purported discharge of his functions as adjudicator unless the act or omission is in bad faith, and that any employee or agent of the adjudicator is similarly protected from liability.

(5) If the contract does not comply with the requirements of subsections (1) to (4), the adjudication provisions of the Scheme for Construction Contracts apply."

Section 108 is not restricted to payment disputes, but includes disputes relating to time, quality and any other matter capable of giving rise to a difference between the parties. Of particular note is the requirement that a party must be enabled to give notice "at any time". This provision effectively removes the traditional authority of the Engineer or the Architect to render decisions which could be challenged only by a subsequent process of arbitration, often after completion of the contract. The new measure entitles the contractor (or the employer) to require immediate adjudication on any matter of difference. This measure also has a profound effect on the procedure formerly contained in cl.66 of the ICE Conditions (now the ICC Conditions) whereby a dispute was to be referred first to the engineer. No such provision can now hold up the right to adjudication. The right to bring adjudication proceedings "at any time" has been held to permit the bringing of adjudication proceedings during the course of litigation. In *Herschel Engineering v Breen*[95] Dyson J. ordered summary enforcement of an adjudication decision where the Referring Party had earlier issued County Court proceedings in which judgment in default had been entered. The Responding Party had succeeded in having the judgment set aside and, while considering an appeal, the Referring Party decided to refer the matter to adjudication. Despite attempts to injunct the proceedings and non-attendance at the hearing, the adjudicator proceeded and the decision was enforced on the basis that no estoppel arose and the normal rule against concurrent proceedings had no application. The judgment included the following:

> "But it is inherent in the Adjudication scheme that a Defendant will or may have to defend the same claim first in an Arbitration and later in Court or in an Arbitration. It is not self evident that it is more oppressive for a Party to be faced with both proceedings at the same time, rather than subsequently. As for the risk of inconsistent findings of fact, on any view, this is inherent to the Adjudication scheme".

Procedure for adjudication

Section 108, set out above, requires either a conforming contractual adjudication scheme or, in default, application of the Scheme for Construction Contracts, which is a Statutory Instrument, introduced by Regulations under delegated powers under the Act shortly before the primary legislation came into force on May 1, 1998.[96] The scheme, which has also been amended by the 2009 Act, contains a detailed procedure for the giving of notice, the appointment, the adjudication procedure, the decision and, to a limited extent, its enforcement. A substantial number of alternative contractual adjudication schemes have been published complying with the requirements of s.108, including those issued by CEDR,[97] and by Construction Industry Council. The JCT Standard Building Contract (2005) provides for adjudication under the Statutory Scheme (art.7 and cl.9.2) as does the JCT Major Project Form, reflecting a growing trend to use the scheme in preference to ad hoc arrangements.

---

[95] [2000] B.L.R. 272.
[96] Scheme for Construction Contracts (England and Wales) Regulations 1998.
[97] Centre for Effective Dispute Resolution.

The statutory Scheme for Construction is in two parts dealing with adjudication and with payment. The provision dealing with adjudication includes the following:

(i) The "Referring Party" may give a written "Notice of Adjudication" of their intention to refer a dispute. The Notice is to set out the nature and brief description of the dispute, the Parties and the nature of the redress which is sought. (Paragraph 1)

(ii) The Referring Party is to identify the Adjudicator who may be: (a) named in the Contract, (b) appointed by a Nominating Body named in the Contract, or (c) appointed by any other Adjudicator Nominating Body. The person so selected is to indicate their willingness to act within two days. (Paragraph 2)

(iii) An Adjudicator Nominating Body is to select an Adjudicator within five days. (Paragraphs 5 and 6)

(iv) The Referring Party, within seven days after the Notice of Adjudication, is to serve a "Referral Notice" on the Adjudicator and on any other Party ("the Referring Party"), to be accompanied by extracts from the Contract and any other documents relied on; and the adjudicator must inform the parties when it was received. (Paragraph 7)

(v) The Adjudicator is to reach his decision not later than: (a) 28 days after receipt of the referral notice; or (b) 42 days after receipt the referral notice if the referring party consents; or (c) such longer period as both Parties may agree. (Paragraph 19)

(vi) The Adjudicator must decide the matters in dispute. They are empowered specifically to open up and revise decisions rendered under the Contract except where they are final and conclusive. The Adjudicator is empowered to decide upon payments due under the Contract and to award simple or compound interest. (Paragraph 20)

Other paragraphs within the scheme provide for the adjudicator to adjudicate, with consent of the parties more than one dispute on the same contract or related disputes under different contracts and for the parties to extend time by agreement. The adjudicator may resign and the parties may agree to revoke the appointment, the adjudicator's right to payment then being dependent on the reason why the adjudication has been terminated. The scheme gives the adjudicator powers to direct the manner in which the adjudication is to be presented and conducted, including directing the timetable and limiting the length of written documents or oral representations. If a party fails to comply with a direction, including a failure to provide documents or written statements requested by the adjudicator, there is express power to continue with the adjudication, to draw adverse inferences and to make a decision based on the information before him (Paragraph 15). These powers are based on similar provisions applying to arbitrators and found in ss.34 and 41 of the Arbitration Act 1996.

By comparison with powers generally available to arbitrators, the following matters are significantly excluded from the powers available to the adjudicator:

(a) The Adjudicator has no power to give a provisional decision: any matter submitted must be decided finally, so far as the Adjudicator is concerned.

(b) The adjudicator, unlike an arbitrator, has no power to dismiss a claim which is not pursued in a timely manner; but time is of the essence in that the adjudicator's powers cease if the time limit expires without an authorised extension.

(c) In the absence of agreement between the parties, the adjudicator has no power to order that one party should pay the legal costs of the other and no power to order security for such costs.

With regard to the award of costs a number of abuses had been reported whereby sub-contractors were, as a term of the sub-contract, being required to pay the costs either of the adjudicator or of the contractor whatever the outcome of the adjudication. The 2009 Act therefore provides, by a new s.108A, that any agreement as to costs is ineffective unless it relates to the apportionment of the adjudicator's fees, and unless it is made after the giving of the notice to refer to adjudication. Where the Scheme for Construction applies, para.25 provides that the adjudicator may determine how his fees should be apportioned between the parties.

Where a dispute referred is the same or substantially the same as one which has previously been referred to adjudication and a decision has been given, the adjudicator must resign (Paragraph 9(2)). This appears to cover both overlapping disputes under the same contract and related disputes arising under separate contracts. Thus, in regard to an issue which potentially affects several parties, such as the cause of particular delay occurring on a project, the first adjudication decision given which will then prevent others dealing with the same or substantially the same dispute. In practice, such situations, if they have arisen, have not come before the court. The issue did, however, come before the court in *Quietfield v Vascroft Construction*[98] where, after an unsuccessful adjudication by the contractor seeking extensions of time (EOT), the employer brought an adjudication seeking an award of liquidated damages. The contractor filed a defence to which was appended a further claim to EOT containing additional grounds. The adjudicator decided not to take account of the further claim to EOT and awarded liquidated damages in consequence. The Court of Appeal decided that the further EOT claim was not the same or substantially the same as that previously decided and that the adjudicator should accordingly have taken it into account. Enforcement of the adjudicator's decision was therefore refused.

The adjudicator, if requested by one of the parties, is required to provide reasons for their decisions. In practice, adjudicators invariably provide reasons, sometimes in considerable detail. While the decision itself may not be challenged for error, the adjudicator is expressly required to "act impartially in carrying out his duties" and to reach a decision in accordance with the Contract and the applicable law. The requirement for "impartially" has led to number of cases in which the losing party has complained or a lack of procedural fairness or breach of "natural justice". The cases show that while the courts have accepted a need to comply broadly with these requirements, they are to be applied to adjudication subject to the limitations necessarily imposed by the Act. In *Discain Project Services v Opecprime (No 1)*[99] H.H. Judge Bowsher Q.C. said:

> "The Scheme makes regard for the rules for natural justice more rather than less important. Because there is no appeal on fact or law from the Adjudicator's decision, it is all the more important that the manner in which he reaches his decision should be beyond reproach. At the same time, one has to recognise that the Adjudicator is working under pressure of time and circumstances which makes it extremely difficult to comply with the rules of natural justice in the manner of a Court or an Arbitrator. Repugnant as it may be to ones approach to judicial decision making, I think that the system created by the (Act) can only be made to work in practice if some breaches of the rules of natural justice which had no demonstrable consequence are disregarded".

Thus, for example, the fact that an adjudicator may come to a decision on a point which has not been brought to the attention of one of the parties,

---

[98] [2007] B.L.R. 67.
[99] [2000] B.L.R. 402.

while ordinarily constituting a breach of natural justice, may not result in a refusal to enforce the decision unless the point is significant and material. In *Balfour Beatty v London Borough of Lambeth*[100] the adjudicator himself carried out a critical path analysis of delay issues without informing the parties of his intended methodology or seeking their observations and without giving the Responding Party an opportunity to deal with his analysis. Enforcement of the decision was refused. Enforcement on the ground of breach of the rules of natural justice was also refused where the adjudicator, although not regarded by the court as biased, had conducted private telephone conversations with one party or its representatives such that a fair minded and informed observer would conclude that there was a real possibility or danger of bias.[101]

Section 108(4) requires that the contract should provide in writing for immunity of the adjudicator. The statutory scheme deals with immunity in para.26, which closely follows s.29 of the Arbitration Act 1996, providing as follows:

"26. The adjudicator shall not be liable for anything done or omitted in the discharge or purported discharge of his functions as adjudicator unless the act of omission is in bad faith and any employee or agent of the adjudicator shall be similarly protected from liability."

While s.29 of the Arbitration Act creates an immunity affective against third parties, the scheme, where it applies, takes effect only as a matter of contract[102] which will not, therefore, bind third parties. Additionally, the scheme will not apply where there is a conforming contractual procedure. It is not clear whether the statutory scheme can apply in part, for example, where immunity only is not dealt with in the contractual procedure.

Enforcement of adjudication decision

The enforcement of an adjudication decision raises a number of potential difficulties which were not addressed in the original Housing Grants etc Act. Section 108(3), set out above, requires the contract to provide that the decision of the adjudicator is to be binding until the dispute is finally determined. No other status is given to the decision. The statutory scheme originally provided for enforcement by peremptory order by analogy with the Arbitration Act 1996. Enforcement by injunction has also been considered. However, in the first disputed enforcement action

---

[100] [2002] B.L.R. 288.
[101] *Discain Project Services v Opecprime (No 2)* [2001] B.L.R. 285.
[102] H'GCRA s.114(4).

in *Macob v Morrison Construction*,[103] Dyson J. adopted a purposive approach, seeking to give effect to the perceived intention of the Housing Grants etc. Act, and held that the usual means of enforcement should be by way of summary judgment on the ground that there was no defence to the claim. In response to the contention on behalf of the defendant that the word "decision" meant a lawful and valid decision and that a decision which was challenged could not be binding or enforceable, Dyson J. said:

> "It is clear that Parliament intended that the adjudication should be conducted in a manner which those familiar with the grinding detail of the traditional approach to the resolution of construction disputes apparently find difficult to accept. But Parliament has not abolished arbitration and litigation of construction disputes, it has merely introduced an intervening provisional stage in the dispute resolution process. Crucially it has made it clear that decisions of Adjudicators are binding and are to be complied with until the dispute is finally resolved".

The judge therefore held that a decision whose validity is challenged is nevertheless a decision within the meaning of the Act and should be enforced summarily.

Macob has been followed in many subsequent enforcement decisions given by judges of the TCC, in the course which the extent of available defences in enforcement proceedings has been progressively established. The position as regards enforcement can be summarised as follows:

(1) Is open to the defendant to contend that the contract in question is not subject to the Act because of the nature of its subject matter, for example, scaffolding intended for particular use.[104]

(2) An adjudication decision is enforceable only in relation to the dispute submitted to adjudication. This will not, however, prevent the parties or the adjudicator considering a wide range of arguments and contentions put forward in opposition to or in support of the claim. In *Cantillon Ltd v Urvasco Ltd*[105] enforcement of a decision on extension of time and prolongation costs was challenged on the ground that the adjudicator had made his decision in relation to a period other than that set out in the original claim. Akenhead J. held that the adjudicator was entitled to consider any argument, evidence or other material for or against the disputed claim and that the decision was to be

---

[103] [1999] B.L.R. 93.
[104] *Palmers v ABB Power Construction* (1999) C.I.L.L. 1543.
[105] (2008) C.I.L.L. 2565.

enforced. In reaching his decision, the judge declined to follow the decision in *Edmund Nuttall v RG Carter*[106] which had held that a referring party was bound by the grounds for extension of time first submitted and a decision based on different grounds was not to be enforced.

(3) An adjudication decision will be enforced despite containing an error, if the matter in question fell within the adjudicator's jurisdiction.[107] Thus, if the adjudicator has answered the wrong question, the decision is not enforceable; while if they have answered the correct question wrongly, the decision will be enforceable.

(4) The losing party cannot resist enforcement on the ground of a cross-claim arising after the adjudication was brought. A cross-claim in respect of which appropriate notice has been given[108] may be raised as a defence in the adjudication and determined by the adjudicator. In principle the responding party may have the right to rely on other contractual provisions, giving a right to resist payment of an adjudicator's award. This might apply in the case of termination of the underlying contract between the parties. In the case of *Ferson Contractors v Levolux*,[109] however, the Court of Appeal held that the responding party was not entitled to resist enforcement on this ground, where the disputed termination had not been raised in the adjudication.[110]

(5) The usual route to enforcement, as laid down in *Macob*, is by application for summary judgment under CPR Pt.24. Where an application does not succeed, it is open to the party seeking enforcement to proceed to a trial of the action upon which the court will give a final judgment either enforcing or refusing to enforce the adjudicator's decision.

(6) The responding party is entitled to say that there was in fact no dispute at the commencement of the adjudication and that the adjudicator therefore had no jurisdiction. Such assertions have been based on the contention that the parties were in

---

[106] [2002] B.L.R. 312.
[107] *Bouygues v Dahl Jensen* [2000] B.L.R. 522 (CA).
[108] Section 111 of the Housing Grants, etc. Act and *Rupert Morgan v Jervis* [2004] B.L.R. 18; and see Ch.9.
[109] [2003] B.L.R. 118.
[110] But see also *Bovis Lend Lease v Triangle Development* [2003] B.L.R. 31 and *Parsons Plastic v Purac* [2002] B.L.R. 334.

negotiation which had not reached a final conclusion.[111] An analogous situation arose in relation to intended arbitration proceedings in *Amec Civil Engineering v Secretary of State for Transport*.[112] In this case, disputes were to be referred to the Engineer under an ICE Contract as a condition precedent to reference to arbitration. Defects had been discovered just within the limitation period, so that the reference to the engineer was made, and his decision given, one day after a non-committal letter was sent by Amec. In the circumstances, including the imminent end of the limitation period, the Court of Appeal accepted that there was a dispute capable of being referred to the engineer. The same reasoning will apply in the case of adjudication, making it unlikely that an argument of "no dispute" would succeed.

(7) The converse of Proposition (6) is that, under the statutory scheme, only one dispute may be referred and the adjudicator cannot, without agreement, have jurisdiction to decide two disputes. The test as to whether there are in fact two disputes is whether the decision in Claim 1 necessarily involves deciding all or part of Claim No.2: *Witney Town Council v Beam Construction*.[113]

(8) Where it appears probable that the claimant will be unable to re-pay the money if the decision of the adjudicator is reversed on final determination of the dispute, the court has a discretion to order a stay of enforcement: *Wimbledon Construction v Derek Vago*.[114]

An important question for the adjudicator is whether he is entitled to payment of fees in the event no enforceable decision is produced. In *Systech International v P.C. Harrington*,[115] the Court of Appeal, reversing the decision of the TCC judge, held that where the decision was unenforceable on the ground of breaching the rules of natural justice, the adjudicator was not entitled to any fee. How far this case will apply to a decision which is unenforceable on other grounds will remain to be argued.

Despite the inability to challenge a finding of fact, and the absence of any appeal on law analogous to s.69 of the Arbitration Act 1996, it

---

[111] See *Edmund Nuttall v RG Carter* [2002] B.L.R. 312.
[112] [2005] B.L.R. 227.
[113] [2011] EWHC 2332.
[114] [2005] B.L.R. 374.
[115] [2012] EWCA Civ 1371.

remains a possibility that the court may be persuaded, within the times-scale of enforcement, to reach a contrary decision on an issue of law decided by the adjudicator. In a number of cases the respondent to enforcement proceedings has brought a cross-action for a declaration on a point of law decided adversely by the Adjudicator and invited the court to give a final decision on the point. In *Geoffrey Osborne v Atkins Rail*,[116] Edwards-Stuart J. gave a declaration under Pt 8 which effectively reversed part of the decision of the adjudicator, thereby constituting a *"final determination"* of one of the issues in the dispute. These cases demonstrate the possibility of effectively appealing on a point of law arising in an adjudication without waiting for a second round of full proceedings. However, in *WW Gear Construction v McGee Group*,[117] an application for a declaration as to the meaning and effect of a contract provision which potentially barred a claim was refused where the application was made during the course of an adjudication and before the adjudicator's decision was known.

Challenges to enforcement on the ground of unfairness were rejected in the original *Macob* decision. However, the matter returned to the courts under the Human Rights Act 1998 in *Austin Hall Building v Buckland Securities*,[118] where the defendant contended that the effect of the adjudication was to deny them a fair trial. They contended specifically that they had not had a proper and equal opportunity to present their case or a reasonable time within which to respond to the claim against them. H.H. Judge Bowsher Q.C. held that the adjudicator had not acted in a way incompatible with the Convention since, by virtue of the 28-day time limit, he could not have acted differently. Further, it was held that an adjudicator is not a "public authority" within the meaning of the Human Rights Act 1998 and that in any event the adjudicator had not breached art.6 of the Convention or failed to comply with the rules of natural justice. This case does not represent the last word on the application of the Human Rights Act, which remains to be considered in relation to adjudication by the House of Lords. Meanwhile challenges to applications for enforcement by summary judgement have continued to rely on contended breaches of natural justice and bias. While this has succeeded in a number of cases the courts have generally taken a robust view of such assertions. In *Amec v Whitefriars City Estates*[119] the Court of Appeal decided, in unusual circumstances, that an adjudicator's decision should be enforced despite palpable objections to the fairness of the

---

[116] [2010] B.L.R. 363.
[117] [2012] B.L.R. 355.
[118] (2001) C.I.L.L. 1734.
[119] [2005] B.L.R. 1.

process. The adjudicator had been appointed in an earlier reference and had given a decision, enforcement of which had been refused because the adjudicator appointment provisions had not been complied with. The same adjudicator was, against the objection of the losing party, re-appointed and gave the same decision. The respondent raised other grounds of bias in attempting to resist enforcement but the court decided that there was no objective appearance of bias and that the second decision should be enforced. Other cases on different facts will continue to come before the courts.[120]

A number of substantial adjudication cases have come before the court in which the responding party has complained that the sheer volume and complexity of the adjudication renders it impossible to conduct the proceedings fairly and impartially. In *London & Amsterdam v Waterman*[121] H.H. Judge Wilcox refused to grant summary enforcement of an adjudication decision in a substantial professional negligence claim, not on the ground that the nature or extent of the claims exceeded what could be dealt with in an adjudication, but on the specific ground that the referring party had, at a late stage submitted a substantial volume of additional evidence which the responding party had not had a fair opportunity to deal with. The responding party had complained of being ambushed, in response to which the Judge said:

> "I agree with the submission of Mr. Akenhead that mere ambush however unattractive does not necessarily amount to procedural unfairness. It depends on the case. It may be an important part of the context in which the Adjudicator is required to operate and in which his conduct may fall to be judged in the light of the fundamental common law requirements statutorily underpinned in Section 108(2)(e) of the Act".

In a further substantial case in which enforcement was resisted, inter alia, on the grounds of procedural unfairness, H.H. Judge Toulmin CMG Q.C. upheld an adjudication decision in a long and complex case in which both parties had acceded to successive requests for additional time by the adjudicator, who considered that he was then able to reach a fair decision on the dispute.[122] More recently it has been suggested that statutory adjudication, given its mandatory effect, is subject to public law rights with the effect that the courts should admit a wider range of challenges including irrationality.[123]

---

[120] See, e.g. *Fileturn v Royal Garden Hotel* [2010] B.L.R. 512.

[121] [2004] B.L.R. 179.

[122] *CIB Properties v Birse* [2005] B.L.R. 173.

[123] Public Law and Statutory Adjudication, Julian Bailey, Const L.J. 2008, v24, p.461 and see Ch.1 under Public Law.

The effect of adjudication

The availability of statutory adjudication deprives a building owner or employer of the right to rely on their appointed architect or engineer to regulate payment, the granting of extensions of time and other matters. The same applies in the case of main contractors vis à vis their sub-contractors. All decisions as to payment or otherwise are potentially open to review by an independent adjudicator within the short time-scale of statutory adjudication. Relatively few adjudication decisions are followed by subsequent arbitration or court proceedings. This is confirmed by a significant reduction in the number of TCC actions. The number of arbitration appointments has similarly declined, but under contracts not falling within the Act, disputes are usually resolved either by arbitration or by contractual adjudication.

Chapter 3

DISPUTE RESOLUTION—ARBITRATION

The term "arbitration" has no fixed or definite meaning. In popular usage, it denotes the placing of a dispute before a third party to obtain a fair or equitable resolution, based on discretion rather than on fixed rules. In industrial law, it refers to a process of conciliation, where attempts are made to find a formula acceptable to two parties in disagreement.[1] In commercial law, arbitration has acquired a more definite meaning, as a process, subject to statutory support by which formal disputes may be resolved in a binding manner by a tribunal of the parties' own choosing. It is in the third sense that arbitration has become widely adopted for the resolution of disputes under commercial contracts, including construction contracts, particularly involving international transactions. It is the principal alternative to determination of disputes in the appropriate national court. In the case of domestic construction contracts falling within the Housing Grants, Construction and Regeneration Act 1996, one or both parties will usually bring adjudication proceedings (see Ch.2) which may render further formal proceedings unnecessary.

Starting an Arbitration

Three things are required before there can be an arbitration. First, there must be a dispute. This requires one party to make a claim or assertion and the other party to deny it. Thus, there can be no dispute about a claim which has not previously been put forward, or which has not been rejected. This requirement is common to adjudication proceedings (see Ch.2). Secondly, there must be an agreement to arbitrate. In the case of adjudication there is a statutory right irrespective of whether the contract so provides. Thirdly, there must be a submission of the dispute to

---

[1] Under the Advisory Conciliation and Arbitration Service (ACAS) set up by the Employment Protection Act 1975.

arbitration, which also applies in the case of adjudication. In these and other respects arbitration and adjudication have many common features and draw upon each other's case law.

In construction contracts, the agreement to arbitrate is often included as one of the clauses of a standard form of contract, such as cl.66C of the ICE form. In such clauses the parties agree to submit future disputes to arbitration. There may also be an agreement to arbitrate made after the dispute has arisen, usually referred to as an ad hoc agreement.

In either case there must be a submission (sometimes called a reference) of a specified dispute to arbitration, by one party serving notice to refer on the other. No particular form is required for a submission but it is an important step, as it usually constitutes the commencement of the arbitration for the purpose of limitation, and is thus equivalent to the issuing of a claim form in court. Subject to agreement of the parties, arbitral proceedings are commenced when one party gives notice initiating whatever step is required in accordance with the arbitration agreement, for example requesting the President of the ICE to appoint an arbitrator.[2] No particular form is required for an arbitration agreement, whether made in advance or after a dispute has arisen. If the agreement is in writing, which is invariably so in the case of a construction contract, the arbitration will be governed by the Arbitration Act 1996. An arbitration can exist at common law outside the Act and could, in theory, be enforced in the same way as any other private dispute resolution procedure agreed between the parties.[3]

A reference to arbitration is deemed to be to a single arbitrator unless some other number is agreed.[4] Many commercial arbitrations (such as shipping and commodity disputes) employ three arbitrators who either sit as a court of two arbitrators (one appointed by each side) with an umpire to settle any disagreement; or alternatively as three arbitrators, one acting as chairman or presiding arbitrator. The difference is that an umpire is required to act only where the two appointed arbitrators disagree, upon which they take over as the sole arbitrator.[5] The umpire may or may not attend the hearing with the arbitrators, as the parties may agree. A chairman, on the other hand, acts throughout as one of the arbitrators, usually on the basis that they will make the decision if there is no majority.[6] Multiple tribunals have never been favoured in UK building and engineering disputes. The JCT and the ICE forms of contract have

---

[2] Arbitration Act 1996 s.14.
[3] See under Alternative Dispute Resolution, Ch.2.
[4] Arbitration Act 1996 s.15(3).
[5] s.21.
[6] s.20.

traditionally referred to one arbitrator. The International FIDIC Conditions contemplate that there may be more than one arbitrator, and tribunals consisting of three arbitrators are commonplace under ICC procedure (see below). The function of an umpire is, however, virtually unique to English arbitration law and other laws deriving from it.

The selection and appointment of an arbitrator(s) follows the reference to arbitration. A single arbitrator may be named in the arbitration agreement, but it is more usual to find a requirement that an arbitrator be agreed between the parties and in default appointed by an identified person or body. The JCT and ICE forms provide for appointment, in default of agreement, by the presidents of the RIBA or ICE respectively. In international cases, the arbitration agreement may provide for appointment by the International Chamber of Commerce (ICC) or the London Court of International Arbitration (LCIA). Where the parties cannot agree and there is no mechanism for the appointment, the court has power to appoint an arbitrator.[7] Where there is to be a tribunal of three it is usual for each party to appoint one arbitrator and for the third to be selected by the other two or appointed by an identified person or body. In a recent case which gave rise to issues as to the status of an arbitrator, the Court of Appeal held that arbitrators were employed by the parties, so that an arbitration agreement which provided that only persons of a certain religious belief could act as arbitrator was void as being in breach of UK anti-discrimination legislation (the Equality Act 2010). The issue was finally settled by the Supreme Court, which held, reversing the Court of Appeal, that arbitrators were not employed.[8]

What is arbitration?

Arbitration is to be distinguished from other processes met in construction contracts. The essentials of arbitration are that there must be a dispute, which is referred to an independent arbitrator who is to act in a judicial manner and come to a decision after receiving any evidence and submissions of the parties. Their decision is usually to be final, subject to the possibility of review of points of law by the courts. There are other analogous processes which do not constitute arbitration. Certifying requires the certifier to act professionally and fairly, but there is no dispute and the decision need not be final. Conciliation is used to reach a settlement, but is not usually regarded as arbitration because the parties do not bind themselves to accept the result. Valuation requires that the parties agree to accept an independent opinion, but there need not be a

---

[7] Section 18.
[8] *Hashwani v Jivraj* [2011] UKSC 40.

dispute and the valuer may not receive submissions or evidence. Adjudication (see Ch.2) is the nearest process to arbitration. The result is usually intended to be at least temporarily binding and the process is in many ways similar to arbitration.

It may be difficult to categorise a particular dispute resolution process. For example, the engineer's decision on a dispute under cl.66 of the pre-2005 ICE conditions must be made independently and may become binding. However, there is no duty to hear representations and the process does not amount to arbitration.[9] Arbitrators (like judges) are generally immune from action by the parties.[10] It was suggested in the case of *Sutcliffe v Thackrah*[11] that such immunity would not extend beyond a "quasi arbitration" that is, one to which the Arbitration Act did not apply, but which was an arbitration in all but name. Thus, certifiers, valuers and conciliators may be liable for negligent acts.

Arbitration and the courts

Arbitration is a private alternative to litigation as a means of settling disputes. Inevitably, there are many connections between the two processes. Arbitration must generally be conducted in accordance with the law.[12] The underlying function of the court is to support and enforce the arbitration process through a number of specific powers (see below). Arbitration proceedings are sometimes conducted in a manner analogous to court proceedings, for example, with pleadings, disclosure of documents and evidence closely following the Civil Procedure Rules. This is not a requirement, however, and both arbitrators and parties to an arbitration have a very wide discretion as to the way in which they conduct proceedings, the courts themselves being much more closely restricted by their own rules.

Disputes may generally be brought either in court or in arbitration, so that there is a possibility of conflict. Historically, the courts have been jealous of their supremacy, but the modern approach of the courts is to encourage (and sometimes compel) parties to take disputes to arbitration where they have so agreed. Where a conflict could arise, the courts take the view that it is primarily a matter for the parties whether they wish to proceed with the resolution of their disputes by arbitration or in court. In the case of *Lloyd v Wright*[13] the parties commenced an arbitration but the plaintiff subsequently issued a writ covering the same claims, and the

---

[9] See *AMEC Civil Engineering Ltd v Secretary of State for Transport* [2005] EWCA Civ 291.
[10] s.29 and see also s.74.
[11] [1974] A.C. 727.
[12] But see the Arbitration Act 1996 s.46.
[13] [1983] Q.B. 1065.

question arose as to whether this brought the arbitration to an end. Eveleigh L.J. in the Court of Appeal held:

> "The principle that the court will not allow its jurisdiction to be ousted is at the root of the defendant's argument. However, the court does not claim a monopoly in deciding disputes between parties. It does not, of its own initiative, seek to interfere when citizens have recourse to other tribunals. The court exercises its jurisdiction when appealed to. Until then, the court is not conscious of ignominy if an arbitrator decides a question with which the court is competent to deal. Furthermore, the court will not refuse to allow the subject matter of an action already begun to be referred to arbitration, if the parties so agree. . . . The court, however, will not permit its assistance to be denied to a party who has invoked it except by that party's consent or by its own ruling."

Arbitration and other processes

Arbitration may usefully be compared with other dispute resolution processes as dealt with in Ch.2. In contrast to litigation, arbitration is more final, being subject to challenge only in limited and particular circumstances as detailed below. In contrast to adjudication it is not subject to such stringent time limits, but is more readily enforceable and not susceptible to a rehearing. In contrast to mediation, a party to an arbitration agreement can be compelled to submit to arbitration. Arbitration is to be preceded under some forms of contract (particularly FIDIC—see Ch.13) by reference to a Dispute Adjudication Board (DAB).

This is entirely dependent on the terms of the contract, which provide that the decision of the Board is binding on the parties subject to final arbitration. The process is therefore analogous to statutory adjudication, but the proceedings resemble more of an arbitration. Finally, in contrast to expert determination, arbitration is supported and, to some extent, overseen by state courts, usually limited to those of the country in which the arbitration takes place or in which recognition of the arbitration agreement or enforcement of the award is sought. The function of the English courts in relation to expert determination is limited to enforcement of the decision of the expert, including challenges on the limited grounds available. There are no international conventions supportive of expert determination and its effect in another state is dependent on the local law.

The Arbitration Act 1996

This major piece of new legislation has a long history. Before 1996 the principal arbitration Act was the Act of 1950 which substantially re-enacted the Act of 1934. Many of the provisions dated back to the Arbitration Act of 1889. Owing to its commercial importance, London attracted a large amount of international work, much of this in the maritime, insurance and commodity fields as well as construction. For most of the twentieth century such arbitrations were conducted largely by English arbitrators applying English law. A high proportion of arbitrators in all commercial fields, including construction, were technically and not legally qualified. The system operated satisfactorily through the "case stated" procedure,[14] whereby any point of law could readily be brought before the commercial court. This procedure had the advantage of ensuring compliance with the law and, at the same time, aiding the development of English commercial law through the cases.

Changes began to occur from the 1950s onwards. In 1958 the New York Convention on the enforcement of foreign awards was launched, although only ratified in the United Kingdom by the Arbitration Act 1975. This convention recognised the increasing importance of international trade and the "internationalisation" of commercial arbitration. By the 1970s the view was held that London was losing international business to other foreign centres because of the ease with which appeals could be mounted, whether in domestic or international cases. The lack of finality was regarded as commercially unacceptable. This led to the Arbitration Act 1979 which abolished case stated and substituted a qualified right of appeal, dependent upon leave of the court. Although not made clear by the Act, the House of Lords soon laid down that leave should be sparingly given[15] so that in the majority of cases an award would be final. The next and most fundamental development was the launch in 1985 of the UNCITRAL[16] Model Law on international commercial arbitration. This was intended to be adopted, with or without amendment, in place of national arbitration laws, to produce a harmonised system for international arbitration law, with the option also of adopting the Model Law for domestic arbitration.

A Departmental Advisory Committee (DAC) was established by the DTI, initially chaired by Lord Mustill and subsequently by Lords Steyn and Saville, to consider how England should respond. The first DAC report of 1989 rejected adoption of the Model Law in England and Wales, either to replace existing English domestic law or for international arbitration, but recommended that a new and updated arbitration law be prepared. Subsequently, a DTI committee considering the law of Scotland recommended adoption of the Model Law, which was

---

[14] Arbitration Act 1950 s.21.
[15] *BTP Tioxide v Pioneer Shipping (The Nema)* [1981] A.C. 724.
[16] United Nation Commission on International Trade Law.

incorporated into Scots law in 1990 for international arbitration, Scottish domestic arbitration law remaining unchanged.[17] The DAC produced a number of further reports for England and Wales which led to amendments to the existing Arbitration Acts. Finally, a complete draft Bill was produced in 1994 and substantially revised in 1995. This supersedes with major amendments all the pre-existing Arbitration law. It also codifies the major common law principles of arbitration which had not previously appeared in any of the Acts. Without reversing its earlier decision to reject the Model Law, the DAC nevertheless adopted substantial elements of the Model Law, which has been referred to as the most important influence over the new law. The Act makes major changes in the underlying approach to arbitration and will have a fundamental effect on the process. The Act applies to any arbitral proceedings commenced on or after January 31, 1997. The new Act applies in Northern Ireland. Scotland, since 2010, has had its own Act.[18] While much of the old case law is still of relevance, it must now be applied with reference to the provisions of the 1996 Act.

Effect of an arbitration agreement

Since arbitration is a matter of private agreement, the arbitrator's authority depends upon the scope of that agreement. This may be completely general, such as an arbitration agreement within a contract to refer "any dispute or difference arising under or in connection with the contract"; or it may be limited to specified areas of dispute, for example, an agreement in a lease that disputes as to rent review are to be settled by arbitration. Building and engineering contracts usually contain wide arbitration clauses, but there are usually time limits within which a reference may be commenced, following either the decision of an engineer, or an adjudicator or some other event under the contract. It was also common to provide in construction contracts that disputes might only be commenced after completion of the works, but this requirement has largely disappeared form modern contracts. Such provisions would not in any event affect the right to refer a dispute to adjudication (see Ch.2).

Construction cases before the courts have proceeded on the basis that, where there was an arbitration agreement in the contract, the court would exercise the same powers as the arbitrator, for example by reviewing certificates and extensions of time as necessary. In the case of *Northern*

---

[17] The Arbitration (Scotland) Act 2010 has now brought Scots arbitration law substantially into line with English law, save that it is still possible for parties in Scotland to opt for the UNCITRAL Model Law.

[18] Arbitration (Scotland) Act 2010.

RHA v Derek Crouch,[19] the Court of Appeal held that the court did not have the same powers and interpreted the words "open up review and revise any certificate" in the JCT arbitration clause as creating a power exclusively to be exercised by an arbitrator. The result was that the court was held to have no jurisdiction over such matters. The case was overruled by the House of Lords in *Beaufort Developments v Gilbert-Ash NI,*[20] where it was held that clear and unequivocal words would be needed to deprive a party of recourse to the court and that this was not the effect of the JCT arbitration clause. Lord Hope put the matter this way:

> "If the contract provides that the sole means of establishing the facts is the expression of opinion of an architect's certificate, that provision must be given effect to by the court. But in all other respects, where a party comes to the court in the search of an ordinary remedy under the contract or for a remedy in respect of an alleged breach of it, the court is entitled to examine the facts and to form its own opinion upon them in the light of the evidence. The fact that the architect has formed an opinion on the matter will be part of the evidence. But, as it will not be conclusive evidence, the court can disregard his opinion if it does not agree with it".

Thus, with the exception of any certificate expressed as binding in subsequent proceedings, the courts or an arbitrator have equal and parallel jurisdiction to determine disputes arising under the contract.

Multi-party proceedings

One of the recurrent difficulties of construction industry arbitration is that disputes often involve more than two parties. Ordinarily an arbitration must be limited to the parties to the particular agreement, there being no power comparable to powers available in court to join other parties (see Ch.2). Under the old law (prior to January 1997) it was possible to bring court proceedings against two or more defendants and rely on the discretion of the court to refuse to grant a stay in favour of arbitration. Thus, an owner might bring parallel court proceedings in respect of defects against the contractor and against the designer, alleging alternative claims. This solution, however, is no longer available under the Arbitration Act 1996, because the court no longer has discretion to refuse a stay (see below). Multi-party arbitration proceedings must be based on consent.

---

[19] [1984] Q.B. 644.
[20] [1998] 2 W.L.R. 860.

Multi-party arbitration can take two forms. Consolidation involves treating two or more arbitrations as a single case, to be heard in one set of proceedings and determined by one single award. In effect, consolidated arbitrations merge into a single arbitration in which the arbitrator determines the issues of liability as between all parties. Alternatively, there may be concurrent hearings of two separate arbitrations which remain separate and lead to two separate awards, save that the awards may be expected to be consistent. It is clear that consolidation can never be ordered without the consent of all parties. It is less clear whether an arbitrator when appointed under two related contracts disputes, has a discretion to hold concurrent hearings.[21] An appointing body may decide to appoint the same arbitrator, for example, in a main contract and related sub-contract dispute. The expectation is that there will be consistent findings. Where one or more of the parties objects to concurrent hearings, the arbitrator must adopt a form of procedure which avoids inconsistent findings but which also respects the individual privacy (autonomy) of the parties. Where separate arbitrators are appointed, the problem does not arise.

The position is confirmed by a new provision in the Arbitration Act 1996 as follows:

> "35—(1) The parties are free to agree—
>   (a) that the arbitral proceedings shall be consolidated with other arbitral proceedings, or
>   (b) that concurrent hearings shall be held on such terms as may be agreed
> (2) Unless the parties agree to confer such power on the tribunal, the tribunal has no power to order consolidation of proceedings or concurrent hearings."

This provision does not assist the arbitrator who is appointed in two related disputes involving different parties, where there is no such agreement. In the case *Abu Dhabi v Eastern Bechtel*,[22] the court was asked to appoint an arbitrator in closely related disputes under a main contract and a sub-contract, where the parties had agreed that the arbitrator should be appointed by the English court. The court had to weigh up the competing arguments for and against appointing the same arbitrator. The Court of Appeal concluded that they could appoint the same arbitrator on the parties' agreement that there could be an application to replace the arbitrator if one party thought that it was being prejudiced. Lord Denning M.R. expressed the problem as follows:

---

[21] See *Oxford Shipping v Nippon* [1984] 3 All E.R. 835.
[22] (1992) 21 B.L.R. 117.

"The sub-contractors, for instance, might say that the arbitrator's decision in the first arbitration might affect his decision the second arbitration. If he had already formed his view in the first arbitration, they would be prejudiced. It would be most unfair to them: because he would be inclined to hold the same view in the second arbitration. On the other hand, as we have often pointed out, there is often a danger in having two separate arbitrations in a case like this. You might get inconsistent findings if there were two separate arbitrators."

The solution to these difficulties lies in agreement such as that embodied in the CIMA Rules, incorporated by cl.41B of the JCT 1998 edition. These rules expressly empower the arbitrator to hold concurrent hearings (rule 3.7) when appointed in two or more related arbitrations.

A different type of multi-party problem arose in the case of *Lafarge Redland v Shephard Hill Civil Engineering*[23] where the FCEC form of sub-contract between the parties allowed the main contractor (Shephard Hill) to require that any dispute under the sub-contract should be dealt with jointly with a related dispute under the main contract. The sub-contractor (Redland) gave notice of a number of disputes which Shephard Hill required to be dealt with under the main contract, but failed to appoint an arbitrator, so preventing the sub-contract disputes from proceeding. The House of Lords held there to be an implied term that the main contract arbitration procedure would be initiated within a reasonable time. In default, the sub-contractor was entitled to proceed to separate arbitration under the sub-contract.

Stay of proceedings

If one party to an arbitration agreement brings court proceedings in respect of a matter covered by the agreement they are technically in breach of contract. The court does not order specific performance of the agreement to arbitrate. Instead, the party wishing to enforce the arbitration agreement may apply for a stay of the court proceedings which, if granted, leaves arbitration as the only remedy. If a stay is not granted the action may continue in court.

The court's power to order a stay of proceedings is now contained in s.9 of the Arbitration Act 1996 as follows:

"**9**—(1) A party to an arbitration agreement against whom legal proceedings are brought (whether by way of claim or counterclaim) in respect of a matter which under the agreement is to be referred to arbitration may (upon notice to the other parties to the proceedings)

[23] [2000] B.L.R. 385 (HL).

apply to the court in which the proceedings have been brought, to stay the proceedings so far as they concern that matter.

(2) An application may be made notwithstanding that the matter is to be referred to arbitration only after the exhaustion of other dispute resolution procedures.

(3) An application may not be made by a person before taking the appropriate procedural step (if any) to acknowledge the legal proceeding against him or after he has taken any step in those proceedings to answer the substantive claim.

(4) On an application under this section the court shall grant a stay unless satisfied that the arbitration agreement is null and void, inoperative, or incapable of being performed."

This section gives effect to the provisions of the New York Convention 1958 by which arbitration clauses are required to be enforced (or recognised) save on the grounds set out. English law had previously adopted a difference approach, by which the court had a discretion to refuse to grant a stay (and thereby to refuse enforcement of the arbitration agreement). The grounds on which the court might exercise its discretion included the bringing of alternative claims against two or more defendants, where enforcement of the arbitration agreement would result in multiple proceedings.[24] When the United Kingdom acceded to the New York Convention by the Arbitration Act 1975, it was provided that the mandatory recognition of arbitration agreement, (with no discretion as to stay) applied to international and not to "domestic" arbitration. The availability of the courts' power to refuse a stay of proceedings in domestic arbitration was intended to be preserved by s.86 of the Arbitration Act 1996. Before the 1996 Act came into force, a decision of the Court of Appeal indicated that the provision would be regarded as discriminatory and s.86 was not brought into effect. Consequently, since January 1997, the English courts have been obliged to grant a stay save where any of the grounds set out in s.9 of the 1996 Act are established. In practice, the most important ground is now the taking of "any step in those proceedings to answer the substantive claim". Cases under the old law indicate that any response to the court proceedings, such as filing a defence or even applying for an adjournment of the proceedings, will be regarded as a "step", depriving the defendant of any further right to enforce the arbitration agreement.

Time-bar clauses

Commercial contracts frequently require arbitration proceedings to be commenced within a limited period, being considerably shorter than the

---

[24] See s.4(1) of the Arbitration Act 1950 and *Taunton-Collins v Cromie* [1964] 1 W.L.R. 633.

period of limitation. Periods of months or even weeks are not uncommon. Failure to comply with such limits effectively bars any subsequent right of action. Consequently, a provision was inserted into the Arbitration Acts[25] which empowered the courts to extend the time for beginning arbitration proceedings. Construction contracts tended to include a different type of provision which would render a certificate or decision binding unless challenged by giving notice of arbitration within a specified period. Thus, the engineer's decision under cl.66 of the ICE Conditions was to be binding unless challenged by notice of arbitration; and similarly the architect's final certificate under JCT 98, cl.30.9 (see below).

In *Crown Estate Commissioners v Mowlem*[26] the employer sought to rely on the power of the court to extend time for commencing arbitration proceedings in order to avoid the binding effect of a final certificate in accordance with cl.30.9 of the JCT form of contract (then, JCT 80). The Court of Appeal held that the power to extend the time for arbitration did not empower the court to override the binding effect of the final certificate. The court's power is now somewhat wider under the Arbitration Act 1996, as follows:

> "**12**—(1) Where an arbitration agreement to refer future disputes to arbitration provides that a claim shall be barred, or the claimant's right extinguished, unless the claimant takes within a time fixed by the agreement some step—
> (a) to begin arbitral proceedings, or
> (b) to begin other dispute resolution procedures which must be exhausted before arbitral proceedings can be begun
> the court may by order extend the time for taking that step.
>   . . .
>   (3) The court shall make an order only if satisfied—
> (a) that the circumstances are such as were outside the reasonable contemplation of the parties when they agreed the provision in question, and that it would be just to extend the time, or
> (b) that the conduct of one party makes it unjust to hold the other party to the strict terms of the provision in question."

The new section includes the words "or the claimant's right extinguished", which will permit the court to avoid both a time-bar and a binding certificate, where relief is to be granted, thereby reversing the effect of *Crown Estates*. The new clause further sets out the grounds

---

[25] Previously s.27 of the Arbitration Act 1950.
[26] (1994) 70 B.L.R. 1.

upon which the court may exercise its discretion, which is likely to be sparingly applied.

PROCEDURE IN ARBITRATION

Who is in charge of procedure? There has been long debate as to the proper balance under English law between the powers of the arbitrator and the ability of the parties (or their representatives) to dictate the procedure. Previously, the law stated that the parties should do "all . . . things which during the proceedings on the reference the arbitrator or umpire may require".[27] However, this was usually interpreted as being subject to the agreement of the parties, even if communicated orally during the hearing. The result was that, while the arbitrator was "master of the proceedings"[28] their mastery was subject at any time to an agreement between the parties, for example, extending the length of the hearing.

The result is that arbitration has often been regarded as slow, costly and out of touch with commercial requirements, with the powers of the arbitrator being very limited. The 1996 Act has responded positively to the debate over both the powers of the arbitrator and the efficiency of the proceedings. Section 1 of the Act now states the founding principles as follows:

> "(1)(a) the object of arbitration is to obtain the fair resolution of disputes by an impartial tribunal without unnecessary delay or expense;
>
> (b) the parties should be free to agree how their disputes are resolved, subject only to such safeguards as are necessary in the public interest."

This is supplemented by an important general duty on the arbitrator or tribunal as follows:

> "**33**—(1) The tribunal shall—
>
> (a) act fairly and impartially as between the parties, giving each party a reasonable opportunity of putting his case and dealing with that of his opponent, and
>
> (b) adopt procedures suitable to the circumstances of the particular case, avoiding unnecessary delay or expense, so as to provide a fair means for the resolution of the matters falling to be determined.

---

[27] Arbitration Act 1950 s.12(1).
[28] *Bremer Vulcan v South India Shipping* [1981] A.C. 909.

> (2) The tribunal shall comply with that general duty in conducting the arbitral proceedings, in it decisions on matters of procedure and evidence and in the exercise of all other powers conferred on it."

Further, in setting out the list of procedural and evidential matters requiring decision, it is stated:

> "**34**—(1) It shall be for the tribunal to decide all procedural and evidential matters, subject to the right of the parties to agree any matter."

Section 5 of the Act provides that any such agreement must ordinarily be made in writing. The result is that the arbitrator will be bound by such written agreement (usually comprising the arbitration agreement together with incorporated rules) as exists at the date of their appointment. Subject to this, they have the power "to decide all procedural and evidential matters" unless the parties enter into a further written agreement. In this event, if the further agreement involves fundamental changes or restrictions on the power of the arbitrator, it would be open to them to decline to be bound by the new agreement. This would create an impasse which would require either further agreement as to procedure between the parties and the arbitrator, the parties' agreement to revoke the arbitrator's appointment,[29] or the arbitrator's resignation.[30] While these circumstances are unlikely to arise save in an extreme case, they are a necessary element in establishing, for the first time in English arbitration law, that the arbitrator, subject to the terms of their appointment, is to be in control of the procedure.

Detailed procedural matters

Section 34(2) lists the following matters which are to be decided by the arbitrator in the absence of written agreement:

(a) when and where any part of the proceedings is to be held;

(b) the language or languages to be used in the proceedings and whether translations of any relevant documents are to be supplied;

(c) whether any and if so what form of written statements of claim and defence are to be used, when these should be supplied and the extent to which such statements can be later amended;

---

[29] Arbitration Act 1996 s.23.
[30] s.25.

(d) whether any and if so which documents or classes of documents should be disclosed between and produced by the parties and at what stage;

(e) whether any and if so what questions should be put to and answered by the respective parties and when and in what form this should be done;

(f) whether to apply strict rules of evidence (or any other rules) as to the admissibility, relevance or weight of any material (oral, written or other) sought to be tendered on any matters of fact or opinion, and the time, manner and form in which such material should be exchanged and presented;

(g) whether and to what extent the tribunal should itself take the initiative in ascertaining the facts and the law; and

(h) whether and to what extent there should be oral or written evidence or submissions.

Ordinarily, many of these matters will be the subject of rules incorporated within the arbitration agreement (see below). The 1996 Act also sets out a number of specific powers which the arbitrator may exercise unless otherwise agreed by the parties. These are as follows:

- power to appoint experts or legal advisors or to appoint assessors to assist on technical matters[31];

- power to order security for the costs of the arbitration; and

- power to give directions in relation to any property which is the subject of the proceedings, including inspection, preservation, taking samples or making tests.[32]

The 1996 Act also contains two powers of great importance to construction industry arbitrations which are stated to be available only if the parties so agree:

- a power to order consolidation or concurrent hearings of two related arbitrations in which the same tribunal is appointed[33]; and

- a power to make a provisional order or award.[34]

---

[31] Section 37.
[32] Section 38.
[33] Section 35.
[34] Section 39.

This latter power is considered further below in relation to the range of decisions available to an arbitrator. All the above powers are supplemented by a general duty of co-operation placed upon the parties themselves as follows:

> "**40**—(1) The parties shall do all things necessary for the proper and expeditious conduct of the arbitral proceedings.
>
> (2) This includes—
>
> (a) complying without delay with any determination of the tribunal as to procedural or evidential matters, or with any order or directions of the tribunal . . .".

Arbitrators are often requested, in the absence of other applicable procedure, to follow court practice in ordering pleadings, disclosure of documents and other matters. While this may be a useful guide, the 1996 Act makes it clear that these rules do not apply to arbitration. The arbitrator should in every case use their discretion as to what is required. There may be cases where, in lieu of formal pleadings, it is sufficient for the claimant to rely on an existing claim document, and for the respondent to be ordered to submit details of grounds of disagreement. This may save considerable time and cost to the parties. Similarly, there is no requirement for an arbitrator to direct a formal hearing following practice in the High Court. The arbitrator might, if appropriate, direct the parties to attend on site and explain their dispute directly to them there, or they might require the parties to deliver documents to them so that they may investigate the dispute before proceeding further; or again, if the arbitrator forms the view there is some issue of principle upon which the dispute will turn, they might order the parties to deal with this issue at the outset. In all such matters, the arbitrator is required to decide upon the procedure to be adopted, taking account of the express duties contained in the 1996 Act.

An issue which arises frequently in international cases, where it may not be possible or convenient for an application to be made to the court, is whether the arbitrator or tribunal should order what are referred to under the ICC Rules as "interim or conservatory measures". These are usually understood to mean measures intended to preserve the status quo pending the decision of the tribunal on the merits of the case, which may be many months or years in the future. It is generally recognised that Interim Measures can assist the parties and all arbitration rules make provision in their own terms for the tribunal to have such powers. This is recognised by the English Arbitration Act 1996 which provides by s.38 that the parties are free to agree on the powers exercisable by the tribunal, providing also default powers including those mentioned above. The powers exercised by tribunals will generally be of a conservatory nature, for example ordering a party to refrain from demolishing works pending examination by an expert for the parties, It is important that, in ordering such measures, the tribunal does not form any view on the merits of the case, which at that stage will be largely undefined. There are proposals to amend the UNCITRAL Rules (see below) to include wide powers to order interim measures.

Duties of the arbitrator

The express requirement under s.33(1)(a) to act "fairly and impartially as between the parties", although derived from the UNCITRAL Model Law[35] expresses in part the common law duty which applies to arbitrators and other tribunals, to comply with the rules of "natural justice". This is an unwritten concept whose boundary can be traced through the cases in which arbitrators have been accused of what was formerly called "misconduct",[36] but will now be known as "serious irregularity[37] (see below). The arbitrator must be impartial and must act so as to convey a continuing impression of impartiality. This does not mean that an arbitrator can have no connection whatsoever with either of the parties—in the construction industry this would be an impossibility since arbitrators and lawyers alike are regularly engaged in disputes involving major players in the industry. The arbitrator should, however, be satisfied that they are in fact impartial in relation to the dispute in question and should disclose any circumstances which, if known, might create doubt. The arbitrator must also ensure that they possess any qualifications required by the arbitration agreement and that they are in all ways capable of properly conducting the proceedings. The 1996 Act provides specifically for the removal of an arbitrator on the grounds:

> "**24**—(1) (a) that circumstances exist that give rise to justifiable doubts as to his impartiality;
> (b) that he does not possess the qualifications required by the arbitration agreement;
> (c) that he is physically or mentally incapable of conducting the proceedings or there are justifiable doubts as to his capacity to do so;
> (d) that he has refused or failed—
> (i) properly to conduct the proceedings, or
> (ii) to use all reasonable despatch in conducting the proceedings or making an award,
> and that substantial injustice has been or will be caused to the applicant."

---

[35] Article 18.
[36] Arbitration Act 1950 s.23.
[37] Arbitration Act 1996 s.68.

This, and other sections as well, apply subject to application first to any institution vested with relevant powers.

Remission and setting aside

The sanction available under s.24 is limited to removal: the court has no power to remit, for example, with a direction that the arbitrator should henceforth conduct the proceedings in some different manner. This emphasises the limited extent to which the courts exercise any overseeing role in arbitration. In the case of *Damond Lock v Laing Investments*[38] an arbitrator decided to maintain a hearing date even though one party had produced a large number of relevant documents at a late stage so that the other party would have no proper opportunity to consider them. The court had no jurisdiction to remit the matter[39] and consequently had to choose between allowing the matter to proceed or removing the arbitrator, in this case choosing the latter.

The power of the court to remit to the arbitrator on the ground of serious irregularity is available only once the tribunal has made an award.[40] The court then has power to remit the award, set the award aside or declare it to be of no effect in whole or in part. The court must also be satisfied that serious injustice has or will be caused to the applicant. The individual grounds upon which an application may be made are:

"**68**—(2) (a) failure by the tribunal to comply with section 33 (general duty of tribunal);

(b) the tribunal exceeding its power (otherwise than by exceeding its substantive jurisdiction: see section 67);

(c) failure by the tribunal to conduct the proceedings in accordance with the procedure agreed by the parties;

(d) failure by the tribunal to deal with all the issues that were put to it;

(e) any arbitral or other institution or person vested by the parties with powers in relation to the proceedings or the award exceeding its powers;

(f) uncertainty or ambiguity of the award;

(g) the award being obtained by fraud or the award or the way in which it was procured being contrary to public policy;

(h) failure to comply with the requirements as to the form of the award;

(i) any irregularity in the conduct of the proceedings or in the award which is admitted by the tribunal or by any arbitral or other institution or person vested by the parties with powers in relation to the proceedings or the award."

---

[38] (1992) 60 B.L.R. 112.

[39] Under s.22 of the Arbitration Act 1950.

[40] The same result was held to apply in the case of an application under s.22 of the Arbitration Act 1950 in *Three Valleys v Binnie & Partners* (1990) 52 B.L.R. 42.

The above provisions are a compendium of many provisions formerly found in the cases. It is a useful checklist for the arbitrator. Some of the provisions are more obviously directed towards remission (for example, failure to deal with all the issues, or ambiguity in the award); while others are likely to give rise to a serious question as to whether remission or removal is most appropriate (for example, failure to comply with the agreed procedure). An application under s.68 may be coupled with an alternative application for removal under s.24, for example on the grounds of lack of partiality.

How should the arbitrator proceed in practice so as to avoid an application to the court? As well as being in fact impartial the arbitrator should take pains to appear impartial at all stages and be seen to treat the parties equally. They should ordinarily act only upon the evidence or other material presented to them in the arbitration. If they wish to take any step which might take the parties by surprise or be regarded as unconventional, they should inform the parties as to what they are doing and give such explanation as will demonstrate that they have proper reasons. Another important practical question is how to control the length of the proceedings. In this regard, they have potentially conflicting duties to give the parties a reasonable opportunity to put their cases, but to avoid unnecessary delay or expense.[41] The important word is "reasonable" and this means that the arbitrator may and on occasions must, set a limit to various stages of the proceedings, unless they are bound by an agreement between the parties.

The arbitrator must take a sufficient note of the evidence and argument to enable them to determine the issues and to deliver a reasoned award, if called for. The parties may agree to provide a shorthand note of the proceedings. Alternatively, some arbitrators choose to make their own tape recordings of the hearing. This should not, however, be regarded as a normal requirement; and it should never be regarded as a substitute for following the argument as it goes on.

An example of an arbitrator falling foul of the general requirements as to conduct is found in the difficult case of *Fox v P.G. Wellfair*.[42] The respondent builders were in liquidation at the time of arbitration proceedings which were about a block of flats which were alleged to contain numerous defects. The proceedings were continued to obtain the benefit of NHBC insurance, but were effectively undefended so that the plaintiff's evidence was unchallenged. Instead of making an award in accordance with the plaintiff's evidence, the arbitrator substantially reduced the sums claimed. He relied on his own opinion about the defects, but did not disclose this to the plaintiff, who had no reason to suppose that their

---

[41] Arbitration Act 1996 s.33(1)(a) and (b).
[42] [1981] 2 Lloyd's Rep. 514.

evidence was contested. The Court of Appeal held that the arbitrator had committed misconduct by failing to bring his views to the attention of the plaintiff. The three judgments show a range of views as to what the arbitrator had done wrong. Essentially, the court considered that the plaintiff ought to have had the opportunity of knowing what was in the arbitrator's mind. However, in *J D Wetherspoon v Jay Mar Estates*[43] it was held in the TCC that a rent review arbitrator was not in error in relying on his own assessment of rent without giving parties opportunity for further submission. This reflects the more supportive approach of the courts since the passing of the 1996 Act.

Power of the courts

Traditionally the courts have exercised a wide range of powers in support of the arbitration process.[44] In recent years, however, there has been a policy of progressively reducing these powers to those regarded as essential. The 1996 Act has continued this policy through a number of express provisions which encourage the transfer of powers to the arbitrator or to an arbitral institution. The remaining essential powers of the court fall into the following categories:

(1) appointment and removal of arbitrators,

(2) extension of time and stay of proceedings,

(3) supportive powers during the proceedings, and

(4) challenges to and enforcement of awards.

In regard to category (1), the courts have always had power to step in when necessary to ensure that appropriate arbitrators are appointed and this continues under the 1996 Act.[45] Category (2) is dealt with above and category (4) below. This section deals with the remaining supportive powers in the 1996 Act, which are all subject to any agreement of the parties to exclude such powers.

It is to be noted that s.1(c), following the UNCITRAL model law, now provides expressly in relation to Pt I of the Act (ss.1–84) that "*the court should not intervene except as provided by this Part*". It might appear that the court had no remaining inherent powers. However, in *Al Naimi v Islamic Press Agency*[46] the Court of Appeal, faced with an issue as to whether or not

---

[43] [2007] B.L.R. 285.
[44] Arbitration Act 1950 s.12(4)(5) and (6).
[45] Sections 17, 18.
[46] [2000] B.L.R. 150.

disputes fell within an arbitration agreement, decided that the court had an inherent power to stay the proceedings so that an arbitrator could decide both the issues of jurisdiction and the substantive matters, if falling within the arbitration agreement. In *J Jarvis & Sons v Blue Circle*[47] the court, while accepting that the power to grant an injunction remained available,[48] held that it would be exercised rarely and refused to stay an arbitration where the respondent anticipated the issue of a parallel claim in court.

Section 44 of the 1996 Act provides for the court to have power to make orders in relation to the following matters, unless otherwise agreed by the parties:

> "(a) the taking of the evidence of witnesses;
> (b) the preservation of evidence;
> (c) making orders relating to property which is the subject of the proceedings or as to which any question arises in the proceedings—
>
>> (i) for the inspection, photographing, preservation, custody or detention of the property, or
>> (ii) ordering that samples be taken from, or any observation be made of or experiment conducted upon, the property;
>
>> and for that purpose authorising any person to enter any premises in the possession or control of a party to the arbitration;
> (d) the sale of any goods the subject of the proceedings; and
> (c) the granting of an interim injunction or the appointment of a receiver."

The courts' powers are further limited to acting in cases of urgency, or otherwise with the permission of the tribunal or agreement of the parties. The court will not act if the tribunal or any arbitral institution has the power and is able to act. These provisions emphasise the extremely narrow circumstances in which the court will now take "supportive" action. All the above measures are within the list of powers that may, in the absence of contrary agreement, be exercised by the arbitrator (see s.38) save for the powers under (e) to grant an interim injunction or to appoint a receiver. The parties must therefore consider at the outset whether they wish the court to retain these potentially valuable powers. In addition, s.43 permits a party to make use of the powers of the court to secure the attendance of a witness, but only with the permission of the tribunal or the agreement of the parties. Again, this is a matter to be considered in the arbitration agreement or in any incorporated rules.

---

[47] [2007] B.L.R. 439.
[48] Under s.37 of the Senior Courts Act 1981.

Powers in case of default

The 1979 Act allowed a party to apply to the court to vest the arbitrator with enhanced powers to deal with default.[49] This is now replaced by s.41 of the 1996 Act which provides that the parties are free to agree default powers. In the absence of agreement, the tribunal has power, where a party fails to comply with an order or direction without sufficient cause, to make a "peremptory order", giving a time for compliance. If the party then fails to comply, the tribunal may do any of the following:

(a) direct that the party in default shall not be entitled to rely upon any allegation or material which was the subject matter of the order;

(b) draw such adverse inferences from the act of non-compliance as the circumstances justify;

(c) proceed to an award on the basis of such materials as have been properly provided to it; and

(d) make such order as it thinks fit as to the payment of costs of the arbitration incurred in consequence of the non-compliance.

Alternatively, unless the parties have excluded the power, either the tribunal or the other party with the permission of the tribunal, may apply to the court for an order requiring compliance with the peremptory order. In addition to the peremptory order procedure, s.41 re-enacts the power[50] to dismiss a claim where the claimant has been guilty of inordinate and inexcusable delay; and also confirms the power of the tribunal to continue with the proceedings in the absence of a party after being duly notified.[51]

ARBITRATION RULES

No uniform system of procedure applies in arbitration comparable to the Civil Procedure Rules of the courts. It is therefore natural that various trade and professional bodies should consider creating their own rules of procedure. The courts have adopted a supportive approach to rules in the

[49] Section 5.
[50] Originally s.13A of the Arbitration Act 1950.
[51] *Bremer Vulcan v South India Shipping* [1981] A.C. 909, per Lord Diplock.

past. Under the 1996 Act they are essential to make effective use of the available powers.

The need for procedural rules is also shown by the wide diversity of arbitrations. At one extreme, there are commodity arbitrations concerning consignments of goods, where the arbitrator may be required to form a rapid opinion as to the quality of perishable goods (sometimes referred to as a "look-sniff" dispute). At the other extreme there are commercial disputes, for example in the field of re-insurance, involving contractual argument, many documents and lengthy evidence, which may be conducted in a manner similar to disputes in the High Court. While many construction disputes tend to resemble more the latter, there is often a substantial element of the former, and it is therefore more important that construction arbitrators should be in a position to exercise effective control with flexibility. Under the pre-1996 legislation several sets of rules existed for construction disputes, particularly the ICE Arbitration Procedure (1983) and the JCT Arbitration Rules (1988). With the impending arrival of the Arbitration Act 1996, steps were taken to draw up a set of rules for adoption throughout the UK construction industry. The Construction Industry Model Arbitration Rules were published in February 1998 with the endorsement of all the major bodies within the construction industry. The Rules are reviewed below. Other industries have adopted or adapted their own rules and other sets of rules may occasionally be encountered. Thus, the Chartered Institute of Arbitrators has drawn up a set of rules which are partly based on the CIMA Rules. The ICE, prior to the introduction of CIMAR, produced an amendment to its procedure, now known as the ICE Arbitration Procedure 1997, which is available as an alternative to CIMAR.

Construction Model Arbitration Rules

The Rules are arranged in roughly the same logical order as the Act, although preliminary matters such as joinder are necessarily dealt with at the outset. After Rules 1-3 concerning the setting up of the arbitration, Rules 4, 5 and 6 deal generally with powers and procedure. Rules 7, 8 and 9 set out three alternative forms of procedure. Rule 10 deals with provisional relief and Rule 11 with default powers. Rules 12 and 13 deal with the award and costs. The following particular points may be noted:

> RULE 1: OBJECTIVE AND APPLICATION—repeats the general objectives of the Act and provides that the parties may not, without agreement of the arbitrator, amend the rules after their appointment.

RULE 2: BEGINNING AND APPOINTMENT—for the first time, makes provision for a mechanism whereby the appropriate appointer must consider whether or not the same arbitrator is to be appointed in two related arbitrations. This is achieved by a contractual requirement (forming part of the arbitration agreement) that the appointer should "give due consideration". The appointer is not, of course, a party to the agreement. Nevertheless, an effective sanction exists in that a failure to give consideration may result in an appointment which is not in accordance with the parties' agreement.

RULE 3: JOINDER—covers all different forms of joinder—multiple claims brought by the claimant—cross claims by the respondent—additional disputes raised by either party—joinder of related arbitral proceedings in which the same arbitrator is appointed—consolidation of related proceedings (with consent). The objective is to secure the efficient resolution of all related disputes so far as practically possible. The arbitrator is, accordingly, given various discretions to allow (or not allow) additional disputes to be added.

RULE 4: PARTICULAR POWERS—includes provision as to the grounds upon which the arbitrator may order security for costs, based on practice in the courts. The Act itself is silent as to the grounds. Rule 4.7 encourages (but does not bind) the arbitrator to give reasons. The parties may well wish to amend this rule.

RULE 5: PROCEDURE AND EVIDENCE—while providing that the arbitrator is not bound by the strict rules of evidence, requires a formal record to be made of the evidence tendered in cases of: (a) an application for Security for Costs; (b) an application to strike out; (c) an application for Provisional Relief, and (d) any other instance where it is appropriate. Section 34 (2) (which contains wide procedural powers), is incorporated.

RULE 6: FORM OF PROCEDURE AND DIRECTIONS—requires the arbitrator, with information provided by the parties, to consider the appropriate procedure as soon as they are appointed. This may involve adopting the procedure set out in Rules 7, 8 or 9, or any part of those procedures, or any other procedure they consider appropriate. The arbitrator is thus given the widest possible discretion.

RULE 7: SHORT HEARING—is appropriate where there is to be a hearing of not more than one day, the award to be made within one month of the conclusion of the hearing.

RULE 8: DOCUMENTS ONLY—is appropriate where there is to be no hearing. The arbitrator is nevertheless empowered to direct a hearing of not more than one day, but must otherwise make their award within one month.

RULE 9: FULL PROCEDURE—sets out a formal procedure involving exchange of pleadings, statements and expert reports. The arbitrator is to fix the length of the hearing and may require any matter to be put into writing.

RULE 10: PROVISIONAL RELIEF—puts into effect the machinery of s.39, whereby the arbitrator is empowered to order on a provisional basis any relief which they would have power to grant in a final award. This rule contains equivalent powers to those in CPR, Pts 24 and 25 which, in the light of *Halki Shipping v Sopex*[52] now represent the only means of obtaining a summary decision which is: (i) clearly enforceable, and (ii) not subject to appeal save in the course of subsequent arbitration proceedings (see further below).

RULE 11: DEFAULT POWERS AND SANCTIONS—this puts into effect the provisions of s.41—power to dismiss a claim for inordinate delay and power to proceed in the absence of a party in default; also the power to give a peremptory order which may be enforced by the court under s.42. Rule 11.3 empowers the arbitrator to order direct sanctions against non-compliance, including the drawing of adverse inferences.

RULE 12: AWARDS AND REMEDIES—gives effect to ss.47, 48, 49 and 57 empowering the arbitrator to make awards on different issues, to grant a wide range of remedies, to award simple or compound interest and to correct an award.

RULE 13: COSTS—gives effect to ss.63 and 65 (power to limit costs). The rule also sets out the matters which the arbitrator should have regard to in awarding costs, on the general principle that they should be borne by the losing party. By rule 13.4 the arbitrator, in imposing a limit on recoverable costs, is to have regard primarily to the amounts in dispute. Provision is also made for taking account of offers of settlement.

---

[52] [1998] 1 W.L.R. 726.

RULING 14: MISCELLANEOUS—deals, inter alia, with service and reckoning of time periods.

A review committee has been established which keeps the Rules under review, publishes guidance notes and considers amendments to the Rules.

100 day Arbitration Rules

The popularity of statutory adjudication under Construction Contracts, demonstrates both the desire of potential claimants to have their disputes dealt with in a timely and expedited fashion, as well as the ability of tribunals and parties to accommodate new stringent time limits. There are, however, notable drawbacks to statutory adjudication including the requirement for the same procedure to be adopted irrespective of the size of the dispute. The result has been that a number of large and potentially complex disputes have been referred to adjudication and the resulting decisions challenged through the courts on grounds of natural justice (see Ch.2). Parties have spent substantial sums in costs only to find the decision open to full re-hearing. In order to provide an alternative procedure which capitalises on the ability of parties to conduct rapid proceedings, but also preserves the best features of Arbitration, a new arbitration procedure was launched in 2004 intending to lead to an award within a timescale of 100 days. The main differences between this procedure and statutory adjudication are in the longer period available, greater flexibility in the procedures which can be adopted and in the fact that the time limit commences only after each party, including the respondent, has served its written case. Where a counterclaim is included, the time limit commences when the claimant has served a defence to that counterclaim. The parties are thus treated with equality in the sense that each has a proper opportunity to present its case in writing to the arbitrator. Thereafter the procedure provides a series of "*not more than*" time periods covering the following matters:

- service of outstanding pleadings, witness statements and expert reports;
- service of further documents relied on and reply statements or reports;
- service of documents requested for disclosure;
- an oral hearing not exceeding 10 working days;
- final written Submissions; and
- award within 30 days at the end of the oral hearing.

The award will be final subject to such rights of challenge or appeal as are provided by the Arbitration Act 1996. The procedure is available for use in international disputes where any right of challenge will be dependent on the procedural law of the arbitration. The 100–day procedure may be adopted by agreement at any stage of a dispute. It may be written into a contractual Dispute Resolution Clause, or it may be adopted ad-hoc for an existing identified dispute, including any cross-claim. It may also be adopted where the parties have commenced adjudication proceedings and concluded that the issues require a longer and more considered decision making process. The procedure makes provision for the award of costs, which is not generally available in adjudication. The parties are free to opt out of the power to award costs, once the dispute has arisen.[53] The full procedure is available on the Society of Construction Arbitrators' Website at *http://www.arbitrators-society.org*.

JURISDICTION AND COMPETENCE

Arbitration, unlike litigation, is subject to a number of constitutional difficulties which stem from the essential nature of the process. Foremost among these is the extent of the arbitrator's jurisdiction and the powers they may exercise when challenges are made. What is the position if one party asserts that the arbitrator (or tribunal) does not have jurisdiction over some dispute which the other party wishes to bring forward? At common law, while the arbitrator can and should consider such a challenge in order to decide whether to go on with the arbitration or not,[54] only the court can finally decide on jurisdiction. The same principle applies in a case where the existence of the arbitration agreement is put in issue, which may be because one party contends that the underlying contract was never concluded. In both respects, the 1996 Act contains important powers which support the ability of the arbitrator to continue with the arbitration despite such challenges. The question whether and to what extent an arbitrator can make decisions bearing on their own jurisdiction is often given the German label *kompetenz kompetenz* or, in French *competence de la competence*. The first advance in the 1996 Act is the adoption of a provision from the UNCITRAL model law requiring a party to raise the question of jurisdiction timeously:

[53] Arbitration Act 1996 s.60.
[54] *Christopher Brown v Genossenschaft Oesterreichischer* [1953] 1 Q.B. 495.

"**31**—(1) An objection that the arbitral tribunal lacks substantive jurisdiction at the outset of the proceedings must be raised by a party not later than the time he takes the first step in the proceedings to contest the merits of any matter in relation to which he challenges the tribunal's jurisdiction.

A party is not precluded from raising such an objection by the fact that he has appointed or participated in the appointed of an arbitrator.

(2) Any objection during the course of the arbitral proceedings that the arbitral tribunal is exceeding its substantive jurisdiction must be made as soon as possible after the matter alleged to be beyond its jurisdiction is raised.

(3) The arbitral tribunal may admit an objection later than the time specified in subsection (1) or (2) if it considers the delay justified."

Unless otherwise agreed by the parties, the tribunal is given power under s.30 of the 1996 Act to rule on its own jurisdiction including the question whether there is a valid arbitration agreement or what matters have been submitted to arbitration. This ruling, if given in the form of an award, may be challenged before the court.[55] Alternatively, the court may be asked to rule on the question of jurisdiction under s.32. Where a party does not raise a challenge to jurisdiction timeously, they may lose the right thereafter to raise objection.[56] The 1996 Act thus establishes a means whereby challenges to jurisdiction should be resolved at an early stage, usually by the arbitrator, but must always be raised promptly.

Separability

This is another concept well known under civil law systems but relatively novel under English law. The issue arises most frequently in construction disputes where the parties continue to negotiate a contract despite commencement of the work and end up in disagreement as to whether a contract has been concluded. Simple analysis suggests that if an arbitrator appointed under such an arrangement (or the court) were to decide that no agreement had been made, their jurisdiction would thereby disappear along with the arbitration clause contained in the non-existent contract. Such a conclusion, however, is neither necessary nor even logical. It was held by the Privy Council in *Heyman v Darwins*[57] that an arbitration clause survived termination of the contract through repudiation; and in *Ashville v Elmer*[58] it was held that an arbitration clause might

---

[55] Arbitration Act 1996 s.67(1)(a).
[56] Section 73.
[57] [1942] A.C. 356.
[58] [1989] Q.B. 488, 37 B.L.R. 55.

empower an arbitrator to rectify the contract containing the clause. Both these cases are examples of the arbitration clause being seen as separate from the underlying contract. A more recent application of the same principle occurred in *Fiona Trust v Privalov*[59] where the ship-owner respondent to an arbitration brought by charterers sought to restrain the arbitration of the ground that the underlying contract had been procured by fraud, and that the dispute as to whether the contract had been rescinded for fraud lay outside the scope of the arbitration clause. The Court of Appeal and House of Lords[60] rejected the owner's application on the ground that the whole dispute fell within the arbitration agreement which in any event would survive rescission of the contract. Section 7 of the 1996 Act has now placed the doctrine of separability beyond doubt in the following terms:

> "**7** Unless otherwise agreed by the parties, an arbitration agreement which forms or was intended to form part of another agreement shall not be regarded as invalid, non-existent or ineffective because that other agreement is invalid, or did not come into existence or has become ineffective, and it shall for that purpose be treated as a distinct agreement."

Thus either the court or the arbitrator[61] may, if the matter is placed in issue, decide whether the parties have entered into a separate arbitration clause, in the event that the underlying contract was never concluded.

AWARDS

No particular form is required for an award, but it should be in writing and should set out in a logical form the reasons for the decisions contained in the award, unless the parties have agreed to dispense with reasons. An award needs to be "self contained" and to explain the proceedings as well as the decisions, for the benefit of the parties and the court if necessary, since the court will usually have no further evidence available. It is usual to start with recitals and then cover the events leading up to the arbitration. The award should then set out the issues or claims and the arbitrator's reasoning, ending with the decisions. In practice awards without reasons are now rare. Internationally, fully reasoned (or "motivated") awards are invariably required, with a few exceptions,

---

[59] [2007] 114 Con. L.R. 69.
[60] *Premium Nafta v Fili Shipping* [2007] UKHL 40.
[61] Pursuant to the 1996 Act s.30.

notably in the USA where awards with only short reasons are still found. Once made and delivered, an award cannot be altered, except in the case of a clerical mistake or unintended error, usually referred to as a "slip".[62] The essential requirements of an award are that it should decide the matters submitted and no others. It must be certain in its effect, and it must be consistent with any other findings or awards of the arbitrator in the same matter (see Subsequent Claims, Ch.2). Once the arbitrator has expressed a decision in an award, they cease to have further jurisdiction over that matter and is said to be functus officio. Thus, the arbitrator must be careful not to decide matters which either party may wish to argue further. They should not express decisions on matters where they may wish to alter their view and they should never express an opinion on a matter which has not been brought forward or argued.

The 1996 Act clarifies the range of remedies which the arbitrator, subject to the agreement of the parties, may award. These may include the following:

> "**48**—(3) The tribunal may make a declaration as to any matter to be determined in the proceedings.
> (4) The tribunal may order the payment of a sum of money, in any currency.
> (5) The tribunal has the same powers as the court—
>   (a) to order a party to do or refrain from doing anything;
>   (b) to order specific performance of a contract (other than a contract relating to land);
>   (c) to order the rectification, setting aside or cancellation of a deed or other document."

Under the Arbitration Act 1950 arbitrators were empowered to make an "interim" award, which meant no more than an award which dealt with some but not all of the issues submitted, but was otherwise final as to the matters decided. The term gave rise to confusion and has now been dropped. Section 47 of the 1996 Act provides that, unless the parties otherwise agree, the arbitrator may make more than one award at different times on different aspects of the matters to be determined. All that is required is that the award should specify the issue or claim or part of a claim which is the subject of the award. No particular label is given to such awards. The French version of the ICC rules uses the term "*Sentence Partielle*", which is confusingly translated into English as "Partial award". Again, it means no more than an award on some on the issues, which is final as to those issues. The term "Final award" is usually reserved to the last award in time, i.e. that which deals with all outstanding

---

[62] Section 57(3)(a).

matters. The French version "*Sentence Definitive*" is also potentially confusing, but its meaning is clear.

The question lying behind the somewhat confusing terminology referred to above, is whether an arbitral tribunal can grant a partial remedy, for example, in circumstances similar to those in which the English court can grant summary judgment on the basis that the claim is worth "not less than" the figure ordered. The jurisdiction of arbitrators to grant such a remedy has never been clear, although such a power was contained in the ICE Arbitration Procedure (1983).[63] This particular question has been resolved by the 1996 Arbitration Act where the parties may empower the arbitrator, to grant by "provisional" award or order, any relief which can be granted in an award which is final.[64] The Act makes clear that a provisional award is one which may be varied by the tribunal's subsequent (final) adjudication. To clarify these new powers, the Act states that a provisional award may include "a provisional order for the payment of money or the disposition of property as between the parties". The CIMA Rules (see above) make provision for the exercise of these important powers.[65]

While the question of the arbitrator's jurisdiction to grant "provisional" relief is now clarified, the position of the courts remains less clear. For many years prior to the 1996 Act there had been a practice of applying to the court for summary judgment in respect of claims to which it was contended there was no defence and therefore no dispute. The courts, either on the basis that there was no dispute or in the exercise of the court's discretion to refuse to stay the proceedings, adopted the practice of granting summary judgment in respect of indisputable claims and ordering a stay for arbitration in respect of the balance.[66] After the passing of the 1996 Act and the removal of the court's discretion to refuse a stay (see above) the question remained as to whether the court would regard a claim to which there was no defence as creating a "dispute" which the parties remained bound to take to arbitration. In other words, is arbitration now to be regarded as the exclusive remedy for any claim within the arbitration agreement? In *Halki Shipping v Sopex Oils*[67] the Court of Appeal answered the question affirmatively, by refusing an application for summary judgment. A strong dissenting

---

[63] Rule 14.

[64] Arbitration Act 1996 s.39(2).

[65] For an example of the exercise of the power to give a provisional award, under the LMAA Rules, see *BMBF (No 12) v Harland & Wolff* [2001] 2 L.L.R. 227, EWCA Cl 682.

[66] See particularly, *Ellis Mechanical Services v Wates Construction* (1976) 2 B.L.R. 57, and *The Kostas Melas* [1981] 1 Lloyd's Rep.18.

[67] [1998] 1 W.L.R. 726.

judgment was given by Hirst L.J., but leave to appeal the House of Lords was not pursued. These difficult questions therefore still await final resolution.

Equity clauses

Another major advance of the 1996 Act is to recognise, finally, the validity of an "equity" clause empowering the arbitrator to decide the issues not in accordance with strict legal rules but following equitable principles, "good conscience" or other like expressions. There has been long debate in judicial as well as academic circles as to the acceptability of such clauses and particularly as to whether an award made under such a contract would be enforceable in England.[68] The 1996 Act provides for such clauses in the following terms:

> "**46**—(1) The arbitral tribunal shall decide the dispute—
> > (a) in accordance with the law chosen by the parties as applicable to the substance of the dispute, or
> > (b) if the parties so agree, in accordance with such other considerations as are agreed by them or determined by the tribunal."

During the drafting of the Act consideration was given to descriptions such as *ex aequo et bono*, or the French *amiable compositeur*, but plain English prevailed in the form above. One of the problems generated by equity clauses is the practical impossibility of judicial review of any legal decision embodied in the award. The result of giving statutory recognition to these clauses is that an appeal on law from such a decision will not be available. Such an award would, however, still be open to question on the ground of serious irregularity (see above).

Award of costs

It has always been the accepted practice that, in dealing with costs, the arbitrator should adhere broadly to the principles adopted in the High Court, i.e. the successful party should receive their costs unless there are proper reasons for departing from this order. Where there is a claim and counterclaim, each must be considered in relation to costs, but it is frequently found convenient to reflect all the matters in one global order, such as an order that one party is to recover a proportion of their costs.

The above broad principles are now codified to an extent and the undoubted discretion of the arbitrator clarified in the 1996 Act thus:

---

[68] See *DST v RAKOIL* [1987] 2 Lloyd's Rep. 246, *Home & Overseas v Mentor* [1989] 1 Lloyd's Rep. 473.

"**61**—(2) Unless the parties otherwise agree, the tribunal shall award costs on the general principle that costs should follow the event except where it appears to the tribunal that in the circumstances this is not appropriate in relation to the whole or part of the costs."

By s.60 of the 1996 Act agreement that the parties shall pay the whole or part of their costs of the arbitration in any event is valid only if made after the dispute. This, therefore, precludes such an agreement being placed in a standard form of contract or in an arbitration agreement made in advance of the dispute. However, the parties may enter into such an agreement once the dispute has arisen and the new Act encourages the parties and the arbitrators to adopt measures likely to reduce or control the expenditure of costs. In addition to the general requirements as to avoiding unnecessary expense (see ss.1(a) and 33(1)(b)), s.65 allows the arbitrator to place a limit upon the amount of costs which can be recovered as follows:

"**65**—(1) Unless otherwise agreed by the parties, the tribunal may direct that the recoverable costs of the arbitration, or any part of the arbitral proceedings, shall be limited to a specified amount.
(2) Any direction may be made or varied at any stage, but this must be done sufficiently in advance of the incurring of costs to which it relates, or the taking of any steps in the proceedings which may be affected by it, for the limit to be taken into account."

The process formerly known as "taxation" of costs is now renamed the determination of recoverable costs. Once the arbitrator has determined in principle who should recover costs and in what proportion, the arbitrator may be asked to determine what is recoverable. If they do not do so, either party may apply to the court for a determination. In either event, but subject to any agreement between the parties, the recoverable costs are to be determined in the same way as in court (see Ch.2):

"**63**—(5) Unless the tribunal or the court determines otherwise
(a) the recoverable costs of the arbitration shall be determined on the basis that there shall be allowed a reasonable amount in respect of all costs reasonably incurred, and
(b) any doubt as to whether costs were reasonably incurred or were reasonable in amount shall be resolved in favour of the paying party."

Recovery of interest

In awarding interest, the arbitrator should also follow similar principles to those applied in the High Court. They should normally award interest by allowing a realistic rate on the sum awarded from such date as the money ought ordinarily to have been paid, i.e. for the period the successful party has been deprived of the sum awarded.

The powers of the arbitrator are now set out in s.49 of the Arbitration Act 1996. Subject to agreement of the parties, the power of the arbitrator are as follows:

> "**49**—(3) The tribunal may award simple or compound interest from such dates, at such rates and with such rests as it considers meets the justice of the case—
>   (a) on the whole or part of any amount awarded by the tribunal, in respect of any period up to the date of the award;
>   (b) on the whole or part of any amount claimed in the arbitration and outstanding at the commencement of the arbitral proceedings but paid before the award was made, in respect of any period up to the date of payment.
> (4) The tribunal may award simple or compound interest from the date of the award (or any later date) until payment, at such rates and with such rests as it considers meets the justice of the case, on the outstanding amount of any award (including any award of interest under subsection (3) and any award as to costs)."

The power to award interest on a sum claimed but paid before award is to the same effect as the rule applying in the High Court. In both cases, a defendant gains no advantage by deferring payment. The right to recover interest at common law has recently been comprehensively reviewed by the House of Lords in *Sempra Metals v IRC*[69] which has established that interest can now be awarded as part of a claim for damages and may include compound interest on damages or for late payment of a debt, and may be awarded even after the original debt or damages have been paid.

Section 49 of the Arbitration Act includes two important new provisions. First, the arbitrator may be empowered to award compound interest, a power not available to judges except where interest is claimed as damages or is payable under the terms of the contract (see Ch.2). Secondly, the arbitrator is empowered to award interest to be payable in the future, after the date of the award. Awards previously carried interest automatically, but this is now within the arbitrator's discretion.

JUDICIAL REVIEW OF AWARDS

Sections 24 (power to remove arbitrator) and 68 (challenge for serious irregularity) of the 1996 Act are dealt with above; also challenges on the

[69] [2007] UKHL 34.

ground of lack of jurisdiction. This section deals with appeal on a point of law. This issue has a long history which is bound up with the essential nature of English arbitration.

Before 1979, points of law arising in a reference could be referred to the High Court under a procedure known as "case stated".[70] The decision of the court could be obtained during the reference, or a case could be stated at the end, the award depending upon the opinion of the court. This is the process which allowed English arbitration, unlike most civil law countries, to develop the use of "trade" arbitrators, who were not legally qualified. However, in the 1960s the procedure began to produce a substantial number of references to the High Court, such that the decision of the arbitrator could no longer be regarded as normally final.[71] To remedy the situation and to secure the future of London as a venue for international disputes, the Commercial Court Committee promoted reforming legislation which became the Arbitration Act 1979. This Act provided for appeal on the point of law conditional upon consent of the parties or the court granting leave. Shortly after the Act came into force, the House of Lords decided in *BTP Tioxide v Pioneer Shipping (The Nema)*[72] that leave should be given only in very limited circumstances. The grounds upon which leave would or would not be granted became highly complex in the light of further cases. The 1996 Act has taken the opportunity of codifying (and modifying) the existing rules which are now as follows:

"**69**—(1) Unless otherwise agreed by the parties, a party to arbitral proceedings may (upon notice to the other parties and to the tribunal) appeal to the court on a question of law arising out of an award made in the proceedings . . .
 (2) An appeal shall not be brought under this section except—
   (a) with the agreement of all the other parties to the proceedings, or
   (b) with the leave of the court.
   The right to appeal is also subject to the restrictions in section 70(2) and (3).
 (3) Leave to appeal shall be given only if the court is satisfied—
   (a) that the determination of the question will substantially affect the rights of one or more of the parties,
   (b) that the question is one which the tribunal was asked to determine,
   (c) that, on the basis of the findings of fact in the award—
     (i) the decision of the tribunal on the question is obviously wrong, or

---

[70] Arbitration Act 1950 s.21.
[71] See *Halfdan Greig v Sterling Coal* [1973] 1 Lloyd's Rep. 296.
[72] [1981] A.C. 724.

> (ii) the question is one of general public importance and the decision of the tribunal is at least open to serious doubt, and
>
> (d) that, despite the agreement of the parties to resolve the matter by arbitration, it is just and proper in all the circumstances for the court to determine the question."

Section 70(2) and (3) require respectively that the applicant must first exhaust any available means of correcting the award and that the application must be brought within 28 days of the award. Section 69(3)(c) succinctly expresses the effect of *The Nema* and other decisions under the 1979 Act and simplifies the process of applying for leave, which should now be dealt with, in most cases, without a hearing.[73]

Section 69(1) recognises that the parties may make an agreement to exclude the court's jurisdiction to consider an appeal on law, and an agreement to dispense with reasons for the award is to be treated as having the same effect. Under the Arbitration Act 1979, such an "exclusion agreement" could be made in advance in respect of an international arbitration, and the ICC Rules have been held to contain such an exclusion.[74] As regards domestic arbitration, the 1979 Act required that an exclusion agreement must be entered into after the dispute in question had arisen. It was intended that the 1996 Act would have the same effect[75] but the relevant provision was considered potentially discriminatory (see above) and was not brought into effect. In the result, an agreement to exclude the court's jurisdiction in regard to appeals will be effective whenever made. Similarly, the courts recognise an agreement made in advance for giving consent to the bringing of an appeal. Such an agreement is found in section 41.6 of the JCT Conditions.

An alternative means of obtaining the decision of the court on a point of law is available under s.45 of the 1996 Act. This enables an application to be made during the course of arbitral proceedings to determine a question of law arising. Such application is limited by the following requirements:

> "**45**—(2) An application under this section shall not be considered unless—
>
> (a) it is made with the agreement of all the other parties to the proceedings, or
>
> (b) it is made with the permission of the tribunal and the court is satisfied—
>
> (i) that the determination of the question is likely to produce substantial savings in costs, and
>
> (ii) that the application was made without delay."

---

[73] Section 69(5).
[74] *Marine Contractors v Shell Nigeria* [1984] 2 Lloyd's Rep. 77.
[75] See s.87(1).

This procedure is not greatly used but remains potentially useful. The arbitration proceedings may be continued, if appropriate, while the court is considering the matter.

Reasons

Under the old law, an award could be set aside for "error on the face". Consequently, arbitrators went to great length to avoid giving reasons with the award. This ground of setting aside was abolished in the 1979 Act, and there is now no bar to giving full reasons with an award. Ordinarily the parties will wish to know the arbitrator's reasons and, if there is such a request, the arbitrator may be bound as a matter of contract to give reasons. In any event, it is normally considered desirable so that the losing party can know why their case has failed. The arbitrator retains a wide discretion over the extent of detail which they include in their award. For example, when giving an award on some issues, where others remain to be argued, the arbitrator should avoid giving any reasons which might prejudice one of the parties in arguing subsequent issues. Reasons including findings of fact will be relevant to an appeal on a point of law (see s.69(3)(c), above). The court has power under s.70(4) to order the arbitrator to state reasons or further reasons for the award. Where the parties agree to dispense with reasons, this will be treated as an agreement to exclude the right of appeal.[76]

Privacy

Privacy is said to be one of the major advantages of arbitration over litigation, which must normally be conducted in public. Privacy extends to the proceedings and the deliberations of the Tribunal, to the documents and evidence presented in the arbitration,[77] to the arbitral award and even to the existence of the arbitration. The privacy of the proceedings is reflected in the reluctance of the English courts to sanction the appointment of the same arbitrator in two related disputes which involve different parties, where all parties do not agree.[78] There are, however, many grounds on which one party might wish to make use of an award, and this raises the question of the ambit of privicy and how it is to be enforced.

Where one party wishes to use the award as the basis of further proceedings against a third party (whether in arbitration or litigation) the

---

[76] Section 69(1).
[77] *Dolling-Baker v Merrett* [1990] 1 W.L.R. 1205.
[78] *The Eastern Saga* [1984] 2 Lloyd's Rep. 373.

practice, if opposed by the other party, is to apply to the court for a declaration authorising disclosure to the extent necessary In *Ali Shipping v
Trogir*[79] the Court of Appeal confirmed the privacy rule which was said
to be based on an implied term, subject to exceptions. This case was
distinguished in a subsequent decision of the Privy Council in *Associated
Electric v European Re*[80] where an express confidentiality clause was
held not to prevent the defendant relying on an earlier award in proceedings between the same parties to found a plea of issue estoppel. After
referring to the exceptions to the implied term of confidentiality, the
Privy Council held that

> "Their Lordships have reservations about the desirability or merit of
> adopting this approach. It runs the risk of failing to distinguish between
> different types of confidentiality which attach to different types of docu-
> ment or to documents which have been obtained in different ways and
> elides privacy and confidentiality. Commercial arbitrations are essentially
> private proceedings and unlike litigation in public courts do not place
> anything in the public domain. This may mean that the implied restrictions
> on the use of material obtained in arbitration proceedings may have a
> greater impact than those applying in litigation. But when it comes to the
> award, the same logic cannot be applied. An award may have to be referred
> to for accounting purposes or for the purpose of legal proceedings . . . or for
> the purposes of enforcing the rights which the award confers . . .
> Generalisations and the formulation of detailed implied terms are not
> appropriate . . .".

Disclosure to some extent necessarily occurs through the process of
appeal or challenge. In some jurisdictions (some US states and France)
the award becomes part of the record and is open to be reported. It is
through this process that many of the journals which publish arbitration
awards obtain their material. Publication can have serious consequences.
In a case in the French Cour d'Appel,[81] a party sought annulment in
France before a court which clearly did not have jurisdiction, but with
the result that the award and its contents became public. In dismissing
the application, the Court of Appeal imposed substantial damages on the
appellant for having infringed the privacy of the proceedings in such a
flagrant manner. Court proceedings in England dealing with arbitration
matters are heard in private, with the exception of hearings dealing with
points of law. In *City of Moscow v Bankers Trust Company*[82] the Court
of Appeal were asked to sanction publication of a judgment dismissing
an appeal against an award in which one of the respondents had been

[79] [1999] 1 W.L.R. 314.
[80] [2003] 1 W.L.R. 1041.
[81] *Aiterv Ojjeh* 1986 Rev. Arb. 583.
[82] [2004] B.L.R. 229.

found not liable. That respondent sought to publicise the judgment and, by inference, the award. The Court refused to allow publication, holding that it was a matter for the judge hearing the appeal to balance the public interest in the proceedings against the confidentiality of the arbitration.

It is to be noted that not all countries take the same view of privacy. The High Court of Australia held in the landmark decision in *Esso Australia Resources v Plowman*[83] that the parties to an arbitration were not under an implied obligation of confidentiality preventing them from transmitting documents received in an arbitration to third parties. The effect of the ruling was that the public utilities respondents in the arbitration could not be restrained from handing over documents disclosed in the arbitration to their controlling body, the Minister for Energy and Materials. This case has been much discussed,[84] but has not yet been followed in other common law countries. The DTI Advisory Committee on arbitration law, when drafting the 1996 Act, decided not to intervene and to leave privacy to be covered by agreement or by decisions of the courts.

INTERNATIONAL ARBITRATION

There is no uniform definition of international arbitration; the term is used here to mean arbitrations between parties based in different states. Viewed from the United Kingdom, international arbitration has a number of different aspects. There are wholly foreign cases (for example, an arbitration between Greek and German parties, conducted in Rome) in which a person from the United Kingdom might be appointed as one of a panel of arbitrators. Many foreign construction disputes are conducted in the English language, which is frequently also the language of the contract. Alternatively, the same wholly foreign dispute might be heard in London, perhaps with one or more English arbitrators. In either case, the parties might choose to instruct English lawyers to conduct the arbitration or English experts to give evidence. There may also be arbitrations in either category in which a United Kingdom company is one of the parties.

In any international arbitration, the parties face the same procedural problems as in domestic cases, but the barriers of distance and language, as well as cultural and other differences, give rise to a rich variety of other issues. The arbitration clause in the contract will usually deal with

---

[83] (1995) 128 A.L.R. 391.
[84] see 11 Arb. Int. 337 (1995) (Special Issue on Confidentiality).

the means of appointing arbitrators and may state the venue for the hearing. Often the contract will specify the applicable arbitration rules such as those of the ICC or the LCIA. These and other rules are promulgated by bodies who undertake supervision of arbitrations which are then referred to as "institutional". The ICE and RIBA limit their functions to the appointment of arbitrators and an arbitration under their rules is not institutional. International arbitration institutions exist in many parts of the world including Stockholm, Hong Kong, Singapore, Kuala Lumpur and in the Middle East. A set of rules is issued by UNCITRAL, and these may be administered through one of the existing institutions.

There are in theory four different laws which may affect the conduct of an international arbitration[85]:

(i)   the law governing the underlying contract, applicable to the merits of the case (substantive law);

(ii) the law governing the agreement to arbitrate (which will be the same as (i) if contained in the contract);

(iii) the law governing the arbitration proceedings (the procedural law); and

(iv) the law governing the submission to arbitration (which may in theory be different from (i) to (iii)).

The applicable or substantive law (i) is a matter of the express or implied choice of the parties. In most construction contracts there will be an express choice and this is usually found to be the law of the state of the employer, at least where the contract concerns major construction work abroad (see Ch.1).

Some academics argue that international disputes should be subject to international concepts of commercial law collectively referred to as lex mercatoria. This is a body of principles not deriving from the laws of any particular state. The English courts have shown no enthusiasm for adopting this approach. However, in the light of s.46(1)(b) of the Arbitration Act 1996 (see above) there is now no reason why an arbitration which is subject to the Act should not adopt lex mercatoria. The Channel Tunnel contract adopted a similar approach, stipulating that the contract should be interpreted in accordance with "the principles common to both English law and French law and in the absence of such

---

[85] See *Black Clawson v Papierwerke A.G.* [1981] 2 Lloyd's Rep. 446.

common principles, by such general principles of international trade law as have been applied by national and international tribunals".

The procedural law (iii) is also subject to the express choice of the parties. In theory this may differ from the law of the place of the arbitration, but there are obvious practical difficulties about an arbitration held, for instance, in Brussels but subject to English procedural law, which will include the powers exercisable by the English courts. Under English law a choice of venue prima facie implies a choice of the procedural law of that venue.[86] However, international arbitrations take place at different locations at different times, and a more convenient concept is that of the "seat". This is now recognised by the Arbitration Act 1996 and defined as the "juridical seat of the arbitration" which may be designated by the parties or by any institution having the power to do so, or by the arbitrators if so authorised, or otherwise determined.[87] The seat will thus designate the procedural law and the national court having supervisory jurisdiction. In *Braes of Doune v Alfred McAlpine*,[88] a contract for construction of a wind farm near Stirling provided that the seat of any arbitration should be Glasgow, Scotland, but that the English courts should have exclusive jurisdiction over any dispute and that a reference to arbitration should be deemed to be a reference within the meaning of the (English) Arbitration Act 1996. The claimant applied to the TCC in London for leave to appeal an award of the arbitrator, not having made any application in Scotland (which would at that date have required an application for case stated). On the jurisdiction of the TCC being challenged, it was held that the English courts did have jurisdiction and that the reference to "seat" meant only that the arbitration should be held in Scotland. It may be noted that by the Arbitration (Scotland) Act 2010 the right to appeal on a point of law in a Scottish arbitration is now substantially the same as under the English Arbitration Act 1996.

There remains the possibility that the court of some state other than the true seat might also assert its own jurisdiction over the arbitration proceedings in addition to the court of the seat. The arbitrators may then be faced with inconsistent orders being handed down by different courts, requiring them to decide which to comply with. Such situations may create a serious and currently insoluble conflict.[89] In some circumstances the English courts will restrain a party from bringing proceedings in a foreign court by anti-suit injunction. Such an order was made in *C v D*[90] where a party to a London arbitration sought to appeal the award in the

---

[86] *Miller v Whitworth Street Estates* [1970] A.C. 583.
[87] Section 3.
[88] [2008] B.L.R. 321.
[89] *Rupali v Bunni and others* [1995] Con.L.Yb. 155.
[90] [2008] 116 Con. L.R. 230.

US Federal Court. The Court of Appeal affirmed that the choice of London as the seat gave the English courts exclusive jurisdiction over any challenge to an award. This does not prevent the respondent to foreign enforcement proceedings resisting enforcement on any ground open under the law applicable in the country of enforcement, which in most cases will be the grounds set out in the New York Convention (see below). Within the European Community the question of staying proceedings is more complex and subject to Community law.[91] In *Allianz SpA v West Tankers*[92] the European Court held, contrary to the earlier decision of the House of Lords[93] that it was not open to the English court to order a stay of foreign proceedings brought in breach of an arbitration agreement. There has been much academic discussion on the possibility of floating or "transnational" arbitration, not being subject to the procedural law of any one state. English law has so far rejected this concept on the basis that procedure must be referable to the laws of one state and to the courts of that state. The rulings of the European Court of Justice have also served to emphasise that the EC is to be regarded as comprising separate and autonomous legal systems.

Where an international arbitration is subject to the procedural law of one particular state, it may be found that that state has a separate part of its own law designed to apply to international arbitration. Switzerland and France, which are major centres for international arbitration have such provisions within their own law. England, conversely, has never had any body of distinct rules applying to international arbitration. The Arbitration Acts 1975 and 1979 attempted to create such distinctions in relation to the power of the court to refuse to stay proceedings and in relation to exclusion clauses. Both of those distinctions have now disappeared and there is substantially no difference under English law between the procedures applicable in domestic and in international arbitration. As noted above, Scotland in 1990 adopted the UNCITRAL model law and therefore has a dual law system for international and domestic arbitration. There is no longer any likelihood that England will pass a separate Act governing international arbitration. However, in 2010 the Scottish Parliament passed a new Arbitration Act covering the whole field of domestic and international arbitration under which, although technically repealed, it is still open to parties to adopt the Model Law.

International arbitration has a distinct advantage over litigation in that it avoids the perceived bias of selecting, as the forum, the court of one

---

[91] See Ch. 1 (Jurisdiction in International Disputes) and Arbitration Exclusion in Brussels Regulations 44/2001.

[92] (C-185/07).

[93] *West Tankers v RAS Reunione* [2007] UKHL 4.

state, which is necessarily more closely connected with one of the parties. An international arbitration tribunal of three (or more) members can properly reflect the national and cultural balance of the parties as well as selecting genuinely neutral members. The record of enforcement of arbitration awards is at least as good as that of court judgments being enforced in different countries.

Model Law on International Commercial Arbitration

The United Nations Commission on International Trade Law (UNCITRAL) in 1995 adopted a Model Law on International Commercial Arbitration which was intended to serve as a model both for domestic arbitration legislation and for International Arbitration with the particular objective of achieving a more uniform practice and procedure between adopting states. The law provides for broad party autonomy, a principal now universally recognised in arbitration law. As noted elsewhere, the Model Law has been adopted for international arbitration in states having less well developed Arbitration Laws, (including Scotland) and forms the basis of many provisions of the English 1996 Arbitration Act. Most adopting countries have chosen to implement the Model Law only in respect of international arbitration, sometimes on the basis of giving parties the right to "*opt in*" if they so agree.

Model Law itself comprises 36 relatively short Articles. Chapter I (arts 1–6) covers general provisions including definition of "International Commercial Arbitration" to which the law applies. Chapter II covers the Arbitration Agreement (arts 7–9) including the requirement for a court to stay proceedings between parties to an Arbitration Agreement (art.8). Chapter III deals with composition of the Arbitral Tribunal including grounds for and procedures governing challenge of Arbitrators. Chapter IV deals with jurisdiction of the Arbitral Tribunal including competence to rule on its own jurisdiction (art.16). Chapter V deals with conduct of the arbitral proceedings including an express requirement that the parties be treated with equality (art.18). Chapter VI deals with the award and termination of proceedings including provisions as to the form and content of the award (art.31). Chapter VII deals with recourse against an award, setting out grounds upon which an award may be set aside (art.34). Chapter VIII deals with recognition and enforcement of Awards. These are stated to apply "irrespective of the country in which (the Award) was made" and provides for non-recognition of the Award where set aside "by a court of the country in which, or under the law of which, that Award was made". These provisions are intended to achieve a uniform set of rules applying wherever the Model Law is adopted or recognised. The provisions for challenge, recognition and enforcement mirror the corresponding provisions found in the New York Convention which has also achieved wide international adoption (see below).

A feature of particular interest under the Model Law is art.17 which originally provided that the Arbitral Tribunal may "order any party to take such interim measure of protection as the Arbitral Tribunal may consider necessary in respect of the subject matter of the dispute". The tribunal was also empowered to order appropriate security in connection with such measures. UNCITRAL working groups recommended in 2005, a new version of art.17 making much wider and more explicit provisions for the grant of interim measures of protection. These include the power to grant such measures without notice to the other party, provided that the other party is subsequently given the opportunity to object within a short period. These amendments were not universally supported. Some countries (including England and Wales) taking the view that they were unnecessary and that adequate protection can be provided by the court. The new measures have been adopted by many states but not by all, so that the law of some countries contain the new provisions but others do not. Since England has not adopted the Model Law as such, but only its broad principles, it would be necessary for consideration to be given to enlargement of the more limited powers presently contained in the Arbitration Act 1996 s.38. No such amendment has been proposed.

International arbitration rules

There are several sets of rules which are well known in international practice. Foremost among these are the ICC (International Chamber of Commerce) Rules, the LCIA (London Court of International Arbitration) Rules and the UNCITRAL (United Nations Commission of International Trade Law) Rules, each of which may be referred to in the arbitration agreements contained in international forms of contract. The ICC headquarters is located in Paris. In addition to other commercial interests, it administers a substantial body of international arbitration, much of it in the field of construction. ICC arbitration is different in a number of essential respects from English domestic arbitration. The ICC Rules were revised in 2012 require the service of a "Request for Arbitration" and "Answer", which may be accompanied by a counterclaim (arts 4, 5) before the tribunal is fully constituted, these steps being taken under the administration of the ICC Secretariat. These initial documents are intended to contain a full statement of each party's case and other matters including the nomination by each party of an arbitrator. After these steps have been taken, a chairman is appointed (or in an appropriate case, a sole arbitrator). The full tribunal is then required, with the parties, to draw up terms of reference (art.23). This document, which is to be signed by the parties, defines the jurisdiction of the tribunal, the applicable procedural rules and other matters that may be necessary or desirable. Thus, unlike English domestic arbitration (where the arbitrator is appointed at the outset with jurisdiction deriving from the notice of arbitration), an ICC tribunal defines its jurisdiction through the terms of reference after the parties have stated their cases and may therefore include all issues raised by either party up to the signing of the document.

The procedure is left for the parties and the arbitral tribunal to decide. Depending on the wishes and expectation of the parties, there may be formal oral hearings, or the case may be conducted largely or entirely on documents. The question whether full or partial disclosure is to be ordered will again depend on the procedural rules to be agreed or settled by the arbitrators (art.19). The place or seat of the arbitration is to be fixed by the court unless the parties agree (art. 18). When the arbitrators make their award, it must be submitted to the ICC Court for scrutiny (art.33). The ICC controls the administrative costs and arbitrators' fees, by requiring deposits from the parties at the outset. The arbitrators are given power to award costs (art.33). The ICC Arbitration Rules are published together with "Emergency Arbitrator Rules" and ADR Rules covering mediation or any other settlement technique that may be agreed.

In addition to rules for arbitration, the ICC administers and issues documentation for other forms of dispute resolution. These include the provision of technical expertise analogous to expert determination (see above); and different forms of Dispute Review procedure. The latter comprise either a Dispute Review Board which is to issue recommendations, a Dispute Adjudication Board which issues decisions or a Combined Dispute Board which may issue either a recommendation or a decision. Construction contracts are particularly suitable for such forms of interim dispute resolution, which may obviate the need for a full-scale arbitration.

The LCIA is of even longer standing than the ICC, having been founded originally as the London Court of Arbitration in 1893 but having been re-launched to focus on international arbitration in more recent years. The LCIA Rules were revised in 1998 to emphasise the international nature of the institution, which can administer arbitrations in any part of the world. The LCIA Rules similarly require the initial service of a Request for Arbitration and Response with, in each case, the nomination of an arbitrator where a panel of three is to be appointed. The third arbitrator (or sole arbitrator where so required) will be nominated in accordance with the agreement of the parties. However, in all cases, the rules require that the LCIA is to appoint the arbitral tribunal, having regard to but not necessarily following the nominations of the parties. The ICC Rules contain a similar provision. This method of appointment follows the decisions of the French court in the *Dutco* case[94] in which enforcement of an ICC award was refused on the ground that two joint parties had been compelled to appoint a single arbitrator, and had therefore not been afforded equal treatment with the other party to the arbitration, who had appointed its own arbitrator. The LCIA Rules differ from the ICC Rules in that they do not require (but do not preclude) Terms of Reference; the LCIA does not require deposits from the parties at the outset, but only at stages as the arbitration proceeds; and there is no provision for scrutiny of awards by the LCIA court.[95]

The UNCITRAL arbitration rules are intended to be free-standing but may also be used under the auspices of most arbitration institutions, including the LCIA. The rules were issued by the United Nations Commission to accompany the Model Law on international commercial arbitration and were revised in 2010. Section I of the rules provides for the initial Notice of arbitration (art.4) and for the Response to the notice to be issued within 30 days (art.4). The other sections deal with the composition of the tribunal (II) the Arbitral Proceedings (III) and the Award (IV). As regards the tribunal, in the absence of agreement on a single arbitrator, the tribunal is to consist of three, with the presiding arbitrator chosen by the two party-appointed arbitrators. The arbitral tribunal is empowered to conduct the arbitration in such manner as it considers appropriate "provided that the parties are treated with equality and that at an appropriate stage of the proceedings each party is given a reasonable opportunity of presenting his case" (art.17). The rules deal with the service of a statement of claim and defence and with amendments if required (arts 20, 21 and 22). The rules are generally permissive but require that each party shall have the burden of proving the facts relied on (art.27). The tribunal is empowered to grant interim measures at the request of a party including measures for the preservation of assets or evidence. A request for interim measures addressed to a court is not deemed incompatible with the agreement to arbitrate (art.26). The tribunal is empowered, as under other rules, to appoint experts and to receive their testimony. The tribunal is empowered to deal with costs of the arbitration which may include legal and other costs incurred by the parties (art.40). There is a wide discretion over costs but as a general principle the costs are to be borne by the unsuccessful party (art.42).

---

[94] Cour de Cassation, January 7, 1992, *BKMI v Dutco* XVIII YB Com. Arb. 140 (1993).
[95] For further comparison between LCIA and ICC Rules see *International Commercial Arbitration*, ed. Berkeley and Mimms, CCLM King's College London, 2001.

IBA Rules of Evidence

The International Bar Association (IBA) issued a freestanding set of Rules on the Taking of Evidence in International Commercial Arbitration, which can be incorporated into an arbitration agreement or, more usually, adopted ad hoc by agreement during the course of an arbitration. The preamble states that the rules are intended to provide an efficient, economical and fair process for the taking of evidence in international l arbitrations, particularly those between parties from different legal traditions. The taking of evidence should be conducted on the principle that each party should be entitled to know, reasonably in advance of any evidentiary hearing, the evidence on which the other party relies.

The Rules were revised in 2010. They are drafted by lawyers from both common law and civil law jurisdictions, cover documentary and oral evidence, and factual and expert testimony. Article 3 defines the document which each side should disclose in the arbitration. Each party must submit a Request to Produce, including a description of how the documents requested are relevant and material to the case. If the party to whom the request is addressed has objections, these are to be stated in writing to the tribunal which is to consult with the parties and issue a ruling. The Rules cover also requests for the production of documents from a person or organisation not a party to the arbitration. Article 4 deals with witnesses of fact. Each party must identify the witnesses relied on and the subject matter of their testimony. The tribunal may order the filing of written statements which are to be in prescribed form. Further statements may be served in response to the initial statements. Where a notified witness fails to appear without valid reason, the tribunal is to "disregard" that witness statement unless in exceptional circumstances the Arbitral Tribunal determines otherwise.

Article 5 deals with the contents of party-appointed expert reports and empowers the tribunal to order meetings of experts on common issues. Article 6 empowers the tribunal, after consulting the parties, to appoint its own independent experts, who may request parties to provide material information or access to documents or to property. Article 8 lays down a procedure for evidentiary hearings and art.9 sets out rules for the admissibility and assessment of evidence including grounds on which the tribunal may exclude evidence or refuse to order disclosure of documents. The rules provide a helpful platform for dealing with evidentiary issues where the expectation of parties from different jurisdictions may vary to a material degree. It is also important for the tribunal to maintain its overall discretion and in practice tribunals often incorporate the rules by a provision such as "The Tribunal will generally follow the IBA Rules of Evidence, subject to its overriding discretion."

International Treaty arbitrations

The last 20 years has seen a remarkable development in the bringing of International Arbitration claims under Bilateral Investment Treaties (BITs). These are treaties entered into between individual states for the purpose of protecting investment made by nationals of one state in the "*host*" state which benefits from the investment. In the past decade the number of BITs in existence has increased enormously to a figure now in excess of 2,000 so that investors will be likely to find a BIT in existence with most prospective host states. BITs are individual but follow a pattern in providing protection for investors usually including guarantees that investments will be accorded "fair and equitable treatment", that investments will not be subject to nationalisation, expropriation or equivalent measures, and that investors will receive treatment not less favourable than that accorded to investors of any other state. As a further protection, some BITs include a provision termed an "umbrella clause" by which the state party undertakes to observe obligations entered into with regard to investments of nationals or companies of other states, which is argued to have the effect of converting breach of a commercial contract made by or on behalf of the investor into a breach of the BIT.

Most BITs additionally incorporate provisions referring disputes to an arbitration tribunal established under the rules of the International Centre for Settlement of Investment Disputes (ISCID), an international body established under the Washington Treaty of 1965. ICSID arbitrations are similar to commercial institutional arbitrations (for example, under the ICC or LCIA) usually involving one arbitrator appointed by each party and a chairman appointed by ICSID. BIT arbitrations differ from commercial arbitrations, however, in that the subject matter of the dispute must be a breach or contravention of the relevant treaty, which is accordingly regarded as subject to the principles of public international law. Furthermore, ICSID decisions are usually published on the ICSID website, so that they become widely reported and may form the subject matter of academic analysis and comment. The result has been the rapid development of jurisprudence in BIT arbitrations which has dealt with a number of distinctive and recurrent problems including primarily the extent to which the tribunal will accept jurisdiction over a particular dispute. This involves a number of separate issues, initially as to whether the claimant is required first to exhaust any alternative remedy such as that under a commercial arbitration agreement that may be contained in the underlying contract. Further, the claimant party must establish that the subject matter of the claim relates to an "investment" within the definition contained in the BIT. These tend to be widely drawn and have been accepted as applicable in a number of reported cases relating to construction activities. If these hurdles can be overcome the tribunal will proceed to deal with liability and quantum of the claim. There are now a large number of cases which have reached final decisions involving substantial awards of damages. The ICSID Rules require an award to be accepted by the state as a final judgement of the court and not subject to any appeal. The rules also provide, however, that there may be an effective appeal by annulment on the grounds that the tribunal has manifestly exceeded its powers or has departed from a fundamental rule of procedure.[96] Annulment leads to a rehearing by a second tribunal which may similarly be challenged. Most awards are, however accepted as final by the state in question.

Two notable cases have given rise to much comment. The case of *SGS v Pakistan*[97] involved a claim brought pursuant to the Switzerland–Pakistan BIT which contained an umbrella clause elevating contractual breaches by a state party to breaches of the treaty. SGS provided inspection services for goods to be imported into Pakistan. The dispute concerned performance of the contract and the effect of purported termination by Pakistan. The BIT claim had been preceded by court proceedings in Switzerland which were unsuccessful and commercial arbitration proceedings brought in Pakistan. It was in these circumstances that SGS decided to bring a claim under the BIT asserting that the termination was unlawful and that SGS had suffered damage as a result. The tribunal rejected on various grounds the contention that the BIT with its umbrella clause had the effect of elevating contractual claims to breaches of the treaty. The tribunal therefore dismissed the claims to the extent that they amounted to purely contractual claims. This case was followed a short time later by a related claim, *SGS v Philippines*,[98] which similarly concerned the provision of supervision and other services in support of customs, for the Philippines. The tribunal had available to it the decision in *SGS v Pakistan* but reached a different conclusion. The tribunal concluded that failure to pay sums indisputably due to SGS under the commercial contract would constitute a breach of the BIT. The sums were, however, to be determined by the contractual arbitration tribunal and the ICSID tribunal therefore decided that it had no jurisdiction to determine the claim brought. The two cases are not reconcilable and create a further issue as to whether any "principles" applicable to BIT claims can be constructed from the reported decisions, given that no system of precedent exists.

---

[96] Article 52 of the ICSID Convention
[97] ICSID Case No. ARB/01/13, decision rendered August 6, 2003.
[98] ICSID Case No. ARB/02/6 decision rendered January 29, 2004.

These cases were followed by a further case in which a Turkish contractor, whose employment under a FIDIC contract had been terminated, alleged that the termination was motivated by political interference amounting to breaches of the relevant BIT between Turkey and Pakistan. In *Bayindir v Pakistan*,[99] the respondent government argued that the dispute was rooted in the terms of the FIDIC contract and the claim should be brought in a commercial arbitration forum. The ICSID Tribunal ruled, in an initial jurisdiction hearing, that the fact that a state may be exercising a contractual remedy in termination the contract did not exclude the possibility of a treaty breach. While the essential basis of the claims were contractual, treaty claims and contractual claims were, as a matter of principle, independent. The contractor had a self-standing right to pursue any remedy accorded by the treaty. The tribunal further accepted that the contractor, in taking on and financing the project in part ranked as an investor for the purposed of jurisdiction.

It remains to be seen whether the scope of BIT claims will continue to develop. At present they offer the possibility of bringing pressure to bear on recalcitrant government parties or state-controlled entities where more orthodox commercial routes have failed. The relative unpredictability of jurisdictional decisions will remain a stumbling block but there will undoubtedly be further developments in this field. In addition to arbitration under Bilateral treaties, mention should be made of another growing field of arbitration under Multilateral Investment Treaties, which include the North American Free Trade Agreement (NAFTA) and the Energy Charter Treaty (ECT).

ENFORCEMENT OF AWARDS

An arbitration award does not of itself compel the losing party to comply with its terms. The aid of the court must be invoked, and this may be done in two ways. First, under s.66 of the Arbitration Act 1966, the award may, by leave of the High Court, be enforced as a judgment. Secondly, the party seeking enforcement may bring an action on the award as a contract if the award is for a sum of money, the claimant may seek to enter summary judgment for the amount awarded. In either case the losing party may object to enforcement, for example, on the ground that the arbitrator had no jurisdiction.[100]

---

[99] ICSID Case No.ARB/03/29.
[100] Arbitration Act 1996 s.66(3).

Where enforcement of a foreign award is sought, either in England or abroad, the right of enforcement depends upon the domestic law of the country in which enforcement is sought. It depends in particular on whether that country has acceded to the relevant international conventions on enforcement which limit the grounds on which an award may be challenged. The Geneva Convention of 1927 was the first such convention, which was ratified by the United Kingdom and many European countries. It provides for enforcement of awards in convention countries provided that both parties are subjects of, and the award is made in, convention countries. These do not include much of the Middle East and Africa, where a great deal of international construction work is carried out. Although the Geneva Convention remains in force, the principal instrument through which international enforcement is now sought is the New York Convention of 1958, which was drawn up by the United Nations and ratified by the United Kingdom in 1975.[101] It provides for reciprocal enforcement where an award is obtained in a convention country. Enforcement is possible only in a convention country, but the nationality of the parties is immaterial. Thus it can be used to enforce an award against a non-convention national who has assets in a convention country. The list of states which have acceded to the New York Convention is more extensive than those which have adopted the Geneva Convention, and now includes the great majority of countries which engage in international trade.

The New York Convention is arguably the single most important instrument in the whole sphere of international arbitration. Without the convention international arbitration would hardly exist, having regard to the difficulties of enforcement of awards and the variety of national concepts of arbitration. The convention provides an exhaustive definition of the grounds upon which enforcement may be refused. The grounds are[102]:

(a) a party to the arbitration was under some incapacity;

(b) the arbitration agreement was not valid under the applicable law;

(c) the party against whom enforcement is sought had no proper notice of the proceedings;

(d) the award is outside the terms of the submission;

---

[101] Arbitration Act 1975.
[102] Arbitration Act 1975 s.5, re-enacted as the 1996 Act s.103.

(e) the tribunal or the procedure was not in accordance with the agreement or with the law of the country where the arbitration took place; and

(f) the award has not become binding or has been set aside in the country in which or under the law of which it was made.

Recognition or enforcement may also be refused if the subject matter of the award is deemed not capable of settlement by arbitration or if it would be contrary to public policy.[103]

Ground (f) has given rise to some international conflict. The courts in India have purported to question and refuse enforcement to an international award made under a contract whose substantive law was the law of India,[104] the arbitration having been conducted abroad and subject to other procedural law. It is clear that ground (f) refers to the country whose procedural law applies, and not that whose substantive law applies, the object of the convention being to restrict the influence of the courts of the country in which enforcement is sought. A further international controversy exists in relation to the phrase "may be refused", which has been interpreted in a number of cases as giving the enforcing court a discretion, even when the award has been set aside in the country in which it was made. Thus, awards which had been made and subsequently set aside in Switzerland and Egypt have nevertheless been enforced under the New York Convention in France and in the United States.[105] The exception in respect of public policy has been recognised in English law since at least the early 19th century.[106] In some overseas jurisdictions,[107] it is reported that foreign awards are regularly refused enforcement on this ground. In England, the Court of Appeal refused enforcement of an award of the Beth Din Rabbinical Court in a dispute under a contract which was illegal under English law as well as the law of the country of performance (Iran). Enforcement would be contrary to English public policy.[108] However, in *Westacre Investments v Jugoimport*,[109] an award was enforced in England despite the contract being contrary to public policy in Kuwait, the place of performance. The dispute was subject to Swiss law, under which the contract was not contrary to public policy. The effect of enacting the New York Convention

---

[103] New York Convention art.V.2, Arbitration Act 1996 ss.68(2)(g) and 103(3).
[104] *National Thermal Power v Singer*, Supreme Court of India, 1992 ICCA Yb XVIII.
[105] See Paulsson "May or must under the New York Convention: an exercise in syntax and linguistics" Arb. Internat. 1998, No.2, p.227.
[106] *Richardson v Melish* (1824) Bing. 229, 252.
[107] Particularly Russia.
[108] *Soleimany v Soleimany* [1999] Q.B. 785.
[109] [1999] 3 All E.R. 864.

into English law is illustrated by the case of *Minister of Public Works of Kuwait v Sir Frederick Snow & Partners*,[110] in which enforcement was sought in England of an award made in Kuwait in 1973. The United Kingdom acceded to the convention in 1975 and Kuwait in 1978. The House of Lords held that the subsequent accession of Kuwait nevertheless had the effect of making the existing award "a convention award" so that direct enforcement in the United Kingdom was then available.

An enforcement issue more basic than those set out in the New York Convention arose in *Dalmia Cement Ltd v National Bank of Pakistan* in respect of an arbitration conducted in Paris in which the respondent government disputed that it was a party to the arbitration agreement. The tribunal ruled that Pakistan was a party and made an award against it on the merits. Pakistan resisted enforcement in London, which was eventually refused by the Supreme Court which held, applying French law, that it was not a party to the agreement.[111] Similar proceedings in Paris, however, subsequently resulted in a decision of the Cour d'Appel ordering enforcement on the ground that Pakistan was a party to the agreement. There is nothing to prevent multiple enforcement proceedings, the decision in each state being applicable only to enforcement in that state.

Enforcement of a foreign award without the benefit of either the Geneva or the New York Convention depends on the domestic law of the country in which enforcement is sought. An international award may be enforced in England under s.66 of the Arbitration Act 1996.[112] The conventions, generally, provide more restrictive grounds for objection. Where the conventions do not apply, courts in some foreign states may allow the award to be reopened on the merits, thereby negating the process of arbitration. This has been the situation in a number of countries in the Middle East, Africa and Asia many of which have, however, now adopted the New York Convention.

---

[110] [1984] A.C. 426.
[111] [2010] UKSC 56.
[112] *Dalmia v National Bank of Pakistan* [1975] Q.B. 9.

CHAPTER 4

PARTIES AND STATUS

The principles of substantive law apply to an individual of full age and legal capacity. While most persons concerned with the construction industry will have attained the age of majority (now 18) they will usually be involved as employees or representatives of some larger body whose legal capacity and liability is limited. In this chapter the role and status of the different parties who may be involved with the construction industry is examined. Then the legal capacities and liabilities of those bodies most commonly encountered is discussed.

PARTIES IN THE CONSTRUCTION INDUSTRY

The client

The most essential person is the client, who commissions the work. They may be referred to as the building owner or promoter, but the term "employer" is used in the JCT and ICE forms of contract. The employer may have practically any status. They may be a private individual, partnership, limited liability company, part of local or central government or any other incorporated or unincorporated body. Today many large projects are undertaken by two or more entities acting in "joint venture". In law this usually amounts to a partnership or a specially formed company, with the joint venturers acting as the partners or shareholders and management being undertaken through a board empowered to run the joint venture. Contractors will always need to be concerned with the status of the client since, in the absence of special provisions, the contractor has no security in the work once it becomes attached to land owned by another person (see Ch.14). Invariably a construction contract will contain provisions for stage payments (or payments on account) so that the contractor's exposure is limited. However, there will be no security in respect of a claim or the final account, beyond the financial worth of the employer. Often the "employer" will be a specially formed company, set up to run the project on behalf of other backers, but legally distinct from them. In PFI projects, the PFI contractor, who acts as employer under the construction contract, is usually a specially formed company or SPV (Special Purpose Vehicle), owned in whatever proportions the promoters (including contractors) may agree. The viability of any such scheme depends on the creation of a chain of appropriate security. Another recent trend in speculative development work is for the nominated "employer" to assign its interest in the project during the course of the work, sometimes more than once. Contractors must be alive to the consequences of such events.

Contractors and sub-contractors

A large proportion of building work in the United Kingdom and abroad is still carried out under the system referred to as traditional general contracting. Under this system, the person who carries out the works is the main contractor, also referred to as the builder, building contractor, civil engineering contractor, etc. The employer and the main contractor are the two parties to the main or head contract, which may also be called the construction contract, or the building or engineering contract according to the nature of the works. Professional services, including design, are provided by other persons who may be named in the main contract, but they are not parties to it. Their relationship is by separate contract with the employer.

The contractor, in all but the smallest jobs, sub-contracts (or sub-lets) parts of the work to one or more sub-contractors. Indeed, most of the larger contracting companies now see their role as being managers of the sub-contractors who will perform the physical work. Main contracts commonly provide for certain sub-contractors to be chosen by the employer to carry out particular work, usually identified as "prime cost" (PC) work. They are usually called "nominated" sub-contractors and their status gives rise to particular issues under the standard forms of contract.[1] Sub-contractors who are not nominated are sometimes called domestic sub-contractors. Both the contractor and the sub-contractor will usually be a limited liability company although small concerns may be partnerships or even sole traders. A practical problem often met is that the contracting "company" is a group consisting of a "holding" company and several "subsidiary" companies. The holding company owns the shares in the subsidiaries, and often has most of the assets of the group. This arrangement has taxation advantages, but means also that a subsidiary can be allowed to be wound-up to the detriment of creditors,

---

[1] See JCT, cll. 35, 36, ICE/ICC, cl. 59.

without financial harm to the group. In such circumstances the employer (in the case of a contractor) will normally require a parent company guarantee, and the same will apply to contractors in respect of their intended sub-contractors. In some civil law countries the courts recognise the "doctrine of groups of companies" under which a holding company may be automatically liable for the actions of its subsidiary companies. No such doctrine exists under English law and those dealing with subsidiaries must ensure that a chain of recognised legal liability is in existence.

The professional team

In traditional general contracting, the task of designing the works and supervising their construction is usually carried out by the same person or body. Under a building contract they are the architect, and under a civil engineering contract, the engineer. The title "architect" is, in England, reserved by statute for those professionally entitled to it.[2] The same is not true for engineers, although in some countries, such as Italy, Germany and USA, the title is protected. Statutory registration for engineers has been considered in the UK but not accepted by government. Instead a uniform system of qualification has been created for all professional engineers, by award of the title Chartered Engineer, abbreviated as "C.Eng." Chartered status for UK engineers is conferred by some 35 separate engineering institutions. Also, under European Community legislation, engineers throughout the community can register and use the title "Euro. Ing." Usually a specific person or firm is designated as the architect or the engineer under the main contract. The person so designated will be given certain powers and duties by the contract which they must exercise as the construction work proceeds.

The architect or engineer is not a party to the main contract nor to any sub-contract, but is engaged under their own contract with the employer. In building contracts where the employer engages an architect, a civil or structural engineer may be required to carry out part of the design work. They may be engaged either by the employer or by the architect. Similarly, an architect may be brought in to assist in the design of civil engineering works. Engineers and architects have traditionally practised as partnerships. Many firms of engineers and architects have, however, set up as limited liability companies, which is now permitted by the professional bodies. The result is that some former professional firms are now "owned" by the their shareholders; the shares can be bought and sold and they are subject to take-overs and mergers. The latest

[2] Architects Act 1997, re-enacting and amending earlier legislation.

development, aimed at preserving professional status, is the creation of a "limited liability partnership" or LLP now made possible by the Limited Liability Partnership Act 2000.

A quantity surveyor (QS) is often found on larger contracts. Their traditional function has been to take off quantities from the drawings and other technical descriptions of the intended work, and to prepare from them bills of quantities; and subsequently to carry out measurements and valuations. In the JCT form a quantity surveyor is named and given certain duties. They do not appear in the ICE/ICC form. Their duties there are placed on the engineer, but are usually carried out by a QS. The quantity surveyor may be engaged by the employer, by the architect or by the engineer under a separate contract. Again, quantity surveyors have traditionally practised as individuals or partnerships; many have set up as limited companies and some may be expected to form limited liability partnerships. Quantity surveyors also provide advice pre-contract on matters such as costing and procurement; and post-contract on claims and contractual issues. In the latter role they are sometimes referred to as "claims consultants" or more politely as "construction cost consultants".

In their capacity under the main contract, the architect or engineer is required to carry out functions as the employer's agent, when they must represent the interest of their employer. In addition, the architect or engineer may be required to carry out particular duties, such as certification, on the basis of their professional opinion, sometimes loosely referred to as acting "independently". In such cases while they remain the employer's agent, they are under a duty to hold the scales fairly between the two parties (see Ch.9).

Project manager

In recent years new forms of procurement for construction works have emerged, involving new types of contract under which the roles of the parties differ from traditional general contracting. These are discussed in Ch.8. The new contract forms have given rise to a new professional known as the project manager. Although their position may be defined in a particular case, they do not fulfil a fixed role in the way that the designer or supervisor does. Project management can be a separate professional role, dedicated to the achievement of cost, time and performance requirements, using programming and monitoring techniques. This type of service will be performed under a separate contract of engagement with the employer. A project manager is also appointed by the contractor under a management contract; and the contractor's agent under a conventional construction contract is sometimes called the project manager.

There is, therefore, no single definition of the role and status of the project manager.

In addition to these major participants, there is a group of persons who appear in building and engineering contracts with particular functions and powers. These include the engineer's representative, the clerk of works, the agent and the foreman. All these persons are individuals who represent one or other of the major parties; thus, the engineer's representative and the agent represent on site the engineer and the contractor.

Joint ventures

Joint ventures between promoters are mentioned above. With new forms of procurement and the ever larger construction projects, it is increasingly common for two or more parties to combine as a joint venture to act as contractor or to fulfil any other role in a construction project. The simplest form of joint venture involves two companies who contract on the basis that each of them takes on full, joint and several liability, so that one of them could drop out and the other complete the project. The two joint venturers themselves will enter into a contract regulating their internal rights and liabilities. In the simplest case this may involve equal pooling of resources and sharing of costs and profits. However, there may be a much more elaborate division of responsibility and sharing of profit or loss. For example, two contractors may divide up the project, each taking on a defined area of the work, with each company being jointly and severally liable to the employer. In either case there will be a need to set up a joint management structure, for making decisions which affect both parties. Such joint ventures operate as a partnership, limited to a specific project. Joint venture partners need not make the same type of contribution to a project. A joint venture can be set up to perform a design and build contract between a design company and a construction company. An alternative to joint venturers entering into contracts in their individual names is to set up a jointly owned company (or Special Purpose Vehicle), whose shares and assets are held in agreed proportions. In this event, the employer will invariably require guarantees from the owners of the SPV.

Effect of status

The differing legal capacities and liabilities of those bodies most often encountered in the construction industry are discussed below. The most common is the limited company, while some professional bodies still operate as partnerships. There is a significant difference in the ability to enforce debts. For example, where a building owner has a claim against the contractor (a limited company) for bad workmanship, and against the architect (a partnership) for bad supervision, if the contractor is without assets, pursuit of the claim will lead to winding-up the company with no benefit to the building owner, even though the shareholders and directors may have personal assets. Conversely, the architect's firm will have no such protection. Even if the firm as such is insolvent, the partners will be liable to the limit of their personal possessions. A limited liability partnership shares some of the characteristics of partnership and some of a company.

Many of the potential liabilities incurred in relation to construction projects will be covered by insurance. Professional firms must maintain professional indemnity insurance, ostensibly for the protection of the partners but in practice also representing a further "asset" available, should a loss occur either during or after completion of the project. Insurances provided by a contractor are for the most part maintained in force only during the course of the work, so that claims for latent defects will usually be dependent on the contractor's own assets (see Ch.10). While the great majority of claims will be against the company or partnership which enters the relevant contract, the possibility exists that a claim involving professional negligence may be brought against the individual employee where the company or partnership is without funds.[3]

LIMITED COMPANIES

The word "company" can embrace any body of persons combined for a common object, whether incorporated or not. However, its commercial use is narrower and refers to an incorporated company, as opposed to a partnership. While a partnership is the product of an agreement between partners, an incorporated company is entirely the product of statute, which provides for the essential ingredient of limited liability. In the case of most commercial companies, limitation of liability relates to the issued shareholding. Incorporated companies may, as an alternative, be limited by guarantee, which is often a convenient device for non-profit making companies.

The essential feature of a limited company is that it exists as a separate legal entity, distinct from its shareholders (members). The assets and debts belong to the company, which has perpetual existence until it is

---

[3] See *Merrett v Babb* [2001] 3 W.L.R. 1.

dissolved. Changes of the directors or the members (shareholders) do not change the company. When a company contracts only the company can sue or be sued on the contract. If a wrong is done by or to a company, the proper party in any action is the company itself. A shareholder is not entitled to conduct an action on behalf of the company, even if they hold a majority or all of the shares. Reference to companies being taken over or bought and sold means only that the purchaser has acquired a majority of the shares in the company. Companies are taken over because of their assets, including their business. But they also take with them all debts and liabilities.

Ownership of companies

The assets of a new company are contributed by the members, who subscribe to purchase the shares or "equity" of the company. The main advantage of a limited company, as opposed to a partnership lies in the ability to acquire a financial interest in the success of a commercial venture while limiting the risks of failure. The liability of shareholders is ordinarily limited to the money invested.

The operation of companies is closely regulated by statute. Most of the law is found in the Companies Acts 1985 and 1989, now amended and consolidated by the Companies Act 2006.

There are two types of company limited by shares: public and private. Private companies are usually small, often family businesses and they comprise by far the greater number of registered companies. In a private company the number of members is limited and the shares cannot be freely transferred. However, a private company enjoys certain privileges which make its operation simpler. A public company must be identified by the letters "plc" after its name. Its membership is unlimited; shares are quoted on the stock exchange and are freely transferable. Successful private companies often seek to capitalise their assets by "floating", or transferring themselves into public companies. Both private and public companies must file annual accounts which are open to public inspection. The Companies Act 1989 introduced extensive new provisions relating to company accounts.

Any legal person, including another company, can buy shares. Subject to certain restrictions, a company may purchase its own shares, thereby reducing the issued capital. The capital of a company has a nominal or authorised limit, which in a small private company is often £100. Shareholders are paid dividends out of the company's profits. Additional capital can be raised by selling unissued shares, or by a fresh issue of shares. The re-financing of companies by public share issues often attracts publicity in the financial press, where there will be interest in the quoted price and underwriting arrangements to ensure the shares are taken up. Companies borrow money in their own right but lenders, whether banks or investment institutions, will require security. In the case of small companies, this is likely to be in the form of a personal guarantee given by the major shareholders, which may effectively defeat the objective of incorporation. In the case of companies with substantial assets, a loan may be secured by a debenture, which is a charge over the company's assets. A person putting money into a company set up to pursue some new business (venture capital) has to choose between the higher security but lower reward offered by a debenture loan as against the risks and rewards of buying equity.

The company's business

Every company must have written rules for its operation, set out in the articles and memorandum of association. The articles regulate the internal management of the company, including the appointment and powers of directors. The memorandum sets out, inter alia, the objects for which the company was formed. A company is entitled to do only those things set out in the memorandum, and anything reasonably incidental to them. An act outside the company's objects is ultra vires and void. The effect of the ultra vires rule is substantially amended by the European Communities Act 1972.[4] Where a person deals with a company in good faith, a transaction is deemed to be within the capacity of the company. The practice is, nevertheless, to draft the objects clauses of commercial companies very widely, so that a building company, for example, may if it wishes, carry on business in property development or plant hire or financing.

Management of companies

A company is run jointly by its board of directors and by the members in general meeting. Prima facie, only the board has power to act for the company. But subject to the articles, it will usually delegate powers to a Managing Director or Chief Executive Officer and to other directors, who will usually hold paid employment in the company. Employed officers of a construction company will usually include a finance director and a contracts director. Directors who are not employed by the company are sometimes called "non-executive" directors. They contribute their expertise to the running of the company in return for fees. Subject to the ultra vires rule a company makes contracts in the same way as an individual

[4] Section 9.

and will be equally bound by written or oral agreements provided they are entered into by an agent with authority (see Ch.7). Subject to delegated powers, a company generally acts through its secretary who must put into effect decisions of the board. The secretary is also responsible for keeping proper records. A company may be liable for torts, although they must necessarily be committed through its servants or agents. Certain statutory offences expressly provide for directors to be held personally liable including the possibility of imprisonment, for example under the Environmental Protection Act 1990 (see Ch.15). Directors or employees of a company whose reckless conduct causes death may be prosecuted for manslaughter and the company may also be prosecuted under new corporate manslaughter legislation.[4A] It remains unclear whether a company may be held liable for manslaughter at common law.[5]

The primary duty of a director is to the company rather than to the shareholders. They must act in the best interests of the company, and must disclose their personal interest in any contract made. A director must act with reasonable skill and care, although they may delegate their duties to employees of the company. While the liability of members is limited, a director may become personally liable for claims against the company if they commit fraud of breach of duty. The members exercise their powers by voting in general meetings. The company must hold an annual general meeting to consider the accounts, the payment of a dividend, election of new directors and other matters. Any other meeting is called an extraordinary general meeting, and may be held to consider, for example, changing the name of the company, issuing new shares or winding-up. Meetings must be conducted strictly in accordance with statutory procedure. Company management has in recent years become more closely controlled by statute. Particular matters covered include regulation of the conduct of directors who have personal interests. "Insider" share dealing is now unlawful. Directors are also required to have regard to the interests of employees in carrying out their functions.

Winding-up

When a company is wound-up its business is concluded by a liquidator who takes over the powers of the board. They collect in the debts which are owed to the company and, so far as they are able, pay off the creditors. They may have to decide whether an alleged liability should be

---

[4A] Corporate Manslaughter and Corporate Homicide Act 2007.
[5] The attempt to bring manslaughter charges against Great Western Trains Plc following the Southall train crash was rejected in 1999 on a preliminary point of law and an appeal was subsequently dismissed.

settled, such as a pending action for damages against the company. When the debts are paid, any money left is distributed among the members. Finally the company is dissolved and ceases to exist. Winding-up may be compulsory or voluntary. Compulsory winding-up is by order of the court, upon the petition, usually, of a creditor. In most cases the ground for winding-up is that the company is unable to pay its debts. A company may be wound-up voluntarily for any reason by the passing of a resolution in general meeting. This may be done, for example, to amalgamate with another company. If the company is insolvent the creditors control the winding-up. For the consequences of insolvency see Ch.9.

If a company is insolvent, secured debts such as debentures will be paid first upon winding-up, and they may consume all or most of the assets. Ordinary debts include an unsatisfied judgment against the company. Thus, if a creditor is owed an undisputed ordinary debt, a judgment for the debt is of no advantage if the company goes into liquidation before it can be executed. Often, debenture holders will pre-empt a winding-up by appointing a receiver to protect their security (see Ch.10). The subsequent liquidation is then more of a formality.

Foreign companies

Many foreign companies operate within the UK, and many UK companies operate abroad. Some foreign countries apply restrictions to those entitled to carry on business. In England and Wales (Scotland and Northern Ireland have separate legal systems) any foreign company may carry on business and may sue or be sued in the English courts. The constitution of a foreign company is subject to the law of the place of incorporation.

Some provisions of English company law apply to any foreign company carrying on business within the jurisdiction, but particular provisions apply where a company sets up a place of business in England and Wales. The company must then register and file certain publicly available documents similar to those required of English companies. This includes a list of directors and their interests, accounts and company reports and details of the means of serving notices or legal process on the company. A registered foreign company may then be subject to winding-up proceedings in England.

Particular provisions apply to companies within the European Community. The idea of a "European company" is still under development but regulations provide for a new form of entity called a European Economic Interest Grouping.[6] This is intended to be an amalgamation of

---

[6] EC Regulation 2137/85.

companies, or other bodies, located in different EC Member States, based on similar provisions under French law.

PARTNERSHIPS

A partnership is an unincorporated body of persons combined for a common object. While the incorporation or dissolution of a company is an unequivocal act, it can be difficult to determine whether or not a partnership exists. There is often a written partnership agreement or articles of association, usually in the form of a deed. Professional firms such as architects or consulting engineers will invariably have their constitution set out in such a document. However, a partnership agreement may be oral or even inferred from the acts of the parties. The essential feature which distinguishes a partnership is the carrying on of a business in common with a view to profit. There must be a sharing of net profits, although the shares need not be equal and it is unnecessary for all the partners to take part in running the firm.

Unlike a limited company a partnership, under English law, is not a separate legal entity. It is owned by the partners in common, and the partners are liable for the firm's debts. The capital of the firm is contributed by the partners in any proportions they agree, so that one partner may contribute only capital and another only their expertise. They may agree to share profits in any proportions and prima facie losses must be shared in the same proportions. The question whether a partnership exists may have important consequences, for instance, in relation to loans. If A lends £1000 to B to help finance B's business, then depending on the circumstances, there may be a partnership between A and B so that A might, in addition to losing his £1000, become liable for B's business debts.

In the absence of a contrary agreement, a partnership ceases on the death, bankruptcy or retirement of a partner and must be dissolved. A partnership agreement therefore usually provides for the firm to be carried on by the surviving or remaining partners. Partnership law was codified in the Partnership Act 1890 which continues in force, despite far-reaching changes which have occurred in company law.

Management of a firm

Partners, as between themselves, must act *uberrimae fides*, i.e. with the utmost good faith. A partner may not make a private profit from the firm's business. Decisions must be made by a majority of the partners, but changes in the constitution of the firm, such as taking in a new partner, must be made unanimously. Every partner is prima facie the agent of the firm and can make binding contracts on its behalf. If a partner commits a tort in the course of the firm's business, the firm, i.e. all the partners, will be liable.

When a firm is liable in contract or for a debt the partners are jointly liable. All or any of the partners may be sued in their own names. A judgment may be enforced against any of the partners who have been sued. Alternatively, court rules allow all partners to sue or be sued by bringing proceedings in the name of the firm.[7] Where a firm is liable in tort, a judgment against one partner may be enforced against all others.

Dissolution

A partnership, unlike a limited company, may be dissolved without the assistance of the courts. If formed for an indefinite period, a partnership is dissolved by one partner merely giving notice to the other of their intention to dissolve it. If the partnership is for a fixed and unexpired term it can be dissolved only by order of the court on the grounds, for example, that one of the partners is guilty of prejudicial conduct, or that the business can only be carried on at a loss. While the dissolution of a company takes place after winding-up and distribution of assets, the dissolution of a partnership is the first act. This is followed by the winding-up of the business, for which purpose the partner's authority continues, but may be limited by the appointment of a receiver.

Limited liability partnerships

This is the creature of the Limited Liability Partnership Act 2000, which represents the final response of the Government to the long-standing debate on professional liability. The Act creates a new corporate entity referred to here as an LLP, which itself represents a new concept, since a conventional partnership does not have legal status separate from that of its members. While a partnership needs no formal steps for its creation, an LLP can be created only through registration at Companies House. Once registered, the LLP can hold property and become subject to legal rights and duties and survives changes of its participants or "members". The members, unlike true partners, do not have a general agency and they are not personally liable for the LLP. Insolvency of the LLP may involve some risk of "clawback" in respect of transfers of capital from the LLP within the previous two years (similar to company insolvency) and LLP members may acquire personal liability for

---

[7] RSC Ord. 81, which continues in force.

wrongdoing. However, the personal assets of members are not at risk in regard to claims. Unlike companies, an LLP is not itself subject to taxation and members are treated generally, for tax purposes, as though they were partners, and remain technically self-employed. The partnership deed is replaced by a "Members Agreement". While the finances of partnerships are entirely private and those of companies open to public view, an LLP is required to file relatively simple accounts.

LLPs will be attractive to professional partnerships in any area capable of giving rise to substantial liability, certainly including all the professions relating to the construction industry. An LLP may also be suitable for use as the Special Purpose Vehicle for joint venturers participating in PFI or other complex project structures. LLPs represent the only substantial development in legal business structures for over a century and align the UK with developments elsewhere in the world.

OTHER CORPORATE BODIES

Local authorities

Local authorities are corporate bodies whose constitution and powers derive directly or indirectly from statutes. Constitutional and general matters are found principally in the Local Government Act 1972. The powers and duties of local authorities are laid down in many statutes. Examples of particular importance are the Public Health Acts 1936 and 1961, the Education Act 1944, the Highways Act 1980, and the Town and Country Planning Act 1990. Every part of the country is within the jurisdiction of one or more local authority. The distribution of functions between different local authorities and between the authorities and central government varies according to district and according to the service in question. Different local authorities may combine to provide services by setting up joint committees or a permanent joint board. Like central government, local authorities function through elected members (the Council) and employed officials and staff (Officers).

The Local Government Act 1972, brought about a massive reorganisation of local government. In addition to the re-drawing of boundaries, the Act created a two-tier structure of local government throughout England and Wales. In any area, the primary local authority was either a county or a metropolitan borough council. Below this were district councils, many having as their base the former county boroughs or boroughs. Further changes introduced in 1996 have abolished some second-tier councils and re-established unitary authorities largely based on the old counties.

London has traditionally occupied a special position. Its local authority system was laid down in the London Government Act 1963. It consists of 32 London Borough Councils, including the City. The Greater London Council, which formerly presided over the London Boroughs, was abolished and wound-up in the 1980s, together with the metropolitan county councils. More recently, London has re-acquired its own governing body and mayor, and will be followed by other cities.

The powers of a local authority to enter into contracts are similar to those of an incorporated company. A local authority will be bound by a contract whether written or oral, provided it is made by an agent acting with authority. However, since the powers of all local authorities derive directly or indirectly from statute, their capacity to contract is limited by these powers in the same way that an incorporated company is limited by its objects. Any contract which a local authority purports to make for a purpose beyond such powers is ultra vires and void. In entering into a contract a local authority must also comply with its own standing orders, unless they have been suspended for the purpose. In the case of *R. v Hereford Corporation, Ex p. Harrower*,[8] the Council sought to negotiate a contract with the Electricity Board and failed to invite tenders in accordance with the standing orders, because the Board were to prepare the design. The Court of Appeal rejected this as a ground for non-compliance, holding that there was a statutory duty to observe the standing orders. The question then arose whether the applicants had the right to apply to the court. Lord Parker C.J. held:

> "The mere fact that these applicants were electrical contractors does not, in my judgement, of itself give them a sufficient right. But if, as I understand they or some of them are rate payers as well, then, as it seems to me, there would be a sufficient right to enable them to apply for mandamus."

A contract once entered into is valid despite any breach of standing orders, but the court has power to prevent a local authority from entering into a contract in breach of its rules.[9] Any member of a local authority having an interest in a contract made or proposed must disclose the fact in the same way as a director of a company. Such a member may not take part in discussion or voting connected with the contract.

As an alternative to using commercial contractors for construction work, many local authorities have set up "direct labour" organisations whereby they employ their own workforce to carry out construction work. In some cases this has led to major projects being undertaken by

---

[8] [1970] 1 W.L.R. 1424.
[9] *Letting International v Newham LBC* [2008] EWHC 1583.

councils acting, in effect, as their own main contractor. Direct labour organisations also carry out work for bodies other than their parent authorities. The practice is now controlled by the Local Government Planning and Land Act 1980, which restricts the power of local authorities to enter into agreements to carry out work for other bodies and regulates the way in which direct labour organisations carry out work for their parent authorities. Competitive tenders must be obtained, and authorities are required to publish accounts and to show a return on capital employed. Recent developments in local government financing have led to "privatisation" of many traditional local government services, which are now provided through competitive tendering. In these areas, local authorities have become much more active as employers of services. Conversely, in the construction field, changes in local government financing have severely reduced local authority housing and construction projects.

The Crown

The word "Crown" has several different meanings. It is used here to denote the sum of governmental powers exercised through the various ministries of central government, as opposed to local government. It is not synonymous with the monarch but historically, governments have found it convenient to invest themselves and their executive departments with the privileges and immunities attaching personally to the monarch, and so the term "Crown" is apt. Formerly the Crown enjoyed general immunity in tort and could only be sued in contract by a special process. This was radically changed by the Crown Proceedings Act 1947, which allows the appropriate government department, or the Attorney-General, to be sued by ordinary process of law. This is subject to limitations which, for example, prevent proceedings for summary judgment against the Crown.

In contract the Crown is bound by any agreement made on its behalf by an agent having authority. But if a contract provides for funds to be voted by Parliament, an affirmative vote is a condition precedent to liability. With some exceptions, principally relating to the armed forces, the Crown is liable in tort as if it were a private person of full age and capacity, and it can be made liable for the acts of its servants or agents. By virtue of its residuary immunities the Crown cannot be restrained by injunction, nor can it be deprived of property. The Crown also has a far-reaching privilege to restrain disclosure of documents in legal proceedings, whether or not it is a party to the proceedings.

Building and engineering contracts in which the employer is a government department are often subject to one of a series of standard forms known as GC/Works. In keeping with government privatisation policy, the latest edition of the forms has been produced commercially and is offered for general use in a private version known as PC/Works (see Ch.11). Some government departments favour the use of private sector standard forms, notably the Department of Transport (operating through the Highways Agency) has for many years favoured the use of the ICE Form of Contract but with a number of its own amendments.

All governments throughout the world operate through departments or ministries presided over by Ministers or Secretaries of State. The question sometimes arises whether different ministries comprise separate legal entities or whether they are equivalent, for example, to different departments of the same company. In some countries, notably France and others whose constitution derives from that of France, government departments do indeed comprise separate legal entities. In the United Kingdom, however, the Crown and the government are regarded in law as indivisible. While the Crown Proceedings Act stipulates for particular ministers or Secretaries of State to be sued they are, in law, one with the government. The authority of a Secretary of State extends, in law, over other ministries so that one can represent others. This is, however, now subject to the effects of devolution and the separate constitutions of the Welsh Assembly and the Scottish Parliament. Northern Ireland has always had its own government, although controlled directly, at times, from Westminster.

There are other important contrasts between the constitutional position of the Crown and that of the government of other countries. In the United Kingdom, despite the recent upsurge of public law rights, many of which are exercisable against the government (see Ch.1), the Crown, in general, exercises no rights in regard to commercial contracts beyond those exercisable by any ordinary legal person. Where the government wishes to exercise special powers, it does so through Parliament by passing legislation granting such powers. There are many examples which have operated, for instance during war-time or other emergencies. In general, however, the government has no special commercial powers. This is in sharp contrast to the position in most other countries. In France there is a well-developed body of rights which the government is entitled to exercise in the national interest. For example, under the doctrine of *imprévision*, where unforeseen circumstances arise which might result in a contract not being performed, the government is entitled to require performance to continue on different terms. In *Compagnie Generale d'Eclarage de Bordeaux*[10] the contract for gas supply to Bordeaux became economically impossible to perform owing to huge increases in

---

[10] Conseil d'Etat, March 30, 1916.

coal prices as a result of French coal fields being occupied by the German army during the First World War. The result would have been to cut off lighting to the city. The company was ordered to continue to perform the contract, but at a substantially increased price to take account of the price of coal.

Whenever it is sought to bring an action against a foreign government, whether the action is brought here or abroad, the position may be very different from an action against the British government. As a general rule a foreign sovereign state is immune from action brought in this country, whether in civil or criminal law. Further, if there is no local equivalent to the Crown Proceedings Act, it may not be possible to bring proceedings in the country in question. Parties contracting with foreign states should therefore give serious consideration to the question of guarantees or securities.

Public utilities, privatisation and regulation

Until 1945 "public" services throughout the United Kingdom were provided by private enterprise, although many of the major industries such as coal, steel and the railways had been taken over by the government during the two world wars. The new government of 1945 introduced, for the first time, the concept of "nationalisation" under which these major industries were formally brought under permanent state control in the form of public corporations with a monopoly, under the responsibility of a Minister answerable to Parliament. Subsequent governments de-nationalised certain industries, such as steel and the airlines. During the 1980s, however, an entirely new policy was embarked upon by which virtually the whole of the former public utilities have been systematically "privatised" by breaking them up into commercial organisations for sale as public companies. In some cases the government has temporarily retained a substantial shareholding. But in the main the process has involved the government entirely divesting itself of ownership and setting up, in place of the former government control, a series of regulators intended to exercise controls in the public interest. Such bodies include OFWAT (Water Services), OFTEL (telecommunications) and OFGAS (gas). Each regulator is given powers under statutes which also prescribe the duties of each operator. In the case of the water industry these are the Water Industry Act 1991 and the Water Resources Act, 1991. In the case of the railways, which have given rise to substantial amounts of construction work, privatisation involved a complex split of resources and operations between Railtrack, the train operators and rolling stock owners. Railtrack, subsequently replaced by the not-for-profit company Network Rail, are the principal employers of construction and design services, through works of maintenance, replacement and new build. Their operations are subject to regulation through the Office of the Rail Regulator and, formerly, the Strategic Rail Authority. Matters of safety are regulated by the Railways Inspectorate, which is now part of the Health and Safety Executive. Regulation continues to be an area of growth and development.

The result of the privatisation programme is the setting up of a large number of substantial companies, which operate the utilities and other basic industries on a commercial basis, and whose constitution does not differ essentially from that of any other public limited company. Shares are quoted and traded in the same way as other commercial companies and, as has been seen in recent years, the companies are susceptible to takeovers and mergers. Where an apparent monopoly has existed, government policy has been to insist on the creation of competition, which now applies (despite the use of common facilities) in the field of telecommunications, electricity and gas supply. Many of these newly emerging commercial enterprises are in process of developing appropriate commercial forms of contract and dispute resolution procedures for their operations. Many of these are based on the principles of construction law.

CHAPTER 5

THE LAW OF OBLIGATIONS

In English law, obligations arise in a variety of ways which sometimes overlap. For purposes of analysis they are divided into discrete categories and they are so dealt with in this book. However, it is important to be aware that these categories can be artificial or, more strictly, are imposed as part of a logical order. In this chapter, obligations are considered more broadly and some of the areas of overlap are explored. An example of the overlap of obligations is in the field of professional negligence, where a body of principles has grown up spanning the law of the contract and tort in their application to duties of skill and care. The duties of engineers, architects, and surveyors are dealt with in this book separately in relation to contract and tort, since the former involves specific duties in relation to the construction contract. In the field of medical negligence, however, the difference between contract and tort may be of little relevance.

In this chapter obligations are divided primarily between those arising as a matter of agreement and those imposed by virtue of status. Within the former, it is necessary to distinguish between circumstances in which the law will imply a "contract" which conventionally must have ascertainable terms, and those in which, in the absence of contract, the law imposes an obligation, for example to account for benefits received. In the latter category are obligations arising under the law of tort and through statutory duties imposed on defined persons or bodies. Also included is the law of trusts, a wholly separate area of law which continues to be of considerable utility in the world of commerce and business.

OBLIGATIONS THROUGH AGREEMENT

English law in general rarely finds difficulty in constructing a contract from any circumstances which evidence a mutual exchange of obligations. It may be said that English law is more concerned with identifying circumstances in which an apparent exchange of obligations does not create an enforceable contract (as to which see Ch.6).

The way in which the law identifies and categorises agreements was described in *New Zealand Shipping Co. v Satterthwaite & Co.*[1] This case concerned whether a negligent stevedore could rely on the terms of the Bill of Lading issued by agents of the carrier for whom the stevedore carried out unloading. The question was, therefore, who were the relevant parties to the transaction. Lord Wilberforce's judgment included this:

> "It is only the precise analysis of this complex of relations into the classical offer and acceptance, with identifiable consideration, that seems to present difficulty, but this same difficulty exists in many situations of daily life, e.g. sales at auctions; supermarket purchases; boarding an omnibus; purchasing a train ticket; tenders for the supplies or goods; offers of rewards; acceptance by post; warranties of authority by agents; manufacturers' guarantees; gratuitous bailments; bankers' commercial credits. These are all examples which show that English law, having committed itself to a rather technical and schematic doctrine of contract, in application takes a practical approach, often at the cost of forcing the facts to fit uneasily into the marked slots of offer, acceptance and consideration."

In the construction field, the case of *Shanklin Pier v Detel Products*[2] is regarded as a landmark decision establishing that oral representations about a product made to a prospective user could found a claim in breach of warranty. The user, who was the pier owner, specified the product under a contract made with the main contractor, who placed an order for the product. This has given rise to the now common practice of employers entering into express direct warranties with suppliers or sub-contractors. But in a number of cases both preceding and following the *Shanklin* case, the courts have held that statements may give rise to an enforceable contract without the need for any other direct relationship between the parties in question. In *Andrews v Hopkinson*[3] a second hand car dealer made the memorable statement "It's a good little bus. I'd stake my life on it. You will have no trouble with it". This was followed by the plaintiff entering into a hire purchase contract with a finance company to whom the dealer sold the car. The vehicle had a serious steering defect which led to an accident. The statement was held to be an enforceable warranty which entitled the plaintiff to recover damages both as to the difference in value of the car and damages for personal injury. The *Shanklin* case can therefore be seen as an application of existing principles.

---

[1] [1975] A.C. 154.
[2] [1951] 2 K.B. 854.
[3] [1957] 1 Q.B. 229; approved in *Yeoman Credit v Odgers* [1962] 1 W.L.R. 215; and see also *Brown v Sheen* [1950] 1 All E.R. 1102.

Unilateral contracts

Despite the importance of mutuality in the law of contract there are many situations in which the law has to find a consistent and rational answer to transactions which lack mutuality. They are sometimes referred to as unilateral contracts, although they must be bilateral in the sense that there must be two parties and obligations which each of them takes on. The classic unilateral contract is one in which an offer is made to the world through advertisement expressed to be capable of acceptance by any individual who fulfils the stated requirements. A common example is offers of reward, which may lead to dispute if, for example, several people fulfil the stated conditions. The leading case, now over a century old, is *Carlill v Carbolic Smoke Ball Co.*[4] in which the defendant, who sold a patent cure, offered to pay £100 to any person who used the cure and then caught influenza. This was held to be an offer capable of acceptance particularly as the defendant also advertised that £1000 had been deposited with their bankers. More difficult questions arise where there are multiple claims, or where the person fulfilling the condition was unaware of the offer.

An example of a unilateral contract in the field of construction is the instruction of an estate agent to negotiate the sale of a house on commission. The estate agent does not undertake to do anything and will not be under any liability for failing to achieve a sale. Unless a separately enforceable option is granted, the client can revoke the agent's instructions at any time. Yet if a sale is negotiated, the client becomes liable for the fee: it is a matter of construction whether the fee is to be payable upon sale or upon introduction of a willing purchaser. A person appointed sole agent may be entitled to maintain a claim for damages if the client then sells through another agent.

A common device used in the construction field is the "call off" contract by which the client or employer enters into what appears to be a formal contract containing rates and prices for specified and described items of work or goods and materials. There are usually detailed provisions regulating the ordering of work and there may be a retainer or other fee payable in any event. The obligation to do the work or supply the goods, and the corresponding obligation to pay, arises only as and when orders are placed.[5] An example of this type of contract is one for routine repairs to public services, such as water pipes and apparatus beneath the highway. Water companies, as an alternative to employing their own maintenance gangs, currently let term contracts on this basis within defined areas. Such arrangements are also known as "Framework

---

[4] [1893] 1 Q.B. 256.
[5] See *Brogden v Metropolitan Railway* (1877) 2 App. Cas. 666.

Agreements", a term used in the context of procurement, which is subject to European procurement law.[6]

Letters of intent

Frequently, parties create a situation in which they intend no contract to come into existence, sometimes by expressly stating their intention to enter into a contract in the future. Such an intention, provided that it was honestly held, creates no obligation. Nevertheless, it is common for such a letter of intent to be accompanied by words authorising certain work to be carried out and this may give rise to what is sometimes called an "if" contract, i.e. a contract under which A requests B to carry out work on the basis that if they do so they will receive appropriate payment. This is another example of a particular type of unilateral contract. In *British Steel v Cleveland Bridge*[7] the defendant wrote a letter to the plaintiff stating that it was their intention to enter into a sub-contract, on the basis of which the plaintiff arranged for the manufacture of steel work. The parties continued to negotiate and the steel work was progressively delivered, later than the dates in the contract under negotiation, which was never signed. It was held that there was no "if" contract. Both parties expected there to be a formal contract which would have governed their rights. However, in the absence of a contract being signed, there was simply an obligation in law on the defendant to pay a reasonable sum for work done at its request.

In a number of more recent "letter of intent" cases the issue for the court has been whether the instruction to carry our work satisfied the definition of a "construction contract" in the Housing Grants, etc., Act sufficient to give jurisdiction to an adjudicator appointed to rule on disputed claims for payment. Given the time-scale of adjudication, the adjudicator's decision will be given first and the question of their jurisdiction resolved later on enforcement proceedings in court. Cases where enforcement has been refused on the ground that there was not a sufficient contract in writing[8] will be overtaken by the amendments to the Housing Grants, etc., Act introduced in 2009.[9]

Good faith, best endeavours and fair dealing

The question examined here is whether and to what extent the law of contract recognises enforceable obligations as to the way in which the

---

[6] See Ch.6.
[7] (1981) 24 B.L.R. 94.
[8] See *Hart Investments v Fidler & Larchpark* [2007] B.L.R. 30.
[9] Local Democracy, Economic Development and Construction Act 2009 and see Ch.2.

parties are to behave. Where the parties act in a manner which conveys an intention to be bound, can there be an enforceable obligation to negotiate in good faith? In *Walford v Miles*[10] the defendant was negotiating with a number of people, including the plaintiff, for the sale of a company. The defendant orally agreed with the plaintiff that he would terminate negotiations with any other prospective purchaser in return for the plaintiff furnishing a "comfort" letter from the bank stating that all necessary resources were available for the purchase. The defendant, however, unilaterally decided not to proceed with the plaintiff and sold to another party. The plaintiff brought proceedings alleging, inter alia, breach of an enforceable obligation to negotiate in good faith. The House of Lords rejected the claim, Lord Ackner holding:

> "The reason why an agreement to negotiate, like an agreement to agree, is unenforceable, is simply because it lacks the necessary certainty. The same does not apply to an agreement to use best endeavours. This uncertainty is demonstrated in the instant case by the provision which it is said has to be implied in the agreement for the determination of the negotiations. How can a court be expected to decide whether, objectively, a proper reason existed for the termination of the negotiations? The answer suggested depends upon whether the negotiations were determined in 'good faith'. However, the concept of a duty to carry on negotiations in good faith is inherently repugnant to the adversarial position of the parties when involved in negotiations. Each party to the negotiations is entitled to pursue his (or her) own interest, so long as he avoids making misrepresentations. To advance that interest he must be entitled, if he thinks it appropriate, to threaten to withdraw from negotiations or to withdraw in fact, in the hope that the opposite party may seek to re-open negotiations by offering him improved terms."

The obligation to use best endeavours referred to by Lord Ackner may be thought equally vague. But such an obligation may be enforceable, given the existence of other *indicea* of contract, on the basis that the parties are not in opposed (adversarial) positions but rather taking on obligations of mutual support. The difficulty of proving breach of an obligation to use best endeavours, and the difficulty of establishing damage flowing from such a breach do not prevent such an obligation being given legal effect. This was the case in *Medirest v Mid Essex NHS Trust*[11] where a long-term PFI contract contained an express obligation of good faith, which fell to be interpreted in the context of a contract in which each party had serious commercial interests, coupled with an important common purpose in providing medical services to the public. The court held the

---

[10] [1992] 2 A.C. 128.
[11] *Compass Group UK and Ireland Ltd (t/a Medirest) v Mid Essex Hospital Services NHS Trust* [2012] EWHC 781 QB.

trust to be in material and continuing breach though adopting an unreasonable attitude to contended service failures and associated payment issues as well as attempts to resolve disputes which arose.

Another aspect of the question arises in the context of competitive tendering. Does this create any obligation on the party soliciting the tenders to act fairly or properly? In *Blackpool & Fylde Aeroclub v Blackpool B.C.*[12] the defendant, which operated the local airport, invited tenders for a concession to operate pleasure flights. The form of tender stated that the Council "do not bind themselves to accept all or any part of any tender. No tender which is received after the last date and time specified shall be admitted for consideration". The plaintiff submitted a proper tender but owing to a mistake by the Council it was not considered and the defendant accepted a less favourable tender. The plaintiff claimed damages for breach of contract. Bingham L.J. commented on the fact that a tendering procedure was heavily weighted in favour of the invitor. He went on to say:

> "But where as here the tenders are soliciting from selected parties all of them known to the invitor, and where a local authority's invitation prescribes a clear orderly and familiar procedure—draft contract conditions available for inspection and plainly not open to negotiation, a prescribed common form of tender, the supply of envelopes designed to observe the absolute anonymity of tenderers and clearly to identify the tender in question, and an absolute deadline—the invitee is in my judgement protected at least to this extent: if he submits a conforming tender before the deadline he is entitled, not as a matter of mere expectation but of contractual right, to be sure that his tender will after the deadline be opened and considered in conjunction with all other conforming tenders or at least that his tender will be considered if others are."

More recently it has been by the Canadian Supreme Court, that there was a breach of an implied contractual undertaking where an employer accepted a non-compliant tender, despite a provision that "the lowest or any tender shall not necessarily be accepted"[13]; and in other cases the courts have begun to accept the term "tender contract" to describe the mutual obligations created by the tender process.[14]

For the position under European public works contracts, see Ch.6 and particularly *Harmon Façades v House of Commons*.[15] It should be emphasised that there is no general principle of good faith under English law outside particular contracts such as those of insurance (see Ch.7). In *Interfoto v Stiletto*[16] (see Ch.6 for facts) Bingham L.J. said:

---

[12] [1990] 1 W.L.R. 1195.
[13] *MJB Enterprises v Defence Construction* [1999] 1 S.C.R. 619.
[14] See *Gerald Martin Scott v Belfast Education Board* (2007) C.I.L.L. 2510, NI Ch. Div.
[15] (1999) 67 Con. L.R. 1.
[16] [1989] Q.B. 433.

"In many civil law systems, and perhaps most legal systems outside the common law world, the law of obligations recognises and enforces an over-riding principle that in making and carrying out contracts, the parties should act in good faith . . . English law has, characteristically committed itself to no such over-riding principle but has developed piecemeal solutions to demonstrated problems of unfairness. Many examples could be given, thus equity has intervened to strike down unconscionable bargains. Parliament has stepped in to regulate the imposition of exemption clauses and the form of certain hire purchase agreements. The common law has also made its contribution, by holding that certain classes of contract require utmost good faith, by treating as irrecoverable what purport to be agreed estimates of damage but are in truth disguised penalty for breach and in many other ways."

Third party rights in contract

The spectrum of "obligations" includes the possibility of one party to a contract being under a duty to perform or to pay damages for non-performance to a third party who is not an original party to that contract. The existence of such a duty in tort is mentioned below. A duty of this sort also arises as a result of an express or implied collateral contract with the third party (see above). What is considered here is the creation of contractual "third party rights", by which the contract itself could be enforceable by a stranger.

English common law has consistently rejected the notion of third party rights in contract. Substantially the only rights acknowledged were those arising under the law of trust (see below). In *Beswick v Beswick*[17] a nephew bought his uncle's coal business and promised to pay £6–10s per week for life and thereafter £5 per week to his widow. The nephew refused to pay the widow who was held, under the doctrine of privity, to be unable to recover the money in her own name. However, the House of Lords held that, as the aunt was also the personal representative, she could enforce the contract in the name of her deceased husband. The case represents the high point of the doctrine of privity, and seems an affront to common sense.

However, two recent developments have made major inroads into this area in which English law appears to stand aloof from the rest of the world. First, after some years of deliberation the Law Commission's proposals for the creation of a general right for a third party to enforce a contract expressly or impliedly made for his benefit have been enacted as the Contracts (Rights of Third Parties) Act 1999 (see further Ch.6). A contract may, however, provide that no such rights are created. Where

---

[17] [1968] A.C. 58.

the new Act does not assist, it may be necessary to refer to the underlying common law.

The second development has been in the common law, where three construction cases have dealt with rights of action where damages had become separated from the legal right of recovery. In *Linden Gardens v Lanesta Sludge*,[18] it was held that a purported assignment of the benefit of a large construction contract was ineffective in the absence of consent from the contractor. The result was that the party entitled to enforce the contract (the original employer) was not the party who had suffered the loss. The House of Lords rejected a submission that the loss therefore disappeared into a "black hole" and held that the parties were to be treated as having entered into the contract on the basis that the employer would be entitled to enforce rights against the contractor on behalf of those who would suffer from deficient performance. Lord Griffiths proposed a wider test as follows:

> "In everyday life contracts for work and labour are constantly being placed by those who have no proprietary interest in the subject matter of the contract. To take a common example, the matrimonial home is owned by the wife and the couple's remaining assets are owned by the husband and he is the sole earner. The house requires a new roof and the husband places a contract to carry out the work. The husband is not acting as agent for his wife, he makes the contract as principal because only he can pay for it. The builder fails to replace the roof properly and the husband has to call in and pay another builder to complete the work. Is it to be said that the husband has suffered no damage because he does not own the property? Such a result would in my view be absurd and the answer is that the husband has suffered loss because he did not receive the bargain for which he had contracted with the first builder and the measure of damages is the cost of securing the performance of the bargain by completing the roof repairs by the second builder."

In *Darlington v Wiltshier*[19] the building owner faced a similar difficulty arising, not from commercial transfer of rights but from the well-known device of using a separate financier (Morgan Grenfell) to enter into the building contract which was then to be assigned to the local authority as the true owner. There were defects in the work, but the contractor contended that the loss was suffered by Morgan Grenfell prior to the assignment and the local authority had therefore acquired no rights. The Court of Appeal held the plaintiff entitled to recover, applying the *Lanesta* case.

The third case of *Alfred McAlpine v Panatown*[20] involved the making of a building contract with a nominee company within the same group as

---

[18] Heard with *St. Martin's v McAlpine* [1994] 1 A.C. 85.

[19] [1995] 1 W.L.R. 68.

[20] [2000] B.L.R. 331.

the company which owned the site, for reasons of VAT liability. Again, the right of action appeared to be vested in a party other than the party which had suffered damage. The House of Lords, reversing the decision of the Court of Appeal, held that the case did not fall into any of the exceptions to the common law privity rule. Part of the reasoning turned on the existence of a direct warranty giving a right of action to another company in the same group against McAlpine. As will be seen below, a similar conclusion was reached in the case of *Greater Nottingham Co-op v Cementation*[21] in regard to duties owed in tort. In cases based on similar facts, the first question will now be whether a right of action is provided by the Contracts (Rights of Third Parties) Act 1999. The way in which the Act impacts on common law rights, remains to be considered by the courts.

Status of offers

The principles of offer and acceptance are normally applied with some rigidity so that the parties move at the moment of acceptance from there being no contract to full and binding contractual relations. There are, however, a number of situations in which actions short of acceptance of an offer may give rise to enforceable rights. Some of these are discussed below in relation to quantum meruit and equity. In addition, under the law of some countries the offer itself is regarded as giving rise to legal obligations if relied upon. In *Northern Construction v Gloge Heating*[22] and a number of similar cases the Canadian courts have held that an offer made by a sub-contractor to a main contractor could not be withdrawn (save on grounds which would vitiate a contract) after the main contractor had relied on the offer in making his own tender. Similar principles exist in some civil law countries. Under English law, however, an offer creates no obligation unless accompanied by an enforceable option or an agreement not to revoke the offer.

RESTITUTION AND QUANTUM MERUIT

The absence in English law of any general principle of fair dealing or good faith is commented on above. Yet in two respects at least, English law does afford remedies based on such principles. One is in the area of law loosely referred to as Equity and more specifically the law of trusts,

---

[21] See n.38, below.
[22] (1986) 27 D.L.R. 265; 1 Const. L.J. 144.

which is dealt with below. The other, dealt with here, is an area of law which has come to be referred to compendiously as Restitution or unjust enrichment. This area of law has grown out of the common law principle of quasi-contract in which the law afforded the remedy of repayment of money received or payment of a reasonable sum, in the absence of a contract. The principle has now developed into a general principle of affording restitution where other remedies are unavailable.[23]

The leading cases in the construction field start with *William Lacey v Davis*[24] in which a contractor, having tendered for building work and in anticipation of obtaining the contract, prepared further calculations and particulars for use by the employer in obtaining a ward damage claim. No contract was awarded and the contractor sued for compensation for the services rendered. Barrie J. held:

> "In my judgement, the proper inference from the facts proved in this case is not that the work was done in the hope that this building might possibly be reconstructed and that the plaintiff company might obtain the contract, but that it was done under a mutual belief and understanding that this building was being reconstructed and that the plaintiff company was obtaining the contract. . . . The court should imply a condition or imply a promise that the defendant should pay a reasonable sum to the plaintiff for the whole of these services which were rendered by them."

This principle must be limited, however, to circumstances in which a benefit is conferred subject to a mutual implied expectation of payment. In the old case of *Sumpter v Hedges*,[25] a building contractor who became insolvent abandoned a contract leaving partly completed work, some of which had not been paid for. His action to recover payment for the work failed on the basis that the defendant had no choice but to accept what was attached to his land. In the case of *Regalion Properties v London Dockland Development Corporation*[26] the plaintiff had incurred substantial costs in anticipation of a development contract which did not materialise. These costs would have been recovered out of the income from the development. Rattee J. held:

> "Each party to such negotiations must be taken to know (as in my judgement Regalion did in the present case) that depending on the conclusion of a binding contract any cost incurred by him in preparation for the intended contract be incurred at his own risk, in the sense that he will have

---

[23] See generally Goff and Jones, *The Law of Unjust Enrichment*, 8th edn (London: Sweet & Maxwell, 2011) and *Legal Obligations in Construction* (CCLM, King's College), papers 11 and 12.

[24] [1957] 1 W.L.R. 932.

[25] [1898] 1 Q.B. 673.

[26] [1995] 1 W.L.R. 212.

no recompense for those costs if no contract results. I accept . . . that by deliberate use of the words "subject to contract" with the admitted intention that they should have their usual effect, LDDC and Regalion each accepted that in the event of no contract being entered into, any resultant loss should lie where it fell."

In relation to a subsisting contract, the terms may well be inconsistent with a claim for unjust enrichments. For example where the contract price is lower than the market price, the contractor could not bring an action for the value of the employer's enrichment, since that is what the parties have contracted for. In *Costello v MacDonald*,[27] the defendant builder contracted, with a company of which the plaintiffs were the sole shareholders, to build houses. After a dispute the builder left the works incomplete but with the company owing money. The plaintiffs took possession of the houses without further payment. The builder's action in restitution for unjust enrichment failed on the basis it would undermine the contractual arrangement the parties had entered into.

A potentially important question in relation to work performed in the absence of a formal contract, where the contractor is entitled simply to payment for the work done, is whether the person commissioning the work (the would-be employer) is entitled to credit for defective performance of the work. In the absence of a contract, there could not be a cross-claim, but there could, in theory, be a set-off (see Ch.2). As regards physical defects in the work, there is no difficulty in principle about reflecting this in the value of what is to be paid for. Difficult questions of fact might arise where the defect relates to suitability rather than quality. Such issues would depend on what the contractor had been requested and had agreed to undertake. More difficult is the question of delay. In the absence of any contract there cannot be terms controlling the performance of the work in question. There could not, therefore, be a fixed completion date nor can there be any implied obligation to perform within a reasonable time.[28] The possibility that the value of the work should be reduced by reason of tardy performance cannot, however, be ruled out.[29]

Quantum Meruit under contracts

Where no price is stated for work carried out within an existing contract, the employer will be obliged to pay a reasonable sum, which may be regarded as a species of quantum meruit. More difficult, and of

[27] [2011] B.L.R. 544.
[28] *Sanders & Foster v Monk* (1980) [1995] Con.L.Yb. 189.
[29] *Crown House Engineering v AMEC* (1990) 48 B.L.R. 32.

considerable importance in relation to construction contracts, is whether and in what circumstances, the contractor may be entitled to claim quantum meruit when there is an existing agreed pricing mechanism. Such a remedy is occasionally claimed on the footing that "the basis of the contract has changed" or that circumstances have arisen which were not contemplated by the parties. Some support for this approach appears in the old case of *Bush v Whitehaven Trustees*[30] where variations led to a summer contract being turned into a winter contract. However, the authority of the case has been soundly repudiated by the House of Lords.[31] The case was again relied on by the official referee in *McAlpine Humberoak v McDermott*, but again repudiated by the Court of Appeal in the same case.[32] There is, it is submitted, still a basis in law for such a contention. In *Thorn v London Corporation*[33] the House of Lords recognised, obiter, that circumstances might arise in which the contractor was effectively being required to perform a different contract: "*non haec in foedera veni*". In *Parkinson v Commissioners of Works*,[34] the Court of Appeal allowed a contractor to recover quantum meruit in part where the original contract, which had been subjected to extensive variations, was renegotiated with a provision for a fixed profit. This was held to limit the amount of work which could be ordered so that work in excess of such limit gave rise to a quantum meruit.

An important and unresolved question is whether a contractor, whose contract is brought to an end by repudiation by the employer which is accepted by the contractor, may claim quantum meruit in respect of the whole of the contract works, as an alternative to claiming the value of work done together with loss of profit. There is high authority in support of such right, specifically the Privy Council decision in *Lodder v Slowey*.[35] However, the principle has been doubted in *Keating on Building Contracts*[36] as being inconsistent with both earlier[37] and later[38] authority. The issue is of the highest commercial importance, since it would in theory permit a contractor to escape entirely from an unprofitable contract. The issue can be resolved only by a decision of the Supreme Court. It is to be noted that United States and commonwealth decisions have upheld the right to quantum meruit without question[39];

---

[30] *Hudson's Building Contracts*, 4th edn (London: Sweet & Maxwell), Vol.2, p.120.
[31] *Davis Contractors v Fareham UDC* [1956] A.C. 696, 732.
[32] (1992) 58 B.L.R. 1.
[33] (1876) 1 App. Cas. 120.
[34] [1949] 2 K.B. 632.
[35] [1904] A.C. 442 and see *Chandler Bros v Boswell* [1936] 3 All E.R. 179.
[36] 9th edn (2012), para.9–039.
[37] *Ranger v G.W. Railways* (1854) 5 H.L.C. 72.
[38] *Johnson v Agnew* [1980] A.C. 368, per Lord Wilberforce at p.396.
[39] See *Morrison-Knudsen v British Columbia Hydro Authority* (1978) 85 D.L.R. 3d 186; 7 Const. L.J. 227.

while on the other hand, the principle appears to rest on the theory that a contract which has been terminated following repudiation disappears, relieving the parties from any onerous obligations thereunder. This principle is demonstrably contrary to many authorities which have held that the contract terms survive repudiation.[40] However, decisions supportive of the right to quantum meruit have been in the New South Wales Court of Appeal[41] and in the Supreme Court of Victoria.[42]

OBLIGATIONS THROUGH STATUS

The most common circumstance in which the law imposes obligations on a person by reason of status, rather than agreement, is under the law of tort. The essence of tortious obligations is that a person is required to avoid causing harm to another. The widest area of duty is in relation to the law of negligence where persons in particular circumstances are regarded in law as owing a duty of care in relation to particular types of loss. Thus, a person will be regarded as owing a duty of care not to cause physical harm to anyone whom they ought reasonably to foresee as being affected by their actions. This test will readily cover drivers of motor vehicles and people in many other circumstances. A person will owe a duty to prevent economic harm to a much more limited class, typically those with whom there exists some special relationship of proximity. This was the situation in the celebrated case of *Hedley Byrne v Heller*[43] in which it was held that a bank might be liable in tort (but for a disclaimer) in circumstances close to, but falling short of contract.[44] In all such cases, the obligation is to take reasonable care to avoid causing harm. Other areas of tort impose absolute obligations to make good loss, for example, where it arises from intentional rather than accidental acts. This is the subject of the law of trespass to goods and nuisance in relation to land (see further Ch.14).

An important question which has been the subject of much apparently conflicting authority is whether a claimant may take advantage of a potential right in tort when there exists a contract between the same parties. The question is important because it may be possible to bring a claim in tort after the limitation period in the contract has expired. Before

---

[40] e.g. *Heyman v Darwins* [1942] A.C. 356, *Suisse Atlantique v M.V. Rotterdamsche Colen* [1967] 1 A.C. 361.
[41] *Renard Constructions v Minister for Public Works* (1992) 26 NSWLR 234.
[42] *Sopov v Kane Constructions* [2009] VSCA 141; [2009] B.L.R. 468.
[43] [1964] A.C. 465.
[44] See Ch.14, Negligent Misstatement.

the rapid expansion of the tort of negligence in the 1970s, the law appeared to be that rights in contract and tort were mutually exclusive. However, there have been a number of cases in which parallel remedies have been allowed.

An example of this is the case of *Batty v Metropolitan Realisations Limited*,[45] where a developer was held liable in breach of contract for having sold to the plaintiff a house which was not fit for habitation because it had been built at the top of a potentially unstable slope. When the question arose whether the plaintiffs were entitled also to have judgment entered in tort Megaw L.J. held:

> "In my judgement the plaintiffs were entitled here to have judgement entered in their favour on the basis of tortious liability as well as on the basis of breach of contract, assuming that the plaintiffs had established a breach by the first defendant of the common law duty of care owed to the plaintiffs. I have no doubt that it was the duty of the first defendants, in the circumstances of this case, apart altogether from the contractual warranty, to examine with reasonable care the land, which in this case would include adjoining land, in order to see whether the site was one on which a house fit for habitation could safely be built. It was a duty owed to prospective buyers of the house."

This case has subsequently been doubted by the House of Lords, because the plaintiffs in *Batty* had suffered no physical damage; but the decision as regards parallel duties in contract and in tort remains applicable. The existence of parallel duties has been considered in other situations, widely different from that of building developer and purchaser. In the leading case of *Lister v Romford Ice & Cold Storage*[46] the House of Lords had to consider the following facts. A lorry driver employed by the defendant company took along his father to act as mate. While negligently driving the lorry, the son injured his own father who succeeded in recovering damages against the company for the son's negligence. The company claimed indemnity against the son, and because of the then restrictive rules on contribution the court had to consider whether the potential liability of the son arose in contract or in tort. The majority opted for contract and held the son liable to the company and not entitled to be indemnified by them or their insurer (so that in the result the family recovered nothing). In a dissenting judgment, Lord Radcliffe said:

> "Since in any event the duty in question is one which exists by imputation or implication of law and not by virtue of any express negotiation between the parties, I should be inclined to say that there is no real distinction

---

[45] [1978] Q.B. 554.
[46] [1957] A.C. 555.

between the two possible sources of obligation. But it is certainly, I think, as much contractual as tortious."

This case was considered in *Tai Hing v Liu Chong Hing Bank*,[47] where the Privy Council had to consider the position of a bank customer where a bank clerk had fraudulently drawn and cashed cheques against the customer's accounts, and the customer had failed to detect or notify the bank about the losses. It was argued that, apart from the terms of contract between the customer and the bank, the customer owed a duty in tort to prevent such losses to the bank (on the footing they were otherwise liable to repay the money). The Privy Council decided the case in contract, holding that the bank's terms were not sufficient to impose liability on the customer for the loss. In regard to the tort claim, it was said:

"Their Lordships do not, therefore, embark on an investigation as to whether in the relationship of banker and customer it is possible to identify tort as well as contract as a source of the obligations owed by the one to the other. Their Lordships do not, however, accept that the parties' mutual obligations in tort can be any greater than those to be found expressly or by necessary implication in their contract . . . the bank cannot rely on the law of tort to provide them with greater protection than that which they have contracted."

This observation is in line with a number of other cases, including *Junior Books v Veitchi*,[48] a case much criticised for its decision, but interesting in having raised the question of the possible impact on tort of terms in another contract. In that case, Lord Roskill said:

"During the argument it was asked what the position would be in a case where there was a relevant exclusion clause in the main contract. My Lords, that question does not arise for decision in the instant appeal, but in principle I would venture the view that such a clause according to the manner in which it was worded might in some circumstances limit the duty of care just as in the Hedley Byrne case the plaintiffs were ultimately defeated by the defendants' disclaimer of responsibility."

Two other construction cases have touched on another aspect of the contract-tort relationship. In *Greater Nottingham Cooperative Society v Cementation Piling & Foundations Ltd*[49] a piling sub-contractor had caused damage to an adjoining property, and this had resulted in losses and claims between the main contractor and the employer. The question arose whether the employer could claim these losses against the sub-contractor

[47] [1986] A.C. 80.
[48] [1983] A.C. 520.
[49] [1989] Q.B. 71.

in tort, where the sub-contractor had been required to enter into the usual direct warranty covering design but not the execution of the work. The Court of Appeal held that the fact that these parties had deliberately made a contract (the warranty) which excluded the work in relation to which the tortious duty was alleged, was sufficient to exclude the existence of a duty in tort to fill the gap. Conversely, in the case of *Warwick University v McAlpine*,[50] a similar point was resolved the other way. The unusual facts of this case were that McAlpine were carrying out remedial work arising from an earlier contract. During the course of the work it was decided to bring in Cementation Chemicals Limited (C.C.L.) to carry out specialist work. The university had the opportunity of employing C.C.L. direct, but instead requested McAlpine to employ them, without taking a warranty. The tortious duty alleged was "failing to warn the plaintiffs or the defendants of the damage that would result from the use of such materials and services." Garland J. held as follows:

> "If this is the duty, then the university are not seeking to establish an essentially contractual one, fitness for purpose, but a normal tortious one-to take reasonable care to avoid reasonably foreseeable damage to a sufficiently proximate plaintiff. The fact that the university might have created a contractual duty by an express warranty is not something which in my view should negative the existence of any duty. Where there is a direct warranty which omits to provide for a particular category of damage, the omission may lead to the conclusion that any duty in tort or the consequences of a breach should be correspondingly restricted. In my view there was a duty in the terms I have set out."

The decision in this case was reversed by the Court of Appeal on the facts but the legal discussion in the judgment remains relevant.

A further development occurred in the House of Lords' decision on claims brought against underwriters by Lloyds "names", some of whom had direct contracts and others not, so that their claims were in tort. It was held that claims could proceed on either basis but that the contractual arrangements in other cases might prove inconsistent with an assumption of responsibility in tort. Lord Goff drew an analogy with attempts by a building owner to bring a claim in tort against a sub-contractor:

> "But if the sub-contracted work or materials do not in the result conform to the required standard it will not ordinarily be open to the building owner to sue the sub-contractor or supplier direct under the Hedley Byrne principle, claiming damages from him on the basis that he has been negligent in relation to the performance of his functions. For there is generally no assumption of responsibility by the sub-contractor or supplier direct to the building

---

[50] (1988) 42 B.L.R. 1.

owner, the parties having so structured their relationship that it is inconsistent with any such assumption of responsibility."[51]

In addition, the House of Lords held in *White v Jones*[52] that a solicitor who negligently failed to draw up a will owed a duty, not only in contract (and tort) to the intended testator, but also in tort to the intended beneficiary. The testator, before his death, had given instructions to the solicitor who failed to prepare a new will. Lord Goff held as follows:

"Your Lordship's House should in cases such as these extend to the intended beneficiary a remedy under the Hedley Byrne principle by holding that the assumption of responsibility by the solicitor towards his client should be held in law to extend the intended beneficiary who, (as the solicitor can reasonably foresee) may, as a result of the solicitor's negligence, be deprived of his intended legacy in circumstances in which neither the testator nor his estate will have a remedy against the solicitor".

Statutory duty

This is an area of law closely related to tort in which an injured claimant seeks to rely on breach by the defendant of a duty under statute, rather than breach of duty imposed by common law. In fact, there are many statutory duties which represent codified common law duties, such as the duty of occupiers to take reasonable care (see Ch.14). The discussion here is concerned with duties which arise only by reasons of some duty or power created by statute.

The modern trend is to state expressly in a statute whether it is intended to create any, and if so what, right of action in favour of individuals who may suffer loss. This applies in the case of the Building Act 1984 where s.38 provides expressly for breach of a duty imposed by building regulations to be actionable. However, this section has not yet been brought into force so that no direct right of action presently exists. The debate at present is whether there is a duty at common law in relation to the exercise of statutory powers. Health and safety legislation creates statutory duties and also provides criminal sanctions for breach. There is generally also a civil right of action in favour of individual workmen injured through breach of the relevant statutory duty (see Ch.16).

Building control legislation places upon local authorities powers to enforce compliance with building regulations. In *Murphy v Brentwood D.C.*[53] the House of Lords left open the question of whether these statutory

[51] *Henderson v Merrett Syndicates* [1995] 2 A.C. 145.
[52] [1995] 2 W.L.R. 187.
[53] [1991] 1 A.C. 398.

powers gave rise to a common law duty to owners or occupiers (see also Ch.14). However, in a New Zealand case[54] it was held that the local authority was liable for the negligent exercise of such statutory powers of inspection. The decision was upheld by the Privy Council[55] who emphasised, however, that the common law could adapt itself to the different circumstances of the countries in which it had taken root. In New Zealand there was a significant expectation of reliance on the local authority. The case does not, therefore, resolve the question of whether local authorities in England will be held to owe the same duty.

The House of Lords further held, by a majority, that the powers available under the Highways Act 1980 (see Ch.16) did not give rise to a duty on the highway authority. The authority could not, therefore, be held liable for a major accident arising from a danger of which it had knowledge.[56]

The law of trusts

A trust is a binding arrangement under which property is held by trustees for the benefit of specified beneficiaries. The law of trust is the creation of equity which has developed a substantial body of law, initially through decisions of the courts, much of which is now codified, notably in the Trustee Act 1925. The objective of the law is to impress a high degree of security on the trust property and corresponding duties on the trustees, such that the trust fund is insulated from the rights of the trustees and, for example, survives intact despite their bankruptcy. In order for a trust to be created there must be identified or appropriated trust property together with a declaration or other act creating or setting up the trust.

As in other areas of the law where the court will, for instance, imply the existence of a contract, the courts may declare the existence of an "implied trust" where one person receives money or property which is to be held for the benefit of another. Thus where a person is possessed of property of another, as an alternative to the court declaring the recipient under a duty to make restitution of the property, it may declare the property subject to an implied trust and therefore insulated from adverse claims against the trustee in their personal capacity. One of the novel aspects of the law of trusts is that it permits wholesale departure from the common law rule of privity in that A may transfer property to B on trust

---

[54] *Invercargill City Council v Hamlin* (1994) 3 N.Z.L.R. 513; 11 Const. L.J. 249.
[55] [1996] 2 W.L.R. 367.
[56] *Stovin v Wise* [1996] A.C. 923.

for C who may themselves declare a sub-trust in favour of D and so on. These arrangements are enforceable at the suit of the beneficiary.

The mere holding of property on trust is sometimes called a "bare" trust. Expressly created trusts will be subject to conditions laying down the powers of the trustees and the rights of the beneficiaries, for example as to the conditions under which they are eligible to receive the trust funds. In the construction industry express trusts have become a familiar device for seeking to secure the interest of a contractor or sub-contractor in the retention fund. This is referred to in cl.30.5 of the JCT form of contract which states that "the employer's interest in the retention is fiduciary as trustee for the contractor and for any nominated sub-contractor". The words impose an obligation on the employer to appropriate and set aside a sum equivalent to the retention money in a separate trust fund.[57] Once created such a trust will survive employer's insolvency. However, in *MacJordan Construction v Brookmount*[58] it was held that there was no trust until a sum of money was set aside in a separate account and until that was done the contractor was merely an unsecured creditor. While the contractor could obtain a mandatory injunction ordering the employer to set up the trust,[59] no rights in the fund were required until this had been done. In the case of a retention trust fund, the contractor's interest remains subject to the terms of the contract. The trust funds are therefore not payable until the retention becomes payable under the contract, and the employer retains all rights of set-off available under the contract. This topic formed part of the proposals of the Latham Report[60] but was not carried forward into the Housing Grants, etc. Act 1996. The law of trusts can have a wider application in relation to construction work. In *Hussey v Palmer*[61] a mother-in-law who lived with the family paid for building work to the house. Although there was no enforceable loan, it was held that the value of the work done was held on trust for the mother-in-law. In giving judgment, Lord Denning said:

> "By whatever name it is described, it is a trust imposed by law whenever justice and good conscience require it. It is a liberal process founded upon large principles of equity, to be applied in cases where the legal owner cannot conscientiously keep the property for himself alone, but ought to allow another to have the property or the benefit of it or a share in it. The trust arises at the outset when the property is acquired, or later on, as the circumstances may require. It is an equitable remedy by which the court can enable an aggrieved party to obtain restitution."

---

[57] *Wates v Franthom* (1991) 53 B.L.R. 23.

[58] (1991) 56 B.L.R. 1.

[59] *Rayack Construction v Lampeter Meat Co.* (1979) 12 B.L.R. 30.

[60] *Constructing the Team* (1994).

[61] [1972] 1 W.L.R. 1286.

Another application of the principles of equity being applied in a contractual situation is the Australian case of *Walthons v Maher*[62] in which the plaintiff builder was the owner of an old building. The defendant proposed to take a lease of a new building to be erected on the site and contracts were drawn up which the plaintiff thought had become binding. He demolished the old building and began constructing the new one. The defendant then pulled out of the arrangement. The High Court of Australia held that the defendant had so acted as to encourage in the plaintiff an assumption that a contract would come into existence and that it would be unconscionable to permit the defendant to depart from that assumption. Compensation was awarded for the detriment suffered by the plaintiff.

[62] (1988) 164 C.L.R. 387.

Chapter 6

CONTRACT: GENERAL PRINCIPLES

English law of contract is contained principally in case law. It is only during the present century that statutes have begun to play any significant part. Historically the law of contract has been built up by the judges as a coherent whole so that there exists a body of principles which apply generally to all contracts including building and engineering contracts. In this chapter the general principles are discussed under the headings: (1) the formation of a contract, (2) contracts which though validly formed may not be binding, and (3) the discharge of contracts. In later chapters there are considered some particular types of contract including building and engineering contracts. These particular contracts, in addition to the general principles set out in this chapter, have their own characteristics, and some are governed by individual statutes.

The law of contract is based on the mutual exchange of obligations, in that each side must contribute something to the agreement to make it binding. The only exception to this principle is a contract made by deed. Such contracts were formerly referred to as "under seal," but seals are now abolished[1] and have been replaced by the simpler requirement for signature in the presence of a witness. It may be that references to contracts under seal will continue for some time in view of their long history. A contract by deed binds its maker without need of any exchange of obligations. Contracts other than those made by deed are called simple contracts, whether made orally or in writing. Although the practice is not universal, the term "agreement" can be used to denote a mutual understanding between the parties, and the term "contract" for an agreement which is binding in law. In such terms there can be an agreement without a contract, but every contract must embody an agreement, except a contract by deed.

Parties to a contract are in general free to make any terms they choose, but certain limits may be placed upon them by the common law and by statute. For example, terms may be implied into a contract which will mitigate the severity of an agreement; or one party may have relief

---

[1] Law of Property (Miscellaneous Provisions) Act 1989.

against the other for a misrepresentation outside the terms of the contract itself. Apart from such limits, the function of the courts is to enforce contracts according to the terms agreed. However unjust the terms are, or however unjust they may become, the courts have no power to rewrite the terms of an agreement. Thus, if a contractor has contracted to carry out works at such prices that they are bound to make a loss, they must still carry out the works or pay damages for breach of contract.

FORMATION OF CONTRACT

If a simple contract is to be legally binding, there must be an offer from one party which is accepted by the other, and each party must contribute something to the bargain. The contribution is called consideration. If a contract exists, the courts will determine what its terms are, for instance, when part of the agreement is in writing and part oral, or when there are implied terms. These points are considered in order.

Offer and acceptance

An offer must consist of a definite promise to be bound on specified or ascertainable terms, and it may be made to a particular person or class of persons, or even the public at large (see Ch.5). The exhibition of goods for sale is not an offer but an invitation to make an offer. A shopkeeper may therefore accept or reject an offer from a customer to buy. They are not bound to sell the goods at the price shown. The same applies to an invitation to tender for the construction of building works. The invitation to tender, whether to the public or to an individual builder, is no more than an offer to negotiate. The contractor's tender constitutes an offer which the client may accept or not. Once accepted it forms a binding contract. This is so, despite any provisions as to subsequent execution of formal documents.[2] A proviso that the client is not bound to accept the lowest or any tender is generally unnecessary.

The offer and the acceptance may be in writing or oral, or may even be inferred from the parties' conduct. A person who gets into a taxi will be bound to pay for the service even though no words are spoken except the destination. If a particular method for communicating acceptance is prescribed, it must normally be adopted. However, an equally expeditious method may be sufficient. For example, if an offer requires acceptance by return of post, a fax is likely to be held sufficient. Email raises

---

[2] See ICE, cl.9.

particular issues which the courts have not yet settled, but there is no reason why parties should not expressly agree to accept email communications. When the post is used the rule is that the acceptance is effective and the contract made at the moment of posting. Silence cannot normally constitute acceptance. But there is an exception when goods are taken on a sale or return basis. There will be an implied acceptance if they are not returned within a reasonable time.

An acceptance must be unqualified. A conditional acceptance is, in law, a counter offer which may destroy the original offer so that it cannot be accepted later. The traditional form of acceptance "subject to contract" is not binding at all.

Essential terms

Frequently a contract will be concluded after a period of negotiation involving offers which are accepted in part, so that the applicable terms are gradually agreed. Particularly in the case of construction contracts, it is often found that the parties begin to perform the contract on the assumption there is, or will shortly be, a concluded agreement. Subsequently, the parties may contend that an important term has not been agreed and that there is, in consequence, no contract. The attitude of the courts is that a contract will be upheld if the parties have agreed upon the essential terms, such as the price, scope of works, commencement date and duration, etc. Minor omissions will not prevent a contract coming into existence. In a number of cases the TCC judges have upheld apparently binding contracts even though terms which might be considered important were not agreed. In *Drake & Scull v Higgs & Hill*,[3] lengthy negotiation between the parties resulted in agreement of all matters except Drake & Scull's daywork rates. It was held that a contract came into existence despite this, on the basis that a term could be implied that the sub-contractor would be paid a reasonable sum. In *Mitsui Babcock Energy v John Brown Engineering*,[4] negotiations led to the signing of a contract despite the failure to agree on a term covering performance tests and liquidated damages. The clause was struck out and noted as "to be discussed and agreed". It was held that a contract nevertheless came into existence on the basis that the parties had "made a coherent and workable contract". Failure to agree on one or more terms regarded as essential may prevent an apparent agreement from having legal effect. However in *RTS Flexible Systems Ltd v Molkerei Alois*

---

[3] (1995) 11 Const. L.J. 214.
[4] (1996) 51 Con. L.R. 129.

Muller GMBH,[5] a dispute as to whether a contract had come into existence following a letter of intent, partial agreement of terms and substantial performance led to a decision of the High Court that a contract had been agreed, a decision of the Court of Appeal that it had not, and a decision of the Supreme Court that it had, albeit for different reasons. The Supreme Court decided that even if significant terms had not been agreed, an objective appraisal of the parties' words and conduct may lead to the conclusion that they did not intend the terms to be a pre-condition to the agreement becoming legally binding. In this case the parties had, by their conduct, waived a clause providing that the agreement would not become effective until each party had executed it.

Retrospective acceptance

Acceptance of a contract may have retrospective effect if this is the intention of the parties. In a case where a contractor was instructed to proceed and started work while the contract for the works was still under negotiation, it was held that the parties had intended such works to be governed by the contract as eventually made: *Trollope & Colls v Atomic Power Construction*.[6] The judgment of Megaw J. included the following:

> "Frequently, in large transactions a written contract is expressed to have retrospective effect, sometimes lengthy retrospective effect; and this in cases where the negotiations on some of the terms have continued up to almost, if not quite, the date of the signature of the contract. The parties have meanwhile been conducting their transactions with one another, it may be for many months, on the assumption that a contract would ultimately be agreed on lines known to both the parties, though with the final form of various constituent terms of the proposed contract still under discussion. The parties have assumed that when the contract is made-when all the terms have been agreed in their final form-the contract will apply retrospectively to the preceding transactions . . . I can see no reason why, if the parties so intend and agree, such a stipulation should be denied legal effect."

In some types of building contract (and many other commercial transactions) the principles of implied or retrospective acceptance need often to be applied to identify the legal basis of a contract which neither party has ever doubted was binding. A problem which frequently occurs is where the parties enter into correspondence as to the precise terms on which they are to contract. This happens often between main contractor and sub-contractor. The contractor places an "order" on their standard terms

---

[5] [2010] B.L.R. 337.
[6] [1963] 1 W.L.R. 333.

and the sub-contractor "accepts" on their standard terms, which are inconsistent with the order. Correspondence follows in which some terms are agreed and others not. At some point the sub-contractor starts the work. The principles to be applied to such problems are that the last letter is deemed to be accepted if the recipient then starts or continues the work (or permits the other party to do so). But if the parties show by their continuing negotiation that they do not regard themselves as bound, there may be no contract. Equally, if the parties are not agreed as to some important term there will be no contract. In the absence of a binding contract, a party who has carried out work at the request of the other will be entitled to payment of a reasonable sum (see Ch.5).

Revocation

Revocation of an offer is effective only when it reaches the offeree. A promise to keep an offer open for a certain period does not prevent the offer from being revoked prematurely, unless the promise is itself a binding contract, such as an option to purchase shares. An agreement for the periodic supply of goods to order has the legal effect of a standing offer from the supplier which creates a binding contract each time goods are ordered. The offer may accordingly be revoked by the supplier except in respect of orders already placed. If there is no fixed period an unaccepted offer may lapse after a reasonable time. In some countries there exists a doctrine under which an offer may not be revoked once the offeree has relied on it, for example, through a main contractor tendering on the basis of sub-contract tenders. No such doctrine exists in English law, under which contracts are either binding or not and parties to would-be contracts seeking redress must bring their claims within other legal principles (see Ch.5).

Standard terms of business

Most construction work is undertaken through tendering based on one party's standard conditions of contract. Questions which arise regarding formation of the contract are often concerned with whether other documents (such as programmes or qualifying letters) have been incorporated, in addition to the standard terms. In other transactions, typified by sub-contract orders, wider questions arise when standard terms of business are used by both parties. These may be incorporated by reference or printed on the back of order forms or "acceptance" forms. Such terms may compete with each other, for example, each purporting to exclude the other; and there may be particularly onerous provisions hidden within such standard clauses.

The attitude of the courts to such problems has a long history, covering many types of transaction involving tickets, receipts and the like which contain or refer to standard conditions. The courts have evolved principles requiring that particularly onerous clauses should be brought fairly to the attention of the party adversely affected. This area of law is now fundamentally affected by the Unfair Contract Terms Act (see below), which refers to the question whether the "customer" knew or ought reasonably to have known about the terms being relied on. Where the Act does not apply the common law principles will still be effective, permitting the court to refuse to enforce onerous conditions. In a case decided before the Unfair Contract Terms Act,[7] Lord Denning remarked that:

"Some clauses which I have seen would need to be printed in red ink on the face of the document with a red hand pointing to it before the notice could be held to be sufficient."

The notice principles were applied in the case of *Interfoto v Stiletto*,[8] in which the defendant hired 47 transparencies from a lending library, the transaction being subject to printed conditions which required return within 14 days or a fee of £5 a day plus V.A.T. for each one retained. The defendant, who had not read the conditions, returned the transparencies four weeks later and was given a bill for £3783.50. Judgment was given for the plaintiff in the County Court, but the Court of Appeal held that the plaintiff had failed to show that the relevant clause had been brought fairly to the defendant's attention, and therefore substituted a reasonable charge of £3.50 per transparency per week. Dillon L.J. in giving judgment said:

"In the ticket cases the courts held that the common law required that reasonable steps be taken to draw the other party's attention to the printed conditions or they would not be part of the contract. It is, in my judgment, a logical development of the common law into modern conditions that it should be held ... that if one condition in a set of printed conditions is particularly onerous or unusual, the party seeking to enforce it must show that that particular condition was fairly brought to the attention of the other party. In the present case, nothing whatever was done by the plaintiffs to draw the defendant's attention particularly to condition 2; it was merely one of four columns' width of conditions printed across the foot of the delivery note. Consequently condition 2 never, in my judgment, became part of the contract between the parties."

[7] *Spurling v Bradshaw* [1956] 1 W.L.R. 461.
[8] [1989] Q.B. 433.

Battle of forms

Where each of the parties is trying to impose its terms on the other, the question of notice is unlikely to be relevant. This exchange of standard conditions is sometimes referred to as "the battle of the forms" and the principles which are applied here are simply those of offer and acceptance which, however, may be complicated by the conditions themselves.

The general principle was stated in *Butler Machine Tools Co. v Ex-cell-o Corp*,[9] where the plaintiff gave a quotation providing that orders were accepted only on terms of the quotation, which included a price variation clause. The defendant gave an order subject to their own terms and conditions, having no price variation clause, but having a tear-off acknowledgement for signature and return which accepted the order "on the terms and conditions thereon." The plaintiff signed and returned the acknowledgement but with a covering letter stating that delivery was to be "in accordance with our revised quotation." The Court of Appeal construed the acknowledgement as an acceptance which did not bring back the plaintiff's price variation clause. Lord Denning M.R. explained the law as follows:

"It will be found that in most cases where there is a "battle of the forms" there is a contract as soon as the last of the forms is sent and received without objection being taken to it ... the difficulty is to decide which form, or which part of which form, is a term or condition of the contract. In some cases the battle is won by the man who fires the last shot. He is the man who puts forward the latest terms and conditions: and if they are not objected to by the other party, he may be taken to have agreed to them ... in some cases the battle is won by the man who gets the blow in first. If he offers to sell at a named price on the terms and conditions stated on the back: and the buyer orders the goods purporting to accept the offer-on an order form with his own different terms and conditions on the back-then if the difference is so material that it would affect the price, the buyer ought not to be allowed to take advantage of the difference unless he draws it specifically to the attention of the seller. There are yet other cases where the battle depends on the shots fired on both sides. There is a concluded contract but the forms vary. The terms and conditions of both parties are to be construed together."

A further matter of potential difficulty is provisions which are inconsistent with or repugnant to the remainder of the document. The leading case is *Glynn v Margetson*,[10] which concerned the shipment of oranges from Malaga to Liverpool. The bill of lading provided for liberty to

---

[9] [1979] 1 W.L.R. 401.
[10] [1893] A.C. 351.

proceed to a variety of other ports for any purpose. The port of shipment was left blank and was filled up in writing. The ship deviated to another Spanish port with the result that, when the oranges were delivered to Liverpool, they were damaged. The case is authority on the question of a written clause prevailing over printed clauses. However, the House of Lords also dealt with the question of clauses inconsistent with the main purpose of the contract. Lord Halsbury said:

> "It seems to me that in construing this document, which is a contract of carriage between the parties, one must in the first instance look at the whole of the instrument and not at one part of it only. Looking at the whole of the instrument, and seeing what one must regard . . . as its main purpose, one must reject words, indeed whole provisions, if they are inconsistent with what one assumes to be the main purpose of the contract. The main purpose of the contract was to take on board at one port and to deliver to another port a perishable cargo."

The repugnancy principle is not to be applied lightly, but does provide authority for enforcing the main purpose of a contract where other provisions are inconsistent.

Consideration

Each party to a contract (other than one made by deed) must provide consideration if the contract is to be binding. The most common forms of consideration are payment of money, provision of goods, or performance of work. But it may also consist in any benefit accruing to one party or detriment to the other. For example, A may promise to release B from a debt if he will dig A's garden. The courts are not concerned with whether the bargain was a good one. If B's debt was £1,000 and the garden small, that is still good consideration.

There are, however, certain acts and promises which cannot constitute good consideration. Anything which has already been done is no consideration. If B voluntarily dug A's garden yesterday, today's promise of reward is not binding because B gives no fresh consideration to the bargain. Further, if a party promises to do nothing more than they are already bound to do they provide no consideration. If B is A's gardener, A's promise of additional reward is not binding.

The courts have, however, on many occasions shown a highly liberal attitude towards what may constitute consideration. In *Williams v Roffey Bros.*[11] the defendant, the main contractor, concerned that the plaintiff, a carpentry sub-contractor, might not be able to complete on time, orally

[11] [1991] 1 Q.B. 1.

promised additional payments if the work was completed on time. The Court of Appeal upheld the decision of the trial judge that this promise was enforceable, the consideration being the benefit, or the avoidance of detriment to the defendant. In any such case, the defendant may argue that the plaintiff has done nothing more than he was already bound to do. But if the sub-contractor agrees, for example, to accelerate (which he may have no obligation to do) this could amount to good consideration, and the court would not be concerned with the adequacy of the bargain.

Intention to be legally bound

Sometimes, despite the undoubted existence of offer, acceptance and consideration, one party may allege that the contract is not binding because there was no intention to create legal relations. This is not uncommon in family arrangements and it is presumed that domestic agreements are not intended to create legal relations. It is therefore up to the party seeking to enforce such a contract to rebut the presumption.[12] In commercial agreements there is naturally a strong presumption that there was an intention to create legal relations. Nevertheless, the intention may be rebutted. The parties may go further and make it an express condition that the contract is not to be binding in law. This is invariably a condition under which football pool companies accept entries, and the effect is to prevent an enforceable contract coming into existence. A similar result is achieved by a clause purporting to exclude the parties' rights to bring actions in the courts upon the contract. Such a clause will be treated as of no effect by the courts, but may make the contract void and unenforceable. It is to be noted, however, that the new Arbitration Act 1996 permits the parties to agree that their dispute is to be decided in accordance with "such other considerations as are agreed by them or determined by the tribunal",[13] as opposed to the principles of law. This refers to so-called "equity" clauses or other provisions permitting arbitrators to apply principles of fairness of good conscience. The result of such an arbitration will be enforceable[14] but in court the parties are bound by the law as it stands, or by nothing.

Form of contract

Simple contracts may, in general, be in any form and are enforceable despite a complete absence of documentation. However, a few special

---

[12] See *Hussey v Palmer* noted in Ch.5.
[13] Section 46(1).
[14] See Ch.3 generally.

types of contract are unenforceable unless evidenced in writing. These are, principally, contracts for the sale or disposition of land or an interest in land, and some others such as a contract of guarantee. Such a contract need not be made in writing, but some written evidence is necessary which must be signed by or on behalf of the defendant and which states the material terms. However, a contract which does not comply with these requirements may sometimes be enforceable in equity if there has been a part performance of the contract by the person seeking to enforce it, such as a buyer who has entered into possession of a house.

Terms of a contract

The final step in the formation of a contract is the identification of the terms and their effect. If the contract is wholly in writing, the problem is one of construction. But often there are additional terms. Statements made by the parties during their negotiations may have contractual effect. There may also be terms implied in the contract. An express term purporting to exclude or limit liability may raise special problems of interpretation. These points are discussed below.

A statement made during the negotiation of a contract may amount to a representation (see below) or it may become a term and have full contractual effect. There is no decisive test, but a statement is more likely to become a binding term if it is made immediately before agreement is reached, if the maker of the statement had special knowledge, or if the contract itself was not reduced to writing.

Implied terms

In addition to the express terms, there may be other terms implied into a contract which, although not specified by the parties either in writing or orally, are nevertheless as binding as express terms. The leading case on the general implication of terms into contracts is *Liverpool C.C. v Irwin*,[15] in which tenants in a multi-storey council block sought to establish against the local authority a duty to repair and maintain common parts, including lifts and staircases, which were frequently unusable because of vandalism and defects. The House of Lords, in holding the Council under a duty to take reasonable care, considered the contractual basis of the arrangement, which was based on a tenancy agreement silent as to the matters in issue. Lord Wilberforce dealt with the question of implication of terms as follows:

[15] [1977] A.C. 239.

"To say that the construction of a complete contract out of these elements involves a process of 'implication' may be correct; it would be so if implication means the supplying of what is not expressed. But there are varieties of implications which the courts think fit to make and they do not necessarily involve the same process. Where there is, on the face of it, a complete bilateral contract, the courts are sometimes willing to add terms to it, as implied terms: this is very common in mercantile contracts where there is an established usage: in that case the courts are spelling out what both parties know and would, if asked, unhesitatingly agree to be part of the bargain. In other cases, where there is an apparently complete bargain, the courts are willing to add a term on the ground that without it the contract will not work . . . There is a third variety of implication, that which I think Lord Denning M.R favours, or at least did favour in this case, and that is the implication of reasonable terms. But though I agree with many of his instances, which in fact fall under one or other of the preceding heads, I cannot go so far as to endorse his principle; indeed, it seems to me, with respect, to extend a long and undesirable way beyond sound authority. The present case, in my opinion, represents a fourth category or I would rather say a fourth shade on a continuous spectrum. The court here is simply concerned to establish what the contract is, the parties not having themselves fully stated the terms. In this sense the court is searching for what must be implied."

An example of an attempt to imply a term in the third category, namely one that would be reasonable, occurred in the case of *Trollope and Colls v N.W. Met. Hospital Board*,[16] where the parties had made a contract for construction work to be carried out in phases, but had omitted to make any provisions for the consequences of the first phase overrunning. It would doubtless have been reasonable to introduce a term which regulated the timing of subsequent phases, but the contract made no such provision and the judgment of the House of Lords illustrates the limitations on the power of the Court to do what is reasonable. Lord Pearson expressed himself thus:

"The court does not make a contract for the parties. The court will not even improve the contract which the parties have made for themselves, however desirable the improvement might be. The court's function is to interpret and apply the contract which the parties have made for themselves. If the express terms are perfectly clear and free from ambiguity, there is no choice to be made between different possible meanings: the clear terms must be applied even if the court thinks some other terms would have been more suitable. An unexpressed term can be implied if and only if the court finds that the parties must have intended that term to form part of their contract: it is not enough for the court to find that such a term would have been adopted by the parties as reasonable men if it had been suggested to them; it must have been a term that went without saying, a term necessary to give

---

[16] [1973] 1 W.L.R. 601.

business efficacy to the contract, a term which, though tacit, formed part of the contract which the parties made for themselves."

An example of the application of established usage or trade custom occurred in the case of *William Lacey v Davis*[17] (see also Ch.5) where, in relation to the contractor's claims for costs of tendering work, the judge said:

"Mr. Daniel rightly conceded that if a builder is invited to tender for certain work, either in competition or otherwise, there is no implication that he would be paid for the work-sometimes the very considerable amount of work-involved in arriving at his price: he undertakes this work as a gamble, and its cost is part of the overhead expenses of his business which he hopes will be met out of the profits of contracts as are made as a result of tenders which prove to be successful. This generally accepted usage may also—and I think does also—apply to amendments of the original tender necessitated by bona fide alterations in the specification and plans."

In more recent cases the courts have emphasised that the implication of an unwritten term is close to and often an alternative to the process of construction of the written terms. In *Attorney General of Belize v Belize Telecom*,[18] the Privy Council held that an implied term should be seen as spelling out in express words what the contract, read against the relevant background, would reasonably be understood to mean.

There are certain types of contract into which terms are implied by statute, such as under the Sale of Goods Act (see Ch.7). The principles of this Act have been extended to contracts for the supply of services, by the Supply of Goods and Services Act 1982 which applies, whether or not goods are also transferred, so that it will govern ordinary construction contracts. Sections 13, 14 and 15 of the Act provide that such contracts are subject to implied terms that the supplier will carry out a service with reasonable care and skill and that, in the absence of agreement, the service will be carried out within a reasonable time and for a reasonable charge. These terms may be negatived or varied by express agreement subject, however, to the effect of the Unfair Contract Terms Act (see below).

Implied terms in building contracts

Terms which have been implied in decided cases may act as precedents for similar contracts and therefore give rise to what may be called

---

[17] [1957] 1 W.L.R. 932.
[18] [2009] 1 W.L.R. 1988.

a common law contractual duty, beyond the express terms of the contract. There are some important terms which are usually to be implied into building and engineering contracts. Such terms require that the building owner shall give possession of the site within a reasonable time, and give instructions and information at reasonable times.[19] Similarly the contractor must carry out their work with proper skill and care or, as sometimes expressed, in a workmanlike manner. Goods and materials must normally be of good quality and reasonably fit for their purpose.[20] However, there will be no implied term where the matter in question is dealt with by express terms. Some of the matters mentioned may be covered by express provisions in the building contract, so that there may be no case for further implication.

There are some notable terms which are normally not to be implied into building and engineering contracts. Whilst there may be an express term to this effect, there will normally not be an implied term that the contractor will progress the work regularly and diligently,[21] since the contractor is obliged to complete by the completion date and is entitled to arrange his programme of work within that overriding obligation. The employer gives no implied warranty of the nature or suitability of the site or subsoil, or as to the practicability of the design. Thus, where a contractor agreed to build a new bridge over the Thames using caissons, it was found they could not be used and the work proved much more expensive. There was held to be no implied warranty that the bridge could be built according to the engineer's design: *Thorn v London Corporation*.[22] In giving judgment the Lord Chancellor, Lord Cairns, observed:

"Can it be supposed for a moment, that the Defendants intended to imply any such warranty? My Lords, if the contractor in this case had gone to the Bridge Committee, then engaged in superintending the work, and had said: You want Blackfriars Bridge to be rebuilt; you have got specifications prepared by Mr. Cubitt; you ask me to tender for the contract; will you engage and warrant to me that the bridge can be built by caissons in this way which Mr. Cubitt thinks feasible, but which I have never seen before put in practice. What would the committee have answered? Can any person for a moment entertain any reasonable doubt as to the answer he would have received? He would have been told: You know Mr. Cubitt as well as we do; we, like you, rely on him-we must rely on him; we do not warrant Mr. Cubitt or his plans; you are as able to judge as we are whether his plans can be carried into effect or not; if you like to rely on them, well and good;

---

[19] *L.B. Merton v Leach* (1985) 32 B.L.R. 51.
[20] *Young & Marten v McManus Childs* [1969] 1 A.C. 454.
[21] *Leander Construction v Mulalley & Co* [2011] EWHC 3449 (TCC), per Coulson J.
[22] (1876) 1 App. Cas. 120.

if you do not, you can either have them tested by an engineer of your own, or you need not undertake the work; others will do it.

My Lords, it is really contrary to every kind of probability to suppose that any warranty could have been intended or implied between the parties; and if there is no express warranty, your Lordships cannot imply a warranty, unless from the circumstances of the work some warranty must have been necessary, which clearly is not the case here, or, unless the probability is so strong that the parties intended a warranty, that you cannot resist the application of the doctrine of implied warranty."

The general question of responsibility for the site is dealt with in Ch.9. The other side of the coin is that where a contractor builds in accordance with detailed instructions, they will give no implied warranty as to the fitness of the finished product. Thus, where a builder constructed, as specified, a solid brick wall without rendering which allowed rain to enter the house, it was held that the builder was not liable for the defect: *Lynch v Thorne*.[23] In giving judgment, Lord Evershed held:

"If a skilled person promises to do a job, that is, to produce a particular thing, whether a house or a motor car or a piece of machinery, and he makes no provision, as a matter of bargain, as to the precise structure or article which he will create, then it may well be that the buyer of the structure or article relies on the judgment and skill of the other party to produce that which he says he will produce. That, however, is only another way of formulating the existence in such circumstances of an implied warranty. On the other hand, if two parties elect to make a bargain which specifies in precise detail what one of them will do, then, in the absence of some other express provision, it would appear to me to follow that the bargain is that which they have made; and so long as the party doing the work does that which he has contracted to do, that is the extent of his obligation."

Where the builder, in similar circumstances, is under an obligation to comply with the Building Regulations, it may be contended that there is an express obligation to ensure that the works are adequate. However, this is a matter of construction of each contract (see Ch.16). In *Jewson v Kelly*[24] the claimant sought to recover the cost of a number of electric boilers supplied to the defendant who was in course of converting self-contained flats for resale. The defendant was initially satisfied with the boilers after installation, but found subsequently that they contributed to the properties being designated as having low energy efficiency and the defendant lost money on selling the properties. The evidence was that there had been no discussion about the comparable merits or costs of

[23] [1956] 1 W.L.R. 303.
[24] (2003) C.I.L.L. 2042.

different boilers or their effect on the energy efficiency of the flats. It was held that the boilers were fit for their purpose as boilers and there was no reliance on the skill and judgment of the supplier in relation to the particular flats into which they were to be installed. Consequently, the claimant was not in breach of contract.

Exclusion clauses

It is common in standard form contracts, for there to be a term excluding or limiting the liability of one party in the event of breach. This often applies in the case of supply of goods or services to exclude or limit liability for defective materials or work. Such provisions may be unenforceable by statute. However, the courts have always been ready to find grounds on which exclusion clauses could be avoided at common law.

An exclusion clause must be carefully drafted since it will be construed against the party seeking to rely upon it (see Ch.8). General words are unlikely to exclude specific liability. If the term is contained in a document forming part of the contract then the party assenting to such a document is bound by its terms, whether or not they read them and whether or not they sign the document. But a written exclusion clause may be over-ridden by an oral statement. Thus, where a customer took a dress to be dry cleaned, she was asked to sign a document excluding all liability; the assistant, however, said that the exclusion covered only damage to buttons. It was held that the cleaners could not rely on the clause to exclude liability: *Curtis v Chemical Cleaning Co.*[25] Denning L.J. in the Court of Appeal held:

> "By failing to draw attention to the width of the exemption clause, the assistant created the false impression that the exemption related to the beads and sequins only, and that it did not extend to the material of which the dress was made. It was done perfectly innocently, but nevertheless, a false impression was created. . . . It was a sufficient misrepresentation to disentitle the cleaners from relying on the exemption, except in regard to the beads and sequins. In the present case the misrepresentation was as to the extent of the exemption. In other cases it may be as to its existence. For instance, if nothing was said by the assistant, this document might reasonably be understood to be, like a boot repairer's receipt, only a voucher for the customer to produce when collecting the goods, and not to contain conditions exempting the cleaners from their common law liability for negligence."

[25] [1951] 1 K.B. 805.

Standard terms are often designed to avoid this result by providing that no statement is to affect the conditions unless confirmed in writing. But such a term is likely to be effective only where the parties communicate primarily in writing; it would be unlikely to affect the decision in the *Curtis* case above.

Where an exclusion clause is exhibited in an hotel or a garage stating "The management accepts no responsibility . . ." the term is not binding unless the party must be taken to have known of, and agreed to it, before entering into the contract. Even when such a term is effective, it can normally protect only the parties to the contract, so that the negligence of servants, agents or sub-contractors may not be excluded. Nevertheless, the terms of the contract may be relevant to duties in tort undertaken both by the immediate parties to the contract and by others (see Ch.14).

While liability may be limited or excluded, it can generally be done only by contract or in situations akin to that of contract. The exhibition on a motor car of a sign saying "no liability for negligent driving" would not prejudice the rights of the public at large. However, where liability in tort would arise, for example, from free advice given negligently, such liability may be excluded or limited by an appropriate written or oral statement.[26] While clauses excluding all liability are construed most strictly by the courts, clauses which seek only to cap liability at a specified or determinable sum, (for example, the contract price) will be construed more liberally and are more likely to be given effect.

Statutory alteration of terms and unfair terms

The above represents the common law position on exclusion and limitation clauses. The fundamental principle of freedom and enforceability of contract terms has been the subject of statutory intervention. Provisions introduced in 1973[27] require that clauses excluding or restricting the implied obligations of the seller of goods as to their conformity with description or sample, quality or fitness, should be void in a consumer sale; and in a non-consumer sale, i.e. one between commercial parties, such terms are enforceable only in so far as it is fair and reasonable (see Ch.7).

By the Unfair Contract Terms Act 1977 these provisions were extended in their application to other contracts involving the provision of goods (s.7), which include building contracts. The Act contains other far-reaching provisions governing exclusion clauses and notices. Liability for death or personal injury may not be excluded where resulting from

---

[26] *Hedley Byrne v Heller* [1964] A.C. 465.
[27] Re-enacted in the Sale of Goods Act 1979.

negligence, which includes an obligation to exercise care or skill in contract or tort (s.2(1)). Liability for other loss resulting from negligence may be excluded only so far as it is fair and reasonable (s.2(2)). The effect of a contractual term excluding or restricting liability for breach of contract depends on the relative position of the parties. Where the innocent party deals as a consumer or on the other party's written standard terms of business, such a term is enforceable only so far as it is fair and reasonable (s.3). A private employer under a building contract may deal as a consumer, and therefore be entitled to the protection of s.3. It is not clear to what extent other employers under building contracts would be regarded as dealing on the contractor's standard terms where, for example, these are the JCT or ICE conditions. See, however the case of *Langstane v Riverside and others*[28] referred to below under Joint liability and contribution.

Where an exclusion clause is required to be fair and reasonable, it is to be given effect even when the contract has been terminated by acceptance of repudiation (s.9). The application of the Act is restricted in regard to certain types of contract, including contracts of insurance, and contracts with a foreign element. The Act is not to apply where English law applies merely as a choice of proper law in a foreign contract. However, the Act cannot be excluded by stipulating a foreign proper law in an otherwise English contract.

An example of the application of the test of fairness occurred in the case of *George Mitchell v Finney Lock Seeds*,[29] where similar provisions in earlier legislation were considered in relation to a contract for sale of late cabbage seed. The seed delivered was of the wrong variety, and had to be ploughed in, after 60 acres had been planted and had germinated. The buyer claimed loss of profit. The contract limited the right of the buyer to replacement or refund of the price paid. It was shown in evidence that the sellers could have insured against the risk of crop failure at little additional cost, and that it was the practice of seed merchants to attempt to negotiate and settle claims by farmers. The buyers had no opportunity to negotiate the terms offered, which were common to all seed suppliers. In those circumstances, the Court of Appeal and the House of Lords held the clause limiting liability to be unfair and consequently unenforceable. Lord Bridge also observed:

> "The only other question of construction debated in the course of the argument was the meaning to be attached to the words 'to the extent that' in sub-section (4) and, in particular, whether they permit the court to hold that

---

[28] [2009] CSOH 52.
[29] [1983] 2 A.C. 803.

it would be fair and reasonable to allow partial reliance on a limitation clause and, for example, to decide in the instant case that the respondents should recover, say, half their consequential damage. I incline to the view that, in their context, the words are equivalent to 'in so far as' or 'in the circumstances in which' and do not permit the kind of judgment of Solomon illustrated by the example."

An application of the Unfair Contract Terms Act in the context of construction occurred in *Smith v E. S. Bush*,[30] a case concerning the purported exclusion of liability by surveyors, acting for a building society, whose report was shown to and relied on by the house purchaser. Both the Court of Appeal and the House of Lords held that it would not be fair and reasonable to allow reliance on the disclaimer included in the report. Lord Griffiths in the House of Lords observed that while it was impossible to draw up an exhaustive list of factors to be taken into account, the following matters should always be considered:

(1) where the parties are of equal bargaining power the requirement of reasonableness will be more easily discharged than in a case where the purchaser has no effective power to object;

(2) in the case of advice, it is relevant to consider whether it is reasonably practicable to obtain advice from an alternative source;

(3) where the task undertaken is difficult or dangerous, with a high risk of failure, that is a pointer towards exclusion of liability being reasonable; and

(4) the practical consequences of excluding liability should be considered, including the question whether either party can insure, and at what difficulty and cost.

Further provisions apply in the case of "consumer contracts" by virtue of the Unfair Terms in Consumer Contracts Regulations 1999. The Regulations were created in response to an EU Directive on consumer protection and have the effect of providing additional protection to a person who contracts outside their trade business or profession, which will generally include residential occupiers contracting for construction works. While residential occupiers are excluded for the application of the Housing Grants, etc. Act 1996, the JCT minor works contract provides for contractual adjudication. In a series of cases culminating in

[30] [1990] A.C. 831.

the decision of the Court of Appeal in *Bryen & Langley v Boston*[31] it was held that even if the adjudications provisions made it procedurally unfair for a contractor to rely on them, they did not cause a significant imbalance on the parties' rights and were not, therefore, rendered unfair and not binding. This decision was applied in *Steve Domsalla v Kenneth Dyason*[32] where Mr Dyason had contracted as agent for insurers who had agree to pay for reinstatement of his house. However, although the adjudication proceedings were binding, it was held that the withholding notice provisions were unfair and the failure to served notices could not be relied on by the contractor.

CONTRACTS WHICH ARE NOT BINDING

A number of situations exist where, although a contract has been made, one or even both parties cannot enforce the agreement. Those most commonly encountered are when one or both parties make a mistake of fact, or when the contract is induced by misrepresentation or economic duress. Other contracts which may not bind the parties include those which involve illegality, and contracts where one party is under some legal incapacity. These are discussed below.

Mistake

There are two distinct categories of mistake. First, where both parties make the same common mistake, the existence of an agreement is undisputed, but one party may say that the mistake has deprived the contract of its efficacy. Where the mistake relates to the existence of the subject matter the contract is void, as in the case of a sale of goods which have perished at the time of sale, or which never existed. But less fundamental mistakes may not be sufficient. Thus, the sale of a painting by Constable was held not to be void when the picture turned out to be by a lesser artist: *Leaf v International Galleries*.[33] Denning L.J. in the Court of Appeal observed:

> "There was a mistake about the quality of the subject-matter because both parties believed the picture to be a Constable; and that mistake was in one essential or fundamental. But such a mistake does not avoid the contract: there was no mistake at all about the subject-matter of the sale. It was a

---

[31] [2005] EWCA Civ. 973.
[32] (2007) C.I.L.L. 2501.
[33] [1950] 2 K.B. 86.

specific picture 'Salisbury Cathedral.' The parties were agreed in the same terms on the same subject-matter and that is sufficient to make a contract."

The second category of mistake arises when the parties have different intentions. Whether they are both mistaken or whether the mistake is unilateral (one party merely acquiescing in the other's mistake) the law considers this as a question of offer and acceptance. The contract is void only if the mistake prevents one party from appreciating the fundamental character of what they are offering or accepting. A mistake which affects only motives, as when one party thinks they had a much better bargain than was the case, cannot affect the validity of the contract.

If the parties had different intentions the court will, if possible, ascertain the true meaning of the contract. If this cannot be done the contract is void. Thus, where parties contracted for the sale of cotton identified as being delivered by a ship named Peerless from Bombay, it transpired that there were two such ships out of Bombay; the buyer intended one and the seller the other. It was held there was no binding contract.[34] The difference from the *"Constable"* case above was that the parties there were agreed on one picture as the subject-matter of the contract. Where only one party was mistaken the question is whether there was an acceptance of what was offered. If there was such acceptance the contract is not void, but could still be voidable if induced by misrepresentation (see below).

In addition to common law remedies for mistake, other relief may be available in equity. Principally, if both parties, or even one party, intended something different from that which the documents record, rectification may be available (see Ch.8). The remedy of restitution (see Ch.5) may be invoked to recover money paid under a mistake of fact. However, in *Lloyd's Bank v Independent Insurance Co*[35] the Court of Appeal held that the claimant bank was not entitled to recover sums paid to the defendant under the mistaken belief that cheques paid in by the bank's customer had been cleared. The payment had discharged a debt owed to the defendant, who could not be said to be unjustly enriched.

Misrepresentation

A representation is a statement relating to a contract made by one party which does not become a term of the contract. If it is untrue, whether fraudulent or innocent, it is a misrepresentation and the general effect is to render the contract voidable. A voidable contract may be

---

[34] *Raffles v Wichelhaus* (1864) 2 H. & C. 906.
[35] [2000] Q.B. 110.

renounced by the injured party, but until renounced it is valid and binds both parties. Only when a misrepresentation has induced mistake could the contract be declared void.

In order to constitute a representation, the statement must be made before or at the time of contracting; and it must be a statement of fact, not opinion or mere "puff." An estate agent's description of the desirable qualities of a house is not to be taken as a statement of fact unless it gives specific information such as sizes. Silence may amount to a misrepresentation, as when a previous statement becomes false before the contract is concluded. Further, a misrepresentation does not make a contract voidable unless it induced the contract. Thus, the injured party must have relied on the statement and not on their own knowledge, and it must have been a material cause of their entering into the contract.

The rights and remedies which flow from a misrepresentation depend upon whether it was fraudulent or innocent. If the person who made the representation did not honestly believe it to be true then, whatever his motive, it is fraudulent. This gives the other party a right in tort to damages for deceit, and a further right to elect either to affirm the contract (when it will continue for both parties) or to rescind. Rescission involves cancellation of the contract and restoration of the parties to their situation before the contract was made.

A misrepresentation is innocent if the maker honestly, although carelessly, believed it to be true. The principal remedy for the other party is then under the Misrepresentation Act 1967 whereby damages can be recovered unless the maker proves that they had reasonable grounds for believing that the facts represented were true. In *Howard Marine Dredging v Ogden*[36] mis-statement as to the tonnage capacity of barges was held to found claim under s.2(1) of the Act as there were no reasonable grounds for belief that facts represented were true. The person to whom the innocent misrepresentation is made may also sue for rescission, as well as for damages. But the court (or an arbitrator) may, in its discretion, award damages in lieu of rescission.

The right to rescind a contract for misrepresentation, innocent or fraudulent, is available only if restoration of the parties to their former situation is possible, and if no innocent third party would suffer. A party who affirms the contract loses the right to rescind. An alternative remedy for misrepresentation may be available under the law of tort for negligent misstatement.[37] Further, a representation which has become a term of the contract will give rise to the usual remedies for breach of contract if it proves untrue (see below).

[36] [1978] Q.B. 574.
[37] *Hedley Byrne v Heller* [1964] A.C. 465.

Economic duress

A contract in which one party is shown to have acted under economic duress may be set aside at the suit of that party. Most cases on this topic have concerned relationships between individuals and banks requiring charges over property to secure loans. In the recent decision of Dyson J. sitting in the TCC in *Carillon Construction v Felix*,[38] the principle was applied to agreement of a final account (including settlement of claims) put forward by the defendant cladding sub-contractor, under threat of discontinuing supplies which were critical to completion of the project by the claimant main contractor. Dyson J. summarised the law in the following terms:

> "The ingredients of actionable duress are that there must be pressure, (a) whose practical effect is that there is compulsion on, or a lack of practical choice for, the victim (b) which is illegitimate and (c) which is a significant cause, inducing the claimant to enter into the contract. . . . In determining whether there has been illegitimate pressure, the court takes into account a range of factors. These include whether there has been an actual or threatened breach of contract; whether the person allegedly exerting the pressure has acted in good or bad faith; whether the victim had any realistic practical alternative but to submit to the pressure; whether the victim protested at the time; and whether he affirmed and sought to rely on the contract. These are all relevant factors. Illegitimate pressure musts be distinguished from the rough and tumble of the pressures of normal commercial bargaining".

It was held that the ingredient of duress were established and the "agreed" final account set aside. It was irrelevant that the final account had been embodied into a formal settlement agreement. In *Capital Structures v Time & Tide*[39] H.H. Judge Wilcox held that an adjudicator's decision given under a settlement agreement which was arguably made under economic duress would not be enforced since economic duress would render the contract voidable and, if avoided, the adjudicator would have no jurisdiction.

Illegal contracts

Contracts which contravene the law are in general void and no action may be brought upon them. The illegality may involve doing an act prohibited by statute, such as building contrary to the Building Regulations; or it may consist in a project not as such prohibited, for

---

[38] (2000) C.I.L.L. 1693.
[39] [2006] B.L.R. 226.

example, an agreement to commit a crime or a tort or some immoral act. Such contracts cannot be enforced by either party.[40]

The law draws a distinction between a contract which is illegal in its inception and one which is merely performed in an unlawful way. A contract illegal in its inception is totally void and no action can be brought by either party. Property transferred under the contract cannot generally be recovered. But when a contract is illegal only as performed, the effect depends upon the extent of the illegality. If this goes to the core of the contract then a guilty party will have no remedy, while an innocent party may have the usual contractual remedies. If, however, the illegality is not essential to the performance of the contract, both parties may have their normal remedies. Thus, the illegal overloading of a ship in the course of a voyage did not deprive the owners of their right to recover the freight charges, since the overloading was not an essential incident of the contract.[41] Devlin J. in giving judgment held:

> "There is . . . a distinction between the contract which has as its object the doing of the very act forbidden by the statute and the contract whose performance involves an illegality only incidentally. . . . There is no doubt that the plaintiffs cannot succeed if their claim for freight involves showing that they carried the goods in an overloaded ship. But in my judgment, the plaintiffs need show no more in order to recover their freight than that they delivered to the defendants the goods they received in the same good order and condition as that in which they received them."

Where building work is carried out in contravention of statutory provisions, such as the Building Regulations or Planning Acts, the above principles apply in determining whether the builder can recover the price of the work (apart from the question of statutory powers as to enforcement and penalties). Thus where on the face of the contract the work must contravene the law, the contractor cannot recover payment. In *Townsend v Cinema News*[42] building work which was so designed as to comply with the law was carried out in contravention of a building bye law. It was held that the contractor could recover payment for the work since there was no fundamental illegality. But in such circumstances the building owner will usually be entitled to set off a counterclaim for any work necessary to make the original work comply with statutory requirements. Difficulties will arise, for instance, where the fault lies in the foundations, which can be cured only by demolition and rebuilding of parts which are properly built. Such problems depend upon whether the

---

[40] See also *Soleimany v Soleimany* [1999] Q.B. 785, Ch.3.
[41] *St John Shipping v Rank* [1957] 1 Q.B. 267.
[42] [1959] 1 W.L.R. 119—more fully reported at 20 B.L.R. 118.

local authority seek to enforce compliance, whether the building owner has acquiesced in the breach and also on the express terms of the contract.

Incapacity of parties

Certain parties are restricted in their contractual capacity and liability. The most important of these are corporate bodies and infants. A corporate body (such as a limited company or a local authority) can make contracts only within its specific powers. A contract outside these powers is void (but see Ch.4).

An infant occupies a privileged position under the law of contract. They are, in general, bound only by contracts which are substantially for their benefit. Thus, if an infant contracts to purchase goods, they are only liable to pay for them if they are necessary and suitable for their requirements, and they are liable to pay only a reasonable price. An acquisition of property such as land or shares is binding, but may be avoided by an infant before or within a reasonable time after reaching majority (i.e. 18 years). Despite the infant not being bound, they may still take advantage of the contract, by suing the supplier of defective (though non-necessary) goods. Contracts with infants should therefore be approached with caution.

Privity

The common law rule of privity is that a contract cannot be enforced by or against a person who is not a party to that contract. For example, a clause in a building contract enabling the employer to pay money direct to a sub-contractor may be used by the employer, but cannot be enforced by the sub-contractor, who is not a party to the main contract. There are, however, exceptions both general and specific. The law of agency is a general exception, for the principal may sue and be sued on contracts made by their agent (see Ch.7). Specific contracts on which a stranger may sue include (by statute) a contract under seal respecting land or other property, and a third party insurance policy. Contracts which can be enforced against a stranger are practically limited to restrictive covenants over land, which on certain conditions are enforceable against a person who subsequently acquires the land (see Ch.15).

An important aspect of the law of privity is whether, and in what circumstances, a third party can take advantage of an exclusion or limitation clause in a contract which binds the party seeking to make the claim. The leading case is *Scruttons v Midland Silicones*,[43] in which the House of Lords held that a negligent stevedore was not entitled to rely on a

---

[43] [1962] A.C. 446.

limitation clause in the bill of lading. The House left open the possibility that the head contract containing the relevant clause could be expressed in such terms as to permit the third party, in effect, to set up a contract directly with the party suffering the loss. Such an argument was advanced, unsuccessfully, in relation to the taking over certificate in the Model Form A contract,[44] which states that for the purpose of the clause, the contractor contracts "on his own behalf and on behalf of and as trustee for his sub-contractors." In *Southern Water Authority v Lewis & Duvivier*,[45] Judge Smout said:

> "I must be cautious before extending into a wider field those decisions insofar as they apply the principle of unilateral contract to the specialised practice of carriers and stevedores in mercantile law. To my mind, the principle of unilateral contract does not, taken by itself, fit easily on to the accepted facts in the instant case and it strikes me as uncomfortably artificial."

Judge Smout found that the conditions laid down in the *Midland Silicones* case were not satisfied, but nevertheless held that the taking over certificate could be relied on as a defence in tort (see Chs 5 and 14).

Law reform on privity

For many years, judges and academics have expressed dissatisfaction with the English rule on privity, some suggesting that earlier authorities had been misunderstood, and others drawing attention to more liberal laws applicable in virtually every other country, including Scotland. Reform was called for so that the law on privity should give effect to the reasonable expectations of contracting parties. The issue was passed to the Law Commission whose recommendations led to the Contracts (Rights of Third Parties) Act 1999. The essential features of the Act are as follows:

- Section 1 sets out the circumstances in which a third party may have the right to enforce a term of the contract. This is where the contract confers or purports to confer a benefit on the third party. The third party must be expressly identified by name, class or description. The right can be enforced only subject to other terms of the contract.

- Section 2 restricts the way in which the original contracting parties can alter the third party's entitlement, by cancelling or

---

[44] Clause 30.
[45] (1984) 27 B.L.R. 111.

varying the contract without their consent, but subject to any express terms under which the contract may be cancelled or varied.

- Section 3 deals with defences available to the party against which the third party seeks enforcement.

- Section 4 provides that the right of the original contracting party to enforce the contract is not affected.

- Section 5 deals with the situation in which the original contracting party has already recovered in respect of the third party's loss.

- Section 6 contains restrictions on the rights created by the Act.

- Section 7 provides that other rights of the third party are generally unaffected.

- Section 8 requires that the third party be treated as a party to any applicable arbitration agreement as regards enforcement of their right.

The effect of the Act is to allow parties, other than the immediate parties to a contract, to enforce particular rights where the contract expressly so provides. This aspect of the new law is relatively uncontroversial, given that the third party will effectively stand in the shoes of the original contracting party and be subject to such defences as were available against them. If the original right was subject to arbitration, enforcement by the third party will similarly be subject to arbitration. The controversial element of the Bill is in the possibility of a contract being so construed as to create rights in favour of a third party, where this is not expressly set out. The possibility of disputes as to whether one party or another is entitled to enforce a particular right, perhaps in circumstances where the original contracting party has already enforced or sought to enforce that right, may give rise to complex disputes. Typically, such a dispute will involve three parties (at least), being the original parties to the contract and the third party. There may be more than one potential third party claimant. In these circumstances, the effect of an arbitration clause in the original contract becomes more problematical. Issues which remain to be resolved, ultimately by the courts, include whether an arbitrator can resolve disputes as to whether rights have been acquired by one or more third parties (which may involve disputes between third parties) and what is to happen if different arbitrators are appointed in different proceedings to enforce the same rights. Even where the same arbitrator is appointed it does not follow that they will be empowered to hold concurrent hearings involving all relevant parties.[46]

The Contracts (Rights of Third Parties) Act 1999 has received little direct attention in the construction field as a result of a general policy of providing expressly in contracts that they are not intended to confer rights on any third parties. The construction industry had already in place a well-developed practice for creating direct warranties where it was intended to confer rights on an identified party. An attempt to use the Act occurred in *Avraamides v Colwill and Martin (t/a Bathroom Trading Company Ltd)*[47] where a house-owner who had entered into a contract with a limited company (now insolvent) contended that the owners and principals of the company, under the contract by which they had purchased its assets, had undertaken a liability for outstanding orders (including liability for defects in the work) which the house-owner was entitled to enforce as a third party. The contention was rejected by the Court of Appeal principally on the ground that the contract in question did not expressly identify the house-owner as a third party either by name, class or description as required by the Act.

PROCUREMENT AND COMPETITION RULES

These rules exist primarily through European Community law and have the effect of imposing restrictions or sanctions on parties where they apply.

Procurement

The European Treaty requires free movement of goods and freedom to provide services for the purpose of achieving the Common Market. Specifically, art.30 of the Treaty provides:

> "Quantitative restrictions on imports and all measures having equivalent effect shall, without prejudice to the following provisions, be prohibited between member states."

This article was the subject of direct enforcement in the case of the *Commission v Ireland*[48] which involved the Dundalk Water Supply contract. The contract required pipes which complied with an Irish

---

[46] See s.35, of the Arbitration Act 1996, Ch.3.
[47] [2007] B.L.R. 76.
[48] Case No.45/87, (1988) 44 B.L.R. 1.

standard specification and required Irish certification. A tenderer who offered to use pipes of Spanish manufacture which did not have the Irish certification was rejected. The tenderer complained to the commission who brought proceedings against the Irish government on the basis that they were liable for the acts of the employer, the Dundalk Urban District Council. The European court rejected a series of arguments seeking to justify the actions of the UDC. The judgment of the court included the following:

> "The Irish government further maintains that protection of public health justifies the requirement of compliance with the Irish standard insofar as that standard guarantees there is no contract between the water and the asbestos fibres in the cement pipes, which would adversely affect the quality of the drinking water. That argument must be rejected. As the Commission has rightly pointed out, the coating of the pipes, both internally and externally was the subject of a separate requirement in the invitation to tender. The Irish government has not shown why compliance with that requirement would not be such as to ensure that there is no contact between the water and the asbestos fibres, which it considers to be essential for reasons of public health."

The court went on to declare that the government of Ireland had failed to fulfil its obligations under art.30 of the Treaty.

Specific requirements as to procurement are set out in European Council Directives which require implementation in each Member State. Within the United Kingdom these are implemented by a series of regulations[49] which apply to all works contracts exceeding a specific limit, which is itself revised periodically, and which are to be let by a public body or utility. These regulations make detailed provisions for tendering and award of contracts. Requirements as to advertising for tenders must be complied with, which include placing notices in the *Official Journal of the European Community* (OJ). Breach of the procurement requirements may lead to enforcement measures in the relevant state court, including proceeding for interim measures. Available remedies are prescribed in separate Directives which are implemented in the United Kingdom by regulations[50]. The remedies available for breach include, in additional to damages, automatic suspension of the contract award procedure when legal proceedings are started, and a declaration of ineffectiveness or contract shortening. The action will normally be taken by an aggrieved unsuccessful bidder but may be taken by the European Commission at the request of the bidder.

---

[49] Public Contracts Regulations 2006 and Utilities Contracts Regulations 2006.
[50] Public Contracts (Amendment) Regulations 2009 and Utilities Contracts (Amendment) Regulations 2009.

The effect of the Public Works Directive was brought clearly into focus by the TCC case of *Harmon Façades v House of Commons*.[51] The dispute concerned the construction, under a management contract, of the cladding for the new Parliamentary building at Bridge Street, Westminster. Notice inviting tenders was published, as required, in the OJ stating that the award criterion (other than price) was "overall value for money". A number of tenders were obtained and, owing to their amounts, re-tendering was invited on different options. The contract was eventually awarded to a UK company for one of the options. Harmon (a European company ultimately owned by an American holding company) had been asked to re-tender for another option. The two options were not comparable. Furthermore, Public Works Regulations 12 and 20, which were mandatory, did not permit use of the expression "overall value for money" without specification of selection criteria, none of which were to be found in the contract documents. The defendant's policy of awarding contracts to UK contractors was not permitted by the regulations. It was held by H.H. Judge LLoyd Q.C., that the defendant could not lawfully award the contract to the alternative British tenderer. The defendant was in breach of the regulations and Harmon was entitled to recover its tender costs and its tender margin for risk and profit, both of which would have been recovered had the tender been awarded to them. In the course of the judgment consideration was given to the status of the new or revised tenders which were solicited[52] and the effect of the regulated tender regime, in the following terms:

"[The defendant] in soliciting new or revised tenders under the European public works regime (to which effect is given by the Regulations) impliedly undertook towards any tenderer which submitted a tender that its submission would be treated as an acceptance of [an] offer or undertaking and: (a) that the alternative submitted by any tenderer would be considered alongside a compliant revised tender from that tenderer; (b) that any alternative would be one of detail and not design; and (c) that tenderers who responded to that invitation would be treated equally and fairly.

These contractual obligations derive from a contract to be implied from the procurement regime required by the European directives, as interpreted by the European Court, whereby the principles of fairness and equality form part of a preliminary contract of the kind that I have indicated. *Emery* shows that such a contract may exist at common law against a statutory background which might otherwise provide the exclusive remedy. I consider that it is now clear in English law that in the public sector where competitive tenders are sought and responded to, a contract comes into

---

[51] [1999] 67 Con. L.R. 1.
[52] See *Blackpool & Fylde v Blackpool BC*, Ch.5.

existence whereby the prospective employer impliedly agrees to consider all tenderers fairly (see the *Blackpool* and *Fairclough*[53] cases)."

A common cause of complaint by unsuccessful tenderers if that the award critera were not adequately disclosed. The issue of award criteria arose in *Emm G Lionakis v Dimos Alexandroupolis*[54] where the European Court of Justice held that a Greek municipal council had contravened the Directive by further defining the weighting factors within the award criteria during the tender evaluation proess; and in *Letting International v L B Newham*[55] the English Court of Appeal granted an injunction preventing Newham from entering into a contract with another company where an unsuccessful tenderer contended that the weighting of award criteria had not been disclosed and the criteria incorrectly applied. More recently, however, an unsuccessful bidder failed in a challenge to the award of a contract by the UK Ministry of Overseas Development, where the court held challenges to the procurement process did not merit the award process being restrained; and other challenges to the policy applied by the Ministry were matters of public law and not procurement law.[56]

Competition law

The objective is again to promote the free movement of goods and provision of services as required by the European Treaty. Agreements in restraint of trade are subject to the common law[57] and to statute law, principally the Fair Trading Act 1973, and the Competition Acts 1980 and 1998 under which the Competition Commission is given powers of investigation.

Article 101 (formerly numbered art.81) of the European Treaty prohibits agreements and practices which prevent or distort competition and further prohibit abuse of a dominant position having this effect. Breach of these principles may be enforced directly under English law by virtue of the Competition Act 1998; or by the European Commission which may itself investigate, issue directions and impose substantial fines. The task of investigating the breach of competition legislation within the United Kingdom now falls on the Office of Fair Trading, established by the Enterprise Act 2002[58]. Advanced protection for poten-

---

[53] *Fairclough Building Ltd v Port Talbot BC* (1992) 33 Con. L.R. 24.
[54] (2008) C.I.L.L. 2573.
[55] [2007] EWCA 1522.
[56] *Halo Trust v Minister for International Development* [2011] B.L.R. 229.
[57] *Esso v Harpers Garage* [1968] A.C. 269.
[58] For a recent report on anti-competitive bidding practices see OFT Press Release 22 September 2009.

tially anti-competitive agreements may be sought from the National Competition Authorities and National Courts in each Member State.

DISCHARGE OF CONTRACTS

Discharge is a general term for the release of contractual obligations, when the parties become freed from the obligation to do anything further under the contract. This must generally be brought about by some act of the parties. Contracts do not end automatically, unless perhaps by becoming statute barred (see below). Once a contract is discharged neither party can rely on its terms but can only enforce whatever rights may arise from the discharge. It is therefore important to know whether or not a contract is discharged (this may well be an issue between the parties). Determination of the contractor's employment under a provision in a building contract does not determine the contract itself and the parties remain bound by all its relevant terms.[59]

Discharge of a contract may be brought about in four ways:

(1) if the parties perform all their obligations the contract is said to be discharged by performance;

(2) if an event during the course of the contract renders performance impossible or sterile, it may be frustrated;

(3) serious breach by one party may lead to the contract being discharged; and

(4) where one party commits a breach the other party may recover damages in satisfaction of the failure to perform.

These methods of discharge and also the wider topic of recovery of damages for breach of contract are discussed below. A fifth method of discharge is by express agreement; this is discussed later under variation of contracts.[60]

Performance

In general only exact and complete performance of contractual obligations can discharge the contract and a party who has only partially

---

[59] See ICE, cl.63, JCT, cll.27 and 28.
[60] See Ch.8.

performed their obligations cannot recover payment. This rule is mitigated in a number of cases. Where a contract has been substantially performed, payment may be due with an allowance for deficiencies. Further, when a contract is divisible, either expressly or impliedly, payment will be due for parts which have been completed.[61]

A building or engineering contract will be discharged by performance on the part of the contractor when all the work has been completed, including obligations as to maintenance, and when the architect or engineer has issued all requisite certificates; and on the part of the employer when they have paid all sums due. If undisclosed (latent) defects are later discovered the contract has not been performed. The employer will retain the right to sue for breach during the period of limitation, subject to the effect of any final certificate[62] under the contract.

Frustration

As a general rule contractual obligations are regarded as absolute and a party is not absolved because performance becomes difficult or even impossible. A party who contracts to do the impossible is liable for failing to do it, unless they have excluded such liability.[63] If, however, without default of either party, the circumstances change so that performance of a contractual obligation becomes radically different from that undertaken, the contract may be frustrated and thereby automatically discharged.

Examples of situations which have constituted frustration are: (1) a building in which one party is to carry out work for the other is accidentally destroyed by fire; (2) seats are sold to view a public event which does not take place; and (3) government action which prohibits performance of contract for a substantial period. If a term of the contract provides for the contingency which has occurred, it is a question of construction whether it covers the particular circumstances, and thus keeps the contract in being. In *Metropolitan Water Board v Dick Kerr*[64] the contractor had agreed in 1914 to construct a reservoir in six years, with a provision for extensions of time for various delays. In 1916, due to the war, the Ministry ordered the work to cease. It was held that the interruption was likely to be so long that the contract would be radically different, and the extension of time provision did not prevent frustration. Lord Dunedin, in the House of Lords said:

[61] As to performance of building contracts, see Ch.9.
[62] See JCT Contract, cl.30.9; also Ch.12.
[63] See ICE, cl.13.
[64] [1918] A.C. 119.

"The order pronounced under the Defence of the Realm Act not only debarred the respondents from proceeding with the contract, but also compulsorily dispersed and sold the plant. It is admitted that an interruption may be so long as to destroy the identity of the work or service, when resumed, with the work or service when interrupted. But quite apart from mere delay it seems to me that the action as to the plant prevents this contract ever being the same as it was."

Examples of building or engineering contracts being frustrated are extremely rare. Contracts are not frustrated by the work proving more difficult or costly than could have been anticipated, in any degree, unless the difficulty arises from some change of circumstance or supervening event. In the case of *Thorn v London Corporation*,[65] the contract was not frustrated when the engineer's design for a new bridge over the Thames, with piers constructed inside caissons, proved impossible to construct. The contractor had taken the risk as to the method of construction and remained liable to carry out the work by whatever means were necessary, at no extra cost.

The legal effect of frustration is that the contract is discharged as to the future. Money paid before frustration is recoverable and money payable ceases to be payable. But the court may permit a party to retain or recover a sum to compensate them for any expense incurred, or for any benefit to the other party before the time of frustration.[66] A contractor whose contract becomes frustrated may therefore be unable to recover any payment if the employer gets no benefit from the work which has been completed. These rules are, however, subject to the provisions of the contract, and will usually be mitigated by insurances.

Breach of contract

Breach of contract occurs when a party fails to perform some primary obligation under the contract, for example, when goods are not delivered on the date fixed, or when delivered work does not conform to contractual requirements. Under building and engineering contracts, defective work will not necessarily be a breach of contract when done if the contractor is not bound to execute particular work at a specified time. A breach would, however, occur if the contractor refused to obey a proper instruction to remove defective work or if work were not completed according to the contract by the date when it should have been completed.[67]

---

[65] (1876) 1 App. Cas. 120.
[66] Law Reform (Frustrated Contracts) Act 1943.
[67] *Kaye v Hosier & Dickinson* [1972] 1 W.L.R. 146 and see also *Lintest v Roberts* (1980) 13 B.L.R. 38.

It is important, in dealing with claims under a building or engineering contract, to distinguish between a claim for breach of contract and a claim under the contract. A claim under the contract arises when an event occurs (which may or may not be a breach of contract) for which the contract provides a remedy. The remedy is usually payment of a sum of money to or by the contractor, or it may be some other benefit such as an extension of time. Often the same event will give rise to claims both under the contract and for breach. But the consequences of the two heads of claim are different. For example, consequential damages may be recovered for a breach; but under the contract only such remedies as are provided can be recovered. A claim under a contract is a way of enforcing its provisions. This section is concerned only with breach.

Breach of contract may have two principal consequences. First, every breach entitles the innocent party to sue for damages. Secondly, if the breach is sufficiently serious it gives the innocent party an option to treat the party in breach as having repudiated the whole contract. In this case the innocent party may bring the contract to an end by accepting the repudiation; or they may, at their option, treat the contract as subsisting, when it will then continue to bind both parties.

Repudiation

A repudiation may consist in an express or an implied refusal by one party to perform the contract; or it may be a serious breach which goes to the root of the contract. The latter type of breach may be called a fundamental breach, or breach of a fundamental obligation. In each case the question whether a breach is to be taken as repudiation depends upon the importance of the breach in relation to the contract as a whole. Repudiation of a building contract may occur where a contractor carries out defective work and fails or refuses to comply with a proper instruction to rectify the work. Alternatively there may be a repudiation by failure to proceed with due expedition giving rise to substantial delay.

In both of the examples given, the building contract will contain alternative express remedies, for example, to bring in another contractor to rectify defective work or to deduct liquidated damages. Contracts also variably contain powers to determine the employment of the contractor in cases of such default. In neither instance does the existence of these terms detract from the right of the employer to accept the contractor's repudiation as terminating the contract. The employer may give notice which may operate alternatively under the contract or as a common law acceptance of repudiation.

It is possible for the employer to commit a fundamental breach which may at the same time entitle the contractor to terminate their employment under the contract. The contractor may also in such a case serve notice which will operate on either basis in the alternative (see Ch.9). Conduct by the employer which could, depending on the circumstances, amount to repudiation might be a serious interference with the course of the works or repeated and serious failure to make payments due under the contract. With regard to the latter ground, it was held in *Multiplex Constructions v Cleveland Bridge*[68] that failure by the main contractor to make agreed payments to a sub-contractor did not amount to a repudiatory breach having regard, inter alia, to the fact that the contractor had referred the relevant payment disputes to adjudication. In *Alan Auld Associates v Rick Pollard Associates*,[69] however, the court decided that persistent failure to make payments due for consultancy work did amount to repudiation, entitling the innocent party to terminate the contract. Both in the case of employer and contractor, a repudiation and acceptance thereof brings the contract to an end as to the future, while termination of employment does not, the parties remaining bound by the post-termination terms of the contract.

Under the codified law applying to the sale of goods (see Ch.7) certain obligations, such as correspondence with sample, are designated as "conditions", a breach of which is to be regarded as repudiation allowing the buyer to reject the goods and terminate the contract. Terms whose breach does not amount to repudiation are referred to as "warranties". This simple and convenient division of obligations cannot be applied to construction contracts and it would be necessary in each case to ascertain whether the particular breach could be regarded as fundamental.

It has been held that a fundamental breach could itself bring the contract to an end, on the basis that the other party had no choice but to accept the situation. This was in *Harbutts Plasticine v Wayne Tank*,[70] where a defective pipe led to the destruction of factory premises by fire. The case has been criticised and should not be seen as affecting the primary rule that the innocent party is entitled to elect whether to terminate the contract or not. Where the innocent party does elect to terminate they must expressly or impliedly tell the other party. Their choice is binding and will bring the contract to an end as from the election. If the innocent party chooses to treat the contract as subsisting, all the terms will continue to bind both parties.

[68] (2006) 107 Con. L.R.
[69] [2008] B.L.R. 419.
[70] [1970] 1 Q.B. 447.

A failure by a contractor or supplier to complete or perform on time may amount to a repudiatory breach giving the employer the right to terminate the contract where either the delay has become so gross as to amount itself to a repudiatory breach or alternatively where time is or has been made "of the essence" of the contract. This principle was applied in *Charles Rickards v Oppenheim*[71] where the purchaser of a Rolls Royce car initially agreed and then waived a delivery date. After further delay the purchaser fixed a final delivery date which, when not met, led to cancellation of the order. The Court of Appeal held that the purchaser was entitled, after the initial delay, to give reasonable notice making time again of the essence and to terminate the contract upon the date not being met. Denning L.J. expressed the view that the same principle allied whether the contract was for sale of goods or for work and labour. There are difficulties in applying the principle to construction work, where a proportion of the work will be complete and attached to the owner's land at termination and an employer wishing to terminate for delay should rely on the express terms of the contract or on repudiatory breach if possible. The issues was considered by the Court of Appeal in *Shawton Engineering v DGP International*[72] where a sub-contractor was engaged in a series of design packages which were in delay as a result of variations. As the sub-contracts contained no extension of time clauses the main contractor gave notice of required completion dates. Inconclusive meetings followed, after which the main contractor terminated the contracts for delay. The termination was held wrongful since the sub-contractor was not in breach when the completion dates were notified; there had been no reasonable notice making time of the essence; and the sub-contractor was not in repudiatory breach.

Effect on exclusion clauses

When a contract is terminated by acceptance of repudiation, the question arises whether the party in breach may nevertheless rely on an exclusion or limitation clause. In a number of cases it was held that such clauses were destroyed with the contract. However, it is now settled that this is not so. In *Photo Productions v Securicor*[73] the defendant's employees, who were meant to guard the plaintiff's premises, entered and lit a fire which destroyed the factory. It was held by the House of Lords that Securicor were entitled to rely on the clear words of an

---

[71] [1950] 1 K.B. 616.
[72] [2006] B.L.R. 1.
[73] [1980] A.C. 827 and see *Suisse Atlantique v M.V. Rotterdamsche* [1967] 1 A.C. 361.

exclusion clause which exempted them from responsibility for default of their employee unless due to want of care on their part. In giving judgment, Lord Diplock distinguished between the "primary obligation" of a contract, being the services to be provided, and the "secondary obligations" which arose upon breach of the primary obligations. Every failure to perform a primary obligation would be a breach of contract, and this would give rise to secondary obligations such as the payment of monetary compensation for loss sustained. The termination or rescission of a contract for repudiation brings to an end the primary obligations but leaves intact the secondary obligations. Lord Diplock went on to hold that exclusion clauses were to be applied according to their proper construction:

> "In commercial contracts negotiated between businessmen capable of looking after their own interests and of deciding how risks inherent in the performance of various kinds of contract can be most economically borne (generally by insurance), it is, in my view, wrong to place a strained construction upon words in an exclusion clause which are clear and fairly susceptible of one meaning only even after due allowance has been made for the presumption in favour of the implied primary and secondary obligations."

The continued existence of an exclusion clause is also confirmed by the Unfair Contract Terms Act 1977, which provides that such clauses are still to be given effect even when the contract has been terminated by acceptance of repudiation (see below).

REMEDIES FOR BREACH

If the innocent party properly elects to treat the contract as discharged, they are relieved from further liability. They may then claim damages, both as to loss flowing from the breach and loss flowing from the termination. The latter will usually include the additional cost of completing the contract. If the contract is not discharged, (whether or not they could have elected to terminate) the innocent party may claim damages. The right to recover damages is subject to a number of rules which restrict the monetary loss recoverable which are dealt with below. Alternatively, in very limited circumstances, the court may order specific performance, that is, it will compel the defendant to do what they have contracted to do (see below). The Arbitration Act 1996 confirms that an arbitrator may also award specific performance (s.48(5)).

Damages and remoteness

Not every loss which flows from a breach of contract is recoverable in damages. A claim can succeed only in respect of damage which is, in law, not too remote. Further, the innocent party must take all reasonable steps to mitigate their loss (see below). Damage is not too remote if at the time of the contract the parties ought reasonably to have contemplated that loss of that kind would be likely to occur. The common law has, further, developed two categories into which recoverable damage may fall, deriving from the leading case of *Hadley v Baxendale*.[74] In this case, the plaintiffs, who were mill owners, contracted with the defendant to carry a broken crankshaft to the makers at Greenwich. There was delay in transit which resulted in the mill remaining idle so that the plaintiffs claimed loss of profit. Baron Alderson held that:

> "Where two parties have made a contract which one of them has broken, the damages which the other party ought to receive in respect of such breach of contract should be such as may fairly and reasonably be considered either arising naturally, i.e. according to the usual course of things, from such breach of contract itself or such as may reasonably be supposed to have been in the contemplation of both parties, at the time they made the contract, as the probable result of the breach of it."

This classic formulation led to the two grounds for recovery of damages becoming known as the first and second "limb" of *Hadley v Baxendale*. Thus, the first limb covers such loss as will arise from the natural or usual course of events, each party being deemed to be aware of such matters. The second limb (separated by the word or in the quotation) covers such additional or special consequences as may arise from the actual events provided, however, that the parties were at the time of the contract aware of such consequences. This division of recoverable damages has been accepted throughout the common law world, including the United States of America, where *Hadley v Baxendale* is still cited. The second limb is further illustrated by the more modern case of *Victoria Laundry v Newman*,[75] where the plaintiff ordered a new boiler from the defendant for the purpose of taking on new work of an exceptionally profitable nature. The boiler was not delivered and the work was lost. It was held that the plaintiff could recover only the normal profit to be expected, since the defendant had no actual knowledge, at the time the contract was entered into, of the proposed new work.

---

[74] [1980] A.C. 827 and see *Suisse Atlantique v M.V. Rotterdamsche* [1967] 1 A.C. 361.
[75] [1949] 2 K.B. 528.

Foresight

The defendant is liable only for the foreseeable consequences of their breach. This gave rise to particular difficulty in *South Australia v York Montague*[76] in which the House of Lords considered three appeals relating to negligent valuation of properties where, not only had the defendant surveyors over-valued, but the plaintiff had suffered substantial additional losses as a result of the fall in the property market. In two of the cases where the over-valuation was marginal compared to the sum advanced by the plaintiff, the House of Lords held the surveyors not liable for the additional drop in market value. In the remaining case, the House held that the plaintiff had £10m less security than they thought. If they had had this margin they would have suffered no loss. The whole loss (including the drop in market value) was therefore within the scope of the defendant's duty and was recoverable as damages (see further below).

The rules of remoteness have no application to a claim under a contract as opposed to a claim for breach. Thus if a dealer warrants that a motor car is in good condition and it breaks down, the purchaser may recover the cost of repairs and the cost of hiring an alternative vehicle, as damages for breach of contract. If, however, the dealer promises only to replace defective parts, the purchaser's entitlement under the contract is to the cost of repairs, and no question of consequential damage arises. In contracts of sale, an undertaking to replace defective parts is usually given in lieu of any warranty as to quality or fitness, so that the supplier is not in breach if the article is defective. In building contracts the position may be different. A so-called "defect liability" clause, which obliges the builder to put right defects, does not normally prevent the builder also being in breach so that consequential loss may be recoverable, even though the builder may carry out the necessary repair to the work (see Ch.9).

Causation

The party claiming damages for breach of contract must also prove that the damage was caused by the breach. Such issues arise both under the law of contract and of tort, so that the authorities can apply in both areas. In *The Wilhelm*,[77] the master of a ship, at the onset of winter, delayed departure from port with effect that the ship became frozen in until the spring. The defendant was held liable for the whole of the delay since the possibility was apparent and could reasonably have been

---

[76] [1996] 3 W.L.R. 87.
[77] (1866) 14 L.T. 638.

contemplated. Conversely, in *Associated Portland Cement v Houlder*,[78] another shipping case, the defendant was in delay on a voyage during wartime to load the plaintiff's goods. The day after the due date, the ship was sunk en route by an enemy submarine. The plaintiff recovered damages in respect of the one day's delay; the event which caused the remainder of the damage was not reasonable to be contemplated. The question of causation in a construction case is illustrated by *Quinn v Burch Bros*,[79] where the plaintiff, an independent plastering sub-contractor, was carrying out work for the defendant who was to supply necessary equipment. The defendant failed to supply a stepladder, as a result of which the plaintiff improvised a trestle, which collapsed causing him injury. Although the defendant was in breach of contract, Sellers L.J. in the Court of Appeal held:

> "This cannot be said to be an accident which was caused by the defendant's breach of contract. No doubt that circumstance was the occasion which brought about this conduct of the plaintiff, but it in no way caused it. It was in no way something flowing probably and naturally from the breach of contract."

Measure of damages

The measure of damages awarded is usually the actual monetary loss. The principle is that the innocent party should be restored to the position that they would have been in had the other party performed their obligation. Thus where the plaintiff's factory was burnt down as a result of the defendant's breach and there was no reasonable alternative to rebuilding the factory, the plaintiff recovered the full cost of rebuilding: *Harbutts Plasticine v Wayne Tank*.[80] Lord Denning held, in this case:

> "When this mill was destroyed the plasticine company had no choice. They were bound to replace it as soon as they could, not only to keep their business going, but also to mitigate the loss of profit. They replaced it in the only possible way, without adding any extras. I think they should be allowed the cost of replacement. True it is that they got new for old; but I do not think the wrong-doer can diminish the claim on that account. If they had added extra accommodation or made extra improvements, they would have to give credit. But that is not this case."

The normal measure of damage in respect of a breach affecting goods or property is the loss of value. However, where a contractor in breach of

---

[78] (1917) 118 L.T. 94.
[79] [1966] 2 Q.B. 370.
[80] [1970] 1 Q.B. 447.

contract carries out defective work, the measure of damages is normally taken as the actual or estimated cost of reinstatement; and where the breach consists of not doing work the damages will normally be the extra cost of completing the work at the earliest reasonable time. Additional damages such as loss of rents and profits will depend upon the rules of remoteness set out above. Where the cost of remedial work is disproportionate or where other circumstances dictate that remedial cost is not the true measure of loss, the claimant may be compensated for the loss in value to the property. In *McGlinn v Waltham Contractors*[81] a claimant who demolished and re-built the property defectively built by the defendant was held entitled to recover only damages based on the cost of repairs rather than the higher costs actually incurred, since the defects complained of were aesthetic rather than structural and it was held not to be reasonable to demolish.

An interesting application of these principles arose in the case of *Ruxley Electronics v Forsyth*[82] where the plaintiff contractor built a swimming pool for the defendant. The contract required a depth of 7ft 6in in the diving area but on completion the pool was found to be only 6ft deep. There was no adverse effect on the value of the property nor on diving. The estimated cost of rebuilding to the specified depth was £21,560. Judge Anthony Diamond Q.C. awarded £2,500 for loss of amenity on the counterclaim, holding the cost of reinstatement to be an unreasonable claim. The Court of Appeal reversed the decision, awarding the owner the full cost of reinstatement. The House of Lords restored the original judgment on the basis that the expenditure was out of all proportion to the benefit to be obtained. This was despite the fact that Mr Forsyth had stated his intention to rebuild the pool and offered undertakings as to use of the sum in question, if recovered. Lord Lloyd dealt with the point in the following terms:

> "In the present case the judge found as a fact that Mr Forsyth's stated intention of rebuilding the pool would not persist for long after the litigation had been concluded. In those circumstances it would be "mere pretence" to say that the cost of rebuilding the pool is the loss which he has in fact suffered. This is the critical distinction between the present case and the example given by Staughton L.J., of a man who has had his watch stolen. In the latter case, the plaintiff is entitled to recover the value of the watch, because that is the true measure of his loss. He can do what he wants with the damages. But if, as the judge found, Mr Forsyth had no intention of rebuilding the pool, he has lost nothing except the difference in value, if any."

---

[81] (2007) 111 Con. L.R. 1.
[82] [1996] A.C. 344.

Inflation in building costs often results in argument as to the date at which repair costs should be assessed for the purpose of an award of damages. The position was clarified by the Court of Appeal in *Dodd Properties v Canterbury C.C.*[83] The defendants were liable for damaging the plaintiff's garage premises in 1968. There was a delay in carrying out repairs until 1978, which resulted in a considerable increase in cost, for which the defendants disputed liability. The plaintiffs delayed doing the work because the cost would have resulted in financial stringency, and they were reluctant to lay out money before being sure of recovering it. It was held that the plaintiffs could recover the 1978 price of the work. The general position was restated as follows:

"The general object underlying the rules for the assessment of damages is, so far as is possible by means of a monetary award, to place the plaintiff in the position which he would have occupied if he had not suffered the wrong complained of, be that wrong a tort or a breach of contract. In the case of a tort causing damage to real property, this object is achieved by the application of one or other of two quite different measures of damage, or, occasionally, a combination of the two. The first is to take the capital value of the property in an undamaged state and to compare it with its value in a damaged state. The second is to take the cost of repair or reinstatement. Which is appropriate will depend upon a number of factors, such as the plaintiff's future intentions as to the use of the property and the reasonableness of those intentions. If he reasonably intends to sell the property in its damaged state, clearly the diminution in capital value is the true measure of damage. If he reasonably intends to continue to occupy it and to repair the damage, clearly the cost of repairs is the true measure. And there may be in-between situations.

. . . a case in which the plaintiff has reinstated his property before the hearing, the costs prevailing at the date of that operation which were reasonably incurred by him are prima facie those which are relevant. Equally in a case in which a plaintiff has not effected reinstatement by the time of the hearing, there is a prima facie presumption that the costs then prevailing are those which should be adopted in ascertaining the cost of reinstatement. There may indeed be cases in which the court has to estimate costs at some future time as being the reasonable time at which to reinstate."

This case concerned a claim in tort, but the principles are equally applicable in contract.

Damages against surveyor

There is an apparent exception to the rule of reinstatement of the claimant's loss where a surveyor gives an erroneous report on the

[83] [1980] 1 W.L.R. 433.

condition of the property. The purchaser relying on the report can recover, not the cost of repairing the undisclosed defects, but the difference in value between the property as reported and as it actually was: *Phillips v Ward*.[84] This case is not a true exception to the rule, however. The purchaser's position, had the surveyor performed his contract properly, would be that he knew the true value of the property, and should not pay more. The surveyor could be liable for the cost of rectifying defects only if he had given a warranty that the house was free of such defects.

The potential liability of a negligent valuer was considered in the *South Australia v York Montague* (above). In that case, Lord Hoffman dealt with an argument on behalf of the defendant that damages, following a negligent survey, should be limited to the excess over the highest valuation which would not have been negligent. The argument was dealt with as follows:

"The valuer is not liable unless he is negligent. In deciding whether or not he has been negligent, the court must bear in mind that valuation is seldom and exact science and that within a band of figures valuers may differ without one of them being negligent. But once the valuer has been found to have been negligent, the loss for which he is responsible is that which has been caused by the valuation being wrong. For this purpose the court must form a view as to what a correct valuation would have been. This means the figure which it considers most likely that a reasonable valuer, using the information available at the relevant time, would have put forward as the amount which the property was most likely to fetch if sold upon the open market. While it is true that there would have been a range of figures which the reasonable valuer might have put forward, the figure most likely to have been put forward would have been the mean figure of that range. There is no basis for calculating damages upon the basis that it would have been a figure at one or other extreme of the range."

Mitigation of loss

A claimant seeking to recover damages is sometimes said to be under a "duty" to mitigate. This, however, belies the reality which is that the defendant has the burden of proving failure to mitigate. There are many cases in which the courts have rejected complaints of failure to mitigate, preferring indulgence to the innocent party rather than saving the money of the contract breaker or tortfeasor. An important aspect of this question arises where the innocent party has to decide upon the extent of remedial works to be carried out and the advisors of the defendant are contending that significantly less costly measures would be adequate. This was the

---

[84] [1956] 1 W.L.R. 471. See also *Watts v Morrow* [1991] 1 W.L.R 1421.

case in *Great Ormond Street Hospital v McLaughlin & Harvey*[85] where there was a major and public dispute between experts for the parties as to the extent of remedial piling work which was appropriate to the new cardiac wing. This debate took place before the work was carried out. The plaintiff acted on the advice of their expert. The advice and the expert were subjected to serious attack at the trial. Judge Newey rejected the challenge, holding that the natural consequences of the defendant's breach was that the plaintiff would take expert advice and would act upon it. He further held that the chain of causation might be broken if it were shown that the plaintiff's expert had acted negligently. But short of this, the fact that other experts held different opinions was not a matter which should result in the plaintiff recovering less than the sums actually expended. The principle on which this case was decided has, however, been strongly criticised[86] and in *Scandia Property v Thames Water Utilities*,[87] the plaintiff failed to recover remedial costs incurred as a result of wrong or at least unreasonable expert advice.

Liquidated damages

In many commercial contracts, including construction contracts, provision is made for "liquidated" damages or sometimes "liquidated and ascertained" damages. Where the amount has been freely agreed between the parties, the sum in question will usually be enforced by the court, whether its effect is to obviate the need for proof or, conversely, to cap what would otherwise be a greater loss. In some circumstances, the liquidated damages may be declared unenforceable at the suit of the party being asked to pay (see Ch.8) and it is theoretically possible they could be unenforceable as an exclusion of liability at the suit of the party suffering the loss.[88] Ordinarily, liquidated or prestated damages are a convenient device to avoid the need to prove loss. Other sums appearing in building contracts, for example, rates and prices for elements of work do not constitute liquidated sums. The contractor may be entitled under the contract to be paid particular rates. However, in a claim for damages, the actual loss must be established and the sums stated in the contract will constitute no more than evidence of the loss.

---

[85] (1987) 19 Con. L.R. 25.
[86] TECBAR Review Spring 2012, Charles Pimlott.
[87] [1999] B.L.R. 338.
[88] Unfair Contracts Act 1977.

Joint liability and contribution

Where more than one person is potentially liable in respect of the claimant's damage, affect the claimant's right to recover the full loss from any one of the defendants is unaffected. However, as between the defendants who are each liable, the court has power to apportion liability and for this reason each defendants can be expected to seek to apportion blame onto others. Formerly the power of apportionment was available only between joint tortfeasors (see Ch.14). But it now applies whatever the legal basis of liability (including breach of contract) by virtue of the Civil Liability (Contribution) Act 1978. A defendant may bring another person who may be liable into an action as a third party; or separate proceedings may be brought against the other person later, to recover a contribution. The way in which the law of contribution applies in construction cases has been criticised in the DTI Report on Professional Liability.[89] The application of the rules is illustrated by the case of *Eckersley v Binnie*.[90] The trial judge apportioned liability 55 per cent to Binnie, 30 per cent to the Water Authority and 15 per cent to the contractor. On appeal, the second and third defendants were found not liable at all, so that Binnie had to take 100 per cent of the responsibility. The same result would have obtained if some defendants had been unable to pay their share of the damages: the plaintiff would have been entitled to recover in full from any of them.

As a measure to mitigate this seeming injustice, some professionals and professional bodies have introduced "net contribution clauses" which purport to limit the liability of a professional to the amount that would be apportioned on the basis other defendants also being liable, or to the amount which it is just and reasonable for them to pay. There is no reason in principle why such a limitation of liability should not be effective, subject to the clause otherwise being enforceable. In the Scottish case of *Langstane v Riverside and others*,[91] defendant consulting engineers sought to rely on a net contribution clause contained in the ACE Conditions of Engagement, which was challenged as unreasonable under the Unfair Contract Terms Act (see above). The court held that the parties had not contracted on the consultant's own standard terms of business but on the association's terms which were widely used within the profession. The terms did not therefore have to be shown to be fair and reasonable and should be given effect. The court also observed that it would

---

[89] HMSO 1989.
[90] (1988) 18 Con. L.R. 1; the facts are summarised in Ch.9.
[91] [2009] CSOH 52.

have held the clause to be fair and reasonable had this been a requirement.

Claimant partly at fault

Where the fault lies partly with the claimant the damages recoverable may be reduced by the court if the claim is brought in tort.[92] For many years it was unclear whether contributory negligence applied also where the claimant sued only in contract. The law was finally clarified in *Vesta v Butcher*,[93] where it was held that contributory negligence would apply where the defendant's liability in contract was the same as their liability in the tort of negligence. Where liability in contract was absolute, contributory negligence would not apply so that the claimant would be entitled to recover in full where negligence was proved against them. An intermediate category of obligations was also identified where it would still be open for the defendant to argue that there should be a deduction in respect of the claimant's negligence. In *Barclays Bank v Fairclough*[94] the defendant was held responsible for causing asbestos pollution during building operations, but the trial judge held the plaintiff also to be negligent so that the damages recovered were reduced. The defendant was found to have breached both obligations of reasonable care (equivalent to liability in tort) and also absolute obligations. The Court of Appeal held that the plaintiff was entitled to recover in full for breach of the absolute obligations irrespective of the theoretical reduction in respect of lesser obligations. But in *Sahib Foods v Pashkin Kyriakides*[95] the Court of Appeal held that damages awarded against the defendant architects should be reduced by 66 per cent where the claimant's failure to give accurate information as to the use of a factory was held to be a material cause of its loss by fire. While the claimant owed no duty to the defendant, it was sufficient that his conduct was a cause of the loss

Specific performance

Specific performance is an equitable remedy and is discretionary. It is not normally awarded if damages would be an adequate remedy, or if performance would require supervision by the court. Therefore, as a general rule, specific performance will not be ordered of a contract to build. The remedy may be available, for instance, when the claimant

---

[92] Law Reform (Contributory Negligence) Act 1945.
[93] [1989] A.C. 852.
[94] [1995] Q.B. 214.
[95] (2004) C.I.L.L.

sells or leases land to the defendant with an obligation to build. Specific performance may be ordered if the following conditions are satisfied: (1) the claimant has a substantial interest such that damages would not compensate them; (2) the defendant is in possession of the land so that the claimant cannot do the work; and (3) the work is adequately particularised. Specific performance may be granted of a landlord's repairing covenant in a lease, when the tenant has no right to carry out the work, for instance, because it affects parts retained by the landlord.

LIMITATION PERIODS

A final condition which must be satisfied is that the claim must ordinarily be brought within the period of limitation. The effect of the limitation Acts is to bar the remedy and not to extinguish the right of action. Accordingly, limitation will be relevant only if raised by the defendant in their defence.

The present law of limitation is set out principally in the Limitation Act 1980, which provides that an action founded on simple contract must be brought within six years of the date on which the cause of action accrued (s.5) and a claim upon a contract by deed within 12 years (s.8). Most of the cases concern the date upon which the cause of action is to be taken as having accrued. In contract, the cause of action accrues on the date of the breach. The fact that damage occurs or is discovered at a later date does not give the claimant any further or other cause of action. In the case of a building contract, however, the date upon which the breach occurs may not be the same as the date upon which the acts complained of were carried out. Defective work may create one cause of action when done, but a further breach and a further cause of action may arise if the builder fails to comply with an instruction to rectify the defects. Yet a further breach may occur at the end of the maintenance period. Thus, it is necessary to read the contract and to consider the facts to ascertain the latest date upon which the claimant is entitled to commence proceedings.

There is an exception to the ordinary limitation periods under s.32 of the Limitation Act 1980 which provides for postponement of the limitation period where any fact relevant to the claimant's right of action has been deliberately concealed from them by the defendant. The period of limitation is not to begin until the claimant has discovered the concealment or could, with reasonable diligence, have discovered it. The section provides that deliberate commission of a breach in circumstances where it is unlikely to be discovered for some time amounts to deliberate concealment. The section codifies previous decisions of the court, which are illustrated by the case of *King v Victor Parsons*.[96] In 1962 the plaintiff purchased from developers a plot of land on which the foundations and concrete oversite had already been laid with two courses of brickwork completed. The developers undertook to complete the house to the plaintiff's reasonable satisfaction. The plaintiff went into occupation in 1962. In 1968 large cracks developed and the plaintiff brought an action in breach of contract. The house had been built over a rubbish tip, and the developer had disregarded advice as to the type of foundation needed. It was held that the developer, or the builder as his agent, knew of these facts, and the failure to inform the plaintiff amounted to deliberate concealment, so that the plaintiff's cause of action arose in 1968 not 1962.

The House of Lords has recently affirmed that deliberate concealment did not include the mere failure to disclose a negligent breach of duty of which the person in breach was not aware.[97] In this case a negligent solicitor had failed to answer letters from the client who had found that a document which was intended to secure rights over land was ineffective because it bound only the owner. Lord Millet summarised the point in this way:

> "The maxim that ignorance of the law is no defence does not operate to convert a lawyer's inadvertent want of care into an intentional breach."

---

[96] [1973] 1 W.L.R. 29.
[97] *Cave v Robinson Jarvis* [2003] 1 A.C. 384.

CHAPTER 7

SPECIAL CONTRACTS

This chapter deals with special types of contract which are likely to be encountered in the construction industry, and which are governed by their own special rules in addition to the general principles set out in Ch.6.

The topics covered are the sale of goods, which is perhaps the most universal form of legal transaction; the law of agency, which defines the position of architects and many other persons who act on behalf of another; and contracts of insurance, which are an incident to most building and engineering contracts. Finally, the section on sale of dwellings covers a combination of contractual and other relationships which may be encountered when a recently built house or flat is acquired. In addition to the matters covered in this chapter, reference should be made to Ch.4, which deals with the legal status of parties involved in the construction industry. These may also embody a special type of contract; for example, that between a company and its members or directors, and between the partners of a firm. Chapter 9 should be consulted for the special features of building and engineering contracts.

SALE OF GOODS

Contracts for the sale of goods are governed by the Sale of Goods Act 1979. This field covers a multitude of transactions ranging from retail purchases in shops to the sale of articles of great value or rarity, and may include contracts under which the goods are to be specially made. The Act does not apply, inter alia, to contracts which are in substance to carry out work or which relate to hire-purchase, or the sale of land or "things in action" such as shares or debts. The law applicable to transactions which involve "sale" of articles under a contract which also includes work or design, is considered at the end of this section.

The Act does not displace the ordinary principles of the law of contract except where they are inconsistent with its provisions. Thus, the formation of contract and the effects of misrepresentation and mistake are the same as for any other contract. The Sale of Goods Act is a codification of the common law, so that its principles can apply outside the limited sphere to which the Act strictly applies. The most important part of the Sale of Goods Act lays down a series of terms which, unless excluded or modified, are to be implied into all contracts to which the Act applies. These consist of four terms relating to description and quality and one relating to title. This legislation was originally contained in the Sale of Goods Act 1893, which was amended and is now consolidated in the Act of 1979, which has itself recently been amended by the Sale and Supply of Goods Act 1994.

Implied terms as to quality

Where there is a contract for sale of goods by description, (which is invariably the case when required for construction work) the goods must correspond with their description. Also, if the sale is by sample as well as by description, it is not sufficient if the goods correspond only with the sample; they must also correspond with the description (s.13). Even a small deviation from description, (providing it is not de minimis), will constitute a breach of the term. Where any variation can be permitted a specific tolerance should therefore be stated. Description may extend not only to the goods but also to their packing (see below).

Where there is a sale by sample, the bulk of the goods must correspond with the sample in quality, and the goods must also be free from defects which would not be apparent on reasonable examination (s.15). The use of a sample does not therefore protect the seller from latent defects in the goods. Sections 13 and 15 apply to all contracts of sale, but s.14 (below) applies only to sales which are made in the normal course of business by a dealer. Thus, in private sales, the only terms to be implied are those relating to correspondence with description and with sample. Dealers are additionally bound by two important terms which relate to fitness for purpose and to quality.

If a dealer is expressly or impliedly told of any particular purpose for which the goods are wanted, they must be reasonably fit for that purpose (s.14(3)). However, such an obligation is not to be implied where the circumstances show that the buyer does not rely, or that it is unreasonable for them to rely, on the seller's skill and judgment. Fitness for purpose may extend to the container as well as the goods. Where the condition applies, the dealer's liability is strict. It is no defence that all reasonable care was taken if the goods are still unfit.

In addition to being fit for their purpose, the goods purchased from a dealer must be of satisfactory quality (s.14(2)). The buyer is under no duty to examine the goods, but if they do so the dealer is not liable for defects which that examination ought to have revealed. Nor are they liable for defects drawn to the buyer's attention before the contract is made. Goods are of satisfactory quality if they meet the standard that a reasonable person would regard as satisfactory, having regard, inter alia, to their description and price (s.14(6)).

The type of defect which can render goods of unsatisfactory quality or unfit for their purpose will generally be a more substantial defect than is necessary for a breach of ss.13 or 15. However, the fact that goods are substantially defective does not mean there must be a breach of both ss.14(3) and 14(2). In the *Hardwick Game Farm* case,[1] feeding stuff was supplied to the plaintiffs who bred pheasants. It contained a substance which killed the pheasants. When the supplier sought an indemnity from his supplier it was held that there was a breach of s.14(3) as the goods were unfit for their particular purpose. However, the evidence established that the contaminated feeding stuff was acceptable for the manufacture of cattle foods, and consequently it was held that there was no breach of s.14(2) of the Act.

The law dealing with quality has been further codified and amended by the Sale and Supply of Goods Act 1994. This inserts into s.14 the following further rules:

"(2A) ... goods are of satisfactory quality if they meet the standard that a reasonable person would regard as satisfactory, taking account of any description of the goods, the price (if relevant) and all other relevant circumstances.

(2B) ... the quality of goods includes their state and condition and the following (among others) are in appropriate cases aspects of the quality of goods—

(a) fitness for all the purposes for which goods of the kind in question are commonly supplied;
(b) appearance and finish;
(c) freedom from minor defects;
(d) safety, and
(e) durability."

Right to sell

In any sale, unless a different intention is shown, the seller must always have a right to sell the goods at the time of sale (s.12). The right to sell applies usually to the ability to pass title to the goods, but it may also cover other matters which affect the right to deal in the goods. In the

---

[1] *Hardwick Game Farm v Suffolk Agricultural and Poultry Producers' Association* [1969] 2 A.C. 31.

case of *Niblett v Confectioners' Materials*,[2] the contract was for the supply of tins of condensed milk. Some of the cases supplied were labelled "Nissly Brand," which was considered to be an infringement of the "Nestle" trade mark, and as a result the purchasers were forced to resell the goods unlabelled. Scrutton L.J. held, in the Court of Appeal:

"The respondents impliedly warranted that they had then a right to sell (the goods). In fact they could have been restrained by injunction from selling them, because they were infringing the right of third persons. If a vendor can be stopped by proceed of law from selling, he has not the right to sell. Therefore the purchasers . . . have made out a cause of action for breach of section 12."

The more usual application of the section is where the seller cannot pass title, for example because they hold the goods on hire purchase. Where there is a breach of the section, the buyer can recover the whole price even though they may have used the goods.

Formerly, all the implied conditions described above could, in principle, be excluded from the contract of sale by an appropriately worded clause and this was frequently done. The situation now is that any clause excluding or restricting the operation of ss.13, 14 or 15 of the Act is void in the case of a consumer sale, and in any other case, unenforceable so far as it is not fair or reasonable. An exclusion or restriction of s.12 is void. These provisions are now contained in the Unfair Contract Terms Act 1977, which also applies the same principles to other types of contract (see Ch.6).

Other rights and remedies

Remedies of the buyer under the Sale of Goods Act for breach of contract depend on whether the term "broken" is a condition or as a warranty. Breach of a condition gives the buyer a right to reject the goods and treat the contract as at an end, and to sue for damages. Breach of a warranty gives only a right to damages, and the buyer remains liable for the price. The five implied terms set out above are stated in the Act to be conditions so that a breach of any one of them, subject to any exclusion clause, gives the buyer a right to reject the goods. Time of delivery is often made a "condition" so that the buyer may refuse delivery and cancel the contract if the goods are not delivered on time. The expression "time to be of the essence" is often used to establish the right of rejection. It needs to be emphasised that these principles are exclusive to contracts of sale.

[2] [1921] 3 K.B. 387.

Contracts for work and materials

Contracts for the sale of goods are essentially simple transactions, compared to construction contracts. The subject matter of a "sale" is usually ascertained at the date of the contract, and compliance with the terms of the contract can be ascertained with reasonable certainty. Thus, it has been possible for the law to prescribe simple direct sanctions, such as the right of rejection and cancellation of the contract. In contracts where the supplier also carries out work as part of the obligation, the situation is more complex. It may not be possible to discover whether the goods conform to the contract until the work has been carried out, so that the supplier has virtually performed their obligations. Where the contract concerns construction work on the purchaser's land, the goods become fixed and simple rejection is no longer possible. In these circumstances it is necessary to revert to common law principles which underlie the Sale of Goods Act. Since the Act codified the common law in regard to particular types of contract, it follows that contracts outside the ambit of the Act continue to be governed by the same principles.

One of the leading cases concerned a contract for making false teeth. In *Samuels v Davis*[3] the plaintiff alleged that the goods were not reasonably fit for their purpose. It was argued for the dentist, the defendant, that the Sale of Goods Act did not apply, and the defendant's obligation was only to use materials of good quality and reasonable skill and care. The judge at first instance had acquitted the defendant of negligence. In the Court of Appeal, Scott L.J. said:

> "In my view, it is a matter of legal indifference whether the contract was one for the sale of goods or one for services to do work and supply materials. In either case, the contract must necessarily, by reason of the relationship between the parties and the purpose for which the contract was entered into, import a term that, given reasonable co-operation by the patient, the dentist would achieve reasonable success in his work."

A similar point arose in relation to construction work in *Young & Marten v McManus Childs*,[4] where roofing tiles were purchased by a subcontractor and installed during the construction of a number of houses. The question then arose as to whether the main contractor was responsible for latent manufacturing defects in the tiles. In the House of Lords, Lord Wilberforce considered the question of the application of warranties in the main contract:

[3] [1943] 1 K.B. 526.
[4] [1969] 1 A.C. 454.

"Before the Sale of Goods Act 1893, the courts had to consider questions of implied warranty under the common law and they did so, both in relation to sales, and to analogous contracts, not strictly or at least not purely sales, in precisely the same way. Their conclusions as to sales were taken into the Act, but the pre-existing principles remained and continued to be applied ... since the Sale of Goods Act 1893, it has been fully accepted by the courts that suitable warranties, adapted to the nature of the contract, ought to be applied in contracts where there are mixed elements of supply of goods and work to be done."

The Supply of Goods and Services Act 1982 has codified this further area of common law, by analogy with the Sale of Goods Act. The Act creates implied terms, inter alia, of quality and fitness for purpose in a variety of contracts which involve the transfer of property in goods. The 1982 Act has not, it appears, brought about any substantive change in those areas which were previously covered by the common law. In regard to quality, therefore, the Acts of 1979 and 1982, and the underlying common law, may be seen as achieving the same result, overlapping in many cases. In addition, where materials are supplied as part of a contract to carry out work on a dwelling, the Defective Premises Act 1972 requires the supply of "proper materials" and that the work be carried out so that the dwelling will be fit for habitation when completed. The purchaser thus has a further alternative in the event of complaint.

Property in goods

It may be important to decide precisely when property in goods passes from seller to buyer if, for example, the goods are damaged or stolen, or one party becomes insolvent before physical delivery of the goods. No property can pass until the goods are ascertained, such as, by separating the number to be sold from a bulk. Once the goods are ascertained or specified, the property passes when the parties intend it to pass. However, if no intention is expressed or implied, the Sale of Goods Act defines when the property is to pass. In the simplest case where the sale is unconditional and the goods are in a deliverable state, property passes when the contract is made (ss.17 and 18). Unless otherwise agreed, risk passes with the property. Thus, if a contract is made to sell specific goods and delivery is to be suspended until payment, then the risk passes to the buyer on making the contract. If the goods are damaged or destroyed before delivery, the buyer remains liable for the price.

In building and engineering contracts these problems can occur under supply sub-contracts. The construction industry operates on credit. Suppliers have naturally tried to retain some security over their goods until they are paid for. In *Aluminium Industrie v Romalpa*[5] the Court of Appeal upheld a clause which prevented the passing of property in goods until paid for. The argument in this case was as to the effect of the clause, where the goods had been used in the defendant's manufacturing processes, and then sold on to third parties. The Court of Appeal held that there was no objection to the creation, as between seller and buyer, of a fiduciary relationship which entitled the unpaid seller to claim the proceeds of sale, despite the insolvency of the buyer. The effect of the clause was to place the buyer in the position of an agent. Roskill L.J. said:

> "If an agent lawfully sells his principal's goods, he stands in a fiduciary relationship to his principal and remains accountable to his principal for those goods and their proceeds. A bailee is in like position in relation to his bailor's goods. What, then, is there here to relieve the defendants from their obligation to account to the plaintiffs for those goods of the plaintiffs which they lawfully sell to sub-purchasers?"

Since this decision, many contracts of sale have incorporated so-called Romalpa clauses to seek to protect the unpaid seller. The ICE conditions stipulate the opposite effect, namely that all goods when on the site are deemed to be the property of the employer. This provision may run into difficulties when the property in the goods has never passed to the main contractor, since no-one can pass a better title to goods than they have themselves. There is, however, a further overriding principle that anything attached to land (or to buildings) must belong to the owner of the land. Thus, once goods or materials are built into the works the unpaid seller will be reduced to the rank of an unsecured creditor, whatever their contract says.

AGENCY

Agency is a broad term describing the relationship between two parties whereby one, the agent, acts on behalf of the other, the principal. Common situations when this arises are when a person is appointed to buy or sell goods, or to conduct business on behalf of the principal. Examples of persons who act as agents are brokers, auctioneers, architects and engineers. An agency may be either special, that is limited to a particular transaction, or it may be general. An agent may represent their principal in many different ways. They may conduct legal proceedings,

[5] [1976] 1 W.L.R. 676.

or even commit a tort on behalf of their principal. This section addresses the ways in which an agent may affect the contractual position of their principal.

When an agent acting on behalf of their principal makes a contract with a third party the usual result is that the agent drops out, leaving the contract enforceable only between the principal and the third party. Agency is thus a substantial exception to the rule of privity of contract. There may be two or three distinct contracts involved in an agency transaction. First, there is the relationship between principal and agent creating the agency. Secondly, there is the contract with the third party which the agent makes on behalf of the principal. There may also be an implied promise by the agent to the third party that they have authority to contract for the principal. This may be called a warranty of authority.

Formation of agency

An agency may arise under a contract, whereby the agent is appointed by their principal to carry out certain duties. Engineers and architects are frequently so appointed to act for promoters of building schemes. The appointment may be to act expressly on behalf of the employer, as when the engineer is appointed to administer the performance of a contract. An agency may also arise where the engineer is appointed to carry out design work. This may involve acting on behalf of the client, for example, dealing with the planning authority, the public health inspector and with other public bodies. An agency may also arise without an express appointment but by virtue of the relationship between the parties in question. A director of a company or a partner of a firm may hold such an agency.

An agency may also arise without actual authority. If the principal acts so as to clothe a person with ostensible authority, the principal will be bound by acts within such authority. An estate agent who is expressly instructed to find a purchaser may have ostensible authority to accept a deposit. If this is so and the agent defaults, the principal will be liable for repayment. An agency may also arise when it becomes an urgent necessity to perform some action on behalf of another person whose instructions cannot be obtained. This may apply where a person is in charge of goods which are in danger of perishing. In such a situation the person in charge may lawfully sell the goods on behalf of the owner. If a person without authority purports to act as agent for an identified principal, that principal may within a reasonable time ratify the agent's act and become bound by it. Ratification of a contract relates back to the date when the agent purported to make it. However, the principal must be competent to make the contract both at the date of the agent's act and at the date of ratification.

However the agency is formed, there will be some express authority to act. In addition, the agent will have an implied authority to do such things as are reasonably incidental to their express powers. This authority will also bind the principal. Where there is a limitation upon the authority of the agent it is a matter for the principal to give notice of this as is commonly the case under construction contracts where the consent of the employer is needed, for example, to agree to a variation.

Rights of parties

The position of the third party, that is, the person with whom the agent makes the contract, depends crucially upon whether the third party knows that they are dealing with an agent. If an agent with authority discloses their agency, the third party can in general sue and be sued by only the principal. But if the agent does not disclose their agency, either the agent or the undisclosed principal can sue on the contract. Similarly, the third party, after discovering the agency, may choose whether to sue the principal or the agent on the contract. But their choice is binding, and if a judgment obtained against one is unsatisfied, they cannot afterwards sue the other. These rules will apply to a person dealing with an individual builder who is in fact acting on behalf of a company: either the individual or the company may sue for payment, and the client has the option of suing either of them if they are dissatisfied with the work, but they cannot proceed against both.

Where an agent acts without authority, or in excess of their actual or implied authority, the principal will be bound only if they created ostensible authority or if they ratify the contract. Otherwise the agent will be liable to the third party, not on the contract which they have purported to make (which is of no effect) but for breach of warranty of authority. The agent is so liable whether they have acted fraudulently or innocently.

An agent properly appointed is entitled to an indemnity against liabilities properly incurred. They have a lien over the principal's goods in their possession for payment of sums due. If the contract of agency makes no express provision for payment, an agent is entitled to a reasonable fee. It is a matter of construction of the contract of agency when payment becomes due. In the case of an estate agent their commission is usually payable out of the purchase money, so that nothing will be due until the property is sold. If, however, the terms required the estate agent only to produce a ready and willing purchaser, the fee would be payable whether or not the sale took place.

An agent must act honestly and obediently, and exercise reasonable skill and care. The agent must generally carry out the duties entrusted to them. However, there are circumstances in which an agent may delegate. There may be an express or implied agreement to permit delegation; or it may be necessary for the proper performance of the work. In the construction industry, an architect has no power to delegate their duty without express authority. If an architect agrees to design a building but is unable to perform the structural design work, there are two courses open to them. They may request the client to employ a specialist; or they may, while remaining liable to the client, seek advice and assistance. In either event the client will have a remedy for negligent design work: *Moresk Cleaners v Hicks*.[6]

An agent must not take a secret profit from their work, nor must their own interest conflict with their duty to the principal. In *Salford Corp. v Lever*[7] an agent who arranged coal supplies received secret commission from suppliers. The court held that the employer was entitled to recover damages jointly and severally from the agent and from the suppliers, and in addition to recover from the agent the secret commission. Lord Esher said:

> "Hunter [the agent] had received money from the defendant for the performance of a duty which he was bound to perform without any such payment. Nothing could in law be more fraudulent, dangerous or disgraceful and therefore the law has struck at such conduct in this way. It says that, if an agent takes a bribe from a third person, whether he calls it a commission or by any other name, for the performance of a duty which he is bound to perform for his principal, he must give up to his principal whatever he has by reason of the fraud received beyond his due. It is a separate distinct fraud of the agent."

Termination of agency

A contract of agency may be brought to an end by the parties themselves, or by operation of law. Architects and engineers are normally employed, expressly or impliedly, until the completion of the works, although such an appointment may be limited to separate stages of the work and the terms of engagement usually provide for termination. An agency may at any time be terminated by agreement. An agency contract between individuals will be terminated automatically by the death of either party or by the bankruptcy of the principal. It may also be terminated by frustration, such as by destruction of the subject matter, or by the contract becoming illegal.

---

[6] [1966] 2 Lloyd's Rep. 338.
[7] [1891] 1 Q.B. 168.

Architects and engineers as agents

An agency between the promoter of a building scheme and their archi-tect or engineer will arise as soon as there is an appointment to carry out design or investigation work. The extent of the agency will initially be limited, but will be enlarged by subsequent instructions, such as to obtain planning consent and then to obtain tenders for the work. The agency will not normally embrace entering into contracts on behalf of the promoter. Building contracts are almost invariably made directly between the contractor and the promoter. The role of the architect or engineer is usually to represent the interests of the promoter during the course of the works, in addition to their duties as independent certifier under the building contract (see Ch.9).

Architects and engineers are frequently employed under standard conditions of engagement, such as those of the RIBA or the Association of Consulting Engineers. Under such conditions, the work is usually divided into stages, and the authority of the client is necessary before each new stage is commenced. The conditions usually deal expressly with particular duties required to be carried out, such as supervision of the works. However, such appointments rarely deal fully with the authority of the agent, and it is necessary to consider what implied or ostensible authority will exist, where not expressly given.

An express duty to certify payments to the contractor will usually carry with it an implied authority to supervise the works. There is no implied authority to vary the terms of the contract nor to warrant the accuracy of information in the contract documents. There is further no implied authority to order variations or extra works. However, standard building contracts invariably give express powers to the architect or engineer. They will have ostensible authority to exercise such powers under the building contract, unless the contractor has been expressly notified of any limitation of authority. Thus, the employer or promoter will not be able to deny the architect's or engineer's authority when sued by the contractor. Where the architect or engineer is an employee of the promoter their ostensible (or actual) authority is likely to be more exten-sive and may cover negotiation of the contract terms with the builder. This applies particularly to local government officers.[8] This may allow the contractor to sue the employer directly on an oral variation order, if the contract requires an order in writing.

When an architect or engineer negotiates with a nominated sub-contractor they are no longer the agent of the employer, who is not a party to the sub-contract. They must therefore exercise caution when

---

[8] See *Carlton Contractors v Bexley Corp.* (1962) 60 L.G.R. 331.

conducting such negotiations, especially before the appointment of the main contractor, since they may become personally liable for breach of warranty of authority.

The remuneration due to an architect or engineer under standard conditions of engagement is usually based upon a percentage of the cost of the works but subject to other express agreement. One important function of the conditions of engagement is to define with precision the cost upon which the percentage fee is to be calculated. This method of remuneration is somewhat artificial, and often results in payment being made (apparently) for items not carried out by the person receiving payment. An alternative method is to calculate payment on a time basis; this is often used for partial services. Where there is no express agreement as to the means of payment, the engineer or architect will be entitled to a reasonable fee, which may be calculated either by reference to the standard conditions, or to the time spent.

A question which frequently gives rise to disputes is the ownership of work produced by architects and engineers. The formal documents which are prepared for the purposes of a building project, such as the drawings or specification, become the property of the client; but if there is a dispute about payment of fees, the architect or engineer has a lien over such documents in their possession, against the payment of money due. Documents such as working papers, calculations and correspondence, will not become the property of the employer.

Ownership of the designs produced by an engineer or architect is known as copyright. This remains vested in the designer, and may be transferred or sold like other property. The person who employs an architect or engineer has an implied right to make use of the designs produced in constructing the project. But this does not extend to repeating the design. The case of *Meikle v Maufe*[9] concerned the design of premises in Tottenham Court Road for Heals. The original building was designed and built in 1912. Using another architect Heals, in 1935, embarked upon extensions based substantially on the original design. It was held that there was no implied right to reproduce the original design in an extension, and the copyright remained vested in the original architect.

INSURANCE

The nature of a contract of insurance is that the insurer undertakes to make payments to or for the benefit of the assured on the happening of

[9] [1941] 3 All E.R. 144.

some event. The contract may generally be in any form, even oral; but it is usually contained in a document called a policy. The consideration provided by the assured is called the premium.

Insurance and assurance

There are two different types of insurance. Indemnity insurance involves the insurer agreeing to compensate for losses which the assured may suffer in certain events. Non-indemnity insurance provides for the payment of a specified sum on the happening of some event, such as the death of the assured. This is also referred to as assurance. In many ways the two types are governed by the same rules. However, there is an essential difference. On an indemnity insurance the insurer pays out only the actual financial loss. The essence of a non-indemnity policy is that the fixed sum should be paid when the event occurs. Common examples of indemnity policies are fire, motor and third party liability insurance. Non-indemnity policies include life and personal accident insurances. Life Assurance policies are often used as a vehicle for investment, with provision for accumulation and repayment of premiums. The only additional benefit likely under an indemnity policy is a "no claims" bonus.

Insurable interest

An essential feature of practically every insurance contract is that the assured must have an insurable interest. This usually means a foreseeable financial loss or liability resulting from the event insured against. But there is no complete definition. A person has an insurable interest in their own life even though their loss will hardly be a financial one.

A person need not own the thing they seek to insure in order to have an insurable interest. For example a carrier or custodian of goods has a sufficient interest to insure them in their own name. Works under construction may be insured against loss either by the contractor or by the employer, or by both. The parties to an action or arbitration have an insurable interest in the life of the judge or arbitrator, since their death may result in loss of the costs incurred. There are cases in which no insurable interest exists. Thus, in *Macaura v Northern Assurance Co.*[10] the plaintiff, who owned the shares in a timber company, insured the timber in his own name. When the timber was destroyed by fire it was held that he could not recover under the policy. Lord Sumner said of the appellant:

[10] [1925] A.C. 619.

"He owned almost all the shares in the company, and the company owed him a good deal of money, but neither as creditor nor as shareholder could he insure the company's assets. The debt was not exposed to fire nor were the shares, and the fact that he was virtually the company's only creditor, while the timber was its only asset, seems to me to make no difference. He stood in no legal or equitable relation to the timber at all. He had no concern in the subject insured. His relation was to the company, not to its goods."

Insurance is often effected through an agent or broker. Generally, such a person has no authority to make a binding contract on behalf of the insurer. Their duties are limited to issuing and receiving proposals, although a broker may be authorised to issue temporary cover as a separate contract. The broker is, in law, the agent of the assured.

Extent of cover

As the obligation to pay is dependent upon the happening of an event, it is important for any policy to define the time limits between which it is to apply. If the event occurs outside the time limit, for example, if the proposed assured dies before the policy is effected, there can be no liability.

Cover will usually run from the date of the original policy, or from such later date or time as may be specified in the policy. An accident or indemnity policy may be arranged to run for a specified period. Thus, a specific policy covering building works may be expressed to extend to a date which is the anticipated completion date plus a reasonable margin. At the other extreme, a life assurance policy will usually extend during the life of the assured, although such policies may be taken out for a specific and limited period. Most indemnity policies including professional indemnity, are periodic, usually annual. Although such policies have the appearance of being perpetual, the need for annual renewal means that the insurer annually has the opportunity of increasing the premium, of altering the terms of the policy, or of declining to accept a further renewal.

In professional indemnity insurance, it is often important to know in which year a particular claim must be accounted for. In all such policies, the insured is covered not against negligent acts as such, but against claims being made arising from such acts. Consequently, the claim will apply normally during the year in which it is notified to the insurer, irrespective of the fact that the negligent act complained of may have occurred several years earlier. This arrangement is of benefit to the insured person, and to the party making the claim, because they have the advantage of any increased level of cover available under the later policy. There will be a considerable disadvantage, however, to any person who was insured at the time of the event complained of but who ceased to be insured under the policy before the claim was made, for example because they retired from the practice. Such a person will be uninsured against subsequent claims, and must therefore make appropriate arrangements for protection with the remaining partners. A further consequence of annual renewal is that all claims within a particular year must be satisfied out of the indemnity available for that year. Thus, if a professional is insured for £1 million, and three claims arise in the same year for £0.5 million, the liability of the insurer is limited to £1 million, even though there may be no claims at all in the preceeding and succeeding years.

Duty of disclosure

Any insurance contract is said to be uberrimae fidei that is, based upon utmost good faith. Thus, the assured must make full disclosure of every material fact known to them. A fact is material if it would influence the judgment of a prudent insurer. The duty of disclosure continues after filling in the proposal form, up to the making of the contract. Non-disclosure of a material fact makes a policy voidable by the insurer. Thus, in *Roselodge v Castle*[11] diamond merchants had insured their stock without disclosing that their sales manager had a previous conviction for diamond smuggling. It was held that this was a material fact and the policy was therefore voidable. Under a policy which is annually renewable, the duty of disclosure arises upon every renewal. Thus, where a consulting engineer becomes aware of a defect in a structure which could ultimately result in a claim being made, they will be under a duty of disclosure, and failure to bring this to the attention of the insurer may render the next annual policy voidable.

The policy

Policies such as life insurance tend to be neatly printed on thick paper, relatively easy to follow, and of little interest other than financial. Conversely, indemnity policies, particularly annually renewable ones, tend to exist on many different pieces of paper, sometimes physically attached to a standard policy document, and sometimes not. There are often separate endorsements, exclusions and memoranda all of which have to be identified and construed together.

Despite this, there are certain provisions common to most forms of insurance. There must be a definition of the events upon which the

---

[11] [1966] 2 Lloyd's Rep. 113. For a full review of the law on disclosure see *Pan Atlantic v Pine Top* [1995] 1 A.C. 501.

insurer agrees to pay, and this may be accompanied by certain exclusions of liability. In an indemnity policy, such as a house insurance policy, the right to payment will be defined by specifying the property or item insured (such as the house and contents) and the risks insured against (such as fire, flood and subsidence). There may be a term requiring notice of an event which may lead to a claim. Some policies, especially motor insurances, contain an "excess clause" requiring the assured to bear the first £x of any claim. Such a term does not, however, prevent the assured suing the third party to recover the excess. If goods or property are insured for a sum less than their full value, an "average clause" may be inserted to reduce the sum payable by the proportion of their under-insurance. Where there is more than one indemnity policy covering the same risk there may be provisions which prevent full recovery, or even any recovery, on one or other of the policies.

Exclusions

Exclusion clauses are found in most policies, limiting the risk or circumstances in which the insurer becomes liable. For example, the insurance required in respect of the works under the ICE conditions refer to exclusions known as the "excepted risks".[12] These include "any fault defect error or omission in the design of the works (other than a design provided by the contractor pursuant to his obligations under the contract)". The contractor is not responsible for damage due to such cause, and there will be a corresponding exclusion in the insurance policy taken out to cover their liability. It is important that the wording of the policy follows as closely as possible the limitation upon the contractor's liability. Where there is an exclusion in respect of damage due to or caused by a specified risk, the exclusion will apply only where the events excluded are to be regarded as the effective or dominant cause of the loss. Where there are two causes one of which is excluded under the policy, the exclusion will not apply unless the event excluded was the effective or dominant cause. In *Wayne Tank v Employers Liability*[13] the suppliers of equipment to a plasticine factory had been held liable for a fire which destroyed the factory.[14] They now claimed indemnity against their insurer. The insurer, however, relied on an exclusion which provided:

> "the company will not indemnify the insured in respect of liability conse-
> quent upon . . . damage caused by the nature or condition of any goods . . .
> sold or supplied by or on behalf of the insured."

[12] See cll. 20 and 21.
[13] [1974] Q.B. 57.
[14] See *Harbutt's Plasticine v Wayne Tank* [1970] 1 Q.B. 447.

The goods supplied consisted of a pipe intended to carry hot wax, which was unsuitable for that purpose, coupled with a thermostat which did not work. In the result, hot wax escaped and led to the disastrous fire. However, the supplier argued that the cause of the fire was the fact that the factory owner had left the pipe in operation and unattended, before it had been tested. Lord Denning answered the question of causation as follows:

> "I would ask, as a matter of common sense, what was the effective or dominant cause of the fire? To that question I would answer that it was the dangerous installation of a pipe which was likely to melt under heat. It seems to me that the conduct of the man in switching on the heating pipe was just the trigger the precipitating event which brought about the disaster. There would have been no trouble if the system had been properly designed and installed."

The Court of Appeal accordingly held that the cause of the loss fell within the exclusion, and the insurer was not liable.

Rights of parties

Upon the happening of an event insured against, the assured has a right to sue for payment under the policy, irrespective of any rights which may exist against a third party. But under an indemnity policy the sum payable is limited to the actual loss, and subject to any excess clause. The right of the assured is a claim under the contract, and accordingly there can be no claim for losses consequential to the insured risk, unless this loss is itself insured under the policy.

When the insurer pays out on the policy a right of subrogation arises. This is a right to sue, in the name of the assured, any person who could have been sued by the assured in respect of the loss. Thus, a house insurer who has paid out on the policy for a subsidence claim may, in the name of the assured, sue the builder or architect in respect of defective foundations, to recover the sum paid. Where the party insured is legally liable for the loss, the insurer may nevertheless seek, under their right of subrogation, indemnity or contribution from any other party who caused or contributed to the loss. Where insurance of the works under a construction contract is effected in the joint names of two parties, the insurer who pays out to one co-insured party cannot sue the other, who is insured against the loss, as this would lead to circuitry of action.[15]

The attitude of the courts is, therefore, that the existence of insurance policies available to one of the parties, or even to both, is

---

[15] *Petrofina (UK) v Magnaload* (1983) 25 B.L.R. 37.

legally irrelevant. The courts once used to avoid even mentioning insurance, on the basis that it might be seen as prejudicial to a party's case if they were known to be insured. This attitude has now changed, and the availability of insurance is now directly relevant in the application of the Unfair Contract Terms Act. In the case of *Smith v Eric Bush*,[16] a surveyor's negligence case, Lord Griffiths said:

> "There was once a time when it was considered improper even to mention the possible existence of insurance cover in a law suit. Those days are long passed. Everyone knows that all prudent professional men carry insurance, and the availability and cost of insurance must be a relevant factor when considering which of two parties should be required to bear the risk of a loss (under the Unfair Contract Terms Act)."

The assured is under a duty not to prejudice the insurer's right. They must not release a third party from any liability they may be under in respect of the insured loss. Thus, they must not admit the claim, but must preserve the right of the insurer to dispute it. If the insurer pays out a sum on the policy less than the actual loss, and the assured then receives some other payment in respect of the loss, the assured must repay to the insurer anything received in excess of the actual loss.

Third party rights

There is a statutory right by which a third party, who is not a party to the insurance contract, may obtain the benefit of the policy.[17] This applies when the insured person becomes insolvent. If liability is incurred to a third party, either before or after the insolvency, the right against the insurer vests in the third party. The Act imposes duties on the insured person and on the insurer to give information to the third party. Apart from these provisions, the insurer would either escape liability or the insurance money would go to the creditors and not to the injured party. Under a motor insurance policy a third party, having obtained judgment against the assured, may claim against the insurer irrespective of the solvency of the assured.

Insurance in construction projects

There are a variety of provisions and practices in construction work which usually result in there being a considerable variety of policies applying to different aspects of the work, covering different parties and

---

[16] [1990] 1 A.C. 831.
[17] Third Parties (Rights against Insurers) Act 1930.

providing different types of cover. Some of these are compulsory, being required by conditions of contract, while others are discretionary and taken out for the protection of individual parties. The result is often that, when a loss occurs, the disputes between the parties turns into a dispute between those who have insured the parties against their loss or liability. This can have the unintended effect that the parties effectively lose control of the dispute, and the decision whether to fight or settle is that of the insurers. A number of alternatives to this situation have been suggested, which are mentioned below.

Construction contracts invariably make a number of express requirements for insurance. Particular cover required under the JCT and ICE/ICC contracts is dealt with in Chs 11 and 12. In general, construction contracts require two different types of cover. First, insurance is required on the works themselves. The JCT form[18] requires insurance against specified perils only including fire and storm. The JCT form provides, alternatively, for the employer to take these risks, in which case the contractor is not required to insure. Under the ICE/ICC conditions the contractor is required to take out a policy in joint names of the contractor and the employer, in terms stated in the particular contract. The terms[19] require insurance against loss or damage "from whatsoever cause arising" save for the "excepted risks," which include faulty design, war, radioactivity and like perils. The effect of a joint-names policy was considered by the House of Lords in *CRS v Taylor Young Partnership*[20] where the policy was between main and sub-contractor who sought to apportion blame for an insured loss. The House held that the effect of the policy was to exclude the normal rules for compensation for negligence and breach of contract and that the obligation of the insured was to expend the insurance money as dictated by the contract.

The other, separate type of cover, is insurance against third party claims. While insurance of the works is insurance of "property," whether the cover is against all risks or specified perils, third party insurance is against "liability". Thus, the ICE/ICC conditions[21] require the contractor to insure against damage to any property or person arising out of the works; and the JCT contract[22] makes similar provision. One reason for requiring these two types of cover is that, while the contractor (and the employer) have an insurable interest in the works, they have no such interest in third party property, other than through their potential liability for damage to it.

---

[18] Clause 22.
[19] Clause 21.
[20] [2002] 1 W.L.R. 1419.
[21] Clause 23.
[22] Clause 21.

The insurances just mentioned are specific to the contracts in question, although they may be taken out pursuant to standing arrangements with insurers. In addition to these policies, contractors usually maintain a continuing policy covering a variety of matters, called a Contractors' All-Risks (CAR) Policy. The type of cover provided tends to vary, but a CAR policy typically provides some level of cover against liability for design work, for defects in material or workmanship. The usual procedure is for contracts to be noted on the policy, which continues upon annual renewals. The insurances required under construction contracts are usually released at or shortly after completion. The importance of a CAR policy is that it will continue in force, so that claims made, perhaps long after completion, may be covered. In practice, this is often the only cover which the contractor has against latent defects. In addition to a CAR policy, contractors may take out specific insurance to cover particular risks, such as liability to pay liquidated damages.

The other major insurance cover under construction projects, is the professional indemnity (P.I.) cover taken out by engineers and architects. These are continuing annual policies which cover the professional against legal liability, which will usually arise through negligence. P.I. cover operates on a "claims made" basis. That is, each annual policy covers claims arising during the year of its currency. In addition to terms concerning matters such as notification of claims, there will always be a limit of cover, which may be expressed in terms of each claim or the aggregate of claims during the year. This limit will tend to increase with inflation and with expansion of the professional's business, so that the person making the claim will get the advantage of a higher limit being available in subsequent years. The importance of P.I. cover is that, unlike the contractors' policies under the contract, it will continue (subject to renewals) after completion of the project. Thus, in regard to latent defects, the insurance position is often that the professional's P.I. cover is the major insurance available, supplemented by the contractor's CAR policy, if applicable to the claim.

The effect of "liability" insurance is illustrated by the case of *Wimpey Construction v Poole*,[23] where the contractor undertook a design and construct contract for a new anchored quay wall. The wall suffered partial failure which was found to be due to softening of the clay at the toe. The contractor had a P.I. policy which covered claims arising from "any omission error or negligent act in respect of design or specification of work." The contractor carried out remedial work at his own expense and sought to recover the cost from the insurer, contending that it had carried out the design negligently. The commercial court held that the

---

[23] [1984] 2 Lloyd's Rep. 499.

plaintiff had failed to establish his own negligence, but nevertheless, the failure of the design to make sufficient provision for softening of the clay amounted to an omission or error in respect of that design, and was therefore prima facie covered by the policy. For other reasons, the plaintiff failed to recover the bulk of its loss. The case illustrates the legal contortions that may arise from insurance of liability rather than property.

The availability of insurance has no effect on the ability of a claimant to pursue a claim against a defendant who is held liable. In regard to claims against contractors, recovery of an uninsured claim will depend upon the company's assets. As regards professionals trading as partnerships, the individual partners are liable, and any judgment may be enforced against their personal assets, to the extent of bankruptcy proceedings. For this reason, many professional organisations have turned themselves into limited companies, although this does not rule out the possibility of a tort action being brought against individuals. In addition to the contractor and the professional team, sub-contractors and others involved in disputes may have their own insurance arrangements.

The availability of different insurances essentially covering the same type of loss creates procedural problems, as the cover under different policies will overlap. Also, where cover is based on liability, it is necessary to establish that liability before the insurer becomes bound to pay. A number of solutions have been put forward to deal with these problems. As regards the overlapping cover provided during the currency of the contract, it is possible to take out a "project" insurance policy which is designed to supersede all the different levels of cover otherwise provided, in theory at a lower cost. A more difficult problem is that of latent defects, i.e. those appearing after completion. Here, the problem is even more complicated because employers, particularly developers of commercial buildings, will aim to sell or lease the premises at or soon after completion, often on terms which place liability for latent defects on the purchaser or lessee. These arrangements have in past years led to tort claims against designers and contractors by purchasers or lessees. With the demise of tort claims, warranties have been created giving other rights of action. Such complex arrangements inevitably lead to lengthy and costly litigation, in which the damaged owner receives no compensation until the claims are settled or resolved through the courts.

This unsatisfactory state of affairs was considered in a government committee set up through the National Economic Development Office (NEDO), which in 1988 produced the BUILD (Building Users Insurance against Latent Defects) Report. This recommends a new type of insurance based on the French decennial system whereby the owner takes out a policy effective from completion of the work, which insures the property against latent defects. The report recommends surrender of the right of subrogation so that litigation will not automatically follow a claim. Policies of this type are now available and many have been effected. It is to be expected that the insurer will need to be identified at the outset, and will take an active interest in the design and construction of the building, as well as its subsequent maintenance, in order to protect his liability. BUILD policies are recommended to run for 10 years and to be assignable or otherwise to cover the interests of subsequent owners and occupiers. The major limitation on these policies is that cover is usually limited to major elements such as the structure and weathershield.

SALE OF DWELLINGS

The term "dwelling" is used to cover any form of residential accommodation. The purchase of a dwelling may form the most important economic transaction which many individuals enter into during their lives. It may involve complex problems relating to the title of the property sold, and to the means of raising finance. This section is concerned solely with problems relating to the quality of the building and the rights of parties where there is a dispute. It is further limited to the sale of new or recently built dwellings, where the sale is of the land and building together. When builders are employed to build a house on a person's own land, the rights of the owner will be governed primarily by the building contract.

The term "sale" is used here loosely. The essential feature of the transaction is that the property should be transferred or conveyed from vendor to purchaser. In the case of a house this is usually done by a conveyance by which the title of the land is vested in the purchaser. In the case of flats and maisonettes, and sometimes houses also, the vesting of title may be by a lease, usually for a fixed period, often 99 years. In either case all that needs to be transferred is the physical space in which the building stands (or is to stand, if not completed). The sale automatically transfers with the land everything attached to it, including buildings, paths, walls, trees, etc. and also necessary legal rights. The conveyance or lease, however, usually creates no rights in respect of the building itself.

The conveyance or lease is almost invariably preceded by a contract of sale. This needs to be in writing or at least evidenced in writing. The contract may (in addition to the agreement of sale) contain terms relating to the building, such as a condition that the work has been or will be carried out in accordance with an identified plan or specification, or in a good and workmanlike manner. However, contracts of sale are sometimes entirely silent as to the building itself. In the absence of contractual terms, the law was previously expressed by the maxim caveat emptor: let the buyer beware. They had no redress if the building proved to be defective.

Substantially, this remains the law in respect of the sale of old houses. Where the building is new or of recent construction, a number of developments in the law have changed the position radically. In *Hancock v Brazier*[24] the Court of Appeal held a purchaser entitled to damages in respect of defective hardcore which had been incorporated into the foundation of a house before the date of the contract of purchase. Lord Denning summarised the law as follows:

> "When a purchaser buys a house from a builder who contracts to build it, there is a three-fold implication: that the builder will do his work in a good and workmanlike manner; that he will supply good and proper materials; and that it will be reasonably fit for human habitation."

However, this did not protect the purchaser of a completed house, nor subsequent purchasers of newly built houses. An important further measure of protection was introduced by a private body now known as the National House Building Council (NHBC). They publish forms of agreement relating to the quality of the building. They also operate a scheme of registration under which builders and developers must undertake to comply with NHBC Rules and Requirements. This gives a wide measure of protection to the first purchaser, which is also intended to protect subsequent purchasers. The scheme is backed by insurance so that purchasers will have a considerable degree of protection in the event of the vendor's insolvency. But, there remains the possibility of purchasers being unprotected, for example, if necessary notices are not given, or because a subsequent purchaser fails to acquire the right to enforce the agreement. In such cases the purchaser may have further rights under statute.[25]

Defective Premises Act

In 1972 Parliament passed an Act to impose duties on all persons taking on work for or in connection with the provision of dwellings. The Defective Premises Act creates a general duty on such persons to see that the work is done in a workmanlike or professional manner, with proper materials so that the dwelling will be fit for habitation (s.1). The duty

---

[24] [1966] 1 W.L.R. 1317.
[25] See generally *Harrison and ors v Shepherd Homes* [2011] EWHC 1811 (TCC).

applies to builders and to professional persons such as architects. It may be enforced independently of any contract which may exist, by any person acquiring an interest in the dwelling. Purchasers' rights under the Act cannot be excluded by contract (s.6(3)).

The new Act, before it ever came into force, was entirely overshadowed by the sudden introduction of apparently general rights under the law of negligence in respect of defective building works following the decision of the Court of Appeal in *Dutton v Bognor Regis UDC*.[26] While some claims were brought under the Act there was little incentive to do so until the demise of the new tortious rights, beginning with *Peabody v Parkinson*[27] and effectively ending with *D. & F. Estates v Church Commissioners*[28] in which the Defective Premises Act figures as part of the reasoning for rejecting the general availability of tort claims in respect of building defects. Since then, the Act has taken its proper place in establishing effective and transferable rights in respect of the quality of construction work for dwellings. Section 1 of the Act came before the courts in *Miles Charles Thompson v Clive Alexander & Partners*[29] where the plaintiff sued as the owner of three houses built to the design of the defendants, who also supervised the work and accordingly were subject to the duties under s.1 of the Defective Premises Act. The plaintiff claimed that the work was subject to many defects, only some of which were alleged to render the houses unfit for habitation. It was held by H.H. Judge Lewis Q.C. that fitness for habitation was a measure of the standard required in the performance of the duty imposed by s.1 of the Act and accordingly the defects which were alleged only constituted failure to use proper material or failure to carry out work in a workmanlike or professional manner and did not give rise to liability. In *Harrison and others v Shepherd* Homes,[30] Ramsey J. came to the same conclusion as Judge Lewis in *Clive Thompson v Alexander* but nevertheless held that defects in foundations which had caused only cosmetic defects to a house still rendered the house unfit for habitation and therefore in breach of s.1.

The Act creates a special limitation provision under which a cause of action is deemed to accrue at the time of completion of the original work or of any further work done to rectify defects (see Ch.14). It has been suggested that the incidence of quality disputes would be greatly reduced if the Act were extended to cover commercial buildings as well.

[26] [1972] 1 Q.B. 373.
[27] [1985] A.C. 210.
[28] [1989] A.C. 177.
[29] (1992) 59 B.L.R. 77.
[30] [2011] EWHC 1811 (TCC).

Home information pack

In 2007 the sale of most dwellings became subject to a requirement on the vendor to provide a "Home Information Pack" (HIP) pursuant to requirements set out in regulations made under the Housing Act 2004, subsequently amended. The contents of the HIP were to include:

(i) An Energy Performance Certificate or a Predicted Energy Assessment if the property is incomplete.

(ii) A "Sales Statement" giving details of the property interest to be sold.

(iii) A copy of the title documents.

(iv) A search report on the Title.

The Legislation was in force only up to May 2010 and was formally repealed as from 2012. In practice, however, the voluntary use of energy performance data on houses offered for sale continues.

PRIVATE FINANCE INITIATIVE

In 1992 the Government announced its support for a new policy known as the Private Finance Initiative. This involved relaxation of previous finance policy, encouragement of public-private joint ventures, and promotion of opportunities for private sector financing. There is no definition of PFI, which has now extended well beyond construction projects, into the provision of services formerly provided through public finance in many different fields. An early and substantial example of PFI is the cross-channel rail link.

PFI projects usually involve the creation of a special purpose vehicle (SPV) company which is intended to undertake the primary contractual obligation, financed through equity and loans in whatever proportions the promoters may decide. The involvement of government or public authorities is usually limited to the provision of land, with operating agreements under which the project is usually to revert back to public ownership (as in the case of the channel tunnel) but may involve outright sale. PFI is currently utilised for the provision of roads, prisons, hospitals and other capital projects and services. The essence of PFI projects is that they involve long-term operation agreements coupled with construction contracts in which the terms are modified to fit the wider roles being undertaken by the parties. For example, contractors are likely to have a financial interest in the project, and to undertake substantially enhanced risks under the construction contract. They may also be involved in the associated services contracts. Payment provisions will be related to the contractor's overall interest in the project. The design will also play an important role in the overall viability of the project, and its provision is likely to be integrated with the arrangements for financing and constructing the capital works. Certain construction contracts entered into under the Private Finance Initiative are excluded from the operation of the Housing Grants, etc. Act 1996[31] and are thus not required to conform to the payment provisions under the Act, nor to include the right to adjudication.[32]

In the developing world much construction work has been financed by the World Bank which has favoured standard procurement methods using the FIDIC form of contract. In more recent years PFI has become widely used in a variety of forms depending on the particular project. The procurement methods employed are variously known as Build Operate Transfer (BOT), Build Own Operate Transfer (BOOT) and latterly, Design Build Finance Operate (DBFO). Projects vary greatly in their financial and administrative detail, but all involve the provision of capital works financed through external private sources. The promoters are granted leases or licenses to provide and operate the capital works, with the objective of recouping their investment and profit, the works ultimately being transferred to the government or other promoter of the scheme. Such projects have included power stations, hydro-electric schemes and all forms of building and construction throughout the developing world. Typically, the design and construction will be split between the major contractors, who also contribute to the finance through a joint venture agreement.

---

[31] The Construction Contracts (England and Wales) Exclusion Order 1998.
[32] Section 108 of the HGCRA.

CHAPTER 8

DOCUMENTS

In most cases an oral contract is as good as a written contract in the eyes of the law. However, there are obvious practical differences. When parties to an oral contract are in dispute they may disagree over the terms or even as to whether a contract was concluded. Building and engineering contracts are usually put into some recorded form. But many problems can arise, for example, as to whether the documents represent the whole agreement, as to the status of various documents, and as to their true meaning. In terms of construing documents, the problem is usually that they have been drafted for a particular purpose or in particular circumstances and the events which have in fact occurred are not those that were foreseen.

In addition to their construction, written documents can give rise to other problems. One of the parties may claim that a document does not record what was agreed. If this is so they may, in certain circumstances, obtain rectification of the contract through the courts or in an arbitration. If the parties agree that they intended something different from the written agreement, or if they change their intentions, they may themselves alter the contract. It may then be necessary to determine the legal effect of the alterations. These problems are discussed in this chapter.

INTERPRETATION

As a general rule a written document is interpreted as the sole declaration of the parties' intention and it is from the words used that the intention must be discovered. It is therefore important to ensure that what is written truly records what the parties have agreed. One way to do this is to use words and phrases which have acquired accepted meanings through precedent. These may make a contract sound archaic but they are more likely to cover an unexpected situation. This is one advantage of using a standard form of contract. A contract will generally be construed as a whole so that no words can have an absolute meaning out of context. However, the meaning of similar words in another document is often a guide to construction, and previous decisions of the courts on the meaning of the standard forms of contract are treated as binding precedents.

Evidence admissible

The general rule that intention is to be inferred from the words alone has several exceptions, when extrinsic evidence (that is, evidence outside the document) is admissible to interpret the terms. Thus, evidence may be admitted to show the meaning of technical terms or to establish a special trade usage, i.e. that a particular word or phrase has a special meaning and not its ordinary meaning. The principal exception to the general rule is in the admission of evidence to prove surrounding circumstances. The precise extent of this exception may be a matter of dispute, since the "circumstances" relied on by one side may be much wider than the other side is prepared to admit. In the case of *Prenn v Simmonds*[1] the House of Lords considered the amount of evidence admissible to construe a share option, the exercise of which was dependent upon the available profits. The issue was whether "profits" meant the separate profits of one company or the group profits. In giving judgment, Lord Wilberforce observed that there had been prolonged negotiations between solicitors leading ultimately to the ambiguous clause. The judgment continued:

> "The reason for not admitting evidence of these exchanges is not a technical one or even mainly one of convenience . . . it is simply that such evidence is unhelpful. By the nature of things, where negotiations are difficult, the parties' positions with each passing letter, are changing and until a final agreement, though converging, still divergent. It is only the final document which records a concensus. . . . It may be said that previous documents may be looked at to explain the aims of the parties. In a limited sense this is true: the commercial or business object of the transaction, objectively ascertained, may be a surrounding fact. . . . But beyond that it may be difficult to go: it may be a matter of degree or judgement how far one interpretation or another gives effect to a common intention: the parties indeed may be pursuing that intention with differing emphasis and hoping to achieve it to an extent which may differ, and in different ways. The words may, and often do, represent a formula which means different things to each side, yet may be accepted because that is the only way to get 'agreement' and in the hope that disputes will not arise. The only course then can be to try to establish the 'natural' meaning. . . . In my opinion, then, evidence of negotiations, or of the parties intentions, and a fortiori of Dr Simmonds' intentions, ought not to be received, and evidence should be restricted to evidence of the factual background known to the parties at or before the date of the contract, including evidence of the 'genesis' and objectively the 'aim' of the transaction."

[1] [1971] 1 W.L.R. 1381.

As indicated in the passage above, extrinsic evidence to construe a contract is usually limited to the factual background at or before the date of the contract. However, in *Maggs Builders v Marsh*[2] the Court of Appeal found that the subsequent conduct of the parties was admissible to construe a contract which was partly written and partly oral. In *Chartbrook v Persimmon*,[3] the Supreme Court were concerned with the interpretation of a development agreement, either as a matter of construction or alternatively of rectification. It was held that, instead of rectifying the agreement, where a provision made no commercial sense, the Court could correct a mistake by construction, provided the mistake and the correction were clear. While reaffirming the decision in *Prenn v Simmonds*, the court found that evidence of pre-contract negotiations, which were inadmissible for the purpose of construction, could be used to establish a fact relevant to the background known to the parties.

The principles by which contractual documents are construed by the courts were reviewed by Lord Hoffmann in *ICS v West Bromwich Building Society*,[4] where the effect of *Prenn v Simmonds* was described as follows:

> "The result has been, subject to one important exception, to assimilate the way in which such documents are interpreted by judges to the common sense principles by which any serious utterance would be interpreted in ordinary life. Almost all the old intellectual baggage of 'legal' interpretation has been discarded."

The principles of construction were then summarised as follows:

> "(1) Interpretation is the ascertainment of the meaning which the document would convey to a reasonable person having all the background knowledge which would reasonably have been available.
> (2) The phrase 'matrix of fact', if anything, understates what the background may include.
> (3) The law excludes from the admissible background the previous negotiations of the parties.
> (4) The meaning which a document would convey to a reasonable man is not the same thing as the meaning of its words.
> (5) The rule that words should be given their 'natural and ordinary meaning' reflects the common sense proposition that we do not easily accept that people have made linguistic mistakes, particularly in formal documents."

This case has been followed by others laying down further refinements in the process of construction including *Cirius International Insurance v FAI General Insurance*[5] in which Lord Steyn's judgement included:

---

[2] [2006] B.L.R. 395.
[3] [2009] B.L.R. 551.
[4] [1998] 1 W.L.R. 896.
[5] [2004] 1 W.L.R. 3251.

"The aim of the inquiry is not to probe the real intentions of the parties but to ascertain the contextual meaning of the relevant contractual language. The inquiry is objective: the question is what a reasonable person, circumstanced as the actual parties were, would have understood the parties to have meant by the use of specific language. The answer to that question is to be gathered from the text under consideration and its relevant contextual scene."

And in *Chartbrook v Persimmon* Homes,[6] Lord Hoffmann added the following to what he had said in ICS

". . . in some cases the context and background drove a court to the conclusion that 'something must have gone wrong with the language'. In such a case, the law did not require a court to attribute to the parties an intention which a reasonable person would not have understood them to have had."

As a further aid to construction of uncertain terms, the Supreme Court held in *Rainy Sky v Kookmin Bank*,[7] that where two possible interpretations of a contract provision were both arguable, the court would adopt that which consistent with commercial common sense.

However, not all common law jurisdictions adopt the same approach to precisely what is admissible as an aid to construction; and different emphases are to be found in cases from other countries. As an example the courts of Singapore have adopted and approach described as construction according to "context" as opposed to "text" as indicated in the following passage from the Court of Appeal's judgment in *Zurich Insurance (Singapore) v B-Gold Interior Design*[8]:

"While we are aware that the impetus towards the contextual approach is in part due to the Europeanisation of the English common law, this shift also accords with common sense and logic. We also note that in several other common law jurisdictions such as Australia, New Zealand and Hong Kong, the contextual approach now prevails over the traditional approach."[9]

The application of these principles to ambiguities is often difficult. The safer course, when drafting a contract or other document, is to define any terms which may give rise to dispute. This is often done by incorporating a "definitions" clause such as that often found at the beginning of the standard forms of contract.

[6] [2009] UKHL 38.
[7] [2011] 1 W.L.R. 2900.
[8] [2008] 3 S.L.R.(R.) 1029.
[9] For an overview of the current Australian position, see J.J. Spigelman "From text to context: Contemporary contractual interpretation" (2007) 81 A.L.J. 322.

Sometimes the body or operative part of the document is preceded by a recital relating what has led up to executing the document. For example, the JCT forms of contract commence with a number of recitals beginning "Whereas . . ." which give a brief description of the works with the name of the architect and a list of contract drawings. In the absence of doubt as to construction, the body of the document alone is effective. But where there is an ambiguity in the body, the recital, if clear, may give the true meaning. Recitals can also be useful in setting out the surrounding circumstances so as to provide an agreed background for the construction of any phrases which may later appear ambiguous.

Where a contract is partly in a printed standard form and partly in terms specially written, the latter will usually prevail in the event of an inconsistency, on the basis that they represent the parties' true intention, rather than a document which was prepared by others (see Ch.9). Thus, provisions of a standard form may be overridden by an inserted clause, or by a contrary provision in the specification or bill of quantities. This is, however, subject to the terms of the contract itself.[10]

There is a long-standing convention that documents marked "without prejudice" may not be referred to in the context of any subsequent dispute, including a dispute as to the construction of any agreement eventually reached as a result of the negotiations. As an apparent qualification to the long-standing rule the Supreme Court, in *Oceanbulk Shipping v TMT Asia*,[11] held that all negotiations, including those marked without prejudice, were admissible and to be construed according to ordinary principles of interpretation, in order to determine whether the parties had concluded a settlement.

Maxims of interpretation

Where doubt as to the precise meaning of a document remains after allowing for such extrinsic evidence as may be admissible, and after giving due weight to the different parts of the document, there are a number of principles or maxims of interpretation which may assist in arriving at a definite or at least a more probable meaning. They are often quoted in Latin but, for the most part, an English rendering is given here.

   (1) The law prefers a reasonable to an unreasonable meaning. This is part of a wider legal principle by which many things are judged against an objective standard of reasonableness. Thus,

[10] See JCT, cl.2.2.1 and ICE/ICC, cl.5.
[11] [2011] B.L.R. 1.

if a document can be read as having a sensible meaning or an absurd meaning, it will more readily be taken to have the sensible meaning. Further, if there is either a lawful or unlawful meaning, the lawful meaning will usually be adopted.

(2) An erroneous description can be given effect as it should have been stated, provided it is clear what was meant. This maxim can be used to correct an obvious error in a document. It may apply, for example, to the statement of a price in pounds when pence was obviously meant, and vice versa. If there is genuine doubt, however, the contract may have to be enforced as written.

(3) Express mention of some things will exclude others of the same class not mentioned. This may assist where it is not clear what is to be included in a list of items. Thus, a contract to sell a house and a factory with the fixtures of the house will be taken to exclude the fixtures of the factory. Further, a contract to supply and lay bricks and to supply paving slabs would not include laying the paving slabs. Uncertainty of this sort would normally be resolved, in a construction contract, by reference to the standard method of measurement, but even that may contain ambiguities.

(4) The meaning of a doubtful word may be ascertained from the words associated with it. For example, the term "general contractors" might include almost any commercial activity; but in the context "engineers and general contractors" it must be limited to the field of engineering. This is part of a wider rule that words are to be construed in their context, which may include looking at the whole document and the admissible surrounding circumstances.

(5) Where a series of words comprises a class and is followed by general words, the general words cover only things of that class. This is known as the ejusdem generis rule, and an example is probably simpler than a statement of the rule. Thus, the words "iron, steel, brass, lead and other materials" could include copper since the class is one of metals; but stone or wood could not be included. However, if the words had been "... and other materials of whatsoever kind" they would preclude the operation of the rule and include any other materials. Further, a list reading "steel, bricks, plywood and other materials" forms no particular class, so that again the rule is excluded.

Contra proferentum

The words of a document are to be interpreted against the person proffering it. This is perhaps the best known maxim of construction, but it is equally capable of being misunderstood. The simple notion that any uncertainty in a contract is to be resolved against the party who drafted it is wrong and can lead non-legally qualified arbitrators seriously astray. As regards ordinary contractual provisions, contra proferentum has limited application. Whoever is responsible for drafting a contract, it is ordinarily to be construed by balancing all the competing arguments as to its construction and ascertaining the meaning which most fairly represents the presumed mutual intention of the parties. The maxim can be applied in the case of an ambiguity (see below), i.e. where the contract can have two possible meanings. In this event it is permissible (after considering all other means of the construction) to construe the document against the person who drafted the contract (the proferens).[12]

There is a separate application of the maxim in relation to exclusion and similar clauses, which are to be construed against the party seeking to rely on them. In such a case, any uncertainty of construction will be resolved in favour of the party against whom the clause is being applied. As an example, there are a series of cases in which exclusion clauses have been held not to cover negligence where the clause could be construed as covering other events. The same principle is applied to an indemnity clause, which is the obverse of an exemption clause. In the case of *Smith v South Wales Switchgear*[13] 'the plaintiff motor manufacturer employed the defendant, an electrical company, to carry out maintenance work upon the plaintiff's standard conditions of contract, which provided that the defendant should indemnify the plaintiff against "any liability, loss or claim or proceedings whatsoever under statute or common law in respect of personal injury to, or death of any person whomsoever. . . ." One of the defendant's employees suffered injury as a result of the plaintiff's negligence and breach of statutory duty. The plaintiff claimed to be indemnified under its standard conditions. The House of Lords held that the clause did not afford indemnity against the plaintiff's own negligence because there was no express provision, and the clause could not be construed as covering negligence by the plaintiff's own servants. Lord Dilhorne said:

---

[12] See *Chitty on Contracts*, 31st edn (London: Sweet & Maxwell, 2012), Vol.1, paras 12–071, 14–009.
[13] [1978] 1 W.L.R. 165.

"When considering the meaning of such a clause one must, I think, regard it as even more inherently improbable that one party should agree to discharge the liability of the other for acts for which he is responsible. In my opinion, it is the case that the imposition by the proferens on the other party of liability to indemnify him against the consequences of his own negligence must be imposed by very clear words. It cannot be said, in my opinion, that it has been in the present case."

This very strict approach to exemption clauses has been modified by a number of factors. First, the law concerning fundamental breach, much of which involved construing exclusion clauses so as not to cover supposed flagrant breaches of contract, has been transformed by the House of Lords' decision in *Photo Production v Securicor*.[14] Secondly, the advent of a series of statutes culminating in the Unfair Contract Terms Act 1977, which permit the courts to override "unfair" exempting provisions, has removed the need for the application of strained methods of interpretation. Thirdly, the courts have recognised the need to apply less exacting standards where the parties have entered into an arrangement which limits, but does not entirely exclude, the right of the injured party to compensation. Thus, in *Ailsa Craig Fishing v Malvern Fishing*[15] the House of Lords held that a security company was entitled to rely on a clause which clearly limited its liability to £1000 even though it was admitted that the loss had been caused by their negligence. Lord Wilberforce held:

"Whether a clause limiting liability is effective or not is a question of construction of that clause in the context of the contract as a whole. If it is to exclude liability for negligence, it must be most clearly and unambiguously expressed and in such a contract as this must be construed contra proferentum. I do not think that there is any doubt so far. But I venture to add one further qualification, or at least clarification: one must not strive to create ambiguities by strained construction, as I think the appellants have striven to do. The relevant words must be given, if possible, their natural, plain meaning. Clauses of limitation are not regarded by the courts with the same hostility as clauses of exclusion: this is because they must be related to other contractual terms, in particular to the risks to which the defending party may be exposed, the remuneration which he receives and possibly also the opportunity of the other party to insure."

Another example of the application of the contra proferentum maxim in building and engineering contracts, is in the interpretation of the extension of time clauses. These are to be regarded as benefitting the employer,

[14] [1980] A.C. 827.
[15] [1983] 1 W.L.R. 964.

who is, therefore, seen as the proferens, because the clause protects their right to recover liquidated damages.[16]

Mandatory or permissive

Many contract clauses which set out procedures to be adopted employ the words "may" or "shall" or other equivalent words. It is frequent to find them used inconsistently and sometimes it is necessary to conclude that one in fact means the other. Once the meaning of a clause is ascertained, however, it will be clear whether the provision is mandatory (sometimes called "directory"), or whether it is permissive. The difference is important in relation, for example, to the service of notices under a contract which are intended to achieve a particular objective. If this is the exercise of a determination clause, the question will be of vital importance. The contractor may be entitled to determine their employment by notice "by registered post or recorded delivery". Such words are likely to be construed as mandatory and the provision will not be validly operated unless the prescribed notice is given. Conversely a clause reading "notice may be served by post or by actual delivery" would not rule out other equally expeditious means such as delivery by (legible) fax or perhaps email.

Building contracts tend to make excessive use of "shall", sometimes leading to unnecessary dispute as to whether one party is bound to do something which common sense would suggest to be optional. For example cl.51(1) of the ICE conditions states that "the Engineer shall order any variation . . . that is in his opinion necessary for the completion of the work". While this clause can be given a rational meaning, the JCT form does not purport to bind the architect to give any instruction (cl.3.10).

Ambiguity

This is a term which is often used loosely: it is frequently taken to be synonymous with doubt or uncertainty. In law, however, an ambiguity is a provision which has two (or more) possible meanings, which cannot be resolved by application of the normal rules of construction. Much of the law concerning ambiguity relates to wills and trusts, but the same principles apply to any type of written instrument which has to be construed by the courts. Where construction cannot produce an answer, evidence will be admitted going beyond that which is ordinarily admitted to establish surrounding circumstances (see above). An example of this principle

---

[16] *Peak v McKinney* (1969) 1 B.L.R. 111 and see Ch.9.

occurred in a case concerning a will in which the testator left £100 "to my grand-nephew Robert". There was no such grand-nephew, but there were four of other names. Evidence was therefore admitted which showed that the testator in fact thought that one of his grand-nephews, Richard, was called Robert, and he was held entitled to the bequest.[17]

Clause 5 of the ICC conditions refers to "ambiguities or discrepancies" which are to be explained or adjusted by the engineer. Strictly, these two concepts are different: the former implying two (or more) meanings which cannot be resolved, but the latter not necessarily being incapable of resolution by means of construction. The purpose of this provision, clearly, is to permit the work to proceed by resolving "uncertainty" but in regard to the question of payment the difference could be relevant.

Building and engineering contracts, particularly the latter, are not noted for their clarity and consistency of drafting. Problems often arise because "the contract" is contained in several long and complex documents, often written by different persons at different times. In addition, contract documents are often prepared from standard drafts which are adapted to the particular circumstances. These processes can easily lead to inconsistencies appearing between different parts of the contract. In drafting documents, the contents remain only as clear as the thought which went into them. Where uncertainties arise, it may be impossible to ascribe a definite meaning. If not, the parties may be forced to bring the issue before the court or before an arbitrator, as appropriate, for resolution.

Drafting

The opposite process to interpretation is drafting. Logically it precedes interpreting, but if properly done there should be no room for doubt and therefore little which needs to be interpreted. The rules of interpretation must be kept clearly in mind when putting together a document. The draftsman must constantly ask themselves what their words and sentences mean, but with this added fillip: they will ultimately be read by others, who can be relied on to search out any loopholes they may leave. There are no rules or maxims of drafting. The writer must use his common sense and proceed in an orderly way. They may be assisted by the following considerations, the order of which is not significant.

(1)   What is the object of the document? It may be of assistance to set out in a concise form what is to be achieved by the exercise. This may involve selecting key words or phrases to be

---

[17] *Re Ofner* [1909] 1 Ch. 60.

incorporated in the full draft. The object may also be expressed in diagrammatic or symbolic form. For example, a variation of price clause can usually be written as a simple algebraic formula. The many lines of prose needed to express the formula in words are a purely mechanical exercise.

(2) Is the document dependent on other documents? If it is to stand by itself, it will need to contain or incorporate all necessary material; for example, if the document is to constitute an agreement it must encompass the terms agreed and show the assent of the parties. If the document forms part of another, such as an additional term of a contract, it must be drawn so as to effect all necessary alterations or to prevail over any inconsistency. Examples of the care and thoroughness needed to make effective amendments can be seen in statutes which amend earlier Acts, often by way of detailed schedules.

(3) What is the most appropriate form of document? A formal contract may seem appropriate, containing recitals, articles of agreement, standard conditions, special conditions and other incorporated material. But other ends call for simpler means. If notice is required to be given under a contract, one way is to draw up a formal document stating "WHEREAS . . . NOW WE HEREBY, in exercise of the said. . . ." However, it may be equally effective (and clearer) to write: "Dear Sir, We give you notice under clause. . . ." The appropriate form of document is that which will achieve the object with certainty and efficiency.

(4) What form of drafting is called for? Where the brief is to achieve a stated object the draftsman usually has no difficulty and can use formal language including words such as "notwithstanding" to arrive at certainty. However, there may be objection to this approach. First, the document may be the subject of negotiation and compromise. The other party may not accept language which seems heavily weighted against them (consider the drafting of the standard forms of contract). Secondly, the document may need to be expressed in simple, direct language to fulfil its purpose. A form of contract which places duties on a supervising officer does not fulfil its purpose if the supervising officer cannot understand what is required of them without taking legal advice.[18]

---

[18] Consider the JCT form, Ch.12.

(5) What formal requirements are necessary? A contract should incorporate evidence of the parties' agreement to the terms set out. Formal signature and dating are unnecessary but desirable in the interests of clarity. The most important practical consideration is the identity of the contracting party. Where one party uses a trading name, the true identity of the proprietor should be discovered; and where groups of companies are in evidence, their relationship should be ascertained. In case of doubt or suspicion, a clause prohibiting assignment or sub-contracting may be added to the contract.

(6) Good drafting is an amalgam of clarity, style and choice of appropriate language. Its object is to achieve a result, rather than to hold the interest of the reader. Short sentences are clearer than long ones. They can be more easily adapted if provisos or further clauses need to be added. Where there is doubt in the draftsman's mind there are devices which may assist. Thus, where a clause is to be added to an existing document of less than perfect clarity, the draftsman may add words such as: "For the avoidance of doubt it is agreed that . . ." and add for good measure "notwithstanding anything to the contrary."

(7) Care should be taken to use consistent language where a consistent meaning is intended. This may produce a stilted impression, especially when coupled with overuse of "the said . . .", but greater clarity may result. The legal draftsman has one great advantage over the ordinary user of the English language. They can say with conviction: "When I use a word it means just what I choose it to mean, neither more nor less".[19] Thus, documents may expressly define (often in a separate clause) particular words used. This can be a considerable aid to brevity and clarity, provided the defined meaning is adhered to. If it is not, confusion will result. Where the draftsman is in doubt they may take refuge in the formula ". . . save where the context otherwise requires".[20] A good example of the difficulty of assigning a definition is in use of the word "completion". Most forms of contract permit completion to occur in a variety of circumstances such that it is not easy to define the term without the risk of confusion.

---

[19] Humpty Dumpty in Lewis Carroll, *Through the Looking Glass*.
[20] See ICE/ICC conditions, cl.1(1).

Difficulties, both of drafting and interpreting, lead to the frequent use of precedents, whose meaning and effect is reasonably certain. This applies both to individual clauses and to whole documents (such as contracts, leases, notices, pleadings, etc.). This has become even more prevalent since the advent of the word processor. The problem is then to ensure that the various standard and special parts are consistent.

ALTERATION OF TERMS

Rectification

If, by a mistake, a document does not record the true agreement between the parties, the courts have power to rectify or alter the document so as to give effect to the true agreement. There can be no rectification of a mistake in the transaction, but only of the way in which the transaction was put into writing. Rectification is an equitable remedy, and it is therefore not available as of right, but is a matter of discretion. One consequence of this is that rectification will not be granted if relief can be obtained by other means. The court itself will correct an obvious mistake such as a clerical slip or even an erroneous "not," without recourse to formal rectification. Rectification is not a panacea for badly written contracts, and it is a remedy which is only rarely granted in practice.

In a claim for rectification it must be established that the document was intended to carry out the parties' prior agreement, and not to vary it. If the opposing party claims that the prior agreement was intended to be varied by the subsequent document, a heavier burden of proof falls upon the claimant. However, it is not necessary to prove that a prior concluded agreement was reached before drawing up the document. It is sufficient to show that the parties had a continuing common intention, and that the written contract failed to conform to that intention. Usually the mistake to be rectified is one of fact, but it may also be as to the legal effect of the words used.

Generally the mistake must be common to both parties, but in a few situations a unilateral mistake may be rectified. These situations include the case where one party is mistaken but the other is fraudulent, and also where one party is mistaken and the other party knows of their mistake.

Rectification on the ground of unilateral mistake invariably requires proof of dishonesty or at least sharp practice by the other party. In *Roberts v Leicestershire CC*,[21] when a building contractor had tendered

---

[21] [1961] Ch. 555.

to build a school in 18 months, the employer, after accepting the tender, inserted a period of 30 months into the formal contract without the contractor's knowledge. It was held that the employer knew of the contractor's mistaken belief as to the term, and that the contractor was entitled to have the contract rectified by insertion of a completion period of 18 months.

Voluntary variation

This refers only to variations to the terms of a contract and not to variations made pursuant to an express power in the contract, such as the usual provisions for the variation of the work found in building and engineering contracts. An agreement to vary a contract is like any other contract in that it requires either to be for consideration or under seal in order to be binding. A variation may take the form of an alteration of some of the terms of the contract, or its replacement by a new contract, or even its complete discharge. If the original contract is one which is not required to be evidenced in writing, it may be varied by an oral agreement even if the original is in writing or under seal. An example of a variation is where each side surrenders some outstanding obligation. Each surrender constitutes consideration and the agreement will be binding. Thus, if the employer (without express power) wishes to omit a piece of work and the contractor agrees to the omission, the variation is binding and no action will lie for breach of contract by either party.

Where one party has completely performed their obligations under a contract any variation or release of the obligations of the other party will be binding only if made under seal or if the party being released provides some new consideration, since they have no rights under the contract to give up. The consideration may take any form, and what is commonly surrendered is a potential claim. Thus, where a contractor has completed their work and agrees to accept a sum less than the full amount claimed in return for the surrender by the employer of a claim for defects in the work, the agreement is binding provided that the claims on both sides are bona fide, even though in fact not sustainable. Such an arrangement is called an "accord and satisfaction".

Waiver and estoppel

When one party only agrees not to insist on some right under a contract, the other party gives no consideration. Nevertheless, if the other party has acted on the agreement the court may treat it as a binding waiver. Such a waiver remains effective until reasonable notice of withdrawal has been given. A waiver is a principle which parties in litigation frequently seek to rely on. Its effect may be that, where a party has not insisted on their legal rights, they may be unable to claim the benefit retrospectively. In the case of *Rikards v Oppenheim*[22] the defendant ordered a Rolls Royce from the plaintiff, to be completed by a certain date. It was not finished on time, but the defendant continued to press for delivery. Eventually the defendant stated that if the car was not completed by a specified date he would not accept it; the car was not finished in the time. It was held that the defendant had waived the original completion date. Denning L.J. giving judgment in the Court of Appeal went on to hold:

> "It would be most unreasonable if, having been lenient and having waived the initial expressed time, he should thereby have prevented himself from ever thereafter insisting on reasonably quick delivery. In my judgement, he was entitled to give a reasonable notice making time of the essence of the matter. Adequate protection to the suppliers is given by the requirement that the notice should be reasonable."

There are, however, certain rights which, once waived, cannot subsequently be relied on. This applies, for example, to the right to written notice of a claim within a specified period. If oral notice is received within the period and is acted on, the recipient cannot, after expiry of the period, insist on written notice.

A simpler but distinct doctrine which may effectively vary the terms of a contract is estoppel by convention. Where both parties to a transaction act upon an agreed assumption, both may subsequently be precluded from denying the truth of the assumption. This applies both to questions of fact and to the true construction of a contract. In the *Vistafjord* case[23] an agreement for the charter of a cruise ship was negotiated by agents. Both the agents and owners believed that commission was payable under a previous agreement but no such right existed on the true construction of the agreement. It was held that there was an estoppel by convention binding on the owners by which they were bound to pay commission which both sides assumed to be payable. This form of estoppel is to be distinguished from estoppel by representation, by which a party may be prevented from denying the existence of a fact which has been the subject of representation. Estoppel by representation is a rule of evidence but its effect can be the same as a rule of law.

---

[22] [1950] 1 K.B. 616.
[23] *Norwegian American v Paul Mundy* [1988] 2 Lloyd's Rep. 343.

CHAPTER 9

CONSTRUCTION CONTRACTS

The essence of a construction contract is that a contractor agrees to supply work and materials for the erection of defined building or other works for the benefit of the employer. The detailed design of the work to be carried out is often supplied by or on behalf of the employer, but may also be supplied in whole or in part by the contractor. In legal terms there is no difference between a building and an engineering contract, and the term Construction Contract is adopted to cover both. For the first time under English law, the Housing Grants, Construction and Regeneration Act 1996 Pt II includes a definition of "construction contract" (see below). This is solely for the purpose of identifying types of contract to which the Act applies and does not apply. Many of the excluded activities fall within what is ordinarily understood as a construction contract, and will be subject to the general principles discussed in this chapter.

Almost invariably there will be other parties involved with a construction contract in addition to the contractor and the employer. There may be an architect or engineer who provides the design and supervises the work; and there are likely to be sub-contractors employed to carry out parts of the work. The status and capacity of these parties is considered in Ch.4. This chapter deals with those particular areas of the common law which help to define the rights and duties of the parties and which regulate the performance of construction contracts.

The number of statutory provisions which directly affect construction contracts, as opposed to construction operations, is not great. The number of decided cases which apply to construction contracts has grown very considerably on the past two decades. Since the advent of systematic reporting of construction cases (in the *Building Law Reports, Construction Law Reports* and elsewhere) there has accumulated a large number of decisions on the standard forms and on other principles of construction law. But there remain areas in which there is no direct authority. In such situations assistance may be obtained from the standard textbooks, which are often consulted by, and sometimes expressly approved by the courts in deciding new legal points. Reference is also made frequently to foreign decisions, from the Commonwealth and the United States of

America, where direct authority may be found on areas not yet decided under English law.

In Ch.7 a number of special types of contracts are considered. Each of these contracts has its own particular features; for example, a sale of goods is governed by extensive codified statutory provisions. The special nature of construction contracts arises from the form which most contracts take and from features such as the role assigned to the architect or engineer and the provisions for payment as the work proceeds. These matters are dealt with in this chapter. The following chapter covers factors outside the contract itself which affect the parties' rights. The particular provisions of common forms of building and engineering contracts are considered in Chs 11, 12 and 13.

New statutory definition

As noted above, the Housing Grants, etc., Act provides in ss.104 and 105 an extensive but far from comprehensive definition of "construction contract". Thus, drilling for oil or gas, tunnelling generally, plant or steelwork for nuclear processing, power generation, water or effluent treatment, or chemical, oil, gas, steel or food and drink production are excluded; as are the supply (excluding installation) of components, materials, plant and machinery generally. A contract with a residential occupier is also excluded. The Act does, however, include matters not ordinarily considered subject to construction contracts, such an agreement to do architectural, design or surveying work, or an agreement to provide advice on building, engineering, interior or exterior decoration or the laying-out of landscape in relation to construction operations. Further, by additional regulations, particular types of contract are excluded, such as PFI contracts and highway and sewerage works for adoption. Thus, it is necessary to consider carefully whether particular operations are within the Act. The subject matter of some contracts will be partly within the Act. In this case s.104(5) provides *"where agreement relates to construction operations and other matters, this part applies to it only so far as relates to construction operations"*. This provision may create difficulty in relation to the resolution of disputes by adjudication (see Ch.2) or in regard to the right of suspension.[1]

New forms of contract

While the majority of construction work in the United Kingdom and abroad is carried out under conventional arrangements, with a main

---

[1] s.112 and see below.

contractor, sub-contractors and a professional team, a number of alternatives have emerged in recent years. One of the first alternative forms was the "prime cost" contract under which the traditional "contract sum" was replaced by an accounting procedure by which the contractor's actual costs were to be paid, calculated according to fixed rules and usually subject to a guaranteed maximum price, with additional provision for sharing of savings. Such contracts are sometimes called "cost reimbursable" or "target cost" contracts. Next are management contracts, in which the main contractor, while being ostensibly responsible for the whole of the work, undertakes only management. The contractor's legal liability is substantially restricted in regard to the performance of sub-contractors, who normally perform the entirety of the physical work. A feature of both prime cost contracts and management contracts is that the design can be evolved as the work proceeds, with the main contractor participating in or advising on design decisions. A further development from management contracting is "construction management" (sometimes called a project management) in which the work is carried out under a series of direct or trade contracts. The work of the construction manager is limited to managing and co-ordinating these individual direct contracts.

While these arrangements are referred to as "new" forms of contract, they replicate processes well known in the past. Another form of contracting which has been re-cycled in recent years is "design-and-build", sometimes called "turnkey" contracting, whereby the contractor takes responsibility for the detailed design. Many projects today use bespoke forms of contract which make use of several of these new facets of procurement. Thus a particular project may use a target cost arrangement, with the contractor taking full responsibility for the design, with the traditional role of the engineer or architect being replaced by a project manager, designated as the Employer's Representative. The advent of PFI contracting and the many layers of sub-contracting typically involved, has added to the general climate of change. However, despite such changes, the legal principles by which such contracts are governed remain the same as those which apply to conventional contracts. There are a number of initiatives aimed at producing suites of contract documents capable of covering all the different alternative forms of procurement. Notable among these is the New Engineering Contract (now renamed the New Construction Contract) which claims to promote good management and thereby to avoid confrontation and dispute. Use of the new forms, since their first appearance in 1991, has been somewhat limited. They have been employed on a number of high profile projects but have not yet featured in any reported case before the courts.

PERFORMANCE AND PAYMENT

In a construction contract, the contractor undertakes to carry out and complete the defined works, and to provide all things necessary for completion, which may include outstanding design details. The employer's part of the bargain is usually the payment of money. Problems may arise in deciding when the contractor's obligation is discharged, what amount of money is payable and at what date. In each case the answer depends primarily on construction of the contract, since the parties may make whatever contractual arrangements they choose. There are, however, some general principles which may amplify the parties' intentions and it must be remembered that contracts falling within the Housing Grants, etc., Act are subject to a number of significant statutory terms.

Where the contract is to carry out and complete a specific item of work, the general rule is that only complete performance can discharge the contractor's obligation and no payment is due until the work is substantially complete. In *Sumpter v Hedges*[2] a builder contracted to erect two houses and stables on the defendant's land for a lump sum, but abandoned the contract part-completed. It was held that in the absence of entitlement under the contract, the builder was not entitled to further payment for the unfinished work, despite the fact that the employer retained the benefit: A.L. Smith L.J. giving judgment said:

> "The learned Judge had found as a fact that he abandoned the contract. Under such circumstances, what is the building owner to do? He cannot keep the buildings on his land in an unfinished state forever. The law is that, where there is a contract to do work for a lump sum, until the work is completed the price of it cannot be recovered. Therefore the plaintiff could not recover on the original contract. It is suggested, however, that the plaintiff was entitled to recover for the work he did on a quantum meruit but, in order that that may be so, there must be evidence of a fresh contract to pay for the work already done."

The contractor in such a situation is not, however, always without a remedy. They may recover if they can show that completion was prevented by the employer, or that a fresh agreement to pay for the partially completed work is to be implied. In the above case, the builder did succeed in recovering payment for his materials which had been used by the employer, these not being attached and having remained his property (see also Ch.5).

---

[2] [1898] 1 Q.B. 673.

The contract price

Construction contracts usually state a price for which the work is to be completed. This is invariably subject to modification as the work proceeds on account of ordered variations, allowable price fluctuations, re-valuation of prime cost or provisional sums, claims, and other matters. Where the price of the original contract work remains fixed, the contract may be called a "lump sum" contract. But if the original contract work is based on quantities which are to be recalculated when the work is done, the contract is called a "re-measurement" contract. This is so when there is an express right to have the work re-measured; or where the bills are stated to be provisional or approximate. The JCT form of contract is a lump sum contract, whether or not it is based on quantities (see Ch.12). The ICE/ICC form creates a re-measurement contract; this is emphasised by the fact that the stated price of the work is referred to as the "tender total" (see Ch.11). A further term sometimes used is "fixed price." This is generally taken to mean a contract where the sum payable is not adjustable by reason of price increases (fluctuations). The price may, however, be adjustable on many other grounds. Where the employer wishes to know the exact price of the work in advance, none of the common forms of contract are appropriate. While it is possible, an "invariable price" contract would be uneconomic and difficult to draft.

Stage payments

In most construction contracts of any substance there are express provisions for interim or stage payments to be made as the work proceeds. In more traditional contracts the contractor is to be paid the value of the estimated quantities of work done and materials supplied less a retention which the employer holds as security for completion of the works. In such cases the rule of payment on substantial completion (see above) may still apply to each payment, but subject also to the provisions as to certificates. Even where there is no provision for interim payments there may be, in the absence of express provision to the contrary, an implied term for reasonable interim payments as the work proceeds.

Contracts within the Housing Grants Construction and Regeneration Act 1996[3] must provide for stage or other periodic payments, unless the duration of the work is to be less than 45 days.[4] The contract must also provide a mechanism for determining what payments become due and

---

[3] As now amended by the Local Democracy, Economic Development and Construction Act 2009.

[4] s.109(1).

when, and provide a final date for payment. The contract must provide for the giving of notice not later that five days after the payment due date, specifying the sum considered to be due and the basis on which that sum is calculated. Amendments introduced by the Local Democracy, Economic Development and Construction Act 2009[5] (the 2009 Act) now permit the payee to give such notice, if not given by the payer. If the contract does not comply with any of the statutory requirements, the Scheme for Construction Contracts Pt II is to apply[6]. This provides for calculation of instalments by reference to the value of work done and materials supplied, less previous payments. Section 111 of the original Act dealt with the problem of set-off against sums otherwise due to a contractor (or sub-contractor) by requiring the timely service of a "with-holding notice" by the payer, in the absence of which the full sum would be payable on the final date for payment. The 2009 Act replaces this provision with new requirements (contained in the re-drafted s.111) by which the payer must pay the sum which is notified by either the payer or the payee, or, subject to giving notice seven days before the final date for payment, the payer may pay a lesser sum. The objective is to facili-tate cash-flow and to achieve timely payment.[7] Where the sum payable in accordance with s.111 is not paid by the final date for payment, s.112 (as amended) provides for the right to suspend performance[8] of all or any of his obligations under the contract until payment is made, the party in of all or any of his obligations under the contract until payment is made, the party in default being liable to pay the costs of suspension. Section 113 prohibits "pay when paid" clauses except where the person from whom the payer is receiving payment is insolvent (see Ch.10).[9]

Stage payments based on measurement can be regarded as unneces-sarily complex, requiring more or less detailed measurement, usually on a monthly basis. There is usually nothing to prevent the contractor artifi-cially adjusting the rates and prices under the bill to achieve inflated early payments, which also has the effect of reducing the contractor's incentive to complete. It has been suggested (by Latham and others) that a fairer and more efficient system is to agree lump sum instalments in advance, dependent only upon the contractor's rate of progress. Such sums are referred to as "milestone" payments. They are found routinely in construction contracts in the United States of America and elsewhere, where bills of quantities are rarely incorporated into the contract and are

---

[5] Now comprising ss.110, 110A and 110B.
[6] As also amended by the 2009 Act.
[7] For set-off generally, see Ch.2.
[8] See below under "extension of time".
[9] And refer to case of *William Hare v Shepherd Construction* [2010] B.L.R. 358.

becoming increasingly common in large-scale projects, particularly where measurement would be costly and inconvenient.

No price agreed

In most substantial contracts, the sums to become payable are provided for in detail. There are, however, many situations in which sums are to be paid where the contract terms are inapplicable. In an extreme case this may arise from the absence of a contract, or from a contract making no provision for payment. In such case, the contractor is entitled to a reasonable sum (see Ch.5). However, it is frequent to find provisions under the standard forms, where the pricing mechanisms provided, after eliminating various provisions which do not apply (for example, application of contract rates or analogous rates) lead to the conclusion that the contractor is entitled to payment of a sum based on "a fair valuation"[10] or a sum which is "reasonable and proper".[11] There are many similar provisions in the forms. In each such case it is for the court, or arbitrator or adjudicator, to decide a reasonable sum based on: (1) any materials which the contract may require to be taken into account, and (2) such other material as is placed before the tribunal. There are no rules as to what is admissible and what is not. A fair or reasonable price may be based on rates quoted by other contractors for similar work; or on time and materials plus other allowances. A reasonable sum must include both profit and overheads. A claim limited to "cost" will generally include overheads but not profit.[12]

CONTRACT DOCUMENTS

A common feature of most construction contracts is the incorporation of a variety of different types of document. These are not limited to documents expressed in words: drawings appear in most contracts and have to be interpreted and given legal meaning and significance. Typically, a construction contract of any importance will contain a set of conditions of contract, a specification, a bill of quantities, a set of drawings, and other documents of varying sorts. There may also be a separate "agreement" in which the parties formally bind themselves to perform the terms of the contract. The question necessarily arises, how these

[10] ICE/ICC, cl.52(1).
[11] ICE/ICC, cl.52(2).
[12] ICE/ICC, cl.1(5).

documents fit together, which (if any) are to have precedence, and what is to happen if they conflict.

A further related question, is the definition of "the works" to be performed. Is this governed by all the contract documents, or some of them only, or is there an independent definition? These questions need to be addressed to decide, for example, whether particular work constitutes a variation, and whether completion has been achieved. Every contract is different, and the definition of what is to be performed depends upon its particular provisions. However, there are two distinctly different approaches to the question. The first, and simplest, is to make all contract documents of equal weight and significance. This is the solution adopted in the ICE Conditions of Contract (cl.5). The problem that is then thrown up is, what happens in the event of discrepancies? The ICE/ICC conditions provide that these are to be "explained and adjusted" by the engineer, but it is not clear whether, in doing so, the engineer will vary the contract. Another solution sometimes found, is to provide that the contract documents shall have an order of precedence, i.e. a conflicting requirement in two documents is to be resolved in favour of that having the higher priority.

The second solution is adopted in the JCT forms, which typically provide that the quality and quantity of the work to be carried out is that contained in the contract bills (or in the case of a contract without quantities, in the specification).[13] The effect of these provisions is that the bill (or specification) is given a limited function, and may not override the contract conditions. This type of provision has given rise to some unusual results. For example, a sectional completion provision written into the bills is likely to be ineffective if there is no corresponding amendment to the conditions of contract and the appendix. The principle was applied in *English Industrial Estates v Wimpey*,[14] where, under a JCT form of contract, the contract bills provided for the employer to take possession and occupy parts of a factory being constructed by the defendant. But there had been no relevant amendment to the conditions of contract, which laid down a procedure for the employer to take possession of completed parts, and to become responsible for such parts. The employer in fact took over part of the works which were then destroyed by fire. The question arose, who was responsible? The Court of Appeal (relying on clauses equivalent to those given above) held that, despite the provisions in the bill, the contractor remained responsible for the parts taken over, because the procedure under the conditions had not been followed. Stephenson L.J. said:

---

[13] See cll.14.1 and 2.2.1.
[14] [1973] 1 Lloyd's Rep. 118.

"It follows from the literal interpretation of clause 12[15] that the court must disregard—or even reverse—the ordinary and sensible rules of construction and that the first of the documents (the conditions of contract) . . . expressly prevents the court from looking at the second of those documents (the bills) to see what the first of them means. But that is because the second document is . . . a hybrid document and part of it deals with matters which should have been incorporated in the first."

Contract conditions

Most contracts incorporate a set of conditions whose primary purpose is to lay down procedures of general application to a variety of types of work. It is often convenient to use a set of standard conditions, such as those dealt with in more detail in Chs 11, 12 and 13. There is no rule as to what should be included in conditions of contract, but most sets of conditions follow a standard pattern. Typically, conditions deal with:

(1) general obligations to perform the works;

(2) provisions for instructions, including variations;

(3) valuation and payment;

(4) liabilities and insurance;

(5) provisions for quality and inspection;

(6) completion, delay and extensions of time;

(7) role and powers of the certifier or project manager; and

(8) disputes.

One of the main objects of the conditions of contract is to facilitate the efficient control and administration of the work, while at the same time providing certainty so that, for example, queries as to the nature of the work to be done are dealt with timeously. One of the recurrent problems under UK forms of contract is the extent to which the works are fully specified at the outset and the assumptions of the contract in this regard.

Frequently, there are additional conditions variously described as "special conditions" or "conditions of particular application." Such conditions will generally be construed on an equal footing with "general" conditions, but there is a rule of construction that greater weight should be given to conditions which have been particularly drafted against those which are of a standard nature. The principle is sometimes expressed as

[15] Now cl.2.2.1.

"type" prevailing over "print" and it can also be applied to handwriting prevailing over typescript. Lord Denning, giving a dissenting judgment in the *English Industrial Estates* case, above, described the principle thus:

> "In construing this contract we should have regard to provisions C and D (of the bills). They were carefully drafted and inserted in type in the bills of quantities. They were put in specially so as to enable the contractors to make their calculations. It was on the basis of these that the contractors made their tender and the employers accepted it. They were incorporated into the formal contract just as much as the conditions in the RIBA form. In contrast, conditions 12 and 16 were not specially inserted at all. They were two printed conditions in the middle of 23 pages of small print. It was in quite general terms. On settled principles they should have taken second place to the special insertion."

However, the other two Lords Justices did not agree that, by this means, the bills could be allowed to override the conditions. Had it not been for the express provision that the conditions were to prevail, the typed bill would have decided the meaning of the contract.

Specification

This is the document which describes the work to be carried out, often in great technical detail. There are, however, many ways in which work may be specified without such detail. For example, one of the standard specifications used in many parts of the construction industry may be incorporated. There may also be reference to appropriate British standards or codes of practice. Alternatively, the specification may describe the performance required, leaving the details to the contractor. Although in this case if a JCT form of contract is used, a performance specification is in danger of being held ineffective in seeking to override the conditions of contract (see above). This was the case in *Mowlem v British Insulated Callenders*,[16] where the bills required "waterproof concrete". This provision was held insufficient to impose a design liability on the contractor. In a JCT contract without quantities, the specification is the overriding description of the quality and quantity of the work required.

The specification may make requirements for the method of working to be adopted. In such a case, where it has full contractual effect, a change in the specified method may require a variation order, with the contractual consequences that that entails (see below). In a design-and-build contract, the specification acquires particular significance, because

---

[16] (1978) 3 Con. L.R. 64.

it must set out the employer's requirements to which the contractor's design, or detailed design, must comply. There are often additional "contractor's proposals" as submitted with the tender, and these will also need to be incorporated as part of the specification (see below).

Bill of quantities

These documents originated historically as non-contractual measurements, taken off drawings to assist tenderers in quoting lump sum prices. The practice developed for tendering contractors to retain a quantity surveyor to draw up a bill which all tenderers could use as the common basis for their pricing. Bills subsequently acquired another use, namely for assessing interim payments by approximate measure under a lump sum contract. This is today the primary use of bills under a JCT form of contract. Under engineering contracts, conversely, a different practice developed of using the rates quoted, but recalculating (or remeasuring) the actual quantities of work carried out for the purpose of the final payment. A refinement of this process, effectively limited to civil engineering contracts, is the provision for adjustment to the quoted rates, where the actual quantity of any item of work of itself makes the quoted rate unreasonable or inapplicable.[17]

A further refinement in the use of bills of quantities is standardisation of the descriptions of work and of what those descriptions are deemed to include. The applicable rules are set out in a separate document known as a standard method of measurement, separate versions of which exist for different types of work. For JCT contracts, the RICS method is generally used; while ICE/ICC contracts use either the ICE method or, for some government contracts, the method of measurement for road and bridge works. These documents are not part of the contract, but it is provided that the bill of quantities is "deemed to have been prepared in accordance with" the appropriate standard method; and any error or omission in relation to the standard method becomes a "deemed variation" (see Chs 12 and 13).

The substantive effect of the RICS and ICE standard methods may be quite different, reflecting the contrasts between building and civil engineering work. Civil engineering bills tend to be much shorter and often include many complex and difficult operations rolled up into one simply described item. For example, construction of a tunnel may be measured as a single item, per metre of length. Under the RICS method, although the JCT form of contract does not permit or recognise claims for unforeseen ground conditions, the method of measurement requires separate items to be provided for "excavating in rock" and "excavating in running

[17] ICE, cl.56(2).

silt or running sand." Thus, if such material is encountered, and has not been billed, the contractor is entitled to payment for such work as an extra. Under both methods, the normal way of describing work items is in terms of the work or the product, for example concrete or brickwork. An alternative way of producing bills, sometimes used in civil engineering work, is to use "method related" items, which are not to be paid by measured quantity, but by fixed charge or time-related charge.

Drawings

All construction contracts have some drawings. It is usually necessary to distinguish between those which have been incorporated into the contract (the contract drawings) and those which follow, which may be amendments of the contract drawings or further details necessary for the construction of the work. For example, in a contract for the construction of a building with a reinforced concrete frame, the contract drawings may show the dimensions of the structural frame, and the bill of quantities will record the quantities of concrete and reinforcing steel. The details of the design, including drawings showing the placement of reinforcing bars, and bending schedules showing the shapes of individual bars, will usually be issued at a later stage, when the contractor is approaching the point at which these details are required. In practice, this type of detailing will often lead to large numbers of drawings coming into existence after the work has started. This situation sometimes leads to contractors claiming that the details are more complex than had been envisaged or that they are not issued in sufficient time, in either case giving rise to claims for additional payment. Ideally, all drawings and details would be issued at the date of the contract (except in the case of design-and-build, or management contracts).

Drawings often contain notes and other written material, which is to be construed as part of the drawing. Difficult questions of construction can sometimes arise from such notes where they conflict with provisions elsewhere in the bill or in the specification. A particular problem for designers in large complex buildings is the interaction between the different elements of the design, for example, the services and the structure. Modern building services, particularly heating, ventilating and air-conditioning (HVAC), often require the provision of physically large ducts, which may interact with the structure and with other services and components. Design work is often carried out by different specialist teams; for example, HVAC design may be undertaken in part by a prospective nominated sub-contractor. The problems of integration may not always appear until the work is put in hand. These problems are typical of those which give rise to construction disputes.

Method statement

Recently a practice has grown up, particularly under civil engineering contracts, of requiring contractors to specify their intended method of construction. This was originally regarded as affording protection to the employer, by ensuring that they would have the benefit of the contractor's particular method (which could otherwise be changed at the contractor's option). However, in two recent cases, this principle has been applied in reverse, by contractors contending that a specified method has become impossible, leading to a requirement for the engineer to order a variation, so that the employer is required to pay the additional cost of changing the method. In the case of *Yorkshire Water Authority v McAlpine*[18] the contractor gave a method statement, which was approved by the engineer, and incorporated into the contract. The method statement provided for pipe jacking to be carried out working upstream. The contractor maintained that the work was impossible within the meaning of cl.13 of the ICE conditions. It was held that, on the assumption that the work was impossible, the contractor was entitled to a variation order to carry out the work by some other method. This case was followed by the Court of Appeal in *Holland Dredging v Dredging and Construction Co.*,[19] where the plaintiffs were dredging sub-contractors to the defendant, the main contractor, for the construction of a sea outfall pipeline under conditions of contract substantially the same as the ICE fifth edn. The sub-contract incorporated a method statement which defined the area from which material could be excavated for backfilling. There proved to be insufficient material within the specified area, and the plaintiffs incurred extra cost in winning additional material from elsewhere. The Court of Appeal held that the method statement was to be given full weight as a contract document. Purchas L. J. concluded:

> "The occurrence of the shortfall and the consequential necessity to look elsewhere for material necessary to backfill the trench to the pre-existing levels disclosed an omission in the specification and bill, unless it is to be accepted that the sub-contract is impossible to complete on its terms as agreed."

Employers should, therefore, be clear as to the effect of a method statement if they wish to have such a document incorporated into a contract. While these cases were decided under the ICE conditions, the same principles could apply under a JCT or other lump sum contract on the basis

---

[18] (1985) 32 B.L.R. 114.
[19] (1987) 37 B.L.R. 1.

that the bills and other description of the work restrict the means by which the contractor may carry out the work.

Other documents

The contract itself is likely to be formed by signing a specially prepared "form of agreement" or "articles of agreement" which may be provided with the printed form of contract, or drawn up specially. This gives the opportunity of having the contract executed under seal, thereby increasing the limitation period. Another function of a formal contract is to list the contract documents themselves, and this gives the opportunity of including any other documents to be incorporated. Additional documents may include the contractor's tender and correspondence in which the parties have negotiated the final agreement (this may qualify the tender or the conditions of contract). Many contracts contain "conditions of tendering" or like documents which set out matters which may become relevant to contractual disputes. These are usually not incorporated, but each contract depends on its own terms.

A document frequently referred to, but usually not incorporated, is the site investigation or other data concerning soil conditions. These are usually provided for the contractor's information, and frequently contain a statement disclaiming responsibility or requiring the contractor to form their own judgement. Such documents will still be relevant to a claim for unforeseen ground conditions and it is unnecessary for this purpose for the investigation to be a full contract document. Even when incorporated, it usually adds little to the contractor's protection: a typical ground investigation consists of factual statements which are highly specific to the particular probes or tests that have been carried out, and any interpretation that may be offered will be no more than a statement of opinion.

The works

This expression appears in most construction contracts as part of the stated obligation undertaken by the contractor. It is always a matter of construing the contract to discover the meaning of the expression, and whether the term contains the whole of the contractor's obligation. For example, the contractor may be obliged to carry out "the works" as defined, but also be liable for their performance, in which case the contractor will be bound to carry out any other work necessary to comply with such requirements. Each contract depends on its own terms.

Under civil engineering contracts, there is a potentially important distinction between "permanent works" and "temporary works," both expressions being included within the overall term "works." The precise distinction between the two expressions is often unclear, and there may be an overlap, for example, in relation to steel sheet piling intended to facilitate the construction process, which then becomes incorporated and left in as part of the permanent works. The importance of the distinction relates to the placing of responsibilities for different categories of work. Also, under standard methods of measurement, temporary works are not usually included or priced in the bill, unless they are designed by the engineer or are otherwise of sufficient importance to justify inclusion in the bill. Temporary works are not included at all in building contracts, it being assumed that the contractor will carry out all such necessary works within the prices quoted for the measured work.

VARIATIONS

One of the common features of construction contracts is that the design of the work contracted for may require variation as the work proceeds. The magnitude of variations tends to be greater in engineering works, reflecting the greater element of the unknown in such operations. But it is still a rare event for even the smallest of building jobs to be completed exactly according to the original contract provisions. Strictly the contractor is not bound, without express provision, to execute more than the contract work; and the employer will be in breach of contract if they omit a part of the work included in the contract without a contractual provision enabling them to do so. Construction contracts, therefore, provide that the employer (or their agent) may require alterations, additions or omissions to the contract work and bind the contractor to carry them out.[20]

When there has been a departure from the work specified in the contract, it is necessary to decide whether there is, in law, a variation under the contract; if there is a variation, whether the contractor is entitled to be paid extra; and if so, the amount of the extra payment. These questions are considered below.

The contract work

Extra work for which the contractor is prima facie entitled to be paid must constitute something additional to the work contracted for. It is, therefore, necessary to construe the contract to ascertain whether work claimed as extra is covered by the contract. The shorter and simpler the

---

[20] See JCT, cl.3.10; ICE, cl.51.

description of the work to be carried out, the more difficult it will be for the contractor to contend that work is extra. Thus, in a contract to construct "a three bedroom house," the scope for variations may be limited to extra bedrooms. In *Sharpe v San Paulo Railway Co.*[21] the contractor had agreed to build a railway in Brazil between fixed termini for a stated sum. Re-design became necessary as a result of difficulties in completing the work. There was no extra to the contract, and the contractor was entitled to no additional payment. James L.J. said:

> "The (plaintiff) says that the original specification was not sufficient to make a complete railway and that it became obvious that something more would be required to be done in order to make the line. But their business, and what they had contracted to do for a lump sum, was to make the line from terminus to terminus complete, and both these items seem to me to be on the face of them entirely included in the contract. They are not in any sense of the word extra works."

Where the contract is to carry out itemised works without an overall obligation to deliver a finished product, the contractor may then contend that any items omitted from the contract description are extras. In each case, this depends upon the contract documents reasonably interpreted. Many items will be taken as necessarily included even though not specifically mentioned. In *Williams v Fitzmaurice*,[22] where the contract was to build a house for a fixed sum, the specification omitted to mention the floorboards, and the contractor claimed the boards were an extra. It was held that they must be taken to be included. Pollock C.B. said:

> "It is clearly to be inferred from the language of the specification that the plaintiff was to do the flooring, for he was to provide the whole of the material necessary for the completion of the work; and unless it can be supposed that a house is habitable without any flooring, it must be inferred that the flooring was to be supplied by him. In my opinion the flooring of a house cannot be considered an extra any more than the doors or windows."

Where the contractor is obliged to carry out the whole project, they may nevertheless be entitled to payment for additional items under the terms of the contract, as automatic or "deemed" variations. This is usually the case where there is a bill of quantities drawn up by reference to a standard method of measurement. Items which should have been included in the bill, so that they would have been priced by the contractor, are to be paid for as extra work.[23] In addition, under the ICE/ICC conditions, increases

---

[21] (1873) L.R. 8 Ch. App. 597.
[22] (1858) 3 H. & N. 844.
[23] See JCT, cll.14.1, 2.2 and ICE, cl.55(2).

or decreases in the actual quantities of work required are to be treated, for the purpose of payment, as variations (cl.56(2)).

Cost-plus contracts

In addition to these traditional forms of contract, there are many alternative forms where the concept of a "variation" may be of less importance. The simplest type is an agreement to pay the contractor the cost of the work (usually by some specified means of calculation) plus a further sum which may be called profit, overheads, or a fee. The statement of quantities or a contract sum will be of little significance. An example of this type of contract is the JCT Fixed Fee Form of prime cost contract. An alternative form is the "target" contract under which the contractor is paid the cost of the work together with an additional sum which varies according to how close the final cost is to the pre-stated "target." This is intended to give the contractor an incentive to adhere to a particular figure, there being no such incentive under the "fixed fee" form. These contracts, however, tend to become more difficult to operate when made subject to a "cap", beyond which the contractor is to accept all financial liability.

Payment for extras

If the contractor carries out work which is an extra to the contract, they will be able to recover payment for that work only if they can show that the employer is bound under contract to pay. The mere doing of extra work, or doing work in a way different from that specified, does not of itself bind the employer to pay for extras. If the building contract provides for the ordering of and payment for extras, the contractor may claim payment under the contract, provided that any condition precedent to payment is satisfied. Most contracts provide that a written order is necessary. However, there may be an implied promise to pay if an appropriate order is refused. In *Molloy v Leibe*[24] a building contract provided that no payment for extras would be made without a written order, it was held that there was an implied promise to pay for the works if they were extras. Lord Macnaughten held:

> "As Molloy insisted on the works being done, in spite of what the contractor told him, the umpire naturally inferred ... that the employer impliedly promised that the works would be paid for either as included in the contract price or, if he were wrong in his view, by extra payment to be assessed by

[24] (1910) 102 L.T. 616.

the architect. It is difficult to see how the umpire could have drawn any other inference from the facts as found by him without attributing dishonesty to Molloy."

As an alternative, the question whether a variation order should be given for work which the employer insists on having done, will usually be within the powers of an arbitrator appointed under the contract, so that the requirement for an order in writing is a formality only.

If a promise is made to pay for extra works, that promise may be enforceable as a separate contract whether or not the extras are claimable under the construction contract. This will not avail the contractor if the "extras" are in fact no more than they were bound to do under the building contract, since the promise is then unsupported by consideration. But the court took a different view in *William v Roffey*.[25]

Most contracts which make provision for extras also lay down means of valuation and these will determine what the contractor is entitled to be paid. In the absence of such provision, extra work will be paid for at the contract rates or at reasonable rates. In addition, it is common for building contracts to provide for some additional payment (or "claim") if the ordering of variations causes expense beyond the payments allowed. The JCT form allows recovery of loss or expense not recoverable elsewhere in the contract (cl.4.23). The ICE/ICC form permits a refixing of the rates for any items of work in addition to those varied (cl.52(2)). The International (FIDIC) form allows the contractor to recover additional payment if variations exceed 15 per cent of the net contract sum.

Limit of permissible variation

Contracts do not usually place any limit on the permissible extent of variations. The usual provision that no variation is to vitiate (or invalidate) the contract, makes it difficult to imply any limit. However, there must always be some limit to what may be added to a contract. If work exceeding such limit is ordered, the contractor may be entitled to be paid on a quantum meruit basis (see Ch.5). The question of such entitlement arose in the case of *Thorn v London Corporation*.[26] In that case, the Lord Chancellor said:

"Either the additional and varied work which was thus occasioned is the kind of additional and varied work contemplated by the contract, or it is not. If it is the kind of additional or varied work contemplated by the contract, he must be paid for it, and will be paid for it, according to the

---

[25] [1991] 1 Q.B. 1: see Ch.6.
[26] (1876) 1 App. Cas. 120; see Ch.6.

prices regulated by the contract. If, on the other hand, it was additional or varied work, so peculiar, so unexpected, and so different from what any person reckoned or calculated upon, that it is not within the contract at all; then, it appears to me, one of two courses might have been open to him; he might have said: I entirely refuse to go on with the contract—*Non haec in foedera veni*: I never intended to construct this work upon this new and unexpected footing. Or he might have said, I will go on with this, but this is not the kind of extra work contemplated by the contract, and if I do it, I must be paid a *quantum meruit* for it."

This principle was applied in *Blue Circle v Holland Dredging*[27] where it was held, in relation to cl.51 of the ICE Conditions (5th edn) that the construction of an artificial island in Lough Larne, Eire, could not be the subject of a variation order in a contract for dredging the Lough. A further aspect of the limit on what may be ordered applies in the case of omissions. Generally, a power to order a variation will be taken to apply only where the work is not required. In *Commissioner for Roads v Reed & Stuart*[28] the High Court of Australia held that the supply and placing of top soil under a roads contract could not be omitted where the employer intended to have the work performed by others at lower cost.

Responsibility for the site

Contractors sometimes make claims on the basis that the site conditions have turned out to be more difficult than was anticipated. This is not a variation and the contractor is entitled to no extra payment unless they can establish a proper ground to claim for additional payment. The general rule is that, when the contractor has undertaken to carry out and complete the work for a stated price, they are bound to do so, however difficult or expensive the work may prove to be. Thus, in the old case *Bottoms v Mayor of York*[29] the contractor undertook to build sewerage works in unknown ground which turned out to be marshy. He abandoned the works when the engineer refused to authorise additional payment. It was held that since there was no express warranty as to the nature of the site, the contractor was entitled to no additional payment. Lord Esher said:

"In such circumstances, contractors sometimes seek to rely The corporation insisted upon his observing the contract and going on with it. But he resisted and refused to have anything more to do with it. If that be true, he brought himself into a very difficult position, and was not able to enforce

---

[27] 1987 37 B.L.R. 40.
[28] (1974) 12 B.L.R. 55.
[29] (1892) *Hudson's Building Contracts*, 4th edn, Vol.II, p.208.

any payment whatever. . . . I take it that the real reason why he has come to this misfortune, indeed, is that he would go and tender when there was no guarantee given to him as to the kind of soil, and when there was no information given to him as to what the soil was- when there was no contract entered into by the people who asked him to tender as to what the nature of the soil was, and that he either too eagerly or too carelessly tendered and entered into the contract without any such guarantee or representation on their part, and without due examination and enquiry by himself. That is what has produced the difficulty."

In such circumstances, contractors sometimes seek to rely on any instruction or direction which may be given by the engineer or architect.[30] However, an instruction relating to an existing obligation will not entitle the contractor to additional payment.[31] In the case illustrated, the contractor may well have had a claim under the modern version of the ICE/ICC Conditions, for unforeseen conditions. Alternatively, in a number of cases it has been held that employers may have a duty to disclose vital information in their possession where the contractor is unlikely to discover it.[32] In *Bacal Construction v Northampton Development Corp*,[33] where the contractor designed foundations on the basis of ground information supplied by the employer, it was held there was an implied warranty that the ground would accord with the information provided.

CERTIFICATES

A common feature of construction contracts is a provision for an independent third party to issue certificates signifying particular events and usually embodying administrative decisions. The events range from sums becoming due to one party to extensions of time and other matters. A certificate is merely a manifestation of the parties' private agreement and its effect is no more than the parties have agreed it to be. The duty of issuing certificates is usually given to the architect or engineer under the contract, either as a personal appointment or as a firm. In this section such a person is referred to as the certifier. In modern building contracts the role of the certifier is invariably to act impartially between the employer and the contractor. This is distinct from the other role of the engineer or architect as the employer's agent, when they must act as

---

[30] *Simplex Concrete Piles v St Pancras B.C.* (1958) 14 B.L.R. 80.
[31] *Howard de Walden v Costain* (1991) 55 B.L.R. 124.
[32] *Morrison-Knudsen v State of Alaska* (1974) 519P (2d) 834.
[33] (1975) 8 B.L.R. 88.

agent in the best interests of their principal. The role of the certifier was clarified in the case of *Sutcliffe v Thackrah*,[34] where Lord Reid said:

> "The building owner and the contractor make their contract on the understanding that in all such matters the architect will act in a fair and unbiased manner and it must therefore be implicit in the owner's contract with the architect that he shall not only exercise due care and skill but also reach such decisions fairly, holding the balance between his client and the contractor."

The role of the certifier, whether called the engineer, architect, project manager or construction manager, has been clarified in two recent cases from the TCC. First in *Costain v Bechtel*[35] contractors on the CTRL project sought an injunction to restrain alleged improper interference by Bechtel with their employees acting as project managers for the purpose of disallowing contractors' costs in payment certificates under an NEC Contract. While refusing the injunction for other reasons, Jackson J. was not persuaded by Bechtel's argument that there was no duty of impartiality. Secondly, in *Scheldebouw v St James*[36] the same judge dealt with a contract under which the employer proposed to appoint itself as replacement construction manager to exercise certifying functions. The judgment drew a distinction between the "agency function" such as issuing variation instructions and the "decision-making function" such as issuing certificates. It would add an express term in the contract to permit the empoloyer to appoint itself to perform the latter function, given expectation that the role would be performed in an impartial manner.

The function of a certificate is usually to record factual events only. But this frequently involves the certifier forming a judgment or giving an opinion, for example as to the value of work performed or whether it complies with the terms of the contract. In some cases they can impose their own standard, such as where particular items of work are required to be to the "approval" or "satisfaction" of the engineer. These phrases can create difficulty in their application. Depending on the context, the engineer's approval may be to no more effect than that the work complies with the express terms of the contract, but more often it will have the effect of imposing some further unstated requirement. There may also be a dispute as to whether material which has been "approved" can subsequently be rejected for latent defects. Generally such approval does not preclude subsequent rejection.[37]

[34] [1974] A.C. 727.
[35] [2005] EWHC 1018, C.I.L.L. p.2239.
[36] [2006] B.L.R. 113.
[37] But see *Rotherham v Haslam* (1996) C.A. 78 B.L.R. 1.

A certificate may be conclusive as to what it purports to certify. However, most modern construction contracts draw a firm distinction between "interim" and "final" certificates, with the latter only being given qualified finality.[38] What is more difficult is the status of a certificate which is "interim," when the contract provides for no review other than at the end of the contract, for example an interim extension of time.[39] Generally, the certifier will be entitled to exercise the function once only but there may be a right of immediate challenge by adjudication.

A requirement for any certificate is that it must be properly made in order to have effect as provided in the contract. Thus, a certificate which is not in the correct form or which is given by the wrong person is of no effect. Subject to this the courts will uphold the parties' agreement as to the effect of a certificate. Thus under the JCT form the House of Lords have held that the courts are bound by a final certificate which is to be conclusive evidence that the work has been properly carried out. In *Kaye v Hosier & Dickinson*[40] an architect gave his final certificate under a JCT contract during the course of court proceedings concerning defects. The certificate was held to have the effect of preventing the employer from continuing to contend that the work had been executed defectively. Lord Pearson said:

> "The architect's function is not primarily or essentially an arbitral function. The works have to be carried out to his satisfaction, and accordingly he must give or withhold his expression of satisfaction. He may notify defects and require them to be made good. He has to issue certificates showing how much money is owing. Incidentally, his certificates and instructions may resolve some controversial points, and he has to act fairly, but he is not primarily or characteristically adjudicating on disputes. If in a contract such as this the parties agree that the architect's final certificate shall be conclusive evidence of certain matters, I do not think that there is any invasion of the court's jurisdiction or any affront to its dignity. The court's function in a civil case is to adjudicate between the parties, and if they have agreed that a certain certificate shall be conclusive evidence the court can admit the evidence and treat it as conclusive."

It is not a ground of objection to the certifier that they are engaged and paid by the building owner, as is often the case in local authority contracts. Construction contracts, both within the United Kingdom and abroad, have in recent years developed a number of alternatives to the traditional certifier. Some contracts appoint only an "employers'

---

[38] See JCT, cl.30.9. The ICE/ICC final certificate involves no finality.
[39] See ICE, cl.44.
[40] [1972] 1 W.L.R. 146.

representative" who may nevertheless be required to give decisions on matters in dispute between the parties. In the United States of America, many substantial contracts operate without an appointed certifier, leaving matters such as extension of time to settled by agreement. At the same time, particularly in foreign contracts based on the FIDIC form, employers have sometimes sought to appoint themselves as the certifier, effectively creating a right for one party to change the terms of the contract.[41] In the UK and in other countries which have introduced a statutory right to adjudication, certificates, including the failure to issue a certificate in due time, may be the subject of immediate challenge. This right will be limited, however, to challenging the proper exercise of powers contained in the contract.

Types of certificate

Certificates may be of three types. First, interim or progress certificates are those which are issued periodically during the course of the work to signify quantities of work carried out and interim payments due to the contractor. The most usual contractual provision is for a monthly valuation and certificate. Such payments form a vital part of the economics of contracting, sometimes referred to as the "life-blood" of the industry. An interim certificate, properly given, creates a debt due from the employer. In a series of cases, starting with *Dawnays v Minter*,[42] the Court of Appeal held that an interim certificate was payable without set-off, save for liquidated or established claims. This case was disapproved by the House of Lords in *Gilbert Ash v Modern Engineering*,[43] which held that the general right of set-off was available against sums certified in favour of the contractor or a sub-contractor. In this case, the main contractor had refused payment due to a sub-contractor upon an architect's certificate, relying on a cross-claim. Lord Dilhorne held:

> "Consideration of the terms of the main contract leads me to the following conclusions: There is nothing in it to justify the conclusion that it excludes the contractor's right to counter-claim and set-off under the common law and in equity. . . . An interim certificate does not create a debt of a special nature. It is a certificate of the value of work properly executed and it is only for the work properly executed, less any deduction that may properly be made, that the employer has to pay the contractor and the contractor to pay the portion attributed to the sub-contractor. . . . I see no ground for holding that . . . the contractor cannot seek to deduct from the amount claimed from him the amounts bona fide claimed by him from the

---

[41] See *Balfour Beatty v DLLR* (1996) C.I.L.L. 1143.
[42] [1971] 1 W.L.R. 1205.
[43] [1974] A.C. 689.

sub-contractor. Even if the subcontract does not give, as it does, an express right to make such deduction, I can see nothing in it to exclude the contractor's common law and equitable rights to set off and counter-claim."

Thus, where there has been delay or defective work, the employer may generally withhold the amount of their cross-claim from certified sums due to the contractor, and the contractor may similarly withhold from a sub-contractor. The right of set-off, however, is now subject to the additional requirement of timely service of a withholding notice under contracts which fall within the Housing Grants, etc., Act.[44]

A different aspect of "finality" arose in the case of *Lubenham v South Pembroke D.C.*[45] where an architect had wrongly deducted liquidated damages from an interim certificate. The error was patent but the employer refused to pay the difference and the contractor terminated his employment on the grounds of non-payment. The court treated the certificate as effective even though demonstrably wrong. May L.J. delivering the judgment of the court said:

> "We can for our part see no sufficient reason for differentiating as suggested between certificates which contain patent errors and those which contain latent errors. Whatever the cause of the undervaluation, the proper remedy available to the contractor is, in our opinion, to request the architect to make the appropriate adjustment in another certificate, or if he declines to do so, to take the dispute to arbitration under clause 35. In default of arbitration or a new certificate the conditions themselves give the contractor no right to sue for the higher sum. In other words we think that under this form of contract the issue of a certificate is always a condition precedent to the right of the contractor to be paid."

It is clear that such a certificate may be challenged, but only by invoking the available contract machinery, and until revised, the certificate must stand. In *Rupert Morgan Building Services v Jervis*[46] the Court of Appeal held that, in the absence of a withholding notice complying with s.111 of the Housing Grants, etc., Act, the owner had no right to resist payment of an architect's certificate by challenging whether the work covered by the certificate had been properly performed. A case which also turned on the status of certificates in new circumstances was *Reinwood v Brown*[47] in which a contractor had determined his employment under a JCT contract on the ground of non-payment. The payment in question had been properly withheld on the ground of delay, supported by a proper with-holding

[44] Section 111 and see Ch.2.
[45] (1986) 33 B.L.R. 39.
[46] [2004] B.L.R. 18.
[47] [2008] UKHL 12.

notice. Before the payment became due the architect granted a further extension of time, which would have the effect of reducing the damages which the employer could set off. The Court of Appeal and House of Lords held that the subsequent extension did not have the effect of depriving the employer of the right to rely on the original with-holding notice, which was validly given at the time.

The second type of certificate is the final certificate which may be issued after completion of the works. A final certificate may fulfil either or both of two functions. It may state the sum finally due to or from the contractor; and it may certify approval of the works. The final certificate issued under the JCT form (cl.1.10) fulfils both functions. Under the ICE/ICC conditions, the final certificate is merely a document of account (cl.60(4)) and the maintenance certificate signifies final completion of the work (cl.61).

The third type of certificate is that which records some event for the purposes of the contract. Examples of this type are certificates of substantial completion[48] or practical completion[49] of the works; and a certificate of non-completion where the work is delayed.[50] An extension of time given by the architect or engineer, although not so called, has the effect of a certificate.

Recovery without a certificate

There is a substantial amount of case law concerning the recovery of money under construction contracts where no certificate has been given. This situation arises only when, on the construction of the contract, the certificate is a condition precedent to recovery; but in contracts subject to the Housing Grants, etc., Act there may be an immediate claim by adjudication where a certificate is not issued in due time. There are many cases concerning alleged improper conduct by the certifier, for example, by colluding with the client. In such circumstances, the courts have, in a number of judgments, held the certifier to be disqualified so that the contractor was entitled to recover payment in the absence of a certificate. In the leading case of *Panamena Europa v Leyland*[51] the certifier was alleged to have considered extraneous matters before coming to his decision. The certifier insisted upon being satisfied that the work had been done economically, but it was held that the contract limited his function to deciding whether the work was satisfactory. The contractor was

[48] ICE, cl.48.
[49] JCT, cl.2.30.
[50] JCT, cl.2.31.
[51] [1947] A.C. 428.

accordingly entitled to recover payment without the certificate. In giving judgment Lord Thankerton held:

> "[The surveyor] declined to proceed with the matter unless he was provided with the information to which on his erroneous view of the contract he held himself entitled; in this view [the employer] concurred and this position was maintained up to and after the issue of the writ. This means that an illegitimate condition precedent to any consideration of the granting of the certificate was insisted on by [the surveyor] and by [the employer]. It is almost unnecessary to cite authority to establish that such conduct on [the employer's] part absolved [the contractor] from the necessity of obtaining such a certificate and that [the contractor] is entitled to recover the amount claimed in the action. . . . If [the employer] had taken the contrary view of their surveyor's function under clause 7, it would have been their duty to appoint another surveyor to discharge that function."

In most construction contracts the actions and decisions of the certifier are expressly open to challenge by arbitration or litigation, and in contracts under the Housing Grants, etc., Act, also by adjudication. The question of disqualification, therefore, rarely arises today in relation to payment issues. It may continue to be relevant, for example, in relation to a disputed termination based on certificates and decisions rendered by the certifier. A different aspect of certificates and their effect arose in *Henry Boot v Alstom Combined Cycles*[52] where it was contended that the cause of action in respect of unpaid work arose, under the ICE Conditions, when the work was carried out and not when later certified, so that some claims were statute barred. The Cout of Appeal held that the right to payment arose upon the issue of a certificate and not when the work was done. It did not follow, however, that absence of a certificate barred the right to payment since the engineer's decision was open to review by an arbitrator or by the court.

Immunity of certifier

It has long been the law that judges and those performing judicial functions, including arbitrators, are generally immune from actions in negligence. The immunity of arbitrators, except where acting in bad faith, is confirmed under the Arbitration Act 1996 (s.29). In the leading case of *Sutcliffe v Thackrah*[53] the House of Lords ruled that an architect had no such immunity in respect of an interim certificate which including work not properly done. The builder, having been overpaid for the work, became insolvent so that the employer could not recover the loss. In

[52] [2005] B.L.R. 437.
[53] [1974] A.C. 727.

holding the architect liable for negligence, the court found no inconsistency in owing a duty to the employer to act with due care and skill, while being under a duty to hold the balance fairly between his client (the employer) and the contractor. The rule giving immunity applied only where there was a dispute which called for a judicial decision. Such immunity is not confined to formal arbitration proceedings, and might include a person acting as a contractual adjudicator. An adjudicator appointed under the Housing Grants, etc., Act is entitled to contractual immunity.[54]

ENGINEERS AND ARCHITECTS

A particular feature of construction contracts is the position in law of the engineer or architect. This varies according to the function being performed. It is important for them, and for those affected by their decisions, to know their status. The engineer or architect may perform functions as the agent of, or as an independent contractor engaged by the employer, or as an impartial certifier. They may also do things which incur a duty under the law of tort to other persons. The position of the certifier (see above) and the relationship between principal and agent generally (see Ch.7) are considered elsewhere. In this section specific duties and liabilities to the employer and to others are considered. An additional factor to be considered in some construction contracts is the imposition by the employer of constraints upon the exercise of the functions of the certifier. This may take the form of placing limits upon the power to certify, or requiring impartial decisions to be confirmed by the employer. This creates an internal inconsistency in the contract which may result in the contractor no longer being bound to obtain a certificate which the certifier is prevented from giving.

Duties to the employer

The scope of the work normally performed by the engineer or architect may be divided broadly into pre-contract duties and duties which arise under or by virtue of the construction contract. In the pre-contract stage, the duty is to prepare skilful and economic designs for the works, acting as an independent contractor for the employer (unless the designer happens to be the employee of the building owner). When the work is in progress, the duties arising under or by virtue of the contract are likely to

[54] s.108.(4).

include the supervision and administration of the carrying out of the works in the best interests of the employer. Such functions will generally be performed as the agent of the employer. In each case the duty is owed in contract and the common law requires such duties to be exercised, subject to the terms of the contract, with reasonable skill and care. Whether particular conduct will incur liability for any resulting loss depends primarily upon established practice, that is, whether the conduct falls within the range regarded by peers as acceptable. The required standard was laid down in *Bolam v Friern Hospital*,[55] which was a medical negligence case decided by a jury (like many building cases in the USA). The summing up in the case is still regarded as the classic exposition of the appropriate standard of case. McNair J. described the standard as follows:

> "Where you get a situation which involves the use of some special skill or competence, then the test as to whether there has been negligence is not the test of the man on top of the Clapham Omnibus, because he has not got this special skill. The test is the standard of the ordinary skilled man exercising and professing to have that special skill. A man need not possess the highest expert skill; it is well established law that it is sufficient if he exercises the ordinary skill of an ordinary competent man exercising that particular art."

This is ultimately a question (in the absence of a jury) for the judge to decide. But in practice unless the failure is gross and obvious it is necessary to call an expert practising in the same technical field to present evidence as to the accepted practice and as to the breach of duty alleged.[56]

There may be occasions on which the court will find that the parties intended a different standard of duty. Where the engineer or architect is employed by a contractor who is liable for the fitness for purpose of the works, the court may impose a higher duty. In *Greaves Contractors v Baynham Meikle*[57] an engineer was employed in such circumstances to design the structure of a building known to be subject to vibrating loads. The floors were not adequately designed to resist the vibrations. The court accepted that the engineer had not failed to exercise reasonable skill and care, but found there to be an implied term of his engagement that the building would be fit for its purpose. The engineer was therefore held liable. Lord Denning held:

> "The law does not usually imply a warranty that (a professional man) will achieve the desired result, but only a term that he will use reasonable care and skill. The surgeon does not warrant that he will cure the patient. Nor

---

[55] [1957] 1 W.L.R. 582.
[56] See *Lusty v Finsbury Securities* (1991) 58 B.L.R. 66.
[57] [1975] 1 W.L.R. 1095.

does the solicitor warrant that he will win the case. But when a dentist agrees to make a set of false teeth for a patient, there is an implied warranty that they will fit his gums. What then is the position when an architect or an engineer is employed to design a house or a bridge? Is he under an implied warranty that, if the work is carried out to his design, it will be reasonably fit for the purpose? Or is he only under a duty to use reasonable care and skill? This question may require to be answered some day as a matter of law. But in the present case I do not think we need answer it. For the evidence shows that both parties were of one mind on the matter. Their common intention was that the engineer should design a warehouse which would be fit for the purpose for which it was required. That common intention gives rise to a term implied in fact."

This decision has not, been followed in a number of other reported cases where the ordinary duty of a professional person has been re-stated as a duty to use reasonable skill and care.[58] In the recent case of *Platform Funding v Bank of Scotland*,[59] however, the *Greaves* decision was followed in a case where a surveyor, instructed to value a property as security, had mistakenly valued the wrong property. The Court of Appeal, by majority, held the surveyor to be in breach of contract in the absence of negligence.

Design duties

What constitutes reasonable skill and care in the design of work depends upon the circumstances of each case. The duty may normally be discharged by following established practice, but there is no rule that doing what others do cannot give rise to liability. There may be situations where there is no established practice, such as where a new construction technique is used. In such cases the duty of reasonable skill and care may be discharged by taking the best advice available and by warning the employer of any risks involved. In an old case, *Turner v Garland & Christopher*[60] the employer had instructed his architect to use a new patent concrete roofing which proved to be a failure. It was held that where an untried process was used, failure might still be consistent with reasonable skill. This case was also tried with a jury. Earle J. said, in summing up:

"The plaintiff will merit your verdict if the defendant was found to be wanting in the competent skill of an ordinary architect. If he possesses competent skill and was guilty of gross negligence, although of competent skill, he might become liable. If of competent skill, he had paid careful

[58] *George Hawkins v Chrysler* (1986) 38 B.L.R. 36.
[59] [2008] EWCA Civ. 930.
[60] (1853) *Hudson's Building Contracts*, 4th edn, Vol.II, p.1.

attention to what he undertook, he would not be liable. You should bear in mind that if the building is of an ordinary description in which he had had abundance of experience, and it proved a failure, this is an evidence of want of skill or attention. But if out of ordinary course, and you employ him about a novel thing, about which he has had little experience, if it has not had the test of experience, failure may be consistent with skill. The history of all great improvements shows failure of those who embark on them; this may account for the defect of roof."

However, when a novel design is to be undertaken, or where tried and traditional methods are to be superseded by cheaper processes, the risks involved must be brought to the attention of the employer, who is to bear such risk. It is the employer, who must decide the course to adopt, and they must be given all necessary information to enable them to reach a proper and considered decision.

When dealing with the liabilities of the parties and with insurances, the standard forms of contract often refer to loss or damage being caused by the design of the works.[61] Such a criterion does not necessarily coincide with that of whether the designer has exercised sufficient skill and care. In *Queensland Railways v Manufacturers Insurance*[62] a river bridge failed during erection because the piers were subjected to forces beyond those which could be predicted by existing knowledge. It was held that the failure was in fact caused by faulty design, even though there might be no fault attributable to the designer.

Delegation of design

There may be many situations where design work is undertaken by persons other than the engineer or architect named in the building contract. Problems may then arise as to who can be sued for a design defect. If the employer directly employs a consultant, or even the contractor, to do design work, they will have a remedy for design defects, depending upon the terms of the contract. Where the engineer or architect delegates design work, there is no contract between the employer and the designer. As a general rule the engineer or architect will remain liable for the design unless the employer concurs in a delegation of responsibility. Thus, in *Moresk Cleaners v Hicks*[63] an architect delegated the design of a reinforced concrete structure to the contractor. The design proved to be defective and it was held that the architect was liable. The official referee in his judgment said:

---

[61] ICE/ICC, cl.20.
[62] [1969] 1 Lloyd's Rep. 214.
[63] [1966] 2 Lloyd's Rep. 338.

"If the defendant was not able, because this form of reinforced concrete was a comparatively new form of construction, to design it himself, he had three courses open to him. One was to say: 'This is not my field.' The second was to go to the client, the building owner, and say: 'This reinforced concrete is out of my line. I would like you to employ a structural engineer to deal with this aspect of the matter.' Or he can, while retaining responsibility for the design himself seek the advice and assistance of a structural engineer, paying for his service out of his own pocket but having at any rate the satisfaction of knowing that if he acts upon that advice and it turns out to be wrong, the person whom he employed to give the advice will owe the same duty to him as he, the architect, owes to the building owner."

However, delegation may be permissible in the case of specialist processes. In the case of *Merton LBC v Lowe*[64] an architect was held to have a design responsibility in respect of a proprietary plaster system used for a swimming pool ceiling, but was found not to be in breach because he was entitled to rely on the specialist manufacturer's expertise, where details of the design were not revealed. Waller L.J. held:

"It was submitted (by the plaintiffs) that the fact that Pyroc (the sub-contractor) maintained secrecy was immaterial, and reliance was placed on the case of *Moresk Cleaners v Hicks*. I entirely agree with the judgment in that case. There the architect had literally handed over to another the whole task of design. The architect could not escape responsibility for the work which he was supposed to do by handing it over to another. This case was different. Pyroc were nominated sub-contractors employed for a specialist task of making a ceiling with their own proprietary material. It was the defendant's duty to use reasonable care as architects. In view of successful work done elsewhere, they decided that to employ Pyrok was reasonable. No witness called suggested that it was not at the beginning."

The architects were, however, held liable under their general design responsibility, for failing to take adequate steps to remedy the design deficiency which subsequently became apparent.

Direct warranty

If the design work is done by a nominated sub-contractor, the employer may protect themselves by obtaining a direct (or collateral) warranty from the sub-contractor. This constitutes a separate contract under which the sub-contractor warrants their work, usually in consideration of their nomination by the employer. The warranty must be given before the sub-contract is entered into, otherwise there is no consideration and the warranty may be unenforceable. The principle was first applied to a

[64] (1982) 18 B.L.R. 130.

construction contract in *Shanklin Pier v Detel Products*.[65] In this case a supplier stated to the employer that his paint had a life of seven to 10 years. The particular paint was specified by the employer and duly used by the contractor. The paint in fact lasted for about three months. It was held that the statement made concerning the quality of the paint constituted a warranty so that the employer was entitled to damages from the supplier for breach. Payment of a fee will be equally effective as consideration to support any such warranty.

Standard forms of warranty have been issued by the RIBA and now the JCT. The general subject of warranties has become more important since the retrenchment which has occurred in the law of negligence. Developers and purchasers who hitherto relied on tort claims against those with whom they had no contract are now, in general, unable to advance such claims. Lawyers have responded by producing a new generation of assignable warranties intended to replace such rights by creating directly enforceable contractual obligations. No new principle of law is involved in these documents, but the following points should be considered when preparing or giving a warranty:

(1) *Who is to give the warranty?* Frequently warranties are requested from a variety of parties involved in a construction project, sometimes from all parties. Where professional organisations take on work as a partnership or limited company, care should be taken not to allow individuals to sign warranties, so losing any corporate protection.

(2) *Terms of the warranty*: the warranty may be made to cover any part of the work, not limited to that which is the responsibility of the person giving the warranty. The party signing should be careful to understand what they are taking on.

(3) *Standard of duty*: warranties requested from professionals sometimes require a promise that the work will be reasonably fit for its purpose, going beyond the ordinary duty of reasonable skill and care.

(4) *Limitation period*: warranties may be expressed so as to extend the ordinary limitation period in contract, either by requiring the warranty to run for a stated period or by requiring an indemnity.

(5) *Assignment of rights*: warranties frequently provide that the recipient (usually the developer) may assign the warranty or

[65] [1951] 2 K.B. 854.

rights in it to third parties who acquire an interest in the building or works. This is a substantial enlargement of potential responsibility and the terms should be reviewed with care.

(6) *Contribution rights*: a party who gives a warranty has a right to expect that those who may share responsibility for any loss will be capable of being sued for contribution, if also shown to be liable. The most convenient way of ensuring this is to provide that the warranty is not to become effective unless and until other (identified) parties involved in the project have also given similar warranties. In addition it is possible to limit liability to the net amount after deducting contributions owed by others liable for the same loss, where such potential contributors are insolvent.

(7) *Indemnity insurance*: professionals in particular must check with their insurers as to whether they are covered in respect of the wider responsibility created by the warranty; many insurers will not cover duties beyond reasonable skill and care.

(8) *Fee*: there is no reason why the person giving the warranty should not charge a realistic fee, although some developers will offer design commissions only on condition that the professional will agree to give warranties at no additional cost.

(9) *Standard forms*: a number of these have evolved, issued by professional bodies and by insurers. There are, however, many ad hoc forms in circulation, often drafted for individual projects or clients.

The effect of a contractual warranty on a claim in tort was considered in two cases. In *Greater Nottingham Cooperative Society v Cementation Piling & Foundations Ltd*[66] the Court of Appeal held that the taking of a warranty from a sub-contractor covering design but not performance of the work, precluded a duty in tort relating to the performance of the work, on the footing the parties had had the opportunity to create a direct duty and had not done so. Conversely, however, in *Warwick University v McAlpine*[67] Garland J. held that the failure to place any direct duty in contract on a sub-contractor did not prevent the existence of a duty of care in tort. The reduction in the ambit of tort claims makes it unlikely that there will be further developments in this area of the law (see further, Ch.5). It may be noted that the use of warranties has not, as anticipated

[66] [1989] Q.B. 71.
[67] (1988) 42 B.L.R. 1.

by the Law Commission, been replaced by use of the Contracts (Rights of Third Parties) Act 1999, since the UK construction industry has generally adopted the policy of contracting out of the Act (see Ch.6).

Supervision and quality assurance

The purpose of supervision is to ensure that the works are carried out by the contractor in accordance with the requirements of the construction contract; and the engineer or architect must provide reasonable supervision for this purpose. The amount of supervision required depends on the nature of the works. The building of a house may require visits every two weeks; while engineering operations may require constant attention from a resident staff. The duty of supervision was considered in *East Ham v Bernard Sunley*,[68] a case concerning the meaning of "reasonable examination" under the JCT form of contract. Lord Upjohn said:

> "As is well known, the architect is not permanently on the site but appears at intervals, it may be of a week or a fortnight, and he has, of course, to inspect the progress of the work. When he arrives on the site there may be many very important matters with which he has to deal: the work may be getting behind-hand through labour troubles; some of the suppliers of materials or the sub-contractors may be lagging; there may be physical trouble on the site itself, such as, for example, finding an unexpected amount of underground water. All these are matters which may call for important decisions by the architect. He may in such circumstances think that he knows the builder sufficiently well and can trust him to carry out a good job; that it is more important that he should deal with urgent matters on the site than that he should make a minute inspection on the site to see that the builder is complying with the specifications laid down by him. . . . It by no means follows that, in failing to discover a defect which a reasonable examination would have disclosed, in fact the architect was necessarily thereby in breach of his duty to the building owner so as to be liable in an action for negligence. It may well be that the omission of the architect to find the defects was due to no more that an error of judgement, or was a deliberately calculated risk which, in all the circumstances of the case, was reasonable and proper."

But whatever the frequency of inspections, they must be sufficient to check important items, especially those which will be covered up by later work. In the old Scottish case of *Jameson v Simon*[69] the architect had made weekly visits to a house under construction, but failed to inspect the bottoming of the floors, which was defective. He was held liable to the employer for the failure. The Lord Justice Clerk said:

---

[68] [1966] A.C. 406.
[69] (1899) 1 F. 1211.

"There may, of course, be many things which the architect cannot be expected to observe while they are being done-minute matters that nothing that daily or even hourly watching could keep a check upon. But as regards so substantial and important a matter as the bottoming of a cement floor of considerable area, such as this is shown by the plans to have been, I cannot hold that he is not chargeable with negligence if he fails before the bottoming is hid from view by the cement to make sure that unsuitable rubbish of a kind that will rot when covered up with wet cement has not been thrown in quantities as bottoming contrary to the specification."

The whole subject of supervision of building and construction works has been the subject of numerous reports and proposals aimed at introducing procedures based on Quality Assurance and self-supervision. Such arrangements are now regularly required, but in addition to existing contractual obligations. The problem which still confronts the drafters of contracts is to devise appropriate means whereby external supervision and its attendant sanctions is replaced by quality control procedures, involving entirely different sanctions.[70] Such procedures are well known in other industries, including the offshore oil industry, but require further development for land-based construction.

Administration

The term is here used compendiously to describe the various functions which the engineer or architect may or must perform under a construction contract. Administration is part of the duty normally included under the umbrella description "supervision." However, it includes many matters not related directly to superintendence on the site. The most important of these are: issuing certificates and ordering variations, which are considered above; and issuing instructions and drawings. In each case the scope of the particular powers or duties depends on the express or implied terms of the contract.

In the absence of express terms[71] the contractor is entitled to have instructions and drawings supplied in reasonable time. Whether the express or implied obligation has been complied with is often difficult to determine, for example, when instructions are needed to enable a subcontract to be placed so as to permit timely completion. This is often a source of contention between contractor and employer. Under the standard forms the contractor is usually required to give notice of any instruction which they consider to be necessary.

---

[70] See J.N. Barber, *Quality Management in Construction*, S.P. 84 CIRIA (1992).
[71] See ICE, cl.7 and JCT, cl.2.12.

During the course of carrying out construction work the engineer or architect may sometimes issue instructions permitting a deviation from the contract to assist the contractor, when strictly the employer is entitled to rely upon the contract. In such a case the instruction should be carefully distinguished from a true variation order. In *Simplex v St. Pancras B.C.*,[72] the contractor undertook to install piles of specified capacity. This proved impracticable and the contractor offered alternative, differently priced, schemes. The architect accepted one of these "in accordance with quotations submitted." It was held that although the contractor would have been liable for the failure of the first scheme, the architect's acceptance of the alternative amounted to a variation. The contractor was therefore entitled to be paid the price of the alternative scheme and not the (lower) price originally tendered. Edmund-Davies J. held:

> "The architect's letter of 30th July contained an instruction involving a variation in the design or quality (or both design and quality) of the works which the plaintiffs were being instructed to perform, and I have already indicated my view that he did so in circumstances in which he was accepting on the employers' behalf that they would be responsible for the extra cost involved. Such an action fell, in my judgement, within the 'absolute discretion' vested in him by clause 1 and was motivated by his great desire 'to get the job moving' as he put it, and regardless of the legal position of the plaintiffs under their contract. It was an action which led to the plaintiffs doing something different from that which they were obliged to do under their contract, and it was an action which involved the defendants in responsibility for the extra expense which it entailed."

This case has been criticised and was not followed in *Howard de Walden v Costain*.[73] The issue is also dealt with expressly under the ICE conditions, 6th edn, where it is provided as follows:

> "51(3). . . The value (if any) of all such variations shall be taken into account in ascertaining the amount of the Contract Price except to the extent that such variation is necessitated by the Contractor's default."

This provision would not necessarily reverse the effect of the *Simplex* case. The best course is for any instruction for alternative work made necessary by default of the contractor, to be given expressly on the terms that it will not involve additional payment. The instruction should also deal with the impact of any change on timing of the work, since the varied work may still constitute a variation, even though no payment is due.

---

[72] (1958) 14 B.L.R. 80.
[73] (1991) 55 B.L.R. 124.

Quantity surveyors

The duties of a quantity surveyor include taking off quantities from drawings, preparing bills of quantities and measuring the works in progress. The quantity surveyor is named in the JCT forms of contract, where they are engaged by the employer. In the ICE/ICC form such duties are placed on the engineer, but in practice are usually carried out by quantity surveyors employed by the engineer. On most construction works of any substance there will, in addition to those employed by or on behalf of the employer, be quantity surveyors employed by the contractor. In smaller construction contracts, a surveyor alone may be appointed as certifier, and may also be given the functions of supervising and administering the contract. The training of quantity surveyors includes contract administration and legal studies. Consequently, they frequently become involved in claims and disputes. A number of firms have been established specialising in these areas. Quantity surveyors as such are less frequently encountered outside the United Kingdom and the Commonwealth. In the United States of America, for example, bills of quantities rarely become contract documents and interim valuations are generally based on pre-agreed milestone payments.

Other liabilities

The duties of engineers and architects to the building owner arise by virtue of their employment under contract. Acts performed for or on behalf of the employer may at the same time give rise to duties and liabilities to other persons. This may arise by virtue of the position as agent for the employer, when there may be personal liability on a contract or liability for acting without authority. In addition, architects and engineers are subject to the Defective Premises Act 1972. Under s.1, they owe a duty to any present or future owner of a dwelling to see that their work is done in a professional manner (see Ch.7).

The question of liability in tort has been subject to retrenchment (see Ch.14). There are, however, many circumstances in which professionals may still be under tortious liability in relation to construction work. In *Clay v Crump*[74] an architect had failed to examine a dangerous wall and allowed it to remain in the belief that it was safe. He was held liable in negligence to a workman who was injured when the wall collapsed. The contractor who employed the man and the demolition contractor were also liable. In this case Ormerod L.J. held:

[74] [1964] 1 Q.B. 533.

"It may be that there was negligence in some degree on the part both of the demolition contractors and builders. If there was such negligence, it may be that it was a contributory cause of the accident. It cannot however, in my judgement, absolve the architect from a share in the blame. To hold otherwise would be to hold that an architect, or indeed anyone in a similar position, could behave negligently by delegating to others duties he was under an obligation to perform and escape liability by the plea that the injuries caused were caused by the negligence of that other person and not of himself. I do not accept that as being the true position in law."

While this case is of interest as regards the type of duty which may be owed, there will be difficulty in recovering loss not resulting from physical damage to person or property, unless the case is brought within the principles of *Hedley Byrne v Heller*[75] (see Ch.14).

A more significant case concerning tortious liability is *Eckersley and Others v Binnie & Partners*,[76] the *Abbeystead* case. Owing to the undetected presence of methane gas in an underground pumphouse, an explosion occurred, killing or injuring many visitors who had been invited to a view by the Water Authority. The trial judge found fault on behalf of the designer (Binnie), the contractor and the Water Authority and the loss was apportioned between them. The Court of Appeal found no liability on the part of the contractor and the authority, but by a majority held Binnie alone liable. The trial judge suggested that the designer might be under a continuing duty, after completion of the project, to advise on new information which might indicate a danger. Bingham L.J. while not prepared to rule out any possibility of such a continuing duty, said:

"What is plain is that if any such duty at all is to be imposed, the nature, scope and limits of such a duty require to be very carefully and cautiously defined. The development of the law on this point, if it ever occurs, will be gradual and analogical. But this is not a suitable case in which to launch or embark on the process of development because no facts have been found to support a conclusion that ordinarily competent engineers in the position of (Binnie) would . . . have been alerted to any risk of which they were reasonably unaware at the time of handover."

While a continuing duty to review a design has been recognised in other cases,[77] it was held in *New Islington HA v Pollard Thomas & Edwards*[78] that any duty to review the design on a completed project would only arise where something occurs to put the architect on notice of the need for such review. The duty owed in regard to the carrying out of the works

---

[75] [1964] A.C. 465.
[76] (1988) 18 Con. L.R. 1.
[77] See *Brickfield Properties v Newton* [1971] 1 W.L.R. 862.
[78] [2001] B.L.R. 74.

will be more limited. In the case of *Oldschool v Gleeson*[79] it was contended that consulting engineers were liable to contractors who suffered loss through the collapse of a party wall. Sir William Stabb, the senior Official Referee, held:

> "The duty of care of an architect or of a consulting engineer in no way extends into the area of how the work is carried out. Not only has he no duty to instruct the builder how to do the work or what safety precautions to take but he has no right to do so, nor is he under any duty to the builder to detect faults during the progress of the work. The architect, in that respect, may be in breach of his duty to his client, the building owner, but this does not excuse the builder for faulty work.
>
> I take the view that the duty of care which an architect or a consulting engineer owes to a third party is limited by the assumption that the contractor who executes the works acts at all times as a competent contractor. The contractor cannot seek to pass the blame for incompetent work onto the consulting engineer on the grounds that he failed to intervene to prevent it.
>
> . . . The responsibility of the consulting engineer is for the design of the engineering components of the works and his supervisory responsibility is to his client to ensure that the works are carried out in accordance with that design. But if, as was suggested, here, the design was so faulty that a competent contractor in the course of executing the works could not have avoided the resulting damage, then on principle it seems to me that the consulting engineer responsible for that design should bear the loss."

Duties of contractors

Contractors sometimes refer to themselves as "engineers" and it is not lost on the courts that they invariably employ professional engineers, architects and surveyors. They are experts not only in construction techniques and management, but usually also in matters of design. The expertise possessed by contractors leads to particular duties being placed upon them, outside the express terms of the contract. Implied terms in building contracts are discussed in Ch.6. Duties arising in the law of tort are illustrated by *Clay v Crump* (above) in which the contractor was also held liable to the injured man and by the *Abbeystead* case in which the contractor was initially held liable for the injuries and damage which occurred (this finding was reversed on appeal). A particular aspect of the "professional" liability of a contractor is in what has become known as the "duty to warn". In what circumstances should a contractor warn the employer, their engineer or architect that the works to be performed under the contract are inadequate or dangerous?

---

[79] (1976) 4 B.L.R. 103.

This issue has been considered in a number of TCC decisions starting with *EDAC v Moss*,[80] where H.H. Judge Newey Q.C. found there to be an implied term that the contractor would warn of design defects as soon as they came to believe that they existed, either as a result of experience or on examination of drawings. The issue came before the Court of Appeal more recently in *Plant Construction v Clive Adams Associates (first defendant)* and *JMH Construction (second defendant)*[81] which concerned works carried out by the plaintiff for the Ford Motor Company, the plaintiff employing the first defendant as its consulting engineer and the second defendant as its sub-contractor.

JMH were instructed by a representative of the owner to place Acrow props in specified positions to support roof trusses. Both JMH and Clive Adams realised that the propping was inadequate, as would any competent engineer or contractor. They carried out the work, however, which subsequently led to a major collapse after heavy rain. Clive Adams settled the claim against them, leaving the issue as to the contractor's liability for having failed adequately to warn of the perceived danger. May L.J., in his judgment stated:

> "These temporary works were, to the knowledge of JMH, obviously dangerous to the extent that a risk of serious personal injury or death was apparent. JMH were not mere bystanders and, in my judgment, there is an overwhelming case on the particular facts that their obligation to perform their contract with the skill and care of an ordinary competent contractor carried with it an obligation to warn of the danger which they perceived.
>
> The fact that the design and details of the temporary works had been imposed by Ford and that Plant had Mr Adams as their consulting engineer do not, in my view, negative or reduce the extent of performance which the implied term required in this case. The fact other people were responsible and at fault does not mean, in my judgment, that on the facts of this case JMH were not contractually obliged to warn of a danger. Nor in this case is the extent of performance negated by the fact that JMH were expressly obliged by contract to do what [Ford] instructed."

But in *Aurum Investments v Avonforce*[82] the opposite conclusion was reached by Dyson J in contribution proceedings between the defendant Design and Build Contractor and *Advanced*, specialist underpinning contractors. *Advanced* carried out underpinning works to a flank wall and were aware that extensive works were subsequently to be carried out adjacent to the flank wall. When these works were carried out, without providing propping, the flank wall collapsed. It was held that *Advanced*

---

[80] *Equitable Debenture Assets Corporation v Moss* (1984) 1 Const. L.J. 131.
[81] [2000] B.L.R. 137 CA.
[82] (2001) C.I.L.L. 1729.

were not under a duty to warn merely on the ground that it was possible that the Design and Build Contractor would carry out the excavation as it did. *Advanced* were not bound to assume the work would be carried out negligently, when it could have been carried out in a safe alternative way. The judge added:

> "I consider that it is relevant to the question of whether there is a duty to warn that the client is being advised by a professional person. Why should the contractor assume that the client will act negligently, particularly when he being independently advised by an engineer?"

DESIGN-BUILD CONTRACTS

In traditional construction contract practice there is a more or less rigid distinction between design and construction. Design is the task of the engineer or architect and is taken to be excluded from the contractor's function. This distinction is entirely removed in certain modern forms of contract, sometimes described as "package" or "turnkey" or design-build contracts. Before dealing with the particular difficulties of these forms, it is necessary to examine the extent to which the contractor's traditional responsibility also includes design.

First, the word "design" has no precise meaning in building contracts. It certainly encompasses the planning of the form of the finished works. The ICE/ICC conditions draw a distinction between design of permanent and temporary works (cl.8(2)), the latter normally being the contractor's responsibility. Under the JCT forms, temporary works are entirely the contractor's responsibility unless otherwise provided for. In regard to the permanent works, no contract can lay down every detail of the "design," for example, the precise positioning of screws or the mixing of mortar. Each such operation involves an element of design, which is left to the contractor. In simpler forms of contract, this design element may be extensive and important. In addition to a term of good workmanship, there will generally be an implied term that the work and materials will be reasonably fit for their purpose, to the extent they are not fully specified. The contractor should thus be responsible for elements of "design" left to them.[83]

This principle may be limited by the form of the contract. Both the ICE/ICC and JCT forms entitle the contractor expressly to be given

---

[83] *Young & Marten v McManus Childs* [1969] 1 A.C. 454; *Cammell Laird v Manganese Bronze* [1934] A.C. 402; but see *Rotherham v Haslam* (1996) C.A. 78 B.L.R. 1.

instructions necessary to complete the works.[84] The ICE/ICC conditions require any design responsibility for the permanent works to be expressly stated (cll.8(2), 58(3)). Under the JCT form, the contractor's obligation is limited to the work shown in the contract drawings and bills (cl.1.3). Thus, in *Mowlem v BICC*[85] the bills stipulated "waterproof concrete," leaving the means of achieving the result unspecified and unpriced. This was held insufficient to make the contractor responsible when the concrete (otherwise constructed in accordance with the contract) leaked. Sir William Stabb held:

> "I should require the clearest possible contractual condition before I should feel driven to find a contractor liable for a fault in the design, design being a matter which a structural engineer is alone qualified to carry out and which he is paid to undertake, and over which the contractor has no control. I agree that the construction for which (counsel for the employer) contends places the contractor in an impossible position. He cannot alter the faulty design without being in breach of contract, for this fault in the design is not, in my view, a discrepancy or divergence between the contract drawings and/or the bill of quantities, and yet if he complies with the design he would still be in breach. I decline to hold that the specification in the bill of quantities makes the contractor liable for the mistakes of the engineer and, in so far as they may purport to do so, I think that it is ineffective by reason of clause 12(1) of the [JCT form of] contract."

Drafting a design-build contract

Where it is intended to make the contractor fully responsible for the design, the standard forms require substantial amendment, beginning with the clauses mentioned above. A simple design-build contract could be written in the form "Build a house with six bedrooms." Difficulties will arise when the owner seeks to elaborate the contract to retain control over the appearance, lay-out and cost of the work. A method of overcoming these problems is for the employer to issue tender documents with outline requirements and to invite tenderers to submit their own designs with a lump sum price. Difficulties arise if, having selected a design, the employer wishes to vary it. Standard form design-build contracts usually allow the contractor to object to a variation which may affect their design responsibility.

The procedure usually adopted in design-build contracts for determining the design is for the tender documents to contain particulars of the "Employers' Requirements" and for the contractor's tender to include "Contractor's Proposals". These two documents then become

---

[84] ICE, cl.7(1); JCT, cl.2.12.
[85] (1978) 3 Con. L.R. 64.

incorporated into the contract which makes provision for generation of the necessary details of the work, in general by the contractor exclusively. The contractor must always retain some level of discretion and choice in regard to unspecified details. The contractor is entitled by these means to achieve economies in the work. Employers sometimes seek to circumvent this by the provision of considerable detail in the employer's requirements. There will, however, always be areas of choice for the contractor.

A design-build contract should include provision expressly making the contractor responsible for the design. It should make clear that responsibility is for the adequacy (and not mere provision) of the design. In principle, the responsibility should be on the basis of fitness for purpose, and this can often be achieved conveniently by incorporating performance requirements, for example, for mechanical plant. In some contracts, the obligations of the designer will be found to be limited to reasonable skill and care. This creates potential difficulty where liability for individual components may be on a higher basis. In the absence of express or clear provision the courts have resolved doubts in favour of the building owner where it was clear that the design had been carried out by the contractor, or their sub-contractors. This was the case in *L.B. Newham v Taylor Woodrow*,[86] where the contractor disputed liability arising from the partial collapse of a tower block known as Ronan Point. A modified JCT form of contract had been used, which was nevertheless held sufficient to put the contractor under an absolute responsibility to comply with Building Regulations. The contractor was therefore liable despite being absolved of negligence. Conversely, in *Independent Broadcasting Authority v EMI and BICC*,[87] the sub-contractor who designed the Emley Moor T.V. mast (BICC) was held liable in negligence for its collapse. The House of Lords, however, expressed their view on the basis there was no negligence. They held that the main contract included design responsibility, although this was to be carried out by the sub-contractor alone. Lord Fraser went on to say:

> "If the terms of the contract alone had left room for doubt about that, I think that in a contract of this nature a condition would have been implied to the effect that EMI had accepted some responsibility for the quality of the mast, including its design, and possibly also for its fitness for the purpose for which it was intended. . . . It is now well recognised that in a building contract for work and materials a term is normally implied that the main contractor will accept responsibility to his employer for materials provided by nominated sub-contractors. The reason for the presumption is the

---

[86] (1981) 19 B.L.R. 99.
[87] (1980) 14 B.L.R. 1.

practical convenience of having a chain of contractual liability from the employer to the main contractor and from the main contractor to the sub-contractor—see *Young & Marten Ltd v McManus Childs Ltd.*[88] . . . In the present case it is accepted by BICC that, if EMI are liable in damages to IBA for the design of the mast, then BICC will be liable in turn to EMI. Accordingly, the principle that was applied in *Young & Marten Ltd* in respect of materials, ought in my opinion to be applied here in respect of the complete structure, including its design. Although EMI had no specialist knowledge of mast design, and although IBA knew that and did not rely on their skill to any extent for the design, I see nothing unreasonable in holding that EMI are responsible to IBA for the design seeing that they can in turn recover from BICC who did the actual designing. On the other hand it would seem to be very improbable that IBA would have entered into a contract of this magnitude and this degree of risk without providing for some right of recourse against the principal contractor or the sub-contractors for defects of design."

A number of standard design-build contracts are now available including those published by the JCT and by the ICE/ICC. They all possess similar characteristics in terms of the design mechanism while retaining essential features from the parent form of contract. Both of these forms involve difficulties over the degree of liability which the contractor accepts in respect of the design (see Ch.11). A common device often used in commercial development work is for the employer initially to employ a design team, and subsequently to require the building contractor to take on responsibility to the employer for the design, together with assignments of all the design contracts. The contractor thus takes on the burden of pursuing any claim against the actual designer arising from a design defect.

Among the advantages claimed for design-build contracts is the rapidity with which contracts can be let and performed and the avoidance of delays and disputes arising from late or changed design details. The building owner can look to a single point of responsibility rather than several. Conversely, the owner necessarily relinquishes control over detailed design matters and does not have the protection of independent quality control as provided by separately retained engineers or architects. Additionally, the tender process can create problems where the project is offered as a "design competition", where the owner selects the preferred design and rejects all others. This can be avoided in a number of ways. For major projects the competition takes place in stages with only one preferred tenderer going forward to the final design stage. Design-build is invariably used in projects under the PFI scheme, where the detailed design is agreed between the PFI Contractor and their design-build contractor. The input of the end-user will then be through

---

[88] [1969] 1 A.C. 454.

performance requirements or "output specification" rather than design details of the buildings to be provided.

COMPLETION

This covers the time period within which the work must be carried out and the consequences of delay; what is necessary to achieve completion of the work; and the effect of maintenance or defects liability clauses. Generally building contracts do not require the contractor to carry out individual items of work at particular times and a programme of work, while usually required under the terms of the contract, is not itself a contract document. Consequently, the contractor will not be regarded as in breach by reason of delay during the course of the work unless there is a failure to comply with a term requiring expedition or "due diligence". Similarly the contractor is not necessarily in breach by reason only of defective work, provided he can complete in accordance with the contract.[89] Conversely when defects appear within the maintenance period, although the contractor has the right and duty to make good, they are nevertheless in breach so that the employer may sue for damages, through being deprived of use of the works. In this event, the damages recoverable will not be limited by any provision for liquidated damages, which are recoverable for delay in achieving completion.

Time for completion and damages

The time within which the work is to be performed is a matter of economic importance both to employer and contractor. In most contracts dates will be specified for the start and completion of the work. The contractor is bound to do the work within the period set, and will be liable in damages if they fail to complete, subject to entitlement to extensions of time. The contractor also has an entitlement to carry out the work. Thus, if the employer prevents completion, for example by failing to give possession of the site, they will be liable in damages to the contractor. Where no time period is specified, the same principles apply, save that the contractor is obliged and entitled to complete within a reasonable time.

Damages recoverable by the employer for delay are usually limited to "liquidated damages".[90] When the delay is caused partly by the

---

[89] *Kaye v Hosier & Dickinson* [1972] 1 W.L.R. 146; *Lintest v Roberts* (1980) 13 B.L.R. 38.
[90] See JCT, cl.2.32, ICE/ICC, cl.47.

employer's default, it has been held that no liquidated damages may be recovered unless the contract allows an extension of time to be granted on the ground of the default, and such extension is in fact granted. Thus, in *Peak v McKinney*[91] building works were suspended after the discovery of defective piles, for which the contractor was responsible. The employer caused further delay before work restarted. The contract did not provide for an extension of time for the employer's default. It was held that no liquidated damages could be recovered for any of the delay. Salmon L.J. held:

> "The liquidated damages and extension of time clauses in printed forms of contract must be construed strictly contra proferentum. If the employer wishes to recover liquidated damages for failure by the contractors to complete on time in spite of the fact that some of the delay is due to the employers' own fault or breach of contract, then the extension of time clause should provide, expressly or by necessary inference, for an extension on account of such a fault or breach on the part of the employer."

The grounds of this decision were that liquidated damages may be recovered only from a date fixed under the contract. Where the original completion date cannot be met as a result of the actions of the employer, and if no later date can be fixed under the contract, time is "at large." This is sometimes referred to the "prevention principle". For this purpose the liquidated damages and extension of time clauses are regarded as being for the employer's benefit and are construed against them, so that general words cannot be relied on. These issues were recently considered by the TCC in *Multiplex Constructions v Honeywell Control Systems*[92] where Jackson J. decided that an act of prevention by Multiplex did not set time at large where Honeywell, the sub-contractor, had not complied with conditions precedent under the sub-contract. The decision followed recent Scottish authority[93] and did not adopt a controversial Australian authority to the contrary effect.[94]

The advantage of liquidated damages is that the employer may deduct or recover them without proof of loss. It is for this reason that contractors seek to argue that they are not recoverable, despite the fact that pre-determined damages are as likely to benefit the contractor as the employer. Liquidated damages may be challenged on the ground they constitute a penalty. There are very few cases in which recovery of liquidated damages has been refused on this ground. There was such an

---

[91] (1970) 69 L.G.R. 1; 1 B.L.R. 111.
[92] [2007] B.L.R. 195.
[93] *City Inn v Shepherd Construction* (2003) S.L.T. 885.
[94] *Gaymark Investments v Walter Construction* [1999] NTSC 143, (2005) 21 Const. L.J. 71.

unsuccessful challenge in *Alfred McAlpine v Tilebox*,[95] where Jackson J. reviewed the law, holding that damages would be not a penalty unless there was a substantial difference between the pre-stated damages and the actual damages. However, in *Braes of Doune v Alfred McAlpine*, leave to appeal against an award was refused where the arbitrator had held that no liquidated damages could be recovered because the contract could make the contractor liable for delay caused by another contractor.[96] If damages for delay are not "liquidated," the employer may sue for their actual loss. In *Chattan Developments v Reigill Civil Engineering*,[97] Ramsey J. held that where parties had agreed to exclude liquidated damages they were to be taken as having also agreed to exclude general damages for delay.

A further aspect of liquidated damages was examined in the case of *Bath District Council v Mowlem*[98] in which the contractor under a JCT form of contract for refurbishment of the Bath spa rooms refused to comply with an instruction to remove work deemed by the architect to be defective. The employer accordingly instructed another contractor to do the work. Mowlem, however, refused them access and resisted an application for an interim injunction (in advance of trial) contending that liquidated damages under the contract constituted an adequate remedy for the delay. The Court of Appeal disagreed, holding that liquidated damages would not adequately compensate the Council for loss which they might suffer during the period up to the trial.

Extension of time and acceleration

Construction contracts usually provide for extensions of time to be granted by the architect or engineer on a variety of specified grounds.[99] Where the ground of extension would otherwise be the contractor's risk, the extension is purely a concession, such as for inclement weather. Where the extension is based on some act or default of the employer, for example, the ordering of variations or giving late instructions, the contractor may be entitled also to extra payment. For this reason, the contractor may seek to attribute the actual delay to grounds carrying reimbursement in respect of the period granted.[100] While the employer may not be entitled to rely on general words to protect their right to

---

[95] [2005] B.L.R. 271 and see also *Liberty Mercian v Dean & Dyball Construction* [2009] B.L.R. 29.
[96] [2008] B.L.R. 321.
[97] [2007] EWHC 305 and see also *Temloc v Errill* (1989) 39 B.L.R. 30.
[98] [2004] B.L.R. 153.
[99] JCT form, cl.2.28; ICE form, cl.44.
[100] JCT form, cll.2.28 and 26.

liquidated damages, such words will benefit the contractor. Thus under cl.44(1) of the ICE/ICC conditions, the contractor is entitled to an extension on the ground of "other special circumstances of any kind whatsoever."

It is a matter of construction of the extension of time clause whether the contractor must establish that the event relied on will cause the works to be delayed beyond the completion date under the contract. In this event, a further problem arises if the contractor has programmed to finish early.[101] Alternatively, where the clause entitles the contractor to be granted an extension by reference to "the delay that has been suffered by the contractor as a result of the alleged cause"[102] it may be unnecessary for the contractor to demonstrate any net delaying effect to the contract. The operation of these clauses will be important where a bonus is to be paid for achieving early completion.

Most contractors now utilise standard computer software to generate programmes which calculate the "critical" elements and show additional time available for non-critical work as "float". Software will again be used to "calculate" extensions of time (EOT) due to the contractor. This exercise is dependent on many factors including the particular method of analysis and it is frequently the case that scheduling experts employed by the two parties to a dispute on EOT will arrive at very different conclusions. Such differences arise first from the assumptions made when inputting data to the computer programme: for example, this may involve decisions as to whether particular variations or instructions have the potential to prevent other work from proceeding; and secondly, differences arise from the method of analysis. There are many different methods. Those most commonly encountered are known as:

(i) *As-planned v As-built.* This is the simplest method which compares the originally intended and actual events.

(ii) *As-planned, impacted.* This method takes the planned programme at a particular point and adds new activities to represent delaying events at the point of impact.

(iii) *As-built, but-for.* This is the opposite of (ii) which takes the actual programme achieved and subtracts delaying events to find the date which could have been achieved had the relevant events not occurred.

(iv) *Time-impact analysis.* This method takes the achieved programme at a particular point and adds all delaying events,

---

[101] See *Glenlion Construction v Guinness Trust* (1987) 39 B.L.R. 89.
[102] ICE, cl.44(2).

irrespective of which party is responsible. The analysis is repeated as necessary and determines delays for which each party is responsible.

Where an event occurs which would potentially impact on the contractor's progress, but the activities impacted are not critical to progress, the questions arises "who owns the float?" In other words, is the employer (or contractor in the case of a sub-contract) entitled to be credited with the available float and to use it without granting an extension of time? An answer to the question was given in *Ascon Contracting v Alfred McAlpine*[103] where HH Judge Hicks Q.C. held that the main contractor (McAlpine) was entitled to use float to avoid his own liability for liquidated damages to the employer. The judgment continued:

> "He cannot, however, while accepting that benefit as against the employer, claim against sub-contractors as if it did not exist. That is self-evident if total delays as against sub-programmes do not exceed the float. The main contractor, not having suffered any loss of the above kinds, cannot recover from sub-contractors the hypothetical loss he would have suffered had the float not existed, and that will be so whether the delay is wholly the fault of one sub-contractor, or wholly that of the main contractor himself, or spread in varying degrees between several sub-contractors and the main contractor. No doubt those different situations can be described, in a sense, as ones in which the 'benefit' of the float has accrued to the defaulting party or parties. But no one could suppose that the main contractor has, or should have, any power to alter the results so as to shift that 'benefit'."

Other views have been expressed, however, regarding ownership of float. Many project managers hold the view that float "belongs to the project". This is the view adopted in a Protocol for Determining Extensions of Time and Compensation for Delay and Disruption, issued by the Society of Construction Law.[104]

There are a number of questions that regularly arise when operating extension of time clauses which can be, but rarely are, given definitive answers in the contract terms. Some of these have been addressed by the courts but others remain matters of expertise upon which planning experts tend to hold differing opinions. The ownership of float is one such question. Another is the way in which an extension is to be computed when the work is already in delay. This question has two possible answers: the extension may be to the date on which the work can now be completed having regard to the relevant cause of delay; or it may be to the current completion date extended by the number of days delay

---

[103] (2000) C.I.L.L. 1583.
[104] Published October 2002.

resulting from the relevant cause. In *Balfour Beatty v Chestermount Properties*[105] Colman J. held the answer to be the latter, i.e. the net method rather than the gross method. Other questions on which assistance is to be gained from the cases include the effect of concurrent delays, one of which is a ground for extension of time, and concurrent delays, one of which is a ground both for extension of time and compensation.[106]

In *City Inn v Shepherd Construction*, the Scottish Court of Session, both at first instance[107] and on appeal[108] held that a where there were two concurrent causes of delay operating at the same time, the contractor was entitled to an extension of time apportioned between the two causes on a "fair and reasonable" basis, reflecting the words of the extension clause. The case is not binding in the rest of the United Kingdom where the contrary view may prevail.[109] This is that the contract contemplates that, as there will often be competing causes of delay, the grant of an entitlement to extension on a specified ground entitles that contractor to extension of the full amount of delay, provided the specified ground has at least equal "causative potency" as a delaying event. This view was upheld in the recent decision of Akenhead J. in the TCC in *Walter Lilly v Giles Macka*,[110] where it was held that a full extension of time was merited where one of two effective causes of delay was a relevant event. However, the entitlement to compensation for delay may, depending on the wording of the contract, require a different test of causation, analogous to the right to recover damages. In such a situation the contractor may be entitled to an extension of time and relief from liquidated damages but without further compensation.

Claims for acceleration may arise where the employer wishes to have the work completed earlier than the projected completion date. Provisions to this effect are included in a number of contracts[111] but usually on the basis of agreement with the contractor. Alternatively, the contractor may contend that as a result of express or implied instructions, the engineer or architect has ordered acceleration measures. This may arise where the contract is held subsequently to be entitled to an extension of time, but at the time of the delay the extension is denied and the contractor is required to adhere to the original completion date. This is sometimes referred to

---

[105] (1993) 63 B.L.R. 1.
[106] See *Henry Boot v Malmaison Hotel* (1999) 70 Con. L.R. 32, J. Marrin QC, "Concurrent Delay" (2002) Const. L.J. 436 updated 2013 and *Keating on Construction Contracts*, 9th edn (London: Sweet & Maxwell, 2012), paras 8-025-8-028.
[107] [2008] B.L.R. 269.
[108] [2010] B.L.R. 473.
[109] *Keating on Construction Contracts*, 9th edn para.8-026.
[110] *Walter Lilly v Giles Mackay and DMW Developments* [2012] EWHC 1773.
[111] ICE/ICC, cl.46(3), GC/Works/1, edn 3, cl.38.

as "constructive" acceleration. There is no direct English authority on such claims but they have been recognised in the United States of America[112] and in the Commonwealth.[113]

Right to suspend work

At common law, there is no right of suspension outside the terms of the particular construction contract. The contractor will be justified in suspending work where a ground of delay exists which gives rise to an extension of time; and suspension may be ordered under most forms of contract by the engineer or architect. There is normally no right to suspend work for non-payment or other breach by the employer. For a construction contract falling within the definition in the Housing Grants, etc. Act 1996, s.112 provides that where a "notified sum" (as defined by substituted s.111 of the Housing Grants, etc. Act) is not paid by the final date for payment (see stage payments above), the contractor has the right to suspend performance until payment is made, subject to first giving seven days notice and stating the grounds. Any such period of suspension is to be disregarded in computing any contractual time limit. It is thought that the right must apply to the whole of the works, even though non-payment relates to part. Section 111 deals inter alia with the effect of a dispute as to the contractor's right to payment which is referred to adjudication (see Ch.2).

Meaning of completion

Generally, full and complete performance is required to discharge contractual obligations. However in construction contracts the purpose of signifying completion is not to release the contractor, but to permit the employer to take possession of the works and to allow the contractor to leave the site. Contracts, therefore, use terms such as practical completion[114] and substantial completion.[115] While such terms do not permit the contractor to achieve completion without finishing the whole of the work (save for permitted exceptions), it is thought they allow completion to be certified despite the existence of non-material departures from the contract.

Completion is not affected by the existence of latent defects.[116] If defects are discovered after apparent completion (whether during or after

---

[112] See *Norair Engineering v U.S.* (1981) 666 F. 546.
[113] *Morrison-Knudsen v B.C. Hydro & Power* (1978) 85 D.L.R. 3d. 186; 7 Const. L.J. 227; *Perini Pacific v Commonwealth of Australia* (1969) 12 B.L.R. 82.
[114] JCT, cl.2.30.
[115] ICE/ICC, cl.48(1).
[116] *Jarvis v Westminster C.C.* [1969] 1 W.L.R. 1448.

the maintenance period) the employer is entitled to sue for damages, including loss of use.

Defects clauses

These oblige the contractor to rectify faults appearing within a specified period, often six or 12 months following completion. They may also oblige the contractor to maintain the works and to put right defects not due to their default, the latter at the employer's expense.[117] When a default is due to the contractor's failure to comply with the contract, they are in breach. The maintenance clause permits the contractor to mitigate the effect of the breach by carrying out rectification himself. A provision which entitles the employer to have defects rectified within a specified period does not absolve the contractor from liability for defects appearing after expiry of the period. Clear words are required to make a maintenance clause operate also as an exclusion clause. Such words are found in the standard form of contract for mechanical and electrical works, MF/1, where the contractor is expressly absolved of further responsibility after carrying out the rectification of defects.[118]

---

[117] Compare JCT, cl.2.38 and ICE/ICC, cl.49.
[118] Clause 36: see Ch.11.

CHAPTER 10

VICARIOUS PERFORMANCE AND INSOLVENCY

Chapter 9 deals with the operation of construction contracts and the parties' rights arising from them. This chapter covers a number of matters outside the contract itself which may affect the parties' rights. Vicarious performance refers to the carrying out of contractual obligations by a person not party to the contract. This may be either by sub-contract or assignment. Sub-contracts are found in most construction work, since very few contractors have the resources to carry out the whole of a project themselves. Particular problems arise when the sub-contractor is nominated. Assignment is the means by which a party may transfer to another the whole or part of their rights or duties under a contract. When the contractor assigns part of their obligation to perform the work, the effect is similar to a sub-contract save that the assignee is in direct contract with the employer. Finally, insolvency and bonds deal with the rights of the parties when one of them becomes unable to perform the contract by reason of financial difficulties.

SUB-CONTRACTS

In the traditional system of contracting in the construction industry the whole of the work is initially let to the main contractor. Subject to the provisions of the main contract, the contractor is entitled to sub-let portions of the work, save where the contract is let by reason of some special skill or quality of the contractor. Thus, a contract for specialist site-investigation work is likely to be one which may not be sub-let without consent of the employer. Performance by a sub-contractor constitutes vicarious performance on behalf of the contractor, who remains fully responsible for the work, save where the main contract provides otherwise.

The standard forms usually contain terms restricting the right of sub-letting. The JCT form prohibits sub-letting without the architect's consent, which is not to be unreasonably withheld (cl.3.7). The withholding of consent may be challenged, if considered to be unreasonable.

Under the ICE/ICC form sub-letting of parts of the work is permitted without the need for consent, but sub-letting the whole requires consent (cl.4). If sub-letting occurs without any necessary consent, this may give the employer no right beyond nominal damages. However, a refusal to resume performance by the contractor may constitute repudiation. The better course is to provide express remedies in the contract, such as determination. The employer may waive their right to object, and would be held to do so by making payment for the sub-contracted work with knowledge of the sub-contract.

Engineering sub-contractors tend often to be specialists who carry out limited parts of the works, such as piling. In building, it is not uncommon for the majority of the work on a substantial contract to be carried out by a large number of trade sub-contractors. As an alternative to the traditional main contract, under a management contract the whole of the work is sub-contracted, the contractor's role becoming that of a manager. Payment is usually made on the basis of prime cost together with a fee which is retained by the contractor. One advantage claimed for the management contract is flexibility in development of the design.

Rights and obligations

A sub-contract creates no privity of contract between the sub-contractor and the employer. This has remained the position despite the Contracts (Rights of Third Parties) Act 1999, since construction industry contracts usually contain express exclusions of such potential rights. The sub-contractor can thus sue only the main contractor for the price of the sub-contracted work. The advantage to the employer is that while the work may actually be performed by various specialists, the main contractor alone remains responsible for the whole operation and, perhaps most important, for the co-ordination of their own work and that of sub-contractors. Sums included in the main contract and designated as prime cost (PC) usually represent work intended to be sub-let. This may be called prime cost work, since the employer must pay the actual cost. Prime cost work often represents an important part of the project which has not been designed in any detail, and which is to be sub-let to a nominated specialist who will furnish the design. Prime cost work may be the subject of special provisions in the conditions of contract. A provisional sum usually represents work of uncertain scope which may be sub-contracted.

A common feature of main contracts is for the employer to retain the right to make direct payments to a nominated sub-contractor.[1] These

---

[1] See JCT98, cl.35.13 and ICE/ICC, cl.59(7) and see below. There is no provision for nominated sub-contracting in JCT05.

provisions are appropriate where payments due to the sub-contractor are to be determined by the architect or engineer, so that the contractor acts merely as a channel for payment. However, neither nomination nor direct payment to sub-contractors gives a sub-contractor the right to sue the employer and no privity of contract is thereby created. There may be an exception to this principle where the employer obtains a collateral warranty from the sub-contractor. A warranty as such gives the sub-contractor no right to sue for payment, but the JCT forms of warranty oblige the employer to operate the direct payment provisions. Such rights will generally be subject to any cross-claim which the employer may have against the contractor.

When making a sub-contract, the main contractor will usually wish to ensure, so far as is possible, that the arrangements are "back to back", that is that the sub-contractor automatically becomes liable for any act or omission which causes breach of the main contract. This is sometimes attempted by seeking to incorporate the whole of the main contract into the sub-contract. But this may create problems of interpretation and may not achieve the effect intended. A more useful device, adopted by the standard forms of sub-contract, is to require the sub-contractor to perform so that the contractor is not caused to be in breach of the main contract. This is likely to be effective as regards the standard or quality of work. However, as regards time, it is much more difficult to devise obligations which will ensure that the sub-contractor performs to a programme entirely conformable to the needs of the main contract. Any programme fixed in advance is vulnerable to the need to make adjustments before or even during the performance of the sub-contract work. A device which is likely to be effective is to require the sub-contractor to start only as and when instructed to do[2] but it may be difficult to secure the sub-contractor's agreement.

Payment to sub-contractors

A sub-contract falls within the definition of "construction contract" under the Housing Grants, etc. Act 1996 and the sub-contractor is, as against the main contractor, entitled to the benefit of all the payment provisions contained in ss.109–111, including the right to suspend performance for non-payment without effective notice under s.112 (see Ch.9). In addition, sub-contracts of all kinds have for many years contained provisions commonly known as "pay-when-paid" clauses, by which the main contractor could withhold payment from the sub-contractor until the sums in question were received from the

---

[2] *Kitson's Sheet Metal v Matthew Hall* (1989) 47 B.L.R. 82.

employer. Depending on the terms of the contract, such clauses could take effect as meaning "pay-if-paid". The same provisions are frequently found in sub-sub-contracts and contracts of supply.

Under s.113 of the Housing Grants, etc. Act 1996, such clauses are rendered ineffective unless the condition of payment is that the payer (or any other person payment by whom is under the contract (directly or indirectly) a condition of payment by the payer) is insolvent. Thus, it is permissible for the main contractor (or sub-contractor in the case of a sub-sub-contract) to provide that payment may be withheld where the provider of the funding becomes insolvent; otherwise any withholding of payment must be made in accordance with s.111 of the Housing Grants, etc. Act 1996 by service of an effective notice. The validity of any such withholding may then immediately be challenged by adjudication under s.108 of the Act.

Nomination

The usual procedure for letting a nominated sub-contract is for the architect or engineer to obtain competitive quotations for the work in question directly from prospective sub-contractors, and then, under powers contained in the main contract, to instruct the contractor to place an order with the chosen tenderer. The terms of the sub-contract will largely be settled before the nomination, usually by incorporating a standard form, but both the contractor and sub-contractor may seek to amend or alter the terms. The main contract usually gives the contractor some protection by entitling them to object to a nomination which does not contain certain beneficial terms.[3] JCT 98 requires the sub-contractor's bid to be given on a standard form of tender. Note that nomination is omitted from JCT 05 and subsequent editions.

Liability for defects

One of the problems relating to sub-contracts is that of determining the obligations of the main contractor in respect of materials and work of nominated sub-contractors, and thus determining the rights of the employer in the event of default by a nominated sub-contractor. There is generally no problem in regard to the express description of the work. This will become incorporated in the main contract by virtue of the nomination. The problem arises when the sub-contractor's work, while complying with the express terms of main and sub-contract, is alleged to

---

[3] See ICC, cl.59(1).

be in breach of an implied term requiring good quality or fitness for purpose.

Generally, the main contractor will be responsible both for the quality and for the fitness of materials used, unless there are circumstances which are such as to negative the existence of either term. Where there is a nomination, the materials will be specifically chosen by the architect or engineer, so that the main contractor will not be responsible for their fitness or suitability. In *Young & Marten v McManus Childs*,[4] the House of Lords held that the choice of tiles made by only one manufacturer excluded the warranty of fitness but was not sufficient to exclude the implication of a warranty of quality in the main contract, so that the main contractor was liable for latent defects in the tiles. Lord Pearce expressed his view thus:

> "It is frequent for builders to fit baths, sanitary equipment, central heating and the like, encouraging their clients to choose from the wholesalers' display rooms the bath or sanitary fittings which they prefer. It would, I think, surprise the average householder if it were suggested that simply by exercising a choice he had lost all right of recourse in respect of quality of the fittings against the builder who normally has a better knowledge of these matters. Of course, if a builder warned him against a particular fitting or manufacturer and he persisted in his choice, he would obviously be doing so at his own risk. And a builder can always make it clear that he is not prepared to take responsibility for a particular kind of fitting or material."

In the case of *Gloucestershire County Council v Richardson*,[5] the main contractor discovered, during the course of construction works, defects in pre-cast concrete columns provided by a nominated supplier. The form of contract (RIBA form, 1939 edn) did not permit the contractor to object to the terms of the nominated supply contract, which was subject to a limitation of liability. It was held that the main contractor was not liable for the quality (or the fitness) of the components, and was not therefore in breach of contract. Lord Wilberforce held:

> "The design, materials, specification, quality and price were fixed between the employer and the sub-supplier without any reference to the contractor: and so far from being expected to secure conditions or warranties from the sub-supplier, he had imposed upon him special conditions which severely restricted the extent of his remedy. Moreover, as reference to the main contract shows, he had no right to object to the nominated supplier . . . In these circumstances, so far from there being a good reason to imply in the contract . . . a condition or warranty binding the contractor in respect of

---

[4] [1969] 1 A.C. 454.
[5] [1969] 1 A.C. 480.

latently defective goods, the indications drawn from the conduct of the contracting parties are strongly against any such thing."[6]

A further problem arises if a nominated sub-contractor repudiates or "drops out". Is the contractor obliged to complete the work at their own expense, so far as this exceeds the agreed sub-contract price, or must the employer pay the additional cost of finding an alternative sub-contractor? In *N.W. Metropolitan Hospital Board v Bickerton*[7] it was held that under the 1963 JCT form the architect was obliged to re-nominate, so that the employer must bear the loss. The decision was based on the fact that the contract contemplated that prime cost work would be carried out only by a nominated sub-contractor. The decision may therefore apply, depending on the particular wording, to other forms of main contract such as the ICE 4th edn. The ICE 5th and later editions including the newly designated ICC form, contain express provisions dealing with parties' rights upon the default of a nominated sub-contractor, so that there is little application for the *Bickerton* principle. JCT 98 and earlier versions dealt expressly with re-nomination in respect of sub-contractors.

A combination of the above problems occurs if a nominated sub-contractor repudiates leaving defects in partly completed work. If the facts are similar to the *Young & Marten* case above, the main contractor would be liable for the quality of the sub-contractor's work. In *Fairclough v Rhuddlan B.C.*,[8] the main contractor was prima facie liable for the work of the sub-contractor, but was held not to be under any responsibility for defects discovered after the sub-contractor had repudiated, relying on the principle established in the *Bickerton* case, that the main contractor had neither the right nor the duty to carry out work within a PC sum.

Liability for delay

If a nominated sub-contractor causes delay without repudiating, the contractor generally remains liable and may pass on the employer's claim to the sub-contractor in default. However, the JCT form provides expressly for an extension of time on the grounds of delay by a nominated sub-contractor.[9] This effectively deprives the employer of remedy, save under any direct warranty.

Where the nominated sub-contractor repudiates, it appeared to follow from the *Bickerton* case that the employer would remain responsible for

---

[6] See also *IBA v EMI* (1980) 14 B.L.R. 1 and Ch.9.
[7] [1970] 1 W.L.R. 607.
[8] (1985) 30 B.L.R. 26.
[9] 1963 edn, cl.23(g); JCT 80, cl.25.3.7.

the delay in providing a replacement sub-contractor. However, it was held by the House of Lords in *Percy Bilton v GLC*[10] that such delay was not the responsibility of the employer. Lord Frazer held:

"Withdrawal of a nominated sub-contractor is not caused by the fault of the employer, nor is it covered by any of the express provisions of clause 23 . . . accordingly, withdrawal falls under the general rule and the main contractor takes the risk of any delay directly caused thereby."

Where a nominated sub-contractor has achieved apparent completion and defects are thereafter discovered in the work, the question arises, under the JCT forms of contract, whether this can constitute "delay on the part of nominated sub-contractors". These facts occurred in the case of *Jarvis v Westminster Corporation*,[11] where defects were discovered in bored piles after the sub-contractor had withdrawn from the site. The necessary remedial work resulted in substantial delays to the main contract. Lord Dilhorne held:

"A practical completion certificate can be issued when owing to latent defects the works do not fulfil the contract requirements and . . . under the contract works can be completed despite the presence of such defects. Completion under the contract is not postponed until defects which became apparent only after the work had been finished had been remedied . . . I conclude that the [sub-contractor] had completed the sub-contract works to the reasonable satisfaction of the architects and the [main contractor] and so were not guilty of delay."

Accordingly, as in the *Percy Bilton* case, the subsequent delay was not covered by the extension of time clause, and the main contractor remained responsible for the delay. Nomination under modern contracts is often avoided because of the difficulties outlined above. However, the advantage of using specialists to perform particular and often significant parts of a project remains and has led to alternative devices being used. These include "listing" of potential specialist sub-contractors, where the main contractor is to make the choice, remaining fully responsible for their performance. Other forms of contract employ nomination, but on terms rendering the main contractor generally responsible for performance. Where this approach is taken, it remains important to take into account the principles established in the *Bickerton* cases lest the contract, by inadvertence, releases the main contractor from an intended full responsibility.

[10] [1982] 1 W.L.R. 794.
[11] [1969] 1 W.L.R. 1448.

It is to be noted that the term "vicarious liability" is applied also to the tort of negligence where one party, typically a contractor or sub-contractor, employs another to carry out particular work. The question is whether and in what circumstances the employer is liable to a third party who suffers loss as a result of the negligence of the employed person. This question is addressed in Ch.14.

ASSIGNMENT

An assignment is a transfer, recognised by the law, of a right or obliga-tion of one party to another. Most rights and obligations are capable of assignment. This may be achieved in a number of ways. Assignments are sometimes brought about by operation of law. This section is concerned primarily with assignment of rights and obligations under building contracts, but the principles involved cover many other things. An assignment, in common with other legal transactions, is distinct from a contract to make an assignment. An assignment does not generally require consideration but a contract to assign, in order to be enforceable, must comply with the same requirements as any other contract, including the need for consideration. An assignment of a right or obligation arising under a contract is a further exception to the doctrine of privity in that rights or burdens are conferred upon persons who are not party to the contract (see Ch.5).

Assignments not permitted

Building contracts and sub-contracts often contain terms restricting or prohibiting assignments:[12] such terms have the effect of making any purported assignment invalid as against the other party to the contract.[13] However the right to prevent an assignment may be lost by waiver. Thus, if the contractor assigns their right to receive payment, the employer will waive their right to object if payment is made to the assignee. Where the contract permits assignment with consent, such consent not to be unrea-sonably withheld, it has been held that an assignment made without requesting consent remains invalid, even where consent could not reasonably have been withheld.[14]

---

[12] JCT, cl.19; ICC, cl.3.
[13] *Linden Gardens v Lanesta Sludge* [1994] 1 A.C. 85.
[14] *Hendry v Chartsearch* [1998] EWCA Civ. 1276.

There are some rights which may not be assigned. It is a fundamental principle of English law that a "bare" right to sue for damages cannot be assigned. Thus, a party who has suffered personal injury must pursue the claim for compensation themselves: they cannot sell that right to another. However, in commercial transactions, there may be a good reason for transferring a right of action. The law on this topic was reviewed by the House of Lords in *Trendtex v Credit Suisse*,[15] where a bank sought to uphold the validity of an assignment of a claim for damages arising out of a transaction which had been financed by the bank. Lord Roskill stated the law as follows:

> "The Court should look at the totality of the transaction. If the assignment is of a property right or interest and the cause of action is ancillary to that right or interest, or if the assignee has a genuine commercial interest in taking the assignment and in enforcing it for his own benefit, I see no reason why the assignment should be struck down as an assignment of a bare cause of action or as savouring of maintenance."

In *Camdex v Bank of Zambia*[16] the Court of Appeal extended the principle by upholding the validity of an assignment of a bona fide debt in circumstances where litigation for its recovery was in contemplation. In the result, it can now be taken that claims under construction contracts may generally be assigned. It is thus possible, for example for a sub-contractor who has suffered loss to take over the rights of the main contractor to enforce claims under the main contract, including their own claim.

Methods of assignment

A legal assignment is one which complies with s.136 of the Law of Property Act 1925. This requires that the assignment is in writing and is absolute, and that notice in writing is given to the other party. No particular form is needed and the document need not be under seal. An assignment which is conditional, for example, until a loan is repaid, is not absolute. The assignment takes effect and becomes enforceable against the other party only on receipt of notice. A transfer which does not comply with the requirements of a legal assignment, such as one made orally, may be enforceable as an equitable assignment. But an equitable assignment will require to be evidenced in writing if it relates to an interest in land.

[15] [1982] A.C. 679.
[16] [1998] Q.B. 22.

In either type of assignment it is necessary to draw a distinction between a benefit and a burden. In a construction contract the benefit to the contractor is the right to be paid and the burden is the obligation to do the work. Subject to any restriction in the terms of contract, a benefit may be assigned irrespective of the wishes of the other party. The burden, conversely, may generally be assigned only with the consent of the other party. Thus the contractor may not assign the obligation to carry out the work without the employer's consent; and the employer may not assign the duty to make payments without the contractor's consent.

Apart from the above methods, the assignment of certain rights are governed by statutory provision. These include transfers of shares and debentures in companies, and assignment of life insurance policies. In addition to transfers brought about by act of the parties some assignments take place by operation of law. Thus on death, the rights of the deceased person vest generally in their personal representative. Upon bankruptcy, the rights of the bankrupt vest in the official receiver and, upon appointment, in their trustee in bankruptcy. In the case of corporate insolvency, a liquidator has power under the Insolvency Act 1986 to assign causes of action to which the company was entitled (see further below).

Effects of assignment

Upon a valid assignment, the assignor loses their rights in the things assigned. The assignee acquires the right to sue in their own name. However, if the assignment is equitable, the assignor may need to be made a party to the action. The right acquired is subject to any rights of the other party against the assignor, including the right of set-off. Thus if a contractor assigns money payable under a certificate, the employer may set-off against the assignee any claim for defects or delay. They cannot counterclaim, but the set-off may reduce or extinguish the debt.

Assignment does not generally discharge the party assigning from their own contractual obligation. Thus when a lease is assigned, the land-lord is entitled to look to the assignee or to the original tenant for payment of rent. Similarly if the contractor assigns the obligation to carry out work, they may still be liable to the employer for breaches, such as defective work. From the contractor's point of view, a more satisfactory arrangement is that there should be a substitution of the new contractor. This is referred to as a novation. Where both the benefit and the burden of a contract are assigned, the latter requiring express consent, this may operate as a novation. Where a new contractor is substituted in the course of a construction contract, difficulties may arise as to existing matters which may later give rise to disputes as, for example, where the work is behind programme or there are grounds for a claim. These matters are best dealt with by express agreement.

The effect of purported assignments in breach of contract was considered by the House of Lords in the consolidated appeals in *Linden Gardens v Lanesta Sludge* and *St Martin's Property v McAlpine*.[17] It was held that there was no reason for holding a contractual prohibition on assignment to be contrary to public policy and that purported assignments in breach of cl.17(1) of the 1963 JCT form of contract[18] were invalid. The result, in each case, was that the purported assignee who had suffered damage was not entitled to enforce rights under the contract. However, the House held that the original contracting party could recover damages on behalf of the party suffering loss, thereby rejecting the submission that the party otherwise in breach should escape liability. Lord Browne-Wilkinson held:

"McAlpine had specifically contracted that the rights of action under the building contract could not without McAlpine's consent be transferred to third parties who became owners or occupiers and might suffer loss. In such a case it seems to me proper, as in the case of the carriage of goods by land, to treat the parties as having entered into the contract on the footing that [the original employer] would be entitled to enforce contractual rights for the benefit of those who suffered from defective performance but who, under the terms of the contract, could not acquire any right to hold McAlpine liable for breach. It is clearly a case in which the rule provides a remedy where no other would be available to a person sustaining loss which, under a rational legal system, ought to be compensated by the person who has caused it."

Lord Griffiths was in favour of expressing the principle even more widely (see also Ch.5).

Assignment of warranties and other duties

This topic has acquired currency through the creation of contractual warranties intended to replace claims previously available in tort. The assignees are those subsequently acquiring an interest in construction works. Thus, parties involved in carrying out a construction project, particularly the designers and other professionals, may be asked to give forms of warranty (see Ch.9) with the intention that these may be assigned to subsequent owners or leases. In accordance with the principles discussed above, the benefit of such a warranty is generally assignable without need of express provision or consent. However, an

[17] [1994] 1 A.C. 85.
[18] Now cl.19.1, JCT 80.

assignment can do no more than to transfer rights available to the assignor; it is not capable of creating new rights in favour of an assignee. Thus, while the client can in theory assign the right to have a building adequately designed, it is unclear what right would be transferred to sue for damages in the event of breach. If the developer/assignor has sold the building or created a full-repairing lease, then their right would be to nominal damages only. A further difficulty would arise where a building is sold or leased to a number of different purchasers. The assignment to each of a right to have the building properly designed creates a number of problems as to what enforceable right has been transferred to each purchaser. These problems are capable of resolution, in principle, by the terms of the document to be assigned, particularly if created by deed (so as to avoid problems of consideration). Thus, the nature and extent of rights to be transferred may be defined, as well as the damage that may be claimed in the event of a breach. This approach is gaining support and contractors and designers are increasingly being required to enter into warranties which are expressly assignable to purchasers and tenants of buildings being designed and constructed. Such a warranty is now found in the 2005 JCT form of contract (Sch.5, Pt 1).

Another solution which seeks to avoid the above problems is to draft the document in the form of a novation, whereby an assignee may take over the full contractual rights of the employer as though named as an original party to the transaction. The effect of a contract expressly made with the intention that its benefit be assigned to another party was considered by the Court of Appeal in *Darlington v Wiltshier Northern*.[19] This concerned the financing of local authority development works by use of a bank (Morgan Grenfell) as the primary employer. Unlike the *Linden Gardens* case (see above) the contract package provided expressly for assignments. After completion the development (a recreational centre) was alleged to be subject to serious defects. Darlington then took an assignment of rights under the original contract and brought proceedings in their own name. The Court of Appeal held the council entitled to recover the damages, following the *Linden Gardens* case. They also held that the bank could, before any assignment, have recovered damages as a constructive trustee for the council (see Ch.5), providing another route by which the council could recoup its losses. An appeal to the House of Lords was compromised before hearing. The result of *Darlington* and *Linden Gardens* is that it is now much less likely that the courts will uphold a "no loss" argument where contractual rights and damages have become separated.[20]

---

[19] [1995] 1 W.L.R. 68.
[20] See also *Alfred McAlpine v Panatown* [2001] 1 A.C. 518.

In the context of design-and-build contracts, it has become fashion-
able for developers to employ a design team expressly on terms that their
design contracts will be assigned to the successful tenderer who is then
to take full responsibility both for the construction work and the design.
The assignments take the form of a "novation" by which the agreement
is effectively re-executed with the name of the contractor substituted for
that of the original employer. Novations typically include a provision
stating that liability of the designer *"whether accruing before or after the
date of this Novation shall be to the contractor"* and that the designer
agrees to be liable to the contractor in respect of any breach of the terms
of the appointment occurring before the date of this novation "as if the
contractor had always been made as a party to the appointment in place
of the employer". These and similar phrases are intended to give the
agreement effect as though it had originally be entered into between the
contractor and the designer. In the Scottish case of *Blyth & Blyth v
Carillion*,[21] it was held, despite wide wording such as that above, that the
contractor was not, prior to tendering, entitled to rely on the design
contract being novated and therefore that any defects in the pre-novation
design work could not affect their tender. Consequently, the contractor
had no right to claim its own losses, nor any losses that might have been
suffered by the employer, in respect of breaches prior to the date of novation. Since this case, forms of assignment and novation have sought to
take such matters into account, but there remains the difficulty of creating
a contractual right to recover losses which cannot be linked to breach of
a duty owed to the parties suffering such loss at the time the loss occurred.
In a more recent case, *Technotrade v Larkstore*,[22] the Court of Appeal
held that rights and benefits under a site investigation report commissioned by the owner of development land and subsequently assigned to
the purchaser of the land, could be enforced by the purchaser including
recovery in respect of damage which occurred between the date of sale
and the date of the assignment.

INSOLVENCY

Insolvency is not a term of art, but means, in practical terms, inability
to pay debts. The effects of this depend on whether the debtor is an individual or a company, but in either case the consequences are severe, both
for the debtor and for the creditor who is unpaid. The laws of bankruptcy

[21] (2001) C.I.L.L. 1789.
[22] [2006] 1 W.L.R. 2926.

and of winding-up companies provide for the realisation and distribution of assets, with certain debts having priority for payment. In construction contracts the insolvency of one party will usually bring the work to an end. The law on both bankruptcy and winding-up are contained mainly in the Insolvency Act 1986 and the Insolvency Rules, amended by the Insolvency Act 2000 and the Enterprise Act 2002.

The fact that an individual or a company is insolvent does not mean that there will be a bankruptcy or winding-up. This depends on the action of the creditors (and of the debtor). The creditors may simply defer the enforcement of their rights; or they may agree to a formal arrangement or moratorium by which the debtor attempts to pay off or reduce the debts. This shows that the concept of insolvency is uncertain. Insolvency is often brought about not by the loss of assets but by the loss of credit facilities or, particularly in the building industry, by temporary adverse cash-flow. This reflects the fact that construction companies often have a large cash turnover against comparatively small assets.

Where a contractor is bound to make a payment (to a sub-contractor) under a sub-construction contract within the Housing Grants, Construction and Regeneration Act 1996 as now amended[23], s.113 of the Act allows the payer to rely on a "pay when paid" clause (which the Act provides is otherwise ineffective) where the party who is to pay the contractor is insolvent. However, in *William Hare v Shepherd Construction*,[24] the Court of Appeal held that this provision did not, as a matter of construction of the pay when paid clause, allow the contractor to refuse payment where the employer had gone into "self certified" administration pursuant to the Insolvency Act 1986 Pt II. A suitably drafted clause could have this effect.

Winding-up of companies

When a company is wound up its business is concluded by a liquidator who takes over the powers of the board. He collects in the debts which are owed to the company and, so far as he is able, pays off the creditors. He may have to decide whether an alleged liability should be settled, such as a pending action for damages against the company. When the debts are paid, any surplus is distributed among the shareholders. Finally the company is dissolved and ceases to exist.

Winding up may be compulsory or voluntary. Compulsory winding up is by order of the court, upon the petition, usually, of a creditor. In most cases the ground for winding up is that the company is unable to pay its debts. A company may be wound up voluntarily for any reason by the

---

[23] By the Local Democracy, Economic Development and Construction Act 2009.
[24] [2010] B.L.R. 358.

passing of a resolution in general meeting. This may be done, for example, to amalgamate with another company or for re-structuring a business.

In a winding up, the liquidator's duty is to collect in the assets and apply them in discharge of the company's liabilities. The liquidator has powers to carry on the company's business, to sell the assets and to compromise claims. This includes the right to sell debts and claims to third parties who take on the risk of non-recovery. In *Norglen v Reeds Rains Prudential*,[25] the House of Lords upheld an assignment of a claim by a liquidator of an insolvent company to former directors. The defendants complained of prejudice in that the directors could apply for legal aid, which they could not, and that there could not be an application for security for costs, which would have been available against the insolvent company.

The liquidator must use the collected assets to discharge the company's debts in a fixed order as follows:

1. debts secured by fixed charge such as debentures;

2. expenses of winding up;

3. preferential debts, principally relating to employment and pensions;

4. debts secured by floating charge;

5. unsecured (ordinary) debts;

6. interest on debts;

7. unpaid dividends; and

8. shareholders funds.

Ordinary debts include an unsatisfied judgment against the company. Thus, if a creditor is owed an undisputed ordinary debt, a judgment for the debt is of no advantage if the company goes into liquidation before it can be executed. In many cases, debenture holders will pre-empt a winding up by appointing a receiver to protect their security. The subsequent liquidation is then more of a formality with few remaining assets for other debt classes.

Administration

As an alternative to winding-up in the case of potential insolvency, the Insolvency Act 1986 as amended by the Enterprise Act 2002 creates a

[25] [1999] 2 A.C. 1.

further regime of company "Administration", by appointed administrators who have powers to rescue a company as a going concern in the best interests of creditors, or alternatively to control the sale of assets so as to realise the best return. In an administration, the company's business is taken over and the company protected from the ordinary consequences of insolvency. Administration may be ordered by the court, but an alternative procedure is available by which the directors may swear a statutory declaration and may then enter voluntary administration. The administration will lead either to a scheme allowing the company to continue or to winding-up. These procedures may be contrasted to the insolvency laws in the United States which allow companies faced with large debts, often through court actions, to file for "Chapter 11" protection, which allows the company to continue trading while attempts are made to settle outstanding claims and liabilities.

Bankruptcy proceedings

Bankruptcy applies to individuals and is a process under which possession of the debtor's assets is taken for the benefit of creditors. The process has similarities with and is governed by the same legislation as liquidation of companies. The debtor obtains release from their debts and liabilities, but is subject to restrictions. A petition may be brought by a creditor, but often the debtor applies. When the court makes a Bankruptcy Order, the assets and affairs of the bankrupt pass to the official receiver and then to a trustee in bankruptcy, for the purpose of realising and distributing the assets. The bankrupt is allowed to retain tools, vehicles and equipment necessary for employment or business, and basic household equipment. These provisions are harsh, but it should be remembered that the statutory bankruptcy process has evolved as the alternative to imprisonment for civil debt, graphically described in a number of the novels of Charles Dickens. The bankrupt person can usually obtain discharge after 12 months.

Receivers

A receiver is a person appointed to collect and preserve property. The courts have wide jurisdiction to appoint receivers[26], such as in a pending action to protect the subject matter of the dispute. A receiver may also be appointed, as a matter of contract, by a party under a security, such as a mortgage or debenture. The receiver's duty in this case is to take possession of the assets mortgaged or charged in order to protect and realise the

---

[26] CPR Pt 69.

security. Such an appointment is usually indicative of the debtor's insolvency or financial difficulty. The appointment and exercise of the receiver's powers may have an important effect on the debtor's ability to perform a subsisting contract.

Receivers appointed under mortgages or charges may exercise statutory powers.[27] However, these are invariably enlarged by the terms of the instrument itself. This may provide for powers of management and for the receiver to be the agent of the debtor company. The instrument under which the receiver is appointed will also specify when the right to appoint arises. When the company is being wound-up, a receiver may be appointed either before or after the appointment of a liquidator. When a liquidator is appointed after a receiver, any powers as agent of the company will be terminated, since the liquidator takes precedence in managing and winding-up the company. But in other matters concerning the right to the company's assets, the liquidator and the receiver may be in conflict.

Insolvency under a construction contract

If the contractor becomes insolvent, the first effect is usually that the work is brought to a stop by the inability to continue financing the work. If the employer is the insolvent party, their inability to meet interim payments will stop the work. In either case, this produces a potentially serious financial loss for the other party, which will not be satisfied by the insolvent party. Such loss may be reduced or even avoided by an employer appropriating retention money or the contractor's plant and goods or by enforcing a bond. A contractor is likely to fare less well. Their work and materials, whether paid for or not, pass to the employer and to the employer's trustee or liquidator on insolvency, when they become attached to the land. Thereafter they cannot be removed. The parties' rights are usually regulated by provisions of the contract which operate upon various events indicative of insolvency. When one party intimates that they cannot continue with a contract by reason of insolvency, they will repudiate the contract and the other party has no real choice but to accept. The standard forms of contract usually provide that the innocent party may terminate the contractor's employment without bringing the contract to an end, so that advantage may be taken of contractual terms applying after such termination, for example, as to the rights in goods and plant, and claims. In *Melville Dundas v George Wimpey UK Ltd*[28] the employer terminated the contractor's employment

---

[27] Law of Property Act 1925 ss.101, 109.
[28] [2007] B.L.R. 257.

under a JCT Design and Build contract on the ground of insolvency of the contractor (Melville), but at a time when application had been made for an interim payment, the final date for payment had passed and no withholding notice complying with s.111 of the Housing Grants, etc., Act had been served. The House of Lords therefore had to decide whether the contract provision, which stated that no further payment was due upon termination, prevailed over the right to payment provided by the Act. The House decided by majority that the unpaid sum was not payable once the contract's employment had been properly terminated.

As an alternative to termination, PFI contracts and other projects involving outside "funders" provide "step-in" rights whereby banks and other funders are entitled, in defined circumstances including an impending termination, to take over all the rights of the employer and to continue the contract in order to preserve their investment. Such right may be accompanied by corresponding "step-out" rights, by which the funder may release themselves and leave the project to continue without the additional obligations involved in stepping in.

The ICE form seventh edn and the ICC form now gives the contractor a right of determination under the contract for insolvency (cl.64). Under earlier editions it would be necessary to rely on common law repudiation. The employer is given the right to terminate the contractor's employment in the event, inter alia, of the contractor becoming bankrupt or having a receiving order or administration order made against them or going into liquidation. The employer then has the right to complete the contract by other contractors and to claim or set-off the additional cost of completion (cl.65).

The JCT forms have traditionally given rights of determination to both employer and contractor. The contractor may determine for non-payment of certificates, whether or not due to insolvency (cl.8.9). The contractor may then claim their loss from the employer. However, such claim is not secured since goods and materials, when paid for, become the employer's property (cl.4.17). The employer has similar rights if the contractor, inter alia, becomes bankrupt or has a Winding-Up Order made or a receiver of their business appointed. In such cases the contractor's employment is automatically ended, subject to reinstatement. The employer may claim the additional costs of completion from the contractor (cl.8.7), but the only security for such a claim is the retention of money and any performance bond (see below). The new JCT 05 forms contain step-in rights available to funders upon an impending termination (Sch.5).

All of the above provisions take effect subject to the laws of insolvency. The principles which may conflict with such contractual rights are:

(1) provisions which vest the debtor's property, upon insolvency, in a particular creditor may be void; and

(2) the statutory right of disclaimer of a trustee in bankruptcy or liquidator cannot be excluded.

The impact of insolvency law is illustrated by the case of *British Eagle v Air France*[29] in which the House of Lords held the International Air Transport Association (IATA) scheme to be subject to the laws of insolvency. The scheme provided for settlement of debts and credits between airlines and precluded direct claims between them. Upon the insolvency of British Eagle it was held that claims could be brought directly against other airlines. The case has given rise to concern generally about the ability of contractual provisions to survive insolvency. A recommendation in the Latham report that the *British Eagle* principle should be reversed has not been acted on.

Under the 6th and earlier editions of the ICE conditions, cl.53 provided that the contractor's plant and equipment, when brought to the site, was deemed to vest in the employer. While such a provision may be enforceable on insolvency,[30] it was held in *re Cosslett (Contractors)Ltd*[31] that the clause was ineffective to pass title in the contractor's plant. The effect of the clause depends also on property in goods and materials having passed to the contractor (see Ch.7). The 7th edn contains no such vesting requirement, but similar provisions are found in other forms and may be added in ad hoc drafts. Determination following insolvency is not contrary to the insolvency laws and it is thought that a determination correctly carried out under the above clauses will be effective against a liquidator. In *re Cosslett (Contractors) Ltd* it was also held that the employer had the right to use the contractor's plant after determination on the ground of insolvency, even though property in the plant had not passed to the employer. But there is doubt as to the validity of a determination where the trustee or liquidator seeks to exercise their right to complete the contract and the employer may not be entitled to recover their loss where the trustee or liquidator exercises their right of disclaimer. Insolvency of the main contractor may raise issues as to whether the employer may make a direct payment to a sub-contractor of a sum otherwise due to the insolvent main contractor. In *re Tout & Finch*[32] it was held that a direct payment provision under the JCT form[33] could be

---

[29] [1975] 1 W.L.R. 758.
[30] *Re Walker, ex p. Barter* (1884) 26 Ch. D. 510.
[31] [1998] 2 W.L.R. 131.
[32] [1954] 1 W.L.R. 178.
[33] See cl.35.13.5 of JCT 80.

operated where the conditions of the clause were satisfied, namely that the contractor had failed to provide proof that a previous payment in respect of the sub-contractor had been discharged. The right of direct payment did not become available upon the contractor's insolvency but by reason of his previous default.

BONDS

When the contractor fails to complete the contract, whether by reason of their own default or the employer's determination, and the employer is unable to recover their loss from the contractor, the employer may have some further protection if the contractor has provided a bond. A bond is an undertaking by a surety to make payment upon the contractor's default. The usual form of bond guarantees the contractor's performance of the contract with an undertaking to be bound in a specified sum until (and unless) such performance is achieved. Upon the contractor's failure to perform in full, the employer is entitled to call on the surety (or bondholder) to make good the loss, up to the maximum amount of the bond. Since a bond is a contract of guarantee, it requires to be evidenced in writing. Further, since the employer gives no consideration (save that the contractor must include the cost of the bond in their price for the work) the bond must be made by deed. A call on a bond must be in proper form. In *AES-3C Maritza v Credit Agricole*,[34] it was held that future liabilities could not be the subject of a demand, so that a call including such sums was invalid. The ICC has issued as set of Uniform Rules for Demand Guarantees which can be incorporated into bonds.

A surety may be discharged from liability by a material alteration in the contractor's obligation which has been guaranteed,[35] such as extra works being ordered or an extension of the contract period being granted; but this is subject to the terms of the bond which will usually make provision for such alteration, which is inevitable under construction contracts.[36] In *Hackney Empire v Aviva Insurance*,[37] the employer and contractor entered into a side agreement intended to assist the contractor by inter alia making on account payments for claims. When the contractor defaulted and the employer claimed under a bond, the insurer argued that the side agreement had the effect of discharging the bond. It was held

[34] [2011] B.L.R. 249.
[35] *Holm v Brunskill* (1877) 3 Q.B.D. 495, CA.
[36] See also *Beck Interiors Ltd v Russo* [2010] B.L.R. 37, where a personal guarantee was held arguably not to cover variations.
[37] [2011] B.L.R. 726.

that the side agreement had not altered the terms of the contract guaranteed and the bond remained in force. The employer is under a duty to mitigate their loss, since otherwise it may be said the loss is not caused by the contractor's non-performance. The ICE/ICC form of contract incorporates a form of bond which provides:

> "The Surety shall not be discharged or released by any alteration variation or waiver of any of the terms and conditions and provisions of the contract or in any extent or nature of the works and no allowance of time by the Employer under or in connection with the contract or the works shall in any way release reduce or affect the liability of the Surety under this Bond."

These provisions are designed to overcome the above difficulties. The ICE/ICC conditions (cl.10) and tender provide that the contractor may be required to obtain a bond in a specified sum, not exceeding 10 per cent of the tender total. The JCT form provides for bonds covering advance payments, payment for off-site materials and the retention fund, but not for a general performance bond. Such a requirement may be incorporated into the tender documents. The provision of a bond may be made a condition precedent to the execution of the contract or to the contractor's right to payment.

A bond of the form under discussion is in the nature of a guarantee. The bondsman is not an insurer, and consequently there is no automatic duty of disclosure (see Ch.7). The terms of the bond may, however, require that notice be given of relevant events. A further matter which should be dealt with in the bond is its intended duration. This may be, for example, until the end of the maintenance period or for some further stipulated period. It is a matter of some difficulty for contractors if bonds do not provide for release, since banks may be unwilling to continue to provide further bonds while those given earlier remain in force. The law on bonds took an unexpected turn in the case of *Trafalgar House v General Surety*.[38] A groundworks sub-contractor had given a bond for 10 per cent of the value of the sub-contract. The terms of the bond included the following archaic but traditional language:

> "If the sub-contractor shall duly perform and observe all the terms provisions conditions and stipulations of the said sub-contract on the sub-contractor's part to be performed and observed according to the true purport, intent and meaning thereof or if on default by the sub-contractor the surety shall satisfy and discharge the damages sustained by the main contractors thereby up to the amount of the above written bond then this obligation shall be null and void . . .".

[38] [1996] A.C. 199.

The contractor completed the work and issued proceedings against the bondsman. The Court of Appeal held the contractor entitled to summary judgment without a full hearing,[39] on the claimant's assertion that it had suffered loss exceeding the value of the bond. The Court of Appeal considered that the commercial purpose of the bond was to provide immediate funds in the event of a failure by the sub-contractor. The House of Lords, however, held that the bondsman was entitled to raise any matter of defence or cross-claim and that the contractor would have to establish liability against the sub-contractor before payment on the bond could be demanded. In effect, the House of Lords rejected the Court of Appeal's attempt to treat the guarantee bond as an on-demand bond (see below).

On-demand bonds

As an alternative to a conditional bond, the effect of which is to guarantee payment of loss once established, there has been great development in recent years in a different type of instrument, still called a bond, but having a totally different effect. The on-demand bond usually entitles the holder (the employer) to call for payment by the bondsman (usually a bank) upon giving a particular form of notice. The notice usually requires no more than an assertion of default on behalf of the contractor. The bond money will then be paid irrespective of any disputes that may exist, either in relation to the underlying contract generally, or in relation to the purported reason for calling the bond in particular. The law relating to this type of bond has developed in the English courts through a series of cases in which contractors or sellers have sought injunctions from the court to prevent the bank from paying the bond or to prevent the other party to the contract calling for payment. The courts have consistently refused such injunctions, in line with decisions of courts in many other countries. The only material exception to this rule is where the contractor is able to establish (not merely allege) fraud. In *Edward Owen Engineering v Barclays Bank*,[40] the plaintiff, English suppliers to a Libyan customer, gave an on-demand bond. The customer, when himself in default, called the bond and the plaintiff sought an injunction against the bank to restrain payment. Lord Denning explained the procedure: the customer claims from the bank (there may be an intermediary bank involved also), the bank pay "on first demand without proof or conditions", and the bank then claim against the English suppliers. Lord Denning continued:

---

[39] R.S.C. Ord.14, see Ch.2.
[40] [1978] Q.B. 159.

"It is obvious that that course of action can be followed not only where there are substantial breaches of contract, but also when the breaches are insubstantial or trivial, in which case they bear the colour of a penalty rather than liquidated damages; or even when the breaches are non-existent. The performance guarantee then bears the colour of a discount on the price of 10 per cent or five per cent or as the case may be. The customer can always enforce payment by making a claim on the guarantee and it will then be passed down the line to the English supplier. The possibility is so real that the English supplier, if he is wise, will take it into account when quoting his price for the contract."

However, in the recent TCC case of *Simon Carves v Ensus UK Ltd*, an injunction restraining call of an on-demand bond was granted where the contractor established a strong case that the call was in breach of the underlying contract, which provided that the bond was to be treated as null and void.[41] In the great majority of cases, fraud will be the only available ground upon which payment may be resisted.

The demand for this type of bond has increased as international trade and construction work in particular have grown. Considerable problems remain for a contractor seeking to recover the proceeds of a bond which has been wrongly called, or even claiming credit for the value of the bond in any subsequent dispute. It is a matter of considerable importance that these issues should be dealt with fully in the underlying construction contract, so that they may be brought before arbitrators who may become seized of a dispute under that contract.

[41] [2011] B.L.R. 340.

CHAPTER 11

STANDARD FORMS OF CONTRACT

The widespread use of standard printed forms of contract is one of the hallmarks of the UK Construction Industry. Until the Housing Grants, etc., Act of 1996 there had been no statutory provisions governing the rights of parties in relation to construction works, in contrast to the position in Civil Law countries where detailed legislation is usually be found covering the rights of parties to construction projects. For this reason standard form contracts are not found in most Civil Law countries, while in the UK and in most common law jurisdictions the rights and liabilities of the parties are set out in detail in contracts. Historically it has been found convenient to use standard printed forms for this purpose. The obvious advantage is that they become well-known and predictable, and their provisions can be interpreted by the courts, providing added guidance to users. The same situation is found in other areas of commercial law, such as insurance and shipping, where standard documents exist which become well-known both to practitioners and to the courts.

Standard forms of construction contract can be traced back into the nineteenth century when most major building projects were undertaken by public authorities. These early forms of contract tended to be drafted by lawyers following a format which would now be seen as unduly harsh towards contractors. In the twentieth century standard forms were developed by a number of professional bodies, notably the RIBA and the ICE and during the past few decades many other institutions have developed their own forms. At the same time large main contractors issued their own standard forms, particularly for sub-contracts, leading to a major proliferation of different forms. Despite encouragement to produce a smaller number of more widely used forms (for example, in the Banwell Report of 1964) the trend continued in the opposite direction. In addition, the building industry and the engineering industry have each continued to produce their own separate forms, despite the close similarity of subject matter. In the 1980s a number of standard forms appeared dealing with alternative forms of procurement, e.g. management contracts and design and build forms. There then developed a practice of producing suites of contracts which could be used or adapted for many different circumstances including different form of procurement. Notable amongst these was the New Engineering Contract (NEC) produced by the ICE. More recently the emphasis on private finance for major projects has led to a new generation of standard forms and accompanying documentation of increasing complexity and length.

Construction Contracts in the UK, with some exceptions, are now subject to statutory rights and restrictions as a result of the Housing Grants, etc. Act 1996 covering stage payments, the right of suspension, prohibition of *"pay-when-paid"* clauses and the statutory right to adjudication. In some cases these rights are covered by express provision in the Standard Forms, and in other cases the parties are left to their statutory rights. However, most of the contents of the standard forms, dealing with matters such as management of the project, claims and extensions of time, remain subject to whatever the parties may agree. To this extent the standard forms of contract continue to operate as a private code of law governing the majority of the economic rights of the parties to the contract.

This chapter reviews some of the better known forms of contract that are likely to be encountered. The available standard forms are being amended and re-issued with increasing frequency. Consequently forms will be encountered in many different versions. For new projects the latest editions will generally be used; but when dealing with disputes under projects which have been under way for perhaps some years, older versions of the forms will be found. In seeking to cover the current forms this poses an editorial problem. In order to cover the field the forms of main contract reviewed in Chs 12 and 13 are those most recently issued, including the new JCT form published in mid-2005. This chapter, however, contains a mixture of current and older editions, including the new JCT Standard Building sub-contract, which replaces the former JCT domestic sub-contract forms. Where later versions exist or are in course of publication, this is noted in the text.

FORMS OF MAIN CONTRACT

Despite the huge proliferation of contract forms, the standard documentation issued originally by the RIBA and subsequently the Joint Contracts Tribunal (JCT) and those issued by the ICE have remained dominant in their respective areas of building and civil engineering construction. These forms are of importance, both in their own rights and as influencing many derivative forms of contract. The following two chapters present an outline commentary on the JCT and on the ICE standard forms. In this chapter the major alternative standard forms are reviewed, comprising the GC/Works form, Model Form MF/1 and the FIDIC forms, which are now dominant in the field of International Construction. When analysing the rights of the parties in relation to a matter covered by one of the standard forms it must be borne in mind that, in addition to the rights created by the printed form, the general principles of contract and of construction law will apply; the rights of the parties may also be governed by statutory provision, including mandatory requirements under European law; and for international contracts the governing law is likely to be other than English law.

The ICE/ICC Conditions

The Institution of Civil Engineers (ICE) has, since 1945, issued a form of contract works of civil engineering construction. The form was latterly issued jointly with the Association of Consulting Engineers (ACE) and the Civil Engineering Contractors' Association (CECA). The latest edition was the 7th, issued in 1999 and subsequently revised to take account, inter alia, of the Housing Grants, Construction and Regeneration Act 1996. In 2011, the ICE decided to sever its links with the form, which was taken over by the other sponsoring bodies under the new title of the Infrastructure Conditions of Contract (ICC). Alternative versions of the form now exist for design and build, for a "Term Contract", for Target Cost, for minor works, for ground investigation and for archaeological investigation. A form of sub-contract exists known as the "ICE Blue Form". While intended for use for domestic subcontracts with the ICE contracts, it is issued solely by the CECA.

The principal version of the ICE/ICC Contract remains the measurement version, which creates a "measure and value" contract by which the contractor is to be paid at the contract rates (which are themselves subject to variation) for the actual quantities of work executed. There is thus no "contract sum" but instead a "tender total". The work is to be carried out to the satisfaction of the engineer who is given wide powers of control and direction. When acting as agent of the employer, the engineer must act in the best interest of his principal. Conversely, when certifying or deciding on matters of entitlement under the contract, the engineer must act impartially. The conditions contain wide-ranging provisions under which the sums payable to the contractor are subject to alteration, usually in favour of the contractor.

The conditions contemplate that the form of contract will be accompanied by drawings and a specification in which the work is described, and by bills of quantities in which the work is measured and priced. By cl.9 of the conditions, the contractor undertakes to execute the contract agreement, which may be under seal. Clause 5 of the conditions states that the documents forming the contract "*are to be taken as mutually explanatory of one another and in case of ambiguities or discrepancies the same shall be explained and adjusted by the Engineer*". If necessary the engineer is to issue an instruction in writing. The engineer is given the power and duty to issue such further details as may be necessary. By cl.7, instructions which require a variation are deemed to be issued by the engineer pursuant to cl.51.

The contractor is required to provide all necessary superintendence during the construction of the works and to give the engineer access to inspect the work. The contractor's general obligation, by cl.8, is to construct and complete the works, provide all labour materials and equipment whether temporary or permanent for the construction and completion so far to be inferred from the contract. The contractor is not, however, to be responsible for the design or specification of any part of the permanent works, except as may be expressly provided in the contract. The contractor is to take full responsibility for the adequacy stability and safety of all site operations and methods of construction.

Where the contract provides for the contractor to be responsible for part of the design, by cl.7 the contractor is to supply drawings, specifications, calculations and other information to satisfy the engineer that the contractor's design generally complies with the requirements of the contract. The engineer may require further documents as necessary for the proper and adequate construction completion and maintenance of the works. Acceptance by the engineer is not to relieve the contractor of his responsibilities under the contract, but the engineer is responsible for the integration and co-ordination of the contractor's design with the rest of the works.

The contractor is required to take the risk of the site and the sub-soil. By cl.11 he is deemed to have inspected and examined the site and is responsible for the interpretation of information provided by the employer. As a significant exception to this responsibility, cl.12 allows the contractor to claim additional payment for work to overcome "*physical conditions (other than weather condition or conditions due to weather conditions) or artificial obstructions which conditions or obstructions could not in his opinion reasonably have been foreseen by an experienced Contractor*". Clause 12 is widely used as a vehicle for presenting claims for additional cost arising from constructional difficulties, usually relating to sub-soil conditions. The Court of Appeal upheld an award in which a transient combination of soil strength and stress was held to constitute a physical condition within cl.12.[1] In an Australian case similar wording has been held to permit a claim for an unforeseen condition in material within a

---

[1] *Humber Oil v Harbour & General* (1991) 59 B.L.R. 1; and see [1995] ConL.Y.B. 98.

borrow area[2]; and in the Technology and Construction Court, H.H. Judge Havery QC accepted that the words of cl.12 were wide enough to cover "*a substantive element of the works themselves*".[3]

A further significant qualification to the contractor's obligation to carry out and complete the works appears in cl.13 which states that the contractor is to construct and complete the Works "save insofar as it is legally or physically impossible". The degree of impossibility required to absolve the contractor from further performance was considered in *Turriff v Welsh Water Authority*,[4] where it was held sufficient that the work was commercially impossible in a practical sense. The contractor was attempting to join rectangular pre-cast sections of culvert, whose design tolerances prevented a seal being achieved. It was held the contractor was not under a duty to re-design the work to render it capable of being constructed. This principal has been applied in Hong Kong where government conditions of contract contain similar words.

Clauses 21–25 contain important requirements as to insurance and liability for losses. Clause 21 requires the contractor to insure the works and his materials and plant against loss from any cause, other than specified "*excepted risks*", so as to cover his responsibility for the works under cl.20. This insurance is to be in the joint names of employer and contractor. It is important for the employer to be aware that the works are not insured against damage caused by any fault in the engineer's design. The employer's ability to recover for such loss will depend on the limit of the engineer's professional indemnity policy (see Ch.7). Clause 22 apportions liability for third party claims which arise out of or in consequence of the work. Clause 23 requires the contractor to insure his own liability. Clause 24 deals with injuries to workmen and cl.25 gives the employer the right to effect any insurance which the contractor fails to take out.

Clause 14 deals with programme and method. The contractor is generally responsible for the method of working, but cl.51(1) includes a method change within the definition of a variation. Clauses 36–39 deal with workmanship and materials, inspection, testing and removal non-compliant work. Upon completion the engineer is to issue a Certificate of Substantial Completion which may be in respect of any substantial part of the works which have been substantially completed and have passed any final test. Completion is followed by the defects correction period. The later discovery of hidden defects does not invalidate the completion certificate and the contractor remains responsible for any breach of the contract within the period of limitation.

---

[2] *Atlantic Civil Pty Ltd v Water Administration Corp* (1992) 83 BLR 113 (HCNSW).
[3] *Associated British Ports v Hydro Soil Services* [2006] EWHC 1187.
[4] (1979) [1995] ConL. Y.B. 122.

The appendix to the contract specifies the time for completion, but there are extensive provisions under which the engineer may extend the completion date. The engineer also has powers to require expedition of progress under cl.14(4), or under cl.46 where the contractor is in default. Repeated failure to proceed at an adequate rate may lead to determination under cl.65.

The engineer has a wide power to issue a variation order which may include changes in quality or character or in any specified sequence, method or timing of construction. Valuation of variations, and of changes in quantities of the work are dealt with in cll.52 and 56. The contractor is fully liable for "domestic" sub-contractors. Where the contract requires a nominated sub-contractor, cll.58 and 59 lay down provisions governing the parties' rights, particularly in regard to default by the sub-contractor. Such work will be designated as either a provisional sum or a prime cost item. Clause 59 provides that, where a nominated sub-contract is terminated, the engineer must either make a re-nomination or order a variation, in the first instance at the employer's expense. These provisions are based on clauses in the JCT management.

Clause 60 sets out the monthly accounting procedure for interim payments. Measurement is dealt with in cll.55–57. The contractor is to be paid for the actual quantities of work executed at the contract rates, which may themselves be varied under cl.56(2). Clause 60(7) provides for payment of compound interest on certificates withheld or unpaid. In addition, there may be incorporated optional fluctuations clauses based on formula adjustments. Payments to the contractor may include claims, on numerous grounds, if accepted by the engineer. If not accepted, they may be the subject of a dispute. At the conclusion of the accounting process the engineer issues a final certificate which is a matter of account only and does not signify acceptance of the work.

For disputes, the conditions provide, by cl.66, a multi-tier system for resolution. In place of the former mandatory reference to the engineer, there are now three alternatives viz amicable resolution, adjudication and arbitration, from which the parties may choose. Clause 66B provides an adjudication procedure in accordance with s.108 of the Housing Grants, Construction and Regeneration Act 1996.

Clause 66C provides for arbitration in accordance with either the Construction Industry Model Arbitration Rules (CIMAR) or the ICE Arbitration Procedure (1997).

GC/works/1

This form has a long history as the standard government document for placing building and civil engineering contracts (works). Earlier editions were produced by government and, while published for information, use was restricted to government projects. After the demise of the PSA, production of the 3rd edn in 1990 was undertaken as a "privatised" project, although the document continued to be published by HMSO. A new edition was issued in 1998, also privately produced and published by HMSO. This exists in different versions: With Quantities, Without Quantities and Single Stage Design and Build Conditions. A model form and commentary are also published separately.

Under GC/Works/1, the work is to be carried out subject to instructions given by the PM (Project Manager) who is to be a person employed in that capacity by the employer "to act on his behalf in carrying out those duties described in the contract". The PM may issue a wide range of instructions (cl.40). They are to be valued, whether amounting to variations or not, by the QS (Quantity Surveyor), who is also appointed for the time being by the employer. The PM is empowered to grant extensions of time (cl.36). Provision is made for claiming expense by reason of delay or disruption from specified causes, and the QS is to value the claim (cl.64). Both the PM and the QS are, therefore, required to exercise their professional judgement in the same way as the engineer or architect under other forms.

The contract provides a wide range of measures which the employer may utilise at their option, including agreed measures for acceleration or cost savings (cl.38) and payment of a bonus for early completion (cl.38A). Provision is made for design work carried out by the contractor (cl.10). Where a programme is submitted, the contractor is taken to warrant that it shows the events that are critical to the satisfactory completion of the works, and that the programme is achievable and conforms with the requirements of the contract (cl.33). The contract expressly requires regular progress meetings and reports on progress and delay (cl.35). The contract allows for additional payment in respect of ground conditions or artificial obstructions which could not reasonably have been foreseen, having regard to information which ought reasonably to have been ascertained (cl.7), in terms similar to those appearing in the ICE Conditions of Contract. The Conditions of Contract are specifically tailored to the requirements of the Housing Grants, etc. Act 1996, e.g. providing expressly for suspension for non-payment (cl.52) and for adjudication (cl.59). Disputes (other than relating to enforcement of any adjudicator's decision) are to be referred to arbitration, but no reference is to be made until after completion, unless the parties otherwise agree (cl.60). Consequently, the decision of an adjudicator will be binding until the award of an arbitrator is subsequently given. Upon a reference to arbitration a timetable is to be set for the hearing, which is not to exceed a period of six months from the date of the preliminary meeting; and the award is to be made within three months thereafter.

One of the recommendations of the Latham report, which was not carried forward into the Housing Grants, etc. Act 1996, is included within the contract: cl.1A expressly requires the employer and the contractor to "deal fairly, in good faith and in mutual co-operation with one another". The contractor is required similarly to deal with all of their sub-contractors and suppliers. As the law currently stands, this would be unenforceable by sub-contractors (who are not parties to the contract) but as between employer and contractor the obligation of good faith and, possibly co-operation, might well lead to substantive allegations of breach.[5] The contract makes provision for nomination (cl.63) but the main contractor is to remain fully responsible and the employer is not to be required to pay any greater sum arising from any determination or re-nomination except on the ground of the sub-contractor's insolvency (cl.63A).

Form GC/Works/1 is intended for large scale building and civil engineering works. Alternative versions of the form are also issued known as GC/Works/2 for medium-sized projects, GC/Works/3 for M&E contracts, GC/Works/4 for small projects and GC/Works/10 for facilities management. Non-governmental forms are also issued known as PC/Works based on the government versions.

Model Form MF/1

A set of conditions known as the "Model-Form" has been issued by the Institutions of Mechanical and Electrical Engineers for many years. The edition of 1988 is issued with the Association of Consulting Engineers. The form is intended for contracts involving substantial elements of plant and machinery. In such forms of work, it is traditional for the supplier to perform much of the detailed design work but there is an appointed engineer with important powers. A notable feature of the form is the extensive provisions for completion and performance tests and for release of the contractor's liability at the end of the "defects liability period", a term which is correctly employed under this form.

The contractor is required, with due care and diligence, to "design manufacture deliver to site erect and test the plant, execute the works and carry out the tests on completion within the time for completion". The works are to be to the reasonable satisfaction of the engineer but the contractor is responsible for the "detailed design of the plant and of the works in accordance with the requirements of the specification" (cl.13). The contractor is also required to submit to the engineer drawings as called for in the contract or as may be required by the engineer. Drawings, etc. are to be approved and signed by the engineer (cl.15). The contract

---

[5] See Ch.5, Good Faith, Best Endeavours and Fair Dealing.

contains provisions for gaining access to the site, co-operation by the employer and for the contractor to maintain progress (cll.11, 13). The contractor may make a claim if obstructions are found on the site which could not reasonably have been ascertained from an inspection (cl.5.7).

The bulk of the form is directed towards installation and testing of plant and machinery. Thus, by cl.23, the engineer is given extensive powers to inspect, examine and test the plant at the contractor's premises where they may reject the plant which they consider defective, or not in accordance with the contract (cl.23). The contractor must obtain permission before delivery of plant and in default the engineer may suspend the work at the contractor's cost (cll.24, 25). After installation the engineer may carry out further tests and reject any plant considered defective, or not in accordance with the contract (cl.26). When the works are complete, and after notice the contractor is to carry out the tests of completion which may lead to rejection of the works (cl.28). By cl.29.2, "when the works have passed the tests on completion and are complete (except in minor respects that do not affect their use for the purpose for which they are intended) the engineer shall issue a certificate to the contractor and to the purchaser". This is the "Taking Over Certificate" which signifies effective completion and passing of the risk to the employer. However, this may be followed by the performance tests, if included in the contract, which are to be carried out after the works have been taken over. In the event of failure to pass the performance tests, the contract may stipulate liquidated damages for failure to achieve any guaranteed performance (note that these are not related to delay but to failure of the works to comply with the contract requirements). Alternatively, the purchaser may accept the works subject to abatement of the price (cl.35.8).

The contract contains provisions of far reaching importance as to latent defects. By cl.36 the contractor is required to make good any defects appearing within the defects liability period (usually 12 months), a similar liability period attaching to any repaired work. These obligations are expressed to be in lieu of any other obligation for the quality or fitness of the works and no further liability is to attach after the expiry of the defects liability period (cl.36.9). The only exception is in respect of "gross misconduct" where the contract may be liable within a period of three years after taking over (cl.36.10). The exclusion of liability is expressed to apply to sub-contractors. The equivalent clause has been held ineffective to protect sub-contractors by virtue of the doctrine of privity, but nevertheless effective to bar a claim in tort.[6] In addition, the contract provides for a final certificate which is to be exclusive evidence that the work is in accordance with the contract and that the contractor

---

[6] *Southern Water v Duvivier* (1985) 27 B.L.R. 111.

has performed all of their obligations. The certificate is also final as to the value of the works, with the exception of fraud or dishonesty, or proceedings brought within three months after the certificate (cl.39.12).

The engineer is given extensive powers under the contract, including a general power to order variations. This is, however, limited to a net additional value of 15 per cent (cl.27). Decisions, instructions and orders of the engineer may be disputed within 21 days, whereupon the engineer must confirm, reverse or vary the same, with reasons. Thereafter, the contractor must challenge the decision within a further 21 days otherwise it is binding (cl.2.6). A supplement containing amendments required by the Housing Grants, etc. Act 1996 was published in 1999. This is inappropriate where the form is used for work situated abroad.

MANAGEMENT CONTRACTS

This refers to main contracts in which the contractor offers "management" services in lieu of full responsibility for the performance of the work. The interest in these forms of contract does not centre on the management services to be provided, but on the extent of the main contractor's responsibility for performance by sub-contractors. The usual arrangement is that the whole of the physical work is to be carried out by sub-contractors. The contractor is usually entitled to be paid the actual cost, onto which may be grafted incentive payments or penalties. Where default occurs in relation to quality or time, it is usually provided that the management contractor is liable only if the sub-contractor can also be held liable, so that the main contractor's risk is very limited.

JCT Management Contract

This is the best known standard form of management contract, which was first issued in 1987, revised in 1998 and re-issued as a management contract "suite" in 2008 including a dedicated "works" agreement and contract conditions, a works contractor-employer agreement and sets of warranties to be given by the management contractor and/or the works contractors in favour of a purchaser or tenant and/or a funder. The essence of the contractual arrangement is that all physical work is to be performed by works contractors (who are sub-contractors but no longer so called). The management contractor is to be paid the prime cost of the work (which includes amounts payable under works contracts) plus a management fee. The prime cost to be paid is to exclude costs incurred as a result of any negligence by the management contractor.

The obligations of the Management Contractor include the requirement to:

> "2.3.1 ensure that the Project is carried out in a proper, workmanlike, economical and expeditious manner and in accordance with the Contract Documents and the Construction Phase Plan".
>
> 2.3.6 ensure that all work to be carried out by Works Contractors . . . carried out in accordance with the Project Specification and with the Works Contracts, using materials, goods and workmanship of the quality and standards therein specified . . .".

As regards default by a sub-contractor the management contractor is to take steps in consultation with the architect/contract administrator to enforce the sub-contract or otherwise secure the satisfactory completion of the project. The employer is required to pay the management contractor all amounts properly incurred by them in fulfilling these obligations (cl.5.2.1). The employer is then given the right to recover amounts so paid or credited, including liquidated damages, from the management contractor. The liability of the Management Contractor is, however, qualified as follows:

> "3.7 The Management Contractor shall fulfil all the duties required of him under each Works Contract and, subject to claused 5.1 to 5.4, the Management Contractor shall be fully liable to the Employer for any breach of the Terms of this Contract including any breach occasioned by any Works Contractor's breach of a Works Contract.
>
> 5.2 In the case of any breach or non-compliance as referred to in clause 5.1 and notwithstanding clause 3.7 the Employer shall:
>
> .1 be entitled to recover from the Management Contractor all amounts that the Employer pays, reimburses or credits to the Management Contractor . . . and where relevant the amount of liquidated damages referred to in clause 5.2.3 but only to the extent that such amounts have been recovered by the Management Contractor from the defaulting Works Contractor."

The difficulty which arises from such provisions (there are variants in other management forms) is that it can be argued that if the management contractors' own liability to the employer is contingent on recovery from the works contractor, they cannot show loss for the purpose of such recovery, with the result that the employer must always bear the loss. The point has not been before the courts but in the light of "no loss" arguments raised in other cases, the argument seems unlikely to succeed. In *Copthorne v Arup*[7] the Court of Appeal, considering a different aspect of cl.3.21 of the 1987 form (equivalent to cl.5.2.1 above), held that it did not exempt

---

[7] (1997) 85 B.L.R. 22.

the management contractor from liability for his own breach of obligations under the contract. The other point of interest under management
contracts is the nature and definition of the services to be provided by the
management contractor, in return for the management fee. In the JCT
management contract these are listed in cl.2.3 and include the following:

(1) preparing all necessary programmes,

(2) entering into Works Contracts timeously,

(3) providing site facilities,

(5) providing continual supervision and management,

(6) securing compliance with and giving statutory notices, and

(7) keeping necessary records.

Schedule 1 contains a detailed definition of Prime Cost. Schedule 2 (if
applied) stipulates for limited adjustment of the Construction Period
Management Fee where the prime cost achieved exceeds or falls below
the Project Cost Plan Total by more than 5 per cent, or any other
percentage agreed and stated in the Contract Particulars. Thus, if the
prime cost increases by 10 per cent the construction period management
fee increases by 5 per cent and similarly reduces by 5 per cent for a
reduction in prime cost of 10 per cent. This may be seen as the opposite
of a target cost arrangement, with no incentive adjustment at all if the
actual prime cost falls within 5 per cent of the target. No doubt these
provisions will be renegotiated in many contracts.

DESIGN AND BUILD CONTRACTS

As with management contracts, these come in many forms, often
being ad hoc drafts. The form of the contract is dependent on the degree
of design liability to be undertaken by the contractor. For example, if the
employer wishes to specify the overall design, with the contractor being
responsible only for detailed drawings, then the contract will need to
contain performance requirements only for the elements that the
contractor is to design, and these can be accommodated within a relatively conventional construction contract. Conversely, if the contractor is
to undertake the conceptual design as well as the details, then there needs
to be a carefully drafted list of employer's requirements, which may go
beyond technical performance. Further, the contractor, on submitting a

tender, will usually put forward specific proposals, and these will need to
be incorporated. Consideration needs also to be given to the submission
of details for approval as the work proceeds, and what is to happen if the
employer is not satisfied or changes their mind.

JCT Design and Build Contract

The latter type of contract is reflected in the JCT Design and Build
Form, previously known as the Standard Form of Building Contract with
Contractor's Design. Under the earlier name the form was last re-issued
in 1998. This review covers the newly named form issued in 2005, along
with revisions of most of the JCT suite of contract documents. The
Design and Build form provides for a statement of the employer's
requirements and the contractor's proposals, each of which are primary
contract documents. Clause 2 of the conditions then provides:

> "2.1.1 The Contractor shall carry out and complete the Works in a proper
> and workmanlike manner and in compliance with the Contract
> Documents the Health and Safety Plan and the Statutory
> Requirements and for that purpose shall complete the design for the
> Works including the selection of any specifications for any kinds
> and standards of the materials and goods and workmanship to be
> used in the construction of the Works so far as not described or
> stated in the Employer's Requirements or the Contractor's
> proposals, and shall give all notices required by the Statutory
> Requirements".

In the case of *Co-operative Insurance v Henry Boot* [2002] EWHC 1270
(TCC),[8] it was held that the obligation to "*complete the design*" rendered
the contractor liable for an inherent defect in the design taken over. This
result has, however, been reversed by an additional cl.2.17, which also
qualifies the contractor's design obligation generally. There is no
appointed architect and instructions are given directly by the employer
(cl.3.5) or the employer's designated agent. The employer may issue an
instruction which constitutes a variation (in the form called a change),
which includes change to the employer's requirements, or changes to
access, working space, working hours or the order of execution. The
contractor has the right to object as follows:

> "3.9.1 ... provided that the Employer may not effect a change which is or
> makes necessary, an alteration or modification in the design of the
> Works without the consent of the Contractor which consent shall
> not be unreasonably delayed or withheld."

[8] [2002] EWHC 1270 (TCC).

Where objection is raised by the contractor and the matter is not settled by agreement, the parties must invoke the dispute resolution procedure contained in s.9 and arts 7, 8 and 9. Clause 9.1 provides for mediation, cl.9.2 and art.7 for adjudication, cll.9.3–9.8 and art.8 for arbitration if chosen in the contract particulars, and art.9 for legal proceedings as the default mechanism. The contractor is under no further obligation to seek the employer's consent or approval to the details of the design, provided they comply with the requirements and proposals and are subject to any instruction the Employer may give. In regard to the contractor's design work, the contract provides:

> "2.17.1 . . . the Contractor shall in respect of any inadequacy in such design
> have the like liability to the Employer, whether under statute or
> otherwise, as would an Architect or, as the case may be other appro-
> priate professional designer holding himself out as competent to
> take on work for such design who, acting independently under a
> separate Contract with the Employer, had supplied such design for
> or in connection with Works to be carried out and completed by a
> Building Contractor who is not the supplier of the design."

This is to be contrasted with the position in the absence of any such provision, where there would ordinarily be an implied term that the work would be fit for purpose (see Ch.9). Where the contract involved work for or in connection with the provision of a dwelling, cl.2.17.2 contains a saving in respect of the higher liability placed on a designer by the Defective Premises Act 1972.

JCT Major Project Form

This form contrasts both with the 1998 edition of the JCT standard form and the 2005 revision. While it covers broadly the same topics as the standard form, the drafting is terse and direct so that the form achieves its objectives in about half the length of the 1998 form. Despite the designation "major" there is no suggested limit on the size of the project. The form creates a design and build contract in which there is no appointed architect or project manager. As with the design and build form, administrative decisions are made by the employer or employer's representative.

The contractor's basic obligation is:

> "1.1 The Contractor shall execute and complete the project in accordance
> with the Contract, including the completion of the design, the specifi
> cation or selection of materials and the execution of the construction
> works.
> 2.1 The Contractor shall comply with all written instructions issued by the
> Employer in connection with the design, execution and completion of

the project, except to the extent that the terms of Contract restrict the Employer's right to issue any particular instruction.

2.2 Where the Contract provides that an instruction is not to be treated as giving rise to a change, the Contractor shall not be entitled to any additional payment or adjustments to the completion date as a consequence of complying with the instruction and the issue of the instruction shall not relieve the Contractor of any of its obligations under the Contract."

Clause 39 contains a list of defined terms including:

"*Requirements*: the documents identified in the appendix that had been prepared by the employer in order to set out its requirements for the project and identify the boundaries of the site."

As regards design liability the conditions provide:

"5.1 The Contractor shall not be responsible for the contents of the Requirements or the adequacy of the design contained within the requirements.

6.1 The Contractor shall prepare the design documents.

6.2 The Contractor shall submit the design documents to the Employer."

Clauses 6.2–6.10 contain a design submittal procedure by which the design documents are to be submitted to the employer who returns the documents appropriately marked with the employer's comment. Clause 18 provides for the parties, upon entering in to the contract, to execute a Model Form of Novation Agreement in respect of all pre-appointed consultants. Responsibility for their work is then provided for as follows:

"18.4 Subject to clause 5.1 the Contractor shall be solely responsible under the Contract for the services provided by any pre-appointed consultant whether before of after the date of the Contract and for the works undertaken by any named specialist or replacement specialist appointed in accordance with clause 18.8.

18.8 Either before or as soon as possible after the termination of the Contract of a pre-appointed consultant or named specialist, the Contractor shall notify the Employer of its proposed replacement consultant or specialist. Where possible the replacement specialist shall be selected from any list contained within the Requirements. The proposed replacement consultant or specialist shall be appointed by the Contractor unless the Employer raises reasonable objection within seven days of the notification . . .".

The Contractor is entitled to extensions of time subject to providing notices to the employer who is then required to notify the contractor of such fair and reasonable extension or why it considers the completion date should not be adjusted.

Changes (variations) are dealt with conventionally by notification from the contractor or employer with provision for the contractor to provide quotations for acceptance by the employer, in default of which the employer is to make a fair valuation including an allowance for loss and expense in consequence of the change (cl.20). Clause 21 provides for loss and/or expense in respect of other causes including:

> ".1 A breach or act of prevention on the part of the Employer or its repre-
> sentative or advisers appointed pursuant to clause 15.2 other than any
> matters or actions that are expressly permitted by the Contract and
> that are stated not to give rise to a change.
> .2 Interference with the Contractor's regular progress of the project by
> others on the site.
> .3 The valid exercise by the Contractor of its rights under section 112 of
> HGCRA 1996 (Suspension)."

Claims to additional payment also include cl.8: Ground Conditions which provide:

> "8.1 If the Contractor encounters ground conditions or manmade obstruc-
> tions in the ground that necessitate an amendment to the Requirements
> and/or Proposals it shall notify the Employer of the amendments it
> proposes for the agreement of the Employer, such agreement not to be
> unreasonably delayed or withheld. Unless Clause 8.2 applies, such
> amendment shall not be treated as giving rise to a change.
> 8.2 When the Appendix states that Clause 8.2 is to apply, any amendment
> agreed by the Employer under Clause 8.1 shall be treated as giving
> rise to a change to the extent that ground conditions or manmade
> obstructions in the ground could not reasonably have been foreseen
> by any experienced and competent Contractor on the base date, having
> regard to any information concerning the site that the Contractor had
> or ought reasonable to have obtained."

This clause plainly owes its origin to the ICE Conditions of Contract.

Payment in respect of the works are to be made on a interim basis, including the value of the changes, reductions and claims. The appendix to the contract contains a pricing document which provides particulars of the manner in which the contract sum is to be paid with alternative methods of valuation comprising

> Rule A—interim valuation.
> Rule B—stage payment.
> Rule C—progress payments.
> Rule D—some other (specified) method.

The contract also contains a Third Party Rights Schedule which obliges the contractor to notify and take account of the interests of funders and contains restrictions on exercise of the contractor's rights, including the right of termination.

Clauses 35–37 provide for the resolution of disputes alternatively by mediation, adjudication or legal proceedings. The parties may agree to arbitration should they consider it appropriate, but the requirement for legal proceedings leaves the parties free to join in any sub-contractor, designer or funder who may have an interest in the outcome of any dispute.

The contract represents a modern reaction to the realities of contracting, first in that contractors are increasingly required to design substantial elements of major projects, including taking over responsibility for the employer's earlier consultants and advisers; and the fact that contract administration can effectively be operated by the employer or their representative, bearing in mind the immediate right of the contract to adjudicate upon any matter of dispute. The form represents a welcome alternative to the JCT Standard Form of Building Contract. The form is published together with a dedicated form of sub-contract.

ICE/ICC Design and Construct Conditions

The ICE produced their own Design and Construct Conditions in 1992 based closely on and using much of the drafting of the 6th edn of the main conditions. A second edition was issued in 2001, which is now updated and adopted as part of the ICC suite of contract forms. Some of the conditions are identical to, and many are simply adapted from, the main form. Conditions considered inappropriate to a design and construction contract are "not used" (cll.13, 17, 27, 34, 57 and 59). Administration of the contract is through the employer's representative with no independent engineer. The employer's representative carries out many of the functions otherwise performed by the engineer including certification (cl.60) and granting extensions of time (cl.44).

The contract operates in the same manner as the JCT Contractor's Design Form. The contract documents incorporate the employer's requirements and the contractor's submission, the latter being defined as "the tender and all documents forming part of the contractor's offer together with such modifications and additions thereto as may be agreed between the parties prior to the award of the contract" (cl.1(1)(f)). The contractor's basic obligation is to "design construct and complete the works and provide all design services, labour materials . . . and everything whether of a temporary or permanent nature required . . . so far as the necessity for providing the same is specified in or reasonably to be inferred from the contract" (cl.8(1)). As regards the completion of the design (which often gives rise to dispute or at least dissatisfaction under design and build contracts), cl.36(2) provides that materials and work-manship, where not described in the contract, are to be "appropriate in all the circumstances". By cl.8(2), the contractor's design obligation, including checking the employer's design, is to "exercise all reasonable skill care and diligence". As with the JCT form, this effectively operates as a limitation of liability, which would ordinarily be one of fitness for purpose (see Ch.9).

The employer's representative is given no general power to issue instructions. Their power to alter the works is conditional upon first having consulted with the contractor's representative, who is required to submit a quotation for the work as varied and their estimate of any delay, these matters to be agreed before the order is issued "wherever possible" (cll.51, 52). The variation must be to the employer's requirements, leaving the contractor to complete the design details in accordance with the contract.

The ICC, based in Paris, issued in 2007, a model turnkey contract for major projects intended to be used internationally. The form includes detailed obligations of good faith in line with other model forms of contract issued by the ICC.

HYBRID FORMS OF CONTRACT

This term refers to forms of contract intended for use in a wide range of situations, covering different forms of procurement as well as the complete range of projects falling within the description of construction. Indeed some projects involve primarily the provision of services, with construction being an ancillary part of the undertaking.

Engineering and Construction Contract

This form comprises a full suite of contract documents intended to cover a wide range of procurement options as well as all the different activities within the project. The form was first produced by the ICE in 1991 as the New Engineering Contract (NEC). Following the prominent support given in the Latham Report, it was renamed the Engineering and Construction Contract. A number of editions have been produced and the component documents have been updated individually. The notes below relate to the new 3rd edn published in June 2005. The documents make use of core clauses which are common to all versions and the forms are intended for use with a wide range of projects, not limited to building and civil engineering. The drafting of all the documents follows the same somewhat unconventional style, making use of the present tense.

A notable feature of the form is that the functions conventionally fulfilled by the engineer, are split into three. Inspection and checking functions are carried out by the "supervisor"; certifying and other administrative functions are carried out by the "project manager"; and decisions on disputes are given by the "adjudicator", a concept introduced into the NEC which predated both the Latham report and the Housing Grants, etc., Act. In later versions of the form the provisions for adjudication are modified to comply with requirements of the Act, where it applies. The forms are intended to be used for the full range of engineering and construction activities, much of which is not subject to the Act.

The core clauses are contained in nine different sections. A logical but unconventional numbering system is also adopted by which the first group of clauses is numbered 10,11,12,13, etc. The core clauses cover:

> (cll.10,11, etc.)—general, including definitions and requirements as to communication. The contractor and project manager are each to give the other "early warning" of matter which could increase the price or cause delay;

> (cll.20,21, etc.)—contractor's main responsibilities, including provisions for submission of design details;

> (cll.30,31, etc.)—time, including provisions for the programme, possession and acceleration by agreement;

> (cll.40, 41, etc.)—testing and defects, including provision for tests before delivery;

> (cll.50, 51, etc.)—payment, including provision for interim certificates;

> (cll.60, 61, etc.)—compensation events, including a long list of matters giving rise to adjustment of the costs or programme. The contractor is required to quote for such events. The project manager may accept the quotation or require a revised one or assess the consequences themselves;

> (cll.70, 71, etc.)—title, covering ownership of plant and materials;

> (cll.80, 81, etc.)—risks and insurance, providing for either the employer or the contractor to carry and insure risks arising under the contract; and

> (cll.90, 91, etc.)—termination by either party.

Despite the unconventional drafting, many of the detailed contractual provisions are similar in effect to those of other standard forms, particularly the ICE conditions. Examples of core clauses falling within the above sections are the following:

"16.1 The Contractor and the project manager give an early warning by notifying the other as soon as either becomes aware of any matter which could

- increase the total of the prices
- delay completion
- delay meeting a Key Date or
- impair the performance of the works in use

21.2 The Contractor submits the particulars of his design as the works information requires to the project manager for acceptance. A reason for not accepting the Contractor's design is that it does not comply with either the Works Information or the applicable law.
The Contractor does not proceed with the relevant work until the project manager has accepted his design.

31.1 If programme is not identified in the Contract data, the Contractor submits a first programme to the project manager for acceptance within the period stated in the Contract data.

45.1 If the Contractor is given access in order to correct a notified defect but he has not corrected it within its defect correction period, the project manager assesses the cost to the Employer of having the defect corrected by other people and the Contractor pays this amount. The Works Information is treated as having been changed to accept the Defect.

50.5 The project manager corrects any wrongly assessed amount due in a later payment certificate.

60.1 The following are compensation events
(12) The Contractor encounters physical conditions which

- are within the site
- are not weather conditions and
- which an experienced Contractor would have judged at the Contract date to have such a small chance of occurring that it would have been unreasonable for him to have allowed for them

Only the difference between the physical condition encountered and those for which it would have been reasonable to have allowed is taken into account in assessing a compensation event.

72.1 The Contractor removes equipment from the site when it is no longer needed unless the project manager allows it to be left in the works.

81.1 From the starting date until the defects certificate has been issued the risks which are not carried by the Employer are carried by the Contractor."

Many of the standard clauses, despite the unconventional drafting, are clearly based on the standard ICE conditions and the result is, in many cases, the same. The organisation of the ECC can be seen in the index to the conditions. Thus, the main contract document is printed with the full set of core clauses and with optional clauses to be substituted in order to produce the following main option form;

Option A   Priced Contract with Activity Schedule
      B   Priced Contract with Bill of Quantities
      C   Target Contract with Activity Schedule
      D   Target Contract with Bill of Quantities
      E   Costs Reimbursable Contract
      F   Management Contract

For disputes the contract provides two options, W1 if the Housing Grants, etc., Act does not apply and W2 if it does. Both provide similar adjudication procedures, W1 being subject to time limits before a dispute may be referred. In both cases the adjudicator's decision must be challenged further within 28 days and may be referred to arbitration if so provided in the contract data.

Each of the main options contains a set of "secondary options" which are equivalent to appendices which cover the following matters: X1 Price adjustment for inflation; X2 Changes in the law; X3 Multiple currencies; X4 Parent company guarantees; X5 Sectional completion; X6 Bonus for early completion; X7 Delay damages; X12 Partnering; X13 Performance bond; X14 Advanced payment to the contractor; X15 Limitation of design liability; X16 Retention; X17 Low performance damages; X18 Limitation of liability; and X20 Key Performance Indicators. In addition to the six main forms of contract the NEC package contains a "short Contract" containing similar compressed wording; a form of sub-contract containing a set of core clauses, main option clauses and secondary option clauses following the pattern of the main contract; a short sub-contract form and a professional services contract. The forms are published as a boxed set, together with extensive guidance notes and flow charts covering all the different options available.

Following the example of the NECC, which was promoted by the ICE, the Insitution of Chemical Engineers, which had previously published only a form of main contract, issued a full suite of forms designed for use on process plant projects. The suite includes sub-contracts, a minor works contract and main forms for target cost, cost reimbursable and lump sum contracts. A set of forms for dispute resolution is also included.

PFI Forms of Contract

Since the launch of the Private Finance Initiative in 1992 the Government has issued numerous guidance documents setting out recommended practice, including the Standardisation of PFI Contracts (SoPC). Version 4 of the recommendations was issued in March 2007.

The documentation can be accessed on the Government website *http://www.hm-treasury.gov.uk/documents*. A separate local government supplement is also available and individual standardised versions can be found on linked sites for school, housing and specialised construction works such as highways.

The full documentation consists of over 300 pages incorporating specimen clauses, including definitions. The important distinction between a PFI contract and a construction contract is that the latter provides, in addition to conventional design and construction obligations, provisions as to the "service period", that may typically continue for 25 years after completion and occupation of the building or facility. During the initial construction or development phase all the necessary finance is provided via the PFI contractor by "funders" whose rights will be set out in a suite of ancillary documents linked into the primary PFI contract. At the end of the construction phase the PFI promoter, who in public works schemes is usually termed "the authority", occupies and uses the building or facility and pays fees ("service charges") which are intended to permit the funders to recoup the investment. A PFI project therefore operates in some ways as a 100 per cent mortgage of the scheme with repayments stipulated so that the funders become entitled to make a profit overall. Where the new facility is to be used by the public, for example, a motorway, bridge or tunnel, the service charge will be replaced by a right to charge tolls during the concession period.

The construction phase of the project requires all the conventional provision of a construction contract, including sanctions and compensation provisions which may result in sums becoming payable by or to the authority. There will be provision allowing extension of time for specified causes ("relief events") which tend to follow conventional construction contracts. Provisions for raising technical issues must cover matters arising during two distinct periods, namely the initial design and construct period followed by the period of occupation, during either of which corrective or additional work may be required. Likewise provisions for termination of a PFI contract must deal with the design and construct period and separately, with the subsequent period of occupation and use of the facility.

The PFI contract will contain many project-specific clauses and it is for this reason that the extensive Government PFI Code is in the form of examples and specimen clauses together with guidance and recommendations. As regards payment, the Treasury Guidance document includes the following:

"7.2.1 The key features of a payment mechanism must be:

• no payment should be made until the service is available.

- there should be a single Unitary Charge for the service which is not made up of separate independent elements relating to availability or performance.
- the level of payment should be linked to the level of service. For a payment method based on availability with an overlay of performance deductions, this will mean linking payment to both the availability and the quality of the service
- the Unitary Charge should never be paid in advance of the period to which it relates
- . . .".

Provisions for additional payment to or by the PFI contractor should be accounted for only at completion when delivery of the service commences. The guidance notes also recommend incentives to performance, both financial and non-financial. Provisions are commonly made for changes of circumstances, including change of law both during the design and construction period and during the service period. For the resolution of disputes, PFI contracts usually provide for disputes initially to be referred to a form of ADR which may require, as a first step, meetings between senior executives. PFI contracts are excluded from the Housing Grants, etc., Act and therefore are not subject to a mandatory right to adjudication. Contracts often provide, however, for contractual adjudication based on statutory adjudication, and this may be as an alternative to mediation. Where not resolved by any of these means, parties are then bound to refer the dispute to private arbitration.

PFI contracts and their ancillary documents typically provide for different types of "step-in" rights. Under the PFI contract itself the authority may reserve step-in rights to be available during the service period where there is a need to prevent or mitigate serious risk to health and safety or to the environment. This is usually seen as a limited and short-term measure. In addition, under the financing arrangement, Senior Lenders may retain step-in rights by which, under a direct agreement with the authority, they may take over and exercise rights under the PFI contract, for example following a termination, in order to revive the project and thereby protect their investment. Particular provision will be needed to govern the liabilities thereby acquired by the Senior Lenders and the ability to step-out and reinstate pre-existing contractual arrangements.

PFI contracts are intended to operate without an appointed third party administrator, such as an architect or engineer. Certain matters requiring positive decision, particularly as to the achievement of completion, may be referred to a specially appointed "independent certifier" charged with the duty to give specific decisions. Other matters such as claims or extensions of time may be dealt with under the dispute resolution procedure, or alternatively provision may be made for an independent person to give a decision as an expert, which will not generally thereafter be open to review. A typical provision in a PFI contract relating to the performance of the design and construction work is as follows.

> "The PFI contractor shall procure the performance of the works in accordance with
> (1) This agreement (including all annexures and appendices).
> (2) All law.
> (3) Any relevant design documents.
> (4) Any relevant planning approval and planning agreement.
> (5) In the case of the Initial Works, the schedule of phases and key dates.
> (6) The requirements of ISO 9000.
> (7) Good industry practice.
> (8) The reasonable instructions of the authority."

The key to understanding of the structure of a PFI contract lies in the need to provide adequate protection and security to all parties in respect of a substantial and long-term investment which is dependent initially on the proper performance of design and construction obligations and subsequently on the adequate delivery over many years of the services contracted for. Essentially the long-term contract is made between the authority or user and a combination of the design/building contractor and the intended service provider, in each case acting through the PFI contractor and funded by the senior and subsequent lenders. The so-called "PFI contractor" is usually a specially formed company (special purpose vehicle) without substantial asset, whose funding is entirely dependent on the companies which undertake to provide services and funding to operate the project. For an illustration of disputes arising under a local authority PFI project, see *Biffa Waste Services v Maschinenfabrik Ernst Hesse Gmbh*.[9] While PFI contracts substantially originated in the UK they have been increasingly used internationally. For schemes in developing and transition countries UNCITRAL has, with the backing of the European Bank for Reconstruction and Development (EBRD) issued a set of rules and model laws for infrastructure projects intended to promote the best internationally accepted standards.

Framework Agreements

A novel form of agreement which has recently been adopted by a number of Institutions is the so-called framework agreement by which the parties set out terms which will apply to orders placed over a defined

---

[9] [2008] B.L.R. 155; [2009] B.L.R. 1.

future period. One such form is the JCT standard Framework Agreement (FA 2007). This operates in conjunction with an underlying contract to provide a mechanism for calling off building work or services. There is an optional guarantee of a stated volume of work within the term of the agreement. The agreement is compliant with EU public procurement rules[10] and may therefore be used by public or private sector clients.

PARTNERING FORMS

Partnering as a concept has been in existence for many years, but only during the last decade has the principle become formalised with the production of various guides and, more recently, standard documentation. As discussed elsewhere in this book, partnering falls into different categories according to the intention of the participants. Thus, the arrangement may comprise a contract which is intended to have enforceable legal consequences, or it may comprise a non-binding declaration or "charter". Secondly, the arrangement may be bilateral, which will usually be the case with contractual obligations, or it may be made between many parties. A non-binding charter will usually be multilateral and may be signed by any number of participants. Thirdly, the arrangement undertaken may relate to a single project or may comprise a long-term arrangement. In the latter case, the arrangement may consist of nothing more than a long-standing business relationship under which, without legal obligation or any formal terms, repeat orders are placed to the mutual benefit of two parties. Mention should be made of the concept of "Alliancing" which is generally understood to represent a more formal and binding arrangement with financial incentives based on profit and risk sharing.

Recognising the apparent management benefits of the concept of partnering (which is by no means unique to construction), a number of standard documents have been produced, some of which are gaining currency and following in the construction industry. Those reviewed here comprise the PPC 2000 standard form Project Partnering Contract, which was drafted in collaboration with the Association of Consultant Architects (ACA); the NEC partnering option, intended for use in all NEC contracts; the ICE partnering addendum intended for use with the ICE and related conditions; and the JCT partnering charter. The catalyst for each of these documents has been the recommendations of the Latham Report, together with the Construction Task Force Report "Rethinking Construction". Whilst these documents represent current

---

[10] EU Consolidated Directive and Public Contract Regulations 2006.

aspirations for the future direction of the construction industry, their effect, both in management and legal terms, remains to be established.

PPC 2000 ACA Standard Parnering Form

This is a fully developed construction contract drafted in association with and published by the Association of Consultant Architects (ACA). The document comprises 28 substantial clauses and five lengthy appendices comprising a full design and build contract expressed in current partnering language. The contract comprises a project partnering agreement together with "partnering terms" and incorporates other "partnering documents" comprising a partnering timetable, consultant services schedules, payment terms, project brief, project proposals, price framework and Key Performance Indicators (KPI's). The parties to the contract are the "partnering team" who are intended to comprise both client and the contractor (referred to as the constructor) together with consultants (including design professionals) and specialist (sub-contractors). The partnering team comprises those who enter in to initial project partnering agreement and others who may subsequently join.

Essentially, the document creates a conventional construction contract between the client and the constructor (main contractor) to which consultants and specialists become party for the purpose of joint co-operative activities. The stated objective is to generate mutual benefit in terms of the efficient, economic and successful performance of the project, this being the essence of the theory of partnering. The primary legal obligations taken on under the contract are, however, carefully limited to the parties as between which they are intended to apply. These points are set out in the following clauses:

> "1.3 The Partnering Team members shall work together and individually in the spirit of trust, fairness and mutual co-operation for the benefit of the Project, within the scope of their agreed roles, expertise and responsibilities as stated in the Partnering Documents.
>
> 1.5 ... only the client and no other Partnering Team member shall be responsible for making all payments due to each Consultant in accordance with the relevant Consultant Payment Terms.
>
> 1.6 ... only the Constructor and no other Partnering Team member shall be responsible for making all payments due to each Specialist in accordance with the Specialist Payment Terms set out in the relevant Joining Agreement or Specialist Contract."

Clause 3.1 of the partnering terms obliges the Partnering Team members to work together and individually in accordance with the partnering documents to achieve transparent and co-operative exchange of information and to organise and to integrate their activities as a collaborative team.

Clause 3.3. requires the establishment of a Core Group who are to meet regularly and to review and stimulate progress. Likewise the full partnering team are to meet regularly, in each case reaching decisions by consensus. Clause 4 sets out the partnering objectives which include achieving for their mutual benefit:

> "(i) trust, fairness, dedication to common goals and an understanding of each other's expectations and values.
> (ii) finalisation of the required designs, timetables, prices and supply chain for the project.
> (iii) innovation, improved efficiency, cost effectiveness, lean production and reduction or elimination of waste.
> (iv) completion of the project within the agreed time and price and to the agreed quality.
> (v) measurable continuous improvement by reference to the targets described in clause 4.2 and the KPI's, and
> (vi) commitment to people including staff and the users of the project."

Clause 4.2 sets out the partnering targets which are as follows:

> "(i) reduced capital cost and whole life costs.
> (ii) reduced design, supply and construction time.
> (iii) reduced defects and zero defects.
> (iv) reduced accidents.
> (v) increased predictability.
> (vi) increased productivity.
> (vii) increased turnover and profit.
> (viii) improved quality.
> (ix) improved sustainability.
> (x) any other targets identified in the KPI's."

Following upon these objectives, the conventional sections of the contract are also expressed in co-operative terms including the following:

> "8.1 The Lead Designer and the other Design Team Members shall develop the design and process of the Project in accordance with this clause 8, with the object of achieving best value for the client.
> 8.8 At each stage of design development the Lead Designer, with input as agreed from other Design Team Members shall amend designs as necessary to adopt the results of Value Engineering exercises undertaken in accordance with clause 5.1(iii) where such results are approved by the Client after Core Group Consultation."

Payment is dealt in cl.12 and includes the following:

> "12.3 Prices for all aspects of the Project shall be developed and agreed in accordance with this clause 12 by reference to the Price Framework and other Partnering Documents to establish an Agreed Maximum

> Price within any Budget stated in the Price Framework and other-
> wise as low as is achievable consistent with best value and in
> compliance with the Partnering Documents."

The constructor's profit and overheads are to be fixed at agreed amounts
subject to such variations as may be agreed with prices for direct labour
and specialists (sub-contractors), being similarly agreed. In addition:

> "12.10 The Core Group shall investigate the potential for cost savings
> against the Agreed Maximum Price and for added value in the
> design, supply, construction and operation of the Project and shall
> make recommendations to the Client."

As regards variations, cl.17 provides that any member of the Partnering
Team may propose a change in the best interests of the project to be
considered by the client, who may also propose changes which are to be
the subject of agreed price and time consequence. In lieu of agreement
the client's representative is to ascertain the time and cost effects of any
change on a fair and reasonable basis. In this respect, as in others, the
contract makes necessary provisions for the partnering approach to result
either in agreement or not as to the consequences of unavoidable risks.
In a similar vein, cl.18 contains relatively conventional machinery for
granting extension of time in respect of conventional causes of delay
including "exceptionally adverse weather conditions". Clause 18.5 identifies those grounds for extension of time which entitle the constructor to
an addition to the agreed maximum price in respect of the time-based
overheads.

In general terms, PPC 2000 represents a bold amalgam of partnering
principles with established construction contract precedent, aimed at
producing a forward looking document which attempts to require all the
relevant parties to the construction process to co-operate for what is
intended to be their mutual benefit, as well as the benefit of the project.
In many ways the document is an alternative means of achieving the
same objective as the New Engineering and Construction Contract. The
ACA also publishes a version known as SPC 2000 which is intended for
use where specialist sub-contractors are to be involved in project design
and risk management from the outset.

ICE/ICC Partnering Addendum

Unlike PPC 2000 the ICE/ICC Addendum has no independent effect
and operates as a series of common obligations intended to be incorporated into each of the separate Bi-Party Contracts between those who
enter into or "join" the Addendum. The participants are referred as

"partners" and within the partners there is to be core group who are to set up an executive board which operates by unanimous vote (P2 (3)). The details of the partnering arrangement are intended to be set out in Partnering Objectives, in Partnering Operation and Documents, in Partner Risk Managing Arrangements and in Partner KPI/Incentive Arrangements, each of which require to be specially agreed and recorded respectively in Schedules 3, 4, 5 and 6 of the Addendum. It is anticipated that revisions may be made to each of these documents and that new partners or core group members may join or leave as may be agreed. The arrangement is, thus, one of almost complete flexibility. The form is now part of the ICC suite of contract forms.

There are, however, a number of provisions within the Addendum which contain obligations which may be of significance within the individual bi-party contracts which otherwise bind the parties, including the following.

"P4(3) The Partners shall work together as a team in accordance with the Partnering Objectives and in the best interests of the project.

P4(5) Without limitation to the Partners' obligations under the Bi-Party Contracts, each Partner shall give a warning to the other Partners as soon as it becomes apparent that

(a) he will be or may become unable to meet his obligations or requirements under his Bi-Party Contract and partnering Addendum and

(b) he or one of the other partners will or may be likely to incur delay and/or additional cost under his Bi-Party Contract stating the reasons, the party or parties responsible and the likely impact.

And in each case, together with any proposed solutions.

P4(9) A Partner may ask another Partner to provide the information that is needed to carry out the work in his Bi-Party Contract in accordance with the consolidated programme whilst at the same time giving notice of such request to the Core Group. The other Partner shall provide such information to the extent required under his Bi-Party Contract."

It is possible that provisions of this sort may create substantive rights, but these are subject to the following limitations:

"P8(1) This Partnering Addendum shall not (itself) create a legal partnership or any legal relationship between the Partners and does not include direct remedies between Partners who are not party to the same Bi-Party Contract to recover losses suffered by one Partner caused by a failure of another Partner.

P8(2) This Partnering Addendum does not confer any right on any Partner to represent any other Partner or enter into a commitment

> on behalf of any other Partner (without such other Partners' prior written consent)."

The intention of the Addendum is to create a common set of objectives and to foster mutual support and co-operation in the common interests of the project.

JCT Partnering Charter

This document is issued as part of Practice Note 4 and is stated to be the first of what may be a number of JCT documents seeking to embed the culture of partnering both for one-off and repeat clients. The present document is stated to be non-binding and intended for single projects. The Practice Note itself emphasises that partnering is primarily about team-working and establishing good relationships based on co-operation, openness and trust. The Charter itself is contained in three pages only, which provide for a (substantial) list of Team Members who, under the Charter:

> "agree to work together on [the defined project] to produce a completed project to meet agreed client needs, and meet agreed quality standards within agreed budgets/price and agreed programme."

Unlike the ICE model, the JCT Charter does set out the agreement of the signatories to act:

- in good faith;
- in an open and trusting manner;
- in a co-operative way;
- in a way to avoid disputes by adopting a "no blame culture";
- fairly towards each other; and
- valuing the skills and respecting the responsibilities of each other.

The Charter also specifies the objectives to be achieved by the team which are to be measured against performance indicators to be established. These are as follows:

Delivery

     □ right first time with zero defects;
     □ utilise best and safest practice;

☐ encourage innovation and the efficient use of resources; and
☐ maximise the efficiency of our respective contributions.

People

☐ consider neighbours and others affected by the project;
☐ respect each other;
☐ promote an enjoyable and healthy working environment;
☐ provide training and staff development; and
☐ foster tolerance.

Teamworking

☐ focus on the customer;
☐ plan and promote clear and effective communication;
☐ engender a working environment that is conducive to shared problem solving;
☐ provide mutual support; and
☐ involve all members of the supply chain the partnering concept.

Commercial

☐ add value and enhance reputations;
☐ create incentives for maximising the rewards for all parties;
☐ provide transparency and certainty of information; and
☐ provide feedback.

FORMS OF SUB-CONTRACT

Many contractors impose their own standard terms on sub-contractors. These tend to contain one-sided provisions which place the sub-contractors at a disadvantage in a dispute. Conversely some specialists and suppliers impose their own terms on main contractors. A fairer balance may be achieved by using one of the standard forms of sub-contract designed for use with the standard main forms.

JCT Standard Building sub-contract

The 2005 revisions to the full JCT suite of Contract Documents include a Standard Building Sub-Contract which replaces both the former Domestic and Nominated Sub-Contract forms. The new documents also include Standard Sub-Contract forms for use with the Intermediate Building Contract, with the Design and Build Contract and a Management Works Contract for use with the Management Building

Contract. The Standard Building Sub-Contract is available with or without Sub-Contractor's design. The notes below relate to the form including design.

The format of the Sub-Contract Conditions follows the new layout of the Standard Building Contract with topics being divided into "sections". The sections correspond to the Standard Building Contracts save that Section 7 (assignment) is omitted. The Sub-Contract Form is published with a separate Form of Agreement, which includes the Contract Particulars. The conditions are published together with five schedules including Forms of Bonds (Schedule 3) and Fluctuations Options (Schedule 4).

The obligation of the Sub-Contractor is stated to be as follows:

> "2.1 The Sub-Contractor shall carry out and complete the Sub-Contract Works in a proper and workmanlike manner, in accordance with the Sub-Contract Documents, the Health and Safety Plan and the statutory requirements and in conformity with directions given in accordance with Clause 3.4 and all other reasonable requirements of the Contractor (so far as they apply) for the time being regulating the carrying out of the Main Contract Works, and shall in relation to the Sub-Contract Works give all notices required by the statutory requirements".

As regards the Sub-Contractor's Designed Portion:

> "2.2.1 The Sub-Contractor shall, in accordance with the Numbered Documents (to the extent they are relevant) complete the design for the Sub-Contractor's Designed Portion (SCDP) including the selection of any specifications for the kinds and standards of the materials, goods and workmanship to be used in the SDP Works, so far as not described or stated in the Contractor's requirements or the Sub-Contractor's proposals;"

and in respect of materials, goods and workmanship:

> "2.4.1 All materials and goods for the Sub-Contract Works, excluding the SCDP Works shall so far as procurable, be of the kinds and standards described in the Sub-Contract Documents. Materials and goods for the SCDP Works shall, so far as procurable, be of the kinds and standards described in the Contractor's requirements or, if not there specifically described, as described in the Sub-Contractor's proposals . . .".

The sub-contractor's design liability, as in the case of the Main Contract, is limited to that of a professional designer, i.e. a duty of reasonable skill and care (cl.2.13.1). As regards delay to the works, the sub-contractor is entitled to claim extension of time on the same grounds as those under the Main Contract. The application must, however, be made to the contractor who is required to fix such revised period for completion as they estimate to be fair and reasonable (cl.2.18).

The sub-contractor is required to comply with directions issued by the contractor save that there is a right of reasonable objection in respect of variation which affects access or working conditions (cl.3.5). Any instructions from the architect which affect the Sub-Contract Works are, when issued by the contractor deemed to be a direction (cl.3.4).

The sub-contractor's right to payment is not tied to the Main Contract but may be either on an adjustment basis using Bills of Quantities, or a re-measurement basis (cl.4.1, 4.2). Variations may be valued on a traditional basis using billed rates or fair rates (cl.5.6) or the contractor may direct the sub-contractor to provide a quotation in accordance with the procedure set out in Schedule 2, which quotation the contractor may accept. Alternatively, the sub-contractor is entitled to object for the procedure under Schedule 2, in which event the contractor must issue a fresh instruction for the work to be valued conventionally (cl.5.3). A Schedule 2 quotation is to include both the costs and time adjustment required and may include the cost of preparing the quotation. If the quotation is not accepted, the cost of preparing it is to be added to the sub-contract sum.

As in the case of the main Form of Contract, the sub-contract contains provisions for resolution of disputes by mediation, adjudication or arbitration. The latter is available only if selected in the Article, the default procedure being legal proceedings.

CECA form of Sub-Contract

This sub-contract document was first issued by the FCEC (now Civil Engineering Contractors Association) for use in conjunction with the ICE Conditions of Contract and is often (misleadingly) referred to as the ICE form of sub-contract. It remains in current use with the ICE conditions, 5th to 7th editions and now the ICC form. A revision was issued in 1998 and reprinted with amendments in 2001. Being drawn up by one body only, the form is a model of clarity, avoiding most of the obscurities and length of the main forms of contract.

The form contains short recitals recording that the sub-contractor has been afforded the opportunity to read the main contract, and five schedules. These are to contain, inter alia, particulars of the main contract, further documents to be incorporated, a description of the sub-contract works, the contract price and the completion period. The most important provisions in the conditions are:

"3(2) Save where the provisions of the sub-Contract otherwise require, the sub-Contractor shall so shall execute, complete and maintain the sub-Contract works that no act or omission of his in relation to thereto shall constitute, cause of contribute to any breach by the Contractor of any of his obligations under the main Contract and the sub-Contractor shall, save aforesaid, assume and perform hereunder all the obligations and liabilities of the Contractor under the main Contract in relation to the sub-Contract works . . ."

3(3) The sub-Contractor shall indemnity the Contractor against every liability which the Contractor may incur to any other person whatsoever and against all claims, demands, proceedings, damages, costs and expenses made against or incurred by the Contractor by reason of any breach by the sub-Contractor of the sub-Contract."

The sub-contractor's obligations are not tied directly to the operations of the main contract. Thus, extensions of time may be granted without reference to the engineer; save that where the delaying event entitles the contractor to an extension, the sub-contractor's extension is not to exceed the extension under the main contract (cl.6(2)). Instructions and variations ordered under the main contract do not bind the sub-contractor, unless the engineer's order is confirmed in writing by the contractor (cll.7, 8). In particular:

"7(2) The Contractor shall have the like powers in relation to the sub-Contract works to give instructions and decisions as the Engineer has in relation to the main works under the main Contract and the sub-Contractor shall have the like obligations to abide by and comply therewith and the like rights in relation to thereto as the Contractor under the main Contract . . .".

There is therefore wide scope, both for the exercise of such powers by the contractor and for making claims by the sub-contractors. The sub-contract provides for vesting of the sub-contractor's equipment, temporary works and materials in the contractor and then in the employer where the main contract so provides (cl.11(1)). Current editions of the ICE Main Conditions do not so provide, but the sub-contract may also be used with older editions that do.

After completion, the sub-contractor is required to maintain their work until completion of the main works and further to maintain them throughout the maintenance period of the main contract (cl.13). The contractor may determine the sub-contractor's employment if the main contract is determined (cl.16) or if the sub-contractor commits specified defaults corresponding substantially to the grounds of determination under cl.63 of the ICE main contract (cl.17). The form is not specifically designed for use with nominated sub-contractors but contains provisions broadly in accordance with the minimum requirements under the ICE form for a nominated sub-contract. The form is used principally for direct sub-contracts.

The JCT issues two forms of contract for smaller works: the Minor Building Works form and the Intermediate form. The range of work suitable for these forms is not defined. The form of contract for Minor Building works, in keeping with its subject matter, is short. The form of contract was amended in 1998 and again in 2005 in line with other JCT documents. The form deals fully with liability for, and insurance against, various risks. This is necessary since the consequential losses which may arise out of building works may bear no relation to the scale of the works. The form contains many of the provisions of the standard JCT contract in an abbreviated form. The architect may vary the works, including the order or period in which they are to be carried out. The contractor is entitled to interim payments at not less than four-weekly intervals. The JCT also issue an "Intermediate" form of building contract known as IFC. This form follows closely the format of the minor building works form, while adopting much of the wording of JCT main form. Like the main form, IFC contains provision for sub-contract work to be placed with a "listed" sub-contractor of the contractor's choosing.

The ICE have also issued a form for minor works, now updated as part of the ICC suite of contract forms, which is accompanied by notes for guidance, stating that the form is intended for contracts of value not exceeding £500,000. This form represents a concise version of the essential elements of the ICE/ICC general conditions, rearranged and expressed in much simpler language. Among features to be noted is the requirement that the engineer is to be a named individual (cl.2.1). The traditional maintenance period was more accurately renamed "defects correction period" (cl.5), an innovation adopted for the ICE, 6th and 7th edns. The contractor is made fully liable for acts or defaults of sub-contractors (cl.8.3).

CHAPTER 12

THE STANDARD BUILDING CONTRACT

The Standard Building Contract, formerly known as the RIBA form, is now issued by the Joint Contracts Tribunal (JCT) comprising the RIBA, RICS, the Association of Consulting Engineers, and bodies representing employers, local authorities contractors and sub-contractors. It is commonly referred to as the JCT form and is intended for use in all types of building work. The form originated early in the twentieth century and has gone through a number of editions most notably those of 1939, 1963, 1980, 1998 and 2005. Formal amendments are issued from time to time with periodic reprints incorporating accumulated amendments. A new edition was issued in 2011, retaining the same format as the 2005 edition, which had departed radically from the 1998 edition, which extended to 42 clauses. The latest edition of 2011 reviewed in this chapter is divided into nine sections (although still referred to as clauses), and is accompanied by seven schedules, articles of agreement and contract particulars (previously known as appendix).

The JCT form has for many years existed in alternative versions including forms with or without quantities and with approximate quantities. Other versions exist and, since the 1980s the JCT has progressively issued other contract forms, sub-contract forms and other documents which now comprise a full suite of procurement documentation. Some of the other JCT documents are covered in Ch.11. The JCT forms traditionally place specific duties on the architect who, given the statutory restrictions upon use of the designation, is referred to in the form as the Architect/Contract Administrator. The term "Architect" is used here for brevity.

The Form is published together with the following schedules: Contractor's Design Submission Procedure (Schedule 1). Procedure for Quotation and Agreement of Instructions (Schedule 2). Insurance Options (Schedule 3), Code of Practice for Opening Up (Schedule 4), Provisions as to Third Party Rights (Schedule 5), Forms of Bonds (Schedule 6), and Fluctuations Options (Schedule 7).

The commentary which follows is intended as an introduction to the basic working of the contract. The most important clauses or sub-clauses are printed with notes as to their effect. Other clauses are referred to where appropriate. Some clauses are omitted as being not essential to the basic scheme of the form. These clauses may, of course, be vital to any particular issue or dispute.

The Contract

The form contemplates that the contract will be made by executing the Articles of Agreement, which may be either under hand or executed as a deed. The latter method will extend the period of limitation from six to 12 years. But neither method is essential and the Conditions of Contract may be incorporated by reference in any other document of agreement provided the essential terms which are identified in the Articles of Agreement are recorded in some other manner.

The Articles themselves state as follows:

"Now it is hereby agreed as follows

Article 1: Contractor's obligations

> The Contractor shall carry out and complete the Works in accordance with the Contract Documents.

Article 2: Contract Sum

> The Employer shall pay the Contractor at the times and in the manner specified in the Conditions the VAT–exclusive sum of (£) ('the Contract Sum') or such other sum as shall become payable under this Contract."

In Articles 3 and 4 the architect and quantity surveyor are to be named. Article 5 identifies the planning supervisor for the purposes of the CDM Regulations (if other than the Architect) and Article 6 names the principal contractor under the CDM Regulations (if other than the contractor). Article 7 provides for adjudication of any dispute or difference (whether or not subject to the Housing Grants, etc., Act. Articles 8 and 9 provide alternatively for arbitration or litigation. The choice of arbitration is required to be noted in the contract particulars with litigation taking effect as the default provision. Detailed procedures for adjudication or arbitration are contained respectively in cll.9.2 and 9.3–9.8. Adjudication is to be conducted in accordance with the Scheme for Construction Contracts and arbitration in accordance with the CIMAR Rules.

By cl.2.1 of the conditions the contractor is required to "carry out and complete the works in a proper and workmanlike manner and in compliance with the contract documents . . .". Clause 1.1 contains an extensive list of definitions including "Contract Documents" which includes the Contract Drawings, the Contract Bills, the Agreement, the Conditions and, where the Contractor takes on part of the design, the Employer's Requirements and the Contractor's Proposals. The relationship between these documents and their function is provided for as follows:

"Work included in Contract sum

4.1 The quality and quantity of the work included in the Contract Sum shall be deemed to be that set out in the Contract Bills and, where there is a Contractor's Designed Portion, in the CDP Documents."

"Agreement, etc. to be read as a whole

1.3 The Agreement and these Conditions are to be read as a whole but nothing contained in the Contract Bills or the CDP Documents shall override or modify the Agreement or these Conditions."

"Preparation of Contract Bills and Employer's Requirements

2.13.1 Unless in respect of any specified item or items it is otherwise specifically stated in the Contract Bills, the Contract Bills are to have been prepared in accordance with the Standard Method of Measurement and any addendum bills to be issued for the purposes of obtaining a Schedule 2 Quotation shall be prepared on the same basis."

"Contract Bills and CDP Documents—errors and inadequacy

2.14.1 If in the Contract Bills, or any such addendum bill as is referred to in clause 2.13.1, there is any unstated departure from the method of preparation referred to in that clause or any error in description or in quantity or any omission of items (including any error in or omission of information in any item which is the subject of a Provisional Sum for defined work), the departure, error or omission shall not vitiate this Contract but shall be corrected. Where the description of a Provisional Sum for defined work does not provide the information required by the Standard Method of Measurement, the description shall be corrected so that it does provide that information."

Clause 2.14.3 provides that, subject to the contractor's obligation to comply with statutory requirements, any such error or omission is to be treated as a variation.

Where the works include a Contractor's Designed Portion the Contractor is required, in accordance with the Contract Drawings and Contract Bills where relevant, to "complete the design for the Contractor's Designed Portion, including the selection of any specifications . . . to be used in the CDP works . . ." so far as not otherwise described (cl.2.2.1).

The effect of the above clauses is that, save for questions of quality or quantity of the work, the conditions override the Contract Bill. A provision intended to amend the conditions (such as one for Sectional Completion) may therefore be ineffective if placed in the Bills. The Contract Bills are, however, permitted to include a limitation on the contractor's access to or use of parts of the site, limitation of working hours or the execution or completion of the work in any specific order (cl.5.1.2). The Bills will also override the Contract Drawings in that, while the contractor must perform all the work shown on the drawings, any part which is not included in the Bills is an extra to be paid for. In addition to the Contract Documents as defined, in contracts of any size there are likely to be extensive documents described as "specifications" or other descriptive schedules. These are conventionally incorporated within the Contract Bills as they contribute to the description of the quality of the work. As stated in cl.1.3, the agreement and the conditions are to be read as a whole and afforded equal status.

The contract provides for the mutual provision of necessary information as between the contractor and the architect as follows.

"Construction information and Contractor's master programme

2.9   .1 As soon as possible after the execution of this Contract, if not previously provided:

.1 the Architect/Contract Administrator, without charge to the Contractor, shall provide him with 2 copies of any descriptive schedules or similar documents necessary for use in carrying out the Works (excluding any CDP Works); and

.2 the Contractor shall without charge provide the Architect/Contract Administrator with 2 copies of his master programme for the execution of the Works and, within 14 days of any decision by the Architect/Contract Administrator under clause 2.28.1 or of agreement of any Pre-agreed Adjustment, with 2 copies of an amendment or revision of that programme to take account of that decision or agreement,

but nothing in the descriptive schedules or similar documents (or in that master programme or any amendment or revision of it) shall impose any obligation beyond those imposed by the Contract Documents.

Information Release Schedule

2.11 Except to the extent that the Architect/Contract Administrator is prevented by an act or default of the Contractor or of any of the Contractor's Persons, the Architect/Contract Administrator shall ensure that 2 copies of the information referred to in the Information Release Schedule are released at the time stated in that Schedule. The

Employer and the Contractor may agree to vary any such time, such agreement not to be unreasonably withheld.

Further drawings, details and instructions

2.12 .1 Where not included in the Information Release Schedule, the Architect/Contract Administrator shall from time to time, without charge to the Contractor, provide him with 2 copies of such further drawings or details as are reasonably necessary to explain and amplify the Contract Drawings and shall issue such instructions (including those for or in regard to the expenditure of Provisional Sums) as are necessary to enable the Contractor to carry out and complete the Works in accordance with this Contract.

.2 Such further drawings, details and instructions shall be provided or given at the time it is reasonably necessary for the Contractor to receive them, having regard to the progress of the Works, or, if in the Architect/Contract Administrator's opinion practical completion of the Works or relevant Section is likely to be achieved before the relevant Completion Date, having regard to that Completion Date.

.3 Where the Contractor has reason to believe that the Architect/ Contract Administrator is not aware of the time by which the Contractor needs to receive such further drawings, details or instructions, he shall, so far as reasonably practicable, advise the Architect/Contract Administrator sufficiently in advance as to enable the Architect/Contract Administrator to comply with this clause 2.12."

In addition, cl.2.10 requires the architect to provide accurately dimensional drawings to enable the contractor to set out the works.

Control of the Work

The Conditions envisage that the work will be under the joint control of the parties. The RIBA Conditions of Engagement provide for periodic but not constant supervision. Day to day supervision is therefore left to the contractor and, to the extent necessary, the employer:

"Access for Architect/Contract Administrator

3.1 The Architect/Contract Administrator and any person authorised by him shall at all reasonable times have access to the Works and to the workshops or other premises of the Contractor where work is being prepared for this Contract. When work is to be prepared in workshops or other premises of a sub-contractor the Contractor shall by a term in the sub-contract secure so far as possible a similar right of access to those workshops or premises for the Architect/Contract Administrator and any person authorised by him and shall do all things reasonably necessary to make that right effective. Access under this clause 3.1 may be subject to such reasonable restrictions as are necessary to protect proprietary rights.

Person-in-charge

3.2 The Contractor shall ensure that at all times he has on the site a competent person-in-charge and any instructions given to that person by the Architect/Contract Administrator or directions given to him by the clerk of works in accordance with clause 3.4 shall be deemed to have been issued to the Contractor.

Employer's representative

3.3 The Employer may appoint an individual to act as his representative by giving written notice to the Contractor that from the date stated the individual identified in the notice will exercise all the functions ascribed to the Employer in these Conditions, subject to any exceptions stated in the notice. The Employer may by written notice to the Contractor terminate any such appointment and/or appoint a replacement.

Clerk of works

3.4 The Employer shall be entitled to appoint a clerk of works whose duty shall be to act solely as inspector on behalf of the Employer under the directions of the Architect/Contract Administrator and the Contractor shall afford every reasonable facility for the performance of that duty. If any direction is given to the Contractor by the clerk of works, it shall be of no effect unless given in regard to a matter in respect of which the Architect/ Contract Administrator is expressly empowered by these Conditions to issue instructions and unless confirmed in writing by the Architect/Contract Administrator within 2 working days of the direction being given. Any direction so given and confirmed shall, as from the date of issue of that confirmation, be deemed an instruction of the Architect/Contract Administrator."

On larger projects the architect and employer may agree to employment of a resident architect on the work. They will have no specific power or duty such as those of the engineer's representative under the ICE Conditions.

GENERAL OBLIGATIONS OF THE CONTRACTOR

The contractor's obligations are to comply with the Contract Documents which define the work and the time within which it is to be carried out, to complete any CDP works included in the contract and to comply with proper instruction of the architect:

"General obligations

2.1 The Contractor shall carry out and complete the Works in a proper and workmanlike manner and in compliance with the Contract Documents, the Health and Safety Plan and the Statutory Requirements, and shall give all notices required by the Statutory Requirements.

Contractor's Designed Portion

2.2 Where the Works include a Contractor's Designed Portion, the Contractor shall:

.1 in accordance with the Contract Drawings and the Contract Bills (to the extent they are relevant), complete the design for the Contractor's Designed Portion, including the selection of any specifications for the kinds and standards of the materials, goods and workmanship to be used in the CDP Works, so far as not described or stated in the Employer's Requirements or the Contractor's Proposals;

.2 comply with the directions of the Architect/Contract Administrator for the integration of the design of the Contractor's Designed Portion with the design of the Works as a whole, subject to the provisions of clause 3.10.3;"

"The Works" are defined by cl.1.1 as "the works briefly described in the First Recital (including where applicable the CDP works) as more particularly shown, described or referred to in the Contract Documents, including any changes made to those works in accordance with the Contract". The contractor's obligation to carry out the works in accordance with the prescribed standards is absolute in general. In regard to CDP Works, however, Contractors obligation is limited under cl.2.19 to that of a "professional designer", i.e. a duty of reasonable skill and care. In respect of dwellings, duty includes that laid down by the Defective Premises Act 1972.

Clause 2.15 requires the contractor to give notice should he find any discrepancy or divergence between the Drawings, the Bills, any Architect's Instructions or further drawings or documents or any CPD documents, and for the architect to issue instructions in that regard. Clause 2.3 requires that materials and goods for the works and their workmanship are to be of the standards described in the Contract Bills or, in the case of CPD works, to the standard described in the Employer's Requirements or the Contractor's Proposal. Where materials or workmanship are matters for the opinion of the architect, they are to be to his reasonable satisfaction. To the extent that no standards are prescribed, materials or workmanship are to be to a standard appropriate to the works.

The architect is vested with a series of specific powers, the widest of which is to require or sanction a variation which, by cl.5.1, may include the addition, omission or substitution of any work or a change to the standards of materials or goods or the removal of work which complies with the contract. The architect's general power to give instructions is contained in cll.3.10–3.21 as follows:

"Compliance with instructions

3.10 The Contractor shall forthwith comply with all instructions issued to him by the Architect/Contract Administrator in regard to any matter in respect of which the Architect/Contract Administrator is expressly empowered by these Conditions to issue instructions, save that:

.1 where an instruction requires a Variation of the type referred to in clause 5.1.2 the Contractor need not comply to the extent that he makes reasonable objection to it in writing to the Architect/Contract Administrator.

.2 where an instruction for a V ariation is given which pursuant to clause 5.3.1 requires the Contractor to provide a Schedule 2 Quotation, the Variation shall not be carried out until the Architect/Contract Administrator has in relation to it issued either a Confirmed Acceptance or a further instruction under clause 5.3.2;

.3 if in the Contractor's opinion compliance with any direction under clause 2.2.2 or any instruction issued by the Architect/Contract Administrator injuriously affects the efficacy of the design of the Contractor's Designed Portion (including the obligations of the Contractor to comply with regulation 13 of the CDM Regulations), he shall within 7 days of receipt of the direction or instruction by notice in writing to the Architect/Contract Administrator specify the injurious effect, and the direction or instruction shall not take effect unless confirmed by the Architect/Contract Administrator.

Non-compliance with instructions

3.11 If within 7 days after receipt of a written notice from the Architect/Contract Administrator requiring compliance with an instruction the Contractor does not comply, the Employer may employ and pay other persons to execute any work whatsoever which may be necessary to give effect to that instruction. The Contractor shall be liable for all additional costs incurred by the Employer in connection with such employment and an appropriate deduction shall be made from the Contract Sum.

Instructions requiring Variations

3.14 .1 The Architect/Contract Administrator may issue instructions requiring a Variation.

.2 Any instruction of the type referred to in clause 5.1.2 shall be subject to the Contractor's right of reasonable objection set out in clause 3.10.1.

.3 In respect of the Contractor's Designed Portion, any instruction requiring a Variation shall be an alteration to or modification of the Employer's Requirements.

.4 The Architect/Contract Administrator may sanction in writing any Variation made by the Contractor otherwise than pursuant to an instruction.

.5 No Variation required by the Architect/Contract Administrator or subsequently sanctioned by him shall vitiate this Contract."

Clauses 3.12 and 3.13 require instructions to be in writing and for the architect to specify the power under which any instruction is given, upon request. Clauses 3.15 and 3.16 empower the architect to order a post-ponement of any work and to order work to be done under a Provisional Sum. Clause 3.18 allows the architect to order the removal of work or material not in accordance with the contract and to open up further work for inspection or test in accordance with the Code of Practice set out in Schedule 4. Under cl.3.19 the architect is empowered to retain work which is not in accordance with the contract, but the contractor in such a case acquires no right to payment or extension of time.

Liability and Insurance

Clause 6 deals with various types of potential liability in connection with the work and insurance in respect of such liability.

"Liability of Contractor—personal injury or death

6.1 The Contractor shall be liable for, and shall indemnify the Employer against, any expense, liability, loss, claim or proceedings whatsoever in respect of personal injury to or the death of any person arising out of or in the course of or caused by the carrying out of the Works, except to the extent that the same is due to any act or neglect of the Employer or of any of the Employer's Persons.

Liability of Contractor—injury or damage to property

6.2 The Contractor shall be liable for, and shall indemnify the Employer against, any expense, liability, loss, claim or proceedings in respect of any loss, injury or damage whatsoever to any property real or personal in so far as such loss, injury or damage arises out of or in the course of or by reason of the carrying out of the Works and to the extent that the same is due to any negligence, breach of statutory duty, omission or default of the Contractor or of any of the Contractor's Persons. This liability and indemnity is subject to clause 6.3 and, where Insurance Option C (Schedule 3, paragraph C.1) applies, excludes loss or damage to any property required to be insured thereunder caused by a Specified Peril."

Clause 6.3 provides that "property real or personal" does not include the Works prior to their completion. Clause 6.4 requires insurance to cover these liabilities and cl.6.5 provides for insurance, if required in the contract particulars, to cover the employer and the contractor against third party liability including damage arising from the Works. As regards damage to the Works, Schedule 3 sets out three options, A, B and C one of which is to be selected in the Contract Particulars. The options are All Risks Insurance of the Works by the Contractor (Option A), All Risks Insurance of the Works by the Employer (Option B), or Insurance by the Employer of existing structures and Works or extensions to them (Option C). Each of the options includes joint names policies covering reinstate-ment of the Works. Clause 6.9 requires that such policies shall either include sub-contractors or provide waiver or any right of subrogation against sub-contractors.

Where the contract includes a Contractor's Designed Portion the contractor is required additionally to take out Professional Indemnity Insurance to cover their design liability. As regards protection of the Works from fire, the Contract Particulars may provide for the application of the Joint Fire Code published by the Construction Confederation and other bodies. Provisions giving effect to the Code are contained in cll.6.14–6.16.

Completion and Possession

The contractor's obligations fall into two separate periods: the period up to the Certificate of Practical Completion, when the work is carried out; and the rectification period, during which the contractor must make good any defects. These are dealt with as follows:

"Practical completion and certificates

2.30 When in the opinion of the Architect/Contract Administrator practical completion of the Works or a Section is achieved and the Contractor has complied sufficiently with clauses 2.40 and 3.25.3, then:

.1 in the case of the Works, the Architect/Contract Administrator shall forthwith issue a certificate to that effect ('the Practical Completion Certificate');

.2 in the case of a Section, he shall forthwith issue a certificate of practical completion of that Section (a 'Section Completion Certificate');

and practical completion of the Works or the Section shall be deemed for all the purposes of this Contract to have taken place on the date stated in that certificate.

Schedules of defects and instructions

2.38 If any defects, shrinkages or other faults in the Works or a Section appear within the relevant Rectification Period due to materials or workmanship not in accordance with this Contract or any failure of the Contractor to comply with his obligations in respect of the Contractor's Designed Portion:

.1 such defects, shrinkages and other faults shall be specified by the Architect/Contract Administrator in a schedule of defects which he shall deliver to the Contractor as an instruction not later than 14 days after the expiry of that Rectification Period; and

.2 notwithstanding clause 2.38.1, the Architect/Contract Administrator may whenever he considers it necessary issue instructions requiring any such defect, shrinkage or other fault to be made good, provided no instructions under this clause 2.38.2 shall be issued after delivery of a schedule of defects or more than 14 days after the expiry of the relevant Rectification Period.

Within a reasonable time after receipt of such schedule or instructions, the defects, shrinkages and other faults shall at no cost to the Employer be made good by the Contractor unless the Architect/ Contract Administrator with the consent of the Employer shall otherwise instruct. If he does so otherwise instruct, an appropriate deduction shall be made from the Contract Sum in respect of the defects, shrinkages or other faults not made good."

Where the employer wishes to take possession of any part of the Works prior to practical completion, they may do so with the contractor's consent (not to be unreasonably delayed or withheld) and the relevant section is deemed to be completed on the date so certified by the architect (cl.2.33). The contract then provides for the making good of defects in the relevant part. The contractor ceases to be responsible and insurance cover on the relevant part is deemed to terminate. For these reasons it is important that any taking of possession by the employer is carried out formally and so that relevant insurance cover is reinstated appropriately.

Time

The speed with which the contractor carries out the work is usually an important element in performance of the contract. The Contract Particulars provide for the date or dates of possession to be specified including deferment of possession of any section; and for the completion date which is subject to adjustment, including dates for completion of sections.

"Date of Possession—progress

2.4 On the Date of Possession possession of the site or, in the case of a Section, possession of the relevant part of the site shall be given to the Contractor who shall thereupon begin the construction of the Works or Section and regularly and diligently proceed with and complete the same on or before the relevant Completion Date. For the purposes of the Works insurances the Contractor shall retain possession:

.1 of the site and the Works up to and including the date of issue of the Practical Completion Certificate; or

.2 of each Section and the relevant part of the site up to and including the date of issue of the Section Completion Certificate for that Section and, in respect of any balance of the site, up to and including the date of issue of the Practical Completion Certificate

and, subject to clause 2.33 and section 8, the Employer shall not be entitled to take possession of any part or parts of the Works or Section until such date.

Notice by Contractor of delay to progress

2.27 .1 If and whenever it becomes reasonably apparent that the progress of the Works or any Section is being or is likely to be delayed the Contractor shall forthwith give written notice to the Architect/ Contract Administrator of the material circumstances, including the cause or causes of the delay, and shall identify in the notice any event which in his opinion is a Relevant Event.

.2 In respect of each event identified in the notice the Contractor shall, if practicable in such notice or otherwise in writing as soon as possible thereafter, give particulars of its expected effects, including an estimate of any expected delay in the completion of the Works or any Section beyond the relevant Completion Date.

.3 The Contractor shall forthwith notify the Architect/Contract Administrator in writing of any material change in the estimated delay or in any other particulars and supply such further information as the Architect/Contract Administrator may at any time reasonably require."

Clause 2.28 sets out machinery for the architect to grant an extension of time by fixing such later date as the completion date for the Works or a section as they estimate to be fair and reasonable. The architect is required to give their decision within 12 weeks but has a further right to review the extension within 12 weeks after practical completion. The grounds entitling the contractor to extension of time or "relevant events" are set out in cl.2.29 as follows.

"Relevant Events

2.29 The following are the Relevant Events referred to in clauses 2.27 and 2.28:

.1 Variations and any other matters or instructions which under these Conditions are to be treated as, or as requiring, a Variation;
.2 instructions of the Architect/Contract Administrator.

    .1 under any of clauses 2.15, 3.15, 3.16 (excluding an instruction for expenditure of a Provisional Sum for defined work), 3.23 or 5.3.2; or
    .2 for the opening up for inspection or testing of any work, materials or goods under clause 3.17 or 3.18.4 (including making good), unless the inspection or test shows that the work, materials or goods are not in accordance with this Contract;

.3 deferment of the giving of possession of the site or any Section under clause 2.5;
.4 the execution of work for which an Approximate Quantity is not a reasonably accurate forecast of the quantity of work required;
.5 suspension by the Contractor under clause 4.14 of the performance of his obligations under this Contract;
.6 any impediment, prevention or default, whether by act or omission, by the Employer, the Architect/Contract Administrator, the Quantity Surveyor or any of the Employer's Persons, except to the extent caused or contributed to by any default, whether by act or omission, of the Contractor or of any of the Contractor's Persons;
.7 the carrying out by a Statutory Undertaker of work in pursuance of its statutory obligations in relation to the Works, or the failure to carry out such work;
.8 exceptionally adverse weather conditions;
.9 loss or damage occasioned by any of the Specified Perils;
.10 civil commotion or the use or threat of terrorism and/or the activities of the relevant authorities in dealing with such event or threat;
.11 strike, lock-out or local combination of workmen affecting any of the trades employed upon the Works or any of the trades engaged in the preparation, manufacture or transportation of any of the goods or materials required for the Works or any persons engaged in the preparation of the design for the Contractor's Designed Portion;
.12 the exercise after the Base Date by the United Kingdom Government of any statutory power which directly affects the execution of the Works;
.13 force majeure."

The completion date as extended becomes the "relevant completion date". Where this is not achieved the contract provides as follows:

"Non-Completion Certificates

2.31 If the Contractor fails to complete the Works or a Section by the relevant Completion Date, the Architect/Contract Administrator shall issue a certificate to that effect (a 'Non-Completion Certificate'). If a new Completion Date is fixed after the issue of such a certificate, such fixing shall cancel that certificate and the Architect/Contract Administrator shall where necessary issue a further certificate.

Payment or allowance of liquidated damages

2.32   .1 Provided:

>   .1 the Architect/Contract Administrator has issued a Non-Completion Certificate for the Works or a Section; and
>   .2 the Employer has informed the Contractor in writing before the date of the Final Certificate that he may require payment of, or may withhold or deduct, liquidated damages,
>
>   the Employer may, not later than 5 days before the final date for payment of the debt due under the Final Certificate, give notice in writing to the Contractor in the terms set out in clause 2.32.2."

Notice under cl.2.32.2 is a requirement that liquidated damages are to be paid or deducted. The recovery of liquidated damages appears to be optional but, where the employer elects to deduct, there is a requirement for a Withholding Notice complying with the Housing Grants, etc., Act.

Sub-Contractors

It is very rare in practice for the contractor to perform the whole of the physical work under a JCT Contract and it is frequently the case that a main contractor will largely provide management services and that all the major trades, as well as specialist items, are sub-let. Sub-contracting does not reduce the liability of the contractor to the employer in respect of the work sub-let. It is equally common for the contractor to sub-let all or part of the design work, but in each case sub-letting requires consent, which may not be unreasonably delayed or withheld.

"Consent to sub-letting

3.7   .1 The Contractor shall not without the written consent of the Architect/Contract Administrator sub-let the whole or any part of the Works. Such consent shall not be unreasonably delayed or withheld but the Contractor shall remain wholly responsible for carrying out and completing the Works in all respects in accordance with clause 2.1 notwithstanding any such sub-letting.
>   .2 Where there is a Contractor's Designed Portion, the Contractor shall not without the written consent of the Employer sub-let the design for it. Such consent shall not be unreasonably delayed or withheld but shall not in any way affect the obligations of the Contractor under clauses 2.2 and 2.19 or any other provision of this Contract."

Sub-letting at the contractor's option is sometimes referred to as "domestic" sub-contracting. In previous editions certain elements of the work have been required to be sub-let to sub-contractors selected by the employer or the architect, typically specialists carrying out significant elements of the work. This process was formally known as "nominating" and both the selection and pricing of the sub-contracted work was taken out of the contractor's hands. The work was usually designed "Prime Cost" work and the price arranged through tendering conducted by the architect. The contractor was then instructed to place a sub-contract with the selected "nominated" sub-contractor. A standard provision of all previous JCT Forms of Contract was an entitlement to extension of time in respect of delay by a nominated sub-contractor. The effect of these provisions and of the requirement for the work to be carried out by the selected sub-contractor was also to relieve the main contractor, not only of responsibility for timely performance by the nominated sub-contractor, but also for responsibility for failure to complete or even to perform the Works as well as responsibility for the quality of any work left incomplete by a defaulting nominated sub-contractor.[1] As a result nomination eventually fell out of fashion, although similar provisions were included in other forms of contracts such as the ICE Conditions. Nomination remains under several other contract forms, but, ironically, has now been removed entirely from the JCT Form.

In place of nomination, a number of earlier editions of the JCT Form introduced an alternative category of "listed" sub-contractors which achieves substantially the same result as nomination, i.e. securing the performance of the work by specialists, but without diluting the liability of the main contractor for the sub-contractor's performance.

"List in Contract Bills

3.8 .1 Where the Contract Bills provide that certain work measured or otherwise described in those Bills and priced by the Contractor is to be carried out by persons named in a list in or annexed to the Contract Bills and selected from that list by and at the sole discretion of the Contractor, the provisions of this clause 3.8 shall apply.

    .2 The list shall comprise not less than three persons. The Employer (or the Architect/Contract Administrator on his behalf) and the Contractor shall each be entitled with the consent of the other, which shall not be unreasonably delayed or withheld, to add additional persons to the list at any time prior to the execution of a binding sub-contract."

Note that the contractor is required to price the work in the tender so that the employer does not take any financial risk. Clause 3.9 contains a list

---

[1] See Ch.10 for a review of the relevant cases.

of conditions to be included in any listed sub-contract document including the requirement that materials or goods paid for in advance shall become the property of the employer.

Default and Determination

The contract contains a number of separate provisions giving one party the right to take action where the other is in default. For example, the architect may serve notice under cl.3.18 requiring the removal of materials or goods not in accordance with the contract; and the contractor may serve notice under cl.4.14 of their intention to suspend performance where a certificate is unpaid. Where the default of either party is more serious, Section 8 provides rights of termination available to either party. Termination brings the rights and obligations regarding performance of the work to an end, but leaves the contract in tact together with particular provisions which are to apply after termination.

Termination by the Employer is dealt with as follows:

"Default by Contractor

8.4   .1 If, before practical completion of the Works, the Contractor.

    .1 without reasonable cause wholly or substantially suspends the carrying out of the Works or the design of the Contractor's Designed Portion; or

    .2 fails to proceed regularly and diligently with the Works or the design of the Contractor's Designed Portion; or

    .3 refuses or neglects to comply with a written notice or instruction from the Architect/Contract Administrator requiring him to remove any work, materials or goods not in accordance with this Contract and by such refusal or neglect the Works are materially affected; or

    .4 fails to comply with clause 3.7 or 7.1; or

    .5 fails to comply with clause 3.25,

the Architect/Contract Administrator may give to the Contractor a notice specifying the default or defaults (the 'specified default or defaults').

.2 If the Contractor continues a specified default for 14 days from receipt of the notice under clause 8.4.1, the Employer may on, or within 10 days from, the expiry of that 14 day period by a further notice to the Contractor terminate the Contractor's employment under this Contract.

.3 If the Employer does not give the further notice referred to in clause 8.4.2, (whether as a result of the ending of any specified default or otherwise) but the Contractor repeats a specified default (whether previously repeated or not) then, upon or within a reasonable time after such repetition, the Employer may by notice to the Contractor terminate that employment."

Additionally, cl.8.5 gives the employer a right to terminate at any time if the contractor is insolvent; and if the contractor or any employee of theirs is guilty of corruption under this or any other contract with the employer, the employer may terminate this and any other contract with the contractor. Where the contractor's employment is terminated, the employer has the right to employ and pay other persons to complete the Works and to claim the additional cost from the contractor. Where the correctness of the employer's termination is challenged, the ensuing dispute may be long and complex. Adjudication is usually inappropriate for such a dispute, since the adjudicator's decision is open to immediate challenge by arbitration.[2]

Section 8 also provides for termination by the contractor on the ground of default by the employer in the following terms:

"Default by Employer

8.9　.1　If the Employer:

.1　does not pay by the final date for payment the amount properly due to the Contractor in respect of any certificate and/or any VAT properly chargeable on that amount; or

.2　interferes with or obstructs the issue of any certificate due under this Contract; or

.3　fails to comply with clause 7.1; or

.4　fails to comply with clause 3.25,

the Contractor may give to the Employer a notice specifying the default or defaults (the 'specified default or defaults').

.2　If before practical completion of the Works the carrying out of the whole or substantially the whole of the uncompleted Works is suspended for a continuous period of the length stated in the Contract Particulars by reason of:

.1　Architect/Contract Administrator's instructions under clause 2.15, 3.14 or 3.15; and/or

.2　any impediment, prevention or default, whether by act or omission, by the Employer, the Architect/Contract Administrator, the Quantity Surveyor or any of the Employer's Persons

(but in either case excluding such instructions as are referred to in clause 8.11.1.2), then, unless in either case that is caused by the negligence or default of the Contractor or of any of the Contractor's Persons, the Contractor may give to the Employer a notice specifying the event or events (the 'specified suspension event or events').

.3　If a specified default or a specified suspension event continues for 14 days from the receipt of notice under clause 8.9.1 or 8.9.2, the Contractor may on, or within 10 days from, the expiry of that

---

[2] See *CIB v Birse* [2005] B.L.R. 173.

14 day period by a further notice to the Employer terminate the Contractor's employment under this Contract.

.4 If the Contractor for any reason does not give the further notice referred to in clause 8.9.3, but (whether previously repeated or not):

    .1 the Employer repeats a specified default; or

    .2 a specified suspension event is repeated for any period, such that the regular progress of the Works is or is likely to be materially affected thereby,

then, upon or within a reasonable time after such repetition, the Contractor may by notice to the Employer terminate the Contractor's employment under this Contract."

Clause 8.10 gives an additional right to terminate upon the insolvency of the employer. Clause 8.11 gives the right to either party to terminate the contractor's employment where the work is suspended by force majeure, architect's instructions, loss occasioned by any of the Specified Perils, civil unrest, or the exercise of statutory powers. Where the contractor terminates their employment or there is a termination under cl.8.11, the contractor is entitled to payment in respect of the work carried out up to the date of termination together with the reasonable costs of removal from the site; and where termination is on the ground of the employer's default (or termination under cl.8.11.1.3 is occasioned by the employer's default) the contractor is also to be paid loss or damages caused by the termination.

CERTIFICATION AND PAYMENT

The sums payable to the contractor are subject to many adjustments under the contract. The Contract Sum itself, however, remains fixed:

"Adjustment only under the Conditions

4.2 The Contract Sum shall not be adjusted or altered in any way other than in accordance with the express provisions of these Conditions and, subject to clause 2.14, any error, whether of arithmetic or otherwise, in the computation of the Contract Sum shall be deemed to have been accepted by the Parties.

Items included in adjustments

4.3 .1 The Contract Sum shall be adjusted by:

    .1 any amounts agreed by the Employer and the Contractor in respect of Variations, as referred to in clause 5.2.1;

> .2 the amounts stated in any Schedule 2 Quotations for which the Architect/Contract Administrator has issued to the Contractor a Confirmed Acceptance and by the amount of any Variations thereto as valued under clause 5.3.3;"

The Contract contains extensive provisions for payment as the work proceeds. Where the parties do not opt for fixed stage or milestone payments linked to defined stages of the work, Interim Certificates are required, usually issued monthly.

"Issue of Interim Certificates

4.9   .1 The Architect/Contract Administrator shall from time to time as provided in clause 4.9.2 issue Interim Certificates stating the amount due to the Contractor from the Employer and specifying to what the amount relates and the basis on which that amount was calculated.

    .2 Interim Certificates shall be issued on the dates provided for in the Contract Particulars up to the date of practical completion of the Works or the date within one month thereafter. Interim Certificates shall thereafter be issued as and when further amounts are ascertained as payable to the Contractor by the Employer and upon whichever is the later of the expiry of the Rectification Period or the issue of the Certificate of Making Good (or, where there are Sections, the last such period or certificate), provided always that the Architect/Contract Administrator shall not be required to issue an Interim Certificate within one calendar month of a previous Interim Certificate."

Interim Certificates are to be based on valuation of the work carried out in accordance with cl.4.16. This requires full valuation of the work properly executed, together with materials and goods delivered to the site. Additional materials and goods not yet delivered to the site may be included in valuations provided they are listed in the contract and subject to conditions including passing of property and adequate security. The employer is entitled to deduct retention in accordance with rules set out in cl.4.18. Alternatively, the contractor, where so provided in the Contract Particulars, may provide a retention bond in respect of the amount otherwise deductible. Fluctuations are to be added to interim payments in accordance with the fluctuation provision identified in the contract. The options are listed in Schedule 7.

Variations are to be valued in accordance with rules set out in Section 5:

"Measurable Work

5.6   .1 To the extent that a Valuation relates to the execution of additional or substituted work which can properly be valued by measurement or to the execution of work for which an Approximate Quantity is included in the Contract Bills and subject to clause 5.8 in the case of CDP Works, such work shall be measured and shall be valued in accordance with the following rules:

.1   where the additional or substituted work is of similar character to, is executed under similar conditions as, and does not significantly change the quantity of, work set out in the Contract Bills, the rates and prices for the work so set out shall determine the valuation;

.2   where the additional or substituted work is of similar character to work set out in the Contract Bills but is not executed under similar conditions thereto and/or significantly changes its quantity, the rates and prices for the work so set out shall be the basis for determining the valuation and the Valuation shall include a fair allowance for such difference in conditions and/or quantity;

.3   where the additional or substituted work is not of similar character to work set out in the Contract Bills, the work shall be valued at fair rates and prices;

.4   where the Approximate Quantity is a reasonably accurate forecast of the quantity of work required the rate or price for the Approximate Quantity shall determine the valuation; and

.5   where the Approximate Quantity is not a reasonably accurate forecast of the quantity of work required, the rate or price for that Approximate Quantity shall be the basis for determining the valuation and the Valuation shall include a fair allowance for such difference in quantity.

Provided that clauses 5.6.1.4 and 5.6.1.5 shall apply only to the extent that the work has not been altered or modified other than in quantity.

.2   To the extent that a Valuation relates to the omission of work set out in the Contract Bills and subject to clause 5.8 in the case of CDP Works, the rates and prices for such work therein set out shall determine the valuation of the work omitted.

.3   In any valuation of work under clauses 5.6.1 and 5.6.2:

.1   measurement shall be in accordance with the same principles as those governing the preparation of the Contract Bills, as referred to in clause 2.13;

.2   allowance shall be made for any percentage or lump sum adjustments in the Contract Bills; and

.3   allowance, where appropriate, shall be made for any addition to or reduction of preliminary items of the type referred to in the Standard Method of Measurement, provided that no such allowance shall be made in respect of compliance with an Architect/Contract Administrator's instruction for the expenditure of a Provisional Sum for defined work."

To the extent a variation cannot properly be measured, it is to be valued on the basis of prime cost or day works. Where a variation relates to CDP work, additional or substituted work is to be valued consistent with the value of similar work set out in the CDP analysis making allowance for significant changes; alternatively a fair valuation is to be made.

As an alternative to this traditional method of valuing of variations, the architect in their instruction may require the contractor to provide a quotation in accordance with the provisions of Schedule 2. This requires both a quotation for the cost of work and its effect on time under the contract, as well as any other amounts payable in respect of the variation. The employer may accept the Schedule 2 quotation; or alternatively the architect may instruct that the variation is to be carried out in accordance with the valuation rules otherwise applying, or they may cancel the variation. In either event, however, the contractor is entitled to be paid the costs of preparing the Schedule 2 quotation.

As under all previous JCT Forms, the Contract provides for the payment of "direct loss and/or expense" not otherwise to be reimbursed, by reason of the regular progress of the Works being materially affected by any of the defined "relevant matters". Subject to the contractor giving proper notice and particulars of the loss and/or expense claimed.

"4.24 The following are the Relevant Matters:

.1 Variations (excluding any loss and/or expense relating to a Confirmed Acceptance of a Schedule 2 Quotation but including any other matters or instructions which under these Conditions are to be treated as, or as requiring, a Variation);

.2 instructions of the Architect/Contract Administrator:

    .1 under clause 3.15 or 3.16 (excluding an instruction for expenditure of a Provisional Sum for defined work);

    .2 for the opening up for inspection or testing of any work, materials or goods under clause 3.17 (including making good), unless the cost is provided for in the Contract Bills or unless the inspection or test shows that the work, materials or goods are not in accordance with this Contract;

    .3 in relation to any discrepancy in or divergence between the Contract Drawings, the Contract Bills and/or other documents referred to in clause 215;

.3 suspension by the Contractor under clause 4.14 of the performance of his obligations under this Contract, provided the suspension was not frivolous or vexatious;

.4 the execution of work for which an Approximate Quantity is not a reasonably accurate forecast of the quantity of work required;

.5 any impediment, prevention or default, whether by act or omission, by the Employer, the Architect/ Contract Administrator, the Quantity Surveyor or any of the Employer's Persons, except to the extent caused or contributed to by any default, whether by act or omission, of the Contractor or of any of the Contractor's Persons."

Loss and/or expense is to be added to Interim Certificates as and when ascertained. Clause 4.26 provides that these rights are without prejudice to any other rights of the contractor, which will include the right to claim damages where the employer commits a breach of contract, for example, a breach of an implied term relating to non-interference with the progress of the Works (see Ch.9). Such claims fall outside the powers of the architect, but may be the subject of adjudication or arbitration proceedings since they fall under the contract.

Final Accounting

The architect is required to issue a Final Certificate within two months of the latest of the end of the rectification period and certificate of making good, or the date on which the architect provides to the contractor a statement of all adjustments to the Contract Sum. The latter document is to be issued not later than three months after receipt from the contractor of all documents necessary for adjustment of the Contract Sum. The timetable therefore depends on the contractor's timely and adequate provision of sufficient details to the architect/quantity surveyor and it is not unusual for this process to take many months and to involve detailed work and potential disputes. Once the calculations have been carried out the contract provides as follows:

"4.15   .2 The Final Certificate shall state:

       .1 the Contract Sum adjusted as necessary in accordance with clause 4.3; and

       .2 the sum of the amounts already stated as due in Interim Certificates plus the amount of any advance payment paid pursuant to clause 4.8;

and the difference (if any) between the two sums shall (without affecting the rights of the Contractor in respect of any Interim Certificate which has not been paid in full by the Employer by its final date for payment) be expressed in the Final Certificate as a balance due to the Contractor from the Employer or to the Employer from the Contractor, as the case may be. The Final Certificate shall state the basis on which that amount has been calculated.

.3 Not later than 5 days after the date of issue of the Final Certificate the Employer shall give a written notice to the Contractor which shall, in respect of any balance stated as due to the Contractor from the Employer in the Final Certificate, specify the amount of the payment proposed to be made, to what the amount of the payment relates and the basis on which that amount was calculated.

.4 The final date for payment of the balance payable by the Employer to the Contractor or by the Contractor to the Employer, as the case may be, shall be 28 days from the date of issue of the Final Certificate. Not later than 5 days before the final date for payment of the balance the Employer may give a written notice to the Contractor which shall specify any amount proposed to be withheld and/or deducted from any balance due to the

Contractor, the ground or grounds for such withholding and/or deduction and the amount of withholding and/or deduction attributable to each ground."

JCT Contracts have traditionally provided for the Final Certificate to bind the parties both as to the valuation of the work and as to the contractor's compliance with the terms of the contract and such provisions have been upheld by the courts on a number of occasions.[3] The present contract makes the following provision:

"Effect of Final Certificate

1.10   .1 Except as provided in clauses 1.10.2, 1.10.3 and 1.10.4 (and save in respect of fraud), the Final Certificate shall have effect in any proceedings under or arising out of or in connection with this Contract (whether by adjudication, arbitration or legal proceedings) as:

    .1 conclusive evidence that where and to the extent that any of the particular qualities of any materials or goods or any particular standard of an item of workmanship was described expressly in the Contract Drawings or the Contract Bills, or in any instruction issued by the Architect/Contract Administrator under these Conditions or in any drawings or documents issued by the Architect/Contract Administrator under any of clauses 2.9 to 2.12, to be for the approval of the Architect/Contract Administrator, the particular quality or standard was to the reasonable satisfaction of the Architect/Contract Administrator, but the Final Certificate shall not be conclusive evidence that they or any other materials or goods or workmanship comply with any other requirement or term of this Contract;

    .2 conclusive evidence that any necessary effect has been given to all the terms of this Contract which require that an amount be added to or deducted from the Contract Sum or that an adjustment be made to the Contract Sum save where there has been any accidental inclusion or exclusion of any work, materials, goods or figure in any computation or any arithmetical error in any computation, in which event the Final Certificate shall have effect as conclusive evidence as to all other computations;

    .3 conclusive evidence that all and only such extensions of time, if any, as are due under clause 2.28 have been given; and

    .4 conclusive evidence that the reimbursement of direct loss and/or expense, if any, to the Contractor pursuant to clause 4.23 is in final settlement of all and any claims which the Contractor has or may have arising out of the occurrence of

[3] See Ch.9.

> any of the Relevant Matters, whether such claim be for breach of contract, duty of care, statutory duty or otherwise."

Clause 1.10.2 provides that the certificate is not to be final as regards any adjudication, arbitration or other proceedings commenced before the issue of the Final Certificate. Clause 1.11 confirms that no other certificate is to be conclusive evidence that the work is in accordance with the contract.

DISPUTES

The architect is empowered to render decisions on various matters of contention as the contract proceeds, notably those relating to payment, time and quality of the work carried out. Where a decision of the architect is not acceptable a dispute or difference arises. This may be at the suit of either party but more usually it will be the contractor who expresses dissatisfaction. In previous editions of the JCT Form, where arbitration has been the exclusive remedy, there have been restrictions on the right to commence proceeding before practical completion. Largely as a result of the Housing Grants, etc., Act, under which adjudication is available "at any time", all such restrictions have now been removed and the parties may proceed to more formal dispute resolution at a time of their choosing, whether before or after practical completion.

Section 9 of the Contract provides four methods of dispute resolution which may be alternative or sequential, generally at the option of the party initiating the dispute. Thus the options are as follows:

(1) Clause 9.1 provides that the parties may refer a dispute to mediation in accordance with a published Guide.

(2) Article 7 and cl.9.2 provide that either party may (at any time) refer a dispute to adjudication in which case the statutory scheme is to apply. The adjudicator or the nominating body is to be that stated in the Contract Particulars.

(3) Article 9 provides that, subject to Article 7 (adjudication) and Article 8 (arbitration) if it applies, the parties may bring legal proceedings in respect of any dispute.

(4) Article 8 and cl.9.3, if so selected in the Contract Particulars, provide for disputes to be referred to Arbitration either as alternative or following mediation or adjudication. The proceedings

are to be conducted in accordance with the Construction Industry Model Arbitration Rules (CIMAR). Other provisions governing the arbitration are set out in the following clauses.

"Notice of reference to arbitration

9.4   .1 Where pursuant to Article 8 either Party requires a dispute or difference to be referred to arbitration, that Party shall serve on the other Party a written notice of arbitration to such effect in accordance with Rule 2.1 identifying the dispute and requiring the other Party to agree to the appointment of an arbitrator. The Arbitrator shall be an individual agreed by the Parties or, failing such agreement within 14 days (or any agreed extension of that period) after the notice of arbitration is served, appointed on the application of either Party in accordance with Rule 2.3 by the person named in the Contract Particulars.

    .2 Where two or more related arbitral proceedings in respect of the Works fall under separate arbitration agreements, Rules 2.6, 2.7 and 2.8 shall apply.

    .3 After an arbitrator has been appointed either Party may give a further notice of arbitration to the other Party and to the Arbitrator referring any other dispute which falls under Article 8 to be decided in the arbitral proceedings and Rule 3.3 shall apply.

Powers of Arbitrator

9.5 Subject to the provisions of Article 8 and clause 1.10 the Arbitrator shall, without prejudice to the generality of his powers, have power to rectify this Contract so that it accurately reflects the true agreement made by the Parties, to direct such measurements and/or valuations as may in his opinion be desirable in order to determine the rights of the Parties and to ascertain and award any sum which ought to have been the subject of or included in any certificate and to open up, review and revise any certificate, opinion, decision, requirement or notice and to determine all matters in dispute which shall be submitted to him in the same manner as if no such certificate, opinion, decision, requirement or notice had been given.

Effect of award

9.6 Subject to clause 9.7 the award of the Arbitrator shall be final and binding on the Parties.

Appeal—questions of law

9.7 The Parties hereby agree pursuant to section 45(2)(a) and section 69(2) (a) of the Arbitration Act 1996 that either Party may (upon notice to the other Party and to the Arbitrator):

> .1 apply to the courts to determine any question of law arising in the course of the reference; and
>
> .2 appeal to the courts on any question of law arising out of an award made in an arbitration under this arbitration agreement.

Arbitration Act 1996

> 9.8 The provisions of the Arbitration Act 1996 shall apply to any arbitration under this Contract wherever the same, or any part of it, shall be conducted."

Article 8 provides that the Arbitration Agreement is not to apply to disputes arising under the Construction Industry Scheme or in respect of VAT where legislation provides for dispute resolution; nor in respect of the enforcement of any decision of an adjudicator.

By Clause 1.10, where adjudication, arbitration or other proceedings have been commenced before the Final Certificate, if neither party takes any further step in the proceedings within 12 months after its issue, the Final Certificate is to become binding, subject to any terms of settlement that may have been agreed. Further, where an adjudication decision is given, that decision becomes binding unless arbitration or legal proceedings are commenced within 28 days.

CHAPTER 13

FIDIC (INTERNATIONAL) CONDITIONS

There has been available since 1956 a form of contract based on the ICE Conditions, for use in engineering contracts having an international element. A fourth edition of this form was issued in 1987 by the International Federation of Consulting Engineers (FIDIC), recommended for use both in international and domestic civil engineering contracts. Up to and including the fourth edition, the clause numbering and much of the content of the FIDIC Conditions followed the ICE Form of Contract. In 1998, however, FIDIC decided upon a new course by publishing, over a period of years, five entirely new standard forms as follows:

(1) Conditions of Contract for Construction of Building or Engineering Works designed by the employer or his representative, the engineer (known as the *New Red Book*);

(2) Conditions of Contract for Plant and Design-build, for the Provision of Electrical or Mechanical Plant and for the Design and Execution of Building or Engineering Works (known as the *New Yellow Book*);

(3) Conditions of Contract for Estimated Prime Cost (EPC) Turnkey Projects, where one entity takes total responsibility for the design and execution of an engineering project (known as the *New Silver Book*);

(4) Short Form of Contract for Building or Engineering Works of Relatively Small Value (known as the *New Green Book*); and

(5) Conditions of Contract for Design, Build and Operate (DBO) (the *Gold Book*).

These forms adopt an entirely new clause numbering pattern, even though much of the wording of earlier editions has been retained. The documents were initially published as a "test edition" and revised after consultation in a formal first edition, issued in 1999. The commentary in this chapter is on the *Red Book* for building and engineering works designed on behalf of the employer. Further versions of FIDIC forms have been published but the *Red Book* remains in its 1999 form. As a departure from previous editions containing 70 clauses, the *New Red Book* has 20 clauses, in which the topics are re-arranged and consolidated.

THE CONTRACT

Clause 1 contains key provisions dealing with the contract documents, in the form of extensive definitions, which also cover other topics, including assignment, delayed receipt of information and compliance with applicable laws. Clause 1.5, as with previous editions, states the order of priority of the contract documents. The main provisions of the clause are as follows:

> "1.1.1.1 '**Contract**' means the Contract Agreement, the Letter of Acceptance, the Letter of Tender, these Conditions, the Specification, the Drawings, the Schedules, and the further documents (if any) which are listed in the Contract Agreement or in the Letter of Acceptance.

> 1.1.2.2 '**Employer**' means the person named as employer in the Appendix to Tender and the legal successors in title to this person.

> 1.1.2.3 '**Contractor**' means the person(s) named as contractor in the Letter of Tender accepted by the Employer and the legal successors in title to this person(s).

> 1.1.2.4 '**Engineer**' means the person appointed by the Employer to act as the Engineer for the purposes of the Contract and named in the Appendix to Tender, or other person appointed from time to time by the Employer and notified to the Contractor under Sub-Clause 3.4 *[Replacement of the Engineer]*.

> 1.1.2.5 '**Contractor's Representative**' means the person named by the Contractor in the Contract or appointed from time to time by the Contractor under Sub-Clause 4.3 *[Contractor's Representative]*, who acts on behalf of the Contractor. . . .

> 1.1.2.8 '**Subcontractor**' means any person named in the Contract as a subcontractor, or any person appointed as a subcontractor, for a part of the Works; and the legal successors in title to each of these persons.

> 1.1.2.9 '**DAB**' means the person or three persons so named in the Contract, or other person(s) appointed under Sub-Clause 20.2 *[Appointment of the Dispute Adjudication Board]* or Sub-Clause 20.3 *[Failure to Agree Dispute Adjudication Board]*. . . .

> 1.1.4.2 '**Contract Price**' means the price defined in Sub-Clause 14.1 *[The Contract Price]*, and includes adjustments in accordance with the Contract.

1.1.4.3 'Cost' means all expenditure reasonably incurred (or to be incurred) by the Contractor, whether on or off the Site, including overhead and similar charges, but does not include profit.

1.1.4.4 'Final Payment Certificate' means the payment certificate issued under Sub-Clause 14.13 *[Issue of Final Payment Certificate]*.

1.1.4.5 'Final Statement' means the statement defined in Sub-Clause 14.11 *[Application for Final Payment Certificate]*.

1.1.4.6 'Foreign Currency' means a currency in which part (or all) of the Contract Price is payable, but not the Local Currency.

1.1.4.7 'Interim Payment Certificate' means a payment certificate issued under Clause 14 *[Contract Price and Payment)*, other than the Final Payment Certificate.

1.1.4.8 'Local Currency' means the currency of the Country.

1.1.4.9 'Payment Certificate' means a payment certificate issued under Clause 14 *[Contract Price and Payment]*.

1.1.4.10 'Provisional Sum' means a sum (if any) which is specified in the Contract as a provisional sum, for the execution of any part of the Works or for the supply of Plant, Materials or services under Sub-Clause 13.5 *[Provisional Sums]*. . . .

1.1.6.1 'Contractor's Documents' means the calculations, computer programs and other software, drawings, manuals, models and other documents of a technical nature (if any) supplied by the Contractor under the Contract. . . .

1.1.6.7 'Site' means the places where the Permanent Works are *to* be executed and to which Plant and Materials are *to* be delivered, and any other places as may be specified in the Contract as forming part *of* the Site.

1.1.6.8 'Unforeseeable' means *not* reasonably foreseeable by an experienced contractor by the date for submission of the Tender.

1.1.6.9 'Variation' means any change to the Works, which is instructed or approved as a variation under Clause 13 *[Variations and Adjustments]*.

. . .

1.4 The Contract shall be governed by the law of the country (or other jurisdiction) stated in the Appendix to Tender.
1.5 The documents forming the Contract are to be taken as mutually explanatory of one another. For the purposes of interpretation, the priority of the documents shall be in accordance with the following sequence:
  (a) the Contract Agreement (if any),
  (b) the Letter of Acceptance,
  (c) the Letter of Tender,
  (d) the Particular Conditions,
  (e) these General Conditions,

(f) the Specification,
(g) the Drawings, and
(h) the Schedules and any other documents forming part of the Contract.
If an ambiguity or discrepancy is found in the documents, the Engineer shall issue any necessary clarification or instruction.

. . .

1.7 Neither Party shall assign the whole or any part of the Contract or any benefit or interest in or under the Contract. However, either Party:
(a) may assign the whole or any part with the prior agreement of the other Party, at the sole discretion of such other Party, and
(b) may, as security in favour of a bank or financial institution, assign its right to any moneys due, or to become due, under the Contract.

. . .

1.9 The Contractor shall give notice to the Engineer whenever the Works are likely to be delayed or disrupted if any necessary drawing or instruction is not issued to the Contractor within a particular time, which shall be reasonable. The notice shall include details of the necessary drawing or instruction, details of why and by when it should be issued, and details of the nature and amount of the delay or disruption likely to be suffered if it is late.
If the Contractor suffers delay and/or incurs Cost as a result of a failure of the Engineer to issue the notified drawing or instruction within a time which is reasonable and is specified in the notice with supporting details, the Contractor shall give a further notice to the Engineer and shall be entitled subject to Sub-Clause 20.1 *[Contractor's Claims]* to:
(a) an extension of time for any such delay, if completion is or will be delayed, under Sub-Clause 8.4 *[Extension of Time for Completion]*, and
(b) payment of any such Cost plus reasonable profit, which shall be included in the Contract Price.

. . .

1.13 The Contractor shall, in performing the Contract, comply with applicable Laws. . . . "

The above provisions need to be read into the clauses which set out the substantive rights of the parties. Thus the definition of "unforeseeable" needs to be read into the provision allowing a claim for "unforeseeable physical conditions" in cl.4.12; and the definition of "cost" needs to be read into this clause and others dealing with claims, including cll.1.9 (Instructions), 2.1 (Access) and 8.9 (Suspension) etc.

THE EMPLOYER AND THE ENGINEER

Clause 2 contains consolidated provisions dealing with the rights and duties of the employer and the functions and powers of the engineer, which include the following:

"2.1 The Employer shall give the Contractor right of access to, and possession of, all parts of the Site within the time (or times) stated in the Appendix to Tender. The right and possession may not be exclusive to the Contractor. If, under the Contract, the Employer is required to give (to the Contractor) possession of any foundation, structure, plant or means of access, the Employer shall do so in the time and manner stated in the Specification. However, the Employer may withhold any such right or possession until the Performance Security has been received. . . .

2.2 The Employer shall (where he is in a position to do so) provide reasonable assistance to the Contractor at the request of the Contractor:

   (a) by obtaining copies of the Laws of the Country which are relevant to the Contract but are not readily available, and

   (b) for the Contractor's applications for any permits, licences or approvals required by the Laws of the Country:

      (i) which the Contractor is required to obtain under Sub-Clause 1 .13 *[Compliance with Laws]*,

      (ii) for the delivery of Goods, including clearance through customs, and

      (iii) for the export of Contractor's Equipment when it is removed from the Site.

   . . .

2.4 The Employer shall submit, within 28 days after receiving any request from the Contractor, reasonable evidence that financial arrangements have been made and are being maintained which will enable the Employer to pay the Contract Price (ac estimated at that time) in accordance with Clause 14 *[Contract Price and Payment]*. If the Employer intends to make any material change to his financial arrangements, the Employer shall give notice to the Contractor with detailed particulars."

Clause 3 sets out provisions dealing with the role of the engineer whom the employer is required to appoint to carry out the duties assigned under the contract. The engineer may delegate his powers to assistants. The engineer's dual role is recognised by the following provisions:

"3.1 The Employer shall appoint the Engineer who shall carry out the duties assigned to him in the Contract The Engineer's staff shall include suitably qualified engineers and other professionals who are competent to carry out these duties.

The Engineer shall have no authority to amend the Contract

The Engineer may exercise the authority attributable to the Engineer as specified in or necessarily to be implied from the Contract If the Engineer is required to obtain the approval of the Employer before exercising a specified authority, the requirements shall be as stated in the Particular Conditions. The Employer undertakes not to impose further constraints on the Engineer's authority, except as agreed with the Contractor.

However, whenever the Engineer exercises a specified authority for which the Employer's approval is required, then (for the purposes of the Contract) the Employer shall be deemed to have given approval.

Except as otherwise stated in these Conditions:

(a) whenever carrying out duties or exercising authority, specified in or implied by the Contract, the Engineer shall be deemed to act for the Employer;

(b) the Engineer has no authority to relieve either Party of any duties, obligations or responsibilities under the Contract; and

(c) any approval, check, certificate, consent, examination, inspection, instruction, notice, proposal, request, test, or similar act by the Engineer (including absence of disapproval) shall not relieve the Contractor from any responsibility he has under the Contract, including responsibility for errors, omissions, discrepancies and non-compliances.

. . .

3.3 The Engineer may issue to the Contractor (at any time) instructions and additional or modified Drawings which may be necessary for the execution of the Works and the remedying of any defects, all in accordance with the Contract. The Contractor shall only take instructions from the Engineer, or from an assistant to whom the appropriate authority has been delegated under this Clause. If an instruction constitutes a Variation, Clause 13 *[Variations and Adjustments]* shall apply.

. . .

3.5 Whenever these Conditions provide that the Engineer shall proceed in accordance with this Sub-Clause 3.5 to agree or determine any matter, the Engineer shall consult with each Party in an endeavour to reach agreement. If agreement is not achieved, the Engineer shall make a fair determination in accordance with the Contract, taking due regard of all relevant circumstances.

The Engineer shall give notice to both Parties of each agreement or determination, with supporting particulars. Each Party shall give effect to each agreement or determination unless and until revised under Clause 20 *[Claims, Disputes and Arbitration]*."

The above provision gives to the engineer's determination (or to an agreement) temporary finality until resolved finally by a subsequent dispute resolution procedure as provided by cl.20.

GENERAL OBLIGATIONS OF THE CONTRACTOR

Clause 4 sets out the general obligations of the contractor. Note that cl.4.4 requires the contractor to take (full) responsibility for acts or defaults of all sub-contractors. Nominated sub-contractors are dealt with in the following cl.5:

"4.1 The Contractor shall design (to the extent specified in the Contract), execute and complete the Works in accordance with the Contract and with the Engineer's instructions, and shall remedy any defects in the Works.

The Contractor shall provide the Plant and Contractor's Documents specified in the Contract. and all Contractor's Personnel, Goods, consumables and other things and services, whether of a temporary or permanent nature, required in and for this design, execution, completion and remedying of defects.

The Contractor shall be responsible for the adequacy, stability and safety of all Site operations and of all methods of construction. Except to the extent specified in the Contract, tile Contractor (i) shall be responsible for all Contractor's Documents, Temporary Works, and such design of each item of Plant and Materials as is required for the item to be in accordance with the Contract, and (ii) shall not otherwise be responsible for the design or specification of the Permanent Works.

The Contractor shall, whenever required by the Engineer, submit details of the arrangements and methods which the Contractor proposes to adopt for the execution of the Works. No significant alteration to these arrangements and methods shall be made without this having previously been notified to the Engineer.

If the Contract specifies that the Contractor shall design any part of the Permanent Works, then unless otherwise stated in the Particular conditions:

(a)   the Contractor shall submit to the Engineer the Contractor's Documents for this part in accordance with the procedures specified in the Contract;

(b)   the Contractor's Documents shall be in accordance with the Specification and Drawings, shall be written in the language for communications defined in Sub-Clause 1.4 *[Law and Language]*, and shall include additional information required by the Engineer to add to the Drawings for co-ordination of each Party's designs;

(c)   the Contractor shall be responsible for this part and it shall, when the Works are completed, be fit for such purposes for which the part is intended as are specified in the Contract; and

(d)   prior to the commencement of the Tests on Completion, the Contractor shall submit to the Engineer the 'as-built' documents and operation and maintenance manuals in accordance with the Specification and in sufficient detail for the Employer to operate, maintain, dismantle, reassemble, adjust and repair this part of the Works. Such part shall not be considered to be completed for the purposes of taking-over under Sub-Clause 10.1 *[Taking Over of the Works and Sections]* until these documents and manuals have been submitted to the Engineer.

. . .

4.4 The Contractor shall not subcontract the whole of the Works.

The Contractor shall be responsible for the acts or defaults of any Subcontractor, his agents or employees, as if they were the acts or defaults of the Contractor. Unless otherwise stated in the Particular Conditions:

(a) the Contractor shall not be required to obtain consent to suppliers of Materials, or to a subcontract for which the Subcontractor is named in the Contract;

(b) the prior consent of the Engineer shall be obtained to other proposed Subcontractors;

(c) the Contractor shall give the Engineer not less than 28 days' notice of the intended date of the commencement of each Subcontractor's work, and of the commencement of such work on the Site; and

(d) each subcontract shall include provisions which would entitle the Employer to require the subcontract to be assigned to the Employer under Sub-Clause 4.5 *[Assignment of Benefit of Subcontract]* (if or when applicable) or in the event of termination under Sub-Clause 15.2 *[Termination by Employer]*

. . .

4.6 The Contractor shall, as specified in the Contract or as instructed by the Engineer, allow appropriate opportunities for carrying out work to:

(a) the Employer's Personnel,

(b) any other contractors employed by the Employer, and

(c) the personnel of any legally constituted public authorities,
who may be employed in the execution on or near the Site of any work not included in the Contract.

Any such instruction shall constitute a Variation if and to the extent that it causes the Contractor to incur Unforeseeable Cost. Services for these personnel and other contractors may include the use of Contractor's Equipment, Temporary Works or access arrangements which are the responsibility of the Contractor.

If, under the Contract, the Employer is required to give to the Contractor possession of any foundation, structure, plant or means of access in accordance with Contractor's Documents, the Contractor shall submit such documents to the Engineer in the time and manner stated in the Specification

. . .

4.10 The Employer shall have made available to the Contractor for his information, prior to the Base Date, all relevant data in the Employer's possession on sub-surface and hydrological conditions at the Site, including environmental aspects. The Employer shall similarly make available to the Contractor all such data which come into the Employer's possession after the Base Date. The Contractor shall be responsible for interpreting all such data.

To the extent which was practicable (taking account of cost and time), the Contractor shall be deemed to have obtained all necessary information as to risks, contingencies and other circumstances which may influence or affect the Tender or Works. To the same extent, the Contractor shall be deemed to have inspected and examined the Site, its surroundings, the above data and other available information, and to have been satisfied before submitting the Tender as to all relevant matters, including (without limitation):

(a) the form and nature of the Site, including sub-surface conditions,

(b) the hydrological and climatic conditions,

(c) the extent and nature of the work and Goods necessary for the execution and completion of the Works and the remedying of any defects,

(d) the Laws, procedures and labour practices of the Country, and

(e) the Contractor's requirements for access, accommodation, facilities, personnel, power, transport, water and other services.

4.11 The Contractor shall be deemed to:

(a) have satisfied himself as to the correctness and sufficiency of the Accepted Contract Amount, and

(b) have based the Accepted Contract Amount on the data, interpretations, necessary information, inspections, examinations and satisfaction as to all relevant matters referred to in Sub-Clause 4.10 *[Site Data]*.

Unless otherwise stated in the Contract, the Accepted Contract Amount covers all the Contractor's obligations under the Contract (including those under Provisional Sums, if any) and all things necessary for the proper execution and completion of the Works and the remedying of any defects.

4.12 In this Sub-Clause, 'physical conditions' means natural physical conditions and manmade and other physical obstructions and pollutants, which the Contractor encounters at the Site when executing the Works, including sub-surface and hydrological conditions but excluding climatic conditions.

If the Contractor encounters adverse physical conditions which he considers to have been Unforeseeable, the Contractor shall give notice to the Engineer as soon as practicable.

This notice shall describe the physical conditions, so that they can be inspected by the Engineer, and shall set out the reasons why the Contractor considers them to be Unforeseeable. The Contractor shall continue executing the Works, using such proper and reasonable measures as are appropriate for the physical conditions, and shall comply with any instructions which the Engineer may give. If an instruction constitutes a Variation, Clause 13 *[Variations and Adjustments]* shall apply.

If and to the extent that the Contractor encounters physical conditions which are Unforeseeable, gives such a notice, and suffers delay and/or incurs Cost due to these conditions, the Contractor shall be entitled subject to Sub-Clause 20.1 *[Contractor's Claims]* to:

> (a) an extension of time for any such delay, if completion is or will be delayed, under Sub-Clause 8.4 *[Extension of Time for Completion]*, and
>
> (b) payment of any such Cost, which shall be included in the Contract Price.
>
> After receiving such notice and inspecting and/or investigating these physical conditions, the Engineer shall proceed in accordance with Sub-Clause 3.5 *[Determinations]* to agree or determine (i) whether and (if so) to what extent these physical conditions were Unforeseeable, and (ii) the matters described in subparagraphs (a) and (b) above related to this extent
>
> However, before additional Cost is finally agreed or determined under subparagraph (ii), the Engineer may also review whether other physical conditions in similar parts of the Works (if any) were more favourable than could reasonably have been foreseen when the Contractor submitted the Tender. If and to the extent that these more favourable conditions were encountered, the Engineer may proceed in accordance with Sub-Clause 3.5 *[Determinations]* to agree or determine the reductions in Cost which were due to these conditions, which may be included (as deductions) in the Contract Price and Payment Certificates. However, the net effect of all adjustments under sub-paragraph (b) and all these reductions, for all the physical conditions encountered in similar parts of the Works, shall not result in a net reduction in the Contract Price. The Engineer may take account of any evidence of the physical conditions foreseen by the Contractor when submitting the Tender, which may be made available by the Contractor, but shall not be bound by any such evidence.
>
> . . .
>
> 4.17 The Contractor shall be responsible for all Contractor's Equipment. When brought on to the Site, Contractor's Equipment shall be deemed to be exclusively intended for the execution of the Works. The Contractor shall not remove from the Site any major items of Contractor's Equipment without the consent of the Engineer. However, consent shall not be required for vehicles transporting Goods or Contractor's Personnel off Site."

Other sub-clauses deal with performance security, the contractor's representative, assignment, safety, quality assurance, access, environmental matters, free-issue material, progress reporting, maintenance of the site and fossils. Clauses 4.11 and 4.12 substantially replicate equivalent clauses of the ICE/ICC Conditions which confirm the contractor's responsibility for the sufficiency of the tender.

Clause 8 deals with commencement, delays and suspension, including detailed provisions as to programmes (cl.8.3) and extensions of time (cl.8.4). Note that, despite appearances to the contrary, the programme never becomes a contract document and never directly binds either party to its provisions:

"8.1 [T]he Engineer shall give the Contractor not less than 7 days' notice of the Commencement Date. Unless otherwise stated in the Particular Conditions, the Commencement Date shall be within 42 days after the Contractor receives the Letter of Acceptance.

The Contractor shall commence the execution of the Works as soon as is reasonably practicable after the Commencement Date, and shall then proceed with the Works with due expedition and without delay.

8.2 The Contractor shall complete the whole of the Works, and each Section (if any), within the Time for Completion for the Works or Section (as the case may be), including:

(a) achieving the passing of the Tests on Completion, and

(b) completing all work which is stated in the Contract as being required for the Works or Section to be considered to be completed for the purposes of taking over under Sub-Clause 10.1 *[Taking Over of the Works and Sections]*

8.3 The Contractor shall submit a detailed time programme to the Engineer within 28 days after receiving the notice under Sub-Clause 8:1 *[Commencement of Works]*. The Contractor shall also submit a revised programme whenever the previous programme is inconsistent with actual progress or with the Contractor's obligations. Each programme shall include:

(a) the order in which the Contractor intends to carry out the Works, including the anticipated timing of each stage of design (if any), Contractor's Documents, procurement, manufacture of Plant, delivery to Site, construction, erection and testing,

(b) each of these stages for work by each nominated Subcontractor (as defined in Clause 5 *[Nominated Subcontractors]*),

(c) the sequence and timing of inspections and tests specified in the Contract, and

(d) a supporting report which includes:

(i) a general description of the methods which the Contractor intends to adopt, and of the major stages, in the execution of the Works, and

(ii) details showing the Contractor's reasonable estimate of the number of each class of Contractor's Personnel and of each type of Contractor's Equipment, required on the Site for each major stage.

Unless the Engineer, within 21 days after receiving a programme, gives notice to the Contractor stating the extent to which it does not comply with the Contract, the Contractor shall proceed in accordance with the programme, subject to his other obligations under the Contract. The Employer's Personnel shall be entitled to rely upon the programme when planning their activities.

The Contractor shall promptly give notice to the Engineer of specific probable future events or circumstances which may adversely affect the work, increase the Contract Price or delay the execution of the Works. The Engineer may require the Contractor to submit an estimate of the anticipated effect of the future event or circumstances, and/or a proposal under Sub-Clause 13.3 *[Variation Procedure]*.

If, at any time, the Engineer gives notice to the Contractor that a programme fails (to the extent stated) to comply with the Contract or to be consistent with actual progress and the Contractor's stated intentions, the Contractor shall submit a revised programme to the Engineer in accordance with this Sub-Clause.

8.4 The Contractor shall be entitled subject to Sub-Clause 20.1 *[Contractor's Claims]* to an extension of the Time for Completion if and to the extent that completion for the purposes of Sub-Clause 10.1 *[Taking Over of the Works and Sections]* is or will be delayed by any of the following causes:

(a) a Variation (unless an adjustment to the Time for Completion has been agreed under Sub-Clause 13.3 *[Variation Procedure]*) or other substantial change in the quantity of an item of work included in the Contract,

(b) a cause of delay giving an entitlement to extension of time under a Sub-Clause of these Conditions,

(c) exceptionally adverse climatic conditions,

(d) Unforeseeable shortages in the availability of personnel or Goods caused by epidemic or governmental actions, or

(e) any delay, impediment or prevention caused by or attributable to the Employer, the Employer's Personnel, or the Employer's other contractors on the Site.

If the Contractor considers himself to be entitled to an extension of the Time for Completion, the Contractor shall give notice to the Engineer in accordance with SubClause 20.1 *[Contractor's Claims]*. When determining each extension of time under Sub-Clause 20.1, the Engineer shall review previous determinations and, may increase, but shall not decrease, the total extension of time.

8.5 If the following conditions apply, namely:

(a) the Contractor has diligently followed the procedures laid down by the relevant legally constituted public authorities in the Country,

(b) these authorities delay or disrupt the Contractor's work, and

(c) the delay or disruption was Unforeseeable,

then this delay or disruption will be considered as a cause of delay under subparagraph (b) of Sub-Clause 8.4 *[Extension of Time for Completion]*."

By cl.8.6, the engineer is entitled to require measures to expedite progress, based on cl.46 of the ICE/ICC Conditions; and by cl.8.7, the contractor is required to pay "delay damages" (liquidated damages) as specified in the appendix, in respect of any period of overrun. Clauses 8.8–8.12 contain somewhat elaborate provisions dealing with suspension of the works (an extremely rare event on any project) on the engineer's instruction and the consequences, which may include deemed omission or termination by the contractor. The causes of delay giving entitlement to extension under the conditions include force majeure under cl.19, which is defined as follows:

"19.1 In this Clause, 'Force Majeure' means an exceptional event or circumstance:

    (a) which is beyond a Party's control,

    (b) which such Party could not reasonably have provided against before entering into the Contract,

    (c) which, having arisen, such Party could not reasonably have avoided or overcome, and

    (d) which is not substantially attributable to the other Party.

Force Majeure may include, but is not limited to, exceptional events or circumstances of the kind listed below, so long as conditions (a) to (d) above are satisfied:

    (i) war. hostilities (whether war be declared or not), invasion, act of foreign enemies,

    (ii) rebellion, terrorism, revolution, insurrection, military or usurped power, or civil war,

    (iii) riot, commotion, disorder, strike or lockout by persons other than Contractor's Personnel and other employees of the Contractor and contractors.

    (iv) munitions of war, explosive materials, ionising radiation or contamination by radio-activity, except as may be attributable to the Contractor's use of such munitions, explosives, radiation or radio-activity, and

    (v) natural catastrophes such as earthquake. hurricane, typhoon or 'volcanic' activity."

Subject to giving of notice, cl.19 provides for extension of time, payment of costs and, in the event of protracted delay, termination by either party and for the consequences of such termination.

CERTIFICATION AND PAYMENT

Measurement, valuation and payment are dealt with compendiously in cll.12, 13 and 14. The work is to be measured and valued, both for the final valuation and for interim payments, at rates or prices specified in the contract, which may themselves be varied if circumstances require (cl.12.3). Note that cl.14 provides for an alternative payment regime, if agreed, comprising a schedule of lump-sum payments. Variations are to be valued in accordance with an agreed evaluation or otherwise in accordance with the provisions of cl.12 (cl.13.3):

"12.1 The Works shall be measured, and valued for payment, in accordance with this Clause.

    . . .

12.2 Except as otherwise stated in the Contract and notwithstanding local practice:

    (a) measurement shall be made of the net actual quantity of each item of the Permanent Works, and

(b)   the method of measurement shall be in accordance with the Bill of Quantities or other applicable Schedules.

12.3   Except as otherwise stated in the Contract, the Engineer shall proceed in accordance with Sub-Clause 3.5 *[Determinations]* to agree or determine the Contract Price by evaluating each item of work, applying the measurement agreed or determined in accordance with the above Sub-Clauses 12.1 and 12.2 and the appropriate rate or price for the item.

For each item of work, the appropriate rate or price for the item shall be the rate or price specified for such item in the Contract or, if there is no such item, specified for similar work. However, a new rate or price shall be appropriate for an item of work if:

(a)   (i)   the measured quantity of the item is changed by more than 10% from the quantity of this item in the Bill of Quantities or other Schedule,

(ii)   this change in quantity multiplied by such specified rate for this item exceeds 0.01 % of the Accepted Contract Amount,

(iii)   this change in quantity directly changes the Cost per unit quantity of this item by more than 1 %, and

(iv)   this item is not specified in the Contract as a 'fixed rate item';

or

(b)   (i)   the work is instructed under Clause 13 *[Variations and Adjustments]*,

(ii)   no rate or price is specified in the Contract for this item, and

(iii)   no specified rate or price is appropriate because the item of work is not of similar character, or is not executed under similar conditions, as any item in the Contract.

Each new rate or price shall be derived from any relevant rates or prices in the Contract, with reasonable adjustments to take account of the matters described in sub-paragraph (a) and/or (b), as applicable. If no rates or prices are relevant for the derivation of a new rate or price, it shall be derived from the reasonable Cost of executing the work, together with reasonable profit, taking account of any other relevant matters.

Until such time as an appropriate rate or price is agreed or determined, the Engineer shall determine a provisional rate or price for the purposes of Interim Payment Certificates."

Where the contract includes a provisional sum, the engineer may instruct work to be executed by the contractor or by a nominated sub-contractor (cl.13.5). By cl.5.2, the contractor is not obligated to employ a nominated sub-contractor against whom he raises reasonable objection. In this event, the employer has the option of agreeing to indemnify the contractor against the consequences of such objection. Otherwise, the contractor is to be fully responsible for the performance of a nominated sub-contractor.[1] By cl.5.4, the employer may make direct payments to a

---

[1] In contrast to the position under successive versions of the JCT Conditions up to 2005, and the ICE Conditions from the 5th edition of 1973.

nominated sub-contractor who has not been paid sums previously certified, and recover such sums from the contractor.

Interim payment certificates may include, if agreed, "*an amount for
Plant and Materials which have been sent to the Site for incorporation
in the Permanent Works*" and for corresponding reduction when the plant
or materials are included the value of the permanent works (14.5) As
already noted, as an alternative to conventional interim payments based
on measurement, cl.14 makes provision for payment according to an
agreed schedule of lump-sum payments, which payments may be
adjusted by the engineer if progress is less than that on which the
schedule was based (14.4). In addition to periodic payments, the parties
may agree to an advance payment, "*as an interest-free loan for mobilisa-
tion*", subject to provision of a guarantee. The advance is to be repaid
through a percentage deduction from interim certificates and the guarantee reduced accordingly (14.2). Clause 14 includes a procedure for the
contractor's final statement and for the engineer to issue the final
payment certificate (14.12, 14.13).

COMPLETION

The contract contains new provisions for tests on completion (cl.9)
and an extended procedure for the employer's taking over and defects
liability (cll.10 and 11), which include the following provisions:

"9.1 The Contractor shall carry out the Tests on Completion in accordance
with this Clause and Sub-Clause 7.4 *[Testing]*, after providing the
documents in accordance with sub-paragraph (d) of Sub-Clause 4.1
[Contractor's General Obligations].
The Contractor shall give to the Engineer not less than 21 days' notice
of the date after which the Contractor will be ready to carry out each
of the Tests on Completion. Unless otherwise agreed, Tests on
Completion shall be carried out within 14 days after this date, on such
day or days as the Engineer shall instruct.
In considering the results of the Tests on Completion, the Engineer
shall make allowances for the effect of any use of the Works by the
Employer on the performance or other characteristics of the Works.
As soon as the Works, or a Section, have passed any Tests on
Completion, the Contractor shall submit a certified report of the
results of these Tests to the Engineer.

. . .

10.1 Except as stated in Sub-Clause 9.4 *[Failure to Pass Tests on
Completion]*. The Works shall be taken over by the Employer
when (i) the Works have been completed in accordance with the

Contract. including the matters described in Sub-Clause 8.2 *[Time for Completion]* and except as allowed in sub-paragraph (a) below, and (ii) a Taking-Over Celiificate for the Works has been issued. or is deemed to have been issued in accordance with this Sub-Clause.

The Contractor may apply by notice to the Engineer for a Taking-Over Certificate not earlier than 14 days before the Works will, in the Contractor's opinion, be complete and ready for taking over. If the Works are divided into Sections, the Contractor may similarly apply for a Taking-Over Certificate for each Section.

The Engineer shall, within 28 days after receiving the Contractor's application:

(a)   issue the Taking-Over Certificate to the Contractor, stating the date on which the Works or Section were completed in accordance with the Contract, except for any minor outstanding work and defects which will not substantially affect the use of the Works or Section for their intended purpose (either until or whilst this work is completed and these defects are remedied); or

(b)   reject the application, giving reasons and specifying the work required to be done by the Contractor to enable the Taking-Over Certificate to be issued. The Contractor shall then complete this work before issuing a further notice under this Sub-Clause.

If the Engineer fails either to issue the Taking-Over Certificate or to reject the Contractor's application within the period of 28 days, and if the Works or Section (as the case may be) are substantially in accordance with the Contract, the Taking-Over Certificate shall be deemed to have been issued on the last day of that period.

. . .

11.9   Performance of the Contractor's obligations shall not be considered to have been completed until the Engineer has issued the Performance Certificate to the Contractor, stating the date on which the Contractor completed his obligations under the Contract. The Engineer shall issue the Performance Certificate within 28 days after the latest of the expiry dates of the Defects Notification Periods, Or as soon thereafter as the Contractor has supplied all the Contractor's Documents and completed and tested all the Works, including remedying any defects. A copy of the Performance Certificate shall be issued to the Employer.

Only the Performance Certificate shall be deemed to constitute acceptance of the Works.

11.10 After the Performance Certificate has been issued, each Party shall remain liable for the fulfilment of any obligation which remains unperformed at that time. For the purposes of determining the nature and extent of unperformed obligations, the Contract shall be deemed to remain in force."

However the continuing rights of the contractor are further limited by the following provision:

"14.14 The Employer shall not be liable to the Contractor for any matter or thing under or in connection with the Contract or execution of the Works, except to the extent that the Contractor shall have included an amount expressly for it:

(a) in the Final Statement and also

(b) (except for matters or things arising after the issue of the Taking-Over Certificate for the Works) in the Statement at completion described in Sub-Clause 14.10 *[Statement at Completion]*.

However, this Sub-Clause shall not limit the Employer's liability under his indemnification obligations, or the Employer's liability in any case of fraud, deliberate default or reckless misconduct by the Employer."

EMPLOYER'S REMEDIES

Clause 15.1 provides a general remedy for non-performance:

"15.1 If the Contractor fails to carry out any obligation under the Contract, the Engineer may by notice require the Contractor to make good the failure and to remedy it within a specified reasonable time."

Where the works fail to pass the tests on completion for a second time or the contractor fails to remedy any defect or damage at the second opportunity, the contract provides the employer with further specific remedies as follows:

"9.4 If the Works, or a Section, fail to pass the Tests on Completion repeated under Sub- Completion Clause 9.3 *[Retesting]*, the Engineer shall be entitled to:

(a) order further repetition of Tests on Completion under Sub-Clause 9.3;

(b) if the failure deprives the Employer of substantially the whole benefit of the Works or Section, reject the Works or Section (as the case may be), in which event the Employer shall have the same remedies as are provided in subparagraph (c) of Sub-Clause 11.4 *[Failure to Remedy Defects]*; or

(c) issue a Taking-Over Certificate, if the Employer so requests.

In the event of sub-paragraph (c), the Contractor shall proceed in accordance with all other obligations under the Contract, and the Contract Price shall be reduced by such amount as shall be appropriate to cover the reduced value to the Employer as a result of this failure. Unless the relevant reduction for this failure is stated (or its method of calculation is defined) in the Contract, the Employer may require the reduction to be (i) agreed by both Parties (in full satisfaction of this failure only) and paid before this Taking-Over Certificate is issued, or (ii) determined and paid under Sub-Clause 2.5 *[Employer's Claims]* and Sub-Clause 3.5 *[Determinations]*.

...

11.4 If the Contractor fails to remedy any defect or damage within a reasonable time, a date may be fixed by (or on behalf 01) the Employer, on or by Which the defect or damage is to be remedied. The Contractor shall be given reasonable notice of this date.

If the Contractor fails to remedy the defect or damage by this notified date and this remedial work was to be executed at the cost of the Contractor under SubClause 11.2 *[Cost of Remedying Defects]*, the Employer may (at his option):

(a) carry out the work himself or by others, in a reasonable manner and at the Contractor's cost, but the Contractor shall have no responsibility for this work; and the Contractor shall subject to Sub-Clause 2.5 *[Employer's Claims]* pay to the Employer the costs reasonably incurred by ihe Employer in remedying the defect or damage;

(b) require the Engineer to agree or determine a reasonable reduction in the Contract Price in accordance with Sub-Clause 3.5 *[Determinations]*; or

(c) if the defect or damage deprives the Employer of substantially the whole benefit of the Works or any major part of the Works, terminate the Contract as a whole, or in respect of such major part which cannot be put to the intended use. Without prejudice to any other rights, under the Contract or otherwise, the Employer shall then be entitled to recover all sums paid for the Works or for such part (as the case may be), plus financing costs and the cost of dismantling the same, clearing the Site and returning Plant and Materials to the, Contractor."

Clause 11.4 (c) and 9.4 (b), above, each provide that the employer may terminate the contract in part or in whole where the defect or failure in performance deprives the employer substantially of the whole benefit of the works or part of the works. Termination is an extreme remedy which is provided for on general grounds by cl.15:

"15.2 The Employer shall be entitled to terminate the Contract if the Contractor:

(a) fails to comply with Sub-Clause 4.2 *[Performance Security]* or with a notice under Sub-Clause 15.1 *[Notice to Correct]*,

(b) abandons the Works or otherwise plainly demonstrates the intention not to continue performance of his obligations under the Contract,

(c) without reasonable excuse fails:
(i) to proceed with the Works in accordance with Clause 8 *[Commencement, Delays and Suspension]*, or
(ii) to comply with a notice issued under Sub-Clause 7.5 *[Rejection]* or Sub-Clause 7.6 *[Remedial Work]*, within 28 days after receiving it,

(d) subcontracts the whole of the Works or assigns the Contract without the required agreement,

(e) becomes bankrupt or insolvent, goes into liquidation, has a receiving or administration order made against him, compounds with his creditors, or carries on business under a receiver, trustee or manager for the benefit of his creditors, or if any act is done or event occurs which (under applicable Laws) has a similar effect to any of these acts or events, or

(f) gives or offers to give (directly or indirectly) to any person any bribe, gift, gratuity commission or other thing of value, as an inducement or reward:

(i) for doing or forbearing to do any action in relation to the Contract, or

(ii) for showing or forbearing to show favour or disfavour to any person in relation to the Contract,

or if any of the Contractor's Personnel, agents or Subcontractors gives or offers to give (directly or indirectly) to any person any such inducement or reward as is described in this sub-paragraph (f). However, lawful inducements and rewards to Contractor's Personnel shall not entitle termination.

In any of these events or circumstances, the Employer may, upon giving 14 days' notice to the Contractor, terminate the Contract and expel the Contractor from the Site. However, in the case of sub-paragraph (e) or (n, the Employer may by notice terminate the Contract immediately.

The Employer's election to terminate the Contract shall not prejudice any other rights of the Employer, under the Contract or otherwise.

The Contractor shall then leave the Site and deliver any required Goods, all Contractor's Documents, and other design documents made by or for him, to the Engineer. However, the Contractor shall use his best efforts to comply immediately with any reasonable instructions included in the notice (i) for the assignment of any subcontract, and (ii) for the protection of life or property or for the safety of the Works.

After termination, the Employer may complete the Works and/or arrange for any other entities to do so. The Employer and these entities may then use any Goods, Contractor's Documents and other design documents made by or on behalf of the Contractor.

The Employer shall then give notice that the Contractor's Equipment and Temporary Works will be released to the Contractor at or near the Site. The Contractor shall promptly arrange their removal, at the risk and cost of the Contractor. However, if by this time the Contractor has failed to make a payment due to the Employer, these items may be sold by the Employer in order to recover this payment. Any balance of the proceeds shall then be paid to the Contractor."

Clauses 15.3 and 15.4 provide for matters of account and payment. Clause 15.5 provides for termination for convenience, in which event the contractor is entitled to full payment for work performed and termination costs under cl.19.6, but such costs (surprisingly) do not include loss of profit on unperformed work. Clause 16.1 permits the contractor to suspend work in consequence of the employer's breach of payment or finance obligations; and cl.16.2 entitles the contractor to terminate for default as follows:

"16.2 The Contractor shall be entitled to terminate the Contract if:

(a) the Contractor does not receive the reasonable evidence within 42 days after giving notice under Sub-Clause 16.1 *[Contractor's Entitlement to Suspend Work]* in respect of a failure to comply with Sub-Clause 2.4 *[Employer's Financial Arrangements]*,

(b) the Engineer fails, within 56 days after receiving a Statement and supporting documents, to issue the relevant Payment Certificate,

(c) the Contractor does not receive the amount due under an Interim Payment Certificate within 42 days after the expiry of the time stated in Sub-Clause 14.7 *[Payment]* within which payment is to be made (except for deductions in accordance with Sub-Clause 2.5 *[Employer's Claims]*,

(d) the Employer substantially fails to perform his obligations under the Contract.

(e) the Employer fails to comply with Sub-Clause 1.6 *[Contract Agreement]* or Sub-Clause 1.7 *[Assignment]*,

(f) a prolonged suspension affects the whole of the Works as described in SubClause 8.11 *[Prolonged Suspension]*, or

(g) the Employer becomes bankrupt or insolvent, goes into liquidation, has a receiving or administration order made against him, compounds with his creditors, or carries on business under a receiver, trustee or manager for the benefit of his creditors, or if any act is done or event occurs which (under applicable Laws) has a similar effect to any of these acts or events,

In any of these events or circumstances, the Contractor may, upon giving 14 days' notice to the Employer, terminate the Contract. However, in the case of subparagraph (I) or (g), the Contractor may by notice terminate the Contract immediately.

The Contractor's election to terminate the Contract shall not prejudice any other rights of the Contractor, under the Contract or otherwise."

Clauses 17 and 18 make provision for risks, indemnity and insurance. Clause 17.1 provides mutual indemnities in respect of third party claims. Clause 17.2 provides for responsibility for the works:

"17.2 The Contractor shall take full responsibility for the care of the Works and Goods from the Commencement Date until the Taking-Over Certificate is issued (or is deemed to be issued under Sub-Clause 10.1 *[Taking Over of the Works and Sections]*) for the Works, when responsibility for the care of the Works shall pass to the Employer. If a Taking-Over Certificate is issued (or is so deemed to be issued) for any Section or part of the Works, responsibility for the care of the Section or part shall then pass to the Employer.

After responsibility has accordingly passed to the Employer, the Contractor shall take responsibility for the care of any work which is outstanding on the date stated in a Taking-Over Certificate, until this outstanding work has been completed.

If any loss or damage happens to the Works, Goods or Contractor's Documents during the period when the Contractor is responsible for their care, from any cause not listed in Sub-Clause 17.3 *[Employer's Risks]*, the Contractor shall rectify the loss or damage at the Contractor's risk and cost, so that the Works, Goods and Contractor's Documents conform with the Contract.

The Contractor shall be liable for any loss or damage caused by any actions performed by the Contractor after a Taking-Over Certificate has been issued. The Contractor shall also be liable for any loss or damage which occurs after a Taking-Over Certificate has been issued and which arose from a previous event for which the Contractor was liable."

Clause 17.3 sets out the employer's risks which include

"(g) design of any part of the Works by the Employer's Personnel or by others for whom the Employer is responsible, and

(h) any operation of the forces of nature which is Unforeseeable or against which an experienced contractor could not reasonably have been expected to have taken adequate preventative precautions."

Clause 17.6 provides for limitation of the liability of either party to the other for the following risks

". . . loss of use of any works, loss of profit, loss of any contract or for any indirect or consequential loss or damage which may be suffered by either party in connection with the Contract other than under clause 16.4 [Payment on Termination] and clause 17.1 [Indemnities]".

Clause 17.3 also provides for limitation of the total liability of the contractor to the employer.

DISPUTES

Disputes amounting to a difference of view between the parties are inevitable under any construction contract, and an important function of the conditions of contract is to regulate those disputes including, if necessary, their determination in a manner that will not impede the further progress of the works. There are many instances where the engineer is called on to make decisions on matters of management, including valuations and the granting (or withholding) of extensions of time. Only where the parties continue to take issue with the decision can there be said to be a dispute. When this arises the engineer is required, pursuant to cl.3.5, to encourage the parties to reach an agreement, in default of which he must make a "determination" by which the parties are to be bound unless and until revised under cl.20 (Claims, Disputes and Arbitration). Clause 20 first sets out contains requirements as to notice of claims:

> "20.1 If the Contractor considers himself to be entitled to any extension of the Time for Completion and/or any additional payment, under any Clause of these Conditions or otherwise in connection with the Contract, the Contractor shall give notice to the Engineer, describing the event or circumstance giving rise to the claim. The notice shall be given as soon as practicable, and not later than 28 days after the Contractor became aware, or should have become aware, of the event or circumstance.
>
> If the Contractor fails to give notice of a claim within such period of 28 days, the Time for Completion shall not be extended, the Contractor shall not be entitled to additional payment, and the Employer shall be discharged from all liability in connection with the claim. Otherwise, the following provisions of this Sub-Clause shall apply.
>
> The Contractor shall also submit any other notices which are required by the Contract, and supporting particulars for the claim, all as relevant to such event or circumstance.
>
> The Contractor shall keep such contemporary records as may be necessary to substantiate any claim, either on the Site or at another location acceptable to the Engineer. Without admitting the Employer's liability, the Engineer may, after receiving any notice under this Sub-Clause, monitor the record-keeping and/or instruct the Contractor to keep further contemporary records. The Contractor shall permit the Engineer to inspect all these records, and shall (if instructed) submit copies to the Engineer.
>
> Within 42 days after the Contractor became aware (or should have become aware) of the event or circumstance giving rise to the claim, or within such other period as may be proposed by the Contractor and approved by the Engineer, the Contractor shall send to the Engineer a fully detailed claim which includes full supporting particulars of the basis of the claim and of the extension of time and/or additional payment claimed. If the event or circumstance giving rise to the claim has a continuing effect:
>
> (a) this fully detailed claim shall be considered as interim;
>
> (b) the Contractor shall send further interim claims at monthly intervals, giving the accumulated delay and/or amount claimed, and such further particulars as the Engineer may reasonably require; and
>
> (c) the Contractor shall send a final claim within 28 days after the end of the effects resulting from the event or Circumstance, or within such other period as may be proposed by the Contractor and approved by the Engineer.
>
> Within 42 days after receiving a claim or any further particulars supporting a previous claim, or within such other period as may be

proposed by the Engineer and approved by the Contractor, the Engineer shall respond with approval, or with disapproval and detailed comments. He may also request any necessary further particulars, but shall nevertheless give his response on the principles of the claim within such time.

Each Payment Certificate shall include such amounts for any claim as have been reasonably substantiated as due under the relevant provision of the Contract. Unless and until the particulars supplied are sufficient to Substantiate the whole of the claim, the Contractor shall only be entitled to payment for such part of the claim as he has been able to substantiate.

The Engineer shall proceed in accordance with Sub-Clause 3.5 *[Determinations]* to agree or determine (i) the extension (if any) of the Time for Completion (before or after its expiry) in accordance with Sub-Clause 8.4 *[Extension of Time for Completion]*, and/or (ii) the additional payment (if any) to which the Contractor is entitled under the Contract.

The requirements of this Sub-Clause are in addition to those of any other Sub-Clause which may apply to a claim. If the Contractor fails to comply with this or another Sub-Clause in relation to any claim, any extension of time and/or additional payment shall take account of the extent (if any) to which the failure has prevented or prejudiced proper investigation of the claim, unless the claim is excluded under the second paragraph of this Sub-Clause."

Clause 20.2 and 20.3 deal with appointment of a Dispute Adjudication Board (DAB) which may be named in the contract or otherwise appointed. The DAB may consist of one or three persons. In the latter case, each party is to nominate one person, whom the other must approve, the third member being agreed by the parties. The DAB is then required, under cl.20.4, to give a decision on any dispute which, in the absence of notice of dissatisfaction by either party within 28 days, will become final and binding upon both parties. After notice of dissatisfaction, the parties are required to attempt amicable settlement, following which the dispute may be referred to arbitration in accordance with the ICC Rules. If the parties omit to appoint a DAB, by cl.20.8 any dispute may be referred directly to arbitration:

> "20.4 If a dispute (of any kind whatsoever) arises between the Parties in connection with, or arising out of, the Contract or the execution of the Works, including any dispute as to any certificate, determination, instruction, opinion or valuation of the Engineer, either Party may refer the dispute in writing to the DAB for its decision, with copies to the other Party and the Engineer. Such reference shall state that it is given this Sub-Clause.
>
> For a DAB of three persons, the DAB shall be deemed to have received reference on the date when it is received by the chairman of the DAB.

Both Parties shall promptly make available to the DAB all such additional information, further access to the Site, and appropriate facilities, as the DAB may require for purposes of making a decision on such dispute. The DAB shall be deemed to be not acting as arbitrator(s).

Within 84 days after receiving such reference, or within such other period as may be proposed by the DAB and approved by both Parties, the DAB shall give its decision, which shall be reasoned and shall state that it is given under this Sub-Clause. The decision shall be binding on both Parties, who shall promptly give effect to it unless and until it shall be revised in an amicable settlement or an arbitral award as described below. Unless the Contract has already been abandoned, repudiated or terminated, the Contractor shall continue to proceed with the Works in accordance with the Contract. If either Party is dissatisfied with the DAB's decision, then either Party may, within 28 days after receiving the decision, give notice to the other Party of its dissatisfaction. If the DAB fails to give its decision within the period of 84 days (or as otherwise approved) after receiving such reference, then either Party may, within 28 days after this period has expired, give notice to the other Party of its dissatisfaction.

In either event, this notice of dissatisfaction shall state that it is given under this Sub-Clause, and shall set out the matter in dispute and the reason(s) for dissatisfaction. Except as stated in Sub-Clause 20.7 *[Failure to Comply with Dispute Adjudication Board's Decision]* and Sub-Clause 20.8 *[Expiry of Dispute Adjudication Board's Appointment]*, neither Party shall be entitled to commence arbitration of a dispute unless a notice of dissatisfaction has been given in accordance with this Sub-Clause.

If the DAB has given its decision as to a matter in dispute to both Parties, and no notice of dissatisfaction has been given by either Party within 28 days after it received the DAB's decision, then the decision shall become final and binding upon both Parties.

20.5 Where notice of dissatisfaction has been given under Sub-Clause 20.4 above, both Parties shall attempt to settle the dispute amicably before the commencement of arbitration. However, unless both Parties agree otherwise, arbitration may be commenced on or after the fifty-sixth day after the day on which notice of dissatisfaction was given, even if no attempt at amicable settlement has been made.

20.6 Unless settled amicably, any dispute in respect of which the DAB's decision (if any) has not become final and binding shall be finally settled by international arbitration. Unless otherwise agreed by both Parties:

(a) the dispute shall be finally settled under the Rules of Arbitration of the International Chamber of Commerce (ICC),

(b) the dispute shall be settled by three arbitrators appointed in accordance with these Rules, and

(c) the arbitration shall be conducted in the language for communications defined in Sub-Clause 1.4 *[Law and Language]*.

The arbitrator(s) shall have full power to open up, review and revise any certificate, determination, instruction, opinion or valuation of the Engineer, and any decision of the DAB, relevant to the dispute. Nothing shall disqualify the Engineer from being called as a witness and giving evidence before the arbitrator(s) on any matter whatsoever relevant to the dispute.

Neither Party shall be limited in the proceedings before the arbitrator(s) to the evidence or arguments previously put before the DAB to obtain its decision, or to the reasons for dissatisfaction given in its notice of dissatisfaction. Any decision of the DAB shall be admissible in evidence in the arbitration.

Arbitration may be commenced prior to or after completion of the Works. The obligations of the Parties, the Engineer and the DAB shall not be altered by reason of any arbitration being conducted during the progress of the Works.

20.7 In the event that:

> (a) neither Party has given notice of dissatisfaction within the period stated in Sub-Clause 20.4 *[Obtaining Dispute Adjudication Board's Decision]*,
>
> (b) the DAB's related decision (if any) has become final and binding, and
>
> (c) a Party fails to comply with this decision,

then the other Party may, without prejudice to any other rights it may have, refer the failure itself to arbitration under Sub-Clause 20.6 *[Arbitration]*. Sub-Clause 20.4 *[Obtaining Dispute Adjudication Board's Decision]* and Sub-Clause 20.5 *[Amicable Settlement]* shall not apply to this reference."

Clause 20.4 provides for two types of DAB decision according to their finality: (i) the decision itself is to be "*binding on both Parties, who shall promptly give effect to it unless and until it shall be revised in an amicable settlement or an arbitral award*"; and (ii) if no timely notice of dissatisfaction is given, "*the decision shall become final and binding upon both Parties*". In either event, the binding effect of the decision is dependent on the existence of a means of enforcement which, in practice, means enforcement through a state court, usually that of the country in which the works are situated. Clause 20.6 requires disputes to be referred to ICC Arbitration, and this will include the disputed enforcement of a DAB decision. After the party seeking enforcement has initiated ICC Arbitration, it is still necessary for the award (if successful) to be enforced by the court.[2] Clause 20.7 expressly provides that enforcement of a Type (ii) DAB decision (which is final and binding) can proceed straight to arbitration without antecedent amicable settlement. In a number of cases, awards ordering enforcement of DAB decisions of both Types (i) and (ii) have been enforced by State courts. However, in a recent case in Singapore,[3] enforcement of a Type (i) DAB decision was refused, inter alia, on the ground that the tribunal should have given a

---

[2] For enforcement of arbitral awards generally, see Ch.3.
[3] *CRW v PT Perusahaan TBK* [2011] SGCA 33.

decision on the merits of the dispute and not merely ordered enforcement of the DAB decision. This judgment has been criticised[4] as misunderstanding the intent and purpose of cl.20 and its predecessors under earlier FIDIC conditions.[5] If correct, however, the effect of a DAB decision under cl.20 is no more than advisory.

Post Note

The *New Red Book*, which has extensive international backing, represents a significant achievement in the modernisation of standard forms of contract, retaining the traditional formula of technical and financial control of the engineer, but without the additional role of settlement of disputes, which has, in the past, led to abuse. FIDIC's latest publication is a Design Build and Operate Form, issued in 2007, which adopts the same format and style as the existing forms but provides new definitions specific to DBO projects. The form provides for the possibility of long-term operation by the DBO contractor, but each contract will be subject to its own financial package as required to achieve economic viability for the project.

---

[4] See [2011] *International Construction Law Review* 388.
[5] Clause 67.

CHAPTER 14

LAW OF TORT

The law of tort is mostly to be found in the common law, but there are some important statutes. Tort can be defined as a civil wrong independent of contract; or as breach of a legal duty owed to persons generally. The practical consequences of the law of tort are concerned with the adjustment of losses. Where the elements of fault and damage exist, the law determines who should bear the resulting financial loss.

There is no complete body of general principles which applies to all torts, in the way that all contracts are governed by the same general principles. Some jurists view torts as a series of separate civil wrongs. For more practical reasons the torts discussed in this chapter are set out in separate sections. There are, however, some principles common to all or most torts, and these are discussed by way of introduction. This chapter covers those specific torts which are most relevant to the construction industry and to those professionally involved in it.

NEGLIGENCE

Negligence is by far the most important of torts, for several reasons. It forms the cause of action in the majority of cases brought in tort; its scope is very wide; and it may also be an element in liability for other torts. The term negligence is also found in the context of breach of contract, for example, where an architect is alleged to have carried out negligent design or supervision. A common type of action in negligence heard in the courts is that between two or more drivers involved in a road accident. In such cases it is not infrequent for all parties to be held to be negligent in some degree.

Element of liability

The claimant in an action for negligence must show: (1) that the defendant owed them a duty of care; (2) that there was a breach of that

430 LAW OF TORT

duty; and (3) that recoverable damage was thereby caused. Considering the first of these elements, it is necessary to decide whether in the particular circumstances one person (the defendant) owed a duty of care to the other (the claimant). The classic test as to when a duty of care might arise was stated in the leading case of *Donoghue v Stevenson*.[1] The manufacturer of ginger beer was held to owe a duty to the ultimate consumer, who found a decomposing snail in the empty bottle. The consumer could not sue in contract because the ginger beer had been purchased by a friend, and in any event the default was that of the manufacturer, not the seller. In a celebrated judgment Lord Atkin held:

> "The rule that you are to love your neighbour becomes in law, you must not injure your neighbour; and the lawyer's question who is my neighbour? receives a restricted reply. You must take reasonable care to avoid acts or omissions which you can reasonably foresee would be likely to injure your neighbour. Who, then, in law is my neighbour? The answer seems to be-persons who are so closely and directly affected by my act that I ought reasonably to have them in contemplation as being so affected when I am directing my mind to the acts or omissions which are called in question."

The law of negligence remained comparatively dormant for some time after *Donoghue's* case and it was not until *Dutton v Bognor Regis UDC*[2] that the courts began to grapple with the questions which subsequently came to dominate this area of law, namely the circumstances in which a duty would arise and the inter-relationship between such duties and the type of damage suffered.

The expansion period

In *Dutton's* case the plaintiff, a second purchaser of a house built on a rubbish tip, was unable to sue in contract. Proceedings were brought in tort against the original builder and against the local authority who had approved the plans and inspected the work on site. The case against the builder was settled but Mrs Dutton proceeded against the local authority. In the Court of Appeal it was argued that the council owed no duty and that there was no physical damage to found an action in tort. It was further pointed out that the council should not be held liable because the builder was not liable in tort. Lord Denning M.R. rejected all these arguments holding not only that the council was liable but, incidentally, the builder would also have been liable in tort.

[1] [1932] A.C. 562.
[2] [1972] 1 Q.B. 373.

Dutton's case had two important consequences. First, claims in tort were potentially available against parties not hitherto thought liable; and secondly, claims in tort could be brought as an alternative to claims in contract. The importance of the second point is that claims in contract become statute-barred within (usually) six years of the date of the breach, whereas claims in tort do not arise until damage is suffered. In addition to more claims being available, *Dutton* created the possibility of bringing claims which would hitherto have been long barred by limitation. This development led to another series of cases on the question when the cause of action in tort arose. In regard to latent defects in buildings, the doctrine was developed that the cause of action arose when the plaintiff ought reasonably to have become aware of the existence of the damage. The courts had, therefore, to consider many stale claims.

In *Anns v LB Merton*[3] the House of Lords, for the first time, considered the principles arising from *Dutton's* case. *Anns'* case concerned allegations of negligence against the local authority's building inspectors, the primary issue being whether the claim was statute-barred. The House of Lords approved, with some modification, the decision in *Dutton* so that the flood of litigation, which had started with Dutton, continued.

On the limitation issue it was held that the cause of action arose only when the state of the building was such that there was present or imminent danger to the health or safety of occupiers. This point was developed further in later cases.

The next development in the law of tort was the case of *Junior Books v Veitchi*.[4] This was a Scottish case (the Scots law of delict was for the purpose of the appeal regarded as identical with the English law of tort), in which the plaintiff owners of a factory brought a claim in tort for economic loss against a nominated sub-contractor who was alleged negligently to have installed flooring, the loss representing the financial consequences of having to replace the defective floor. The House of Lords allowed the claim, holding that there was no good reason to restrict the loss recoverable to the cost of making good physical damage. Lord Brandon delivered a strong dissenting judgment which has subsequently achieved greater currency than the case itself, but the case itself has never been overruled.

[3] [1978] A.C. 728.
[4] [1983] A.C. 520.

The retrenchment period

There followed a number of cases dealing with local authorities. In *Peabody v Parkinson and Lambeth*[5] the House of Lords, held that the local authority owed no duty to the plaintiff owners, and that the appropriate test as to whether there was such a duty, given the existence of proximity, was whether it was just and reasonable. Thereafter, in *Investors in Industry v South Beds DC*[6] the Court of Appeal, following *Peabody*, held that it would not normally be just and reasonable to impose a duty on a local authority where the building owner relied on other professional advisers, and that the duty owed by the local authority would ordinarily be limited to a duty to subsequent owners. Other cases held that the right to sue for damages in tort was available only where the plaintiff had a proprietary or possessory right in the property damaged: it was not sufficient for the plaintiff to have a mere contractual right.[7]

The most far-reaching decision in this period of retrenchment was the case of *D. & F. Estates v Church Commissioners*.[8] Here, the owners of a flat brought a claim in tort, inter alia, against Wates, who were main contractors when the block of flats was constructed, in respect of alleged negligence by their plastering sub-contractor (who was not a party to the action). The plaster was found to be cracked and unsound, and the plaintiffs claimed the cost of renewing it. The House of Lords held that Wates were not under the duty alleged, and approved the dissenting judgment of Lord Brandon in *Junior Books* in which he said:

> "It is, however, of fundamental importance to observe that the duty of care laid down in *Donoghue v Stevenson* was based on the existence of a danger of physical injury to persons or their property . . . the relevant property for the purpose of the wider principle on which the decision . . . was based was property other than the very property which gave rise to the danger of physical damage concerned."

The question of the existence of a duty of care, arose again in the case of *Caparo Industries v Dickman*.[9] The plaintiff had purchased shares in a public company. After publication of statutory accounts prepared by the defendant, the plaintiff, relying on the report, decided to purchase more shares and eventually launched a successful takeover of the company. Subsequently errors were found in the accounts, and the plaintiff claimed

[5] [1985] A.C. 210.
[6] [1986] Q.B. 1034.
[7] *Candlewood v Mitsui* [1986] A.C. 1.
[8] [1989] A.C. 177.
[9] [1990] A.C. 605.

damages in tort from the accountants. *Hedley Byrne v Heller*[10] established that such an action was maintainable, but the particular issue in the *Caparo* case was whether a duty was owed by accountants to shareholders and to investors. The House of Lords held that no duty at all was owed. Lord Bridge described the test as follows:

> "What emerges is that, in addition to the foreseeability of damage, necessary ingredients in any situation giving rise to a duty of care are that there should exist between the party owing the duty and the party to whom it is owed a relationship characterised by the law as one of 'proximity' or 'neighbourhood' and that the situation should be one in which the court considers it fair, just and reasonable that the law should impose a duty of a given scope upon the one party for the benefit of the other."

The latest and decisive stage in the retrenchment of the law of tort in regard to buildings occurred in the case of *Murphy v Brentwood DC*.[11] In that case, the Court of Appeal had upheld the decision of the Official Referee, allowing recovery by a plaintiff house-owner who discovered cracks which were attributable to the negligent passing of plans by the local authority. Instead of carrying out repairs, Mr Murphy sold his defective house and sued for the drop in value. The House of Lords now had the opportunity to reconsider *Anns*, and did so in an unusual court of seven Law Lords, including the Lord Chancellor. The decision, which is of far-reaching importance, established, or restated the law of negligence in the following terms:

(1) a builder owed duty of care within the principle of *Donoghue v Stevenson*, to persons likely to suffer injury as a result of his negligence;

(2) this extended, however, only to injury caused by latent, i.e. undiscovered defects in the building;

(3) where a defect came to light, whether through the existence of cracks or through a survey, expenditure on remedial work was to be regarded as pure economic loss, not recoverable in tort;

(4) contrary to *Dutton* and *Anns*, cracks representing the manifestation of underlying defects were not to be regarded as material damage; and

---

[10] [1964] A.C. 465.
[11] [1991] 1 A.C. 398.

(5) the question of whether a local authority exercising powers to secure compliance with building regulations owed any duty to owners or occupiers of the relevant building was left open.

Ordinarily, such liability in tort will be limited to injury to persons or other property, excluding the property which gave rise to the injury (i.e. the building itself). Lord Bridge, in the *Murphy* case, recognised two possible exceptions. The first was expressed in the following passage, which also summarises the general extent of the builder's liability:

> "If a builder erects a structure containing a latent defect which renders it dangerous to persons or property, he will be liable in tort for injury to persons or damage to property resulting from that dangerous defect. But if the defect becomes apparent before any injury or damage has been caused, the loss sustained by the building owner is purely economic. If the defect can be repaired at economic cost, that is the measure of the loss. If the building cannot be repaired, it may have to be abandoned as unfit for occupation and therefore valueless. These economic losses are recoverable if they flow from breach of a relevant contractual duty, but, here again, in the absence of a special relationship of proximity they are not recoverable in tort. The only qualification I would make to this is that, if a building stands so close to the boundary of the building owner's land that after discovery of the dangerous defect it remains a potential source of injury to persons or property on neighbouring land or on the highway, the building owner ought in principle to be entitled to recover in tort from the negligent builder the cost of obviating the danger, whether by repair or demolition, so far as that cost is necessarily incurred in order to protect himself from potential liability to third parties."

The second exception arises from the possibility of damage to "other property." What is the position if the other property is part of the defective building itself? This was considered in the *D. & F.* case and was dubbed the "complex structure theory." Despite wide and searching academic criticism, the House of Lords in *Murphy* appear to regard the theory as still sound. Lord Bridge re-stated his view of the theory as follows:

> "A critical distinction must be drawn here between some part of a complex structure which is said to be a 'danger' only because it does not perform its proper function in sustaining the other parts and some distinct item incorporated in the structure which positively malfunctions so as to inflict positive damage on the structure in which it is incorporated. Thus, if a defective central heating boiler explodes and damages a house or a defective electrical installation malfunctions and sets the house on fire, I see no reason to doubt that the owner of the house, if he can prove that the damage was due to the negligence of the boiler manufacturer in the one case, or the electrical contractor in the other, can recover damages in tort on the *Donaghue*

v Stevenson principles but the position in law is entirely different where, by reason of the inadequacy of the foundations of the building to support the weight of the superstructure, differential settlement and consequent cracking occurs. Here, once the first cracks appear, the structure as a whole is seen to be defective, and the nature of the defect is known."

Further Cases

The major shift in English law described above is still being developed in new cases. Of particular note is three decisions from the Commonwealth in which the *Murphy* decision has not been followed, demonstrating that much of the earlier law may still have relevance.[12] It is also to be noted that the Defective Premises Act 1972 (see Ch.7) still affords to residential owners rights equivalent to those held in the *Dutton* case. A continuing debate in the construction industry is whether the Act should be extended to cover commercial buildings. New cases have shown the court willing to extend the range of situations in which parties who can be regarded as proffering specialist advice or services, may be held to have assumed a duty of care to avoid economic loss, as re-defined in *Murphy*. Thus in *Storey v Charles Church Developments*[13] a design and build contractor was held to owe a duty of care in tort in respect of structural defects to the client, despite the existence of a contract; and in *Barclays Bank v Fairclough*[14] a specialist sub-contractor was held to owe a duty to the main contractor in respect of economic loss suffered when the specialist so negligently carried out maintenance work that potentially dangerous asbestos dust was spread throughout an industrial site. Even in the case of a local authority, while a claim based on negligent failure to enforce the Building Regulations is unlikely to be open, the courts are continuing to define the circumstances in which a duty of care will be recognised[15]; and in the case of other bodies performing statutory functions, the existence of a duty may depend on the extent to which such functions are prescribed by a statutory scheme.[16]

The inter-relationship of tort and contract duties was further clarified in the decision of the Court of Appeal in *Robinson v Jones*.[17] Mr Robinson had purchased a newly built house on the NHBC terms in 1992 from Jones the builder. In 2004 it was discovered that flues serving gas fires were defectively constructed and an action was brought in tort, which the

---

[12] See I.N. Duncan Wallace Q.C., "*Murphy* Rejected" (1995) 11 Const. L.J. 249.

[13] (1996) 73 Con. L.R. 1, 12 Con. L.J. 206.

[14] (1995) 44 Con. L.R. 35.

[15] See *Barrett v L B Enfield* [2001] 2 A.C. 550.

[16] *Marcic v Thames Water* [2004] 2 A.C. 42, *Hanifa Dobson v Water Services Regulation Authority* [2007] B.L.R. 465.

[17] [2011] B.L.R. 206.

defendant resisted as being statute barred. The court held that, absent a professional relationship, there was no duty of care co-existent with the contract terms and no duty in respect of economic loss. Any claim in contract being statute barred, the action failed.

Who is liable?

The circumstances in which claims in negligence could succeed in relation to reliance on advice in the form of a report, were considered by the House of Lords in *Smith v Eric Bush*.[18] The case concerned claims brought by purchasers of houses against surveyors and valuers who provided reports (at the cost of the purchasers) to mortgagees who, on the strength of the report, approved the purchase and advance finance to the purchasers. Proceedings in negligence were subsequently brought by the purchasers against the surveyors and the question arose as to whether any direct duty of care was owed. Lord Griffiths in the House of Lords held as follows:

> "In what circumstances should the law deem those who give advice to have assumed responsibility to the person who acts upon the advice or, in other words, in what circumstances should a duty of care be owed by the adviser to those who act upon his advice? I would answer—only if it is foreseeable that if the advice is negligent the recipient is likely to suffer damage, that there is a sufficient proximate relationship between the parties and that it is just and reasonable to impose the liability. In the case of a surveyor valuing a small house for a building society or local authority, the application of these three criteria leads to the conclusion that he owes a duty of care to the purchaser."

This case was applied and extended in the decision of the Court of Appeal in *Merrett v Babb*.[19] The circumstances in this case were even more extreme in that a firm of valuers had given a valuation to a building society which had resulted in the claimant purchasing the property which was subsequently found to suffer from settlement cracking of which no adequate warning had been given. The report was drawn up by Mr Babb, a professionally qualified surveyor who was an employee, but not a partner, of the firm Clive Walker Associates. Some two years after the survey report, the sole principal of the firm became bankrupt, the firm went out of business and professional indemnity insurance was cancelled. The action was therefore pursued personally against Mr Babb. By a majority, the Court of Appeal held that Mr Babb had assumed personal

---

[18] [1990] 1 A.C. 831.
[19] [2001] 3 W.L.R. 1.

responsibility and was therefore liable for the claimant's loss. The House of Lords subsequently refused leave to appeal. It will remain to be seen whether this case leads to other actions against individuals where, for whatever reason, an action against the firm or company cannot be pursued.

Losses recoverable in negligence

The law of negligence is now to be regarded as concerned with actual damage in the form, usually, of physical injury to persons or property, necessarily caused by latent defects. Ordinarily, the property must be something distinct from that which the negligent defendant has supplied or constructed. The question whether a local authority will ever be liable for the negligent exercise of its powers in accordance with these principles, remains to be decided under English law. It is to be noted that in all the local authority cases, none involved loss or injury of a type that would now be regarded as recoverable. The *Murphy* case has also settled, for the present, the question of when damage to a building is to be regarded as "purely economic loss" and therefore unrecoverable. In both *Dutton* and *Anns*, it was held that the cracks to the building themselves constituted physical damage. This analysis was decisively rejected in *Murphy*. In the result, expenditure on repairing damaged or defective parts of buildings will not normally be recoverable, unless falling within one of the exceptions referred to above.

In some negligence cases, the question arises as to which losses are properly to be regarded as economic, and where the line is to be drawn. In *Spartan Steel v Martin*,[20] the Court of Appeal had to consider issues arising from the negligent cutting of an electricity cable to a factory. This caused physical "damage" to certain products which were being manufactured in the plaintiff's machinery at the time of the power cut. The plaintiff recovered the value of the material damaged and also loss of profit on this material as consequential (economic) loss. The Court of Appeal refused to allow recovery in respect of other material which the plaintiffs were unable to process during the power cut, regarding this as purely economic. The case has been much discussed, particularly as to whether these distinctions were matters of law or policy. Lord Oliver, in his judgment in the *Murphy* case commented on *Spartan Steel* as follows:

> "The solution to such borderline cases has so far been achieved pragmatically, not by the application of logic but by the perceived necessity as a matter of policy to place some limits—perhaps arbitrary limits—to what

would otherwise be an endless cumulative causative chain bounded only by
theoretical foreseeability."

Debate will continue as to when and on what legal basis certain losses
are irrecoverable. However, the general rule that losses in tort must arise
from physical damage is now firmly established.

Breach and damage

If a duty of care exists, it is necessary to establish a breach of that duty.
The standard of care required is that of a "reasonable man." This is a
legal abstraction which represents a person who weighs up the circumstances, considers the characteristics of the persons endangered, takes
greater care when there is greater danger, and never loses their temper.
They are sometimes epitomised as the man on the Clapham omnibus.
The duty is to guard against probabilities, not bare possibilities. But
where the risk is greater, such as where children are involved, reasonable
possibilities must be guarded against. The required standard of care thus
depends on the circumstances, but in any particular case there is one
appropriate standard below which a person is legally negligent. The
term "gross negligence" is sometimes used in contracts, but the adjective
has no legal significance in the law of tort. There is only one appropriate
standard of care, any breach of which, gross or slight, incurs liability
in law.

Finally, the injury to the claimant must have been caused by the
defendant's act, and the damage must not be too remote (see below). In
a very clear case the court may apply the maxim *res ipsa liquitur* (the
thing speaks for itself). This was the case in *Drake v Harbour & White*[21]
where a house owner had vacated her house to allow access for electri-
cians carrying our re-wiring. When the house burned down overnight,
the court was satisfied that, although the claimant could not demonstrate
the exact mechanism leading to the fire, it was evident that the defendants were complicit in the activities which caused the fire. Conversely, in
Baxall Securities v Sheard Walshaw Partnership[22] the Court of Appeal
held architects not liable to subsequent lessees for a design defect in a
building which ought to have been detected by a competent survey: there
was no duty of care in respect of damage which should have been found
by a survey. Where the claimant succeeds in their action in negligence
but the loss was caused partly by their own default, the court may reduce

[21] [2008] EWCA Civ 25.
[22] [2002] B.L.R. 100.

the damages recovered under the Law Reform (Contributory Negligence) Act 1945. This provides by s.1:

> "Where any person suffers damage as a result partly of his own fault and partly of the fault of any other person or persons, a claim in respect of that damage shall not be defeated by reason of the fault of the person suffering the damage, but the damages recoverable in respect thereof shall be reduced to such extent as the Court thinks just and equitable having regard to the claimant's share in the responsibility for the damage."

Contributory negligence applies also to breaches of statutory duty. The application to a claim for breach of contract is covered in Ch.6.

Negligent mis-statement

Liability for statements has developed, historically, along different lines from liability for acts or omissions. The leading case is *Hedley Byrne v Heller*,[23] where a bank gave a gratuitous reference for a customer in respect of a company with whom they proposed to do business. The reference was favourable but was given "without responsibility." The reference was given negligently, and the customer lost money. The House of Lords held that the bank owed a duty of care and would have been liable, but was protected by the express disclaimer of responsibility. In giving judgment, the House considered the circumstances in which liability might arise for statements. Lord Devlin expressed the matter thus:

> "Wherever there is a relationship equivalent to contract, there is a duty of care. Such a relationship may be either general or particular. Examples of a general relationship are those of solicitor and client and of banker and customer. . . . Where, as in the present case, what is relied on is a particular relationship created ad hoc, it will be necessary to examine the particular facts to see whether there is an express or implied undertaking of responsibility."

Thus, engineers, architects and other professionals must be cautious when making statements to their clients, even concerning matters in which they are not directly instructed. A duty of care may equally arise when giving gratuitous advice to strangers if the circumstances are such that there is an implied undertaking of responsibility.

This branch of the law was further developed in *Esso Petroleum v Mardon*.[24] The defendant had taken a lease of a garage after

---

[23] [1964] A.C. 465.
[24] [1976] Q.B. 801.

representations were made by the plaintiffs as to the likely throughput of petrol. Their figures were based on the original design for the garage, but planning permission was refused and the garage was in fact built fronting away from the main road. In the result, the volume of trade was considerably reduced and the defendant lost money. The question arose regarding whether the plaintiff's statements could be relied on when they were followed by a contract. Lord Denning held that the defendant was entitled to succeed in his counterclaim:

> "If a man who has or professes to have special knowledge or skill makes a representation by virtue thereof to another (be it advice, information or opinion) with the intention of inducing him to enter into a contract with him, he is under a duty to use reasonable care to see that the representation is correct, and that the advice, information or opinion is reliable. If he negligently gives unsound advice or misleading information or expresses any erroneous opinion, and thereby induces the other side to enter into a contract with him, he is liable in damages."

In both of these cases, the defendant had made a relatively simple statement upon which the plaintiff had relied, in the second case the statement being followed by a contract. What is less clear, is the precise ambit of this principle. Before the recent developments in the law of tort this question was of limited importance, but since the retrenchment elsewhere, the *Hedley Byrne* principle may be the only avenue by which pure economic loss can be recovered in tort. It is therefore to be anticipated that there will be further attempts to bring cases within this principle. In *IBA v EMI*[25] the designing sub-contractor responded to a request from the employer concerning the performance of the television mast, stating "we are well satisfied that the structure will not oscillate dangerously." The Court of Appeal treated this as contractually binding, but the House of Lords regarded it as falling within the principles of *Hedley Byrne*. It is difficult to see any logical dividing line between the provision of a design, upon which the building owner will invariably place reliance, and the simple provision of information, particularly if a statement that "our design is adequate" is regarded as sufficient.

A further, unsuccessful, attempt to apply the *Hedley Byrne* principle occurred in *Pacific Associates v Baxter*.[26] In this case the defendant was appointed engineer under a FIDIC contract. As a result of rejecting claims brought by the contractor, arbitration proceedings had to be pursued against the employer, which resulted in a partially successful settlement. The plaintiff contractor then attempted to sue the engineer in

[25] (1980) 14 B.L.R. 1; and see Ch.9.
[26] [1990] 1 Q.B. 993.

tort to recover the remainder of his loss. The engineer applied to strike out the claim as unsustainable. The application succeeded both before the official referee and the Court of Appeal, the latter holding that there was no voluntary assumption of responsibility. The case was complicated by argument based on a clause in the main contract providing that the engineer was not to be liable, but the case is relevant in defining the limits of the *Hedley Byrne* principle.

Fraud

In an extreme case the conduct of one of the parties may be alleged to be fraudulent. This will usually be concerned with statements and the essential element of fraud, whether tortuous or criminal, is that the person making the statement has no belief in its truth. Fraud always involves dishonesty: motive and intention are each irrelevant. In *BSkyB v HP Enterprise Services UK*,[27] claims were brought against a tendering contractor alleging that a contract for the provision of a customer relationship management system had been procured by fraudulent representations. BSkyB took over the contract as a result of non-performance and incurred substantial additional costs in completing the system. The defendants were found to have represented that they had carried out a proper analysis as to whether they could deliver the project, which representation was false and known to be false. The defendants were therefore liable for damages in deceit and there was no duty on BSkyB to carry out their own investigation.

Fraudulent misrepresentation entitles the innocent party to damages for the tort of deceit, as well as other remedies available in the case of an innocent misrepresentation.[28] English law does not allow the award of punitive damages so that there is little difference between remedies for fraudulent or innocent misrepresentation. Fraud may also constitute a criminal act punishable by fines or imprisonment. The offence of conspiracy to defraud was, until recently, governed largely by the common law rules. Fraud is now a statutory offence under the Fraud Act 2006. This defines fraud under three categories:

- Fraud by false representation.

- Fraud by failing to disclose information.

- Fraud by abuse of position.

---

[27] [2010] B.L.R. 267.
[28] See Ch.6.

All three involve dishonesty together with an intention to make a gain for the perpetrator or another and/or to cause loss or expose another to the risk of loss. Dishonesty is to be judged by the standard of a reasonable and honest person and the perpetrator must be aware that their conduct would be viewed as dishonest by such a person.

OTHER ASPECTS OF NEGLIGENCE

Liability of occupiers

Under the Occupiers' Liability Act 1957 an occupier of premises owes a duty of care to all visitors lawfully on the premises. Unless the occupier can and does modify or exclude their obligations by agreement, they owe to any visitor a duty to take reasonable care so that the visitor will be reasonably safe in using the premises for the purposes for which they are permitted to be there. The occupier may escape liability by giving adequate warning of existing dangers, and they may also expect persons such as workmen entering to carry out a job to guard against special dangers of their trade. In *Roles v Nathan*[29] two chimney sweeps had been warned of the danger of fumes, which they disregarded. They were asphyxiated but the occupier was held not liable. An occupier is not liable for the faulty work of an independent contractor (see below) unless they are themselves to blame for the defects.[30] An occupier may avoid such liability if they have taken reasonable steps to ensure that the contractor was competent and the work properly done.

The Occupiers' Liability Act applies to those who occupy land and buildings (including building and construction sites) and any fixed or moveable structure such as a vehicle, vessel, lift or scaffolding. An "occupier" need not be the owner of the premises but is merely a person having some degree of control. There may therefore be more than one occupier of the same premises. In *A.M.F. v Magnet Bowling*[31] both the general contractor and the employer were held to be occupiers with respect to a specialist direct contractor. A sub-contractor may also be an occupier of the whole or part of the site.

The Act does not apply to persons who are not visitors, whether they come onto the land lawfully, such as for the purposes of using a right of way, or unlawfully as trespassers. In the past, this has created great diffi- culty, particularly in the case of children who may stray into dangerous

[29] [1963] 1 W.L.R. 1117.
[30] See also *D & F Estates*, above.
[31] [1968] 1 W.L.R. 1028.

areas. Construction sites are a particular case where children and others may be at risk. The common law extended the principle of the Occupiers' Liability Act 1957 to provide that an occupier might, in such circumstances, owe a limited duty. This development is superseded by the Occupiers' Liability Act 1984, which deals expressly with these difficulties. The 1984 Act provides that an occupier owes a duty to a person who is not a visitor if they are aware (or have reasonable grounds to believe) that a danger exists and also knows (or have reasonable grounds to believe) that the other person is or may come into the vicinity of the danger. The risk must be one against which the occupier may be expected to offer some protection. Where such a duty exists, the occupier must take reasonable care to avoid injury, but the duty may be discharged by giving appropriate warning or discouraging persons from incurring the risk.

The Unfair Contract Terms Act 1977 provides, in respect of a business occupier, that liability as an occupier cannot be excluded (by a contract term or notice), in respect of death or personal injury resulting from negligence. In respect of other loss, liability can be excluded or restricted only so far as it is fair and reasonable. The 1984 Act restricts the operation of this provision to persons who are granted access for the purpose of the business of the occupier, so that, for example, owners of quarries who allow access for rock climbing may now exclude liability for the dangerous state of the premises.

Employers' liability

An employer may be liable for injury caused to their employee in three ways:

(1) if the injury is caused by the negligence of a fellow employee acting in the course of their employment (see below);

(2) if it is caused by the employer's breach of a statutory duty (see Ch.16); or

(3) if it is caused by the employer's negligence. The third possibility is discussed here.

There is no doubt that an employer owes their employees a duty of care. The problem for the common law has been to trace its extent. It has been defined as a three-fold duty: the provision of a competent staff of men, adequate material, and a proper system and effective supervision. However, the duty can be viewed as a single duty to take reasonable care for the safety of employees in all the circumstances. Thus the duty is not absolute, and an employer is only liable for injury caused by their failure to take sufficient care.

The standard of care that is required varies with the circumstances so that where potentially dangerous plant is being used the employer may have to provide safety devices or protective equipment. The employer remains liable for breach of their duty even though they may delegate its performance. In *McDermid v Nash Dredging*,[32] the plaintiff had been employed by the defendant but was required to work on board a tug owned by a Dutch company and under the control of their captain. The plaintiff was injured by an accident caused by the captain's negligence and the issue arose whether the employer remained liable. Lord Brandon in the House of Lords restated the relevant principles of the law as follows:

> "First, an employer owes to his employee a duty to exercise reasonable care to ensure that the system of work provided for him is a safe one. Secondly, the provision of a safe system of work has two aspects: (a) the devising of such a system and (b) the operation of it. Thirdly, the duty concerned has been described alternatively as either personal or non-delegable. The meaning of these expressions is not self-evident and needs explaining. The essential characteristic of the duty is that, if it is not performed, it is no defence for the employer to show that he delegated its performance to a person, whether his servant or not his servant, whom he reasonably believed to be competent to perform it. Despite such delegation the employer is liable for the non-performance of the duty."

However, where an employee is experienced and the danger apparent, the duty upon the employer may be a limited one, particularly where the employer is not in control of the premises. In the case *Wilson v Tyneside Window Cleaning*[33] the plaintiff, an experienced window cleaner, was injured when a handle came away from a window, causing him to lose his balance. He had never received any instructions regarding safety, except that if he found a window which presented unusual difficulty or risk he was to report for further instructions. It was held that there was no breach of duty by the employer. Pearce L.J. observed:

> "The master's own premises are under his control: if they are dangerously in need of repair he can and must rectify the fault at once if he is to escape the censure of negligence. But if a master sends a plumber to mend a leak in a respectable private house, no one could hold him negligent for not visiting the house himself to see if the carpet in the hall creates a trap. Between these extremes are countless possible examples in which the court may have to decide the question of fact: did the master take reasonable care

---

[32] [1987] 1 A.C. 906.
[33] [1958] 2 Q.B. 110.

so to carry out his operations as not to subject those employed by him to unnecessary risk. Precautions dictated by reasonable care when the servant works on the master's premises may be wholly prevented or greatly circumscribed by the fact that the place of work is under the control of a stranger. Additional safeguards intended to reinforce the man's own knowledge and skill in surmounting difficulties or dangers may be reasonable in the former case but impracticable and unreasonable in the latter."

The employee must show regard for their own safety, and if they are injured as a result of their own negligence this may reduce or even extinguish the employer's liability. The employee also owes the employer a duty to exercise reasonable skill and care at his work and may be liable to their employer for causing injury in breach of this duty.

These general common law principles apply equally to work on construction sites. However, in many industries, particularly construction, there exist detailed regulations and this is particularly so following recent directives from the European Union (see Ch.16).

Strict liability

When a person keeps some potentially dangerous object on their land or carries on a dangerous operation there, the ordinary law of negligence may not afford adequate protection. Instead of extending the duty of care, the common law has set apart certain things for which liability is strict, without regard to lack of care. A person who deals in such things does so at their peril. This special type of liability is known by the name of the case in which it was first formulated. In *Rylands v Fletcher*[34] the defendant built a reservoir on his land using reputable engineers and with the necessary permission. However, when the reservoir was filled, the water escaped down through a disused mine shaft and flooded the plaintiff's coal mines on adjoining land. Although the defendant's actions were without fault, he was held liable for the plaintiff's loss. In giving judgment Lord Cairns held:

"On the other hand if the defendants, not stopping at the natural use of their close, had desired to use it for any purpose which I may term a non-natural use, for the purpose of introducing into the close that which in its natural condition was not in or upon it, for the purpose of introducing water either above or below ground in quantities and in a manner not the result of any work or operation upon or under the land-and if in consequence of their doing so, or in consequence of any imperfection in the mode of their doing so, the water came to escape and to pass off into the close of the plaintiff, then it appears to me that that which the defendants were doing they were

[34] (1868) L.R. 3 H.L. 330.

doing at their own peril; and if in the course of their doing it, the evil arose to which I have referred, the evil, namely the escape of water and its passing away into the close of the plaintiff and injuring the plaintiff, then for the consequence of that, in my opinion, the defendant would be liable."

In addition to reservoirs, strict liability has been attached to colliery spoil heaps and inflammable goods. In *Hoare v McAlpine*[35] a contractor was held liable for the escape of vibrations from pile driving operations which caused damage to an old house. Although vibrations may also constitute a nuisance (see below) it may be a defence to nuisance that the property damaged was unusually frail. Liability in *Rylands v Fletcher* is, however, strict.

To incur liability the object or operation must be non-natural, so that while there is strict liability for a reservoir, the owner of a natural lake can be liable only under the ordinary principles of tort, such as in negligence or nuisance. To establish strict liability there must also be an "escape" from the claimant's land which causes the damage, such as a slide of material from a spoil heap. In *Read v Lyons*[36] an explosion in a munitions factory which injured persons on the premises did not incur strict liability since there had not been an escape from the defendant's land. In this case, Lord Macmillan observed:

> "The two prerequisites of the doctrine [of *Rylands v Fletcher*] are that there must be the escape of something from one man's close to another man's close and that that which escapes must have been brought upon the land from which it escapes in consequence of some non-natural use of that land, whatever precisely that may mean. Neither of these features exists in the present case. I have already pointed out that nothing escaped from the defendant's premises and were it necessary to decide the point I should hesitate to rule that in these days and in an industrial community, it was an non-natural use of land to build a factory on it and conduct there the manufacture of explosives."

The principle of strict liability arose in a stark form in the case of *Cambridge Water v Eastern Counties Leather*[37] where the defendants, leather manufacturers, used a chemical solvent. Small quantities seeped through the floor of their premises and into the soil below, eventually entering the ground water from which the plaintiff drew supplies. The escape rendered the water unfit for human consumption and involved substantial losses on the part of the plaintiff without any question of negligence on the part of the defendant. The House of Lords rejected the

[35] [1923] 1 Ch. 167.
[36] [1947] A.C. 156.
[37] [1994] 2 A.C. 264.

claim, taking the view that instead of extending the concept of "natural" use of land, the principle should be restricted by the need to establish foreseeability of harm. The House also recognised the role of legislation in such a sensitive area. Lord Goff said:

> "I incline to the opinion that, as a general rule, it is more appropriate for strict liability in respect of operations of high risk to be imposed by parliament than by the courts. If such liability is imposed by statute, the relevant activities can be identified, and those concerned can know where they stand. Furthermore, the state can, where appropriate, lay down precise criteria establishing the incidence and scope of such liability."

In Australia the principle has been subsumed into the ordinary law of negligence.[38] In the English case of *Transco v Stockport Metropolitan Borough Council*,[39] however, the House of Lords applied the principle to a claim based on the unforeseen failure of a water supply pipe which, without negligence on the part of the owner, had damaged a gas pipeline owned by Transco. The claim failed on the basis water pipes constituted a routine and ordinary use of the land.

Product liability

Claims based on negligence or on the Defective Premises Act (see Ch.7) require proof of fault. An alternative claim may now be available under the Consumer Protection Act 1987, which is based on the European Community Directive on Product Liability. Subject to very limited defences, the Act imposes strict liability for personal injury and also for damage to property, other than the defective product itself. The Act provides special limitation periods of three years from discoverability of the damage with a longstop period of 10 years from the time of supply of the product rather than 15 years from the negligent act as under the Latent Damage Act (see below).

NUISANCE

Private nuisance may be defined as an unlawful interference with the use or enjoyment of another person's land. The interference may result in damage to property, such as by flooding or vibrations, or it may be only an annoyance, such as excessive noise or dust. There must be a

---

[38] *Burnie v General Jones* (1994) 120 A.L.R. 42.
[39] [2004] A.C. 1.

substantial interference. A nuisance is often a continuing state of affairs, although an isolated happening may support an action in nuisance. Neighbours must exercise give and take, but deliberate acts intended to annoy neighbours can create an actionable nuisance. Persons who live in noisy or industrial neighbourhoods must usually put up with the attendant discomforts, although actual damage to property will be actionable.

Usually the only person who can sue for private nuisance is the occupier of the land, although other persons may be able to sue on the same facts, for instance in negligence. The person liable is usually the occupier of the land or premises where the nuisance exists, but the person who created the nuisance may be liable. Thus, prima facie a building contractor will be liable for interference with adjoining land caused by the construction operations, but the employer may also be liable (see below).

Unlike negligence, liability for nuisance does not depend primarily on the standard of conduct of the defendant. Thus, it is not necessarily a defence to nuisance that reasonable care was taken to avoid it. But in the context of building and construction operations, those carrying out such work are under a duty to take proper precautions to see that nuisance is reduced to a minimum. Thus, in *Andreae v Selfridge*[40] where a demolition contractor took no steps to minimise noise and dust near to the plaintiff's hotel, an actionable nuisance was created for which the employer was liable. Sir Wilfred Green M.R. held:

> "Those who say that their interference with the comfort of their neighbours is justified because their operations are normal and usual and conducted with proper care and skill are under a specific duty, if they wish to make good that defence, to use that reasonable and proper care and skill. It is not a correct attitude to take to say: 'We will go on and do what we like until someone complains.' That is not their duty to their neighbours. Their duty is to take proper precautions, to see that the nuisance is reduced to a minimum. It is no answer for them to say: 'But this would mean that we should have to do the work more slowly than we would like to do it or it would involve putting us to some extra expense.' All those questions are matters of common sense and degree and quite clearly it would be unreasonable to expect people to conduct their work so slowly or so expensively, for the purpose of preventing a transient inconvenience, that the cost and trouble would be prohibitive. It is all a question of fact and degree and must necessarily be so."

In the more recent case of *Westminster City Council v Ocean Leisure*[41] a shop proprietor recovered damages for public nuisance where hoardings

---

[40] [1938] Ch. 1.
[41] [2004] B.L.R. 393.

had been erected giving only a narrow access to a shop over a period of more than 30 months. There was no suggestion that the work had been unreasonably prolonged or that the hoardings were unnecessary. The Court of Appeal held that substantial interference over a substantial time with the right of an adjoining owner to use the highway for access constituted a public nuisance actionable at the suit of a member of the public who suffered special damage. The law of private nuisance may be an important underpinning to the rights of individuals faced with potentially damaging but authorised development affecting their properties. The leading authority on the effect of planning permission is *Watson v Croft Promo-Sport*[42] where it was held that while the grant of planning permission as such does not affect the private law rights of third parties, the implementation of planning permission might alter the nature and character of the locality as to shift the standard of reasonable user which governs the question of nuisance. And in regard to licensed activities, it was held in *Barr & Ors v Biffa Waste Services*,[43] that the existence of a Waste Management permit for tipping of pre-treated waste granted by the Environment Agency on conditions which prohibited "odours . . . likely to cause pollution of the environment . . ." did not prevent action in common law nuisance by affected individuals or groups.

A nuisance may be controlled by the local authority under the Environmental Protection Act 1990. Sections 79 and 80 empower the authority to serve an abatement notice in respect of a "Statutory Nuisance" as defined by the Act. This includes:

"(a) any premises in such a state as to be prejudicial to health or a nuisance;
. . .
(d) any dust or effluvia caused by any trade, business, manufacture or process and being prejudicial to the health of or a nuisance to the inhabitants of the neighbourhood;
(e) any accumulation or deposit which is prejudicial to health or a nuisance."

Where a statutory nuisance is not abated, the authority may acquire powers to carry out necessary work. Under the Control of Pollution Act 1974 a local authority has powers to control noise on construction sites. They may serve a notice restricting the use of specified plant, restricting hours of work and limiting the level of noise. The act also permits the

---

[42] [2009] EWCA Civ 15.
[43] [2012] EWCA Civ 312.

contractor to obtain the prior consent of the authority to the methods of work proposed.[44]

Where the matters complained of affect a wider class than adjoining occupiers the possibility exists of a claim in public nuisance. In *Corby Group Litigation v Corby Borough Council*[45] claimants who had been born with physical deformities brought a group action alleging public nuisance through the council's failure to remediate 680 acres of heavily contaminated land, which had formerly been owned by British Steel. The Court of Appeal, without deciding the claim, ruled on a stiking out application, that it was arguable that a claim in public nuisance would lie.

Rights of support

A nuisance may be committed by interference with a right of support of land. There is a natural right of support for unweighted land, and a nuisance is committed if subsidence is caused either by removing the lateral support by excavation, or by undermining. Generally it is unimportant how the withdrawal of support occurs, but as an important exception there is no liability for causing subsidence by withdrawal of subterranean percolating water. Thus, in *Langbrook v Surrey CC*[46] pumping carried out to keep excavations dry resulted in lowering of the water table and settlement of buildings on adjacent land. The adjoining owner was held to have no redress. Plowman J. after reviewing the authorities, concluded that a landowner was entitled to abstract water under his land which percolates in undefined channels, notwithstanding that this may cause neighbouring land to subside. The judge went on to consider whether there could, in such circumstances, be liability for nuisance or negligence, and held:

> "Since it is not actionable to cause damage by the abstraction of underground water, even where this is done maliciously, it would seem illogical that it should be actionable if it were done carelessly. Where there is no duty not to injure for the sake of inflicting injury, there cannot, in my judgement, be a duty to take care not to inflict the same injury."

The right of support for a building, as opposed to the land on which it stands, is not a natural right and must be acquired as an easement by grant or by usage (see Ch.15). Once acquired, the right is usually a right

---

[44] Sections 60, 61; and see Ch.15.
[45] [2008] B.L.R. 411.
[46] [1970] 1 W.L.R. 161.

of support both from adjacent land and from adjoining buildings. The right, however, is one which must be exercised with caution.

In *Redland Bricks v Morris*[47] a landowner, the stability of whose property was threatened by excavation in an adjoining quarry, obtained a mandatory injunction against the quarry owner compelling him to carry out work to restore stability. But, in *Midland Bank v Bardgrove*[48] the plaintiff failed to recover damages for the cost of work which he had carried out to protect his property against threatened instability from excavation on the defendant's adjoining site. The defendant had constructed an inadequate restraining wall which was likely to cause damage at some time in the future, but the claim failed on the basis the plaintiff's cause of action in damages arose only when physical damage was suffered. This conclusion was based on a series of nineteenth century mining cases which held that where property was damaged by undermining (the same principle applied to lateral withdrawal of support) a fresh cause of action arose each time damage was suffered.[49] Consequently, although the claimant whose land is threatened can recover compensation for every occurrence of damage, without the right to claim becoming statute-barred, it follows also that a claim cannot be maintained until the loss has occurred. In respect of coal mining, the rights to compensation is now governed by statute.[50] The common law rule remains and has major implications for claims as between adjacent owners where one wishes to carry out construction works involving excavation. A sensible solution is to enter into an express agreement defining the measures to be taken to preserve stability so that any breach or non-observance will give a right to claim compensation. Where major civil engineering undertakings require special parliamentary authority, the enabling Acts invariably contain express provisions governing compensation claims. These do not, however, generally oust common law rights nor do they preclude the possibility of express agreement where the work may involve a particular risk of damage.

Other rights which may give rise to an action in nuisance for interference include rights of light and air, water rights and rights of way. Where an interference is caused to a wider group of persons than the occupier of neighbouring land, such conduct may constitute a public nuisance. This is primarily a crime, but a civil action may be brought in respect of a public nuisance by an individual who has suffered special damage different from that suffered by the public at large. Common examples of

---

[47] [1970] A.C. 652.
[48] (1992) 60 B.L.R. 1 CA.
[49] *Darley Main Colliery v Mitchell* (1886) 11 App. Cas. 127 and see Ch.2 above.
[50] Coal Mining (Subsidence) Act 1957, amended and re-enacted 1991.

public nuisance are obstruction of the highway, and creating dangers upon or near the highway.

Forseeability

Interference with a right of support is generally actionable irrespective of whether the consequences were foreseeable by the defendant. However, in some cases of nuisance the defendant's conduct will not be actionable unless the consequences were foreseeable. The leading case, as regards damage to land, is *Leakey v National Trust*[51] where two house-owners lived near the foot of a historic mound known as Burrow Mump in Somerset. Over the years soil and rubble had fallen from the mound and the defendant, who was responsible for its upkeep, knew of potential instability that might result in larger falls. After a substantial fall proceedings were brought. An interlocutory injunction was granted ordering the defendant to carry out protective works and at trial modest damages were awarded. The Court of Appeal upheld the judgment stating that, while the action was properly brought in nuisance rather than negligence, the distinction was of no practical importance. The defendant's duty was limited to doing what was reasonable.

Leakey's case figured in an important review of the law concerning natural support and coastal erosion. In *Holbeck Hall Hotel v Scarborough Borough Council*[52] the claimants owned a cliff-top hotel and the defendant owned the undercliff adjoining the hotel grounds, which was subject to coastal erosion rendering the cliffs inherently unstable. After a number of slips, the defendant commissioned investigations and carried out some remedial work. In 1993, however, a massive landslip occurred as a result of which the hotel had to be demolished. In the TCC, the defendant was held liable on the basis that, although they did not foresee the damage which in fact occurred, they owed a duty of care which required them to conduct further investigations which they had failed to carry out. The Court of Appeal reversed the decision and dismissed the claim. Stuart-Smith L.J. stated that the law in these terms:

> "The scope of (the defendants') duty was confined to an obligation to take care to avoid damage to the plaintiff's land which they ought to have foreseen without further geological investigation. It may also have been limited by other factors . . . so that it is not necessarily incumbent on someone in (the defendant's) position to carry out extensive and expensive remedial work to prevent the damage which they ought to have foreseen; the scope

[51] [1980] Q.B. 485.
[52] [2000] 2 W.L.R. 1396.

NUISANCE

of the duty may be limited to warning neighbours of such risk and they
were aware of or ought to have foreseen and sharing such information as
they had acquired relating to it".

The Court of Appeal also considered that Scarborough BC could have
been under a duty to warn the hotel owners of such risk as they did
appreciate and share with them the information available. A local
authority may also become liable in nuisance arising from exercise of its
statutory functions. In *Bybrook v Kent County Council*[53] the defendant
was held liable for a culvert carrying water under a road which, although
not foreseen as likely to cause flooding, had as a result of development,
became an obstruction, which aggravated flooding. But in *Marcic v
Thames Water Utilities*,[54] a water company was held not to be liable to a
house owner for flooding by sewage. The Court of Appeal had held the
water company liable in common law nuisance on the basis that once it
knew of the hazard, it was for the defendant to show that it had taken all
reasonable steps to prevent the flooding. The House of Lords held that
the obligations of the water company were prescribed by the Water
Industry Act 1991, under which their performance was supervised by the
Director General of Water Services. This precluded other remedies both
at common law and under human rights legislation.

Another aspect of rights of support, where forseeability of harm is
relevant, is the incursion of tree roots from neighbouring land. This has
long been recognised as a species of nuisance resulting in settlement of
buildings through desiccation of clay soil. Some older cases were decided
on the basis that liability was absolute. However, it is now clear that
forseeability of damage is an essential element of liability. This was the
result in the first "tree root" case to reach the House of Lords: *Delaware
Mansions v Westminster City Council*.[55] The claimant owners of a block
of flats had incurred the cost of underpinning as a result of structural
damage following the 1989 drought. The damage was caused by desiccation of the soil by the roots of a tree owned by the Council. The tree
had been planted in the early years of the twentieth century and had been
regularly inspected and pruned periodically by the Council. Lord Cooke
stated that it was important that local authorities or other tree owners
should not be under unreasonable and unacceptable burdens. He
continued:

"If reasonableness between neighbours is the key to the solution of problems in this field, it cannot be right to visit the authority or owner

---

[53] [2000] L.G.R. 302.
[54] [2004] 2 A.C. 42.
[55] [2001] UKHL 55.

responsible for a tree with a large bill for underpinning without giving them notice of the damage and the opportunity of avoiding further damage by removal of the tree. Should they elect to preserve the tree for environmental reasons, they may fairly be expected to bear the cost of underpinning or other reasonably necessary remedial works; and the party on whom the cost has fallen may recover it, even though there may be elements of hitherto unsatisfied pre-proprietorship damage or protection for the future. But as a general proposition, I think that the defendant is entitled to notice and a reasonable opportunity of abatement before liability for remedial expenditure can arise. In this case Westminster had ample notice and time before the underpinning and piling, and is in my opinion liable."

Tree owners must, therefore, now be vigilant to anticipate the possibility of damage to neighbouring property and take appropriate steps to avoid its continuance.

VICARIOUS LIABILITY

Vicarious liability in this context means liability for the torts of others. In the construction industry this may arise in two ways. First, the employer may be liable for the torts of the contractor or the contractor, for their sub-contractors; secondly, any of the parties involved in the work may be liable for the torts of their own individual employees.

As to the first type of vicarious liability, as a general rule a person is not liable for torts committed by their independent contractors. However, there are substantial exceptions to the general rule, whereby the employer may be liable. These include:

(1) where the liability is strict, such as under the rule in *Rylands v Fletcher*;

(2) where work involves danger on or near a highway; and

(3) where work will involve danger to other property unless proper care is taken (see above).

Even where the employer is not prima facie responsible they may still be liable for their own negligence in employing an incompetent contractor, or for failing to give adequate directions to avoid damage to another. The employer will also be liable under the law of agency if they authorise or ratify they contractor's wrongful act.

Master and servant

A master is liable for a tort which he authorises or ratifies and is also vicariously liable, in general, for the unauthorised tort of his servant if it is committed within the course of his employment. The terms "master" and "servant" have acquired a special meaning in law which is rather wider than employer and employee. A servant may be said to be a person employed to carry out work other than as an independent contractor. The work of the servant is an integral part of the master's business, while an independent contractor undertakes only to produce a given result. Persons are frequently found on construction sites who are technically self-employed, but who may be difficult to categorise as servants or independent contractors. The master is generally not liable for the latter.

In addition to deciding who is a servant, it may be necessary to decide who is the master, for instance, where a servant is hired by their employer to another employer. It is presumed that the original employer remains liable as the master, unless the right to control the way in which the work was done passes to the temporary employer. Thus, in *Mersey Docks v Coggins & Griffiths*[56] a contractor hired a crane together with its driver to carry out unloading work. The hirer supervised the work but not the management of the crane. The original employer was held to be responsible for the driver's negligence. In this case Lord Porter said:

> "Amongst the many tests suggested I think the most satisfactory, by which to ascertain who is the employer at any particular time, is to ask who was entitled to tell the employee the way in which he is to do the work upon which he is engaged. If someone other than his general employer is authorised to do this he will, as a rule, be the person liable for the employee's negligence. But it is not enough that the task to be performed should be under his control, he must also control the method of performing it."

The approach of asking which of two possible employers should be held liable was found to be unsatisfactory in *Viasystems v Thermal Transfer*[57] where ducting work was being carried out by a fitter and his mate supplied on a labour only basis by a sub-sub-contractor to a sub-contractor, whose fitter also supervised the work. The first fitter's mate negligently damaged the sprinkler system causing extensive damage. The Court of Appeal held that the relevant question was whose responsibility it was to prevent the negligence, and concluded that both sub-contractor and sub-sub-contractor were jointly and equally vicariously liable for the loss. Further, in a case concerning remedial welding carried

---

[56] [1947] A.C. 1.
[57] [2006] Q.B. 510.

out by a sub-sub-contractor, the Court of Appeal held that the employing sub-contractor was not liable for the negligence of welders over whom there was a right of supervision, but not a right of control; nor was the employer liable by reason of the hazardous nature of the operation, since the welding could have been carried out safely.[58]

The master will be liable for the tort of his servant only if the tort is committed during the course of his employment; that is, it must be a wrongful way of doing that which he is employed to do. Thus, an employer will be liable if the employee carries out their duties negligently or fraudulently. The employer may even be liable if the employee does something which they have expressly been forbidden to do, provided it is within the scope of their employment. But in *Conway v Wimpey*[59] a driver, employed on a building site to carry only fellow-employees, carried an employee of another firm on the site. This was held to be an act which he was not employed to perform. The employer was therefore not liable for the driver's negligence. In giving judgment in the Court of Appeal, Asquith L.J. held:

> "I should hold that taking men not employed by the defendants on to the vehicle was not merely a wrongful mode of performing the act of the class this driver was employed to perform, but was the performance of an act of a class which he was not employed to perform at all. In other words, the act was outside the scope of his employment."

Whether or not the master is liable, the servant is generally liable for their own tort and may be sued jointly with the master, or separately. Similarly where an employer is liable for their independent contractor, the contractor may also be sued jointly or separately. The practical importance to a claimant of vicarious liability is that it affords more likelihood of finding a defendant who is either solvent or who has the benefit of insurance cover. Where more than one defendant is held liable, the principles of contribution come into play (see below).

Remedies

The remedy claimed in most tort actions is damages. The successful claimant in an action for damages will generally be awarded a sum which is intended to compensate for the real loss suffered. The sum awarded must take into account future loss since usually only one action may be brought. There is an exception in the case of withdrawal of support (see above). Damages may be proportionally reduced if contributory negligence is

---

[58] *Biffa Waste Services v Maschinenfabrik Ernst Hesse GmbH* [2009] B.L.R. 1.
[59] [1951] 1 All E.R. 56.

found against the claimant. In addition to damages, the claimant may apply for an injunction (see below) and this may in some cases be the only substantial remedy required (see the *Redland Bricks* case, above).

Remoteness and causation

Once liability is established, the question may arise as to whether the damage claimed is too remote to be recoverable. The general test is that compensation may be recovered for damage which is of a reasonably foreseeable kind. If this is so it does not matter if the damage occurred in an unforeseeable manner or to an unforeseeable extent; the defendant will be liable for the whole loss. The rules of remoteness in contract and in tort are not identical. The tortfeasor is liable for loss which is foreseeable as the possible result of their conduct and therefore may bear a heavier burden than the contract breaker, who is liable only for the probable result of their actions (see Ch.6).

The test of foreseeability was discussed in the leading case *The Waggon Mound*,[60] in which the Privy Council had to consider the following facts. A large quantity of furnace oil was discharged through the negligence of the defendants from their ship while moored. The oil spread to a wharf belonging to the plaintiffs who were engaged while refitting work, including welding. Believing there to be no danger, the plaintiffs continued the welding. The oil ignited and caused serious damage. The Privy Council held the defendants not liable. Lord Simonds, after reviewing the authorities said:

"The essential factor in determining liability is whether the damage is of such a kind as the reasonable man should have foreseen. This accords with the general view thus stated by Lord Atkin in *Donoghue v Stevenson*: "The liability for negligence ... is no doubt based on a general public sentiment of moral wrong-doing for which the offender must pay." It is not a departure from this sovereign principle if liability is made to depend solely on the damage being the direct or natural consequence of the precedent act. Who knows or can be assumed to know all the processes of nature? But if it would be wrong that a man should be held liable for damage unpredictable by a reasonable man because it was direct or natural, equally it would be wrong that he should escape liability however indirect the damage, if he foresaw or could reasonably foresee the intervening events which lead to it being done. ... Thus forseeability becomes the effective test."

The question of causation, rejected in *The Wagon Mound* may still be of relevance. In *Barnett v Chelsea Hospital Committee*[61] a night-watchman

---

[60] *Overseas Tankship v Morts Dock & Engineering* [1961] A.C. 388.
[61] [1969] 1 Q.B. 428.

presented himself at the hospital casualty department complaining of
vomiting after drinking tea. He was told to go home to bed, where he
later died of arsenic poisoning. In an action by the widow for negligence,
it was held that the plaintiff had failed to establish that the defendant's
negligence had caused the death. Conversely in *Baker v Willoughby*[62] the
plaintiff sued for injury to his leg caused by the defendant's negligent
driving. But before the claim was heard, he was involved in an armed
robbery in which the injured leg was shot and had to be amputated. The
House of Lords declined to reduce the damages on this account, holding
the second injury a mere concurrent cause. The questions of remoteness
and causation, both in tort and contract, will continue to produce many
complex legal problems.

Contribution

Where there are two or more defendants responsible for the same loss
the claimant is entitled to recover judgment against each to the full
amount of their individual liability. The claimant is then entitled to
enforce the judgment obtained against either, provided that they do not
recover more than the total damages proved. It would be a matter for the
claimant to decide against which defendant first to enforce. To mitigate
this, the court has power under the Civil Liability (Contribution) Act
1978[63] to apportion liability between defendants. The apportionment is
dealt with by the judge after deciding upon the liability of the defendants
to the claimant. The effect is to give any defendant entitled to contribution the right to recover from another defendant the amount of that
defendant's liability. If, therefore, one or more of the defendants is
without the means to pay, the remaining defendants must bear the whole
loss. In many construction cases, this has operated to the disadvantage of
professionals who have indemnity insurance available, when contractors
or sub-contractors may be insolvent. Parties who anticipate the possibility of being joined in disputed litigation, particularly construction
professionals, may seek to protect their interests by including a "net
contribution clause" in their contracts. This is intended to limit their
liability to the contribution that would be due if all other parties were
solvent, thus avoiding potential liability for the contribution due from
other insolvent parties. Such a clause under the ACE conditions of
engagement has been applied in a Scottish case[64] but the principle has
not yet been tested in England.

---

[62] [1970] A.C. 467.
[63] Previously the Law Reform (Married Women and Tortfeasors) Act 1935.
[64] *Langstane Housing Association v Riverside Constructin (Aberdeen)* [2009] C.S.O.H. 52.

The rules as to contribution apply whether or not the other persons liable have been sued by the claimant. A defendant may therefore bring into an action as a third party anyone whom they consider should contribute to the claimant's loss as a joint tortfeasor. Or the defendant may bring separate proceedings claiming contribution after the claimant has obtained judgment.

Injunction

An alternative remedy to damages, which may be appropriate particularly in cases of nuisance, is an injunction, either to restrain the defendant from doing some act or to compel the performance of an act. An injunction is an equitable remedy and therefore lies in the court's discretion. It will usually be refused where damages would be an adequate remedy, or where to grant it would be in vain. A valuable feature of this remedy is the power of the court to give an interlocutory injunction. Temporary relief may be obtained within days or even hours of a cause of complaint arising. The power to grant an injunction is applicable particularly where the defendant is threatening an act which is arguably unlawful and likely to cause damage. An interlocutory injunction may be issued, ex parte, (in the absence of the defendant) in the first place and then reconsidered after a short period when the defendant can be heard. The court will then consider whether to continue the injunction for a further period or even up to trial. The test upon which the court decides whether to give an interlocutory injunction has been restated by the House of Lords.[65] The claimant is required to establish that they have a good arguable claim to the right which they seek to protect. The court then considers the balance of convenience in granting or refusing the injunction.[66]

Limitation

An important consideration in any action must be the period during which the action may be brought. The Limitation Act 1980 provides that an action founded on tort shall not be brought after the expiration of six years from the date on which the cause of action accrued (s.2). There is a further limitation where the claim is for damages in respect of personal injuries arising from negligence, nuisance or breach of duty. Here, the action must normally be brought within three years from the date on which the cause of action accrued (s.11) subject to certain extensions (see below).

---

[65] *American Cyanamid v Ethicon* [1975] A.C. 396.
[66] See also *Bath District Council v Mowlem* [2004] B.L.R. 153.

The main difference between limitation in a contract action and in tort is that in the former case, the cause of action accrues at the date of the breach. In tort, however, the cause of action accrues only when damage is suffered, so that the cause of action may not arise until long after the relevant act or omission occurred. Thus, if a builder negligently erects a chimney stack, a cause of action in contract arises in favour of the employer when the work is done, or when the builder purports to finish it. If the work remains in place and no complaint is made, the right of action in contract will be lost after six years. If, after 10 years, the chimney falls, to injure a passer-by, a right of action in tort then immediately vests in the injured person.

Latent damage

There has been great development in the law of limitation relating to defects in building work in recent years. The impetus came from those cases (see above) which held that a right of action in tort was available, and this led to a series of cases in which local authorities, builders, designers and other professionals were held liable long after the relevant work was carried out. In a number of cases it was held that the cause of action accrued only when the building owner became aware, or ought reasonably to have become aware, of the existence of the defect. A further period of six years was then available to issue proceedings. However, these decisions were contrary to the law of limitation as applied in personal injury cases. Here, the House of Lords held in *Cartledge v Jopling*[67] that the plaintiff's action was statute-barred before the damage (contraction of pneumoconiosis) could reasonably have been known. As a result of this case, an amendment to the Limitation Act was passed,[68] allowing a further three years to bring an action from the date when the plaintiff knew or ought to have known that he had a cause of action for personal injury. The question of limitation in relation to claims for damage to buildings was referred to the Law Reform Commission, but the issue came directly before the courts in *Pirelli v Oscar Faber*.[69] This concerned the design of a chimney, built in 1969. Not later than 1970, cracks developed near the top, but they were not discovered until 1977. A writ was issued in 1978. The House of Lords, while agreeing that the law was unsatisfactory, held that the cause of action arose in 1970 and was therefore statute-barred. *Cartledge v Jopling* applied equally to damage to property and the previous contrary decisions of the

---

[67] [1963] A.C. 758.
[68] Limitation Act 1980 ss.11 and 14.
[69] [1983] 2 A.C. 1.

Court of Appeal were overruled. As a result of *Murphy v Brentwood*[70] it became apparent that a building owner might suffer economic loss before the appearance of physical damage, and that this might affect the accrual of a cause of action for limitation purposes. In *Abbott v Will Gannon*[71] the Court of Appeal held that *Pirelli* was still good law and, until over-ruled by the House of Lords, still determined when limitation commenced.

The general law of limitation was changed by the Latent Damage Act 1986 which introduced new sections into the Limitation Act 1980. The material effect of these provisions is, first, that an action for damages for negligence may be brought within three years of the date upon which a reasonable person would conclude that proceedings could and should be instituted (s.14A). Secondly, a longstop period of 15 years is applied to the bringing of any such action, this period running from the date of the last alleged act of negligence (s.14B). The act also introduces a change to the law where a person buys a house which has a defect such that a cause of action has already arisen. In the case of *Perry v Tendring District Council*[72] the official referee held, in such circumstances, that the cause of action vested in the original owner and could not ordinarily be transferred to a purchaser. Section 3 of the Latent Damage Act 1986 reverses this decision by providing that a fresh cause of action is to accrue to the purchaser on the date that they acquire an interest in the property, that cause of action being treated as having accrued on the same date as the original cause of action of the previous owner (so that, the defendant is not to be placed in any worse position). These cases must all be reconsidered in the light of the *Murphy* case (see above).

It is ironic that, while the Latent Damage Act was going through Parliament, the courts were embarking on the series of tort cases already referred to which, by 1990 finally established that tortious liability would normally be limited to cases of actual physical injury. Thus, the resolution of doubt over the law of limitation in tort has coincided with emasculation of the rights of action.

Defective premises

A further development, overshadowed at the time by changes in the law of tort, was the passing of the Defective Premises Act 1972 (see Ch.7). This Act creates a general duty on persons to see that work is done in a workmanlike or professional manner, with proper materials and so

---

[70] [1991] A.C. 398.
[71] [2005] B.L.R. 195.
[72] (1984) 30 B.L.R. 118.

that the dwelling will be fit for habitation (s.1). For the purpose of limitation, the Act provides that any cause of action in respect of a breach of these duties:

> "shall be deemed . . . to have accrued at the time that the dwelling was completed, but if after that time a person who has done work for or in connection with the provision of the dwelling does further work to rectify the work he has already done, any such cause of action in respect of that further work shall be deemed for those purposes to have accrued at the time when the further work was finished."

The Act, therefore, creates a statutory duty similar to (although rather wider than) that which the courts had sought to impose under the law of tort, and also provides what may be regarded as a fair limitation rule, which has no need of a longstop provision. Since the *D. & F.* and *Murphy* cases the Defective Premises Act represents the principal remedy outside contract in respect of damaged buildings.

Concealment

Section 32 of the Limitation Act 1980 postpones the limitation period in a case where facts relevant to the claimant's right of action have been deliberately concealed from them by the defendant. The section is amended by the Latent Damage Act 1986 with the effect that ss.14A and 14B (see above) do not apply in the case of deliberate concealment, where the normal period of limitation will apply after the claimant has discovered or could reasonably have discovered the concealment. The ambit of deliberate concealment has recently been affirmed as not extending to the mere failure to disclose a breach of duty of which the person in breach was not aware[73] (see also Ch.6).

Normal limitation provisions will also be overridden where a claim for contribution is brought under the Civil Liability (Contribution) Act 1978. Here, by s.10 of the Limitation Act 1980, an action to recover contributions may be brought within two years of the judgment, award or settlement which establishes the liability of the person claiming contribution.

[73] *Cave v Robinson Jarvis* [2003] 1 A.C. 384.

CHAPTER 15

LAND, PLANNING AND ENVIRONMENT LAW

In England the law relating to land has always been different and distinct from law relating to other property. There are many reasons for this. Perhaps the most obvious is that a piece of land is indestructible and unique. No other land is quite the same. On a practical level, it is common for two or more persons to hold simultaneously different interests in the same land, and this is one of the reasons why a sale of land is more complicated and lengthy than a sale of other property.

Although the expression "land owner" is often encountered it requires some qualification in legal terms. It is not possible to "own" land in the absolute way that other property (such as a motor car) may be owned. Instead, the law speaks of owning an estate or interest in land, which gives the owner certain rights over that land. The largest estate which may be owned is called a fee simple absolute in possession. This is what is commonly known as "freehold" and for convenience it is so called in this section, although in legal terms an estate lasting only for the life of the holder may be a type of freehold. Interests in land are termed "real" property as opposed to "personal", which covers other forms of property.

Another type of estate in land is a tenancy. This may be created out of the estate of the freeholder or of a superior tenant. The word "tenancy" refers to a right to possession of land for a limited period. This may be for a fixed term of years (when the tenancy must normally be created by a lease) but also includes periodic tenancies such as a weekly or quarterly tenancy. In practice a building owner is likely to be concerned only with long tenancies created by lease.

Interests in land generally indicate something less than an estate; they may be of many kinds. Two of the most important are easements and restrictive covenants, and these are mentioned further below. Another very common interest in land is a mortgage, where the land is used as a security. Two further provisions may illustrate the special legal status of land. First, an infant, (i.e. a person under 18 years) cannot own an estate in land. Secondly, a contract for the sale of land or any interest in land is unenforceable unless in writing and signed by or on behalf of each party, or in the case of contracts which are exchanged, unless each counterpart is signed.[1]

Throughout its history land law has been profoundly affected by the principles of equity (see Ch.1). The result is that interests in land are for some purposes classified as being either legal or equitable. The practical importance of this distinction is that a legal interest attaches to the land itself and is enforceable against any person. An equitable interest binds only certain persons, and is not enforceable against a bona fide purchaser of the land who has no notice (actual or constructive) of such interest. An equitable interest is, therefore, less secure. An example of an equitable interest is an agreement for a lease. Practically, this is as good as an actual lease but if another person purchases the land without notice of the agreement, it becomes unenforceable against that person.

RIGHTS OF THE OWNER OR OCCUPIER OF LAND

When a person wishes to build on land there are many factors to be considered. They must obtain a sufficient interest to give themselves a right of possession. They must consider what restrictions there are as to what may be done with the land. They will also wish to know who is entitled to ownership or use of things on or in the land. These points are considered below. Another factor, which may be of great importance, is the question of rights which other persons hold concurrently over the land. Such rights are considered in the following section.

Leases

The most common legal device for obtaining possession of premises for business use is by a lease. There is no fixed definition of the term, but it is usually taken to mean a formal tenancy granted by deed. For most purposes a simple written tenancy agreement will have the same legal effect. The process is also colloquially referred to as "letting." Whatever term is used, the process has two separate elements. First, there is conveyance of the property as defined for the period stated (which may be periodic and renewable); secondly, there are terms (sometimes called covenants) which operate as a contract enforceable between the parties. However, because the transaction relates to land, the terms or covenants may be enforceable directly by or against other parties who take over the

[1] Law of Property (Miscellaneous Provisions) Act 1989 s.2.

interest of either landlord or tenant (see below) and there are also statutory restrictions on enforcement.

Leases and tenancy agreements are in many ways more convenient than buying a freehold interest. Commercial buildings are erected as investments, and the letting, subletting, and assignment of such premises are part of the commercial activity of any business community. It is now comparatively rare for commercial companies, at least in inner city areas, to own the freehold of their own premises. The mobility afforded by letting arrangements has allowed the substantial redevelopment of commercial areas which has been carried out over the last decades. Business leases are subject to security of tenure under the Landlord and Tenant Act 1954. At the end of a lease, the tenant may apply to the court for a new tenancy. However, the need to demolish and reconstruct the premises or to carry out substantial reconstruction work is a ground upon which the court can refuse a new lease, the tenant receiving compensation instead; and it is possible to contract out of the provisions for security in the Act.

The detailed operation of leases and their covenants is not dealt with. But mention should be made of two classes of construction dispute which frequently arise out of lettings. Leases invariably contain repairing covenants of some variety. These require the tenant to carry out to defined parts of a building certain works, usually defined in terms of the intended result, such as to keep the premises in "good and tenantable repair." Leases usually require the premises to be yielded up in a repaired state, and when the end of the tenancy arrives, there may be a dispute as to its state. This is referred to as a "dilapidations" claim, which often consists of long schedules and counter schedules settled by surveyors for each party. Such a dispute is concerned only with the assessment and valuation of wants of repair in accordance with the covenants. Sometimes disputes of this sort arise during the term of a tenancy. Here, the position is more complex because, if there are a number of years of tenancy still to run, the landlord usually suffers no damage. Accordingly, where there are three years or more of the term remaining, the landlord must obtain leave of the court before proceeding with any action for breach of a repairing covenant, and the court will grant such leave only on exceptional grounds, such as where it is shown that immediate remedying of the breach is necessary.[2]

In addition to specific covenants covering repairs, payment of rent and other matters, leases usually contain a "forfeiture" clause permitting the landlord to take back the lease, or "re-enter" for breach of covenant. For the protection of tenants, the law has evolved a series of protective

[2] Leasehold Property (Repairs) Act 1938.

measures. First, no such right of forfeiture may be enforced (except in the case of non-payment of rent) unless the landlord has first served a notice specifying the breach and requiring remedy and compensation.[3] When such a notice has been served, and not complied with (perhaps because the tenant disputes that repairs are necessary), the landlord must seek an order from the court for forfeiture, and the tenant can then apply for the equitable remedy of relief (now embodied also in statute) which may be granted on such terms as the court thinks fit. The result of the dispute is, in effect, to decide the rights of the parties under the contractual terms or covenants of the lease, and to enforce them. Only in exceptional circumstances will leases be declared forfeit. Indeed, there is little purpose in the tenant allowing the lease to be forfeited, because they will remain liable for the financial consequences of previous breaches of covenant.

Another type of construction dispute that may arise out of a lease is one relating to the nature of the repairs that the tenant is responsible for. What is the tenant's position under a normal repairing covenant if the premises become defective due to design defects in the original construction? In the case of *Ravenseft Properties v Davstone*[4] a tenant undertook covenants which included an obligation "well and sufficiently to repair, renew, rebuild, uphold, support, sustain, maintain" the premises. The building had been constructed in concrete with external stone cladding, but with no expansion joints to allow differential movement between the stone and concrete. The cladding bowed and needed substantial repair as a result of this inherent defect. It was held that it was a question of degree whether the remedying of an inherent defect was work of repair, and where (as in this case) the work of inserting expansion joints was a comparatively trivial part of the whole building, so as not to involve giving back to the landlord a wholly different building, the tenant was liable for the repairs. In answer to a further argument that the tenant should not be liable for repair necessary to remedy an inherent defect Forbes J. said:

> "It was proper engineering practice to see that such expansion joints were included, and it would have been dangerous not to include them. In no realistic sense, therefore, could it be said that there was any other possible way of reinstating the cladding than by providing the expansion joints which were in fact provided."

Thus, the tenant was held liable for the whole cost of repair, in the only way that it could realistically be done. The effect of this, and other cases

---

[3] Law of Property Act 1925 s.146.
[4] [1980] Q.B. 12.

to like effect, has been to cause tenants to bring claims for their own loss (including loss of use or loss of profit) against contractors and designers. The fact that such claims are now not generally maintainable in tort (see Ch.14) has meant that tenants in particular have sought direct contractual warranties from those responsible for the work (see Ch.9).

Licences

A right to occupation of land which is not sufficient to create a true tenancy is said to create a licence. This is essentially a right to do some act which would otherwise be a trespass. Examples of the operation of licences are a person occupying a cinema seat or an hotel room; or a contractor in possession of a building site. Essentially a licence is a personal arrangement between grantor and grantee which does not bind third parties. There may, however, be circumstances where an interest in the land affecting third parties is created. In *Inwards v Baker*[5] a man allowed his son to build a bungalow on his (the father's) land and then died leaving the land to others. It was held that the son should be allowed to remain in the bungalow as long as he desired. Lord Denning said:

> "All that is necessary is that the licensee should, at the request or with the encouragement of the landlord, have spent the money in the expectation of being allowed to stay there. If so, the court will not allow that expectation to be defeated where it would be inequitable so to do. In this case it is quite plain that the father allowed an expectation to be created in the son's mind that this bungalow was to be his home. It was to be his home for his life, or at all events, his home as long as he wished it to remain his home. It seems to me, in the light of that equity, that the father could not in 1932 have turned to his son and said: 'You are to go. It is my land and my house.' Nor could he at any time thereafter so long as the son wanted it as his home."

A gratuitous licence merely to enter land may be revoked at any time; while a licence coupled with an interest in the property (such as a right to dig gravel) cannot be revoked. A more usual type of licence in business transactions is one given under a contract. Such a licence will be regarded as part of the contract creating it and its revocation in breach of contract may in some circumstances be resisted by injunction. In *Hounslow v Twickenham Gardens*,[6] a contractor's employment under a building contract had been terminated by the employer. The contractor, contending that the termination was invalid, refused to leave the site. The employer claimed an injunction to remove him, which was refused. The

---

[5] [1965] 1 Q.B. 29.
[6] [1971] Ch. 233.

LAND, PLANNING AND ENVIRONMENT LAW

employer was held to be under an implied obligation not to revoke the contractor's licence except in accordance with the contract. In this case Megarry J. said:

"Now in this case the contract is one for the execution of specified works on the site during a specified period which is still running. The contract confers on each party specified rights on specified events to determine the employment of the contractor under the contract. In those circumstances I think that there must be at least an implied negative obligation on the Borough not to revoke any licence (otherwise than in accordance with the contract) while the period is still running."

Having decided that the Borough had not conclusively established the validity of its determination notices, the judge went on to say:

"I fully accept the importance to the Borough on social grounds as well as others of securing the due completion of the contract, and the unsatisfactory nature of damages as an alternative. But the contract was made, and the contractors are not to be stripped of their rights under it, however desirable that may be for the Borough. A contract remains a contract, even if (or perhaps especially if) it turns out badly."

This case, however, has been criticised and the result in other similar circumstances may not be the same.[7]

Rights over the land

The question of what the owner or occupier is entitled to do with the land depends upon many factors. It is subject to numerous statutory provisions, such as the Housing Acts and Public Health Acts. Building work itself is closely controlled by regulations and byelaws (see Ch.16). The occupier of land may become liable to their neighbours under the law of nuisance (see Ch.14). Perhaps the most fundamental restriction upon the user of land arises through statutory planning controls (see below). Rather than to say that land is owned subject to restrictions, it is probably more accurate to say that land is held for the benefit both of the owner or occupier and of the community.

As to ownership of things on or in the land (as opposed to "ownership" of the space occupied by the land), it is presumed that the owner of the freehold owns everything upon or below the land. They are generally entitled to everything which is attached to the land. Such items are commonly called fixtures (as opposed to mere fittings) and they will belong to the freeholder as against a tenant. The question of what

[7] See *Chermar v Pretest* (1992) 8 Cost. L.J. 44.

attachment is sufficient to make an object a fixture is a matter of degree and purpose. Thus in *Webb v Bevis*[8] a corrugated iron building which was bolted to, but not embedded in, a concrete floor was held not to be sufficiently attached to be a fixture. Scott L.J. said:

> "That the concrete floor was so affixed to the ground as to become part of the soil is obvious. It was completely and permanently attached to the ground and, secondly, it could not be detached except by being broken up and ceasing to exist either as a concrete floor or as the cement and rubble of which it had been made. Does that fact of itself prevent the superstructure from being a tenant's fixture? I do not think so. If it had been erected on concrete blocks, one under each post, the top level with the surface of the ground and the attachment of post to block had been plainly removable at ground level, "the object and purpose" of the attachment would have been obvious namely to erect a mere tenant's fixture. In my opinion it was equally so in the actual construction adopted for holding the posts in position on their concrete supports."

Building materials will become the property of the freeholder as soon as they are (like the concrete floor in the case) attached to the land or to the permanent works, whether paid for by the employer or not. As between landlord and tenant there are certain exceptions to the rule, which relate, particularly to trade and agricultural fixtures.

RIGHTS OVER LAND OF OTHERS

Of the many types of interest over land belonging to or in the possession of other persons, the most important so far as a building developer is concerned are easements and restrictive covenants. In this context the building developer is seen as the "other person" over whose land rights exist which may affect its use or development. The short account given below describes the nature of these interests.

Easements

An easement is a right which allows the holder to use, or restrict the use of, the land of another person in some way. Common examples are private rights of way, rights of light and rights of support. An easement can exist only in relation to other land which is nearby, which is said to "benefit" from the easement. A "quasi-easement" (referred to in cl.22 of the ICE conditions) is a term used to describe an habitual right exercised

---

[8] [1940] 1 All E.R. 247.

by a person over a part of their own land, which would be an easement if the two parts were in different occupation, such as a right of support between adjoining buildings. A quasi-easement may become a real easement upon a sale of one or both parts of the land.

Rights of light often restrict development on sites adjoining the land which enjoy the right, called the "dominant tenement." An action to preserve a right of light lies in nuisance. But even where the right has been acquired by long usage, the holder cannot demand unlimited light. The courts have held that the right is to have enough light adequately to light a room "according to the ordinary notions of mankind".[9] It is not the function of a planning authority to guard or preserve rights of light or other easements. Thus, the fact that a right of light is enjoyed does not prevent a developer obtaining planning permission for a building which will block the right. Nor does the grant of planning permission guarantee that the developer will not be prevented from erecting the building in breach of the rights of neighbours. Building in apparent breach of a right of light is a good example of nuisance which could be restrained by interim injunction (see Ch.14).

There are a number of other rights which are similar to, but which do not comprise easements. For example, a profit (or *profit á prendre*) is a right to take something from the land of another person, such as grass or sand. A licence is a private right to go upon another's land (see above). Either of these rights may exist without the holder owning land which is benefited. An easement of support relates only to a building and is distinct from the natural right to have unweighted land supported by adjoining land (see Ch.14).

Covenants

A contractual provision which seeks to constrain the way in which the holder of land may use it is termed a restrictive covenant. An example of the type of covenant which might be relevant to a building developer is one not to build on certain land. As between the original parties a covenant is binding, for instance, when the covenantee and covenantor are respectively landlord and tenant. It will also be binding on successors if it constitutes an easement (see above). Otherwise, only in limited circumstances will a restrictive covenant be enforceable by and against successors in title. A claimant who wishes to enforce a restrictive covenant must show that they have acquired the "benefit" of the covenant and that the defendant has acquired the "burden."

---

[9] *Colls v Home and Colonial Stores* [1904] A.C. 179.

An example of the operation of restrictive covenants occurs where an estate is laid out in lots to be sold or leased for building and each purchaser or lessee agrees to similar restrictive covenants. It is necessary that the area be clearly defined and that restrictions are imposed by the common vendor or lessor which are consistent with the general scheme of the development. The covenants must be for the benefit of all the lots and the sale or leasing must be transacted with this intention. Provided these conditions are satisfied, the covenants will be enforceable by and against the owners or lessees for the time being of any plot on the estate. The covenants therefore constitute a local law for the estate.

Party walls

Problems frequently occur in heavily built-up areas over the rights possessed by adjoining owners in a party wall. This occurs where the boundary line between two premises is built on, or where one adjoining owner has acquired rights in a wall built up to the boundary on neighbouring land. The problem is frequently to define where the boundary lies, and this is often a major problem where there have been alterations and extensions over the years. Having identified the position of the boundary, it is often found that walls vary in line and in thickness, and foundations usually extend out beyond the wall itself, so that there is often no simple answer to the question of ownership.

Assuming that ownership can be established, there are rights at common law to carry out work to a party wall, notwithstanding that part of the wall is not owned by the party wishing to carry out the work. In London, where the problem is most acute, the rights were codified in the London Building Acts 1930–1939.[10] These provisions worked well for London, and have now been extended with some amendments, to the whole country by the Party Wall etc., Act 1996. The Act, for the first time, contains a definition of "party wall", which means:

> "(a) a wall which forms part of a building and stands on lands of different owners to a greater extent than the projections of any artificially formed support on which the wall rests; and
> (b) so much of a wall not being a wall referred to in paragraph (a) above as separates buildings belonging to different owners."

This definition covers both a wall which straddles a boundary and a wall which is built up to a boundary. Section 1 of the Act makes provision for

---

[10] Now repealed.

building new party walls. Section 2 covers the general problem of rights in an existing party wall where one neighbour wishes to build. These rights include underpinning, raising, demolishing and rebuilding or carrying out various work to the wall in question. The person wishing to carry out work must normally serve a "Party Structure Notice" at least two months before the date for beginning the proposed work. No notice is required if the adjoining owner consents in writing, nor if the building owner is required to comply with some statutory obligation, such as complying with a Dangerous Structure Notice. The adjoining owner may serve a "counter notice" and any dispute which is not settled by agreement is to be referred to surveyors under s.10 of the Act. The old London Building Acts required each party to appoint a surveyor. The new Act, consistent with the Civil Procedure Rules (see Ch.2) provides for the appointment of an "agreed surveyor" or two surveyors if there is no agreement. The two surveyors settle the dispute by a "Party Wall Award". If they cannot agree they must appoint a third surveyor to determine the matter. The award is to determine:

(a) the right to execute any work;

(b) the time and manner of executing any work; and

(c) any other matter arising out of or incidental to the dispute including costs of making the award.

Section 10 of the Act further provides that either party may appeal the award to the county court within 14 days; otherwise the award is to be conclusive.

PLANNING LAW

Planning law is substantially a creature of the twentieth century. The first attempts at systematic town planning were introduced in 1909, and since then the scope and complexity of planning law have widened enormously. Very largely unrestricted urban sprawls in the 1930s, together with the destruction brought about by the Second World War with its consequent opportunities for replanning has been responsible for much of this development. The principal enactment is now the Town and Country Planning Act 1990, which consolidates the previous statute law, and the Planning and Compulsory Purchase Act 2004. There are also other important Acts together with regulations, rules and orders made under statutory powers. Parallel legislation has shown increasing interest and emphasis on the conservation of ancient monuments and historic buildings and urban areas.[11]

The practical effect of modern planning law is that the owner's rights to use their land are to a large extent subordinated to the good of the community. In the historic 1947 Act, land use planning was made of general application; and both development rights and development values were effectively nationalised (the latter being returned to landowners by later legislation). In general, a land owner has no right to use their land for any purpose other than its present use and intensity of use, unless they obtain permission. Further, they may be dispossessed of even its present use by authorities exercising powers of compulsory acquisition or discontinuance. The economic importance of planning law to the individual is demonstrated by the direct effect which planning consent has upon the value of land and buildings.

In origin, planning law is entirely contained in Acts of Parliament and the delegated or subordinate legislation made under those Acts. Both the statutes and subordinate legislation are periodically considered and interpreted by the courts. But this occurs in very few cases. Planning decisions usually involve no more than administrative decisions, by the local authority or government department so empowered. An appeal is usually provided to the Minister, and their function is sometimes described as quasi-judicial. However, in neither case is the decision of legal rights (as in the case of a decision in the courts), but of the consistent administration of planning policy. Thus, in a case which arose under the New Towns Act 1946, the Minister stated publicly that Stevenage would be the first new town. He made a draft order to this effect and an inquiry was held into objections. The Minister then confirmed his order. The court, on an application for judicial review, held that there was no judicial duty upon the Minister, but only a duty to consider the objections: *Franklin v Minister of Town and Country Planning* (1948). In this case, Lord Thankerton, in the House of Lords, held:

> "In my opinion, no judicial or quasi-judicial duty was imposed on the (Minister) and any reference to judicial duty, or bias, is irrelevant to the present case. . . . The (Minister) was required to satisfy himself that it was a sound scheme before he took the serious step of issuing a draft order. It seems clear also, that the purpose of inviting objections and, where they are not withdrawn, having a public inquiry, to be held by someone other than the (Minister) to whom that person reports, was for the further information of the (Minister). . . . I am of the opinion that no judicial duty is laid on the (Minister) in discharge of those statutory duties and that the only question

---

[11] Planning (Listed Buildings and Conservation Areas) Act 1990.

is whether he has complied with the statutory directions to appoint a person
to hold the public inquiry and to consider that person's report."

A similar issue arose, more recently, in the context of the Human Rights
Act 1998 (see Ch.1). In *R (Alconbury Developments Ltd) v Secretary of
State for the Environment*[12] the House of Lords had to consider, in three
cases, whether the intervention of the Secretary of State under the Town
and Country Planning Act 1990 was incompatible with the provisions of
art.6(1) of the Human Rights Convention, which provided the right to a
"fair and public hearing . . . by an independent and impartial tribunal
established by law". The issue was whether groups of local objectors in
one case, and the applicant in another, had been deprived of their rights
by the actions of the Secretary of State. The House of Lords held, in each
case, that, although the Secretary of State was not himself an independent
and impartial tribunal, decisions taken by him were not incompatible
with the convention since they were subject to the powers of the High
Court in judicial review proceedings, which were sufficient to ensure
compatibility with art.6(1).

There may be an application to the High Court for judicial review if
the decision of the local planning authority or the Minister involves a
point of law. It is only through such decisions of the court that case law
is created. Otherwise, decisions made by planning authorities or by the
minister are administrative decisions which do not create any precedent.
While these decisions may serve as a guide to enable applicants to assess
the likelihood of planning consent being granted, each decision is a
matter of discretion. The decision must apply relevant local and national
planning policies and guidance, for example, Planning Policy Guidance
(Notes) (PPGs), Regional Planning Guidance (RPGs) or Minerals
Planning Guidance (Notes) (MPGs) which are issued periodically and
updated by the relevant government Departments.

Planning authorities

The administration of planning law and planning control at local
levels is carried out by the local planning authority. This body will be
either a county council, a unitary council or a district council and, in
London, the relevant Borough Council. There is also, as a result of the
2004 Act, a Regional Planning Body for every area. The authority
responsible for central administration is referred to in the Acts as the
Secretary of State (of the relevant Department). In addition to these
authorities, there are other bodies which have specific functions in

---

[12] [2001] 2 W.L.R. 1389.

relation to planning administration. In particular, the Lands Tribunal, among its various functions, has powers to settle disputes over the valuation of land arising out of planning decisions.

Development plan

A primary creative duty of the planning authority is regularly to produce, alter or review plans for future development. A local planning authority must produce a local development plan or scheme, which may be prepared jointly with other planning authorities. The local development plan must be in conformity with the Regional Spatial Strategy prepared by the Regional Planning Body. This regional approach to planning strategy was introduced by the Planning and Compulsory Purchase Act to replace the former structure plans prepared by the county planning authority or other unitary authority. Local development plans are, under the new Act, required to take into account sustainable development principles. Both the regional and local schemes must be given adequate publicity but in place of former procedures for objections and inquiries, each authority must issue a statement of policy as to community involvement of interested parties in drawing up the scheme or strategy. The Secretary of State is also given wider powers of intervention.

A local authority, when considering a planning application is required to "have regard" to the provisions of the development plan so far as material to the application and to any other material considerations.[13] Planning authorities are also required to include measures for improvement of the physical environment and for traffic management. Planning consent may be refused on the ground of adverse interference with surrounding land. The Town and Country Planning (Assessment of Environmental Effects) Regulations, 1998[14] require an environmental assessment for projects which impact on the environment, e.g. a waste disposal installation. Guidance notes are issued dealing with environmental implications of planning decisions.

The ultimate objective of a planning authority is thus to see that its development plan is carried out and its cumulative effects monitored and kept under review. Where this can be achieved by planning restrictions the problem is reduced to one of imposing limits or conditions on consents or of enforcement. But positive development may require more than mere control. One of the most important powers of local authorities in this respect is the power to acquire land compulsorily for planning and

---

[13] T&CPA 1990 s.70(2) as amended by the 2004 Act.
[14] SI 1998/1199.

related purposes, with the authorisation of the Secretary of State. The measure of compensation which is payable upon compulsory acquisition is basically the open market value, but subject to some statutory modifications, for example, where land or buildings are being acquired for a public or non-profitable use. In such cases the notional concept of "appropriate alternative use" is employed for valuation purposes. There are also provisions for additional compensation for such matters as disturbance and severance of lands. Local authorities may compulsorily acquire land within their own areas and also in other areas. They may also revoke planning permission or acquire land by agreement, when the consent of the Secretary of State is generally not required.

Where land has been acquired or appropriated by a local authority for planning purposes, the local authority itself may carry out building or work upon the land; or instead of carrying out development itself the authority may make arrangements with an authorised association to carry out such operations. Alternatively the local authority may dispose of land to others (such as building developers) so as to secure the use or development of the land needed for the proper planning of the area. This method has been used to secure the redevelopment of many inner city and town centre areas. Where land which was acquired compulsorily is to be disposed of, the previous occupants must, so far as is practicable, be afforded an opportunity to return to their land.

Requirement of planning consent

In general any development of land requires a formal application for planning consent to be made to the local planning authority and the development may not be carried out unless such consent is granted. "Development" is defined by the Town and Country Planning Act 1990 as meaning the carrying out of building, engineering, mining or other operations in, on, over or under land, or the making of any material change in the use of any buildings or other land (s.55). The Act contains further definitions of many of its terms, such as "building," "land" and "use" (s.336). There are, however, some classes of exceptions under which things may be done to or with land without the necessity of obtaining planning consent.

The first exception is that no planning permission is required if the project is not within the meaning of "development." The Act states that certain operations or uses of land are not to be taken to involve development. These include most works which do not materially affect the external appearance of a building, maintenance works or works within the public highway. But the division of a dwelling-house into two or more separate units requires planning permission, as does also the extension of a refuse tip, in area or in height, so as to exceed the level of adjoining land (s.55). Where land is being used for a classified purpose[15] the change to another use of the same class does not constitute development. Thus, the change from a grocery shop to a tobacconist does not require planning permission; but a change to a fried-fish shop or to an office is not within the exemption and requires permission.

Secondly, the Secretary of State has power to make Development Orders which permit either particular development in a given place or area or some class of general development. An order may itself grant planning permission or provide for permission to be granted by the local planning authority. An order may be limited in its area of application and may be subject to conditions. The current order sets out the types of operation and change of use which the order itself sanctions.[16] Under powers inserted by the Planning and Compulsory Purchase Act 2004 a local planning authority may issue a local development order.

The third exception is that planning permission is not required in some specified cases relating to the resumption of a former use of land, such as after the expiry of planning permission granted for a limited period (s.57). A fourth exception applies to local authorities and statutory undertakers. Where authorisation is required from a government department for a development, the department may itself grant deemed planning permission (s.90).

Applications for planning consent

If a project requires planning permission to be obtained then the usual course is to make application to the local planning authority. An application must be made in such a manner as is prescribed by regulations,[17] and must be accompanied by plans and other particulars of the project. In some cases the applicant is required to certify that they have given certain notices. For example, where the applicant is not the freeholder or leaseholder of all the land in question, they must take steps to notify the owner of the land of the application. Planning applications (but not listed building consent applications) require payment of a fee, which is periodically reviewed.

Application may be made for "outline permission," in accordance with the provision of a development order (s.92). Such permission will be subject to subsequent approval of "reserved matters" not

---

[15] Town and Country Planning (Use Classes) Order 1987.
[16] Town & Country Planning (General Permitted Development) Order 1995.
[17] Town & Country Planning (General Development Procedure) Order 1995 and TCP(GDP) (Amendment) Order 2005.

particularised in the application. Local authorities increasingly resist the granting of outline planning permission if the site lies within a conservation area.[18] Outline planning permission will only be granted subject to application for approval of reserved matters, and commencement of the development, being made within specified periods. The procedure for outline planning applications may be useful for a prospective developer who does not own the land in question. The procedure does not apply to "change of use" development.

The local planning authority must generally give its decision within two months of an application for planning permission. In coming to a decision the authority must always have regard to the adopted or emergent development plan, and to all other material matters. There are provisions requiring various persons and bodies to be consulted. Where applications require local advertisement, the planning authority must take into account representations received. Where the applicant is not the freeholder or leaseholder the representations of owners of the land must be considered (s.71). In particular, works of demolition, alteration or extension of buildings listed as being of historic or architectural importance are given special consideration, and require separate (usually simultaneous) applications for listed building or conservation area consent.

Effect of planning consent

Planning permission may be granted, refused or granted subject to conditions, and unless it is granted unconditionally reasons must be given for the decision. The conditions imposed may be permanent or of limited duration, although they must relate to the development. For example, a condition that payment should be made to the local authority does not relate to the development, and is invalid. The planning permission itself is granted for a specific period (s.72). As an alternative to planning or listed building consent applications being determined by the local planning authority, the Secretary of State may "call in" for determination particular applications or classes of application. This is particularly common in applications to demolish listed buildings or for controversial or unusual forms of development, where consultees or other interested bodies may have requested this course.

Once planning permission is obtained it attaches to the land for the benefit of subsequent owners. However, there is generally a condition that the development will be begun within five years unless other express time limits are laid down (s.91). The local planning authority is also

---

[18] Planning (Listed Building and Conservation Areas) Act 1990.

given powers to promote timely completion of developments. Thus, the authority may serve a "completion notice" (to be confirmed by the Secretary of State), whereby planning permission will cease to have effect after a specified period in respect of uncompleted work (s.94). The authority also has powers to modify or revoke planning permission, with the confirmation of the Secretary of State (s.97).

Appeals

An appeal against the local planning authority's unfavourable decision or failure to decide may be made to the Secretary of State, generally within six months. He may reconsider the whole application as if made to him in the first place, so that an appeal against the conditions imposed with a consent may result in a refusal of consent. The appeal may be considered on the basis of written representations or by way of a hearing or public local enquiry if either party so requests or the Secretary of State so decides (s.78). There is a final appeal from the Minister's decision to the High Court on a point of law.

Powers of control

If a development is carried out without planning consent, or contrary to conditions imposed with such consent, the local planning authority has the right to enforce their control by serving an enforcement notice, where it appears "that it is expedient to issue the notice having regard to the provisions of the development plan and to any other material considerations" (s.172). The notice must specify the breach of planning control, the precise steps required for their rectification and the period for compliance. The steps required to be taken may include demolition or alteration of buildings or works. Such a notice must be served generally within four years of the offence, or 10 years of the breach of conditions. No time limits are prescribed for listed building enforcement, since the carrying out of works of demolition, alteration or extension are offences of continuing effect. A copy of the enforcement notice must be served on the owner and on the occupier of the land and on any other persons having a sufficient interest. The period for compliance must be reasonable, but development may be stopped on three days' notice by an interim "stop notice" (s.171E). An appeal against a notice may be made to the Secretary of State and the appeal is deemed also to be an application for planning permission in respect of the offending building or works (s.174). There is a further appeal to the High Court on a point of law. If the enforcement notice takes effect and the required steps are not taken then the local planning authority may itself carry out the work and recover the cost from the land owner. The owner is also liable to a fine. The wrongful exercise of enforcement controls or stop orders will entitle the injured developer to compensation.

Compensation

Since permission to develop land has such a direct influence on its value it is obviously right that a measure of redress should be provided for those who suffer loss through planning restrictions. Redress may be available in one of two ways. First, if planning restrictions prevent or hamper development or cause depreciation in the value of the land, compensation may be payable in a limited number of cases. Such restrictions may take the form of a refusal of planning consent or may arise from the exercise of powers, such as those to revoke or modify an existing consent or to order removal of an existing building (ss.97, 102). Compensation may also be payable where land value drops as a result of the future possibility of compulsory purchase.

Secondly, when planning permission is refused, or granted subject to conditions, the owner may in some cases require their land to be purchased by the local authority. But this is possible only if the land is incapable of reasonably beneficial use (i.e. is virtually worthless) in its existing state. The discussion above has been concerned principally with building and construction works. The 1990 Act also contains provisions relating to trees, waste land and advertisements. Buildings of special architectural or historic interest which are so listed are covered by the Planning (Listed Buildings and Conservation Areas) Act 1990 and unauthorised works to them may be a criminal offence and also subject to enforcement measures.

Major infrastructure projects

It has always been the case that some very large projects have required to be dealt with outside the normal planning rules and procedures. In the past, before the advent of modern planning law, projects such as canals and railways were dealt with through special parliamentary Bills. This procedure continues in use and there are now two distinct categories: Hybrid Bills where the development has Government support and in which objections are limited to matters of detail and implementation; and Private Bills introduced by promoters of the project, where the whole question of development may be argued before a select committee. The Channel Tunnel Rail Link was authorised via a Hybrid Bill but many other large scale projects such as the Tamar Bridge have used the Private Bill procedure. In addition, numerous Acts of Parliament supporting particular industries have been introduced containing their own procedures for authorising development. These include the Electricity Act 1989, the Harbours Act 1964 and the Transport and the Works Act 1992. Under such legislation, orders granting consent for development are usually granted by the appropriate Minister. In addition, mention should be made of the New Towns Act 1981, replacing earlier legislation, under which major green field developments have been carried out including a significant number of new towns established in the decades following the end of the Second World War. The New Towns Act establishes new bodies charged with carrying out and managing the new communities during their initial period of life.

Other major infrastructure projects, notably motorways and airports, have in the past been the subject of normal planning control with the issues being considered in great detail at a Public Inquiry at which large numbers of objectors have had the opportunity to make their case. Such procedures have resulted in long delays to important public projects. For example, the Heathrow Terminal 5 Inquiry lasted for some four years between 1995 and 1999 and only at the end of this process, and the Inspector's final report, was the Minister able to confirm the project so as to allow construction to start.

There have been several attempts to speed up the inquiry process. In 2002 new rules were introduced for dealing with major infrastructure projects which had been "called in" by the secretary of state. A further attempt was made in the Planning and Compulsory Purchase Act 2004 which introduced a fast-track procedure under which planning permission could be granted by the secretary of state after a stream-lined inquiry procedure. The latest measures are contained in The Planning Act 2008 under which applications for "development consent" for major new infrastructure projects such as airports, roads, harbours, energy facilities such as nuclear power and waste facilities are to be dealt with by a new Infrastructure Planning Commission (IPC). The important question whether a project falls within the Act is dealt with by the Act itself in terms of defined function and size; and where the Act applies normal planning and other consents are not required.[19] The Act is designed to avoid the lengthy delays of public inquiries by the introduction of new truncated procedures which severely restrict the rights of objectors to major projects. There are two principal elements of the Act: first, national policy statements (NPS) are intended to set out government policy on major infrastructure projects; secondly, the new IPC is both to assess the merits of the project and objections to it and to make the final decision on development consent formerly made by the secretary of state. In place

[19] Planning Act 2008 ss.14, 33.

of the public inquiry system, there is to be a limited "open-floor" hearing, with a public right to serve written objections but with no entitlement to call witnesses or to cross-examine. Detailed procedural rules are contained in the Infrastructure Planning (Applications: Prescribed Forms and Procedure) Regulations 2009. The Act also introduces new measures dealing with the compulsory acquisition of land.

ENVIRONMENT LAW

This term applies to a group of topics formerly existing under titles such as public health. In some areas, the law exists solely as private rights between individuals, for example, under the law of nuisance. There has been a growing trend towards the creation of wider powers and controls over the use of land and the environment, and increasingly this has taken the form of administrative powers exercisable by public authorities. This has naturally relegated the role of the individual to that of requesting public authorities to exercise their powers, and in appropriate cases of seeking public law remedies where the individual is affected (see Ch.1).

Much of the modern structure of environment law goes back to the Public Health Acts enacted over the last hundred years and particularly to the massive Act of 1936. This Act dealt with matters such as domestic water supply and sewerage, collection of refuse, provision of recreation grounds and many other topics. Substantial amendments were made in subsequent legislation. A major environmental impact resulted from the Clean Air Act 1956, which controlled the omission of smoke and other effluent from both industrial and domestic premises. This had a dramatic effect on pollution in all urban communities. The current legislation is the Clean Air Act 1993, which contains further controls over emissions of dark smoke and other effluent from chimneys, and the Environment Act 1995 Pt IV which requires air quality to be regulated. The other major piece of historical legislation on the topic is the Control of Pollution Act 1974.

In the general sphere of environment law and practice the Environmental Protection Act 1990 makes far-reaching changes to the whole field by establishing a new integrated approach to pollution control, to be operated by the Inspectorate of Pollution. In regard to less serious pollution, new functions are placed on local authorities; and in regard to waste disposal, local authorities are given new powers and duties. In some areas, including Greater London, new waste authorities are created. The Act amends and replaces Pt I of the Control of Pollution

Act 1974, with extended controls over waste. There are other provisions for dealing with statutory nuisances and new measures to deal with litter.

Environment law and practice has introduced some new acronyms into the language. Recognising that environment protection must involve questions of priority, controls are often expressed in terms of the principle of Best Available Techniques Not Entailing Excessive Cost (BATNEEC) or the simpler concept of Best Practical Means (BPM). As environment law is a comparatively new concept, there is, as yet, little case law. The following section concentrates on three topics: pollution of land; the control of noise on building sites; and use and abuse of water. In each area, the courts have made some progress in considering the relevant legislation.

Pollution of land

Statutory controls, now under the Environmental Protection Act 1990 Pt II, regulate the disposal of waste which is generally categorised as "controlled" waste or "special" waste. The former covers most types of waste, including that arising from construction, demolition or excavation. Materials do not cease to be waste even though they have use or value. The 1990 Act makes it an offence to deposit controlled waste on any land or to keep it without a waste management licence. There are specific duties to avoid causing pollution to the environment and a general duty of care as respects waste. Licences may be revoked or suspended.[20] No one can now store or deal in waste without complying with the new Act and its regulations.

Special waste is material, designated by regulations, which is considered to be so dangerous or difficult to treat, keep or dispose of that special provision is required for dealing with it (s.62). Regulations also cover treating, keeping or disposal of special waste. Where special waste is discovered on land, for example in the course of carrying out construction work, regulations require the owner to make provision either for its safe retention on the site or for its lawful removal. The 1990 Act makes general provisions for a public register of information concerning waste, for inspectors with powers of entry and taking records, samples, etc. for requiring information to be furnished and for powers to deal with imminent danger of serious pollution (ss.64–71).

Part IIA of the Environmental Protection Act 1990 (which was inserted by the Environment Act 1995) contains a new code for dealing with contaminated land, i.e. land on or under which are substances which create a significant possibility of harm being caused, or of pollution of

---

[20] Environmental Protection Act 1990 Pt II.

controlled waters (see below) (s.78A(2)). Every local authority has a duty to inspect and identify contaminated land (s.78B) and to keep a permanent register (s.78R). The authority has the further duty to require remediation by serving notice (s.78E) on the person who caused or permitted the contamination or, if they cannot be identified, on the owner or occupier (s.78F). Where substances are likely to cause "serious" harm or pollution the land is to be designated a "special site", subject to regulations (s.78C).

Part IIA was brought into force in April 2000 and imposes significant new obligations on local authorities and landowners and occupiers. Contamination will have a serious effect on the value of affected land. The need to identify contamination will place new burdens on those carrying out site investigation and it is vital for persons taking over potentially contaminated land to know whether they also acquire liability for any contamination found on the site. In the recent landmark decision of the House of Lords in *R (National Gas Grid) v Environment Agency*[21] it was held, contrary to the contention of the Environment Agency, that NGG as successor to British Gas was not liable for contamination on a former gas works site which had been sold to developers in 1965 and had never been owned by British Gas.

Control of noise

The Control of Pollution Act 1974 has specific application to noise on construction sites. Under s.60 of the Act the relevant local authority is empowered to serve a notice imposing requirements as to the way in which the works are to be carried out. The Act makes the following provisions about notice:

"60(3) The notice may in particular—

(a) specify the plant or machinery which is or is not to be used;
(b) specify the hours during which the works may be carried out;
(c) specify the level of noise which may be omitted from the premises in question or at any specified point on those premises or which may be so omitted during specified hours; and
(d) provide for any change of circumstances."

Section 60(5) requires the notice to be served on the person who appears to be carrying out or going to carry out the works and on others who appear to be responsible for or have control over the works. The recipient

---

[21] [2007] UKHL 30.

may appeal the notice to a magistrates' court; otherwise, it becomes an offence to contravene any requirement of the notice "without reasonable excuse." Section 61 of the Act makes provision for obtaining prior consent of the local authority to work which is to be carried out. This is a useful device if the contractor needs to know whether they will be permitted to use particular plant and machinery, and if so, during what hours. Although the Act uses only the term "noise," this is defined as including vibration.

Enforcement proceedings

Where contravention of a notice occurs, the local authority may pros-ecute the contractor who, in the event of conviction, will be liable to a fine. If the offences are serious or repeated, consideration may need to be given to other action. This is particularly so where the contractor is under financial or other pressure to continue with the work in contravention of the notice. In such a case, the local authority may invoke the civil juris-diction of the court to grant an injunction to restrain further contraven-tion of the notice. If granted, any further contravention of the injunction would be punishable by all the means available to the court, including imprisonment. The circumstances in which the local authority can take this step is, therefore, of general interest, because it applies in many other areas where a local authority is charged with the proper administra-tion of the law. One example is the proper administration of planning law, which has given rise to a number of cases where there have been flagrant breaches of the law relating to caravan sites, tree preservation orders, and the like. If the relevant enforcement notices have been issued and are being ignored, despite criminal proceedings and the imposition of (modest) fines, the local authority may need to take sterner action. Another example (now historical) is Sunday trading, where fines which could be imposed even for persistent and intentional breaches of the law, were trivial compared to the profits made from illegal trading.

The legal basis for action in these circumstances by the local authority is s.222 of the Local Government Act 1972, which empowers the local authority to take action in their own name where this is expedient "for the promotion or protection of the interests of the inhabitants of their area." In resolving to take such action, the local authority is exercising a public law power, and as such is liable to control through judicial review if it acts improperly (see Ch.1). Further, in deciding whether or not to grant an injunction, the court has to consider whether it is appropriate to grant this civil remedy in aid of enforcement of the criminal law, which provides its own remedy. Thus, over a number of cases, the courts have evolved principles upon which an injunction will be granted. These matters were considered by the Court of Appeal in *City of London v*

Bovis,[22] where the City were seeking an injunction to restrain further breaches of a notice served under s.60 of the Control of Pollution Act. Bingham L.J. stated that the guiding principles were:

> "(1) that the jurisdiction was to be invoked and exercised exceptionally and with great caution;
> (2) there must be something more than mere infringement of the criminal law; and
> (3) the court must conclude that the defendants' unlawful operations would continue unless restrained by injunction."

He also summarised the alternative courses of action that might have been open as follows:

> "Any individual resident of Petticoat Square could have sued in private nuisance. The Attorney General could have sued in public nuisance either ex officio or on the relation of the local authority or a resident of Petticoat Square. The local authority could have sued in their own name for a public nuisance by virtue on section 222 of the Local Government Act 1972 if they considered it expedient for the protection of the interests of the inhabitants of their area. . . . As it was none of these procedures was invoked. Instead, the local authority decided . . . to issue summonses under section 60(8) alleging contraventions of the section 60 notice."

A point argued in the *Bovis* case was whether a construction manager under a form of contract providing for work to be carried out by trade contractors, should be regarded as the appropriate person for service and enforcement of a notice under s.60. Subsection (5) provides:

> "A notice under this section shall be served on the person who appears to the local authority to be carrying out or going to carry out the works and on such other persons appearing to the local authority to be responsible for or to have control over the carrying out of the works as the local authority thinks fit."

The Court of Appeal held that a construction manager came within the section and was properly to be held accountable for breaches of the notice. The categories under s.60(5) were not mutually exclusive, and it was sufficient that *Bovis* under their contract (and under parallel provisions in the trade contracts) were given control of the building operations. Where there is any doubt about the person responsible, the local authority has power under s.93 of the Act to serve notice requiring information.

---

[22] (1988) 49 B.L.R. 1.

This may allow the authority, for example, to obtain copies of relevant commercial documents which will establish who is in control for the purpose of notice abatement.

Use of water

Water-borne pollution may be seen as one of the most serious problems which environment law has to tackle. Off-shore and deep-sea pollution are matters for international law and treaty; but inland and coastal waters are subject to close statutory control of their use as well as to historical common law principles.

A land owner who borders a watercourse is known as a "riparian owner". They normally own the land up to the middle of the stream. At common law the riparian owner is entitled to the use of flowing water for ordinary purposes such as domestic use. They may also use the water for an extraordinary purpose such as manufacturing or irrigation, provided the water is returned in the same volume and character to the stream. However, there are very stringent statutory controls on the right to abstract water from any source of supply, whether it be a watercourse or a well or bore-hole, for other than domestic purposes, contained now in the Water Resources Act 1991.[23]

Most matters concerning use of inland waterways and resources come under the statutory jurisdiction of the Environment Agency.[24] The question of what persons are entitled to put into water is strictly controlled by the Water Resources Act 1991 Pt III, re-enacting earlier statutes. The Act makes it an offence to cause or knowingly permit any poisonous, noxious or polluting matter or any solid waste matter to enter any controlled waters (s.85(1)). In respect of existing discharge of trade effluent, sewage effluent, etc. the Act provides for prohibition notices which may limit the amount or type of discharge or impose conditions, and for any discharge outside these requirements to be treated as an offence (s.86). "Controlled waters" includes rivers, lakes and ponds, ground water, coastal waters and territorial waters (s.104). The possibility of pollution being caused to controlled waters is a ground for taking action to require remediation of contaminated land under Pt IIA of the Environmental Protection Act 1990 (see above).

Where the "person" causing or permitting pollution is a corporate body, an officer of that body (such as a director or manager) may also be liable. A manufacturer was held liable for causing pollution of a river,

---

[23] Pt II, Ch.II.
[24] Until April 1, 1996 the National Rivers Authority: see the Environment Act 1995 and the Water Resources Act 1991 ss.1–23.

even though he had taken elaborate precautions to prevent it and accidental spillage occurred only because of a defect in the apparatus:
Alphacell Ltd v Woodward.[25] In this case, the House of Lords considered
whether an offence under the Act was committed by a person who had no
knowledge of the fact that pollution was occurring and had not been
negligent. Lord Dilhorne held:

> "Here, the acts done by the appellants were intentional. They were acts
> calculated to lead to the river being polluted if the acts done by the appel-
> lants, the installation and operation of the pumps, were ineffective to
> prevent it. Where a person intentionally does certain things which produce
> a certain result, then it can truly be said that he has caused that result, and
> here in my opinion the acts done intentionally by the appellants caused the
> pollution."

Further changes to the operation of the UK Water Industry are introduced by the Water Act 2003 which reforms the system of abstraction
licensing, which is now linked to resource availability and volume
consumed. The Act (in common with other Regulatory legislation) establishes a new Regulatory Framework for the industry, replacing the
former Director General of Water Services with a new Regulatory
Authority. The Act brings in new competition provisions, allowing
opportunities to supply water to large commercial consumers. The Act
also transfers responsibility for reservoir safety from local authorities to
the Environment Agency.

Environment law and Europe

The European Commission has been active in promoting environment
protection measures for many years. A series of environment action
programmes have been issued of which the latest is the seventh. The
programme sets out the general framework in which Directives or
Regulations may be issued by the Commission. The programmes are
authorised by provisions inserted in the Single European Act by which
the Community has a mandate to:

> "preserve protect and improve the quality of the environment . . . contribute
> towards protecting human health . . . [and] to ensure a prudent and rational
> utilisation of natural resources."[26]

---

[25] [1972] A.C. 824.
[26] Article 130 r.(1).

The objective is to respond to rapidly changing external conditions and the increasingly interlinked nature of environmental, economic and social challenges including increased growth in the demand for natural resources and the impacts this has for the environment.

The Commission has adopted a Directive on Environmental Liability under art.174 of the Treaty which provides that "environmental damage should as a priority be rectified at source and that the polluter should pay". The new regime, which is in addition to liability under national law, requires a duty to take preventive action in respect of imminent damage as well as providing for remediation. Enforcement will be through public authorities and is intended to provide for no-fault liability for persons conducting operations involving risk. Implementation of the Directive will depend on national legislation. A further European Initiative which will affect all aspects of the Water Industry is the Water Framework Directive[27] for which the deadline for implementation is 2015. The Directive deals with both water supply and waste management in terms of water quality, pollution and the balancing of environmental needs.

The principle that "the polluter pays"[28] is now commonly adopted both in Europe and elsewhere in the world. It is to be noted that there are other massive developments on a world-wide basis, some of which are in advance of European developments, for example, the United States "superfund". Among the major problems faced by all such schemes is the need for rapid response and prevention measures, as to which ordinary legal processes offer little help. Such problems are exacerbated by the international nature of much water borne and air borne pollution.

---

[27] Directive 2000/60/EC.
[28] See generally, *Construction Law and the Environment*, (Uff, Garthwrite and Barber eds., 1994, King's College, CCLM).

CHAPTER 16

CONSTRUCTION STATUTES AND SAFETY

Contracts under which work is carried out in the construction industry are affected directly by few statutory provisions. However, matters such as the design of the works and the mode of carrying out operations are likely to be subject to many statutory controls. These may impose obligations on one or more of the parties involved. A breach of such an obligation may give rise to statutory penal sanctions and also to consequences at civil law, in tort or for breach of contract (see JCT, cl.6 and ICE, cl.26).

The more directly relevant statutes which affect the construction industry include the Environmental Protection Act 1990, the Health and Safety at Work Act 1974, the various planning Acts and the Building Act 1984. Many of the Acts contain powers for the creation of further delegated legislation in the form of regulations or byelaws, which lay down detailed provisions.

In this chapter three types of statutory provision are discussed, which are of importance to construction work. First, the Building Regulations, which govern the design and construction of building works. Secondly, a short account is given of the law relating to highways, which is primarily governed by statute. Thirdly, statutory provisions relating to health and safety are described.

BUILDING REGULATIONS

Statutory provisions relating to building regulations are now consolidated into the Building Act 1984, which applies throughout England and Wales, including the Inner London Area. Before 1965 the design and construction of buildings was regulated by byelaws made under the Public Health Acts by individual local authorities. There were variations between different authorities, but latterly provisions became based on model byelaws issued by central government. In 1965 the first set of Building Regulations applying throughout England and Wales was issued. These were regularly revised and extended by amending

Regulations. The Building Act has itself been amended to extend the range of matters dealt with by the regulations. The regulations currently in force are the Building Regulations 2010 (SI 2010/2214). All recent sets of regulations are further amended by additional regulations[1] dealing both with technical and administrative aspects of building control.

The current regulations are shorter than previous Building Regulations, and are so expressed that rigid enforcement is not encouraged. The intention is that the regulations should be interpreted so as to achieve reasonable standards of health or safety. A particular innovation in the Building Act 1984 is the use of "approved documents" under s.6. The effect of such documents is defined by s.7 as follows:

> "(1) A failure on the part of a person to comply with an approved document does not of itself render him liable to any civil or criminal proceedings; but if, in any proceedings whether civil or criminal, it is alleged that a person has at any time contravened a provision of building regulations—
> (a) a failure to comply with a document that at that time was approved for the purposes of that provision may be relied upon as tending to establish liability, and
> (b) proof of compliance with such a document may be relied on as tending to negative liability."

Powers and duties of the local authority in regard to passing or rejection of plans are set out in s.16 of the Building Act 1984. In addition, the Regulations contain detailed provisions as to notices and forms. There are, however, provisions by which Building Regulation compliance or approval may be secured other than by a decision of the local authority. These are:

(1) Under ss.12 and 13 of the Building Act 1984, there may be approvals of any type of "building matter", i.e. any matter to which the Building Regulations are applicable. Such approvals may be made with or without specific application.

(2) Under s.17 of the Building Act 1984, "approved persons" may be designated to give a certificate of compliance with Building Regulations. Such a person must also provide evidence of insurance arrangements complying with regulations; alternatively there may be an "approved scheme" to provide insurance.

---

[1] Including the Building (Amendment) Regulations 2011 (201/1515).

The appointment and functions of Approved Inspectors is set out in the Building (Approved Inspectors, etc.) Regulations 2010 (SI 2010/2215) which is also subject to amendment by further regulations.

Content and application of regulations

The Regulations themselves are largely procedural. The technical requirements are set out in Sch.1 (as extended) under the following headings:

Part A—Structure.
Part B—Fire safety.
Part C—Site preparation and resistance to contaminants and moisture.
Part D—Toxic substances.
Part E—Resistance to the passage of sound.
Part F—Ventilation.
Part G—Sanitation, hot water safety and water efficiency.
Part H—Drainage and waste disposal.
Part J—Combustion appliances and fuel storage systems.
Part K—Protection from falling, collision and impact.
Part L—Conservation of fuel and power.
Part M—Access to and use of buildings.
Part N—Glazing—safety in relation to impact, opening and cleaning.
Part P—Electrical safety.

The Regulations themselves provide for the application of the technical requirements. Regulation 4 requires that the building work should be carried out so that it complies with the applicable requirements of Sch.1. As regards extension to or alteration of an existing building, reg.4(3) requires that while the existing building is not required to comply with the requirements it shall be no more unsatisfactory than before the work was carried out.

The regulations apply, inter alia, to the erection or extension of a building or to a material alteration (reg.3). Control is also imposed on a material change of use, defined by reg.5 as including changing to use as a dwelling, the creation of a flat within a building, or changing a building for use as an hotel or public building. Regulation 6 sets out requirements that apply to a material change of use.

In addition to the technical requirements, reg.7 makes provision in respect of materials and workmanship, and requires that building work shall be carried out "(a) with adequate and proper materials . . . (b) in a workmanlike manner". This reflects similar obligations which would arise by implied terms in a construction contract, or by statute, for example, the Defective Premises Act 1972 or the Supply of Goods and Services Act 1982. However, there is a general limitation on application of the technical requirements in that reg.8 provides that particular parts (notably A–D) of Sch.1 are not to require anything to be done:

> "except for the purpose of securing reasonable standards of health and safety for persons in or about the building (and any others who may be affected. . .)."

The regulations do not apply in a number of circumstances. Some buildings and works are exempt from the regulations, including buildings not frequented by people, temporary buildings, greenhouses and agricultural buildings (Sch.2). The technical requirements set out in Sch.1 are accompanied by notes stating the limits to which the requirements are applicable.

Notices and compliance with regulations

A person who intends to carry out building work must submit to the local authority either a "building notice" containing the particulars specified in regs 12 and 13, or they may at their option submit "full plans" complying with reg.14. Alternatively, there may be compliance instead with the "approved persons" procedure (see above). The authority must pass or reject the submitted plans within a period of five weeks, which may be extended by agreement to two months.[2] Where plans are defective or show a contravention the authority may, as an alternative to rejection, pass the plans subject to conditions requiring modification and further deposit of plans.

In addition to obtaining approval under the regulations, a person intending to carry out building work must give notice at various stages of the work. These include two days notice before commencement of the works, one days notice before covering up a foundation, damp-proof course, or drain and five days notice after completing drain work. Notice must also be given within five days of completion of building work (reg.13). During the course of work, the local authority may exercise a right to make tests on drains, or to take samples of materials, to establish compliance with the requirements of the regulations (regs 18, 19). Amended reg.16A makes provision for self-certification by qualified persons and in respect of defined types of work.

---

[2] Building Act 1984 s.16.

Historically, London had its own statutes and building control system, with features differing materially from those applying to the rest of England and Wales. Powers to introduce a uniform system throughout England and Wales, including London, were contained in the Building Act 1984. London has gradually been brought into line with the rest of England and Wales so that few differences now exist.

Civil liability

The Public Health Acts, the Building Act and Building Regulations are enforced primarily through the criminal law. But the regulations are frequently incorporated into building contracts so that failure to comply will be a breach by the builder. The JCT and ICC forms of contract contain general obligations to comply with statutory provisions[3] which include the regulations. A provision for imposing general civil liability for breach of a duty imposed by Building Regulations is contained in s.38 of the Building Act 1984.[4] This has not been brought into effect.

During the 1970s and 1980s there were many cases before the courts where local authorities and builders were held liable in negligence for failing to ensure compliance with Building Regulations. These decisions were based on the case of *Anns v L.B. Merton*,[5] now overruled by *Murphy v Brentwood DC*[6] (see Ch.14). The present law is that, where a building is found to be defective but there is no injury to person or property, money spent in repairing the building must be regarded as a purely economic loss, not normally recoverable under the law of tort. Effectively a whole chapter of litigation has been closed by the *Murphy* decision. The principal right of redress outside the field of contract, is now under the Defective Premises Act 1972 (see Ch.7).

Highways

This section illustrates the operation of statute law in a particular area, which is of importance both to those involved in highway construction and in other fields of construction, such as housing development. The principal governing legislation is now the Highways Act 1980, which consolidates and amends a number of previous Acts. The Act does not

---

[3] See cll.6, JCT, cl.26, ICC.
[4] Formerly Health and Safety at Work Act 1974 s.71.
[5] [1978] A.C. 728.
[6] [1991] 1 A.C. 398.

attempt to define the term "highway," this being a term of some antiquity and of importance under the common law, for example in relation to the acquisition of rights of passage. Generally, a highway is a defined way over land which is exercisable by the public in general, although the right of use may be limited to particular classes of traffic. Highways thus range from a country footpath or a suburban cul-de-sac to motorways. The 1980 Act provides that a bridge or tunnel over or through which a highway passes is to be taken as part of the highway (s.328(2)).

Rights and duties

Questions that arise in relation to construction projects are: who owns or is responsible for a highway? In particular, who is responsible for its maintenance? What rights and duties exist in regard to services or apparatus under a highway? The first question raises interesting issues about rights and easements (see Ch.15) as opposed to legal ownership. There are many possibilities which depend on the way in which the highway was created. There is a general presumption that the owner of land adjoining a highway also owns the soil, and all other rights that go with ownership, up to the middle line of the road. A highway built over land is, in law, no more than a right of passage, together with such rights and obligations as are necessary for maintenance and operation as a highway. These rights and obligations are vested by statute in a "highway authority" who will usually be either a County Council or central government, acting through the relevant Minister of State. Some minor highway functions are vested in District Councils and there are other exceptions.

A highway authority is generally responsible for the construction, maintenance and improvement of highways. A local highway authority may undertake work on behalf of the Minister, either pursuant to an agency agreement or by the provision of services. Different local highway authorities may make agreements between themselves for the carrying out of their functions. The duty to maintain a highway is created by s.41 of the 1980 Act and potentially creates a right of action in respect of loss or injury caused by lack of maintenance. Section 59 creates a statutory defence if the highway authority proves that reasonable care was taken to ensure that the highway was not dangerous. In *Gorringe v Calderdale MBC*[7] it was held that the failure of the highway authority to maintain road markings did not constitute a failure to maintain. An earlier ruling of the House of Lords that the duty to maintain did not include preventing the formation of ice was reversed by an amendment to include a duty to ensure, so far as reasonably practicable, that safe

[7] [2004] 1 W.L.R. 1057.

passage was not endangered by ice or snow.[8] In *Department of Transport v Mott MacDonald*,[9] it was held that the duty under s.41 extended beyond the surface to drainage and its effect on the highway surface.

The creation and designation of major roads falls into two categories. Trunk roads, as defined under s.10 of the Highways Act 1980, are intended to form a network of routes for through traffic, relieved of local traffic. This was the main national road network up to the 1950s. Section 16 of the Act deals with a category known as "Special Roads", which includes motorways. The creation of a "Special Road" requires a scheme to be drawn up by the proposed authority, being either the Minister or the local highway authority, and the Act lays down detailed provisions for publication and enquiry before confirmation of the scheme. Powers and duties of the Department for Transport in relation to managing, maintaining and improving trunk roads and motorways are exercised by the Highways Agency. The Agency also provides design and other technical information and approved contract documents, which must also be compliant with the requirements of the European Commission with respect to public procurement.

Adoption of highways

Builders and developers of housing and industrial estates often construct new road systems to serve the new buildings. When the buildings have been sold or leased off, the question arises, who is to undertake responsibility for continuing maintenance of the new roads? This may go beyond mere resurfacing, as the new highways may include earthworks and structures, including bridges. The same question arises in relation to new sewers constructed to serve an estate.

There is no reason why the developer or the purchasers of the buildings should not keep the roads in their own private ownership and at their own expense. However, a convenient alternative is provided by the Highways Act 1980. Section 38 provides that the highway authority may enter into an agreement with the person responsible for maintenance. The terms of the agreement (colloquially known as a "section 38 agreement") usually provide for the road to be constructed and completed to the highway authority's standard specification or satisfaction, and for the highway then to become a public highway maintained at the expense of the authority. Similar provisions apply to new sewers, which may become vested in the relevant water undertaker.[10]

---

[8] Section 41A inserted by the Railways and Transport Safety Act 2003.
[9] [2006] 1 W.L.R. 3356.
[10] Water Industry Act 1991 Pt IV.

Street works

Many highways, particularly in urban areas, carry services belonging
to public utility companies, such as gas, electricity, water, sewerage,
telephones and others. This gives rise to many potential problems when
the services are to be installed or need repair. Excavations lead to
questions of reinstatement and repair of the carriageway, as well as the
possibility of damage to other services. These matters are now regulated
by the New Roads and Street Works Act 1991 which introduced new
provisions to replace the former Streetworks Code.[11]

In the terminology of the Act, streetworks require a streetworks licence,
which is to be granted by the street authority.[12] The term "undertaker" is
retained from the old Act and means the person by whom the relevant
statutory rights is exercisable or the licensee under the streetworks
licence. A licence is required to place, to retain and thereafter to inspect,
maintain, etc. "apparatus" in the street, which includes a sewer, drain or
tunnel.[13]

The Act requires the undertaker to give not less than seven days'
notice prior to the start of works to any other person whose apparatus is
likely to be affected. There are special provisions for emergency works.
Provision is made for regulations requiring other notices. Notice lapses
after seven days if the work is not begun.[14] The Act places many obligations on the undertaker including a duty to carry on and complete works
with despatch, a duty to reinstate and a general obligation to co-operate
with the street authority and with other undertakers.[15] Regulations may
provide for charges to be levied against the undertaker where work is
delayed.[16] The licensee is required to indemnify the street authority
against third party claims.[17] By subsequent legislation the street authority
now has extended powers to restrict the days or times when street work
is carried out; and power to direct an undertaker to place apparatus in a
different location, in each case in the interest of avoiding traffic disruption.[18] The Act is dealt with expressly under the ICE/ICC conditions,
cl.27. This provides that, for the purpose of obtaining any licence
required for the permanent works, the undertaker is to be the employer,
who is also to be the licensee. For all other purposes the undertaker is the

---

[11] Under the Public Utilities Streetworks Act 1950.
[12] See ss.48, 49, 50.
[13] Section 89(3).
[14] See ss.54, 55, 57.
[15] See ss.60, 66, 70.
[16] Section 74(1).
[17] Sch.3 para.8.
[18] Traffic Management Act 2004 ss.43, 44.

contractor. The employer is to obtain any licence or consent required for the permanent works but the contractor is responsible for giving notices.

HEALTH AND SAFETY

This section deals with the design and implementation of construction projects, and the safety of those engaged on the work. Construction is notoriously dangerous, not through the callous attitude of employers, but usually because workmen take unnecessary risks. This may be seen as a failure by those in control to impose safety requirements on those working on sites. Statistics show that around 100 workers continue to lose their lives annually in construction accidents, and some 10,000 are injured.

As between employer and employee, there is a clear duty of care (see Ch.14), and it is of little importance whether this is regarded as arising in tort or in contract, since the damages for personal injury will be recoverable under either head. Additionally, there has been considerable statutory intervention aimed at imposing positive duties for the protection of workers, formerly through the Factories Acts, subsequently through the Health and Safety at Work Act 1974 and most recently from the European Community. The 1974 Act created the new Health and Safety Executive (HSE), whose inspectors administer the Act and its regulations. These provisions apply throughout industry, but there are particular regulations applying to construction work. The new CDM Regulations also take effect under the 1974 Act and depend upon the HSE for enforcement.

Health and Safety at Work Act 1974

The HSE operates under the direction of the Health and Safety Commission, which is itself charged with the overall duty of achieving the purposes of Pt I of the Act, which are to secure the health, safety and welfare of persons at work (s.1(1)). The Commission may order investigations or enquiries into accidents, which may be carried out by the HSE itself or by others so appointed. This covers also industries for which specialist Inspectorates exist, including the nuclear industry and the railways. Enforcement of the Act and its regulations is carried out through inspectors.

The Act creates general duties on employers to ensure, so far as is reasonably practicable, the health, safety and welfare at work of employees. A similar duty is placed on employers and self-employed persons to ensure, so far as it is reasonably practicable, that other persons are not exposed to risks to health or safety.[19] Persons having control of premises must ensure, so far as is reasonably practicable, that the premises are safe and without risk to health.[20] The European Commission subsequently, in 1989, issued a Directive[21] requiring National Laws to provide for employers to have a duty to ensure the health and safety of workers without restriction. In a test action by the Commission, the ECJ held that the requirement to ensure health and safety "so far as reasonably practicable" did not infringe community law and was therefore in accordance with the Directive.[22]

Powers available to inspectors include the right to enter premises to make examination and investigation, to take samples, and to require the production of documents and information. Where there is a contravention, the inspector may serve an "Improvement Notice"; and where the contravention involves the risks of serious personal injury, they may give a "Prohibition Notice," which may have immediate effect.[23] The Act provides penalties for breach of its provisions. The HSE itself acts as the prosecuting authority. Major accidents, particularly those resulting in death or injury usually result in prosecution under the Act. Alternatively, or in addition, death resulting from gross negligence may lead to the individuals alleged to be responsible being prosecuted.

Manslaughter

There have been a number of attempts by the prosecuting authorities to secure convictions for manslaughter following major accidents, both in the field of rail and maritime transport, most of which have been unsuccessful. This has been due to the difficulty of identifying an individual who could be regarded as the "controlling mind" for the company in matters of safety. Following lengthy debate the Corporate Manslaughter and Corporate Homicide Act 2007 was finally passed, allowing prosecution of companies or partnerships where it can be shown that organisation by senior management amounts to a "gross breach of a relevant duty of care" leading to death. The penalty on conviction, however, is limited to a fine, in contrast to the originally advertised intention to send directors to prison. The result will be that common law manslaughter charges will become even rarer.

---

[19] See ss.2 and 3.
[20] Section 4.
[21] Directive 89/391/ECC art.5.
[22] *Commission v United Kingdom* (C-127/05).
[23] See ss.20, 21, 22.

In *R. v Cotswold Geotechnical Holding*,[24] the proprietor of a specialist site investigation company left a junior employee working alone in a 3.5m deep trial pit. The employee was killed when the pit walls collapsed. He had little training or experience and the trial pit was un-supported. No risk assessment or method statement had been produced. The owner of the company was originally charged with manslaughter and with Health and Safety Act offences which were dropped on the grounds of ill-health. The company was subsequently prosecuted under the Corporate Manslaughter and Corporate Homicide Act, was convicted and fined £385,000 which resulted in the company going into liquidation.

Detailed regulation governing day-to-day activities on construction sites have been issued and amended frequently. The current regulations are incorporated within the CDM Regulations 2007 and are dealt with below.

CDM Regulations

The Construction (Design and Management) Regulations were first issued in 1994 and have had a major impact on the planning of all large scale construction work in the United Kingdom. After some amendment, the Construction (Design and Management) Regulations were re-issued in 2007, replacing both the original CDM Regulations and the Construction (Health Safety and Welfare) Regulations so that one set of Regulations now governs most aspects of construction safety. The Regulations are made under the Health and Safety at Work Act 1974 but derive from a European directive.[25] The CDM Regulations embody new concepts in operational safety planning, as opposed to the previous statutory approach of merely seeking to avoid unsafe situations. The key to the operation of regulations is the appointment and placing of functions upon individuals or parties, referred to as the Client, the CDM Co-ordinator (formerly the planning supervisor), the Designer, the Principal Contractors and other Contractors

Part 2 of the Regulations places general duties of co-operation, co-ordination and the promotion of safety on all persons concerned in a project, and specific duties on the client, the designer and on contractors. The duties of the client include provision of information about the site and the works. Part 3 provides additional duties on all parties with respect to a project which is "notifiable". In particular, the client must appoint a CDM Co-ordinator whose duties include notifying and providing to HSE prescribed particulars of the project. A project is

---

[24] Unreported, 17 February 2011.
[25] Temporary or Mobile Construction Sites Directive.

notifiable if the construction phase is likely to involve more than 30 days or 500 person days of construction work.

The principal duties created by the Regulations with respect to a notifiable project are placed initially on the client, who is required to appoint a CDM Co-ordinator to perform the duties specified in regs 20 and 21, and a principal Contractor to perform the duties in regs 22-24. Furthermore, for any period for which no person is appointed as CDM Co-ordinator or as principal Contractor, the client is deemed to be so appointed and subject to the duties imposed by those regulations (reg.14).

The duties of the CDM Co-ordinator under regs 20 and 21 include giving suitable and sufficient advice and assistance to the client on complying with the Regulations and ensuring that suitable arrangements are made and implemented for the co-ordination of health and safety measures during the planning and preparation for the construction phase. The CDM Co-ordinator must take steps to identify, collect and disseminate preconstruction information and take steps to ensure co-operation between designers and the principal contractor. The CDM Co-ordinator must also prepare or review and update the "Health and Safety file" containing information likely to be needed during any subsequent construction work to ensure health and safety. The duty of notification includes a duty to notify the Office of Rail Regulation where this is the appropriate enforcing authority.

The duties of the principal Contractor under regs 22-24 include planning, managing and monitoring the construction phase to ensure, so far as reasonably practicable, that risks to health or safety are avoided. There are specific duties to liaise with the CDM Co-ordinator, to draw up appropriate health and safety site rules, to ensure that every contractor is given access to the construction phase plan and other information and that workers are given appropriate information and training. There is a specific duty at the start of the construction phase to prepare a construction phase plan sufficient to ensure, so far as reasonably practicable, the avoidance of risk to health or safety and to identify the risks to health and safety arising from the work. Furthermore, the client is placed under a duty to ensure that the construction phase does not start unless the principal Contractor has prepared a construction phase plan and welfare facilities will be provided during the construction phase. Other safeguards designed to ensure compliance with the regulations require that designers shall not commence work unless a CDM Co-ordinator has been appointed; and that contractors shall not carry out construction work unless provided with the names of the CDM Co-ordinator and the principal Contractor.

The regulations are enforceable at the suit of the HSE through penalties and other sanctions under the Health and Safety at Work Act. The importance of the regulations is that, for the first time, they place duties enforceable under the criminal law, on persons other than the contractor, notably the designer.

As noted above, the former individual Regulations affecting construction activities in relation to health and safety have now been replaced by Pt 4 of the CDM regulation: Duties Relating to Health and Safety on Construction Sites (regs 24–44). As part of the new drafting style, the Regulations are expressed in terms of what is "reasonable practicable" or in terms of requiring "all practicable steps". In general, mandatory requirements are limited to specific issues such as prohibiting the use of timber or other materials with projecting nails, but even this requirement is qualified by "if the nails may be a source of danger to any person". Thus, the Regulations in effect address the broad tasks and obligations placed upon persons who control the way in which construction work is carried out in terms of the following matters.

- ☐ Safe Places of Work (Regulation 26).

- ☐ Good Order and Site Security (Regulation 27).

- ☐ Stability of Structures (Regulation 28).

- ☐ Demolition and Dismantling (Regulation 29).

- ☐ Explosives (Regulation 30).

- ☐ Excavation (Regulation 31).

- ☐ Cofferdams and Caissons (Regulation 32).

- ☐ Energy Distribution Installation (Regulation 34).

- ☐ Prevent of Drowning (Regulation 35).

- ☐ Traffic Routes (Regulation 36).

- ☐ Vehicles (Regulation 37).

- ☐ Prevention of Risk from Fire, etc. (Regulation 38).

- ☐ Emergency Procedures (Regulation 39).

- ☐ Emergency Routes and Exits (Regulation 40).

- ☐ Fire Detection and Fire Fighting (Regulation 41).

- ☐ Fresh Air (Regulation 42).

- ☐ Temperature and Weather Protection (Regulation 43).

- ☐ Lighting (Regulation 44).

Regulation 33 makes specific provision for reports following inspections under regs 31 or 32 in respect of excavation or cofferdams and caissons (i.e. excavation within a designed structure). This requires a report to be prepared before the end of the relevant shift complying with Sch.3, which lists matters to be dealt with in the report including details of action taken and any further action considered necessary. As in the case of most modern regulations, these provisions are expressed in terms of the result to be achieved, i.e. safety within the limits of reasonable practicability without attempting (as in earlier regulations) to prescribe the means by which it is to be achieved. In this respect the regulations follow the same course as Building Regulations.

While the revised CDM Regulations govern most aspects of health and safety, special regulations exist in particular areas, notably the Work at Height Regulations 2005.[26] These replace the former provisions which applied to working above a height of two metres. The Regulations now provide an initial requirement that, where reasonably practicable, work is not carried out at height; and that if not practicable, suitable and sufficient measures are to be taken to prevent any person falling a distance liable to cause personal injury.[27]

Civil liability

Regulation 45 of the the CDM Regulations 2007 provides that breach of the regulations does not confer any general right of action in civil proceedings, but this does not apply in the case of an employee nor does it apply to the Health and Safety provisions in regs 26–44. Thus, while the regulations do not provide for civil liability, any breach may be relied on in a civil action for damages by an individual who suffers injury as a result of the breach, in addition to or as an alternative to liability in tort (see Ch.14).

To succeed in a civil action for breach of a regulation in which there is no provision creating civil liability, it must be shown that:

(1) the regulation was intended to protect a class of which the claimant was a member;

(2) the regulation was broken;

(3) they suffered damage of a kind against which the regulation was intended to protect; and

(4) the damage was caused by the breach.

---

[26] SI 2005/735.
[27] Regulation 6(2) and (3).

These requirements may appear self-evident, but their effect in practice may be less than obvious. In a number of cases it has been held that self-employed workmen were not entitled to the protection of the Construction Regulations. Instead of having a right of action in respect of their injuries, self-employed men may themselves be liable to prosecution for breach of the regulations. However, the Court of Appeal has held that the question whether a man is employed or self-employed is to be approached broadly. The fact that he pays tax as a self-employed person is not decisive. In *Ferguson v John Dawson & Partners*[28] a roofing worker was employed expressly as a "self-employed labour only sub-contractor." Despite this, the court found that the reality of the relationship created was that of employer and employee. Megaw L.J. said:

> "The parties cannot transfer a statute-imposed duty of care for safety of workmen from an employer to the workman himself merely because the parties agree, in effect, that the workman shall be deemed to be self-employed, where the true essence of the contract is, otherwise, of a contract of service."

The kinds of damage against which the CDM Regulations are intended to protect will include personal injury, but not, for example, loss of earnings due to unsafe scaffolding preventing work. The damage must also be caused by the breach. In *McWilliams v Arrol*[29] a workman was killed in a fall through not wearing a safety belt. It was found that the contractor, in breach of regulations, failed to provide belts for the men. However, the contractor showed that the deceased would not have worn a belt even if it had been provided, and consequently was held not liable in civil law for damages. Viscount Kilmuir said:

> "The necessity, in actions by employees against their employers on the grounds of negligence, of establishing not only the breach of duty but also the causal connection between the breach and the injury complained of is, in my view, part of the law of both England and Scotland."

Safety on construction sites continue to be an important and developing area of Construction Law.

---

[28] [1976] 1 W.L.R. 1213.
[29] [1962] 1 W.L.R. 295.

APPENDIX

GLOSSARY OF LEGAL TERMS

ADJOURN: To put off the hearing of a case to a later date.

AFFIDAVIT: A written statement sworn on oath which ranks as formal evidence.

AGENT: A person with authority to act for another (the principal).

APPELLANT: The party who brings an appeal to a higher court.

ARBITRATION: Proceedings before a private tribunal to which the parties agree to submit disputes.

ASSETS: Property which is available for paying debts.

ASSIGNMENT: The transfer by agreement of a right or interest to another person.

AWARD: The decision given by an arbitrator.

BAILMENT: Delivery of goods into the possession of another person.

BANKRUPT: A person who cannot pay their debts and who is adjudicated a *bankrupt*.

BAR: The profession of barristers.

BREACH: Non-fulfilment of some contractual (or other) obligation.

BYELAWS: Rules, usually made under statutory authority and having full force of law.

CASE STATED: A statement of facts prepared by a lower court or tribunal for the decision of a higher court on a point of law.

CAVEAT EMPTOR: "Let the buyer beware"; a maxim indicating that any risk is upon the buyer and not the seller.

CHANCERY: One of the three divisions of the *High Court*.

CHARGE: An interest, usually over land, given as security.

CHATTELS: Personal property.

CHOSE IN ACTION: An intangible right which can be enforced by action; such as a debt.

CLAIM FORM: A docoument which initiates a civil claim (formerly a writ).

CLAIMANT: The party who initiates civil proceedings (formerly plaintiff).

COMMERCIAL COURT: A special court in the *Queen's Bench* Division for dealing with commercial actions.

COMMON LAW: Law embodied in case precedent as opposed to *Statute* law or *Equity*.

CONDITION: An important term of a *contract*.

CONSIDERATION: The bargain or inducement provided by a party to a contract.

CONSOLIDATION: Joining of two separate actions so that they may be tried together.

CONTRACT: An agreement which is binding in law.

CONVEYANCE: A written instrument which transfers property (especially land) from one person to another.

COUNTERCLAIM: A cross action brought by a *defendant* or *respondent* against the claimant.

COUNTY COURTS: Local courts which deal with smaller civil claims.

COURT OF APPEAL: The court which hears appeals, civil or criminal, from the *High Court* and *County Courts*.

COVENANT: An undertaking contained in a document, especially in a deed or lease.

CROWN COURT: The branch of the *Supreme Court* which deals with criminal trials (and also some civil cases).

DAMAGES: The money award made to a successful party in a civil action.

DEED: A formal written instrument, signed and witnessed.

DEFENCE: A pleading from the *defendant* in answer to the claim form.

DEFENDANT: The person sued in an ordinary *civil action*.

DETINUE: An action in tort for recovery of a specific *chattel*.

DISCLOSURE: The production before trial of documents relating to a case.

DOMICILE: The country or state with which a person or company is most closely connected.

EASEMENT: A right enjoyed over land belonging to another person.

EQUITY: Law based upon discretion and conscience, derived from the old Court of Chancery.

ESTATE: General term for an interest in land.

EX-PARTE: An application by one side only, now known as "without notice".

EXECUTION: Methods of enforcement of a judgment in an action.

EXHIBIT: A document used in evidence, especially when annexed to an affidavit.

FORCE MAJEURE: Irresistible compulsion, such as war or Act of God.

FORFEITURE: A provision, especially in a *contract* or *lease*, enabling one party to strip the other of their whole interest, in particular circumstances. The term is sometimes applied to termination of a building contract.

FRUSTRATION: Termination of a *contract* as a result of some intervening event, such as war.

GARNISHEE: Proceedings by which a *judgment* debt is enforced by ordering the debtor to pay a debt owed to the him to the judgment creditor instead.

GENERAL DAMAGES: Unascertained damages, to be assessed by the tribunal.

HEARSAY: Testimony by a witness as to a matter not within his personal knowledge.

HIGH COURT: The principal court in which civil actions are heard at first instance.

HOUSE OF LORDS: The highest court of England and Scotland.

INCORPOREAL: Intangible rights and interests, such as debts or shares.

INDORSEMENT: Something written on the back of a document.

INJUNCTION: An order of the court to do or refrain from doing some act.

INTERIM: Provisional, until further direction.

INTERLOCUTORY: A matter dealt with before the trial of an action.

JOINT: Two or more persons sharing a right or obligation such that their interest is not severed, each having an interest in the whole.

JUDGMENT: The order given by a court after hearing a case.

JURISDICTION: Authority of a court or tribunal over matters brought before it.

KING'S (QUEEN'S) BENCH: A division of the High Court.

LAW REPORTS: Authenticated reports of decided cases in the superior courts.

LEASE: A letting or demise of land; also the instrument containing the demise and its covenants.

LEGAL AID: A system for providing free or assisted legal advice or representation, for persons of limited means.

LICENCE: An authority, especially to enter land without having exclusive possession.

LIEN: A right to retain possession of some article until a claim by the holder is satisfied.

LIMITATION: Statutory periods outside which actions may be barred.

LIQUIDATED DAMAGES: Ascertained or calculated monetary loss claimed in an action. *Also* a sum provided by a *contract* as payable in the event of breach.

LIQUIDATION: Winding-up of a company.

LORD JUSTICE OF APPEAL: Title of a judge of the *Court of Appeal*.

LORD OF APPEAL IN ORDINARY: Title of a judge in the *Supreme Court* or *Privy Council*; commonly called a "Law Lord".

MASTER: An official of the High Court who decides many *interlocutory* matters.

MITIGATION: Abatement of loss or damage.

MORTGAGE: A *conveyance, assignment* or *lease* of property as security for a loan.

NEGLIGENCE: Conduct breaching a duty of care.

NUISANCE: Unlawful interference with the use or enjoyment of another person's land.

OBITER DICTUM: Statement of a judge on a point not directly relevant to their decision.

OFFICIAL REFEREE: Former title of a judge in TCC cases.

OFFICIAL SOLICITOR: An officer of the *Supreme Court* who acts for persons under a disability.

PARTICULARS: Details of some allegation pleaded in an action (now called further information).

PARTNERSHIP: An unincorporated association of persons in business with a view to profit.

PENALTY: A sum provided by a contract as payable in the event of breach, which is deemed unrecoverable as *liquidated damages*.

PLEADING: A written statement of a party's case in a civil action.

POINTS OF CLAIM: Pleading served by *claimant* in an arbitration.

PRESCRIPTION: A claim to some right, based upon long user.

PRIVY COUNCIL: The judicial committee of the *Privy Council* is the final court of appeal for some Commonwealth countries.

PROFIT À PRENDRE: A right to take something from another person's land.

QUEEN'S BENCH: One of the three divisions of the *High Court*.

QUEEN'S COUNSEL or Q.C.: A senior barrister.

QUANTUM MERUIT: An action claiming a reasonable price for work or goods.

RATIFICATION: Confirmation, for example of a *contract*, so as to make it binding.

RATIO DECIDENDI: The relevant part of a judge's decision in a case, which is authoritative.

REAL PROPERTY: Certain interests and rights in land; as opposed to personal property.

RECTIFICATION: Correction by the court of a document so as to express the parties' true intention.

REPLY: A pleading from a *claimant* in answer to the *defendant's defence*.

REPUDIATION: An express or implied refusal by one party to perform their obligation under a *contract*.

RESPONDENT: The *defendant* in an arbitration.

RIPARIAN OWNER: An owner of land bordering on a watercourse.

SEQUESTRATION: Order of the *High Court* to seize goods and lands of a *defendant* who is in contempt of court.

SET-OFF: Diminution or extinction of the claimant's claim in an action by deducting a *counterclaim*.

SEVERAL: Where two or more persons share an obligation which may be enforced in full against any one of them.

SHERIFF: A local office of great antiquity, presently relating to the execution of civil *judgments*.

SIMPLE CONTRACT: A written or oral *contract* not made by *deed*.

SPECIAL DAMAGES: Ascertained or calculated monetary loss; as opposed to unascertained or *general damages*.

SPECIFIC PERFORMANCE: An equitable remedy which compels a person to perform their obligation under a contract.

STATUTE: An Act of Parliament.

STATUTORY INSTRUMENT OR SI: A form of delegated legislation, which has full force of law.

SUBPOENA: An order (now called witness summons) requiring a person to appear at court and give evidence or produce documents.

SUBROGATION: The right (often of insurer) to bring an action in the name of a person who has been indemnified.

SUE: To take legal proceedings for a civil remedy.

SUMMONS: An order (now called claim form) to appear before the court.

SUPREME COURT: *The highest UK court, formerly the House of Lords' Judicial Committee.*

TECHNOLOGY & CONSTRUCTION COURT or TCC: The courts in which such cases, formerly known as Official Referee's business, are tried.

TORT: A civil wrong, independent of contract or breach of trust.

TRESPASS: A tortious injury to the person or goods of another, or an unauthorised entry upon their land.

TRUST: An instrument by which property is held by trustees for the benefit of beneficiaries.

UBERRIMAE FIDES: Utmost good faith, required in certain transactions, typically insurance contracts.

ULTRA VIRES: Beyond their powers; especially of a limited company or statutory body.

UNLIQUIDATED DAMAGES: Damages which cannot be calculated as a monetary loss, and which are assessed by the court, such as damages for personal injury.

WARRANTY: A term of a *contract* which is not a *condition*; especially a statement by the vendor as to the quality of goods.

WITHOUT PREJUDICE: Correspondence in connection with a dispute so headed, is privileged and cannot be referred to in the action.

INDEX